Janie's Journal

VOLUME 5

2005-2009

Also by Janie Tippett

Four Lines a Day

Anthology Appearances

*Talking On Paper: An Anthology
of Oregon Letters and Diaries*

*Crazy Woman Creek:
Women Rewrite the American West*

Janie's Journal

Volume 5

2005-2009

Janie Tippett

Lucky Marmot Press

www.luckymarmotpress.com

Wallowa, Oregon

JANIE'S JOURNAL, VOLUME FIVE: 2005-2009
was originally published in the weekly Agri-Times NW.
These columns are collected here with permission of the publisher.

All photos were taken by Janie Tippett as part of her photojournalism for
Agri-Times NW, with the exception of Virgil Rupp on the adjacent page
and where noted in the captions. All photos are used with permission.
The cover photo was taken WHERE AND WHEN

ISBN 978-1-7334833-8-4 (paperback)
ISBN XXX-X-XXXXXXX-X-X (ebook)

Cover design by Jenner Hanni.

This volume was collected, digitized, edited, and published by
Lucky Marmot Press in Wallowa, Oregon.
https://www.luckymarmotpress.com

Cowgirls

Famous twins

(.) Sharon (R) Sherry Llewllyn Jane(R)
Gibson
Catherine ~~the~~

turnout the hills

heading to the hills

Crow Creek Road

~~almost to the~~

of the

East Crow Creek

almost to the

Dorance Place

A Wallowa County ranch from top of Sheep Creek Hill looking down to upper Prairie Creek under a layer of fog, Chief Joseph Mountain in the background.

2005

January 7—Here on Prairie Creek, where there's no buffer to the wind and it's 15 degrees outside, it doesn't feel much warmer inside. So, here I sit, sipping hot tea, scarf wrapped around my neck, long johns under my jeans, and a blanket draped over my knees, writing this column. I don't think they make a house tight enough to keep out that kind of wind, a wind that seeks ways to penetrate these scattered ranch houses.

My flock of chickens—hens still on strike—spend their days inside their house, which is airy enough to ruffle their feathers in this wind. I wonder what fowl find to talk about during these dark days of winter? "Ari" the Aracuna rooster arched his massive colorful neck this morning and crowed so loudly, it nearly broke my eardrums. I was just opening the door to toss a can of wheat on the straw-covered floor.

"Calm down," I said, "spring's months away."

No winter depression evident here: happiness is a can of wheat! Our older cows, the only ones we have left, hearing the sound of Ken's pickup, know their daily ration of hay, will soon be forked onto the surface of their sparsely snow-covered pasture. I watch the cows now, later in the day, traveling to and from the heated, automatic water trough.

Ken, Rowdy, Chad, and Doug, mounted on their quarter horses, gathered the cows in the hills last week. Those cows were ready to come home, but not so the bulls. Rowdy had to hunt them down. The herd made it to the holding pasture along the Crow Creek road that first day, and straggled on into the valley, arriving here at the ranch around 1 o'clock the next afternoon. Because the bulls were getting pretty footsore, Ken hauled them to the ranch in the cattle truck. I fed the "boys" hot soup and homemade bread, and visited with Rowdy about my milk cows.

"Wintering well, Grandma. Got the heifers nearly broke to lead."

"I still miss them," I said, "but not so much when the weather is this nasty."

On December 27, Phyllis and I decided to hike up Locke's hill and beyond, to a large, frozen pond, which turned out to be quite a long trek as we made our way over large clumps of bunch grass and scattered patches of hardened snow. Rewarded by a stunning view of the white-washed Wallowas and a herd of fleeing white-tails, we returned via a rocky draw to the ranch. The dutch oven of beans simmering with a ham bone on the old Monarch tasted good that night.

Doug and I had a pleasurable visit from 9-year-old grandson Ethan over the holidays. He gave us a jar of homemade cocoa he'd made himself, complete with the following directions: *Three tablespoons cocoa, stir in water, your done.* Ethan enjoyed helping me feed the chickens, but couldn't catch the wild kitten in the woodshed. The highlight of his visit to the ranch was a ride with grandpa on the four-wheeler.

Daughter Jackie's family arrived safely from Challis, Idaho, after visiting Buck and bride, Chelsea, in their home in Clarkston, Washington, on the way. I busied myself that day repeating another one of those prime rib dinners, after which I set out myriad leftover Christmas desserts.

Daughter Ramona's family didn't make it back from California in time for that second feast. They had hauled a steer clear to Lodi for great-grandson Clayton's 4-H project. Home again on upper Prairie Creek, Ramona reports her Suffolk ewes have begun to lamb. Thank goodness all of our children on the road over the holidays arrived home safely.

Of course it never ends: grandson James leaves tomorrow to return to college in Dillon, Montana. With him is Emily, who attends the same school. We invited James and Emily—who hails from St. Ignatius, Montana—over for supper the other evening. James had put in an order for blackberry pie and beef, so I pan-broiled the first of our homegrown sirloin steaks in a large cast-iron skillet on the wood stove. I'd spent the day baking french bread and the blackberry pie.

James had given Emily a tour of some of our wild country that day, so they really chowed down. Emily is a dairyman's daughter and majors in wildlife management, as does James. We always enjoy having young folks around. And, Wilmer, you'll be happy to know they played several rounds of checkers; it seems everyone who visits is drawn to your checkerboard.

Doug headed to the canyons this week to fish the Imnaha, and re-turned with a "keeper" steelhead, which he smoked in the shop. Mighty fine eating.

Last week I decided to walk off some of those holiday meals and ended up hiking around our country block—Tenderfoot Valley Road to Bicentennial Lane, south on Liberty Road, east on Bird Lane, north on Tenderfoot again—more than four miles. The afternoon was mild and the sun streamed between dark clouds. Snow squalls played over the mountains, but there was no wind.

Approaching a stubble field, I heard numerous babblings and realized the entire field was full of feeding ducks. I mean, the ground was dark with them. When the wild mallards detected my presence, they took to the air in squadrons of a hundred or so. As they circled the hill and the skies overhead, I heard that wild wind rushing through their wings, until, after I passed, they swept lower and lower and then fell back like leaves onto the stubble to resume feeding. What a welcome home, after such a long walk.

On New Year's morning Doug and I cruised Joseph's deserted main street searching for a place to eat breakfast. The Mountainaire's neon read OPEN so we walked in out of the cold and ordered platters of ham for Doug, sausage for me, and eggs served with homemade whole wheat toast. Soon others joined us, as the town woke up to begin a New Year.

Doug, who's been suffering from a bad cold, is better now, and back to joining the "boys" playing cribbage at the Range Rider. Sure glad he's on the mend, because it became my job to split and haul wood to satisfy the voracious appetite of our wood cook stove.

Phyllis called this morning, wanted to go for a walk or cross-country ski. My snow shoes wait patiently by the front door; haven't had enough snow to make it worthwhile. Kathy, just back from Alaska, calls also. Perhaps tomorrow I can take off through the snowy woods somewhere.

The good news is that a friend is helping me with my book about Imnaha Mary, and real progress is being made. Lately, every spare moment has been spent on that project, which is even more pleasant now, because of the gift of a new laptop word processor, my Christmas gift from Doug.

January 24—Seems eons away when Phyllis and I were making our way up the snowy road toward the Hurricane Creek trail head, she on skis, me wearing snowshoes. The day was bright and clear on that early January Sunday. Refreshed, I'd returned to bake a squash pie for the cowboys who arrived with the cows later that afternoon.

Monday morning Doug and I packed all our "stuff" into the van, and, in spite of dire weather predictions over the Sierra Nevada, we left the ranch, heading for California. No "Daisy dog" looking sadly at our departure. Ken would feed the cows and Ben would see to my chickens and feed the cats.

On our way out of the valley we breakfasted at the Lostine Tavern on a platter of ham 'n' eggs large enough to get us to Winnemucca. The roads were mostly cleared and we refueled ourselves with ice cream at Skinner's Rock House in Jordan Valley. After crossing the border into Nevada, somewhere between McDermitt and Winnemucca, snow fell like feathers from the desert skies.

After a family-style Basque dinner at the old Martin Hotel we retired to Scott's Shady Court for the night. Breakfast consisted of leftover ham and bread pudding eaten in the car. Several inches of new snow had fallen in the night. We headed to Reno and we made our way through narrow lanes, lined with banks of dirty snow, caught in the flow of terrifying traffic.

We zoomed to Boomtown, where we expected to spend the night. Then we noticed a flashing message: *All restrictions lifted over the summit...* and ran to our car to begin the ascent of the snowy Sierra. Bursts of sunlight between rolling clouds illuminated huge drifts of snow; snow that sculpted every rock and tree. Over the top, Donner Summit behind us, we descended the western Slope of the Sierras. Oak trees began to appear. The snow gone! Grass is green! We made our way into the foothills of my youth!

It was 65 degrees and the sun was shining. Doug let me out to walk the narrow county road that winds atop Hubbard Ridge to Fred and Sandra's. I breathed the springtime air, filled with the scent of rain, miner's lettuce, greening mesa and moist granite. After my ears popped, I heard the frog chorus sifting from the swamps.

And thus begins another California adventure. After spending that night above the fog, Doug and I move to Newcastle, guests of sister Caroline and husband, Duane. Here we are in the fog, which dominates our stay. Not to worry: our wheels take us to higher country, to the Mother Lode country in El Dorado County, and on to Auburn, where mom lives. The smile on my 94-year-old mother's face would light up the darkest of days. Noticeably cheered by our long-awaited arrival, mom simply beams.

We treated her to lunch that first day at Marie Callender's, and she savored every bite, taking frequent glances in our direction. The comfortable home mom shares with three other women is warm, clean and happy.

On our frequent visits we were impressed by Davika's' cooking, as well as by the friendly family atmosphere. The days following have been filled with activity, including long walks past early California-style homes built next to mansions, through quiet cul-de-sacs filled with ponds and citrus groves, where oak trees still thrive and quail inhabited a few wild areas where I discovered the first pussy willows. Narcissus grew wild there, and oranges, lemons and grapefruit hung heavy on the trees. Camellias, pansies, primroses and flowering quince announced the beginning of a California spring.

Sandwiched between their jobs, my three sisters treated me to all sorts of serendipity experiences, including four movies at the cinema— one at the old State Theater in Auburn; an elegant afternoon tea at a tea house in Newcastle, a Wilson family reunion at Lau LaBonte's, which included mom; two trips to Roseville Galleria, where this country girl gawked at a court yard filled with trees and bronzed animals, and Caroline and I spent an hour in Borders' Books, and Mary Ann and I had lunch at "Awful Annie's" in old town Auburn.

One day Doug and I drove out of the fog to Auburn, thence down to the American River, and followed the winding road up to the cool. Over the rolling hill country, steaming in sunshine, we drove to Coloma, where gold was discovered, and on to "Hangtown" and Placerville, which is located in El Dorado County.

We lunched on seafood at the "Steamer" and ambled up and down the sunny streets, perusing the shops. We looked into the oldest continuously operated hardware store west of the Mississippi, and crossed the street to "the Bookery," where I found an old copy of the collected works of Alfred Noyes I'd been searching for.

Spent one night with sister Kathryn—the one with the tangerine tree—and we walked the neighborhood, along a creek, down tree-lined streets where 15 turkey buzzards roosted for the night. The next morning we walked in the fog to Starbucks and sipped hot mocha.

Later, K.J. and I met chum Sandra at mom's and we lunched at a bistro in lower Auburn. Caroline and Duane never turn on the TV. We spend our evenings reading good books, and I've not missed it.

Yesterday Caroline and I drove mom to the old pioneer Manzanita Cemetery so she could visit the graves of her first husband, our daddy, and her second husband, Bill.

Although it was foggy and cold, there was a surreal beauty to the quiet oak grove, beyond which cattle grazed green fields and ponds held wild geese.

On the back roads to the ranch where we were raised, we spotted nearly 100 wild turkeys feeding on corns under the oak trees. A stop at our old ranch there in "Hungry Hollow" to visit my brother Jim and his wife, Joyce. Later that afternoon K.J. joined us and we drove to Forest Hill to visit Caroline's son and family. It was 70 degrees. Jeff gave me a 3-foot beaver he'd carved out of cedar with his chain saw.

On the way home, we parked at a trailhead and hiked a worn path maintained by the Bureau of Land Management that wound through oak trees, manzanita, madrone and Toyan berry. Across the canyon, studded with a thick growth of chaparral, we gazed at miles of steep country inhabited only by wild animals.

Suddenly, between the trees and down a steep hillside, we gazed at blue lake Clementine. Numerous mountain bikers, all polite and friendly, whizzed past us. The air was light and balmy, and the last rays of the sun lit up the Digger Pines.

And now, here at Caroline's in rural Newcastle, the skies have cleared of fog to reveal rain clouds. Doug is checking out the Thunder Valley Indian Casino and I must mail this hand-written column.

February 6—Home again. I've just returned from walking off the biscuits and gravy Doug and I shared at the Cheyenne Cafe this morning. A most refreshing hike it was, following fresh coyote tracks in fresh snow across the fields to Hough's hill, then wandering above an irrigation ditch where ice, resembling thin panes of glass, skimmed the water and broke in gentle cracks as the morning warmed.

Breathing in that clean, sage-scented air, I fondly recalled those final days of our visit to California. We had a memorable dinner at the Roseville Gourmet, with all four of my siblings and their spouses sitting at the same table. I recalled the clear, warm morning Doug and I took mom for a ride out in the country, to the old Fruitvale school where I used to walk to school in the first grade. No wonder I like to walk. I started early walking, in all sorts of weather, to and from where we lived at Clovertop Ranch to that one room schoolhouse.

"See those oak trees," I told mom and Doug. "Those are the same trees, bigger now, that the boys used to tie us girls to. Teacher would ring the bell after recess, and there we were, tied with ropes to the trees."

Nice to see the original building is being renovated, and used for a community meeting place. Peeking through the window, I could see the old blackboard still on the wall.

How mom loved that drive. There's nothing as green as that particular shade of Placer County's new grass, especially after all that rain. We took her to lunch at a tiny eatery called "Simple Pleasures," in our old hometown of Lincoln.

"You'd think I'd remember this place," mom commented, "but I don't."

"Not a wonder," I replied. "It's changed over the years." Indeed it has. The Stanford Ranch isn't sprawling ranch land anymore, it's the name given to an enormous housing development. And then there's Del

Web's Sun-City-Lincoln-Hills, not to mention the Thunder Valley Casino. Jansen's Feedstore is now specialty shops and cafes. Mom relished her turkey sandwich and ordered ice cream...her favorite food.

It was hard to say goodbye that next day, knowing it'd be awhile before we saw her again.

Hiking over the snowy hills this morning, lost in thought, I wondered if the amaryllis bulb I'd given mom was blooming yet, and if she gets out on the deck to soak up a little sunshine now and then.

When we were ready to pack up, I mentioned to Doug that we must save room for the "Beaver."

"Beaver? What beaver?" he said. "How big is it?"

"Three feet, carved out of cedar. My nephew Jeff gave it to me," I said timidly.

"We can't take that thing home," he said. But being the good hubby he is, he did make room, and now my beaver is in the shop waiting for the weather to warm enough to apply several coats of preserving oil.

After we moved back to Fred and Sandra's place, Sandra and I squeezed in one last movie at the old State Theater in lower Auburn, which turned out to be "Phantom of the Opera." Munching popcorn, sitting between Bev—another childhood chum—and Sandra, I was blown away by this marvelous production.

The next morning Sandra and I got in one last hike along Hubbard Ridge before Doug and I headed up and over the still snowy Sierras to lunch at Boomtown. I drove from Fernley through thick fog to Fallon, to visit the livestock auction, and thence to Winnemucca.

By next morning the fog had lifted, and the skies—and roads—remained clear all the way back to Wallowa County. After being in the midst of that clogged California traffic, it was very relaxing driving through eastern Oregon's high desert. We stopped in Rome for tea and coffee, and again in Jordan Valley for ice cream at Skinner's Rock House.

At dusk we pulled into Wallowa town, noting the absence of snow. We made our way past the bar of the Backwoods Saloon and into the dining room, where a dance hall girl mannequin sat atop a piano and antiques adorned the walls. The beef I ordered in Beef Country was tender and juicy. Kudos to the cook.

The big news back at the ranch, other than a total lack of snow on the valley floor, was my chickens laying! Must've heard rumors about those dumplings. I complimented Ben on taking such good care of my critters.

Ken is here each morning now to feed the cows on the hill. Sure good to have cows around again, with the promise of new calves not far off. Lately I've been dealing with all those squashes, raised in my Slope garden and stored in the root cellar. After baking them, I scoop out the sweet pulp and freeze it for future pies. There's nothing better than baked squash with brown sugar and butter.

Last Sunday Kathy and I drove to Imnaha to deliver several of those squashes to Mary and Lyman. The day was unseasonably warm, and I was able to photograph Lyman's big, healthy calves in that canyon setting.

Later, we lunched on home-canned tuna sandwiches and tea while observing a cow through the window, pacing around her enclosure. Stomach protruding, bag swaying, the old girl seemed ready to drop her calf. From their kitchen, Mary can keep an eye on the calving cows, which are put in a straw-filled pen with a heat lamp. This cow, however, didn't calve until a day or so later.

We so enjoyed our trip to Imnaha, which was a bit like California in that signs of spring were everywhere; in the reddening limbs of the osier dogwood, the tender green grasses, and in the balmy air itself. Mary tells us her snowdrops have already bloomed, and piles of manure are rotting into the rich soil of her garden.

On the way home, we turned up Camp Creek to visit Andy and have a cup of tea. Her chickens were enjoying the sunshine and scratching in a pile of straw. We ended up transporting—in a box—an Aracuna hen to add to Kathy's flock.

On Monday Carol Wallace, who lives on Trout Creek, and I served at the senior meal site in Enterprise for the CowBelles. Even though there are no more CowBelles, as such, a few of us carry on the tradition of community service.

February appeared on a frosty-clear, 15-degree morning, and I joined other members of our writing group at Fishtrap House for our weekly session, after which we met at "Friends" for lunch. It's also been back to work on the book, which has been sandwiched between the income tax.

Then there was an evening with the gals of "Stitch and Bitch," where we showed up bearing ingredients for pizzas. Later we tended to our knitting. Only I couldn't knit; so Sally put needles and yarn in my hands and showed me how...and now I take lessons from Lori in Enterprise on Tuesday nights. So, there we are, Liz, Lori and I, in a small shop, the only one lit up in our small town, which buttons up at 6 p.m. We did see one car go by.

Although I read voraciously, our winter evenings are long and knitting provides a nice diversion. It's just that when one is 71 and just learning, you feel like a klutz. The scarf I'm fashioning out of soft lavender Alpaca wool is a bit lopsided.

Kathy and I drove to Wallowa to pick up the old saw I'd left for local artist Eugene Hayes to paint a scene on. I wasn't disappointed. Gene had created several Maidu Indians harvesting and grinding acorns in a fall setting amid the oak woods I'd grown up with in Placer County, California. I'd taken him some photographs to work from. As children, we kids used to lay among the old "Indian Rocks," as we called them, with their grinding holes carved into the granite. The old rusted saw was found over 20 years ago by my father, not too far from one of these sites.

When we were leaving, I asked Gene, a native Wallowa Countian, if he remembered a winter this mild.

"1934," he replied.

On Thursday, I gathered ten residents of Alpine House around me and read them Alfred Noyes' poem, "The Highwayman." They were on the edge of their seats, and afterward recalled how they'd memorized poems so long ago in those one-room schools. Every Thursday morning we members of Fishtrap take turns reading in our local assisted living facility. This time I was surprised to see my neighbor Dorothy Waters among the newer residents.

Steelhead, lurking in the cold waters of the Imnaha, proved elusive to Doug when he stole away one day to test his luck. Now he is recovering from another one of those nasty colds. So a kettle of Thanksgiving turkey broth, frozen earlier, simmers on the wood stove.

Later I'll make egg noodles using an old recipe from a tattered cookbook given to me by Mary. Dropped in that meaty broth to cook, noodles and soup are still the best medicine.

February 20—If the *hoo... hoo... hoo*-ing of owls precedes a weather change, the noisy air in our willows were pretty accurate in predicting snow. Because that's what it did on the 13th: it snowed. Six inches. Which was followed by several clear, cold days when the thermometer didn't rise above freezing, and mornings when the mercury lodged near zero. Consequently, we still have snow, and a little more fell last night. So, now, Prairie Creek looks like normal calving weather.

As many as 14 bald eagles have taken up residence in the cottonwoods that line Prairie Creek south of Enterprise. Son Todd, who is calving out the Marr Flat cows on the Mt. Joseph Ranch, called the other morning to tell me about the eagles. Seems our national bird knows which ranches to stake out.

Below the snowline, which stays on the highest ridges, these cross-bred cows and calves, belonging to Lyman Goucher, enjoy nearly spring-like weather on the Upper Imnaha River.

Calving is well under way there, with the first babies arriving before the cold spell. Placentas provide easy meals for these birds of prey, who don't have to prey, but simply wait until patience pays off and a cow expels her meaty afterbirth.

Our cows grow big in the belly, and a few look as though they could drop a calf anytime. Now's when I miss my milk cows the most. Grandson Rowdy and wife, Kasey, sent photos last week of their varied menagerie, and there was "Hollyhock the Holstein," her nose buried in a hay feeder. Will she have twins this year? Suppose I'll have to make a run down to Mt. Vernon later to see my "offspring."

Doug and I had breakfast this morning at the "Mountainaire" in Joseph, and because of wolfing down a platter-sized hot cake, topped with whipped cream and blueberries, I've just returned from walking around our "country block," a four-mile jaunt over snow-covered country roads, past cow dogs that don't bite, ranchers—like Hank Bird—out feeding their cattle in snowy pastures, a black guard llama nibbling hay amidst Larry and Juanita Waters' flock of sheep; past the old Liberty Grange Hall, Hough's bellowing bulls, who are impatient to rejoin the girls, and past our own cows on the hill.

Closer to home, I identify the varied crowings of my three roosters, Ari the Aracuna, the chicken scramble Flash, and Fred's feather-footed Cochin.

On my daily walks I still find myself peering ahead, or behind, for my longtime companion "Daisy dog." She wasn't there to share the surprise of finding the first buttercups this year, the earliest I ever spotted them, high on a hill between patches of snow.

A week later, just before it snowed, Phyllis and I were on another one of our adventures, hiking the entire five-mile length of the east moraine. And there, on that steep boulder-strewn ridge, Phyllis exclaimed, "Lookee there!" and we stumbled into a patch of buttercups. The only ones we saw.

Wearing a film of ice, except where the channel flowed, the lake below gleamed dully. To the east, the blue-white Seven Devils reared their peaks to the sun, and far out on the Zumwalt rose the Buttes—Findley, Harsin and Brumback. Chief Joseph Mountain's massive bulk was mirrored in the open waters of the lake. Not an easy climb, but once we attained the top, the going was pure pleasure.

Nearly 40 mule deer, several bucks missing one antler and others wearing both, grazed across from us on the smaller second moraine. We were surprised to see the remains of an old bucking chute still standing in the natural bowl between the moraines. The crude rodeo chutes had been built back in 1946 to stage a rodeo that was held to celebrate the opening of the Joseph Airport.

That long-ago event was to become the forerunner of the now famed Chief Joseph Days annual rodeo.

The hike brought back memories of when Doug leased 1,600 acres, which comprised most of the east moraine as well as the slopes of Mt. Howard, to graze our fall-calving cows. I remembered all those years we'd spent up there on horseback gathering in the fall and turning out in June. I showed Phyllis where we'd held camp outs when I led my Sourdough Shutterbug 4-H Club. Now, all these years later, I look at a photo taken there on the moraine, of those kids, which included grandsons Rowdy and Chad, as well as Becky, Willie and Jenny, whose names come to mind.

On a recent evening, Doug and I attended the district wrestling tournament at Enterprise High, and although we didn't have any grand-children in school this year, Chad was one of the coaches. Time has a way of slipping by...

Doug finally whipped his cold and made numerous trips to the hills, reporting he'd seen up to 800 elk grazing the tender grasses emerging early due to our mild January.

Taking advantage of our new snow, Phyllis and I snowshoed and skied up Hurricane Creek last week. Great clouds of snow sifted from laden fir boughs, the sun held real warmth, and we were surrounded by clean, cold snow. Below, the creek wandered around snow-covered rocks, and the path of sky above was robin's egg-blue.

We had a surprise visit on Super Bowl Sunday. Buck and Chelsea stopped by on their way to visit friends Luke, Callie, and baby daughter Adeline, who live on Little Sheep Creek. Buck says he's halfway through calving, and Chelsea's nursing school is going great.

Received a long-awaited letter from granddaughter Adele, who is a Rotary exchange student spending eleven months in Argentina. Adele writes, *I was in the southern part of Argentina in the middle of a 19-day trip with 29 other exchange students (15 Americans, 7 Canadians, 3 South Africans, 2 Austrians, 1 Hungarian, and 1 Brazilian).*

After climbing on a large glacier, the guide set up a table, produced glasses, filled them with ice from the glacier (which was supposed to contain magic) and unpacked a box of bon bons. So there we were, in the middle of a glacier in Argentina, on Thanksgiving Day. I missed the turkey and mashed potatoes but WOW!

Adele just turned 17 the day before Valentine's Day.

Her brother James called from Dillon, Montana. "Happy Valentine's Day, grandma!"

"How's fishing?" I asked.

"Caught a five-pound trout," he said. James, majoring in wildlife management, loves his college...as well as the accessibility to good fishing streams.

Later that afternoon, Mary called from Imnaha. "Lyman's making a speed run to Joseph, he'll drop me off at your place soon."

"Great," I said, "You can stay for supper." And they did. While visiting Mary, I whipped up a kettle of shrimp linguine. Too bad Lyman didn't like the chocolate cake I'd baked in the shape of a heart, topped with cream cheese frosting and cherries. After three helpings, he gave up hoping it would taste better!

My sweetheart gave me a sentimental card, which was most appreciated, but to my embarrassment I picked out the same card I'd given him last year. Oops.

Yesterday, Phyllis had to get her annual "lamb fix," so we drove up to daughter Ramona's, where she hugged lambs to her heart's content. Ramona begins lambing her Suffolk ewes in January, which is lucky because that month was incredibly mild.

As it turned out, there were four generations out there in the lambing barn yesterday. Granddaughter Carrie arrived with great-granddaughter Brenna while we were there. Little Brenna was pretty wide-eyed when grandma Mona let her bottle feed a bummer lamb.

I've been working diligently on Mary's book and the long evenings are spent knitting and reading. Winter Fishtrap writer's conference begins Friday. See you next time.

March 8—This afternoon I seem to have a case of spring fever, which brings to mind words to the song, *And it isn't even spring.* Might not be spring by the calendar, but it sure is here on the ranch. Hawks nest in the tall cottonwoods by the creek, buttercups color the hills, 18 newborn calves sun themselves in our snow-less pasture, crocuses bloom alongside the house, blackbirds sing in the willows, and wild geese fly overhead, two by two. Clothes dry on the line, the wood stove (lit to take off the morning chill) has gone out, the bulls are still bellowing, and Doug is harrowing our fields.

We've had day after day of afternoons in the mid-60s, a few clouds forming but dissipating by nightfall. Star-filled, frosty nights give way to windless mornings so sun-drenched you have to squint and shade your eyes, or be blinded by the snowy mountains.

Such was the weather during our Winter Fishtrap Writers' conference. Folks traveling from faraway places were amazed. Sun streamed through the windows of the historic Wallowa Lake Lodge and dulled the frozen surface of the lake. It was a wonderful weekend as we explored the theme "The Tender Age: Remembering Childhood, and Nurturing Children," with our presenters Brian Doyle, Craig Lesley, and Tina Kotek; we all came away richer for the experience.

On a whim, Kathy and I decided to stay at the lodge. Why not? Just because we live in a beautiful area, doesn't mean we can't enjoy staying in places tourists travel miles to see. Our second floor room featured twin beds, a window facing north commanding a view of spacious lawns leading to the lake, and framed prints from a bygone era adorning the walls. Even though we were only a few miles from home, it didn't seem like it. Since I didn't have milk cows calving, and did have Doug to tend my chickens, I decided to go for it.

Staging the writers' conference at the old lodge was a first. In the past, we've crowded together in the small Eagle Cap Chalet's conference room, where our breakfasts and lunches were catered in and we got acquainted really fast by balancing plates on our laps and eating knee to knee with other attendees. Of course, for years, Mike and Maggie Vali served us their yummy pizzas on Friday night, and we would walk down to Russell's for dinner on Saturday.

What a treat to be seated at long tables in the spacious dining room. The food was elegant and plentiful. Wordsmiths work up appetites, and words mixed with well-prepared food is a winning combination.

Saturday morning found most of us seated in front of the old fireplace listening to Ellie Waterston, who gave us prompts to stimulate writing about this year's theme. And let me tell you, Ellie got the job done.

Sunday morning's open mic time was the highlight of the weekend. Dredged from the heart, these stories, read by our attendees, were most impressive. Returning home, it took a long walk around the ranch to recover from those stories. That evening I treated Doug to supper at the R. and R. in Joseph.

By Monday morning, reality had replaced remembering. Ken drove over from the Slope to feed the cows and tend their newborn calves. One cow, overdoing her protective motherability, attempted to tromp Ken into the ground, while another old girl grannied other calves.

Tuesday morning Ken came to the house for some colostrum I'd frozen from one of my milk cows. I wasn't surprised, as earlier I'd discovered calf at the far end of the pasture all by itself. As I'd suspected, it was a twin. And wouldn't you know, mama didn't have enough milk.

Playing "King of the Mountain," these Suffolk lambs romp during a sunny afternoon on Upper Prairie Creek. They are part of a flock owned by Ramona Phillips.

The old Eggleson barn is a familiar landmark on Highway 82, between Enterprise and Joseph.

Presently, all's going well. Certainly one couldn't ask for better calving weather, but we're all concerned over the lack of moisture. March came in like a lamb, and if things don't change it'll be going out the same way.

Wallowa County lost another one of its old-timers, Shorty Lathrop, a neighbor here on Prairie Creek. Shorty survived some pretty hard times in his youth, and gained the respect of many folks over the years.

Daughter Linda and her two boys, Jordan and Brady, showed up Friday evening and spent the weekend with us. Ken put Brady to work helping him feed, and even had him giving the baby calves their shots. Jordan spent most of the time on grandpa's quad. I spent a lot of time in the kitchen cooking.

Grandson James had called earlier in the week. "Hi, Grandma, I'll be home for spring break, bringing four of my friends with me. Been telling them about your pies."

"What kind do you want?" I asked.

"What about gooseberry and apple?" he asked.

"I'll do my best," I told him.

"Thanks, grandma, see you Saturday."

After he hung up, I went to the freezer and found one package of gooseberries and several packages of frozen apple slices. Then, when Jordan and Brady showed up, I decided to bake a large deep-dish peach pie.

How fun to see James' friends. Such nice young men, very polite and appreciative of my efforts. As were Jordan and Brady, when I cooked them a roast beef dinner and sent them back to Salem with sourdough waffles in their tummies.

Son Todd took advantage of those husky college boys and branded a small bunch of calves while they were here. Sure made short work of that. By the time I drove over to snap some photos, they were working the last calves.

Doug just came in from the fields, and I must prepare supper. Bye for now.

March 22—Two days past the vernal equinox finds us here on Prairie Creek feeling a bit more optimistic about the weather. The inch and a half of wet snow that fell Sunday night sure helped not only the land, but our spirits as well. Now if it would just continue. We're not particular what form moisture takes...rain, sleet, snow...but let it happen.

Sunday afternoon, on the first day of spring, I rode with Doug out to the hills. Never had we seen things so dry. No water in East Crow and Dry Salmon creeks, and the roads, normally full of mud holes, were dusty. No snowbanks to water the explosion of buttercups and emerging yellow cous. A fierce prairie wind blew across the lonely hills, sucking up whatever moisture there had been.

We were amazed that some of our ponds contained any water at all, but they did. Not enough to last the summer for sure, but some were half full. Doug unloaded his quad and took off to check those ponds we couldn't see from the road. After he disappeared into the vastness, I not only felt like the only person for miles—I was. Driving the pickup slowly to our buildings on Wet Salmon Creek, I remembered all the years we'd driven cattle over these roads, all those springs and late falls, in all kinds of weather. Waiting there for Doug, listening to the wind, I thought about how it must've been for those early homesteaders...how the sound of that wind defined the word loneliness. Save for the song of the meadowlark woven in the wind, there was no other sound.

Doug returned, only to leave again to inspect more ponds, and elk-damaged fences.

"Meet me at Deadman," he said. "I'll be gone quite a while."

Using my binoculars, I spotted our two horses, who appeared to have wintered well in this winter-that-wasn't. Growing from a mere speck on distant hill, Doug materialized. How welcome the soft motor sound of the quad...another person!

That first day of spring held surprises. Glassing the deep draw and undulating landscape, we saw no wildlife until sunlight on the tawny rumps of a moving herd of elk caught my eye. There they were, streaming up a draw to a high plateau, where they formed a wavering single file line. Above Pine Creek, heading south, we splashed through mud puddles and standing water. The ground was wet! The ponds were full. Apparently a rain cloud had cut a swath across the Zumwalt, leaving other areas dry. Wild mallards appeared to be nesting near some of the ponds. We spotted a smaller herd of elk, bedded down, oblivious to the wind.

Coming down OK Gulch, we noticed a hawk bravely defending her nest from several ravens.

In more than 50 miles of traveling that day, only one other rig did we see!

A couple of weeks ago Doug and I attended the Old Time Fiddlers Show in Cloverleaf Hall in Enterprise. There's just something about those folks who make this show happen that renews your faith in humankind. They don't make a big deal of it, no flashing lights or amplifiers or fancy clothes. But oh man, could they make music! Take Charley Trump for instance, the organizer, well into his 80s, and Lester Kiesecker (87?) out there waltzing the ladies, then climbing the platform to play his fiddle. So proud of his son and great-grandson, who also play the fiddle.

Lots of generations were there that night. The Samples family, and three generations of Dave Murrill's. Spencer Bacon, a beloved fiddle player from way out on Lost Prairie who is no longer with us, would have been proud of his grown grandson, Alan, that night. It was nearly 11 p.m. and there we were... still tapping our toes.

Ken is nearly through calving our little herd... down to the last 20 head or so. Although I still miss my milk cows, I've been getting my "baby calf fix" almost daily. This morning I went to the freezer and found a plastic bag of frozen colostrum marked "Stargirl 2004." It was comforting to know my old cow was, in this way, nurturing a calf that needed a little boost.

On my afternoon walks I love watching the calves romp around the pastures. I head south on Tenderfoot Valley Road and spot another sign of spring: a flock of newborn lambs running rampant in Waters' pastures. Cavorting about on a sunny morning, these lambs bring joy those of us lucky enough to be neighbors.

A week or so ago, Phyllis and I drove to the upper Imnaha and took Mary to her little house. It was our pleasure to not only visit Mary, but enjoy the sight of blooming daffodils, forsythia, and flowering quince, and discover her colorful primroses had made it through the winter. Phyllis and I unpacked our picnic, Mary made tea, and we visited over lunch in Mary's cozy kitchen.

"I'll be your neighbor soon," I said, after we left her off at Lyman's, "when I return to the Writers' Retreat in April." Spending time watching spring happen in the canyons is something I always look forward to. This time my goal is to emerge with Mary's book ready for the publisher.

It snowed a little on St. Patrick's Day and, naturally, there were calves born. I spent the day preparing the traditional corned beef/cabbage boiled dinner. Nine of us around the table that night. Thanks to Linda's Irish soda bread, Phyllis' apple pie, and Kathy's Irish bread pudding with whiskey sauce, we enjoyed a great meal. This, in addition to family and guests, who enlightened us on a diverse range of topics.

The same day my hens laid 10 eggs, the little Cochin rooster Fred gave me really went at it with Flash, the chicken scramble rooster. Feathers were flying until Ari the Aracuna, who rules the roost, broke it up. More signs of spring.

Before grandson James and his friend Kyle left to return to college in Montana, they stopped by for lunch. And then granddaughter Mona Lee was here for a roast beef dinner Saturday night. All our grandchildren

This pet fawn grew up on the Fluitt ranch on upper Prairie Creek. It's right at home with the cattle as it nibbles on a wild rose bush.

live such busy lives these days, it's very special when they take time to visit. Must serve up the beef barley soup I made from that leftover roast...looks like it could snow again tonight. Hope it does.

April 4—The dusting of spring snow we awoke to this morning has completely evaporated. Retreated, just like spring has. Actually, what we are experiencing weather-wise now is typical of April. Icy winds, snow squalls often shot with sunlight, low clouds over the mountains, and occasional patches of storm-scoured blue sky. Since my kitchen window affords a view of Upper Prairie Creek, I can see the snow-line, which begins below the timbered slopes of Ferguson Ridge and the McCully Creek drainage, up there in the vicinity of where Chuck and Chris Frazier live.

I suppose if a person must be sick, this period of "un-spring" would be the time. 'Cause that's what I've been. Sick...ten days sick with whatever bug has been making the rounds. When I finally realized my pneumonia-like symptoms weren't going away, I went to see the doc (a she) who informed me I had a very bad case of bronchitis.

So I canceled all those dates on my calendar, took my pills, drank gallons of water and canned soup, put my feet up, and (when I wasn't having a coughing fit) read. Boy did I read...finished three books. Of course I staggered around and prepared meals, washed clothes, and made weak attempts to clean house. Cleaning, I must admit, was very low on my list of priorities, while up at the top was getting well. This is important—one of those dates I canceled was leaving yesterday for the Writers' Retreat on the upper Imnaha. Although that aggravating cough is still with me, I feel much better today. Otherwise, this column would have joined my list of cancellations.

No hikes to describe this time; no adventures other than the ones I read in books. Due to the "spring-like" weather I've only ventured outside the confines of the house twice. Consequently, I spent a good deal of time peering out the windows. This morning I spied a coyote trotting across Locke's field, the snowy wind blowing his tail. Yesterday several Rufus-sided towhees pecked around under the raspberry canes. And then there's always drama of some sort unfolding down in the calving pasture. I watch Ken feed his pickup load of hay to the cows and toss hay to the bulls.

My son informs me that grandson Rowdy says my cows—Hollyhock the Holstein and her daughter, Flora—have calved. Sure would love to see those babies.

Every morning, Doug tends my chickens and leaves me plenty of

*The only cows left on the Tippett Ranch on Prairie Creek much their break-
fast. These cows began calving in March.*

split wood for the cook stove before heading into his "office" at the Range
Rider. Later, when he returns for lunch, he'll climb on the tractor and
resume his job of "feeding the gophers."

Mary and I send each other sympathy and encouragement over the
Imnaha phone line. She is also suffering from this bug, complicated by
asthma.

"Get well," I say. "I'm leaving Friday for the canyons."

Looked out the window just now to see a mini-blizzard sweep across
Prairie Creek, flakes of snow swirling in the wind. Cuddle up to your
mamas, baby calves and lambs.

Out here in the country the mail is always looked forward to, but
lately it's broken the monotony of my housebound existence. One afternoon Doug came in with a large manila envelope that contained an
advance copy of Jane Kirkpatrick's latest book. Fans of Jane's will enjoy
this novel, entitled *A Land of Sheltered Promise*, which was inspired by
true stories of the Big Muddy Ranch.

The book is divided into three sections that take the reader back to
1901 and a story of a sheepherder's wife, followed by the era of Rancho

Rajneeshpuram and ending with a woman's dream in 1997. This is a good read for book groups, and in the back of the book Jane has included an "author discussion and questions for reflection." Our book group looks back fondly on the time we traveled to Jane's "homestead" on the John Day River. Jane has intimate knowledge of the country she writes about, because she lives there.

Another mailbox treasure was the package that arrived from my sister Mary Ann, who attended the photography conference "Shooting the West" in Winnemucca last month. Because I opted to stay home this year, to work on Mary's book, I was interested to hear how it went.

"You would have loved the presenters," M.A. told me. "I purchased Richard Menzies' new book for you." Menzies is not only a fabulous black and white photographer, he is a great writer. He has combined those talents and produced a book he calls *Passing Through,* wherein he has documented a few of Nevada's eccentrics who live in some of the most desolate places in the West. Fascinating reading and the best medicine for anyone suffering from bronchitis.

Yesterday there was a knock at the door. My Upper Prairie Creek neighbor Bernice handed Doug a container of homemade chicken soup and rice. "For Janie," she said. At noon, I especially appreciated that act of neighborly kindness, as today was the first time I could taste again. The soup was delicious.

April 26—All night long, the April moon (the pink moon, so named for the pink flowers, like the wild phlox that blooms in our hills and canyons this time of year) illuminated Prairie Creek. Perhaps it was the pull of this moon that triggered the birth process in our late-calving cows. Cows calved within minutes of each other, shortly after dawn. Through binoculars I beheld both births through our bedroom window. No matter that I have witnessed many births during my lifetime, it's still a miracle.

In our valley, after winter, and seemingly endless days of unspring, another miracle is the coming of SPRING. I mean, it's so dramatic! Like this morning here on Prairie Creek, where the air is soft, and the warm sun, rising over Hough's hill, burns away the mists that trail above the greening cow pastures. Where killdeers skitter this way and that, loudly protecting their nests; where daffodils bloom, hawks sit patiently in high stock nests, and Doug complains that the lawn needs mowing.

On such a morning, it takes all the discipline I can muster to sit down and write this column. I ache to be out and about. After eight days of coughing I began to heal, and by the following Monday I was back to working on Mary's book, attending our weekly writer's group, and packing up to leave for the Writer's Retreat on Imnaha.

What a joy to have my car loaded and headed for the canyons. Who cared if it was snowing all the way from Sheep Creek Hill to Lightning Creek. The Sarvis berry was in bloom, and at the confluence of Big Sheep creek there was a fresh new greenness on alder, dogwood and willow.

Before I reached the store it began to rain. I could feel the bunch grasses responding to the soft April showers as I continued my way up river to Lyman's where I pulled in to deliver milk and eggs to Mary.

Later, as I pushed by cart across the swinging bridge that spans the Imnaha, I noticed the river was up. Although the first group of writers had left that morning, the gals had left a fire in the wood furnace, so the house was warm and cozy. I settled in, set up my word processor, and went to work.

Through the rain I gazed upward to the highest rims, cloaked in misty clouds that hid a dusting of snow. Cherry trees were just a froth of white blooms above brilliant yellow sprays of forsythia; pink flowering quince, red tulips and orange Crown Imperials added their colorful accents to my green world. Spring had sprung on the Imnaha. The river swirled around the bend, birdsong filled the air, and two wild turkey hens suddenly appeared in my line of vision.

I went right to editing the final chapters of my book, working straight through the afternoon until 4:30 at which time Diane Josephy Peavy appeared in the door way. That evening the two of us dined on baked potatoes with all sorts of creative toppings Diane had purchased in the big CITY of Boise, Idaho.

The next day Cheryl Roberts and Kathleen Dean Moore arrived. I fixed a hearty ranch supper consisting of roast beef, mashed potatoes, gravy, and baked squash harvested last fall from my Slope garden. After Kathy Hunter showed up, we were five around the dinner table that evening.

There followed over a week of intense writing, broken only by short walks whenever the sun came out, and often when it did not. Even as spring continued to burst forth all around us, the rain began to thicken and soon it was snowing! Through the window above my word processor, I loved watching those fat flakes as they floated down and landed on white cherry blossoms. Mostly though, the snow line stopped short on the rims above Indian Creek. The weather remained on the cool side, which was conducive to writing.

Since I was the Retreat "Mom" and in charge of stoking the wood furnace, I was most grateful when Chuck Roberts, Cheryl's husband, arrived with a sharp maul and later departed having left us a stack of split wood and kindling. Thank you Chuck!

Doug called one afternoon.

"Why don'tcha meet me at the Store and Tavern for the oyster feed tonight."

So…I did, driving the 14 miles down river to join my husband over a platter of Sally's fried oysters. At that lower elevation it was dry and balmy, and on my way back, just as the last of that golden April light lingered on the eastern rims, I spotted a small herd of elk grazing a green field alongside the road. At that hour, it seems most of Imnaha's wildlife was out and about. I saw wild turkeys as well as numerous deer. My tummy full of oysters and my senses filled with the magic of spring on the upper Imnaha, I fairly skipped across the bridge and back to work.

I must say it was a treat spending time with Kathleen Dean Moore and Diane Josephy Peavy. Diane, the daughter of Alvin Josephy, has written a book entitled *Bitterbrush Country,* wherein she has compiled essays written about the ranch life in Carey, Idaho. Diane and her husband John operate a large sheep and cattle operation.

Kathleen, the well-known author of *The Pine Island Paradox* and *River Walking,* is the chair of the Department of Philosophy at Oregon State University. You can see I was in the company of very stimulating writers. Both gave me much-needed encouragement on my book.

By Sunday everyone had left except for Kathleen. She would be spending another week. Packing up my "stuff" was hard to do, but I worked on my project until the four new writers arrived. It was their first time for all of them, and it was a glorious day. Among them were Molly Gloss, who wrote *Jump Off Creek,* and former Joseph English teacher Betty Husted, author of *Above the Clearwater.* After they were settled in, I unplugged by word processor, and pushed it and my manuscript across the bridge to my car.

On my way out that afternoon, I stopped to say goodbye to Lyman and Mary, who convinced me I should stay for supper.

"I'm broiling salmon," said Lyman. How could I refuse? Mary and I fried up some spuds and we had us a nice visit before I headed up "on top."

Leaving the canyons behind, I topped out on Sheep Creek Hill, where the sight of those snowy mountains always takes my breath away. Prairie Creek, spread out below, had greened in my absence. Let me tell you, I highly recommend spending a week without a TV, newspaper, or radio, and with very limited use of the phone. It restores your soul.

Last Saturday, on my way to deliver a grocery order to the Imnaha Retreat, I stopped to pick up Mary and take her to her little house upriver from Lyman's. After delivering the groceries to the writers, I returned to help Mary. We spent all morning working in her yard, pulling up dead marigolds and cosmos, raking, pruning, and hauling it off. What fun it was, working with Mary, who will be 88 next month and who continues to provide the needed inspiration for my book.

Later, after a cup of tea and a piece of cake with Mary and Lyman, I was heading up Sheep creek when I remembered the stack of magazines in the back seat that I'd been saving for the Moores who live up Bear Gulch. So I drove in and had a great visit with Myrna and daughter Jennie. Just as I was leaving, Melanie McCadden drove in with her two kids, Alex and Will.

"Is this where the branding is?" And right away I knew she was looking for Big Sheep, so I said, "I know the way. I'll show you."

Not only did I show Melanie the way, I jumped in with her and the kids, as she was driving a high clearance rig, and as a result I spent the rest of the day at the branding my son Todd had organized up the canyon of the Big Sheep. I wouldn't have missed it for the world. Kids everywhere. Border collie dogs, their tongues hanging up, happy like the kids. Cowboys honing their skills; heeling calves, the smell of burning hair, the ground crew, which included many of those youngsters, full of friends and neighbors lending a helping hand.

Daughter-in-law Angie, with help from Melanie and Charlene, were in charge of the food. After the last calf was worked and burned out to join the herd of bawling mamma cows, Angie bar-b-cued hamburger and fed everyone.

All through that April afternoon, clouds periodically spilled a few light showers which were followed by bursts of sunlight. No one seemed to mind. There, in that magnificent canyon setting, seeing those families working and joking together makes me both happy and sad. Sad because all over the West the old traditions are fading. We're seeing it happen with increasing frequency lately, every time a large corporation buys out the family ranch. But I was happy that some of these young folks cling to the old ways simply as a way of life. The only pay those neighboring cowboys received that day was the satisfaction of helping a friend...as well as their obvious enjoyment of participating in preserving a way of life they love.

Young and pretty Alex McCadden summed it up best, as her mom drove me back to where my low clearance car was parked. "I guess my most favorite thing in the world is going to be branding," she said.

April 27—Oldest son Ken is keeping another tradition alive. He and his sons will start trailing out cows and calves to the hills tomorrow. And last evening, at the Outlaw restaurant, Doug and I were selected as the Grand Marshals of the 25th annual Hells Canyon Mule Days to be held September 9-11, 2005, at the Wallowa County Fairgrounds in Enterprise, Oregon. Ya all come! They say Doug and I will be leading the "non-motorized" parade.

April 29—Son Ken and grandson Chad started the cows and calves to the hills today. The day was cloudy and cool, ideal trailing weather. Great for walking, too, which is what I did. Nine miles on foot behind those cows and calves. Well...that is, I stayed behind them for a mile or so, until the herd's pace quickly outdid mine. Every so often, I'd glimpse Ken and Chad on horseback as they disappeared over a distant hill. No matter, I loved waking alone, taking time to enjoy the country.

Actually, I wasn't alone. I was thinking about all my years on horseback, riding alongside Ben or Mike McFetridge, and later, Sherry, Sharon, and Sandy, our cowgirls, as well as more recent times when I was on foot and pushing those tired little calves out of the borrow pits. That was work. Today, however, I traveled with memories, savoring the sounds of the meadow lark, the smell of bruised new grass, and the silence of the hills. Walking along I realized how my faithful old dog Daisy must've felt that day she joined a herd of cattle being driven to the canyons. Even though she could barely walk, my faithful little dog couldn't resist doing what she loved most.

Folks passing by today must have wondered at this old grandma, lagging so far behind that bunch of cows and calves. Our old cows knew where they were going, and Ken held them up often so they'd "mother up," and since their calves were strong and healthy, they traveled right along.

Since we'd gotten an early start this year, the herd made it to the corrals at the old Circle M before noon. Noon, however, came and went for me, still walking that long stretch past Birkmaier's. At the nine mile mark I glanced back to see the trail of dust from an approaching rig, which turned out to be Doug. A welcome sight, as the sack lunch I'd put together that morning was in his pickup.

Joined by Chad's wife, Amy, and two of my great-grandchildren—two-and-a-half-year-old Ronan and year-old Gwenllian—we all picnicked there at the old corrals where the cattle would spend the night...as would the cowboys and their families. A camp trailer was parked nearby for their use.

"Better join us," said my son.

Wishing I were younger, I declined, knowing I needed a hot soak in the tub, after which I'd only have enough energy left to fix supper and turn in early if I was to renew myself for the final lap.

April 30—Early the next morning found me driving our pickup out that long road, searching for the cows and calves. I caught up with the herd near East Crow. Climbing up on a bank, I photographed them just beyond where we used to overnight the cattle. But this year East Crow was dry. I remembered all those wet springs when water filled the creek, as well as a nearby pond, so our cattle, along with the horses we left there overnight, could water up. After driving on ahead, I left my pickup parked at the old Dorrance place and began hiking up the grade.

It was a lovely morning and I was relieved to know I wasn't sore from yesterday's hike. In fact, I felt invigorated by what lay around me; those greening hills, mule deer does and fawns staring at me from a cluster of ponderosa pines, the whistle of a rock chuck below the road, birdsong, and a pair of red-tails circling overhead.

As I neared the top, where I'd planned to photograph the cowboys and the herd making its way up the hill, a sudden wind nearly blew away my hat, and great clouds rolled around above me. Looking back, I was disappointed to see the distant Wallowas were obscured by low clouds. Not wanting to get caught in a thunderstorm, I hurried over the top and started down the winding road toward an old loading chute which would provide shelter in the event of rain.

Just as suddenly as it materialized, the storm swept away. The sun came out and the vast rolling prairie lay before me. My heart was gladdened by the sight of pink grass widows and patches of phlox. Yellow cous blanketed the scab rock, and lush bunch grasses waved in the breeze. Greenwood Butte loomed beyond, and I savored those miles of rockjack fences that enclose that familiar landscape we call "the hills."

As I approached Dry Salmon Creek—normally wet this time of year; bone dry this day—I glimpsed the lead cows making their way down the road. It was a good time to rest against a rock jack, take off my pack, and capture a shot of my grandson, son, and great-grandson Ronan, who waved at me from the saddle, perched in front of grandpa. Also a good time to eat lunch.

After walking a bit farther, I opted to ride ahead with Amy and the children to open the gate and head the cows and calves into Deadman.

Then it was back to the valley ranch to resume my life. Looking back at the photos I took that day, I realize my son Ken made an effort to give to his family those experiences that will create memories for them. Memories of a lifestyle that is fast fading.

May 8—Mama kitty's four kittens have their eyes open now, my mare Morning Star is grazing the horse pasture, Doug's brother Biden's steers and heifers are pastured on the other side of the ranch, my hens are laying well, the rhubarb is ready to pick, and I got a nice letter from grandson Rowdy in today's mail.

Grandson James stopped by the other day. Home for the summer from college, he'll be going to work on a fire crew soon.

Spring is such a busy time for Wallowa County.

Last week Ann Hayes, curator of the Wallowa County Museum, joined me at Alpine House when I read to some of the residents. It was good to visit with Irene McFetridge and Kate Wilde, both ranch wives who love to recall those earlier years. Irene told me she enjoyed walking behind their cows, and how she missed that life. Kate remembered the years she cooked up Big Sheep Creek. She still misses her husband, Will.

What precious old-timers we have.

Later, after a brown bag lunch, I helped Ann with some displays in the Nez Perce room at the museum, which will open Memorial Day weekend.

Then there was the annual meeting of the Alder Slope Pipeline Association, held this year at the newly remodeled home of Ted and Sue Juve. Good to visit my old neighbors, including Wilmer Cook.

On Friday two of my sisters, Kathryn and Caroline, and C's husband, Duane, will arrive from California for a visit. That means I must clean house. Thank goodness it's raining or I'd be out mushrooming. They ought to really pop up now when the sun comes out.

I called Mary the other day and told her how busy I was, meeting myself coming and going, but the book was coming along. She said Dave Warnock used to say, "Never holler whoa in a bad spot." Enjoy your spring.

May 9—There is a wet heaviness in the air this morning. Prairie Creek seems to be waiting for something to happen. Our mountains are swathed in low, moisture-laden clouds. It is warm, and earlier, when I ventured out to feed the chickens, wisps of steam curled above the bare ground in the garden. It is a time for growing and greening. Clover is lush, tender leaves are sprouting on the Northwood maple, apple blossoms are bursting through their buds, and the ancient willows that line out irrigation ditches wear halos of the softest green.

Dark purple clouds merge silently overhead, and our local radio announcer just issued flash flood warnings. This absolutely calm, green morning is in complete contrast to the dryness we've been experiencing—that is, were experiencing until a week ago, when it POURED. Wonderful life-giving rain.

We had just read in our local paper that our county had been declared a drought disaster area. And rightly so. Ponds in the hills are only half full, creeks which normally run this time of year are dried up, and great clouds of dust swirled skyward as we drove the Crow Creek Road. Dry winds sucked up whatever moisture there was. You could read the same story on every rancher and farmer's face.

But that's Wallowa County! Where, it is said, only newcomers and fools predict the weather. And if you don't like the weather, wait around 20 minutes and it'll change. Also, don't go anywhere, even in summer, without your coat. At any rate, those of us who make our living from the land are smiling at the moment.

Yesterday was a memorable Mother's Day. It began with Doug treating me to breakfast at the Mountain Aire Cafe in Joseph, where, it appeared, many other locals had the same idea. Returning to the ranch, Doug filled his thermos with coffee and headed for the hills to check on things: cows and calves, fences, elk, grass, ponds, and bulls. I would have loved to have gone with him, but opted to take advantage of the quiet, and finish editing the last chapter of my book.

As the Prairie Creek wind was blowing ok and my clothes would dry on the line, I started up the washer. While working on Mary's book, wherein she writes in her diary, *My washer quit me today,* I heard a dreadful noise coming from the service porch. You guessed it: that 30-year-old washer died...DEAD.

On Mother's Day yet. Of course, I had to call Mary, and we had a good laugh.

Now, at 9:30 a.m. the silence has ended. A steady downpour of rain pummels our roof and pools in our lane.

Our children and grandchildren showered me with visits, gifts, cards, flowers, phone calls, and love. And guess what? I was able to finish editing that last chapter of the book.

Doug returned late that evening from the hills. He'd spent Mother's Day repairing elk-damaged fences, driving an errant bull back to his pasture, and checking out those ponds, which have improved considerably due to the rain.

May 10—Doug just returned from his cribbage game to announce he was headed for La Grande to purchase a new washing machine.

May 23—This morning's air is saturated with birdsong—swallows, robins, sparrows, killdeer, meadow larks and starlings, who have apparently emerged from wherever birds go when it's raining. They have lots to sing about. The sun is shining after a moonlit night, and even though the clover is coated with frost, our snowy mountains are visible again, rising into a storm-scoured sky. It's enough to make anyone burst into song. Especially since we've been living in a watery green world for so long. No complaints, you understand.

Our ponds are now full, those dry creeks are running, and if you don't stand back the grass will engulf you. Two rhubarb pies cool near the open kitchen window, we savored our first feed of tender green asparagus from the garden last evening, and my friends say the woods are full of morels. Biden's yearling steers are grazing the high grass that's threatening to strangle the machinery yard—my milk cows used to have this job. My little "chicken scramble" hen is setting, and the lilacs are bursting into bloom. The Prune Plum tree son Todd gave me for Mother's Day can now be planted and, hopefully, it'll dry out enough to till the garden.

The new washing machine was installed in time to launder rugs before the Californians arrived, and Doug, just back from his cribbage game, is cleaning out the shop.

On Friday the 13th, around 4:30 p.m., sister Kathryn called.

"Hi sis, we're in Marsing, Idaho, don't wait supper, we're stuffed…had hamburgers and ice cream in Rome."

"See you in about four hours," I said, and hung up.

Since Ken had scheduled a branding the next morning, I'd spent the day cooking. A humongous macaroni salad chilled in the bunkhouse frig, a large ham baked slowly in the oven, and a rhubarb pie reposed on the kitchen table.

Travel-weary, with barely enough energy left to rave about their scenic trip into the Wallowa Valley, the trio arrived around 8 o'clock. I fed them ham and macaroni salad before they fell into bed.

Arising early, my sisters and I made some cookies, fruit and plenty of water, and headed for the "hills." As we made out way out the Crow Creek road, rain clouds gathered and thickened.

My sisters, raised on a small dairy farm in the foothills of a very rural California back in the 40s and 50s, reveled in the vastness of Wallowa County's outback. Accustomed now to freeways and throngs of people, they loved being out on that high grassy prairie where mule deer does, heavy with fawn, stared at us from a thorn brush thicket below Dorrance grade. They gazed off across the miles of silent, wildflower-strewn hills to Greenwood Butte, and beyond to the timbered fringes of the Chesnimnus country. We only passed one rig—a rancher—in over 20 miles.

By the time we pulled into the ranch on Wet Salmon Creek, the cowboys had already corralled the cattle and were sorting calves from cows. Doug and Duane had gone ahead of us in the pickup, and Duane was busy snapping photos. Grandson Chad, wife Amy and two children Ronan and Gwenllian were there as was son Todd and wife Angie.

To free Amy to work with the ground crew, Kathryn and I each took a child...at which time, it began to rain a warm spring rain, good for the country and miserable for branding. Retreating to the old barn, we perched on long wooden planks to view the action taking place in the adjacent corral. In light of the persistent rain, the decision was soon made to drive the calves into the barn, where, hopefully, their hides would dry out enough to accept a brand.

Two Great Horned owls peering down at us from high rafters, not in the least concerned with cowboys and kids. Unlike the owls, the children took flight. So there we were, three white-haired sisters with babies on our hips, traipsing through mud, wet grass, and rain to open up our old house. Whereupon we kindled a fire in the wood cook stove, put on a pot of coffee, and played with my great-grandchildren.

Meanwhile, the crew (getting muddier by the minute) carried on with the branding. Presently, daughter Ramona and son-in-law Charley, along with granddaughter Carrie and daughter Brenna arrived, bearing a large potato salad and bags of chips.

"Where's Annie?"

"She's bringing fried chicken, beans and cake, she should've been here by now," said Ramona. And then we realized it had been over 20 years since Annie had been to Wet Salmon creek. One wrong turn, and she'd be clear out to Billy Meadows, which—we found out later— was precisely what happened. Frustrated and confused, our Annie had returned to the old Dorrance Barn and waited until Todd and Angie, on their way home, found her there.

Of course, another picnic was in order. Although we'd brought along enough to feed the hungry crew, Todd told Annie her fried chicken was mighty welcome. And wouldn't you know, just as the last calf was branded, the sun came out and that rolling green prairie was bursting with wild things. Taking a walk, Caroline surprised a pair of wild geese and their family of goslings; and at the edge of the meadow she was "dive-bombed" by a parent hawk protecting her nest of babies in a nearby Hawthorne. The willows along the creek erupted with Red Wing Blackbirds.

Driving back as great cloud-shadows raced across the hills, I reflected on our day. How I'd enjoyed spending time with little Ronan, the two of lying on the old wooden bridge, staring down at the swimming minnows and skittering skaters, just as I used to do with my own sons and their sons. Despite the rain, the day had proved to be an "Adventure" for my sisters, and the ride back to the valley ranch was incredible, what with the Wallowas visible again, all bright with fresh snow behind those green pastures sprinkled with dandelions.

That evening we were pleasantly surprised by a visit from grandson Buck and bride Chelsea, who had driven over from Clarkston to attend another branding. We talked them into staying for supper. You guessed it...ham, macaroni salad, and rhubarb pie.

Sunday morning I served our guests fried "mountain oysters," scrambled eggs and hot cakes for breakfast. And that evening found nine of us, including Doug, Todd and Angie, plus Mary and Lyman, seated in the dining room of the Imnaha River Inn Bed and Breakfast, enjoying a birthday supper for Lyman. The surprise had been weeks in the planning and was mostly thanks to Mary, who managed to pull it off by telling lies to get him there, Lyman didn't have a clue.

Hosts Nick and Sandy Vidan has gone out of their way to make our time there pleasurable. No matter that it rained, the canyons in May are lovely. Sandy had baked a cake, with candles yet. We dined on roast Cornish game hens, salad, rice, sweet carrots, and homemade rolls. Later we relaxed on the deck, staring down at the rising river and up toward the mist-covered rim rocks that rose before us like tiered wedding cakes.

After everyone left—my sisters, Duane, and I would spend the night—we settled in our rooms upstairs. Caroline and Duane had the room with the fishing theme, while Kathryn and I chose the Bear Den. The rooms were decorated accordingly. This enormous log structure, beautiful in every detail, made us feel like we were in Yellowstone, not Imnaha. Last fall, I'd called in the winning bid for an overnight stay at this Bed and Breakfast during the 4-H auction.

It rained all night and by morning the river was a roiling froth of malt-colored water. Logs and other flotsam spun past as we watched from the deck. After a ranch-style breakfast, the rain ceased long enough for a walk downriver, where we enjoyed the blooming arrowleaf Balsamroot, baby burro, chukars, and deer that were out enjoying the brief respite from the rain.

Returning, we were treated to a rare sight: two Wild Mountain Sheep ewes, their lambs cavorting about on a high ledge. All this we viewed through out binoculars from the deck. The evening before, we'd spotted four wild turkey gobblers on the opposite side of the canyon as they flew to roost in tall cottonwood trees.

Reluctantly we left the Imnaha River Inn with its blooming iris, spacious lawns, and rustic log rooms. Raining again, pouring actually, as we drove up Sheep Creek, we stopped to share a cup of tea with the Moores at Bear Gulch.

That evening I fixed a kettle of chowder using more of that leftover ham, corn, potatoes and onions, and the next morning Doug, Duane and Caroline came down with colds. We had scrambled eggs and ham for breakfast, and Kathryn put a pot of beans to simmer for supper, adding the ham bone, of course. Later I baked a batch of biscuits in hopes they would revive the sickies, and it did seem to help. We all joked about how many meals we'd gotten out of that ham.

My sisters and Duane left early Wednesday morning. Their visit was too brief, but they had jobs waiting at home.

On Saturday I traveled to La Grande to attend great-granddaughter Brenna' second birthday party. What fun to see two more great-granddaughters Riley Ann and Ashlynn, as well as young Ronan, who all arrived with grandma Annie. As one busy day melts into another and I close this column, I can hear Doug roto-tilling the garden.

June 15—If we weren't living in such a green world, you'd think it was March. That is, with the exception of last March, when the weather was considerably warmer than it is now. As I write, a cold rain drenches an already soggy Prairie Creek. Looking out the living room window, I see mama kitty, who's been hunting squirrels, run for shelter.

Hough's black cattle are moving north, bunching up along the fence line, while the horses, their heads down and rumps to the wind, endure the cold soaking. The lilac bush, laden now with fragrant blooms, droops, and our pipe changers must be soaked. In spite of these earlier rains, our pastures began to dry out after the sun and the Prairie Creek winds sapped most of that moisture from the ground. It's time to irrigate. Consequently, no matter the rain, irrigation, once begun, continues.

Doug says irrigating does the most good when it's raining. Pipe changing time significantly alters our lifestyle. Whereas Doug normally leaves early of a morning for town, to play cribbage with the "boys", he now dons his hip boots and takes off on the four wheeler to the far corners of the ranch. He'll return for breakfast anywhere from 7:30 to

9:30, depending on if he has troubles with the pump.

Lately, it's been so cold I've been fixing breakfasts on the wood cookstove, which simplifies things. I keep the sausage and bacon hot in the warming oven, and only fry hot cakes when I see the whites of his eyes. Same deal at night. Never know when to start supper.

Last night I was cooking elk steaks, mashed potatoes and milk gravy at 8:00 o'clock. Now, at 3 :00 o'clock, as sunlight streams through a break in those heavy clouds, the bright new leaves on the Northwood maple glisten with raindrops and there are "whiskers" on the mountains.

Son Todd, who'd been checking cattle on the Divide, just stopped by. "Four inches of hail up there" he said.

Snow fell in the night and frosted the forested slopes above upper Prairie Creek, but thankfully the tomato plants I set out last week didn't freeze. Doug's garden's all in, and last Saturday I worked all morning planting mine on Alder Slope. It was a perfect morning to plant. That black soil was warm and friable, and I loved getting dirt under my fingernails again. Once a gardener, always a gardener.

Daughter-in-law Angie's border collie bitch had just given birth to six puppies. These puppies are descended from some of Wallowa County's top cow dogs. In the pasture next to the garden, Mika's new, dun-colored horse colt dozed in the sun, and Redwing Blackbirds sang in the adjacent swamp. Whenever I chose to look up, there was old Ruby Peak, her snow fields gleaming above those evergreen slopes.

On the way home I stopped at the Alder Slope nursery, where Randy and Pam traded me snapdragons for sourdough starter, along with my recipe for pancakes. Can't beat a deal like that!

We celebrated Mary's 88th birthday twice. Once when she caught a ride to town with Cynthia Warnock to have her hair done, I invited her to join our writer's group for lunch at Ming Li's Chinese Restaurant in Enterprise.

Then, on May 26th, her birthday, Lyman called. "Mary and I are in town at Lear's come join us for supper." So we did! Proving that spur of the moment happenings are just as much fun as planned ones. We did a great deal of laughing, as did the couple dining next to us.

Mary said, "They sound like Tee Hee Birds hatching our Haw Haw eggs!"

I moved the kittens to the wood shed. The little Prune Plum tree seems happy planted in the chicken pen, Biden's little steers are keeping those tall grasses growing outside the yard fence grazed down, and I baked two more of those rhubarb pies. These pies were most appreciated by grandson Buck and his wife Chelsea, who spent the Memorial Day weekend here on the ranch. Along with their horses and border collie dogs, the couples arrived after attending a branding on upper Prairie Creek.

Due to the prolonged spring rains, many brandings have been delayed, so, on any given weekend, skilled ropers are in demand. Their only pay: a free meal This particular meal was memorable, according to Buck, who had a hard time finding adjectives to describe King Crab legs.

The next morning found Buck and Chelsea loading up their horse to help at a branding organized by son Todd, who manages the Marr Flat Cattle Co. There on the Buhler place, the Mt. Joseph Ranch just southwest of Joseph, cowboys, cowgirls, kids and dogs, and this grandma, armed with her camera, converged. Under the scenic mountain that gave the ranch its name, the cattle were corralled.

Since it was a clear, sunny morning—hot, actually—I found myself seeking the shade. That is, after I shot up two rolls of film Lots of action, what with all that head'in and heel'in going on. For once, it didn't snow on Memorial Weekend, so Joseph and Wallowa Lake were teeming with tourists. Actually, the high altitude sun bore down with such intensity that there were quite a few sunburns that day.

After the last calf was worked, Todd treated his hungry crew to pizzas at the Embers, located on Highway 82, which is also Main Street Joseph. As Joseph High School's graduation was scheduled that afternoon, I opted not to join them.

Later, on my way up to the school, I stopped to visit the branding crew, who were enjoying those pizzas while seated on a tree shaded deck above the brick sidewalks of Joseph's busy street. I can imagine those manure-splattered cowboys and cowgirls must've provided plenty of local color to those throngs of shorts-clad tourists.

It was unseasonably hot, which meant it was sweltering in the Jo High gym, but worth the discomfort to see Clayton Lowe, who changed pipes for us one summer, and Michael Marks, Lyman's grandson and Mary's nephew, receive their diplomas. I was so proud of both of them. Fine young lads.

Michael is heading for OSU where he will study engineering and play football. Clayton will attend Treasure Valley Community College and major in Agriculture. These ranch boys know about work. It is my prayer, now that these two are headed away from our canyons and valleys, that their Wallowa County roots will provide the stability needed to face an uncertain world.

Cory Miller gets some horseback help from a future cattleman, son Harley.

16-month-old Harley, sone of Cory and Dena Miller, grins for the camera as he sits in his father's saddle at a branding near Enterprise.

Ryya Fluitt, a cowgirl from Upper Prairie Creek, helps with the branding.
Ryya and her sister, Lexi, helped drive Marr Flat cattle from Enterprise to
Big Sheep Creek.

Talked on the phone to grandson James, home for the weekend, who reports training to be on a fire crew is demanding, but says he's getting in shape. He said those rhubarb pies were tempting, but he was sure his dad and cousin Buck could handle them. He's been busy attending graduations, too, before returning to camp.

Last week, Pete Donovan and I drove to Imnaha to do an oral history of Mary Marks for our local museum. After picking her up at Lyman's, we drove upriver to Mary's tidy little house, where Pete tape recorded her. Such an interesting life Mary has led, over 70 years on Imnaha.

The canyons were still green from the rain, and it was cold enough for Mary to turn on her stove to take the chill off the house. While Mary told her stories, the sun escaped from those clouds and, voila, it felt like a summer day.

At noon we sat at Mary's table and ate our lunches, including one I'd packed for Mary. Over cups of tea and some ginger cookies I'd baked for the occasion, we visited more about Mary's life. Finally, we drove her upriver to the Imnaha Grange Hall, where Peter snapped a photo of Mary and I on the porch. Mary says she's a 50-year member of the Grange.

In the book I'm writing about her life, Mary mentions the Grange frequently. She remembers how they had such fun at all those dances...dances which were, however, held in the former hall, no longer there, located on the edge of a field that is planted to grain today.

Huge thunderheads boiled up over the high canyon rims, and the river ran full of snowmelt and run-off. Driving down into the canyons, we noticed the first blooming Syringa bush and, upriver, entire hillsides covered with the purple-blue Bugloss weed.

One evening Phyllis called, wondering if I wanted to go to Kinney Lake while she fished. Since I didn't have a license, I said sure, I'd go along for the hike. It was one of those rare, warm evenings when the wind dies down and the sun burst through dark clouds, bathing those emerald green hills in golden light. The light illuminated several pairs of wild honkers, downy goslings between them, swimming across the far end of the lake. Wildflowers bloomed profusely amid the lush grasses.

After Phyllis caught three trout, we ambled slowly around the lake, savoring the savoring, back to the car. Like we had so often in the past, Phyllis and I had to agree, those of us lucky enough to live here in this lovely valley are fortunate indeed. We just need to get our of our houses more often and enjoy it. And that's what I 'm going to do now, after I walk out the mail box to post this column.

July 1—After a sleepless night, due in part to the bright-as-day light of the summer solstice moon and the throbbing blisters on my toes, I must begin and end this column before noon. You see, like yesterday, I must feed the hungry haying crew. Luckily there are enough leftovers to create another meal. Today there will only be three, not five men to feed.

I'm not complaining, however. You see, I really enjoy cooking for men. They're always so appreciative of an old-fashioned home-cooked meal. So when Doug left me a note—*Could you fix lunch for my haying crew? There will be five of us*—I went right to cookin'.

One of our home-raised beef pot roasts went directly from freezer to oven. While it roasted slowly all morning, surrounded by carrots and onions, I took my camera out to the hay field and photographed the haying crew at work. An interesting procedure, this making of haylage. Such a crop this year. With no fertilizer yet! Three tons to the acre of grass hay. Incredible yield.

Last week I'd watched, fascinated, as upper Prairie Creek rancher Terri Tienhaara, operating a state of the art swather, roared up and down our beautiful hay field, leaving great waves of grass and red clover in her wake. Camera in hand, I walked up the road to zoom in the action, which proved too much for my viewfinder.

Doug, up on the hill raking; Mike Fluitt baling 3x4-foot-long bales that weigh up to 2,200 pounds; Dick Hammond, 75, operating a forklift transporting those bales to the bagger, where young Ethan Lowe supervises the bagging process; 80-year-old Tex Miller driving truck, hauling bales in from the field. Factor in the ever-present background of Chief Joseph Mountain, the purest of rain-washed skies, and the fragrance of meadow hay, and really...there's no way to capture the reality.

I grab a bag of sprouting potatoes from our cellar on the way back to my kitchen. By noon the table is set for six. A pan of rich gravy simmers in the roaster pan, the aroma of home-cooked meal I've spent all morning preparing fills the warm air on this first day of summer. Here they come...trooping in, washing their hands on the back porch, sweating, hungry, like hay hands down through the ages...anticipating a good meal. And I have one.

Home canned green beans with bits of fried bacon, mashed potatoes, gravy, roast beef, baked carrots, pickled beets, bread, butter, and a jar of jam made from some of Sam Loftus' Camp Creek apricots. A pot of cowboy coffee perks on the stove and glasses of ice water accompany each setting.

I love hearing their stories as they eat, as I love watching young Ethan soaking it all in. I love watching them enjoy this food, the same food their own mothers prepared. These capable old hands, way beyond the years when most folks retire, are still putting in a day's work. No naps for these guys. Finished eating, they head back out to the field to make hay while the summer sun shines.

The phone rings. Daughter Jackie in far-off Challis, Idaho.

"Hi, mom. How you doin'? Are your blisters healing?"

I leave the dishes piled in the sink—I don't like dishwashers—and visit with my daughter. My toes are very sore, I tell her, but have no doubt they will heal. You see, on Sunday, there I was on Freezeout Saddle, gobbling down a delicious salad prepared by Stanlynn Daugherty, resting up for the final lap of a three-day backpack trip that had taken me along the Summit Trail above Hells Canyon.As I write it now, the trip seems like a dream...until I look down at my bare feet and see those blisters.

From McGraw to Himmelwright Springs the first night, then a side trip to Barton Heights, three miles down and three back, through hanging gardens of arrowleaf balsamroot, Indian paint brush, mountain blue bells, and entire hillsides of penstemon, their color so intense that words fail.

Through sleet, hail, snow, and rain, I gazed down upon the Snake River and the Seven Devils in Idaho, so close they took my breath away. I remember dark purple clouds, zigzags of lightning, booming thunder, and scrambling off that high point, dripping wet, and many more miles to the Marks cabin: a place I'd never been, but wanted to be, to see the country Mary talked about in her diaries, to make her stories come to life.

I remember drinking that cold spring water, building a fire in the wood stove to dry out, fixing supper, and sleeping in a real bed. All the clouds were gone that final morning, as I walked past sleek cattle and noticed the last snow banks, the grass coming on now.

Words again fail when it comes to describing this high canyon country, perched on the lip of Hells Canyon on one side and the breaks of the Imnaha on the other. From there, you can look west to the snowy Wallowas, east to the Seven Devils, and south and north across miles and miles of unpeopled country, rugged beyond belief. Humbling, even. How much more I appreciated Mary's life, as well as the lives of the other Marks and Warnocks. The younger generation, still in the cattle business, carries on. Their range has got to be some of the most beautiful in the world.

Stumbling down the final switchback to the trailhead at Freezeout Creek, even though I was totally used up, I felt good. I'd done it; accomplished the dream of a lifetime. At age 71, I'd proven I could still survive the country, even as it is the country itself that gives me the strength.

It was that surreal, spiritual sunset on the hill above Himmelwright Springs; the snow falling on a hillside of Mule Ears, the coyote watching at the edge of the timber, the view from Lookout Mountain, and the cabin itself—a haven in the wilderness at 9 p.m. on a cold, wet evening; it was the song of the thrush and the crickets among hillsides covered with biscuit root, a campfire kindled in the rain and wind, and how it felt sleeping under the moon and the stars. This is called LIVING...in the real world, the world that's always been here. And my blisters are like medals, well earned.

And there, on Freezeout Saddle, were my dear friends, waiting with band aids, food, and sympathy. God love them.

My childhood chum Sandra and her husband, Fred, are—at the moment—on their way here from Klamath Falls, where they spent the night. The haying crew will be in for the noon meal soon, and I must drag myself away from my laptop.

Time is always getting away from me, but there is so much more to write about, like the traditional birthday lunch Kathy and I treated our friend Sharon to at the Rimrock. Delicious food, eaten whilst you gaze off into the breaks of Joseph Creek Canyon. I highly recommend this place, located between Clarkston and Enterprise on what we locals refer to as the "North Highway," near the Flora turnoff, which is another route to Troy.

I tell you, there is so much to see here in our country, we could spend a lifetime and still not see it all. But I'm going to keep trying before I die.

Time to feed the chickens, who must think I abandoned them. Must cook lunch for the haying crew and get this in the mailbox before our company arrives.

Saturday evening, Fred and Sandra will join us at Vali's at Wallowa Lake, where Doug and I will celebrate our 27th wedding anniversary. The old-fashioned yellow rose that grows alongside the old bunkhouse is in full bloom, just like it was on our wedding day.

July 6—As so often happens during these busy summer months, I sat myself down to begin this column when my LIFE intervened. First off I became involved in the cleanup of our big 4th of July picnic on the lawn. Doug and I had removed most of it by 11:00 Monday night, and after hubby fell, exhausted, into bed, I doggedly dealt with leftovers. After midnight, I too succumbed to sleep.

Arising at 5:00 the next morning, I hung in there and managed to finish in time to make my weekly Writers' Group by 10:00. The picnic, however, was worth it. Over 30 of us. Two sons and daughters-in-law, a daughter and son-in-law, along with great-grandson Jackson visiting from southern California. Then there was grandson Buck and his bride, Chelsea, who celebrated their first anniversary up on Cayuse Flat. The rest were friends and neighbors who, thanks to daughter Ramona's planning, arrived bearing watermelon, salads, beans, homemade bread, cookies, and cobblers.

Then here came my friend Kathy, carrying a masterpiece of a coconut cake decorated with real flowers. A cake she'd spent all morning on so we could honor not only Buck and Chelsea's anniversary, but also friend Phyllis and her hubby's birthdays.

Around three o'clock Monday afternoon, daughter-in-law Angie had called from Marr Flat where she and son Todd were still on horseback, moving cattle.

"Hi, Janie. Todd will be there with the meat around 3:00. Do you have some cheap wine to marinate the beef?"

Cell phones are great; that is, if you're someplace like Marr Flat. But if Doug is 25 miles out on our summer range on Salmon Creek, forget it.

Back to the picnic: Todd has a reputation hereabouts for barbecuing beef, so that was his contribution. Mine was preparing a platter of deviled eggs, putting together a punch, setting up tables, and preparing the makin's for two freezers of homemade ice cream.

That morning Doug had picked up a huge bowl of fresh strawberries from our garden, so that went into one batch. The other flavor was vanilla; both mixtures contained Fluitt's Jersey cream and six of our fresh eggs. No way could we go wrong.

I had no trouble rounding up Lexi and Ryya Fluitt to take turns cranking the hand-cranked wooden freezer, and the other freezer was one of those electric jobs...which, in my opinion, doesn't make the best ice cream. Or perhaps it's just a nostalgic notion I have, remembering my wonderful uncles, supervising and letting us young'uns take a turn at the crank...and, perhaps, unknowingly teaching us how to layer the ice and salt, how to remove the dasher, drain off the salty water, and pack it in more ice to "season." Amazing what a small child remembers.

My last uncle, uncle Marshall, died a few months ago. I'll always hold all of them forever in my heart, and thank them for the legacy they left, which repeatedly expresses itself in the turning of a hand-cranked ice cream freezer. My wish is that our children, their children, and our great-grandchildren will continue to hand-crank ice cream, and in doing so, remember our family get-togethers. Family traditions are very important in our family. Not only do they connect us to our past, they point the way to our future.

Son Todd's barbecued sirloin was juicy and flavorful. BEEF...it's what's for dinner at most of our family get-togethers. Beef in beef country. We grow it, we eat it. Beef fuels our busy bodies.

What a joy to observe the youngsters at picnics: wandering afield, picking yellow roses, plaiting them into their long brown braids, petting the horses. Little ones trailing after older ones, dragging toys. We were blessed with one toddler, little Adeline, who lives with her mom and daddy up Little Sheep Creek. Addie learned to say "buck, buck" when she saw my chickens. With the exception of six-year-old Jackson, our "herd" of great-grandchildren wasn't able to attend.

Sad that most of our grandchildren must leave the valley for lack of employment. We did, however, manage to keep our traditional 4th of July picnic alive. In years past we've held them on Ramona and Charley's grass ranch on Sheep Creek Hill, or on their upper Prairie Creek ranch.

In recent years, Doug has taken family and friends out on Wallowa Lake in our boat, where we were able to view those thrilling fireworks flowering above us. Well, the 4th just sneaked up on us this year, and we were all so busy, it was just a last-minute thing. Tummies stuffed, we all walked up on our hill, where Doug and Fred had a campfire going, and the view of our Wallowas was just breathtaking.

Add haying season going on all around us.

Beautiful hay this year. Duane Voss had just opened up one more of our lush fields. There was the east moraine of Wallowa Lake, where, while our own fireworks exploded, we could view the display at the foot of the lake. It was all so wonderful.

Ryya, Lexi and Hannah played their fiddles in the hayfield whilst the firecrackers popped and the campfire crackled. There were the stars coming out, one by one, until the entire dome of the night sky was filled with them. We picked out the big dipper, and the milky way, and wondered why they had blown a hole in Temple Tuttle, the chunk of celestial whatever that sheds the falling Perseids during our midsummer nights.

The grand finale at the lake exploded, the children yawned, and we wearily carried our lawn chairs down the hill. A great way to celebrate Independence Day. The cars left and, tired as I was, I felt good.

Well, anyway, those a few of the reasons I'm late with this column.

Others include going on a birthday hike with Phyllis yesterday, where we observed a pileated woodpecker, three wild tom turkeys, and an entire hillside of clarkia. I returned to drive our ancient tractor while Doug bucked "little" bales of hay onto a handmade flat wooden trailer. You see, Doug hayed this little patch of hay near my chicken pen using his old swather, rake, and baler, and now he's fixin' to pick the rest up with the first loader-stacker in the county, one he purchased years ago.

We don't have Ben anymore. It's just us chickens, plus pipe changers and an occasional hired man, the average age being over 70, like us.

I ran into Ben yesterday at the Grain Growers. He looks great. He and wife Jackie live at the foot of the lake where, he said, they had a great view of those fireworks. Ben is the ditch tender now, a much easier job than the one he had here all those many years.

Buck and Chelsea reported having a great anniversary up on Cayuse Flat. Buck wanted to show Chelsea where he grew up. They rode horseback from Imnaha, leading a pack horse. Buck knew the country, as he should. He and sister Mona spent their summers living there in the Cayuse Flat cow camp, as well as in a tent on Sleepy Ridge, a scale house on Monument Ridge, and places in between, when their daddy worked as a cowboy for Will Wilde. Will's gone now, and his wife, Kate, age 94, lives in Alpine House.

Speaking of Alpine House, I must wind up this column. I'm scheduled to read to those folks by 10:30 this morning. I hope Sam Loftus will be there, because I made him some apricot jam last night. Had to open two quarts of canned apricots I picked last summer down on his place on Camp Creek to make the jam. It's a long story.

Last time I read to these folks, I took Sam a sourdough biscuit. It had been a long time since he'd had one, he said. Well, Sam called up a few nights later and said he'd sure like some apricot jam, and wouldn't you know? I'd fed my last pint to the haying crew. But how could I not take Sam his jam?

Doug said I could just buy some jam and give it to him, but there is no way I'd deceive Sam. This way, he can taste those same apricots he grew all those years ago at his beloved little place on Camp Creek. Growing old is bad enough, but hopefully our Fishtrap Board members can bring a bit of cheer into our precious old-timers' lives as we continue to read to them every Thursday. We never know when we'll be joining them, and I'd sure like someone to bring me some apricot jam, wouldn't you?

So much left out, but the chickens haven't been fed, I've had no breakfast, and the bed's not made. My Summer Fishtrap writer's workshop begins Monday morning and lasts all week. I can't wait. Think of me in Kathleen Dean Moore's class. I'm so excited.

P. S. My blisters healed enough to allow me to "walk" the annual Lostine River Run/Walk. I finished the 5K. Great morning!

July 25—Wow! I need to take a big breath. These past few weeks have been so filled with "summer stuff" I scarcely know what day it is. If it weren't for my notes, hastily scribbled at the end of each exhausting day, I would not remember what, when, or even IF this "stuff" actually occurred.

Our neighbor Don Hough, whose fields lie just east of ours, is making hay. He and his crew finished swathing only yesterday, but due to dry winds and warm temperatures, the hay is already cured. While one hired man rakes, two more, including 70+ Don himself, drive two John Deere tractors, pulling "bread loaf" stackers up and down the field. It is a lovely sight. Large, purple-bellied clouds float overhead, casting their shadows on Hough's sage-covered hills, which I've recently learned comprise the end of the great Palouse Prairie.

Doug is mowing the lawn, red poppies bob in the breeze, and short ribs braise in the oven. Doug has just finished the second irrigation basically by himself, as pipe changers are an endangered species, and tomorrow, after hooking up a flat-bed trailer-load of port-a-potties to his pickup, he'll head for Cold Springs Ridge—hopefully ahead of the Asotin-to-Joseph Trail riders who will come ridin' in to camp later in the day.

"Woe be it," says Doug, if those port-a-potties. aren't there!

Meanwhile…back at the ranch will be me. Just me, that is until Wednesday eve, when son Steve, his wife, Jennifer, and our two "hats" grandchildren arrive, all the way from Alabama. Stetson, three, and Bailey, four, sent me handmade Mother's Day letters with help from mom, letting us know just how much they're looking forward to visiting.

Doug won't return until Friday, and since there'll be no one here but us chickens, literally, I wasn't able to join my "Syringa Sisters" this year. A first. As I write, they are gathered in a remote cabin without electricity somewhere in the wilds east of Idaho City. I think of them today, and envy them, but one cannot be everything to everybody. Besides, next summer, my "sisters" will come to the Wallowas.

Barb and Bobbie, from Portland, who arrived Saturday afternoon, treated Doug and me to one of Vali's famous steak dinners at the lake, after which we three "sisters" slept on our hill. We watched the moon rise over Locke's hill, stared at stars, breathed in sweet red clover scent, and slept like babies, snuggled in our sleeping bags.

At first light I awoke just in time to make eye contact with a wandering skunk, which, thankfully, wandered away, only to startle a white-tail doe, which leaped straight into the air before spotting us (on her hill) and, with flag flying, bounced out of sight. As the sun burst over Hough's hill, the moon was still riding high over Chief Joseph Mountain. Barb and Bobbie missed it all. They also missed the other sounds of Prairie Creek waking up for another summer day: my three roosters crowing, the call of a cock pheasant, screams of two red-tail hawks perched in the cottonwoods along the irrigation ditch, and the brief blushing pink light that bathed the Wallowas.

Barb woke up in time to watch the wild honkers arise from where they'd been feeding in the hayfield, and fly low above us, against the rising sun.

After a hurried breakfast of leftover steak, scrambled eggs, toast, and apricot jam, my "sisters" left for Idaho, without me for the first time in nine years.

I left for the Friendship Feast at TamKaLiks in Wallowa, where I attended a Sunday worship service for all faiths. I joined other friends and listened as one of the elders said we should pray every day, not just on Sunday; be grateful every day to the God who created our world. He said early morning is the best time of the day, when it is cool and the wildlife are about and the sun comes up fresh each morning. And I thought how true that was, having just experienced such a morning. The Indians have a great lesson to teach us about living and loving our natural world. Ranchers know this, because they are out irrigating and working the land.

My dear friend Mary Marks has often told me, "Early morning...the best part of the day."

William Stafford, poet laureate of Oregon, wrote every day before daylight. His son Kim wrote a book about his father entitled *Early Morning*.

And here is me, early Tuesday morning, continuing my column. All is quiet now. But not for long!

Last evening found Phyllis and me in my Alder Slope garden. While I hoe, hoe, hoed, Phyllis picked a bowl of raspberries. The weeds that got ahead of me after Summer Fishtrap week are now under control. We've picked the first zucchini, and in spite of son Todd's mare "Alice," which earlier tromped through the garden, everything is flourishing...especially the SQUASH, as in baking squash. Yep, that same variety one of my fans sent me years ago. This year, I gave it plenty of room.

Speaking of Summer Fishtrap, space and time limit my telling of this incredible gathering of writers from all over the U.S. The Monday-to-Friday workshop I took, along with eleven other writers, conducted by Kathleen Dean Moore, was extremely productive. We all learned so much from this inspiring woman, whom we now call our friend. Kathleen is a nature writer and a doctor of philosophy, who taught us to combine nature and science in our writing.

With the exception of the last morning, all classes were held outside. One day we gathered near the West Fork of the Wallowa River. Another time we caravaned out the Zumwalt Road to Nature Conservancy land, and hiked up on Findley Butte, where we wrote under the welcome shade of a ponderosa thicket. We were inspired by sky, acres of lush bunch grasses, wildflowers, badger holes, a herd of elk grazing a nearby hill with their newborn calves, and, yes, from this rancher's perspective, dried cow pies and the other desirable effects of grazing cattle.

For over a hundred years, cattle have grazed what we refer to as the "hills," now dubbed "The Zumwalt Prairie Preserve." Why is it so precious? Because the ranchers were good stewards, because it was grazed by cattle, even before large herds of elk adapted, encouraged by the shorter, more desirable forage afforded by grazing cattle.

At any rate, we all need to learn from each other. And I learned that day...about the many different kinds of grasses, about the ground beneath the prairie, about how all things are connected: the grass, the animals, and us. Phil Shepard of the Nature Conservancy was most helpful.

You're never too old to learn. Fishtrap is the college I was denied.

Fishtrap mourned this year. We mourned the untimely death of Frank Conley, who contributed so much to our organization, who wrote his own obituary. *In lieu of flowers, take yourselves out into the great outdoors and look around you.* Well, we did just that, Frank, and thank you for the best of gifts.

Speaking of gifts, those of us fortunate enough to take Kathleen's class consider that a gift also. The weekend Gathering was equally inspiring, what with presenters, as well as advisory board members present; such as John Daniel, Valerie Miner, Heidi Muller, Albert M. Andrews/Redstar, Pete Fromm, Jane Vandenburgh, Jack Shoemaker, Frank Walker, Marc Jaffe, John Rember, Alvin Josephy, Susan Armitage, Kathleen Tyan, Jim Hepworth and Craig Lesley.

The theme this year was "Roots," and the writing that came out those workshops, read at open mics, was awesome. As was the music on Saturday night by Heidi Muller and Bob Webb, who taught the song writing workshop and played dulcimers and other non-acoustic instruments. What a treat, especially after a great meal served by the staff of the Methodist Camp. All of our meals were super, prepared with help from members of the Joseph United Methodist Church.

This, our 18th annual Summer Fishtrap conference, was—in this writer's opinion—the culmination of what we've been striving for. After attending every one of the past eighteen conferences, I feel deserving of an opinion.

I have reveled in great-grandchildren and hugged granddaughter Adele, just now home after eleven months in Argentina as a Rotary exchange student. My days have been filled with so many things that my mind is a blur, but I must end this column. Chief Joseph Days is upon us, and soon our house will fill with two of out out-of-town children and their children. Bye for now.

P.S. So good to finally meet Sterling Allen, who appeared on our ranch last week.

August 8—Seated here at our kitchen table on this hot, smoke-hazed afternoon, staring at a blank screen, attempting to describe these past three weeks…seems (at the moment) daunting. What I really need is a nap. A long one. But there are others out there, like Sharon Livingston—president-elect of the Oregon Cattlemen's Association, from Long Creek—who will understand how it is in the summer on a ranch.

After reading my last column, Sharon called in to pay her respects to the passing of Frank Conley. In the small-world department, it seems Frank and Sharon attended the same school. Like all of those who knew Frank, she was shocked to learn he was a victim of melanoma.

Sharon lost her own husband eight years ago to cancer, and she knows how hard it is to be engaged in ranching during these difficult times. Luckily Sharon has a son to help her. Sharon, like me, has a story to tell about our way of life…a way of life that provides not only nutritious, delicious beef, but preserves open space, well-cared-for acres that provide habitat for wildlife and unpeopled places, where one can go to restore the soul; most important in our increasingly complex society.

This way of life has produced generations of families whose children go out into the world shaped by the land, who care passionately about the land. These families put down roots, stay put, and contribute to community. This is the kind of stuff you see at a county fair: volunteer stuff.

But all that is changing, fading into history in all the pretty places in the West. The habitat of the cowboy, as well as the cowboy—the real cowboy—is as endangered as open space itself. The average age of a rancher is creeping up each year. I think it's well past seventy, now. My husband, Doug, will turn 74 next month, and he's tired. His only son has a permanent back injury and lives with his wife and family in Alabama.

Steve likes it that he can take a week's vacation and fly out to visit us over Chief Joseph Days, but if he were running this ranch he would be working seven days a week. I mean, he would be changing hand lines, moving wheel lines, driving 25 miles to the hills to salt cattle, checking drying stock ponds, fixing fence knocked down by elk, hauling "dries" to market, doctoring injured cows, or chasing down errant bulls...all those things his dad is still doing because, unless you're a really big operator, you can't afford a full time hired man. Needless to say, we miss Ben. Ben, the most faithful hand any ranch could ever have.

Phyllis and I fled to the lake one hot afternoon, after our houseful of company left. Gingerly, we waded waist-high into that cold water, before returning to lawn chairs placed earlier under a shade tree in Ben and Jackie's yard. Where, later, Ben joined us. Relaxed, work under control, he visited about all those years he worked for Doug, which included years before Doug and I were married in 1978.

Ben courted his Jackie down on Snake River when he was working for Doug on the Dug Bar Ranch. Jackie had been hired to help with the cooking. If you want to understand about hard work, ask Ben. It gladdens my heart to know that Ben now has time for an evening paddle in his own canoe with Jackie on the lake, and time to go fishing. He earned it.

Ben is now the water master who supervises the vast system of irrigation that originates in the stored water behind the Wallowa Lake Dam; ditches and ditch companies with names like "Moonshine," and "Farmers."

Prairie Creek, where we live, would be just an extension of the dry, sagebrush hills of the Palouse Prairie if it weren't for water from melted snow stored high in the Wallowas, in our land of Winding Waters.

As I mentioned in my last column, they don't make pipe changers anymore. Too much work for too little pay, although minimum wage seems like a lot to me. My children grew up changing pipe. Granddaughter Adele, just returned from Argentina, who now speaks fluent Spanish, is changing pipe, moving cattle, and glad to be back in the saddle again; that is, until she begins her senior year at Enterprise High.

George Kohlhepp's daughters are savvy changing pipe, and I see other youngsters out "building character" in our neighbors' fields. Doug was finally able to enlist several pipe changers, who worked for a while before quitting for various reasons.

Which meant, until he found Adam and Jerry, Doug was changing four wheel lines twice a day and four hand lines once a day, every day. Out at dawn. In for breakfast at 8:00...back for supper anywhere from

7:00 to 9:00 p.m. Add trips to the hills to that already full schedule, and you get the picture. Seventy-four-year-old ranchers are pretty well used up by day's end.

Seventy-six-year-old Lyman Goucher, one of the last ranchers on the upper Imnaha, can tell you about being tired. So can 88-year-old Mary Marks. Not many family-owned ranches left. Every day, one is sold. Our neighbor Don Hough is now in his seventies. Hank Bird, who runs a cattle operation south of us, is in the same situation.

What will happen to our beautiful ranches here on Prairie Creek, like ours? These cow/calf operations, established by generations of cattlemen, like Jidge Tippett, who came before us. What will become of our grass, and our beautiful permanent pastures? These fields of clover whose sweet scent fills the air this August afternoon, what will become of our hayfields? Haying time is a time of work and sweat...and yet, this is another gift of the land, to sustain cattle in winter.

The Nez Perce before us grazed hundreds of cattle and horses on the native bunch grasses. They wintered in the canyons—Imnaha, Joseph Creek, Grande Ronde—and summered "on top," like Doug used to do, and the McClarans still do. It is a beautiful, hard life. Unfortunately, our young, Wallowa County-grown cowboys can't afford to buy local ranches. There's something terribly wrong here.

In Europe, I understand they subsidize and support their family-owned ranches. They encourage ranching because it creates a pleasing-to-the-eye pastoral countryside. It is their pride and joy. Tourists snap pictures of a life everyone longs for. However, here, the throngs of tourists who invade our county this time of year rarely, if ever, leave the highway to Wallowa Lake. That's where the action is: the lanes, the artsy shops, the eateries. But out in Wallowa County's outback is where you'll find the ranches. Others, like ours, are only a few miles from a bronze foundry.

For 27 years I have lived here on Doug's ranch. For 27 years I have watched the seasons come and go, and new folks come and go...and let me tell you, the times, they are a changin'. There are now road blocks set up to destroy our way of life.

Doug just hung up the phone, after talking with old time cattle buyer Wayne Cook. Doug had called to find out when he could ship a bull.

"Can't," said Wayne. "They shut down the killing plant. Have to haul the bull to La Grande."

"Can't do that," says my hubby. "Have to change pipe and stand by with my pumper. Dry lightning last night, might burn up the summer range."

Our ponds are drying up. Doug just loaned his brother Biden a tank this morning. He's hauling water from the valley to the hills. It's tough being in the cattle business. These are just a few of the problems being dealt with on a daily basis. No wonder so many are selling out.

But where will the white-tail birth her fawn? Where will the red-tail roost when the cottonwood trees are cut down? Where will the family of owls nest when the last old barn is torn down or burned up in a prairie fire? Where will the wild geese feed when the irrigated fields are gone? What will happen to the end of the great Palouse Prairie, and to this precious place we call Prairie Creek, when the family ranches are gone?

I know where my grandchildren have gone. As much as they'd love to live here in this valley where they were born, they've had to move away. They can't afford land here. These are good citizens, raised on love, homemade ice cream, family gatherings, 4-H, and FFA; they understand agriculture. Out of our 19 grandchildren, three are—as I write— rappelling out of helicopters on initial attack fire crews, earning money to pay off college expenses, or saving for a ranch.

One is a career Marine and one is home on leave from the Navy. Both have been to Iraq, and might have to go again.

Of the nineteen, only three live in the county. They work hard every day, at whatever work they can find. During winter one grandson is a wrestling coach, boy scout leader, and a leader in his church. He and his wife are expecting their third child, our 13th great-grandchild, soon. Chad's father, my son, is on a fire as well. He dreams of providing a way of life that includes cowboys, cows, and horses, so his grandchildren can experience the life he was raised in.

My other son is a cowboy, a real cowboy, who also has this dream. Not unlike many other sons and daughters born into a ranching life, this is the only life they've ever known. It is a life they've chosen, not for money, but for a way of life outdoors, riding, moving cows, and working hard. Even in the harshness of winter and the heat of summer, even when the pay is low...that life gets in your blood, the way it did for old hands like Sam Loftus and Mike McFetridge who have had to hang up their spurs and store their saddles.

When I go to Alpine House to read my columns to the old-timers, such as Sam Loftus, I see in their old eyes the glint of recognition when I write about life on a ranch. They are back there again, yep, even changin' pipes, swathin' hay, drivin' a bunch of cows, pulling a calf, and smelling that sweet clover scent on an afternoon in August. God bless our old-timers, my hubby included. They are a dying breed. Enjoy their beautiful ranches while you can. Things, they are a changin'.

Chief Joseph Days is over. Doug and I rode as grand marshals of Hells Canyon Mule Days behind Larry Waters' mules, who pulled a buggy down Main Street. We waved at throngs of people, so many that the faces were all a blur, save for grandchildren Ethan, Bailey, and Stetson, who ran up to catch the candy we threw. Grandson Buck, another real cowboy, and his bride, Chelsea, walked in front of us carrying a banner. They'll do it again during the Mule Days parade in September.

Son Steve, wife Jennifer, and their two "hats," ages three and four, spent a week here. Doug was gone that week, hauling port-a-potties on the Asotin Trail Ride. I fed and entertained the Alabamans, watered gardens and lawns, and accompanied the family out to Tippett Corrals when the trail ride camped there Thursday night.

On Tuesday I drove clear out to Frog Pond on Cold Springs Ridge to spend the night in a tent with my husband. I managed to steal away from the horse camp long enough to stare off over miles and miles of canyons while watching the sunset colors. Next morning, I witnessed the sunrise over Hells Canyon.

On the way back to the ranch, early in the morning, I saw three wild turkey gobblers, elk, numerous deer, hawks, a badger, two coyotes, and not one soul in over 40 miles.

And now the raspberries, gooseberries, strawberries, blackberries, and huckleberries are ripening. Dry lightning last night ignited fires in Hells Canyon. Our county fair is in progress. While I was entering my photographs, I looked up to see daughter Jackie standing there. She'd just driven in from Challis, Idaho, for a visit. So good to see her. Now I'll have help with all those berries.

August 23—The owl on our kitchen "bird clock" just announced the midnight hour. Through the open window above my sink I hear the wavering wails and yelps of a family of coyotes. Moonlight floods this place we call Prairie Creek. The scent of newly-mown meadow hay, mostly red clover, permeates the air. Save for the ever-present sound of Hough's diesel motor pumping water into the hand lines across the road, the night is silent. I can't sleep. Perhaps I went to bed too early, or maybe the waning August moon flooding our bedroom woke me up. Who knows? I seem to have a lot on my mind these days.

It's been an unreal summer. Not just for me, but for everyone I talk to in the grocery store. Leaving the dishes piled in my sink—I don't have a dishwasher—I walked up on our hill last evening. I wanted to take a photo, not with my camera, but with my heart. A photo of this place, at this particular time, to store in my mind's eye. I wanted to absorb what

Prairie Creek rancher Don Hough drives a tractor pulling a 'bread loaf' stacker of meadow hay. This is first cutting.

lay before me. And what lay before me, and all around me…well. Once again, words fail. But here goes.

Bathed in evening light were windrows of the most beautiful clover hay I've ever seen. There were the irrigation ditches, lined with ancient willows and cottonwoods, winding their way through the prairie hay fields that comprise our ranch. The old, round wooden silo, maybe 100 years old, its red color faded over the years. Ben's house and outbuildings, and the historic barn across the road, surrounded by permanent pastures, being grazed by Biden's bred heifers.

In that cow pasture, a tiny figure turns out to be Doug, clad in rubber boots, flood irrigating. How I envied him. I remember, as a child, helping my daddy flood irrigate our flat in Northern California. How I loved being out in that alfalfa field, shovel in hand, herding water around, letting it into another check. Water gravity-flowed from a reservoir holding runoff irrigation from the hill pastures above; water from a Nevada Irrigation District (NID) ditch, paid for by the inch, mixed with the manure hosed off in the dairy barn. We didn't need to fertilize!

Gazing westward, my eyes fell on the old Liberty Grange Hall, beyond which lay other ranches, until they stopped short of the mountains. From our hill, one can view the entire Wallowa chain. To the southwest rose the east moraine of Wallowa Lake, with the Prairie Creek cemetery nestled below, and Chief Joseph Mountain rising beyond. Looking north, the wide green prairie wanders beside the dry sage-covered hills that lie

to the east, to the Zumwalt hills. Southward, below East Peak, lies the
McCully Creek drainage, and Ferguson Ridge, our ski area; and farther
southeast, the high timbered perimeter of the Divide.

Turning around, I view Hough's and Locke's hills, home to coyote,
white-tail deer, badgers, ground squirrels, hawks and, in the spring, the
first buttercups. Juvenile red-tail hawks scream in the top of a cottonwood snag as I wander down along the irrigation ditch. The water is
dark and smooth, and mosquitoes, buzzing above the surface, bring trout
to rise.

I remember teaching grandson James how to fish here, letting the
line float down below the overhanging root of a giant cottonwood, where
I knew a big trout would take his grasshopper. There is a photo on our
refrigerator still of that little boy, holding one of those rainbows. Today
James is 19 and a sophomore in college—and an expert fly fisherman.

Memories surface like the fish I see jumping this evening. I crawl
under the electric wire fence and return to the house via the cow pasture
where generations of my milk cows grazed. I remember their names,
beginning with Star, Startch, and my beloved Stargirl…and all those
calves, born in the spring and sold in the fall.

What a summer! Our county fair is history. Since this was the first
fair in 37 years I haven't had a child or grandchild participating, I decided
to adopt other children in our community. And found it just as rewarding.
I do have a great-grandson following the family tradition, however…but
Clayton lives in Lodi, California, and although his grandparents made
the trip to watch him show his steer, great-grandma didn't make it.

Then there was the Redneck Rodeo and chicken scramble, a blur of
kids, shoe races, watermelon, chicken feathers and dust flying in the
wake of cowhide races. Son Todd, pulling Ryya Fluitt, won that event in
17 seconds! Not to mention the museum booth Carol Coppin and I set
up that hot afternoon in Cloverleaf Hall, the blue ribbon yellow zucchini
I entered from Doug's garden, and my red ribbon photo.

Two other series of photos were disqualified because I didn't follow
the rules for size. Oh well, at least it made an exhibit…and exhibits were
down this year, reflecting changes in our rural way of life. One thing that
didn't change, however, were the volunteers; all those unsung heroes,
such as Nancy Carlson and others, who keep Cloverleaf Hall going year
after year.

As in the past, it was Imnaha that shone with pride. Namely Barbara
Warnock's 4-H'ers…like Christina Marks, who won the coveted Junior
Homemaker of the Fair Award. These canyon kids surely embody the
spirit of this year's theme, "It's a Rural Thing." They don't make kids any

more rural than these Imnaha 4-H'ers. Whether it was in the livestock barn or the exhibit hall, Barbara's 4-H'ers made a good showing, not only with their exhibits but with the way they conducted themselves. Didn't matter that they live way down on the upper Imnaha; they brought their steers and eggs, and canned apricots, and quilts, and cookies to town.

As usual, I got a little carried away at the fat stock auction and purchased Stephanie Simpson's 4-H market hog, "Prince Charming", for $3.60 per lb... which computed to $902! And I haven't even paid for the cuffing, wrapping, and curing yet. Stephanie, a sweet little gal, gifted me a bouquet of candy suckers nestled in a pair of rubber boots, the kind 4-H'ers wear to do their "hog chores." Prince Charming was 4-H reserve champion, however, and those pork chops should be mighty tasty.

And, also traditionally, I was a sucker for the UN-wanted chicken scramble chickens. I lucked out this year, however, because this non-ruffled Rhode Island Red pullet not only survived the bedlam of being chased all over the indoor arena, she laid an egg!

And when Doug went to the fairgrounds the next morning to pick her up, she'd laid another one. At daylight the next morning, when I went out to tend my flock, I noticed an increase in the shape of yet another rooster. Well... I guess it's a rooster. Anyway this bit of fluff has a tiny crow and a teeny tiny comb, and as of this writing NO ONE has a clue as to how it got there. But I suspect my son had something to do with it.

I named him "Scramble" and he's lowest on the pecking order. At the top is "Ari," the Aracuna, followed by "Fred" (as in Webb), then "Flash," the escapee from chicken scrambles past, who ran uptown into the Wilderness Inn. I'm sure you remember THAT story.

Anyhoo... it sounds like a chicken farm here of a morning, which is fine with me. And "Rhodie" just keeps on laying an egg a day. Amazing!

Monday morning, following the fair, I flew to Auburn, California, to visit my 95-year-old mama.

It was a rush trip, and I was back home on the ranch by late Wednesday afternoon. Phyllis, who visited her family in Corvallis while I was gone, drove me to the Portland airport. Due to delays, my plane didn't take off until 8:30 p.m., which put me in Sacramento well past my bedtime... not to mention my two sisters' bedtimes.

And when I stepped off the plane it was HOT!

"Cooled down lately," Caroline and Kathryn said. "It's been 103 for days."

Needless to say, I was glad to see them, and after K. drove us to her place in Roseville, Caroline took me home with her. Brother Jim—now retired...about time—picked me up the next morning and drove me to Auburn, where I spent all day with mama.

What a precious time that was. Mama is old. She's tired. She's lived a long life, and she can't paint, read, play the piano, or remember a lot of stuff anymore...and that bothers her. So I tried to cheer her up by just being there.

It was hard to leave, especially when she said, "Sure wish you didn't have to go."

"I'll be back soon," I told her. "Doug is haying, all alone on the ranch. You remember how it was, when daddy was milking cows seven days a week, and haying, when we were young." Mama's beautiful eyes told me she understood.

Mama is very fortunate. She lives with a good family who cares lovingly for her in pleasant surroundings. It was a tearful goodbye.

"Live in the moment, mama," I said. "Enjoy eating ice cream."

And then my childhood chum Sandra appeared to drive me back to Caroline's in Newcastle. My plane took off from Sacramento at six the next morning. I had lots of time to think, flying to Portland. Looking down, I could see Crater Lake, which sparked memories of living along the Rogue River, way back in 1951, when I was 17 and about to give birth to my firstborn.

Last weekend was our Wallowa County Stockgrowers annual meeting, followed by the traditional dinner-dance at Cloverleaf Hall.

Friday evening President Phil Ketscher and his wife, Charity, hosted a social get-together for ranching families out on their ranch in the Zumwalt hills. Since Doug was too tired from haying, I rode out with son Todd and wife, Angie. The road to Ketschers' is long and dusty, but to me there is a charm to the "hills."

I loved seeing the late evening light on the Seven Devils in Idaho, where fires burned in Hells Canyon; where one can look for miles and not see a sign of human habitation, only cattle grazing...fat cattle, in this good grass year.

When we pulled into Ketschers' yard, the sun was going down behind a large cottonwood tree, the only tree in miles; the silence was so complete, you could hear as crickets sang their tiny songs, until we heard the happy sound of playing children.

What a good time those lucky children had that night. We had the potluck outside, eaten on old weathered tables that Charity had covered with tablecloths and decorated with dried wildflowers. Greenwood Butte loomed off to the west, and I could imagine Doug's range on Wet Salmon

Creek, where our own cattle grazed. The rolling dry, grassy hills went on forever, broken only by the timbered Chesnimnus country to the north.

I'd added my dozen deviled eggs to the table already laden with roast beef, salads, bread, and chocolate cakes. It was a younger crowd this year, young ranchers with small children. I loved being with them. We told chicken stories and I stood with the children to watch the full August moon rise over Hells Canyon, huge and reddened from the fires, swelling up and over the vastness that comprises what is referred to as the Zumwalt Prairie. One of those rare moments in time.

Saturday evening, after stuffing ourselves with Randy Garnett's barbecued beef, salads organized by Jean Stubblefield and Barbara Warnock, and dee...licious rolls baked by those same two gals, Doug and I went to dancin'. I mean, you couldn't help it. That toe-tappin' Western swing was hard to resist.

Fun...since we hadn't danced—I mean, really danced like that—in such a long, long time. Fun too, to see our other rancher friends enjoying themselves.

The highlight of the evening was when Mike Lathrop gave a slide presentation in honor of our neighbor Hank Bird, who received the Honorary Cattleman award this year. It couldn't have gone to a more deserving rancher. Congratulations, Hank!

Meanwhile, here on the ranch, helicopters fly over, snorkels dangling, as fire crews continue to fight those Hells Canyon flies. Wild geese fly over too, early of a morning and late of an evening, to feed in our irrigated fields.

Mama kitty birthed four kittens in an old junk pile. Coyotes and cars depleted our cat population, so now we'll have a new generation of mousers. My Alder Slope baking squash is plum out of hand, sending tendrils out into the horse pasture.

Green beans are ready to can, strawberries won't quit, and this weekend is the Tippett family reunion. Our weather has cooled off. Doug is working with his old equipment to hay the second cutting of meadow hay, heavy to red clover. He'll soon be in for supper. Time to print this out.

P.S. At 2:30 a.m. I went back to bed. It is now 8 a.m. on August 25th, and I am finally finishing this column. Life on a ranch is never dull. Because my kitchen table is my "office," I am constantly interrupted. Oh well...

Zeb Hermans is pretty happy about catching his very own chicken in the chicken scramble at the recent Wallowa County Fair in Enterprise.

Grandchildren of Barbara and Grant Warnock, who live on Imnaha, this new generation of Warnocks belong to the Tomahawk 4-H club. Young Riley Warnock is learning from his cousins how to show steers.

Jeannie Mallory (secretary of the Wallowa County Stockgrowers) presents a scholarship to Cayle Krebs at the annual Stockgrowers meeting.

September 7—Swallows fill the air here on Prairie Creek this cool, frostless morning. I pause on the path to the chicken pen to watch them swoop and dive, or perch, side by side, on the power line.

Earlier, before sunrise, when I was just climbing out of bed, a pair of owls who frequent the ancient willows that grow along the irrigation ditch in the horse pasture *hoot, hoot*-ed me awake. Often their calls signal a weather change, either in the form of rain or snow. I sincerely hope these owls are of the wise variety, and that they are predicting rain, because we need moisture. Even though some of our neighbors are still haying, they admit a good rain is long overdue.

Old-timers hereabouts say it's been a long time since they've seen the country this dry. Ponds continue to dry up in the hills, where the coyote-colored bunch grasses wither under the burning afternoon sun, numerous creeks have long since dried up, and the ninebark is beginning to redden in the canyons. Our mountains appear stark, bare-boned, somehow naked as they await that first seasonal snowfall.

We've had day after day of clear skies, with the occasional cloud build-up that dissolves into flaming sunsets. Enormous sunflowers follow the sun's path at the edge of the garden. Each evening I walk the garden rows and "pick" supper. Such a variety. Corn-on-the-cob, squash, carrots, cabbage, potatoes, onions, green beans, lettuce, beets...and, for dessert, strawberries.

Phyllis came over one morning and I tackled the green beans while she picked strawberries. After, we "women talked" our way through the snapping of those beans, which were then processed in my pressure cooker. This time of year finds me in my kitchen cooking applesauce, stirring up strawberry and raspberry freezer jam, pickling, or thinking about shredding the cabbages for sauerkraut.

That is, unless there's a baby shower, like the one for granddaughter-in-law Kasey, who's expecting our 14th great-grandchild in October. Kasey, a veterinarian in John Day, lives with her husband, Rowdy, near Mt. Vernon. This is their first baby. The shower, organized by cousin Carrie and aunt Ramona, was held at Carrie's in La Grande.

That Saturday was also the Tippett family reunion at Wallowa Lake. I didn't want to miss a chance to see some of my great-grandchildren, so I opted to make the 120-mile round-trip to attend the shower, before joining the Tippetts who were, by this time, gathered at the Eagle Cap Chalet lodge...which I had quite a time locating, as Doug had the map.

This recently constructed facility, situated just above the West Fork of the Wallowa River, was buzzing with Doug's relatives. The Tippetts were really into their heritage this year, which proved very interesting to me, because over the years I've managed to collect quite a bit of family history. Thanks to the "Steen gals" paying us a visit Sunday morning, there will be even more history documented for future generations. Interesting to note that three Steens married Tippetts.

Doug's nephews Bob and Mike Tippett spent Saturday night with us, which allowed for a long overdue visit.

The big Granite Creek fire continued to burn, and each afternoon huge billows of smoke rose beyond Hells Canyon to the east of our ranch. Between neighbors Duane Voss, who recently suffered a serious horse wreck, and James Yost, our second cutting of meadow hay got up in good shape. Doug, meanwhile, plugged away at the thick red clover crop and managed to hold his old equipment together long enough to finish the hill pasture. In spite of "that dam clover"—Doug's description—this last, beautiful crop will make fine hay for some lucky cattle this winter.

I say "last crop" because Doug has sold the ranch. Although the new owners, Richard and Mary Frasch, plan to use the land only for agriculture purposes, my beloved hill will likely never grow clover like this again. Richard, a really nice person, assures me the hill will always be mine; a place I can feel free to spread my sleeping bag under an August sky to watch the falling stars.

September 27—It's 1 o'clock...a.m., that is. I'm hoping, by beginning this day early, to beat the enemy...which, as we age, is TIME. Supposedly we now have time on our hands to enjoy the "golden years." Not this gal.

Each day keeps its golden moments, however...like this past Sunday at Alpenfest, sitting with Hope and Harold McLaughlin, listening to Kerry Christensen, perched on the porch of the historic Edelweiss Inn there at Wallowa Lake, sing song after song, accompanied by his accordion. Songs like "Could I Have This Dance," "North to Alaska," "Cattle Call," "Edelweiss," and "Danny Boy," all those dear, familiar sing-along tunes. Add fresh snow on the mountains, crisp clear air, yellowing aspen, and golden sunshine, and you get the picture.

Sunday was in sharp contrast to Saturday when Doug and I strolled from booth to booth, visiting old friends while bundled up to stave off the chill rolling down off Mt. Howard. No complaining, however...we certainly welcomed the moisture. Seated there at long tables, devouring our kraut and German sausage sandwich, we gazed at a snow line not all that far up the mountain.

Looking back through my hastily scribbled notes at the end of each full day, I'm overwhelmed. Did all of this really happen?

Hells Canyon Mule Days grand marshals Doug and Janie Tippett ride in an old carriage owned by Larry and Juanita Waters of Prairie Creek. Larry, in the front seat, uses his team of mules to feed hay to his sheep in winter, and also uses them for many local parades. Seated next to Larry is Sondra Lozier, Mule Days chairman.

Sheryl Curtis of Washington won first place in the non-motorized Hells Canyon Mule Days Parade with her two Brown Swiss oxen.

Did Doug and I spend one afternoon making sauerkraut? Was our 13th great-grandchild born? Did it finally rain? How could I have found time to put up seven-day sweet pickles, applesauce, and pickled beets? Did I really attend those events plastered all over my calendar? Guess I did... says so in my daily journal.

The sauerkraut, sweet pickles, applesauce and blackberry jelly are canned. Baby Kevin Scott was born September 13 to grandson Chad and his wife, Amy, who live here in the county. It finally rained and dusted our peaks with snow, and ever since Mule Days we've been on the go.

It did rain during Mule Days, but not on our parade, and no one seemed to care. The event was a success.

At Friday night's Cowboy Poetry event, held in the indoor arena at our local fairgrounds, Dave Murrill was standing there on the back of a flat bed truck reciting a poem about rain—when suddenly there was this downpour drumming on the tin roof. Thanks, Dave!

Others performing that night included Doug, who recited a poem written by his friend Tom Dorrance entitled "Woman." Doug's cousin, who goes by the name of "Smoke Wade," woke up the crowd when he belted out poems about growing up on the Snake River and working cattle on the "Chesnim."

For my birthday Doug gave me a pair of jeans with belt loops so I could wear my belt buckle, and since it was rainy and cold, I wore my old hat and slicker during the grand entry before the show... and what a show.

My favorite event was the pancake race, where contestants rode their mules to the other side of the arena, built a small fire, mixed pancake batter, heated up a skillet, and, yes, fried a hotcake—all the while holding on to their mule's reins. Then they had to run back to the judge, still leading the mule, and present a "cooked" pancake. The timed event was most entertaining. All through the show mules brayed, balked, and performed, much to the amusement of the crowd.

At Saturday night's big mule and horse auction, Doug purchased "Skeeter," a well-broke quarter horse gelding who now greets me every morning here on the ranch.

One bright morning the "hidden" kittens showed up in the woodshed. Three of them. Mama kitty did a good job of hiding them from the coyotes. Doug has been hauling supplement to the cattle in the hills and cutting wood for winter. In addition to stove wood for our old Monarch range, he found time to deliver a load of split tamarack and pine to our Writers' Retreat on Imnaha. Thanks also to Lyman, who donated several logs from an old corral, we writers will be warm next month.

The Northwood Maple is all a-flame out the kitchen window, and beyond the hayfield rises snowy East Peak and Mt. Howard. It got down in the 20s last week and there went our gardens. Fortunately, I was able to harvest baking squash and boxes of green tomatoes from my Alder Slope garden. Our back porch, front room, and basement are overflowing with produce. How I love this time of year, even though it means work.

There is such satisfaction in putting food by for winter, and also in celebrating it. The local food growers put on the harvest dinner a week ago. My, such a community effort. Cloverleaf Hall was transformed into a Farmer's Market, complete with sunflowers, fall-colored trees growing in pots, colorful platters of locally grown veggies, and grass-fed beef—skewered, marinated and grilled. Yum.

The main course consisted of locally grown lamb, buffalo, and beef, salad greens, and more locally grown vegetables. While folks were served warm, wild blackberry cobbler with a dollop of homemade ice cream, I was supposed to give a talk. Well, have you ever competed with that yummy dessert? Needless to say, my speech was short. Was I going I to let my ice cream melt? My Imnaha blackberries get cold? No way.

Driving home I watched the full Harvest "Corn" moon rise over Prairie Creek. Back at the ranch, I stood outside and listened to a family of coyotes yammering away on the moon-washed hills to the east, and celebrated my own September moon.

On the morning of September 12, son Todd, grandson James and his friend Keith Nantz appeared in my kitchen after bear hunting up Big Sheep. James had called earlier to say he was stopping by for a visit before returning to college, and grandma always has pie... so there I was, peeling apples when they arrived—hungry as bears...with no bear.

James pitched in and fried some of Prince Charming's sausage and bacon while I continued on with the pie. Then, while my versatile grandson took over the pie crust—marking it with T.J.K., brushing it with milk and placing it in the oven. I cooked a dozen eggs and set out raspberry jam to go with the toast. And can you believe, after that pie was baked, they ate half of it? Another one of those golden moments in time. Their visit made my day.

After a long-awaited fishing trip with his dad, James is back in Montana for his sophomore year in college. All of our growing grandchildren make me proud, and the moments spent with them are truly treasured.

Lyman and Mary stopped by that evening for supper and we demolished roasted pork spare ribs from that 4-H hog, along with potatoes, corn on the cob, and green beans from our garden...then polished off the apple pie.

On the 14th, Phyllis and I hiked up Hurricane Creek canyon to the meadow below Deadman Creek. Colors are changing now. Standing there, staring up the Hurricane Divide to where a trickle of water spilled down from the last snow bank, was just what I needed to restore my soul. We who live here are so fortunate in that we have such quick access to wilderness. Phyllis and I poked around in the creek bed where years of flash floods have deposited sand and changed the water's course.

Taking photos with Phyllis' digital camera was fun, and her husband, Fred, printed them out for us when we returned. New snow on Sacagawea Mountain provided a scenic backdrop.

One warm afternoon I had tea at the Wallowa Lake home of Jennifer Bell with Jennifer's 90-year-old mother, Doris, and Mary Frasch and her daughter, who were here visiting from Minnesota. What a delightful time we had... and what a pleasure to meet Doris, who was raised way up the south fork of the Salmon River in Idaho. Talk about stories. Her life is another book, like Mary's.

That evening I joined Wendy, Anne and Kathy for dinner at the RimRock Inn, way out the north highway. My friend Kathy had won the winning bid—on an overnight stay in a tepee—at a silent auction held at the Flora School. Her tepee perched there on the lip of Joseph Creek canyon. Seated at a table, where we could view the rising moon, we savored the chef's special chicken pot pie; this real comfort food was accompanied by poached pears in blackberry sauce.

After Katie, our delightful waitress, fixed us a thermos of coffee for morning, we traipsed off to our tepee, where we tossed our sleeping bags on comfortable mattresses and listened to the quiet of Joseph Creek Canyon. I couldn't sleep in that moonlit landscape, stars silently reeling past the smoke hole in the ceiling, crickets chirping, deer nibbling dry grass, and the nearness of that spiritual canyon, a canyon where the Wallowa band of Nez Perce wintered.

Even knowing our tepee could in no way compare to theirs, I pretended anyway, and finally fell asleep.

Last Saturday night I attended the Nez Perce Art in the Wallowa dinner theater held at the Joseph Community Center. Another one of Joe McCormack's successes, it featured Nez Perce Fisher-caught wild salmon, Raphael's smoked Stangel Ranch buffalo with locally grown veggies, and cheesecake with huckleberries, prepared by special guest chefs and advocate volunteers.

I sat next to a retired doctor and his wife, spending the fall in their cabin at Wallowa Lake, who knew my aunt and uncle, who had a summer home at Echo Lake in the California Sierras.

After that memorable meal, we were treated to a presentation of "York," portrayed by David Casteal, with Susan Hardie directing. This one-man, 2-hour show celebrated the courage York played in the Lewis and Clark expedition.

David also enacted out the vital role played by the Nez Perce. Because, without the aid of a Nez Perce woman encountered by the party as they crossed over the Bitter Root Mountains, warriors would have "rubbed them out." Instead, the Nimiipuu outfitted them and saved them from starvation, and the party was then able to make it to the mouth of the Columbia River. This one-man show was one of the most incredible pieces of acting I've had the pleasure of seeing.

A couple of weeks ago, when the Imnaha fire was still burning, I delivered some milk and medicine to Mary, after which I peeled some windfall apples and made an apple crisp.

It was one of those warm Indian summer afternoons, and while I tended to my baking, Lyman and Mary sat out on the porch shucking corn from their gardens to freeze. All the while a huge helicopter hovered just upriver, filling a bucket with water to dump on the fire, which at that time was burning up a draw just across from us. Mary says she was glad no buildings got burned, and she's glad the rain helped put that fire out…because those "copters" were sure noisy.

Later in the day, I heard this feathery sound above me. Peering upward, I was surprised to see a tiny screech owl perched on a high beam in Lyman's log home.

Before all that fire activity, Lyman and Mary were visited one afternoon by a lone grouse that wandered through an open door. The grouse stayed several weeks on the ranch, following Lyman around as he tended to his chores.

That day spent there with Lyman and Mary was another one of those golden moments to remember.

The goose call on our bird clock reminds me it's now 5 a.m. and I must get some *zzzz*'s. My day is far from over. Doug has just left for town to play cribbage with the boys at the Range Rider.

Tomorrow Doug and I leave for Marr Flat cow camp to help Lyman ship his calves. I'll pick up the steaks late this afternoon.

September 29—Spent all day yesterday near Harral Butte at the Marr Flat cow camp, cooking for the cowboys.

Barbara Warnock brought Mary up. She was the queen. Barb brought along her grandma's rocking chair, and after all those years of "cooking for the cowboys," Mary rested and we waited on her. It was lovely there, with the coral-colored thornbush thickets, the reddening huckleberry bushes, the golden quaking asp, the clean, clear air, frost on the meadows, and bawling cattle in the old corrals that have known so many fall gathers.

I made a picture of the crew there at the corrals, for posterity. The Warnock boys, Sam the vet, the Fluitt family, Doug, and others who came up to help ship the calves and work the cows. Even the fire lookout fellow came down for a steak. It was lots of work, but a day I wouldn't have missed for the world.

It's always sad, somehow, to leave the small cabin in the clearing, knowing we won't see it until next fall. We know how Mary must feel, after all those years spent there, all those entries written in her small five-year diaries, penned after a day of riding or cooking for the "boys."

October 11—As daylight seeps through darkened rain clouds this damp autumn morning, I hear and see a pair of Red-tails circling above our yard where, scattered among the leaves on our lawn, lie bones, flung there by Doug after he finished cutting and wrapping the white-tail buck he shot a week ago. It was a small buck, fattened on Prairie Creek's alfalfa and pea fields. Mama kitty and her kittens, along with several magpies, have been cleaning the bits of meat clinging to those bones. My mare, Morning Star, stares at me through the window, juice from windfall apples dribbling from her mouth. Since she's been turned loose to clean up the tall grasses growing between the house and the garden, my little gray mare seems content. Last evening she relished the corn husks I threw over the fence.

The Northwood Maple has lost its colorful leaves, and the ancient willows are yellowing. Yesterday, Doug dug the potatoes and stored them in the cellar, and covered the carrots with dirt and straw. The last cabbages have been cut and dozens of frozen strawberries hide beneath thick-leaved plants. The sunflowers droop now; their ripening seeds will sustain birds well into winter. My petunias, snapdragons and geraniums have all succumbed to frost.

Last night's gentle rain has freshened up our green fields however, which is in stark contrast to previous mornings when Prairie Creek lay under a thick cover of frost. Looking off to the Wallowas, I see a dusting of new snow over the more permanent layer of white. I love arising early enough to stare through our picture window at coyotes hunting rodents in the hay meadow across the road. Nearby graze the white-tails alongside Hough's black cattle.

Grandson Buck drove in late Friday evening before the opening of buck deer season. Making this his headquarters, he spent the week

88-year old Mary Marks and Dan Warnock inside the Marr Flat cow camp cabin. Dan is the son of Barbara and Grant Warnock of Imnaha. Dan and brothers Joe and Charley grew up on Imnaha. This is one of the cabins where, for years, Mary cooked for the cowboys.

hunting with his buddies Gabe and Luke, with whom he'd attended grades 1 through 8 at the small school on Imnaha. Growing up together in this country, it was only natural that all three of them developed an early love for the outdoors, which would include hunting. They're all married now and, with the exception of Buck, live here in the county.

Of course, I got in and baked a deep dish apple pie, roasted a pork ham roast, and made sure I had plenty of mashed potatoes, gravy, and corn on the cob.

On Sunday, Buck's wife, Chelsea, joined us. Since it rained—and snowed in the higher elevations—raincoats, boots and gloves were hung behind our wood cookstove to dry. The old Monarch was used a lot, simmering a dutch oven full of elk stew while using the warming ovens to set my pans of sourdough biscuits to rise.

Chelsea, a nursing student at Lewis/Clark College in Lewiston, helped me clean house, which was simply wonderful! And quite a shock to my house.

Grandson Ryan drove over from Pendleton to hunt with grandpa, so there was plenty of activity around here.

On Tuesday I attended my weekly Writer's Group at Fishtrap House, after which I met Chelsea and daughter Ramona for lunch at our local hospital. And since I was supposed to meet Mary there after her therapy session, all went as planned.

After assisting Mary during her doctor appointment at Winding Waters Clinic, and making sure Don arrived to drive Mary home to Imnaha, I left for the ranch...after which I hurriedly packed my suitcase and headed for La Grande to spend the night with granddaughter Carrie. After a pleasant evening, which included dinner, and playtime with great-granddaughter Brenna, I hit the hay. The next morning, right on schedule, here came Jessica, who'd driven from Boise to pick me up.

Our destination: Beaverton, Oregon, where we'd join another "Syringa Sister" Bobbie, who had planned an overnight backpack trip in the Cascades before we three attended Barb's wedding on Saturday. After "talking" our way down I-84, we pulled into the Columbia Gorge Hotel, where we lunched on oysters and raved about the blooming petunias, impatiens, and geraniums.

Soon, there we were, entering Portland's maddening traffic. Bobbie's directions in hand, I attempted to guide Jess, who was concentrating on NOT getting us killed. All went well, until Jess missed a vital exit, and there we were, LOST with a capital L...in a neighborhood we knew not where. By some miracle we found a pay phone and placed a call to Bobbie, who assured us we were only ten minutes away from her place.

"Stay there," she ordered. "I'll come rescue you."

Never so glad to see her smiling face, we followed Bobbie home without further incident.

Bobbie and Dick were wonderful hosts. Dick was just taking two loaves of bread out of the oven. The cul-de-sac they live on was quiet and far-removed from traffic, and Jessica and I each had our own bedrooms. Our planned backpack never materialized however, because it rained, which meant snow at the elevations we would be hiking. Never mind. We had a wonderful time anyway.

The next day found us driving up the hill to the lovely historic Pittock Mansion, which was home to Portland pioneers Henry and Georgiana Pittock from 1914 to 1919, whose lives during the late 1800s and early 1900s paralleled Portland's growth, from a small northwest town site to a city of a quarter million population.

In his own words, "barefoot and penniless," English-born Henry L. Pittock came by wagon trail from Pennsylvania to Oregon in 1853, and at the age of 19 began working for Thomas Jefferson Dryer's weekly Oregonian newspaper.

At 26 he married Georgiana, who was 15 years old and from Missouri. Their marriage lasted 58 years and produced six children, and that little newspaper Henry acquired in 1860 is still published today. The mansion is just something you have to see for yourself. And the view of Portland from that hill is awesome, as are the hiking trails that take off from there.

One of the, the Wildwood trail, we took after munching cheese and crackers. Halfway down through this fragrant forest, we spied a young pileated woodpecker. Giant ferns, mossy evergreens, and a quiet path made us feel far-removed from the city.

Late the next morning we walked many blocks through a neighborhood where, Bobbie told us, there used to be large fields of horseradish.

"See that older home over there? That's where the owners lived. Now the fields are gone and there is development all over the place."

Traffic increased, and soon we came to a modern train station where we caught a ride on Portland's light rail. For a country gal, this was quite an experience. Lots of time for people-watching as we sped through long tunnels, then emerged into the light again. All those unsmiling stoic faces...going to and from work...or shopping...or whatever.

We stepped off the light rail a block from Powell's Books, where we wandered the rooms of books, used or new—a rare treat for us bookworms. Hunger drove us to the coffee shop inside the building, where we ordered sandwiches to go with our hot drinks.

Back to the station, and then a walk in the rain, which was really quite pleasant, as it wasn't cold.

The next morning found us several blocks away at Barb's church, helping decorate. It was fun to see Barb, another Syringa Sister, again. Soon we were rolling linen napkins up around sprigs of lavender and tying them with raffia, while other friends dealt with baskets of flowers. Barb served a brunch of Portland pastries, and by noon, all was ready for the wedding that evening.

On the way back to Bobbie's we stopped at a farmer's market, where I purchased some goat cheese and hazelnut brittle. What a colorful place: live music, lovely trees just beginning to color, booths of freshly harvested vegetables and fruit, local vendors cooking up all sorts of ethnic foods, and folks strolling along selecting their week's fresh produce. A very colorful scene. I'll always remember those huge loaves of bread baked at a local bakery.

The wedding was perfect. Barb married her Bob, and then we sat down to a catered dinner for 128 folks, after which a trio of musicians accompanied a young girl with a lovely voice, who sang the "old songs." Songs you could dance to. Only Jessica and I didn't have our husbands, so we were wallflowers, watching Barb and Bob and Bobbie and Dick waltz across the floor.

To assure we were headed out of town on the right road the next morning, Bobbie and Dick led us to 205, where we followed signs to I-84 east. Sure was nice to see Eastern Oregon again. Whew!

Almost forgot...that Sunday we left Portland, my granddaughter Mona Lee and Buck's wife, Chelsea, were running the Portland Marathon. They did it, all 26.6 miles, in a little over four hours. They'd planned this run for nearly a year.

Later that evening, my 14th great-grandchild was born. Another boy, Cutter C. Nash, born to grandson Rowdy and his wife; Kasey. Our little (but mighty) Kasey, a veterinarian in John Day, birthed an 8 lb. 5 oz. baby. This is Rowdy and Kasey's first baby.

Meanwhile, back at the ranch, grandson Ryan got his buck, as did granddaughter Carrie. And Buck shot his buck on the last day of the season. It was quite a week.

Tomorrow, son Ken ships the calves and weans the heifers that have been pastured out in the hills. Doug has been busy out there all week as well.

I'll be leaving Sunday for the Writer's Retreat on Imnaha. Even though my book is written, I'm in need of a little rest, and perhaps I'll come with another project. I'm looking forward to it.

October 21—Seated here in my tiny one-room log cabin on the Upper Imnaha River, as the yellowing leaves of an old apple tree float past my window, is my idea of the perfect place to be in mid-October. There are five of us writers, all women, here at our fall Fishtrap Writer's Retreat.

The cabin, built into the hillside, features a small wood stove, a single bed, a writing table, a worn sofa, a small table and chair, and wooden pegs to hang my clothes on. Access is gained via wooden steps at the front of the cabin, or a back door, which leads uphill to the outhouse.

We refer to this rustic abode as the "tree house." An enormous apple tree grows to the left of the steps, the branches of which have (over the years) created a sort of leafy canopy over the deck. Consequently, in April one can experience living in the midst of pink blossoms, while in October, a roof of apple-laden branches enhances the tree house effect. There is electricity, but no other amenities. I don't miss them.

Since we've been down here during the full moon, several of us have had trouble sleeping. We're turning into lunar moths... or lunatics. Which means we get up in the night to read or write. These fall-colored canyons in moonlight are hauntingly beautiful. Our two poets, Myrna and Eden, have not lacked for inspiration.

Moving in last Sunday morning, my gaze wandered to a high porch beam, where I noticed a tiny screech owl perched. Seemingly unruffled by my comings and goings, the owl stared down at me with sleepy yellow eyes.

After pushing six cart-loads across the swinging bridge that spans the Imnaha River, then toting my "stuff" up those stairs, I'd worked up an appetite, so I fixed myself a sandwich and drug my chair out on the deck to enjoy the autumn sunshine. Every so often I'd glance up to see my little owl still watching me.

Wednesday morning I baked a squash pie and an apple pie—from windfalls here—plus a pork roast, which I took down the river to Mary and Lyman's. Kathy drove the other four gals down later that evening.

There, in Lyman's kitchen, we cooked beans and corn, mashed the potatoes and stirred up a kettle of gravy. Doug, who had shown up that morning with another cord of wood, declined our invitation to stay for supper, so Lyman had to put up with six women. The out-of-county writers were fascinated by the experience. Not often does one get the opportunity to visit a real working cattle ranch, especially in such a remote canyon setting. And, of course, everyone enjoyed visiting with Mary, who is a legend on Imnaha.

We share this lovely, leafy place with a flock of wild turkeys.

Last evening, as I was peeling potatoes at the kitchen sink, I noticed a dark, feathery shape perched on the porch railing, and was surprised to see it fly to the top of the house, after which Glenda reported seeing the turkey—using the roof as a sort of runway—swoop farther up and light in the top of a tall locust tree. Soon, others followed suit, until a dozen of the large birds were roosting high enough to ensure their safety from predators.

Each day they became bolder and more trusting of us. Arising at first light, I hoped to witness the turkeys flying down from their high perch. Fifteen minutes of patience paid off. Landing lightly, for such heavy birds, they stretched their long legs, fluffed their feathers, and trotted off toward Indian Creek.

After starting a fire in my tiny wood stove, I was just sitting down to write when I heard a great cacophony of cluck and gobble. Peering through my window, I was surprised to see nearly 30 turkeys swarm down off the hill into the orchard.

There, under the apple trees, they performed a wild morning "dance." Gobblers fanned out their tail feathers and strutted around, hens leapt straight in the air, then they pursued each other, in what I can only describe as pure joy. There seemed to be no other reason for their actions, other than that they were happy in their surroundings and full of grasshoppers, which swarm all over the canyons this fall.

Other wild visitors include mule deer does and fawns, who appear at dusk to nibble windfalls. Scattered among the dead leaves, we've also noticed evidence of a resident bear, but so far haven't seen one.

There are so many trees around my cabin and the log house, it creates this surreal illusion of living in a world of floating leaves; leaves, backlit by an amber-colored light, swirling in the eddies of the river, and drifting on downstream. Daylight hours are precious, as we are walled in to the west and east by high-tiered rim rocks that end in the bluest of skies. The sun doesn't work its way down to the mouth of Indian Creek until 10:00 o'clock in the morning…and of course, slinks silently behind a high western ridge earlier each afternoon.

On the night of the 17th we five took ourselves outside to gaze in awe as the full October Hunter's Moon cleared the high ridge line to the east. There, beside the river, we glanced down to see the moon's watery reflection simmering at our feet. High up among the scattered rim rocks, the dry canyon grasses glowed like snow.

Each night is a feast. Writers are good cooks. We take turns preparing our specialties. Our kitchen fills with the aroma of freshly baked breads, garlic and olive oil. Days are spent writing, reading or reflecting.

Here, deep in the canyon, there's time to think, or take long walks, to gather Mary's walnuts for her, hike up Indian Creek, or simply wander up and down the graveled country roads, following the river. As the colors deepen each day, the air sharpening and the warmth fading from the sunlight, we sense the need to soak it all in before winter.

The week has flown, and tomorrow we'll all return to our busy lives.

October 25—Leaving was hard, as usual, but we all said goodbye, and after giving Eden a ride down to Mary's, where she would be picked up later, I drove out "on top."

My first task was to put a leg-of-lamb, that Doug took out of the freezer the night before, into my oven. My second: to unload my stuff.

Doug, who had been out in the hills with son Todd, sorting and shipping calves all morning, arrived around noon, only to leave again to

According to Mary Marks of Imnaha, "You just gotta know where these better bucks hang out."

drive to Upper Prairie Creek to where they were weighing and loading calves onto cattle trucks for Scott, who runs cattle on Doug's summer range. After which he'd join the "Apple Pressin' Party" at Chuck and Chris Frazier's place.

When the roast was nearly done, I joined the doin's myself. Since many folks arrived around noon, the apple cider-making process was well under way. Huge piles of fragrant pulp rose beside the garden, and children romped around the top of a low stack of baled hay.

It was another one of those perfect Indian Summer days. A cold creek splashed down beside the house, aspen thickets shimmered in the sunlight, Chief Joseph Mountain reared to the west—the earlier snows nearly melted—and to the north rolled the tawny hills. All manner of mouthwatering meats were cooking, including half a hog, roasting over coals, encased in an enormous handmade barrel-like barbecue constructed by Chuck, our local talented iron smith.

Nearby, a wide grill sizzled with 30 halves of flyers broasting slowly over another handmade affair. Oysters in the half shell or scooped hot out of the coals, fresh prawns from Alaska, and venison skewered over another one of Chuck's inventions. So many folks arrived from miles around, their cars filled an adjacent field.

Lots of visiting. Everyone bringing food: salads, beans, bread, pickled beets, cakes, pies, cookies. The amber-colored apple juice flowing beneath the wooden press, filling bowls that were strained into a huge vat, then drained via a plastic tube to fill the jugs. The smell of ground apples, the taste of the cider, the very air itself, all full of fall.

Into all this I wandered, carrying my roasted lamb. Doug opened the lid of the huge barbecue and placed my roast next to the hog. Chuck basted the meat with the juices in my baking pan, which were flavored with fresh rosemary and garlic.

Doug had been busy grinding horseradish, and already little jars had been filled with ground pulp mixed with white vinegar. Needless to say, we feasted. It was fun to see son Todd there, as well as daughter Ramona, both of whom had been working cattle that day.

To walk off some of that food, several of us took a hike over the hill. Returning, we looked down at that scene: children here and there, making memories they'll never forget. Our young Upper Prairie Creek girls, Ryya, Lexi, and Hannah, played their fiddles on bales of hay. People were still eating and visiting as the sun went down over the Wallowas. The sight made us all feel so lucky to be here...lucky not only for our incredible surroundings, but also for being among the people who choose to live here.

Before I went down to the Writer's Retreat I drove to the hills with Doug to help sort the cows and calves in Butte Creek. Son Ken was there to ship the calves. We three accomplished this by 9 o'clock, as we'd gotten up early that morning. Watching the sun rise over the Zumwalt was worth it all. It was fun being the "gate person," standing there, letting the "ins" in and the "bys" by. It'd been a long time since I was given this responsibility, but I hadn't forgotten.

Our friend Pete arrives this evening. He and Doug will be out on Salmon Creek come morning, hunting their cow elk. My writer's group meets this morning, and I must feed the chickens. Popular Oregon writer Craig Lesley joined our monthly book group yesterday. What a treat. We'd selected his latest book, *Burning Fence,* for our October read. It is a great memoir about growing up in Eastern Oregon. More next time.

November 7—Softly, silently...the snow falls outside my window. Just as silently, the season shifts.

Last week's wild winds have stripped the branches bare of leaves. Beyond the garden, with its frost-bleached corn stalks, there is no other world than white. Everything has slowed. The crops are harvested; the land is allowed to rest. Even my chickens prefer to peck around inside their house, go to bed early, and talk less. The only color left are the bright orange Chinese lanterns growing alongside the house. Predicted high today…36.

Doug is in town, playing cribbage at the Range Rider with "the boys."

While I was down on the Imnaha, 90-year-old Alvin Josephy passed away at his winter home in Connecticut. Much has been written about this famous man who, with his wife, Betty, spent summers at their beloved home at the northern end of the scenic east moraine of Wallowa Lake.

Aside from Alvin's accomplishments, I choose to remember him as a friend; an intelligent, interesting individual who enriched my life. Alvin would tell me stories set in 1933, during the Depression, when I was born. Fascinated by a life I could only imagine, I listened eagerly to every detail. In a way, Alvin reminded me of my four uncles who influenced me greatly during my formative years.

Last Saturday afternoon Doug and I attended a memorial for Betty Cornwell, better known hereabouts as the "Poetess of Upper Prairie Creek." That morning I'd risen early enough to read most of Betty's published poems.

Later, at Betty's memorial, her words, still fresh in my mind, brought tears to my eyes. Betty's sensitive spirit captured the essence of living year round on a small farm, surrounded not only by beauty, but isolation, due to long, cold winters. The loss of Betty's husband, Ken, her daughters all grown and gone, and failing health all forced Betty to move to town, away from the source of her inspiration.

Sometimes, while in Enterprise, I would stop by and visit Betty over a cup of tea. Later, she asked permission to use some of my photos for her last book of poems, *Sprinkle With Stars,* published in 1996.

Betty had a great sense of humor and we laughed together at our life experiences. Eventually, she ended up in our local assisted living facility in Joseph, where, regretfully, I didn't visit as often as I should have. My last memory of Betty is her showing me the new word processor she was just learning to operate.

Pete showed up, as planned, the night before the first cow elk hunt. With leftovers in mind, I cooked up a large, pork roast supper. Pete, who loves my cooking, says his visit here is the most looked-forward-to time of year. Mine too…as Pete does all the dishes.

Early next morning, after one of Doug's famous sourdough pancake breakfasts, we three jumped into the old truck and took off for the hills— me riding in the middle, bouncing over those rough, rocky roads. Not until after we'd eaten our lunches on a high hill did we spot the first elk.

I'd gone along for the ride and the chance for adventure. Which, as usual, turned out to be just that. It began while glassing a timbered butte, where several hundred elk streamed down off the top and disappeared into a deep draw, and ended with Doug helping Jim, Patti and Bill haul an elk Bill had killed downhill from their rig, in a snowstorm yet. Apparently, his shot had spooked the herd we'd seen coming off the butte.

Meanwhile, Pete shouldered his rifle and took off uphill, in hopes of intercepting several elk that suddenly appeared beyond the downed elk! After Bill's elk was laboriously loaded onto our pickup, we switchbacked down that slippery butte. It was still snowing... and, at first, no sign of Pete. Pretty soon, through the falling snow, we saw him heading our way. The elk had given him the slip. The wind began to blow, and it was bitterly cold as we drove to Jim and Pattie's with Bill's elk.

On the way home, Doug picked up some cattle supplement at the Grain Growers and we returned to the ranch on Prairie Creek, where I kindled a fire in the old Monarch and baked a pan of biscuits to go with those yummy leftovers.

The next morning Pete and Doug returned to the hills in hopes of bagging their cows... and returned triumphant. That is, until they had to deal with two carcasses, which translates into WORK. I'd stayed home to read to the residents of Alpine House for Fishtrap. After the men finished eating supper, Pete still had enough energy left to do my dishes before he joined Doug in the living room where they watched baseball on TV.

Friday morning Pete loaded up his elk and left for home. In the mood for baking, I brought up the last jar of mincemeat from my canning cupboard and put together a pie.

Later, after my friend Cathy finished teaching Friday college, I picked her up at Fishtrap House, and we hiked a deserted road on Alder Slope. Even though it began to rain, we enjoyed walking past old apple orchards, shuffling through fallen leaves, and simply soaking in that pastoral countryside.

Driving back to Enterprise, our eyes were drawn to Ruby Peak, which alternately appeared and disappeared in swirling fragments of mists. Sudden breaks in the clouds sent shafts of light streaming down upon evergreen slopes, shot through with golden tamarack; through a curtain of rain we watched a rainbow bloom on lower Prairie Creek.

Saturday morning was the 4-H radio auction. I managed again to secure the winning bid on the gift certificate for the Imnaha River Inn. While staying tuned to our local KWVR radio station, I cooked up a kettle of pasta sauce to use up all those ripened tomatoes I'd picked before the frost. After adding plenty of basil, parsley, garlic and onions, I let the sauce simmer and looked forward to future winter meals from my freezer.

On Sunday Doug treated me to breakfast at the Cheyenne Cafe in Joseph, where we sat at the "locals" table and B.S'd with the rest of them. Then, since it was such a nice day, I decided to drive to Imnaha and purchase a box of apples from Tammy Warnock for the mincemeat I planned to make. After Tammy showed me the spike elk she'd bagged near John Day, and my apples were loaded in the car, I drove upriver to clean out the refrigerators at the Writer's Retreat.

And, of course, the rest of that warm afternoon was spent visiting my friend Mary. Over a platter of cheese, crackers and apple slices, we caught up on most everything. Barbara Warnock drove in later to check on Mary and help cut up the noodles she'd rolled out earlier. Mary said Lyman and the boys were driving the cows down off the ridge.

"He left before daylight," she said.

Reluctantly, I left to drive home; back to Standard time that Sunday, the sun had already slipped over those high rocky rims.

On Monday, Carol Wallace and I, represent the CattleWomen, served the noon meal for the Senior Citizens at the Community Connection in Enterprise. Since it was Halloween we were visited by "witches" who distributed trick or treat candy to everyone. Then it was home to peel, core and chop five bowls of apples for my mincemeat.

That morning I'd risen early to grind up the elk neck that had simmered all night in a large kettle on the wood stove. This old family recipe measures all ingredients in bowls. I must have chosen a larger bowl than usual, because by the time I added the raisins, hand-pressed apple cider, and spices to the apples and ground elk neck, I had the largest kettle in the kitchen full.

Leaving this fragrant concoction to simmer on into the night, I wearily went to bed.

The next morning I got in and canned 12 quarts of mincemeat. Armed with some apple cider and the ginger cookies I'd baked that morning, I joined other friends at Fishtrap House Wednesday evening to attend a book-signing for Marvel Eaves. Marvel, a member of our weekly Writer's Group, had been working on her memoirs for several years, and we're all pretty proud of her.

By November 3 Prairie Creek was white with snow, and our phone went dead over the weekend. Before it snowed, a wild wind storm toppled several old cottonwoods and trimmed dead limbs all over the county.

Had a nice visit with our neighbors Gardener and Tappy Locke recently, in their warm little house, snuggled against the hill. We all

See below

agreed that Prairie Creek was a good place to enjoy our "golden years."

November 23—It is 6:30 a.m. on this day before Thanksgiving. As dawn brightens the clear, cold sky, a pair of horned owls call to each other in the ancient willows, the old Monarch range snaps and pops, and a kettle of water comes to the boil.

On Sunday night, November 13, the phone rang. My sister Caroline. "Mom died 15 minutes ago. Kathryn was with her. Love you, sis."

Sleep was impossible from then on. All night my mind was filled with thoughts of my mother. My mother, who was born in Clarksville, California, on July 10, 1910, and passed away in Auburn, California, at the age of 94 years, four months and three days. Each day counted for her. *5*

The day before mom died, my sister Kathryn had spent the morning with her.

"Mom wanted to be outside," she said, "so we sat out on the patio. It was a lovely, warm Indian summer day, and the leaves were falling...a sudden breeze loosened them, and the pine needles fell in her lap. Mom looked up at the colorful leaves against the clear, blue sky, and commented how lovely they were.

"Afterwards we went inside," Kathryn continued. "Where Mom ate all of her lunch and Davika placed a letter from you next to her plate. Mom had trouble opening it, so I took her hands and helped her." That was the last letter mom saw; the last one I wrote arrived too late.

Living this far away has been very hard on both of us, so I'd been sending daily letters and cards to mom since my September visit.

Doug and I arrived in Auburn a week ago today, and since it had been years since I'd experienced a Placer County fall, it soothed my soul to see Liquid Amber trees again. They were everywhere. And as we passed the Chapel of the Hills where mom's memorial service was scheduled, I noticed a cluster of golden-leaved trees, backlit by the sun. Mom picked a lovely time to die.

Soon we were at sister Caroline's house in Newcastle, where the remainder of that day was spent composing words to aptly describe our mother...words that would convey to others what we, her daughters, thought of this remarkable woman. Dulled by the long trip and not much help, I did manage to contribute, which made me feel better.

Mom's simple service was well attended. Regretfully, not one member of my burgeoning Oregon family could make it. Knowing they were there in spirit helped, as did the large spray of fall flowers I'd ordered from all of us.

Saturday evening our family and friends gathered at Marie Callender's in Auburn for a final meal and to say goodbye, which brought back memories of when Doug and I would take mom there during our January visits. Mom always ordered a hot roast turkey sandwich with mashed potatoes, dressing, gravy, and cranberry sauce. And she always topped her meal off with a bowl of ice cream. It was a joy to watch her eat. I often thought that food reminded her of all those Thanksgivings at Grandma and Grandpa Wilsons…a sort of comfort meal. And now, that is what I must think of. So this column will end.

Today I will bake pumpkin and mincemeat pies, cook cranberry sauce, and cut bread into cubes for dressing. Only this year, we won't have a crowd. For various reasons our large family is scattered. I purchased a small turkey yesterday, and we'll only be five around the table this Thanksgiving. Life is for the living, and we are blessed and thankful for the gift of it, just we are grateful for the gift of having such a special mother, grandmother, great-grandmother and great-great-grandmother for such a long, long time.

December 6—Peering out the front window this morning, just as daylight replaced the long December night, I spied what appeared to be some sort of awry movement in an otherwise motionless landscape. Hough's snowy pastures reposed in silent white, making it easier to spot this movement, which turned out to be two young coyotes chasing each other up and down the field.

All I could see at first were their furry tails and flying paws, which sent clouds of snow scudding in their wake. After about about ten laps, they fell in a heap and nuzzled each other, rolling over in the snow, then leaped in the air and ran in circles. There was so much joy in their play.

It's been so cold lately, the low being about zero, I haven't ventured out much except to feed the chickens. If I don't gather the eggs by noon, they freeze.

Last week I thawed out several eggs and used them to make a pineapple up-side-down cake. Since all of my older hens went on strike, I got on the phone and called Ed Wallace. I got his wife Carol.

"You want some stewing hens?" I asked.

"I'll ask Ed," she said. Later she called back to say they'd be over Monday to pick them up. So, yesterday morning, Carol appeared at my door, cage in hand.

"I'm the chicken catcher," she said.

So…I bundled up, and the two of us trudged up the snowy path to the chicken house. After blocking all means of escape, I positioned Carol at the door and, armed with my handy dandy wire hook, I began to snag those hens by the foot. This caused a great commotion in the hen house, and all that flapping of wings, flying feathers, and squawking alarmed my four roosters, who began to crow wildly. Carol and I began to laugh. We hadn't had this much fun since we'd entered the wild cow milking in the all-girl rodeo many years ago.

While we were in California, son Ken and his family trailed the cows in from the hills, which was a good thing because those ponds are frozen solid by now.

Last week, Doug made several trips out there to haul in the bulls and his tractor. Good to see cows here again, casting their cold shadows on the frozen fields as they patiently wait for the sound of Ken's truck, which means they'll soon be munching their daily ration of hay.

Sometimes it warms up and I head over the hill to see what I can see… and what I see are ducks, hundreds of them, lifting off Locke's stubble field or flying in squadrons toward the lake. And I see white-tail deer, wearing their heavy winter coats, nibbling the tall grasses growing along the irrigation ditches or grazing bare patches of alfalfa. I see tiny tracks of field mice and feathery scuffles in the snow, where I know hawk or owl has made a meal of some warm, little rodent.

One frigid but sunny morning Phyllis and I decided to avoid cabin fever by hiking over Sheep Creek Hill. Bundled to the teeth, we struck off at a good clip and were soon warmed by the exertion.

Such a view from the top. We could see north to the Findley Buttes, eastward to the Divide, the entire Wallowa Chain and the snowy Seven Devils, while below us yawned the breaks of the Imnaha canyons. What wasn't white was blue: blue mountains, blue sky, blue distance. We leaned against a pile of rocks and lunched on elk salami, crackers, fresh Mandarins from California, and chocolate truffles.

Wallowa County loves Christmas. There have been bazaars, a Winterfest parade featuring lighted tractors, tree-lighting ceremonies, and even wagon rides on Main Street Enterprise. Julie Kooch was there, her team of mules hitched to a wagon decorated with colorful lights, the evening Patti, Jim, Bill and Linda treated Doug and I to dinner at Lee's High Country Dining. I must say we stayed in where it was relatively warm, and watched the festivities out the window. Besides, we were so busy retelling all those hunting stories we didn't have time for anything else.

On December 1, I read stories to the folks at Alpine House. It's always fun to visit my friends Kate Wilde, Irene McFetridge and all the other regulars. Especially during the holidays.

Phyllis met me there last Thursday, after which we wandered in and out of Joseph's festively-decorated stores before enjoying a bowl of corn/potato chowder at the Wild Flour Bakery.

Last Saturday Phyllis and I drove to the gym of the old Lostine school, now the Providence Academy, and took in the afternoon performance of the Mid-Valley Theatre Company's production of "The Homecoming." Set on Spencer's Mountain, Virginia, in the year 1933—the year I was born—this play centers around the original story of the "The Waltons." Never mind that there were no fancy seats and the acoustics left a lot to be desired; it was the same spirit of that long ago Christmas Eve, when life was harder. When life was reduced to providing the simplest of gifts, the gift of giving oneself to make others happy.

Bravo! To Craig Stobel, his wife Monica, and the production staff for bringing Theatre to this far northeastern Oregon. Bravo, also, to the local citizenry who memorized all those lines.

Enterprise FFA will be selling local Christmas trees next weekend at the Ag shop, and perhaps granddaughter Adele, home now from Argentina, will be there, warming her hands over the barrel and helping me select a tree.

Although I miss writing to my mother, I still write for her. She has been, and always will be, my inspiration.

December 18—Phyllis and I met other birders at the Wild Flour Bakery in Joseph, where we signed up to tally the birds around town again. It was a sub-zero morning and we bundled in layers of clothes and wearing balaclavas that covered our noses before we began to walk, shortly after 7.

Whenever it is brutally cold and there is snow on everything, and the skies are clear, our valley is incredibly beautiful. The cold December moon still rode on the horizon, and when the sun did burst through the evergreens, growing on the high school hill, it dazzled us with sparkles of frozen filigree. I mean, everything sparkled as we crunched our way around town.

At first the birds were scarce. A chickadee here, a junco, a flutter of sparrows, and then a cold wave of wild honkers flew overhead. Most of the birds flocked to feeders in folks' yards.

We decided to walk up on Barton Heights to check out a mountain ash tree where earlier sightings of Bohemian waxwings had been reported. But after we hiked up the hill to the appointed tree, the only bird that greeted us was a very cold, fluffed-up robin, perched in the middle of the berry-laden tree.

Ironically, we had our own Robin with us. And this pretty young miss used her frozen fingers to record out sightings. Below us, mist trailed above water of the West Fork of the Wallowa River, and the morning light glowed golden white beneath the bare-limbed aspen. The snowy flanks of Mt. Joseph seemed close enough to touch.

Like last year, we bee-lined past the rodeo grounds to the Cheyenne Cafe to thaw out, and were most grateful for the steaming cups of tea, compliments of Doug, who was eating breakfast at the "Locals Only" table. After, the five of us piled in Phyllis' car and drove up Hurricane Creek to her place to count Steller's jays. Although we just missed seeing these bright blue birds, we did spot a hawk and several more chickadees. And we did enjoy the view of the Seven Devils from P.'s kitchen window, and Sacagawea Mountain from her living room. Fred pointed out several birds and informed us later that the blue jays arrived after we left.

Anyway, by noon we returned to the Wild Flour for lunch, where we turned in our list of birds. At least we participated in that 30th annual Wallowa County Christmas Bird Count—and survived the cold!

Then it was home to rest up and return to Joseph by 3 for the Christmas Home Tour, which included Dave and Darlene Turner's festively-decorated home on Walker Lane; the McColgan home on Mill Street, which is in the process of becoming a bed and breakfast; and the Tyreman's Bronze Antler Bed and Breakfast. From there, we drove to Enterprise where Cheryl Kooch showed us around her and Creighton's historic home, which is also home to the famous Kooch Clydesdales.

The last stop was at Steve and Nancy Arment's home on Depot Street. Words fail here. What a treat. Steve is the wood artist who creates whimsical animals, birds, and screen doors. A large Christmas tree stood in one corner of the living room and a wood stove warmed us, as Robin, who had walked around Joseph with us that morning but was now dressed in a Victorian style gown, played sweet tunes on her violin. Steve's creative handiwork was apparent everywhere. He'd transformed an old abandoned house into a unique home that reflected his many talents.

Every evening, just at dusk, a pair of Horned owls stretch their wings and fly from the two Ponderosa pines in our front yard, to spend the night hunting for rodents. I love watching them take off. One night a barn owl, with its heart-shaped face, surprised me by flying nearly into the window.

December 27—On this cold, dreary afternoon, my thoughts are of my oldest daughter Ramona, who has just undergone gall bladder surgery.

Josh

John Nash, home on leave from the Navy, rode his horse from Big Sheep Creek to Prairie Creek behind 320 cows, helping his dad, Todd Nash, trail the cattle to their winter headquarters near Enterprise. Shown in the background are the cows, who spent the night in Doug Tippett's pasture.

I'm also thinking about granddaughter Mona Lee, who left early this morning to drive the wintertime roads to Centralia, Washington. Mona Lee spent Christmas with us and the house seems empty without her.

It was a different kind of Christmas, with no snow on the ground and mild temperatures, at least, that is, until last evening, when it began to snow again.

There were nine of us around the table this year, to chow down on the traditional prime rib dinner. They included grandson James, home from college in Montana; grandson Josh, home on leave from the Navy; granddaughters Becky and Adele; son Todd, his wife, Angie, and, of course, our Mona Lee. Other members of our large extended family were otherwise occupied with their own growing families.

Long-time friends from Montana were here Christmas eve. Pat and Linde shared a kettle of potato soup and homemade french bread with us. They had traveled all that way to lend Ramona and Charley a hand with the lambing. At last count, they had 90 lambs in less than two weeks. Ramona sure appreciated their help at this time

Compared to earlier days of zero temperatures, the weather moderated when the warm breath of a chinook wind melted all our snow and provided a welcome relief from the bitter cold. The days preceding Christmas were filled with varied activities, in spite of the cold.

The morning of the 18th, it was twelve below zero here on Prairie Creek, and that's when son Todd and his crew of cowboys and cowgirls started the cows to the valley from Big Sheep Creek. A three-day drive. They made it to Brushy the first night, and the next morning they headed up the Imnaha highway to Hayden Creek Canyon, and then down Echo canyon to our place. After the cows were turned into the pasture here, I invited the weary, cold crew into the kitchen for steaming bowls of beef and barley soup, and slices of warm mincemeat pie.

The next morning it had warmed up considerably by the time the cowboys saddled up to drive the herd the final miles to their winter quarters on Prairie Creek, just east of Enterprise.

The week before Christmas I invited our Writer's Group out to the ranch for clam chowder, which we enjoyed after our writing session.

On Thursday of that same week Doug and I hosted our Book Group to our traditional potluck, which was followed by readings. Friend Pete had given us a smoked turkey during elk season, and friends arrived bearing potluck. As usual it was a fun evening. We listened to everything from Stubby Pringle's Christmas to Doug's cowboy poem about "Goin' To The Weddin'," which was highly entertaining as Doug got such a kick out of telling the story, he could scarcely get through it.

On the evening of the 21st I drove to Enterprise, boarded—in the rain—a wagon loaded with straw bales, and rode up the hill to the church to view a live Nativity scene. The wagon was pulled by a tractor driven by Harold Jensen. Mrs. Jensen sat next to me on a bale of straw.

Inside the church we listened, enthralled, as granddaughter Amy sang Christmas carols and accompanied herself on the harp. After hot cider and Christmas cookies, I climbed back on the wagon and rode back to my car, parked in the Safeway parking lot. A wonderful way to celebrate both Christmas and the Winter Solstice.

Son Ken shows up each morning to feed the cows, which I can again see from my kitchen window. I often think about all those winters I would bundle up and traipse out to the barn to throw hay to my milk cows. Even though I miss them, I don't miss going out in the cold. My chickens are still laying, which is amazing. And I still bundle up and go out in the cold to tend to them.

How I love receiving Christmas cards and letters from friends and relatives who live far away. This once-a-year contact warms my heart.

Another tradition that warms our hearts is the loving box of freshly-picked tangerines from sister Kathryn's tree in Roseville, California. There is nothing quite as sweet-tasting on a cold winter day, as K's tangerines. And then there's the fragrant fruit cake that arrived in our mailbox from friend Jessica, who lives in Boise.

Before Christmas I made another visit to Alpine House to read to the residents. A treat for me was listening to THEIR stories of long ago, when sleighs pulled by horses slid over snow-covered fences, transporting families across the frozen landscape to visit their far-flung neighbors, back when winters were much worse and the snow much deeper.

This afternoon, grandson James will be here to collect Ari, my old Aracuna rooster. According to James, Ari's neck feathers are quite valuable when it comes to creating flies, and James is really into fly fishing and tying his own flies. In other words, he knows his feathers. So... this grandma is sacrificing her rooster for the art of fly-tying.

Besides, Ari is old, huge, and he eats too much, and it's not like I don't have any more roosters. There's Fred, Flash, and that little but mighty rooster who suddenly appeared in my chicken pen after the county fair chicken scramble. By the way, that mystery was solved: our neighbor Larry Waters finally fessed up.

Happy New Year to all of you out there in Agri-Times land.

Buck Matthews looks for an unbranded calf to rope at a recent branding on Salmon Creek.

2006

January 6—On this Friday morning the temperature here on Prairie Creek stands at 32 degrees, which would explain why, at 10:30, the ground is still frozen. If it weren't for that, you'd think it was early November, what with all the tall, frost-whitened, wind-blown grasses dominating the landscape. Snow, however, blankets the Wallowas, reminding us it is still the dead of winter.

Just called Lyman and Mary's on Imnaha, and they tell me the mud is drying up, the heifers are nearly through calving, and they haven't had any frost! Things are going along pretty well, says Lyman. "Mary hasn't hit me with the mop lately."

Never underestimate the power of a woman...especially Mary. This couple always reminds me that laughter is the best medicine. During these long Wallowa County winters we need all the humor we can dig up.

Daughter Ramona made it through her gall bladder operation and, thankfully, the ewes slowed down with their lambing. Ken shows up each morning to feed the replacement heifers, cows on the hill, his horse, and the bulls. He doesn't have to chop ice in the irrigation ditch anymore, because Doug repaired the automatic heated water trough.

A flock of finches has been feeding on the huge sunflowers in the garden. It is entertaining watching them hang upside down to peck the seeds.

My two horned owls continue to roost, sleeping off their nocturnal hunts in the Ponderosa pines on the front lawn. Every evening at dusk, I watch them stretch their wings and take off to search for rodents on the sagey hills to the east. When frequent Prairie Creek winds blow, and the pine needles swish this way and that, I watch the owls, apparently unperturbed by the violent swaying of their bedroom.

Between wind storms I walk the country roads...still missing my dog Daisy, who would sniff her way along, telling me where a muskrat slid into an irrigation ditch, a coyote trotted, a mouse tunneled under the snow, or another dog had passed that way. But I am not alone. Curious heifers collect along the fences and follow me to the next pasture, hawks sail above, and white-tail deer peer at me, nearly hidden in tall water grass, only the tips of their ears showing. And, once, I spied a solitary bald eagle in one of the ancient willows.

It's not unusual to walk several miles and not meet a single vehicle. If one does pass, it's a local rancher driving an old pickup loaded with hay, border collie dogs perched happily on top.

Well, the deed is done. Grandson James showed up to fetch Ari the Aracuna rooster. It was a cold, windy afternoon, and grandson Ethan and his parents were here for a visit. Doug suggested I should probably keep Ethan and his little brother occupied in the house, so they couldn't witness the rooster killing procedure. Not so. Both little boys, along with their father, put on their coats and trudged up to the chicken pen.

This is the stuff little boys (and big boys) are made of.

Shannon and I stayed inside. In due time, here they came.

"Nothin' to it," exclaimed Ethan. "He's executed!"

Whereupon we all played another game of checkers and ate blackberry pie. James, who was here for supper the other evening, informed me he now has this incredible array of neck feathers for tying fishing flies. And let me tell you, this boy knows his stuff. James will be returning to college in Montana soon, and I wish him the best. One of the joys of life, as we grow older, is seeing our grandchildren mature into adulthood.

It has been interesting, wondering which of my remaining roosters wold rule the roost. It didn't take long. The undisputed leader is Fred, the muscle-bound Cochin rooster given to me by Phyllis' husband, his namesake. It's positively a riot seeing Fred strut around all those hens while the lesser roosters stare enviously from the other side of the chicken pen.

I miss Phyllis. She's in Hawaii visiting grandchildren. Hopefully when she returns, and Doug and I return from California, there will be enough snow for us to go snowshoeing.

But the days pass, and we too enjoy the occasional visits from grandchildren. Like the time granddaughter Chelsie and husband, Justin, popped in with four great-grandchildren over the holidays. Suddenly here they were... Riley Ann, Ashlynn, and the two-year-old twins, Gideon and Jada. Naturally, I had to sit them all down on the sofa for a photograph. Bundled up in matching caps, handmade by grandma Annie, they were helping grandpa Ken feed the cows.

Another day I stopped by to see daughter Ramona, and found granddaughter Carrie there with two-year-old Brenna, who wanted to be outside. So; out we went, to see the chickens, cats, dogs, horses, and baby lambs. Brenna wanted me to push her in a sort of car affair, but this grandma soon petered out.

Doug and I spent New Year's Eve alone. I'd purchased a pizza and rented two movies, which we didn't watch, because they were DVDs and we can only play VCRs. Oh well. We only stayed awake until 9:00 anyway.

The next morning we enjoyed a great breakfast at the Mountainaire Cafe in Joseph, the only one open that morning. Rain the night before had turned to ice, but that didn't stop folks from going to town.

Doug's brother Jack called to wish us Happy New Year from Clarkston, Washington, and we had other phone calls that day as well.

I took down the Christmas tree, which shed needles over three rooms. The next morning I drug the tree up to the chicken pen, to join my Christmas tree graveyard. You can tell Christmases past in my chicken yard. The chickens love getting under the most recent tree, while it still has needles.

Doug drove to the hills to check the horses and reported seeing close to 600 elk.

"Doc" Morgan stopped by with some books I'd loaned him to read. He says the fishin' isn't all that good yet on the Imnaha. I gave him one of my Alder Slope squashes.

Yesterday morning I joined other Wallowa Valley women for "Stitch and Bitch." We all brought food to Kathy's place near Allan Canyon, where we gathered to knit, embroider, or work on some other project, all the while yakking. It was fun, and eating bowls of yam/peanut butter soup was a new experience, but delicious. I'd taken egg salad sandwiches.

Doug is gone, traveling over the mountain to Helix to watch grandson Ryan play basketball. I'm staying home getting this column out early so we can leave for California this week.

January 8—Because the sun was out yesterday, Doug and I drove to Imnaha to get out of the snow that fell Saturday night, and ended up at the Imnaha Store and Tavern, where we were joined by Chris and Chuck Frazier. Nothing like fried chicken mixed with rattlesnake stories to chase away the winter blahs. Hopefully, the next time I write, we'll be in California for our annual visit.

January 9—Daughter Linda and grandson Brady drove in with a friend from Salem Saturday morning about 10 a.m. They pulled into the driveway at the same time Doug returned. Linda was here to pick up our old van, which Doug gave her after he purchased a newer one for us. We spent the remainder of the weekend playing Scrabble and visiting.

Because Brady is a dyed-in-the-wool fisherman, I took him fishing...well, if you want to call casting into a hole in the ice, fishing. But then, 10-year-old boys just love going fishing, which means changing lures, casting, extracting hooks from limbs—all part of the fun.

After breakfasting on sourdough waffles, the family left around noon.

January 25—The window to my world reveals a familiar midwinter scene dominated by hoarfrost. Fronds of summer weeds, raspberry canes, chicken wire, and Ponderosa needles wear a thick coating of ice. As the fog, which creates hoarfrost, begins to lift, so does my heart as blue sky appears. In the bright morning sunlight I see the Horned owls have returned to their perch in the pines. Their dark, feathered shapes are stark against the frost-flocked tree.

Did I just dream that my three sisters, Mary Ann, Caroline, Kathryn, and I were soaking up the late morning sunshine, on a brick patio located on an olive ranch in California's El Dorado County hills? Did I dream that it was 70 degrees in late January? Looking back on my diary entries, I guess not. One entry reads,

We pulled into the Gold Hill Olive Oil Company, which used to be a cattle ranch when I was a girl, and entered a farm shed built in the 1860s, now an olive oil tasting room. This grower raises six varieties of trees in their orchard: Frantoio, Leccino, Lucca, San Felice, Itrana and Mission. These names made me feel like I was in Italy. The first oil was pressed from this young orchard in 2004.

That takes me back.

Caroline drove us to two wineries. I'm sure these spectacular vineyards must have been former ranches as well. The Gold Hill vineyard has been producing fine wines since 1985, and this small family-operated winery sits atop a hill overlooking its 50-acre vineyard, which looks down on the American River Valley and the historic gold-mining settlement of Coloma. Who would have thunk it? These formerly uninhabited chaparral and manzanita-covered hills, growing grapes!

We tasted wines served in sparkling glasses, sipping slowly in sunshine, and gazed upon ponds where ducks swam, and hawks circled overhead. Beyond the vineyards, nothing much had changed. There were the hills above Coloma with their rocky slopes and occasional Digger pines. And there we were: four aging, white-haired, motherless sisters, returning to our youthful haunts...feeling like tourists, only minutes away from where we grew up on a small dairy in the Placer County foothills.

Using leftovers from the Wilson Cousins lunch, held the day before in Sacramento, we located a picnic table along the South Fork of the American River and picnicked near where gold was discovered.

Caroline had made reservations for the four of us at the Coloma Country Inn long before Doug and I headed to California. So, after lunch on Saturday, we'd fled Sacramento and headed up Highway 50 from Folsom toward El Dorado County, where Caroline took us down a winding road that brought us to the small town of Lotus. From there we found our way to the inn, which was built in 1852 by a family seeking gold after the gold rush began. This farm house is connected, via a brick path to the Carriage House. Built in 1898, the rustic building has been turned into a cottage site. Perfect for us!

January is a quiet time in Coloma, and we had the place to ourselves. After settling in, we walked down the hill to the gold discovery site, and wandered around several booths set up to provide an insight into how folks lived during those early times.

In the old blacksmith's shop a fellow was working at the forge, hammering a horseshoe on an anvil. Men wore buckskins, women long dresses and bonnets. An old-timer played a fiddle on a weathered bench near the mill, a family prepared a meal over an open fire, and several young people tried their hand at gold panning along the American River.

As the sun slipped over the piney hills a chill settled over all, and the folks began to pack up and leave. We located the steep switchback trail that led to the James Marshall monument, erected on the top of a hill overlooking the south fork of the river. Signs at the trailhead warned of cougars, rattlesnakes, and poison oak, which didn't discourage us at all.

It was a lovely trail, and crossed one of the historic ditches—built with shovels to provide water for sluice boxes and, later, irrigation—that ran along the hillside. The half-mile jaunt was worth the effort when we gazed upward at the massive bronzed statue of James Marshall, dressed in buckskins, pointing down where he first saw gold glinting in the water at his feet.

My mouth still waters when I think of the meal we had that evening at the Cafe Mahjaic in Lotus. Lotus is smaller than Imnaha, and this old brick building was originally built by Adam Lohry, a German tailor, in 1855, after he accumulated enough money from the gold rush activity to do so. All meals are made from scratch using organic meats, grains, and local produce. What a fun experience!

Back at our Carriage House we played a game of Scrabble before snuggling under warm covers. Were we really in Coloma?

The next morning the sun spilled over the canyon and the mist rose above the river, and hovered over the nearby pond where Malcolm the

Muscovy—a duck—waddles up for a bowl of Cheerios.

After a brisk morning walk I joined my sisters for the breakfast portion of our bed and breakfast, which was served in the old farm house by our hostess, Candi. Sunshine, fresh fruit, biscuits, a steaming egg scramble, and blackberry jam were served at 9 o'clock.

After lingering in the sunshine near our carriage house, we packed up for our tour of the hills which I've already described. Then it was back to Caroline and Duane's, where we'd spent most of our stay. Doug was watching a football game up at Fred and Sandra's when we returned.

We left for home the next day, driving all the way to Ontario, where we spent the night. We arriving here on Prairie Creek yesterday afternoon. *arrived*

While everything is put on hold, I must get this column in the mail.

All three sisters accompanied Doug and me to Lodi, where we visited granddaughter Tammy, her husband Matt, and our three great-grandchildren, Clayton, Cole and Halley. After driving through one rain shower after another, the clouds lifted and the sun shone while Halley showed us her emu, "Moo Moo," which entertained us no end when the big bird, who had been raised with the chickens, was let out of the pen to run about the place.

Then Cole and Clayton showed us the 4-H steer, the burros, the horse, rabbits, "Oreo cookie" cows, pheasants, and other birds, not to mention the dogs and cats…all with stories of how they were acquired. We were amazed to find descendants of our mama kitty living in Lodi. We also took a walk through the vineyards that comprise Matt and Tammy's wine grape operation, some of which were in the process of being pruned that day.

We were fortunate in having good roads coming and going. Traveling through the Sierras going down, the weather was so mild it was raining on the summit. As usual Doug let me walk the country road that follows the ridge to our friends Fred and Sandra. After that hairy ride down Interstate 80 from Donner Pass, it's always nice to get out and stretch my legs.

Our stay at my childhood chum's place is always enjoyable. Fred had a roast beef dinner waiting for us, and Sandra had baked her traditional lemon pie before she went to work that morning. Even though it rained a lot, Sandra and I weren't discouraged. We went shopping, ate lunches at trendy little eateries, and attended the cinema, munching popcorn like school girls again.

I loved watching the blackbirds fly into roost in the Italian cypress tree growing outside the Hubbards' living room. And, every morning, the tall, thick branches of the tree erupted with birds.

Time does not permit recording all our experiences, but a highlight was having dinner at the Chinese restaurant in Loomis, surrounded by my three sisters, brother Jim, and assorted spouses. Another time the clouds fled and the California sun shone down on Caroline, Mary Ann and me as we traveled to Grass Valley to walk around that historic town. Fred and Doug were there too, but we never caught up with them.

Then there were the many walks, one with Mary Ann around her trailer park and another from Caroline's to Mary Ann's at Newcastle. The country roads were lined with Toyan bushes, manzanita, huge granite boulders, ferns, digger pines, and elaborate homes—mansions—on every hill and in between. Even though the blackberry-choked ravines still provide habitat for quail and wild turkeys, those Placer County foothills where I grew up are changing fast.

In everything we did, mama always seemed to be with us. There was her smiling face, encouraging us to be happy and experience life to the fullest. It was refreshing to walk on green grass and pick the first pussy willows, but I must face reality, knowing our spring is many months away.

Time to feed the chickens—which, thanks to son Ken, have survived very well during our absence—and get this column in the mailbox.

February 6—Just when I thought the wind was going to take a vacation, it began to blow again. And since our temps were in the low twenties this morning, Prairie Creek is mighty hilly.

I just hung up from talking to Mary on Imnaha.

"Wind's really blowin' down the river," she said. "Lyman just came in to put on more clothes."

"Not blowing out here," I said. "Cloudy and frozen, but thankfully, no wind."

Wrong again. During a rush trip to Enterprise earlier this morning, I noticed some of the firstborn calves appearing in neighbors' pastures, their tiny black bodies snuggled against the flakes of hay being thrown to their mamas by cowboys riding on the beds of slow-moving pickups. Beyond rose the Wallowas, snowy and coldly beautiful.

In the middle of the night I arose to look out at the swelling "Snow Moon," and there hung the Big Dipper, each star brilliantly defined in the clear night sky. Although February is the time for deep snows and the mountains are buried in a heavy pack, here on Prairie Creek the fields are bare, save for the deep, wind-hardened drifts that fill the borrow pits.

*Enjoying a bit of winter sunshine, these Suffolk ewes and December lambs
nibble hay on Charley and Ramona Phillips' ranch on Upper Prairie Creek.
The lambs started coming during the coldest days of December, but were
kept warm under heat lamps in the barn.*

Returning from my daily wanderings over the eastern hills, I walk
these crusty drifts to clean the gumbo from the thawing ground off my
hiking boots. With the exception of the frozen norths, these sagebrush-
covered hills get pretty greasy by late afternoon.

Cow paths wind beside coyote dens and badger holes, and oftentimes
a great whirring of wings startles me as Hungarian partridge burst from
the tall grasses lining the irrigation ditches.

It's good to be back at the ranch after all those exotic meals we
savored in California. Good to return to cold weather fare: venison
steaks, mashed potatoes, milk gravy, elk stew, beans, ham hocks and
cornbread. Canned green beans, frozen corn, and the quarts of cherries,
peaches and apricots line our canning cupboard shelves.

My chickens are laying again! Just as I was retrieving an egg from
under her, one of my pullets squeezed a warm, brown egg from wherever
eggs come from, practically into my hand.

Finally got in some snowshoeing this past Saturday, when Phyllis
called and we met up Hurricane Creek. After Phyllis donned her cross-
country skis and I strapped on my lightweight snow shoes, we were
off—striding in her case, shuffling in mine—up the snowy road that leads
to the trailhead. It was wonderful to breathe in the cold, sweet air, take in

the snow-laden evergreens, hear the sound of Hurricane Creek pooling and splashing its way down the canyon below, catch the cheery sound of a dipper (water ouzel) bobbing up and down on its mossy rock, and pause to visit other skiers and walkers.

Doug returned from the lower Imnaha last week with three steelhead, one of which we began to eat fresh. Another bright fish was frozen for future meals, while the third fish was smoked. Yum!

The next day I drove to Imnaha with a list of items for Mary and Lyman. How refreshing to encounter green grass at the bridge, and even upriver things looked spring-like. Calving is progressing on Lyman's ranch.

"Had a cow with twins, but she only claimed one," said Lyman. "Calf's out in the barn, needs a bottle." So, after hugging Mary, I warmed up a suckle bottle of milk and headed for the barn. Bedded in clean straw was the smoky-colored calf, who made a beeline for the bottle.

What a pleasant afternoon I spent with Mary. Helping her with several chores that are becoming harder for her, was my pleasure. We visited over tea, putting clean sheets on the bed, folding clothes and peeling potatoes. As usual, it was hard to leave the warmer climate of the canyons.

Driving home I noticed a flock of wild turkeys nibbling the grass at the far end of Lyman's pasture, while new calves absorbed warmth from the canyon's sunny slopes. I chuckled over Mary's telling of how Lyman had carried the wet, chilled twin into the house and laid the shivering calf on rugs in front of the wood stove.

"Barbara Warnock came up and got some milk down it," Mary said. "And pretty soon it struggled up, so we built a barricade so it wouldn't stumble all over the house."

For days, as well as nights, the wind blew. After a while that hollow roar gets to you. To escape I dove into a stack of books that have been collecting next to my recliner in the living room.

While my sisters and I were in Grass Valley, we'd visited a wonderful used book store and I'd come home with a variety of reading material. So... while the wind whistled around the house, I delved into 18-year-old Eric Ryback's account of backpacking from Canada to Mexico along the Pacific Crest Trail.

I devoured four books in all, including Pete Fromm's *Indian Creek Chronicles*, recording the winter he spent alone in Idaho's remote Selway River area. I must say, wrapped in a blanket, seated in a recliner in one's cozy living room, is definitely the best place to experience this type of adventure.

Our reading group—and myriad other Wallowa Countians—is reading Ray Bradbury's *Fahrenheit 451* as part of the annual Big Read. Fishtrap was the recipient of the only grant awarded in the U.S. to a rural community, the purpose of which is to promote reading across the United States.

Jonathan Nicholas, columnist for the Oregonian newspaper and one-time owner of cows, appeared in cowboy boots to deliver a kickoff talk for the Big Read at the Odd Fellows Hall in Enterprise. When Jonathan mentioned how he got into the cow business, he told this story about driving into Madras one night and seeing all the lights at the auction yard. Curious, he attended his first auction, and got so carried away by a heifer he'd seen out back that he ended up purchasing her.

"How do you pick out a good cow?" Jonathan asked a rancher, who told him, "By her eyes. If she has feminine eyes, she'll make a good cow."

"He was right. That cow gave me eleven calves," said Jonathan, who, of course, had to pasture the cow in various locations in Eastern Oregon.

Doug returned from the hills to check on our horses last week and reported seeing many elk. Apparently, these cow-like wild animals prefer to range where cattle have previously grazed. Much preferring new, tender shoots of grass to the rank ungrazed forbs.

Last Thursday, I read to some of the residents of Alpine House. Many new faces appearing these days, taking the place of those no longer with us. Nice to see Irene McFetridge, just turned 90, and Kate Wild, 90-plus, still going strong. Both of them know about life on a cattle ranch.

Son Ken is feeding haylage now to the cows that will calve next month. He uses his backhoe to scoop the large, fragrant bales out of long, plastic bags.

Yesterday I observed two pair of robins pulling worms out of our lawn. Pausing, listening, heads tilted to one side, they suddenly dove downward, their beaks bringing up a wiggling worm. How do they know how to locate them? Sight, sound, smell?

The two Horned owls braved most of the wind, but other times retreated to the protection of the barn. Now they are back in the Ponderosa pines on the lawn. I love watching them throughout the day, their eyes closed, sleeping off their nocturnal meals.

Time to take my daily walk to see what I can see.

February 21—For the firs time in nearly a week, our morning temperatures aren't hovering around zero. When the day's high was only 10-above, things didn't warm up much here on Prairie Creek…and wouldn't you know, that's when the cows began to calve.

Calves are tough little buggers, though; they survived, mostly due to their dams being older cows with experience, who know how to care for their newborns. As long as they can wobble up on all fours and discover a nice warm teat, these amazing babies seem to tolerate the brutal cold.

Now, at 9:30 a.m., the thermometer under the clothesline registers a positively balmy 27 degrees. However, a reminder of that week-long blast of Arctic air are the long spears of ice suspended from bunkhouse, barn, and woodshed, wherever snow thawed and froze. Not to mention the ice-clogged creeks and irrigation ditches. Now that the cows have been moved to the lower calving pasture, Ken must chop an opening in the ice to provide water for the cows to drink.

Every morning I find myself, binoculars in hand, peering out the bedroom window to count calves or search for a cow in labor. Ken is here now, to feed, and I can see him shoving flakes of haylage off the bed of his truck. I imagine the cows savoring this mixture of meadow grass and clover, which has been compressed into large bales and sealed in long rows of white plastic. When first opened, these bags release the sweet smell of summer.

On the 8th, before the cold spell, Phyllis and I decided to climb the steep slopes of the east moraine and, after much huffing and puffing, found ourselves on a long grassy bench that afforded a splendid view of Wallowa Lake and the so-close-you-could-touch-them snowy ramparts of Chief Joseph Mountain. The February sun burned away a layer of gray sky, and warmed our winter-weary souls.

Hiking back to our car, following the highway that borders the lake, we startled hundreds of wild mallards feeding near the shore. What a thrill to see them airborne enough to skim the surface of the lake, then, amid a cacophony of quacking, splash back down into the water. Obviously, these ducks enjoy life.

All through that bitter cold, my hens continued to lay. No explanation, except that I keep the plugged in pet dish full of fresh water, or perhaps they are simply responding to the longer hours of daylight.

On the 10th, our Friends of the Wallowa County Museum put on a spaghetti feed at the Senior Meal site in Enterprise. It was a benefit to raise money toward our capital campaign to help finance the new addition to our museum. The evening before the big event, our committee sliced, diced and grated the ingredients, under the watchful eye of Chef Bombaci, who not only donated his skills for the cause, but stayed up late stirring and simmering the sauce.

The supper was a huge success, complete with music provided by Bob Casey and the local "Ambulatory Revival String Band," so named—

we suspect—because Bob himself, minus a hand (the result of a recent accident) managed to play his "squeeze box." Bob, a very generous person, donates his time to help our community in so many ways. The spaghetti feed was his idea.

That was a busy Friday, as our local "Stitch and Bitch" group of women met at Annie's house up Hurricane Creek for a noon potluck before pulling out the knitting needles. Good to see young gals there... some of whom were teaching the older ones how to knit!

Thank goodness for crock pots. Several of us had cooked our dishes the night before.

Annie gave us a tour of her pottery studio, where she and husband, Jim, create some pretty wonderful stuff.

One cold Saturday evening, Doug and I attended the Elks crab feed in Enterprise, and apparently many other cattlemen and cattlewomen were hungry for crab and talk as well; we met many of our neighbors, such as Reid and Marilyn Johnson, Mack and Marion Birkmaier, Rod and Linda Childers, and Van and Betty Van Blaricom.

For a county so geographically isolated, especially in winter, this remote northeastern tip of Oregon never seems to lack for entertainment—and I mean top-rate entertainment. Like the concert, staged by the Inland Northwest Musicians, held in the Joseph High School gym. I get chills just remembering that live music and being so close to those who have mastered their instruments. The second half of the program, Beethoven's Triple Concerto in C Major, was performed by soloists Heather Lenahan, piano; Rebecca Lenahan, violin; and Austin Lenahan, cello. These gifted young people were accompanied by the orchestra. All three reside in rural Joseph. The hours they must spend practicing!

I had spent that morning down on Imnaha helping Mary, who had other company that day as well.

Last week Lyman called.

"UPS just delivered fresh crab. Gotta come down and help us eat it." So, I baked a "wacky" cake, and soon Doug and I were on our way down, then upriver, where we joined a houseful of neighbors at a table spread with newspapers, and began to crack crab. The winner, with the highest pile of shells, was Doug "Doc" Morgan. That fellow doesn't say much, but he gets really serious when it comes to cracking and eating crab.

Lyman's son Craig, a commercial fisherman in Eureka, California, apparently had a very successful season, so he shipped some to share with his dad's friends.

Barbara Warnock said, "I just knew when I saw the UPS truck go by, we were goin' to eat crab." Imagine, whisking fresh crab on ice fresh from the California coast to Imnaha! Other neighbors contributed salads and we ate chocolate cake for dessert. Thank you, Craig.

Mary just called. "Lyman had his fifth set of twins this morning. Only two more cows to calve." Which is pretty unusual, in that he doesn't have that many cows.

All of this cold weather builds appetites, and it seems like many of our social activities center around food. On Valentine's Day I treated my valentine to dinner out at the Embers in Joseph, after which I listened—minus my valentine—to the lovely voice of Monica Hunter and friends, who presented an Evening of Love Songs at the Indigo Gallery in Joseph. What a wonderful way to end Valentine's Day. Monica's voice was thrilling, and the place was packed. We don't need night clubs in Wallowa County for intimate entertainment.

Daughter Ramona and her husband, Charley, are returning today from back east, where they went to see grandson Shawn before he ships to Iraq. Our prayers are with you, Shawn.

Enjoyed a brief visit with grandson Buck and his wife, Chelsea, over the weekend. The couple drove over from Clarkston to help son Todd with the calving, after he took a tumble off the back of his truck while feeding.

Last Sunday morning, Doug and I drove down to the newly-opened Hells Canyon Roadhouse for breakfast. This cafe, operated by many owners over the years, is situated across the bridge that spans the Imnaha River. We ordered what was described as "Pig Out" on the breakfast menu...and a goodly portion of pig, in the form of ham, was served along with fresh hash browns, two eggs and whole wheat toast.

Doug commented that he had eaten breakfast there over 50 years ago. And we both remembered stopping in for hamburgers on our way home from Snake River, when Doug still owned the Dug Bar Ranch.

Cheerful wallpaper, flowery curtains, and real flowers on each table created a homey effect. The Easley family operates the cafe now; mom cooks, and husband, Sam, and the teenage children help as well. Below the cafe, the river, its waters visible between scattered chunks of ice, made its way down the canyon to join the Snake.

On the hill across the bridge stood the little schoolhouse, and across the street—Imnaha's only street—sat the tiny one-room post office, which has been serving the settlement for over 100 years. Up the street the historic Imnaha Store and Tavern still provides a place for hunters and fishermen, as well as a "Good Old Boys" table. Owners Sally and Dave keep the barrel stove hot and serve the best fried chicken gizzards in Wallowa County.

It was cold down there, too, and a blast of frigid air swirled around our feet every time someone came in the door. Stepping outside, I decided to walk up to visit the Good Old Boys, and give Doc some fishing lures and books to read. As I walked, I gazed up at what makes the canyon country so special: the canyons themselves, those towering tiered rims ending in sky, blocking out a world becoming more complex by the day.

We drove out "on top" past two great white guard dogs protecting a herd of goats, which included several kids. Signs along the Sheep Creek highway warn, *Caution, Slow, Goats.* And you better slow down, as they have the right of way... it's open range down there.

To work off that "pig out" breakfast, I later joined Phyllis and we skied and snowshoed up the snowy road to the Hurricane Creek trailhead. We had to keep moving, as it was bitterly cold after the sun slipped over the Hurricane Divide.

As I wind up this column, it's now Wednesday, February 22. The snow is nearly melted, the roosters are crowing, my house needs cleaning, the eggs need gathering, and it's time to walk out to the mailbox and put the flag up.

March 6—Typical of March is the unpredictability of the weather. A good example being a few nights ago, when I walked up the path to shut the gate to the chicken pen under a clear, black sky, flittering with every star that ever there was. The next morning we awoke to three inches of snow!

Today it's raining, the snow is melted, and its white line has retreated to upper Prairie Creek. Grandson Chad and his son, four-year-old Ronan, were here to feed this morning. Can imagine Ronan got a kick out of "helping" his dad. The gusty winds that have been whipping around Prairie Creek for the past couple of days have run out of breath, and that's a relief.

Grabbing my binoculars to stare through the bedroom window, I note three new calves. I just can't help walking down to check the mama cows. Quite often there is one in labor, and some of these old girls can be pretty creative during the birth process. They'll heave themselves up—calf dangling, nose inches from the ground—and stand there a while, then take a quick turn, and... *whomp!* Out spills the slippery calf.

With mom already on her feet, no time is wasted when it comes to licking the newborns off. Despite this abrupt introduction to the world beyond the womb, these calves are jump-started, up and nursing in jig time. Every few days Ken saddles up his horse, cuts out the new pairs, and drives them across the bridge to join the other mother cows and calves in an adjoining pasture. Oftentimes, on my walks, I watch the babies bucking and playing while their dams chew their cuds, a scene oft repeated this time of year throughout the valley.

Winter Fishtrap conference is now history, but those of us in rural places will live out the reality of this year's theme: "The Old West, New Wealth." In some way it will affect those of us who happen to live in all the pretty places of the West.

It was good to visit with Becky (Hatfield) Hyde, who ranches with her husband in Chiloquin, and listen to presenters such as Laura Pritchett, author of *Hell's Bottom, Colorado,* a collection of short stories, and the novel *Sky Bridge*, who lives in Colorado near the small cattle ranch where she was raised.

Donald Snow, professor at Whitman College, who talked to us about "Ruburbia," where suburbia is taking over rural areas, and how communities need to plan for their futures. Sarah Michael was there to explain how wealth has come to Blaine County, Idaho, the home of Sun Valley. Sarah is a commissioner who proposed an emergency moratorium on new subdivisions that would permanently alter the character of the area. Nils Christoffersen, from Wallowa Resources, offered facts that pertained to Wallowa County's resource-based economy.

All four presenters, plus the attendees who traveled to Wallowa Lake from all over the Northwest, gave us much to think about and mull over in our minds. Like last year, Kathy and I pretended we were from out of the area and shared a room at the historic Wallowa Lake Lodge, where the event was held. It was like a mini-vacation.

The conference ended after brunch on Sunday, and then it was home to frost an orange chiffon cake I'd baked and put in the freezer the week before. Since my hens are laying again, I used eight eggs in the cake and two in the frosting.

The cake? Oh, it was for neighboring rancher Melvin Brink's 73rd surprise birthday party. Wife, Mary Lou, pulled it off.

Doug and Fred finally got off on a fishing trip.

"Thank goodness we didn't catch any fish," said my husband, after they returned late that night. "We'd've had to clean 'em." This after they'd driven clear to Dug Bar on the Snake River. "We sure had a good time. Saw lots of wildlife and ate supper at the Imnaha Store and Tavern," Doug added.

Phyllis and I spent the morning hiking around Wallowa Lake State Park while the guys were fishing. Had the place all to ourselves, and ate our brown bag lunches at the foot of the lake, listening to ice crack into long stretches of open water.

Got a phone call from grandson James, who attends Montana University West in Dillon. Says he'll be home the end of this week for spring break. Guess I'll have to bake a pie or two.

Last week I met James' sister Adele at "Mad Mary's" in Joseph for lunch, and we had much to talk about. We hadn't had a good visit in a long time. Adele is a busy senior and her plans are to attend college at Montana University, too.

Also visited with grandson Buck, who lives in Clarkston. Buck and his wife, Chelsea, want to move back to Wallowa County.

"That's home," says Buck, who was born here. Chelsea will be through with her nursing college this spring, so I sincerely hope it all works out for them.

Saturday evening, Doug and I drove to Cloverleaf Hall in Enterprise and partook of a roast beef supper prepared by members of the Wallowa County Fair Board. We enjoyed visiting several neighbors, including Harold and Ardis Klages, before listening to the Blue Mountain Old Time Fiddlers.

"I just love fiddle music," said Ardis, and I looked around at all the other folks whose lives centered around music. There was Bob Casey, with his artificial hooked hand, packing his little squeeze box instrument; old Charley Trump, wearing a brace as a result of a fall that broke his neck eleven months ago; and Leonard Samples, battling a long illness, the music in his heart keeping him alive; among many others, elderly and slow-moving until they found a fiddle in their hands or piano keys to play.

One after the other they marched up on stage.

"Anyone new here?" asked a husky gal with a twinkle in her eyes. When several hands flew up, she said, "Guess I better keep my shoes on. Don't wanna get too wild here." And then she launched into a tune called "Milk Cow Blues." You could tell she'd played that fiddle since she was a little girl by the way her fingers flew over the frets, and how she drew her bow over the strings.

And old Charley Trump, the organizer all these years, just sat there in his wheelchair, watching every performer...until it was his turn. After he was helped up on stage and settled in a chair, he tucked his old fiddle under his chin and began to play. Four tunes later, Charley limped back to his chair and sat back to enjoy the music again.

Our young Upper Prairie Creek girls—Ryya, Lexi and Hannah—were there again. My, how they've improved. We're so proud of them. A young father played the fiddle while his youngest son wandered around on stage. Earlier, his daughter and son had also taken their turns playing

Old-timer Charley Trump, of Wallowa, who, with wife Nancy, organizes the Fiddler's get-together, plays a toe-tapping tune to a large crowd in Cloverleaf Hall. Bass fiddle (left) is being played by Tyson Samples, guitar (in back) by Tim Collins, mandolin, Dave Murrill, and seated, Bob Casey with his one-handed squeeze box.

the fiddle. Their mom, a former Wallowa County gal, proudly snapped photos of her family.

When Allen Schnetzky drew the bow over the strings of his fiddle and began to play, he reminded me of his grandfather Spencer Bacon, who used to live out on Lost Prairie. Spencer used to play for dances out in Wallowa County's North End, and he was one of the kindest gentlemen I ever knew.

It was good to see the generations carrying on the old-time traditions, such as Leonard Sample's versatile sons, who learned from their old man.

"Plenty of pie left in the kitchen," said Denny, the announcer, who also passed out "Hill Billy" prizes and appointed a sheriff at the beginning of the program. Folks would disappear and reappear with huge wedges of chocolate cream pie.

After the grand finale, where every performer returned on stage to play a hymn, the program ended. I looked at my watch and was amazed to see it was 11:30. We don't stay up that late for New Year's Eve!

Then it was out into the frozen parking lot to scrape frost off the windshield and head back to Prairie Creek with music in our hearts.

March 20—Wild white-tails wound their way up a muddy cow path to the top of Hough's hill, flags flying in alarm as I followed in their wake. And there, between lichen-covered rocks and patches of melting snow, I found them…no, not the white-tail deer, but the first buttercups. The first drops of color after a long winter.

Actually, I'd spotted the first ones yesterday, as Doug and I drove to the hills to check our horses. Heading out the Crow Creek road, we'd noticed numerous squirrels running here and there, standing on their hind feet at the entrance to their burrows, scolding and chittering away. Farther on we saw five golden eagles, some diving down to snatch a squirrel, others perched in the fields while feeding on their prey. That's when I noticed the buttercups, petals of waxy yellow, sprinkled among those scab-rocky hills.

Driving to Salmon Creek, Doug pointed to a nearby hill and said, "Lookee there." Outlined against that enormous sky was a herd of elk. Driving father along we could see they were planning to jump the two fences that line the road right in front of us. Sure enough, here they came, 200 head leaping single file, clearing both fences before running down-slope onto Doug's land, heading toward Greenwood Butte.

I managed to click several shots with my camera without ever having to leave the pickup. What a picture their tawny bodies made against those winter-killed hills! Their color blended so perfectly with the landscape.

We commented on how, in Marches past, one would never attempt to drive this North Pike Creek road. Snow would be drifted several feet deep where those elk had crossed.

We only passed one rig that afternoon, and it belonged to Doug's brother Biden's grandsons, who were out hunting squirrels. A must that day was a four-wheel drive. Where it wasn't rocked, the road was pretty greasy.

Before we reached the Zumwalt road we did run into several snow banks, but they were rapidly melting. And since that day was the vernal equinox, the first day of spring, it seemed appropriate that I should have found the first buttercups.

I could feel the seasonal change on my walk up Hough's hill yesterday. I sensed the softness in the air, the thawing earth, the familiar (not unpleasant) odor of pasture manure as the warmer air releases the fragrance of frozen cow pies, which, composed of grass, will break apart and nurture the soil.

Returning, I thought of my little dog Daisy and how I used to say, "Get the swirls," and she'd take off after the squirrels, which ran in all directions. The rodents were pretty safe, but Daisy sure enjoyed the chase.

It's been a busy two weeks. I attended our weekly Writers Group, after which we met at Mad Mary's for gourmet sandwiches and old-fashioned sodas.

I also played Scrabble up at Christine's cabin perched above the west side of Wallowa Lake. Nothing like a good game of Scrabble while the spring snow dances in the wind and hisses on the white caps of the lake, and nothing like sipping tea, staring out the windows at ducks bobbing up and over the wavelets, picking our brains for words that rack up points. Scrabble was a favorite of my grandma Wilson's as well as my mother. Good for the mind, and for passing the time indoors during the cold months.

On Wednesday evening Doug and I met Ed and Carol Wallace, Dave and Shirley Parker, and John and JoAnn VanBelle at the Top Hand Cafe, which sits atop the hill above Enterprise. It's a homey place to meet. You sit at a long table, and Chet, he's in the kitchen cookin' while wife, Linda, waits the table. Beefsteak is featured every day. As usual, the snow piled up outside while we ate and visited.

A couple of those innocent baby chicks, which I got from Keith out in the Leap area to put under my setting hen last summer, turned out to be roosters. One is a huge white bird with spurs, and another has feathers on his feet. Then there's "Fred" the Cochin and wee "Larry" and "Flash," cast-offs from the county fair chicken scramble.

Well, Fred had long established the pecking order, and he was at the top. All right and good, but one day I noticed that Larry was flying out of the chicken pen and spending more time outside than inside. And then I noticed his head was bloodied, and so was the white rooster's. Too many roosters. So I put water on to boil, Doug went to the woodshed for the axe, and soon two roosters were plucked and gutted and bagged in the freezer. Fred, Larry, and Flash crow on...and seem to get along.

Fishtrap's Big Read ended with a grand finale at the Odd Fellows Hall, where we listened to a wrap-up of Ray Bradbury's book *Fahrenheit 451*, after which we took ourselves out into March's moonlit, windy night to stand around a bonfire and recite poetry or passages from books we'd read and memorized.

Mine was a quote from Henry David Thoreau: *Life is but the stream I go a'fishing in. I drink at it, but while I drink, I see the sandy bottom, and detect how shallow it is. The thin current slides away, but eternity remains.*

On March 13 it was 10 degrees! I called down to Mary and Lyman's, and Mary said Lyman was mad at the elk. "Eatin'in his hay and makin' a real mess." She was mad at Lyman, because "he left the waffle iron lid up. Iron got cold; too many cooks in the kitchen."

Last time I checked, things had improved somewhat.

Doug came down with that bad cold that swept through the county. He's better now and out trimming willows.

On the 15th we had grandson James, his college roommate Kyle, son Todd and his wife, Angie, and grandson Buck and his wife, Chelsea, over for supper.

The week before, James had called and put in an order for pies. So...I'd spent that morning baking one lemon and one huckleberry cream pie, and two loaves of french bread. Later in the afternoon I slid a chunk of prime rib roast (left from Christmas) in the oven, and roasted potatoes, yams and onions. I also roasted garlic in olive oil, butter and parsley, to spread on the bread.

Supper was held up a bit while the "boys" went down to the calving pasture to help Ken with a cow calving. And then Todd was held up for the same reason. You never want to put supper on the table during calving season until you see the white of their eyes.

Anyway, supper was a success. I've seen boys eat pie before, but Kyle wins the prize: two slices each, of both pies. James presented me with a photograph of him holding a fine trout he caught in the Beaverhead River, along with a fly he tied using "Ari" the Aracuna's neck feathers. It was such a pleasure seeing them all again.

One windy morning I hung the flannel sheets on the line and let them flap dry. and replaced them with cotton ones. Good to use the clothesline again.

Phyllis has flown with a friend to tour the Holy Land. Before she left we took a hike up Hurricane Creek canyon. It was a wild, windy day, and to escape the wind we struck off down a trail to the lower campground, which is situated alongside the creek. Here, snow had drifted several feet in places, but we kept from sinking by following a packed ski track.

It was a wonderful hike, and gave us a good workout by the time we trudged up the final trail to the road, and back to the car. We noticed the sap running in the Red Osier Dogwood, and at Phyllis' house she picked me some pussy willows.

Nearly 60 calves sun themselves on the snowless pastures beyond the corrals, and by the looks of things, it may not snow today.

Cut into one of those baking squash I raised on Alder Slope this past summer. The meat is golden-sweet and tastes like fall. I shared some with grandson Chad's family when I visited them last week.

April 3—The weather theme for the past two weeks hasn't varied too much from what our local KWVR radio announcer refers to as "Mostly Cloudy." The weather other than "mostly" has consisted of rain or snow. At any rate, the lavender crocuses have appeared alongside the house, and the sprigs of forsythia I brought home from Lyman and Mary's on Imnaha are downright cheerful.

Doug has been out on the tractor pulling a harrow around our remaining 16 acres, and I suspect he misses having to do more. Ranchers get restless in the spring; their inner clocks know when it's time to get back in the fields. Of course, when it's snowin' and blowin', that provides a good excuse to join the "boys" around the table for cribbage at Ye Olde Range Rider.

Ken has only 10 more cows to calve, and that herd of babies is thriving. Nearly every morning Hough's ancient truck huffs and puffs its way up the road so Ken can load it with haylage. At first I was alarmed at the exhausted truck, whose exhaust sent forth so much smoke I thought the long stacks of hay were on fire. But the old truck just keeps on truckin'.

Doug has nearly finished trimming the willows so a new fence can be built around our property. One afternoon he came to the house for a big band-aid. It seems he was "limbed." He had a fat lip for a couple of days, which caused folks to look askance at me.

Granddaughter Adele, an Enterprise high school FFA senior, sold us two tickets to the annual pork barbecue and auction held last week. Doug and I not only enjoyed the meal, but hung in there and got the bid for Hope McLaughlin's hand-made quilt and a crocheted rug. All goes to a good cause: the FFA senior ag trip.

The next day it was very windy and it didn't snow till afternoon, so I hung a wash on the line.

We've been enjoying the baking squash raised in my Slope garden last summer. No matter that I stored it in the clothes closet. Mary Marks says that's the best place, and she's right.

We sure feel sorry for Bud Birkmaier, who suffered a bad horse wreck recently. Those old bones don't heal as fast as the young ones do. And we locals are mourning the loss of Elizabeth Parsons...but I guess when you get to be 100 years old, that's life well-lived.

I baked a batch of sourdough cinnamon rolls last week, and gave some to our great-grandkids. Cousins Riley Ann, Ashlyn, Ronan and Gwenllian were here "helping" grandpa Ken feed on that cold windy morning. I couldn't resist snapping their photo after they all lined up on the back of the pickup.

I still spend a great deal of time peering through my binoculars in the direction of the cow pasture. It's a wondrous thing, watching the birth of a healthy calf, seeing it stagger to its feet, searching until it finds a warm teat.

What a treat to attend the trial of "The Big Bad Wolf," a very clever operetta/musicale staged by the Enterprise Junior High drama class. A huge part of the production's success goes to volunteer Gail Swart, a retired music teacher.

I so enjoyed seeing neighbor Taylor Darnielle who, just the other day it seems, was a shy little girl growing up on a ranch along Prairie Creek. Now she sings and acts with an assurance far beyond her years. All of the kids were just great!

That young rooster made three meals: fried, souped, and served with homemade noodles. Yum! And now three of my banty hens are setting. Soon I'll be wanting some chicks to sneak under them at night.

After spending one entire morning attending meetings on how to raise funds for our capital campaign to help fund our local museum expansion, I grabbed a bowl of soup at Cloud 9 and made it to the Forest Service Visitors Center in time to view Jan Hohmann's scenic slides of Hells Canyon. Jan recently spent a month caretaking the historic Kirkwood Ranch on the Idaho side of Snake River, and she and a friend backpacked the Snake River trail from Freezeout/Saddle Creek to Dug Bar. Her slides made me homesick for the canyons. Our Museum Board will be taking a boat tour up the Snake in May. I can't wait.

Doug and I did get a chance to see the Snake however, when we traveled to Clarkston, Washington, to help Doug's brother Jack and wife, Blanche, celebrate their 65th wedding anniversary. What a lift to pull down into Clarkston and see blooming trees, tulips, daffodils, and green leaves on trees, especially since we'd driven through a snow storm to get there!

The gala affair was held in the Sternwheel Room at the Quality Inn there in Clarkston. Jack and his bride, Blanche, know all about ranching on the Snake. They raised their family at Rogersburg, not far from the mouth of the Grande Ronde, which was the home place where Doug was raised and attended the one-room school on Joseph Creek. The occasion was full of nostalgia for Doug, who visited several old acquaintances he hadn't seen in years.

Again, we braved a snow storm that materialized on the north highway, where a herd of elk appeared suddenly out of the twilight. After a hot meal at the Top Hand cafe on the hill above Enterprise, we headed home to Prairie Creek, which was white with snow.

Somehow, the latch on the chicken pen door flipped back in its staple the other morning...and there I was, locked in with the chickens. A funny feeling...and no one around, naturally. So I grabbed the long wire hook I use to snag chickens and inched it out through the wire to unhook the thing. I had contemplated climbing over, but the fence is high and hot-wired to discourage coons and skunks...

Kathy and I drove to Imnaha last week to drop some groceries off for Mary and Lyman, and then made our way in the pouring rain across the swinging bridge that spans the Imnaha River, to the Writer's retreat, to inventory and prepare the place for the writers who are now staying there. We noticed the little owl is back, perched on the rafters above the tree house.

On the way downriver we stopped to have tea with Mary before heading back "on top." This coming Sunday I will be staying there for a week myself. I'm looking forward to it.

On the morning of March 30 the birds were at full throttle: robins, red wing blackbirds, starlings, killdeer, sparrows and my roosters. Despite the snow and rain, spring is on the move.

Noticing the goodly amount of frozen raspberries in my freezer, I decided, after finding a recipe in Kathy's Alaska cookbook, to make a batch of raspberry shrub. You simply mash the berries, add vinegar, let the mixture stand four hours in the sun, add sugar, and strain through a cheesecloth and bottle. Two tablespoons of this concoction in a glass of soda water, or just iced water, provides a refreshing drink.

That evening Doug and I drove to Enterprise and Cloverleaf Hall where we partook of a complimentary dinner sponsored by the Wallowa County Grain Growers and prepared by the Liberty Grange. Such a feed: roast beef and chicken, baked potato and cheesecake. The meal was followed by the annual stockholders' meeting. Twenty-eight years ago, I worked at the old Grain Growers feed office.

The next night we had company for supper. I'd spent the afternoon preparing a meal of corned beef, cabbage, potatoes, and carrots that was supposed to have been served for St. Patrick's Day, but it seemed everyone was gone at that time. Hard to get folks together this time of year, what with calving and all. What started out to be 11 people ended up being 7, however, which was just right.

Phyllis and Kathy thought they saw an eclipse of the moon that night, which turned out to be the reflected ring of the new moon...or something. Anyway, we had a great time, and Myrna's sponge cake with lemon curd was mighty tasty, as was P's apple pie and Kathy's herbed cheese bread.

Charley kept us entertained, as did Kathy's chicken—not real—that squawked every time you squeezed its neck. Larry laughed so hard it brought tears.

By 7:45 the next morning, I was boarding a van in the pouring rain and snow with Wallowa County Chamber of Commerce members, where we spent the day traveling a goodly portion of Wallowa County. The purpose was to provide a taste of the county's various economic enterprises for the benefit of a representative of the Rural Design Assistance Team, which will come to the county in the fall to study and recommend economic development actions.

First off, we were treated to breakfast, compliments of the newly-opened Enterprise Bed and Breakfast (the old Warnock home) where our hosts served up great food in a homey atmosphere to warm us up on a cold morning. While we ate, snow drifted softly past the windows. Slides were projected on the wall of scenic Wallowa County, dominated by the Wallowa Mountains...none of which was visible that day. Among the slides I recognized several I'd taken years ago.

We traveled to Wallowa to view the small-diameter wood facility and the Nez Perce Interpretive building. Back to Enterprise to stare out the steamy windows to Stangel's Buffalo Ranch, then into Enterprise to hear the mayor, Irv, talk about the EM&M Building, the library facelift, and the new subdivision on the hill above Safeway. We also toured the new realty offices in the recently remodeled Toma's building, and the new hospital under construction.

After lunch at Lear's—I had great steak sandwich—we headed to Joseph, where Mayor Peggy talked about her vision for that city's future. Then it was down into the canyons to the Hells Canyon road house for more talk, and to introduce our guests to the Imnaha Store and Tavern, with its dollar bills stuck to the ceiling and its rattlesnake count. Yasha, at the road house, served warm cherry and apple pie to those who desired, and soon we were winding our way through a flock of wild turkeys, headed back out on top.

The rest of the late afternoon was spent touring the lake, after which we ended up partaking of a most delicious meal served at the historic Wallowa Lake Lodge. Salmon and beef were on the menu and the cooks did a good job. It had been a long day for all of us, but somehow, being shown around our county as if we too were tourists, was good for us. I was given the opportunity to put my two cents' worth in for ranching and the ag community which always has contributed to the health of our present economy.

My dream, of course, and why I consented to attend this tour, was

Elk leap over two fences in their haste to cross Pine Creek road. Cattle will be turned out to graze on these lands May 1.

for the sake of my grandchildren and their children. I would hope that they too can, in some way, be associated with living and contributing to this unique rural community. There have to be jobs made available, and affordable housing, before they can—and it's comforting to know there are folks working on these issues. They need all the support and cooperation they can get.

April 5—Phyllis and I took our brown bag lunches and spent the morning playing Scrabble with Christine at her cabin on the lake, a pleasant way to pass a windy cold day.

This evening we joined other past grand marshals of Mule Days—Manford and Vera Isley, Fred Talbott, Marcel Walker and Arnold Schaeffer—at the Outlaw Restaurant in Joseph to honor the 2006 grand marshal, Bob Casey. We missed seeing other folks like Mike McFetridge, Mary Marks and Sam Loftus, who couldn't be there.

It was fun dredging up memories of those first Mule Days, like the time Manford got bucked off his spotted mule, and remembering those llamas, and little pup tents (that lifted up at the slightest breeze) used for obstacles in the trail class, which caused several wrecks.

It was a real rodeo, and now 26 years later, the event is still going strong. Y'all come. Hells Canyon Mule Days is always the weekend after Labor Day.

April 6—Read to the folks at Alpine House, then hiked around Joseph with Phyllis where we stumbled onto a vacant lot full of buttercups. After which we split one of those delicious eggplant sandwiches at the Wild Flour Bakery.

Friend Kathy called from the Writers Retreat on Imnaha. "We caught the pack rat in the live trap. Guess the oatmeal and peanut butter did the trick."

A note from grandson Buck and wife, Chelsea: "We're moving here, Buck got a job on a ranch, and when I finish my nurse's college next month, I'm coming too." Good news!

April 7—Doug and I drove to Pendleton. The rivers ran high with snowmelt caused by warm rains and mild temps. We met daughter Lori and grandchildren Ryan and Lacey at Roosters for lunch and a good visit, after which, we looked up old-timer Sam Loftus at Juniper House. We found our old cowboy sitting in the patio in his wheelchair, staring at the blooming daffodils and and wishing he were back at his place on Camp Creek.

Then it was an hour or more to Kennewick, Washington, where we spent the night with sister-in-law Janet and her husband, Jim. A trip long in the planning, we attended the Columbia River CowBoy Gathering at the Benton County Fairgrounds, which was great fun and top entertainment. I mean, those performers—all of them—were some of the best in the U.S.

Of course we'd been drawn there by Doug's nephew, "Smoke" Wade, who calls himself "a legend in his own mind." It was fun to see Bob Fauste, aka "Smoke", again, and listen to him recite poems he's written himself. Bob is fast becoming a legend, aside from in his own mind, and was honored at the event by winning the Top Hand award. Smoke helped line up the entertainers for the event, which played to a packed audience. We sure enjoyed those lip-smackin' ribs before the show, too.

The next morning, after breakfasting on Jim's sourdough pancakes and visiting with daughter Lori and nephew Mike, we headed to Walla Walla and home via Tollgate, where we marveled at the several feet of snow piled alongside the road. The rivers—Grande Ronde, Wallowa, and Minam—were running high with runoff.

April 9—After breakfast with Doug at the Cheyenne Cafe, I was on my way...deep into canyon country. Enormous white clouds formed overhead and cast shadows over the greening hillsides. Sheep Creek dashed downward in a malty froth of snowmelt. At the tiny settlement of Imnaha, I turned upriver where the road was rutty and muddy, but the sight of wild turkeys feeding on grass near the rodeo grounds and blooming fruit trees made up for any discomfort.

Arriving at the Writer's Retreat, I made my way over the swaying bridge that spans the Imnaha with my first cart load of stuff. As I settled into my little one-room cabin, referred to as "the tree house," I noticed the little owl was back on his perch in the rafters above my porch.

Broom in hand, I made my way uphill to the outhouse, where I found a sort of dry arrangement of rose hips to the left of the one-hole wooden toilet seat. After sweeping the chewed up toilet paper on the floor, I left the colorful rose hips as they were.

After I was all settled in, I walked over to the main log home and made myself a sandwich for lunch. Later on, Paula, Fishtrap's writer in residence, appeared at the door.

"I feel like I'm going to throw up," she said. And then I knew she'd just made her first trip across the swinging bridge. Laptop computer in hand, luggage over both shoulders, she appeared pale and shook up.

Howard, a visiting writer, came to the rescue, and showed Paula how to use the cart to carry the next load, and how to relax and develop a sort of cadence, walking in time to the bridge's movements.

I found a thawing chicken in the fridge, filled it with onion, celery and garlic, and stuck it in the oven for supper. Just as we finished supper, here came Tom, all the way from Portland. After he carried all his "stuff" over the bridge, we visited, and later he nibbled on the chicken.

Early to bed for me. I curled up in my nest and slept like a hibernating squirrel. Morning dawned cloudy, but mild. I kindled a small fire to take the chill out of the cabin while I dressed and wrote in my journal.

Walking over to the house, I noticed the blooming forsythia, as well as the lavender and white violets running amuck over the lawn, the golden daffodils, and colorful primroses. I heard the familiar call of the dipper, the cries of the kingfisher and the mergansers, flying two by two; but mostly I heard the sound of the river, a sound that would seep into our very souls for the next week.

No leaves on the trees yet, and the apple blossoms were just beginning to swell. Many crows flew about, their raucous cawing competing with the roar of the rising river. Somewhere, across the river, I hear the *gobble,*

gobble, gobble of three torn turkeys approaching. In the kitchen, Tom is making coffee.

"Going for a morning hike," I say.

"Mind if I join you?" Tom asks, and soon we are breathing in the fresh scent of April greening, and there is no one around, save for Gary Marks' cows and calves.

We walk past Benjamin and Elizabeth's homestead site, with its rocked root cellar; cross the bridge and take the old wagon road that steeply wanders uphill. We make our way past musical waterfalls and through patches of wild rose bushes to the top of some old farm ground. We cross Indian Creek and come to a fence line, where I check Mary's pipeline that carries water from a spring farther up the canyon.

We follow several game trails until they trap us in wild rose bramble, after which we walk around this maze to the top of a hill where we can look down upon the main house and the curve of the river. Then we check Mary's cistern and continue down the old road to where Elizabeth and Benjamin are buried. A mother lilac and her sprouts have all but concealed the final resting place of these early Imnaha pioneers.

Tom and I discuss the book I'm writing about Mary, and how the Markses and Warnocks were the first families to settle here. We return on a different route, stopping to stare down at Indian Creek Falls, cascading down black basalt, spilling upon trembling ferns, coursing to join the Imnaha near our bridge. We witness the rising sun and enjoyed its brief warmth. Good thing, as the rest of the week was either cloudy, windy or raining...which was good, because the beautiful weather would have pulled us away from our work.

Howard left Wednesday. I drove out that morning to join Doug and attend long-time friend Betty Hammond's funeral in Enterprise.

Tom and Paula often completed as many as 19 pages of their novels. I worked at various projects that have been piling up at home. During the long evenings, after supper, we read our work to each other around a blazing fireplace.

Rich came to dinner Thursday evening, and Paula roasted the organic duckling she'd brought from Idaho. I baked sourdough bread and made a fruit cobbler.

On the last evening we took a moveable feast down to Lyman and Mary's: a kettle of kielbasa in homemade sauerkraut, sourdough bread, warm potato salad, and the leftover cobbler. It was great fun. On his fiddle, Tom played old Irish tunes that made Mary tap her toes and stare dreamily off into space, remembering those old Grange dances when she was young and full of life.

We all left on Saturday, save for Paula, who followed me to the mouth of Big Sheep Creek to meet Doug, who gave us a ride to the big branding up-creek about five miles. Paula was wide-eyed, watching as nearly 25 cowboys, cowgirls, kids, dogs and horses worked all those calves in a pouring rain. I managed to photograph the action under the protection of an old slicker.

That was a pretty hardy crew, which included grandsons Josh and Buck, granddaughter Becky, and many friends, all of whom braved a cold, wet Saturday to help son Todd. Daughter-in-law Angie and her crew fed everyone in an old barn down the "crik."

Doug and I drove back to the Imnaha Store and Tavern and ordered chicken strips, and I warmed up with a cup of hot tea.

April 16—Easter Sunday dawned cold, an inch of snow still on the ground from the day before. I baked an Italian Easter bread with colored eggs baked right in the braided loaf, and put a ham from Stephanie's 4-H hog in the oven to roast.

Daughter Ramona, husband Charley, granddaughter Carrie and great-granddaughter Brenna arrived later to feast with us. It was fun having a little one around. She played the piano and jabbered up a storm, once she got used to us. Ramona's asparagus, potato salad and pot of beans went over great, and it was an easy meal for me, considering I wasn't even unpacked from being gone a week.

Other members of our family were just too tired from the big branding to stray far from their own homes. Grandson James called from Montana to wish me Happy Easter. Sounds as if he's really catching the fish, and his college classes are going great. He'll be home soon to work on the fire crew again this summer.

April 17—Our monthly book club gathering. Tomorrow is our Writers group. Back in the swing of spring.

April 20—Sunny, clear and reached 70 degrees, which would have made it a crime to stay inside. Phyllis and I hiked the entire length of the east moraine of Wallowa Lake. Well worth the effort, as the top was covered with buttercups and, when we sat ourselves down on flat rocks to eat lunch, we saw four pairs of bluebirds, grass widows, yellow bells and, from far below, we heard loons. Most are probably migrating, stopping over to rest on the lake. Numerous deer munched the bunch grasses, and over every hump we startled another herd.

Far below spread Prairie Creek and the ranch and farm lands formed a colorful mosaic. To the east rose the jagged snowy crests of Idaho's

Seven Devils. We'd left Phyllis's car parked at the head of the lake so we'd have a way back to mine at the foot.

April 22—I joined friends at Camp Creek, where we were the guests of Andy. After a wonderful hike along the rims above the house, we gorged on potluck, then got down on the living room rug and sorted, traded and discussed garden seeds. Some of us slept over, and Andy prepared a wonderful breakfast of scrambled eggs and blackberry muffins.

Then it was upriver to Mary's for a visit, and to help clean out her garden. The rain of the night before had freshened up the hill sides, and the sarvis and wild plums were white with blooms. I'd prepared lunch of veggie soup, sourdough bread and apple pie, and Lyman joined us.

Hard to leave the canyons in April...but I did, returning to life "on top." Which isn't all that bad, but there's something about being down there that shuts the world out.

The Easter ham is simmering on the stove with split peas, carrots, and onions, and now it's time to add the potatoes. Doug went to the hills to check fences and grass. He'll be hungry!

April 24—We've sprung ahead with spring, time-wise and otherwise. Just came in from mowing the lawn. The daffodils are blooming near the porch steps, the two-week-old chicks I hid under my four setting hens are all feathered out, Ken only has four more cows to calve, the flower beds are cleaned out, I've purchased garden seeds, Doug has pruned the raspberries and the willow tree and continues to clean up around the place, and Mike and Maggie Vali and family are back at the Lake. Good news for Wallowa County.

Later this week, Ken and his crew will start the cows and calves to the hills; the hay piles are shrinking.

Last Friday we had a day of what I call "false spring," which found me up at the Alder Slope Nursery purchasing pansies. Of course after I planted them in the wagon wheel planter, it froze, but pansies are hardy little rascals and they survived.

April 25—Our writers' group met at Idella Allen's today. Idella lives on Barton Heights, where the view of the snowy Wallowas is outrageous. She and husband, Herb, live in one of Joseph's older homes, which they have lovingly restored.

Not only did we feast our eyes on Idella's hundreds of blooming daffodils, we feasted on her chicken soup and homemade noodles. After our writing assignments, we were pretty hungry. And I'd just happened to bring one of my fresh lemon pies for dessert.

Pat Dougherty coils his rope at a recent branding up Big Sheep Creek canyon, near Imnaha. Pat works for Cunningham Ranch near Flora and has just returned from Argentina.

April 26—The fence builders are nearly through fencing off our 16 acres. It pleases me that the ranch will be grazed by cattle at least one more year.

Phyllis and I hiked the West Moraine today. We watched a "fool hen" (Franklin Grouse) for a long time, until it slowly made its way back to its nest. At noon we perched on a rock overlooking Wallowa Lake, opened a can of sardines, and smeared them on some homemade bread. It just don't get any better than this. Especially since it was a "blue bird" day.

April 27—Doug spent the day out in the hills repairing elk-damaged fences before the cattle can be turned in. Ken hauled the bulls to the hills.

We were saddened to learn of the passing of old-timer Howard Johnson of Wallowa. Howard, a descendant of some of the earliest settlers in the lower valley, was a man of integrity and intelligence who will be missed by all of us lucky enough to have known him.

April 28—Clear, mild Friday morning. Up early to help turn the cows and calves at the four corners and then follow them to the hills...on foot.

"Who's your crew?" I asked son Ken.

"Just the family: Chad, Amy and the kids. Ronan, Gwenllian...and six months old Kennon," he said, as he and son Chad slowly outdistanced me on horseback. Didn't matter to me. Once in a while I'd glimpse them trailing the cattle around a turn. I was in no hurry; I had all day. Been there, done that on horseback for over 20 years. Now it was time to relax and enjoy the day...and what a day! Doug came along in the pickup.

"Better get in, they're way ahead, you'll never catch up."

"No thanks," I replied. "I'm fine."

Other ranchers, seeing this old grandma plodding along, offered me rides, but I declined. Out on the Crow Creek road, Phyllis showed up with her two great-grandchildren.

"Do you realize you've already walked nine miles!" she said in alarm. "Better get in and let me take you home."

"Really," I insisted. "Only three more miles and we'll be turning the herd into the corrals at the old Circle M." And I offered to walk with her kids, who were clamoring to get out of the car.

It just happened that Ken had called a rest stop, so we caught up with the cattle, and soon Chad and Ken were giving the little ones rides on the horses.

After Phyllis and the kids left, I enjoyed watching my own great-grandchildren ride with their daddy and grandpa, and when daddy drove the car forward with baby Kennon, Amy got in the saddle. Definitely a "family affair."

It was noon when we corralled the cattle and, holding a little hand in each of my own, we made our way to a sunny bank, sat down, and ate our lunches. Four generations of this family picnicked alongside the Crow Creek road. Baby Kennon waved his chubby fists, obviously loving it all.

Home for me, to soak in the tub, fix a casserole for supper, then load my sleeping bag in the pickup and head out to the corrals, where I found my family roasting hot dogs over an open fire. While the rest of them spent the night in a camp trailer that Ken had hauled out earlier, I slept with my head sticking out of a small tent, dazzled by jillions of stars and listening to a yapping chorus of coyotes. My kind of night.

Larry Waters and Yvonne Petersen drive a four-mule hitch pulling a wagon, all belonging to Kim and Yvonne Peterson of Winnemucca, Nevada, at the Lee Scott Memorial Plowing Bee recently at the Waters' Ranch on Prairie Creek.

Vaden Flock traveled from Anatone, Washington, to participate in the annual Lee Scott Memorial Plowing Bee at the Waters' ranch east of Joseph.

April 29—Saturday morning. A cow bawls, a horse whinnies, and, later, I can hear a meadow lark as a pale light appears beyond the eastern hill. Daylight, and I'm up, pouring a cup of hot Postum out of my thermos and nibbling a homemade sourdough cinnamon roll. At 5:30 I'm behind the cows, all by myself. I experience the awakening of this extraordinary April morning.

New grass trodden by cloven hooves breleases a spring smell, a wandering breeze carries wild scents; willow leaves, thorn brush thickets, aspens, the water smell of springs feeding the creek. The cows graze as they amble along. Ken and Chad help with the family chores back in camp. Ken's wife, Annie, brought out all the food for supper, breakfast and lunches.

Soon, the riders catch up with me, and as we approach the old "pink" barn at the Dorrance Place, Amy lets the two little ones out to walk with me. Here we are, strollinga long, Ronan holding one hand and wee Gwenllian the other. I look down at this great-granddaughter and smile…and from way down there, she smiles, too. Something leaps between us. Some undefinable feeling traveling through four generations. This is a moment I'll always remember. Words fail.

The day warms to over 70 degrees; plodding up Dorrance gulch is a slow process, and the main herd is close to being turned into their pasture. While climbing higher I walk backward, so as to see the distant snowy Wallowas come into view. Then I'm on top! The rest is mostly downward, until the final hill. The last cow has just filed into the Deadman pasture when I arrive, and the rest of the crew is leaving to ferry vehicles.

I opt to stay with the cattle and catch a ride on the return trip. Good thing. A baby calf that lagged behind was corralled at the Dorrance Place, along with an old cow and her calf; the mother to the lazy calf was about to jump the gate and head back! With one eye on the cow, and another on my sandwich, I sat on a grassy bank and ate my lunch. Even managed a nap of sorts.

When Ken returned, we loaded the horses in the trailer and headed for the valley. According to the mileage in the pickup, I'd walked 22 miles in two days.

April 30—Not feeling bad at all today; hardly any stiffness. Even got up enough energy to bake a citrus chiffon cake to take to our writer-in-residence, Paula Coomer, reading at Fishtrap House.

May 1—What a perfect way to spend May Day. Friend Sharon rode down to Imnaha to help me clean the Writers' Retreat. The apple or-chard was a froth of white blooms, the river was running bank to bank, and when we got through with all that scrubbing, the place smelled of cleanliness.

Of course, a trip to the canyon isn't complete without visiting Lyman and Mary. This time the hired man, Robin (the poet) was there, and we all had lunch. Sharon and I had packed our own, and I grilled cheese sandwiches for the rest. Had some of that cake left too.

For entertainment we listened to Lyman and Robin's account of driving the CAT (as in tractor) across that swollen river. A feat not as dangerous (according to Robin) as making their way across the skimpy bridge, just inches from the lapping water.

When we first drove up, Lyman announced he was going to bring the CAT across the river.

"You can't, the river's in flood," I said. To which he replied, "So am I." And off he went.

"If he makes up his mind to do something, he does it," says Mary.

On the way home we stopped at the Hells Canyon Road House for a refreshing root beer float.

May 3—Phyllis and I hiked up Hurricane Creek canyon to the trail-head and returned via the campground which is situated below the road near the creek. I came home with bouquet of budding dogwood, pussy willows and other greenery.

That evening Doug and I attended the Enterprise FFA annual awards banquet. So proud of all those fine Future Farmers of America, and especially of granddaughter Adele, who received the Extemporaneous Speaking award. Can this be our little Adele? She is the last grandchild to graduate from a Wallowa County high school. But, with any luck, we'll be seeing some of those great-grandkids graduating too.

May 4—Read to the folks at Alpine House, whom I always enjoy visiting.

May 5—Cinco De Mayo was memorable.

This afternoon, after picking up Sharon, Doug and I headed to Clarkston, Washington. Grandson Buck and his wife, Chelsea, offered their little house for us to spend the night so we could join other members of the Friends of the Museum on a boat ride up the Snake River the next morning.

Enjoyed seeing all those blooming pink dogwoods and the weather was downright warm. Sharon treated us to a gourmet dinner at Mc-Columns in Lewiston, and I still dream about walleye fish. A bit cloudy, but mild as we boarded Beamer's Snake River Dream, a jet boat with a capacity of 65. Surrounded by familiar faces we took our seats, and Eric, our able young pilot, steered the boat into the wave-tossed waters of the Snake.

We passed the confluence of the Clearwater, and sped under two bridges and headed up the canyon, leaving the small town of Asotin behind. Soon we were at Buffalo Eddy, where ancient Indian drawings are still visible on nearby rocks, just downriver from old "River Rat" Elmer Earl's ranch.

Shortly after 9, we pulled into the dock at Heller Bar where we were treated to biscuits and gravy, muffins, fruit juice and coffee. The sun was out now, as every mile took us into more rugged canyons. We paused at Cache Creek ranch, a lovely spot, with shade trees, neatly painted buildings, and green lawns.

Then Eric made a wide turn, and we were heading up the Salmon River (the River of No Return) where a huge amount of snowmelt was joining the already swollen Snake. We swirled back to the main river, where the high water pretty much washed out the rapids. The Snake narrowed and the canyons began to wall us in where we negotiated a swift rapids and arrived at Eureka Bar.

Lots of history there, and memories of when Doug guided folks through the old mining tunnel. Here the Imnaha rushed in after traveling five miles down its scenic gorge, a hike I'd often taken.

Then, there we were at Dug Bar, where Doug and his family operated a cattle operation for years. There was the winding high road that led to the ranch, the cement block house, the old bunkhouse, the guest cabins, the corrals, the barn, and shop, the locust trees, and Birch Creek splashing down the canyon to fill the watering trough.

Eric pulled up to the Nez Perce crossing sign, explaining how Chief Joseph's band of Nez Perce crossed the river at that spot while the Snake was in spring flood. Doug gave a brief history of the ranch and then we were on our way again.

I was mesmerized by the canyon wildflowers. Pastel pink phlox trickled down steep draws, and brilliant pink clarkia grew between rocks. Golden arrowleaf balsamroot grew everywhere, its sunflower-like blossom scattered up and down the steep green hills. A full-curl ram nibbled lichen from a high cliff; three ewes sunned themselves on a rocky ledge, golden eagles soared above us, and several elk grazed a rockslide on the Idaho side.

"May is the time for bears," Eric said, but we didn't see any that day.

At Pittsburg Landing, we picked up Ace Barton. Like Doug, a walking history book. At Kirkwood Ranch—of Grace Jordan fame, she wrote the book *Home Below Hells Canyon*—we docked near a large rock, scrambled off the boat, and hiked a steep trail that led to a cluster of picnic tables, where we ate the picnic lunch provided by Beamers.

What a delightful place. Even though Doug and I had been there before, it was very interesting going through the old house and the Sterling Cabin, now a museum; and just absorbing the place. Iris bloomed, a water wheel turned in Kirkwood Creek, and the old Moonshine cabin stood just across the bridge.

Back on the boat, we headed up the final rapids to the end of our 95-mile journey. And there, rising thousands of feet above us, was the Hat Point lookout tower, surrounded by snowy ridges.

On the way back we stopped at Copper Creek for a glass of iced tea, which brought back memories of when I took my mother and father up on the mail boat to spend the night in one of those cabins.

The ride back to Clarkston was swift but comfortable. Time and space does not permit the telling of all of this great adventure, which I have recorded elsewhere. The wind had come up and it was cloudy and cold when we got off the boat. But no matter, we'd had a great adventure, we'd ridden the Dream and lived it as well.

May 9—Ken's last three cows have calved, the red tulips alongside the house are in full bloom, we still haven't located mama kitty's kittens, and Scott and Kelly's heifers are grazing what used to be one of our pastures, while Fluitt's cows and calves share the other side of the hill. Ken's heifers are turned out in our field near the chicken house, and Doug trapped the dirty little skunk that dined on several of my new chicks.

This afternoon still has a nip to it, due to this morning's heavy frost, which stunned the fading daffodils and dulled the bright green meadows. Dust rises from neighboring fields as the farmers harrow, seed or roll their acres, and Doug has once again survived the pruning of the old apple tree. It's pretty scary watching him step off the final rung of the ladder, pruning shears in hand, and balance on the highest limb.

Before I forget, Jane Kirkpatrick sent me an advanced copy of her latest book, *A Clearing in the Wild,* which is based on a true story set in the 1850s. Jane's fans will really enjoy this book.

My calendar has been so full, I have to recount my days by thumbing back through my daily journal.

May 10—I joined other members of the Museum Board to help clean the old Wallowa County Museum on Joseph's Main Street in preparation for the Memorial Day opening.

This evening I drove to Enterprise to listen to Bobbie Conner's lecture on "Lewis and Clark through Indian Eyes." Bobbie was promoting the recently released book of the same name, which lets us hear the other side of the story, as told by nine descendants of the Indians whose homelands were traversed. A great book, edited by the late Alvin Josephy, a true friend of Fishtrap, as well as a personal one.

Bobbie, director of the Tamastslikt Cultural Institute on the Umatilla Reservation near Pendleton, is extremely well-versed on this subject.

Found a note on the kitchen table. *Last warning: do something about the chicken scratching in the raspberries, or it's a dead chicken! Doug.* So, aimed with my chicken bucket of scraps from the kitchen, I lured the little hen into the pen, singled her out, snagged her leg with a long wire hook, and clipped her wings.

May 11—We were invited to the upper Imnaha for another one of Lyman's famous crab feeds. I contributed a raspberry cobbler and a tossed salad. Once again we laid out the newspapers on the table, set the large bowl of crab—compliments of Lyman's crab fisherman son, Craig—and joined the neighbors from up and down the river to gorge ourselves.

In addition to all the crab we could hold, we feasted on homemade rolls, corn bread muffins, and Mary's beans. And naturally, no one could beat "Doc" Morgan when it came to cracking and eating crab. He has that down to an art form.

Before we left, I picked a bouquet of fragrant white lilacs to take home. A nearly full moon escaped the canyon walls just before we topped out.

May 12—Doug drove to Stanfield to watch grandson Ryan win the high jump in the district track meet, while I stayed home to make more deviled eggs for the branding that next day, and bake a complicated nut torte, filled with custard, for our Stitch and Bitch potluck that night.

Grandson James stopped by for a surprise visit, and I warmed up some leftover short ribs and sliced him some sourdough bread for lunch. Then we decided to do a "quality control" test on the torte. James is home from college now, once again working on the fire crew at Frazier. It was wonderful seeing him, and he said he planned to help with the next day's branding out on Wet Salmon Creek.

May 13—Branding day dawned clear and mild. Ken's family had spent the night out in the old house near the creek.

On the way out Doug and I spotted a golden eagle and two juvenile barn owls that had flown from their nest up the meadow. As we drove in the ranch, the cowboys were driving the cows and calves into the corral, where two bulls were sparring at each other in the middle of the opened gate. Dust was flying, as it was pretty dry, but finally Ken and his sons, Rowdy and Chad, got the herd corralled. Soon the calves were separated from the cows, the branding fire glowed red, the irons were heated, and cowboys began to rope calves. The older children helped hold syringes and ear tag applicators; others played in the green grass near the old house.

All together there were eight of my great-grandchildren…one of whom, we met for the first time. 7 month old Cutter had arrived the night before from the John Day area with his parents, Rowdy and Kasey.

Other family members arrived: daughter Ramona, son Todd, wife, Angie, and their friends, and of course, the mamas to the children romping around all over the place. There was James in the thick of it, wrestling those hefty calves to the ground as easily as could be, while his cousin Buck roped with a practiced hand. Mixing sweat with dust, the cowboys were soon covered with grime, as well as the two women, Angie and Amy, who persisted until nearly 90 calves were worked.

I helped ride herd on the youngsters who discovered the way to keep cool was to wade in the creek. Luckily it was a shallow body of water, and the only worry was keeping a little one from tumbling off the bridge.

By 12:30 the last calf was branded and the weary, hungry crew headed for the house. Annie and her crew were ready: two hams, baked in the old wood stove oven; a huge kettle of beans, homemade rolls, relishes, my deviled eggs, scalloped potatoes and, for dessert, chocolate sheet cake and deep dish apple pie. Babies conked out, seven-month-old cousins Kennon and Cutter got acquainted in a playpen, and twins Jada and Gideon, mud-caked and happy, continued to play outside.

Of course I shot a whole roll of film, the subjects being mostly great-grandchildren, with a few branding scenes thrown in. Over the years the old corrals there on Wet Salmon Creek have seen many brandings, but I wondered if there had ever been this many wee ones.

After everyone ate we watched a horse race. Cousins Rowdy and Buck, mounted on their steeds, thundered up from the meadow, hollering and grinning. Then the cowboys loaded up their horses and drove to the old Dorrance place to brand 20 more head of calves for son Todd.

Doug and I headed for the valley ranch, but Ken's family would spend another night. I could picture the guitar playing, singing, and roasting of marshmallows around the campfire ring that night, and knew in my heart, that was the real reason son Ken was in the cow business: to give this gift to his family.

The next day was Mother's Day, and after breakfast at the Cheyenne Cafe—my gift from Doug, who always says, "You're not my mother!"—I drove the 60 miles to La Grande to attend great-granddaughter Brenna's third birthday party.

Although it was very hot, we had a great time, and again I got to feast my eyes on the cleaned-up versions of the twins, Gideon and Jana, and their sisters, Riley Ann and Ashlyn, who were on their way home to Nampa, Idaho.

When I returned home there was an apple tree from son Todd, phone messages from other children, a cookbook from daughter Ramona, a hanging basket of flowers from daughter Jackie, and of course, cards. All appreciated.

May 15—Heat is breaking records. Our readers group met to discuss our monthly book this morning at Fishtrap House. Home to set out geraniums, parsley, tomatoes, gather eggs, and water everything in sight. Prepared another batch of deviled eggs to take to granddaughter-in-law Chelsea's graduation tomorrow in Lewiston.

We were all so proud of our Chelsea, as she was pinned by her husband, Buck, at the nurses' ceremony on the Lewis/Clark campus. Chelsea had the loudest cheering section of all, as our extended family is very vocal.

A wonderful tri-tip barbecue with scrumptious salads, Angie's beans, Mona's bread, my deviled eggs, and Jackie's blackberry cobblers, held in Buck and Chelsea's yard, was interrupted by a sudden squall. We fled into the house, plates in hand, where we watched in awe as trees swayed, rain and hail pelted down, and wind hurled itself at all. The town of Clarkston was seen through a sheet of water, its streets rivers, and some of its trees toppled. Then the sun came out, the water drained off, roses glistened, and the air was cooled by the welcome rain.

I finished cleaning the bunkhouse and Doug headed to the dump to use our free pass for the month of May. We're working through twenty-eight years of accumulated junk!

Lyman's chicks finally arrived in the mail. Last I heard, his two setting hens were all fluffed out around them.

Doug treated me to breakfast at the Cheyenne Cafe again last Sunday morning, after which I took off on foot for the ranch to use up the calories in that huge blueberry hotcake. I even turned down a ride from local rancher and neighbor Melvin Brink.

Kevin McCadden, of Alder Slope, tends the fire while the crew works calves at a branding on Wet Salmon Creek in the hills north of Enterprise.

This Thursday we drive to Helix for grandson Ryan's high school graduation, and granddaughter Adele graduates on Saturday in Enterprise. The children grow up, we grow older, and many of our friends pass on...but life goes on.

May 22—Large spring clouds, full of thunder and lightning, darken the skies and spill their contents before moving on down the valley, freshening Prairie Creek with welcome moisture, intensifying the greens, causing rhubarb to bolt, asparagus to push up, lilacs to open, apple trees to bloom, Bleeding Heart to form tiny pink jewels, bulls to bellow, and cats to birth kittens.

It is the magic time of year. Moisture coupled with warmth does it every time.

Doug is roto-tilling the garden, Ken's heifers graze great mouthfuls of lush grass growing outside the yard fences, and the new owners, as well as most of the valley ranchers, have begun to irrigate. Grain crops are sprouting and a new season has begun.

May 23—I donated a load of housewares to our local Soroptimists, a volunteer organization that gives scholarships to young people in the county with the profits from selling items folks no longer have use for. And let me tell you, our bunkhouse was full of leftover pots and pans used by our college kids and then returned to mom and dad.

Vaden Flock (Anatone), Bill Meyers (Hermiston), and Doug Tippett discuss an old Seed Fanner restored by Erl McLaughlin on display on Upper Prairie Creek, near Joseph. McLaughlin has one of the largest collections of old farm equipment in the Northwest.

Erl McLaughlin, left, of Sunrise Iron, a collector and restorer of old farm machinery who lives on Alder Slope, visits with Jim Sackett about an old wagon in Erl's collection.

May 24—Drove to the foot of the lake today, parked the car, and opened the windows to listen to the wind-whipped waves and watch the flotsam, carried down by the rivers draining the snow fields, wash ashore. Recent heavy rains have caused logs, limbs and other debris to come tumbling down the swollen streams into the lake.

I was the only one there, savoring one last glimpse of our lake before tourist season begins.

May 25—Doug to the hills to trim the horses' hooves, then later we drove to Helix to attend grandson Ryan's high school graduation. Arriving early, we decided to stop by the Tamastslikt Cultural Institute on the Umatilla Indian Reservation.

I cannot express enough how beautifully done this facility is, how peaceful and representative of the people themselves. You just have to see for yourselves. However, DON'T BE IN A HURRY, there's too much to learn, and it's so pleasant and quiet there, where you can look out at the Blue Mountains and relax, while becoming informed about a culture that we can learn much from.

Our red-haired wonder, Ryan, graduated with his small class there in the Helix high school gym. The paper backdrop, emblazoned with the words CLASS OF 2006, loudly released its "duct tape" hold and continued to slide downward as the ceremony proceeded. No one seemed to mind, and the graduation of these rural-rooted kids provided a real piece of Americana.

As usual, our family had a large cheering section, and afterward we convened across the street to the city fire hall for a feast put on by the graduates' families. Farm fare: deviled eggs, beans, rolls, cakes and cookies. Despite the rain and chill, everyone seemed happy. After all, Helix is a part of the "bread basket of the country," grain country, and the surrounding fields were brilliant green. Creeks, like Wild Horse, were running and wild roses bloomed along the fence rows.

We returned via Tollgate and noticed snow lingering on top.

May 26—Barbara Warnock and I staged a surprise 89th birthday party for Mary yesterday evening. I baked a maple cake and, on the way upriver, Doug and I stopped by the Imnaha Store for ice cream. Lyman had a good fire in the stove, as it was raining, and snowing on the rims. The snow level is at 5,000 feet.

The younger generation of Warnocks provided entertainment. Young Riley really hid well (between mom and brother) while the boys played hide and seek.

It was cold today, too, when granddaughter Adele graduated from Enterprise High School. When they showed slides of the graduates from babyhood to seniorhood, it brought a tear to my eye to see a photo I had taken of her when she was but a few months old. They grow up in a heart beat.

Miss Adele, a candidate for the Elgin Stampede Court, will be moving to Powell, Wyoming, in the fall to attend college, where she will be a member of the rodeo team.

While Doug moved a tractor from the cellar to the hay shed, a mother robin, who had built her nest in the forklift, never flew off. Such is motherhood.

May 28—I loaded the pickup with Dutch oven, ice cream freezer, butter churn, kraut maker and the sourdough crock, and took off for the Zumwalt. Great cloud shadows raced across the sunlit prairie, and wildflowers—lupine, balsamroot, phlox, larkspur, cous and camas—waved in the breeze. The gumbo-caked road leading to the summer house was pock-marked with puddles that reflected the sky.

After jouncing my way to the head of Camp Creek, there it was. A cluster of habitation. Main house, bunk house, barn, and corrals, all come to life again. Originally built in the 1930s, this has been, for many years, a cattle ranch. A good one too, surrounded by rolling hills of grass and nourished by the cloven hooves of cattle, who have contributed to the fertilization and stimulation of grazing, just as did the Nez Perce cattle and horses not so many years ago.

Camp Creek was happily gurgling along, full of rain and activated springs. I had been asked by the Wallowa Resource folks to participate in a tour that had already been in progress several days before my arrival. Would I demonstrate pioneer ways? Tell stories, along with Julie Kooch, author of *My Life on Joseph Creek*, and Allen Pinkham, a Nez Perce elder, and local rancher Jack McClaran?

"Sure," I replied, always ready for adventure and an excuse to flee to the outback.

Beth Gibans had been hired to do the catering, and together we had fun with the ice cream. She put together the cooked custardy makin's while I provided freezer, ice, salt and instructions to the tour-goers from New York who did the cranking.

"Turn until you can hardly crank the handle," I told them. They did, and the ice cream, served over Beth's dutch oven apple cake, was the best ever.

I arrived early and, after throwing my sleeping bag on an upstairs bunk, I'd had time for a walk down Camp Creek, where I found a flat rock on which to sit, soak up sun, and contemplate water bugs.

Later, Julie arrived and we assisted Beth in shaping rolls and skewering beef kabobs. That evening we listened to, and told, stories from all perspectives: homesteaders, ranchers, and native inhabitants—the first ones, who were here thousands of years before any of us—and present day folks. Today these lands are owned by the Nature Conservancy.

That evening a new moon appeared in the rain-washed skies, just above two tepees pitched up a draw from the main house. Allan and a friend had a fire going in the fire ring and the glow through the walls of that tepee matched the color of the moon. Beth's husband, Leon. took a photo, but it can never convey the feeling on that special night. It was as though the Nez Perce were still here.

I slept well, but dreamt of how it must have been before the coming of the white man, and how it must have been for the homesteaders and the folks who built this very house.

Early the next morning, the sky pink with dawn, I made my way down the narrow stairs to begin my day. I filled my enamel coffee pot with cold, clear water, bringing it to the boil, adding a clean sock full of coffee grounds and letting it simmer, until, like hummingbirds attracted to honeysuckle, folks followed their noses to the bunkhouse for a cup of Cowboy Coffee. Then I prepared elk sausage, bacon and sourdough hot cakes while Beth tended the scrambled eggs and huckleberry sauce for the hot cakes.

After Julie and I briefly touched on how the homesteaders survived, I used aids like the butter churn, the sad iron, and the kraut cutter.

Allan told how his grandmother and ancestors lived. They didn't need refrigeration, he said; they ground camas and dried everything, including wild meat and fish, and made pemmican, a combination of fat, meat, roots or berries. Their diet was healthy, and they were a healthy people, at least until they began to eat the white man's foods. It was a very interesting discussion and provided food for thought.

After the tour-goers left to tour the Buttes with geologist Ellen Morris Bishop, I loaded the pickup and left, stopping along the way to photograph the rolling green hills that led me back to the ranch.

I was just in time to attend a branding in progress on Tucker Down Road at Triple Creek Ranch, which was in complete juxtaposition to my previous experience, but nonetheless is a part of our present culture. Sons, grandchildren and great-granddaughter Brenna along with a daughter and daughter-in-law were all there, roping in a corral recently damped by rain.

As usual, I photographed, this time against the immaculate background of a restored ranch. After the branding, the gracious owners treated their hands to a most elegant feast, albeit not your standard Wallowa County fare, which consisted of King Crab legs soaked in garlic butter, juicy grilled steaks, fruit salads containing whole blackberries from Seattle Pike Market, beans, and a Dutch oven peach cobbler made by one of the sons.

Two new sheepherder wagons graced the lawns in front of the new bunkhouse. Everything was spit and polish, a feast for the eyes. These new folks, attracted to the area like we all were, are providing employment for some of our young folks who grew up here and possess the cowboy skills they need. The name of the West has always been CHANGE.

June 3—Doug and I drove out north to the former ghost town of Flora, I say former, because, as of late you really can't call Flora a ghost town. Not since they've begun to restore the old Flora School House. From the time we arrived until we left, we experienced another era of Wallowa County's rich history. Fiddlers and other old-time instruments were strummed by various locals draped around the entrance to the old two-story school house.

Smells of Dutch oven cooking wafted out over the green grassy fields where a chuck wagon had been set up and light bread, corn bread, ribs and beans simmered or baked. An old Monarch range, smoke pouring from its pipe, was being used to bake cookies, for which a woman, wearing a pioneer dress and bonnet, had ground the wheat and churned the butter before baking. Next to her in the field was a blacksmith bending over a fiery forge, shaping a tool of some sort.

On the north side of the school an enormous draft horse was pulling a "foot burner" plow while a would-be sod-buster wielded the handle as the share bucked its way over and under rocks.

Inside, the Flora women were serving up their famous pies and hand cranked ice cream, while in other rooms, still containing the old blackboards, women struggled with enormous looms to weave rugs and other creations. Upstairs, sewing machines hummed while women worked on squares for the colorful "school house" quilt displayed on the wall. This quilt is being raffled off, with proceeds going to the continued restoration of the Flora School Education Center. A very ambitious project.

Vanessa Thompson checks her pot of beans simmering on an old Monarch wood range. She also baked cookies in the oven for visitors at the "Flora Days" celebration.

Dan Thompson takes a break and praises his draft horse, who pulled a "foot burner" plow in the field of sod to demonstrate how it was done by the first homesteaders at the recent "Flora Days." Dan and his wife Vanessa operate the North End Crossing Bed and Breakfast in Flora, which features old-fashioned farm food.

After partaking of that delicious cookery, friend Kathy and I split a piece of the best chocolate pie we ever tasted. Then it was time to listen to old-time music and marvel at the local talent here in the county.

On the way home we noticed Krebs' ranch is back with its sheep, which always creates a peaceful scene, what with all that lush grass, full ponds, aspen trees and distant Wallowas there along the north highway. I love seeing the herders on horseback with their dogs, working the sheep, or heading to their wagons parked on the hills.

Doug just returned with a can of corn. Does this mean we'll go Kokanee fishing on the lake tonight? Phyllis and I did steal away to hunt morels one afternoon. Got enough for one meal, and enjoyed wandering the woods. Son Todd has roto-tilled the Slope garden; must get to plantin'.

June 5—On mornings such as this, when the lilac Mary gave me droops with dewy lavender blooms, my transplanted petunias glisten with yesterday's rain, the corn pokes through the wet earth in the garden, the sun streams through the living room window onto my planter of Impatiens, the "found" kittens sleep curled around each other in the carport, the air is filled with the sound of baby robins, my wash is pinned on the line, and those mountains, with leftover mists trailing beneath them, their disappearing snow fields gleaming in the rain-washed sky... well, all of it just erases winter. Simple as that!

For those of us who live close to the land, we are rejoicing in these soft, June rains. You should see the hills and the valleys and the canyons. Cattle are indeed belly-deep in GRASS, and the grain crops are jumping up so fast you can measure their daily progress.

Tucker's mare, the snow shape of a horse etched on the peak west of East Peak, is now visible through my kitchen window. If these warm rains continue, its likeness will diminish from a Clydesdale to a thoroughbred.

June 7—I spent the morning preparing a tomato pie, which consisted of a baked crust filled with cheese, tomatoes, basil and buttered bread crumbs.

Later, I joined other members of "Stitch and Bitch" as we savored a fantastic potluck. Nancy's fresh halibut, which they'd just caught in Alaska, Annie's rhubarb-strawberry pie, and Kathy's spinach egg dish and crab salad.

Of course, afterward we stitched and bitched, and mostly talked about our gardens. While the other gals are really into knitting, I've gone back to my childhood love: embroidery. My hands are more suited

Three-year-old Brenna Phillips rides one of uncle Todd's horses at a branding near Joseph.

to milking a cow, pulling weeds, or writing…than "knit one, pearl two," or whatever.

This evening, Dan and Vanessa Thompson drove in from Flora to deliver the silent auction items Doug and I bid on during the Flora School Days celebration. Mine was a gift certificate to a RimRock Inn dinner for two.

Our owls are back, roosting by day in the hay shed and flying by night to hunt under the June moon.

June 8—The morning dawned fresh and clear, after an uproarious thunder storm somewhere in the direction of Hells Canyon last night.

Doug drove to the hills to put out salt and move cattle. He reported seeing elk up the meadow, where several weeks ago Phyllis and I had seen lots of fresh signs when we hiked up Wet Salmon Creek to photograph the Aspen enclosure.

This evening we caught our limits of kokanee again on the lake. Pink brush-stroke clouds were reflected on the water at sunset, and the growing June moon glowed over the moraine.

On the way home we stopped at R&R in Joseph for an ice cream.

June 9—More rain showers, which eliminates the need to irrigate and is making this one of the finest feed years yet, so no complaints. I was asked, along with other "aging" rural women, to participate in a study conducted by OSU on rural women and what they (we) thought about using technology to enable us to stay in our own homes as we grow older.

Well, let me tell you, I don't think they were prepared for us Wallowa County women.

First off they should have selected "older" women. We ranch women in our 70s don't consider ourselves quite ready for TV screens that talk to us, asking how we are, and pill dispensers that cost $800, and monitors on our beds that record when we get up and go down. Goodness. Anyway, I guess these studies are necessary, but I wondered what other rural women in the Northwest thought. We did receive a gift certificate to Safeway for our efforts, and a plastic cutting board that I've stuck in my backpack.

I spent most of the day baking pies for Saturday's annual Wallowa Mountain Cruise in Joseph. Every year at this time, the "Friends of the Wallowa County Museum" offer pies to the hundreds of folks who flock to town for this antique restored car show. I baked two strawberry-rhubarb pies and Sandy Mallory's Flora recipe for chocolate pie.

The next morning we set up in the old fire hall adjacent to the museum. John Isley was there with his butane camp stove, and soon the same old "sock" full of fragrant coffee was simmering away, drawing folks in off the street for Cowboy Coffee and huge slabs of homemade pie. By 2 o'clock we were sold out.

The weather held until the motors started up and the rally *putt-putt*-ed to Enterprise. We here on Prairie Creek were especially proud of local farmer-rancher Tom Butterfield, who walked away with the "King of the Mountain" trophy for his restored 1934 Ford half-ton truck.

Before noon I'd walked down to the Farmer's Market and returned with some of Beth Gibans' fresh spinach, lettuce and honey, as well as a pepper plant and an Italian eggplant.

Beth, who gardens in Joseph, planted her organic garden earlier, and is now harvesting succulent greens. You can purchase this fresh produce on Wednesday afternoons in Enterprise, along with my writer friend Idella Allen's homemade whole wheat bread. Idella uses grains she grinds herself, as well as my eggs. I love these markets; perhaps later, I'll contribute some of my own produce.

This evening Doug and I joined other family members at a potluck held at daughter Ramona's on upper Prairie Creek, the occasion being in honor of visiting long-time friend Debbie Oakes' from California. Debbie grew up with my kids, and we spent many summers at her folks' cabin at Wright's Lake, high in the Sierras, where we packed into the nearby Desolation Wilderness Area with our four children and three burros.

I dug into my photo albums and found some old pictures I'd taken with my little Hawkeye camera in the '60s. A campfire was built, and marshmallows were roasted by great-granddaughter Brenna as well as grandson Buck...who knows how to roast his marshmallows so they're perfect for s'mores.

The great clouds that had been hovering over Prairie Creek pushed off toward the west, which made for a brilliant sunset, followed by the rising of the full June moon over the Seven Devils in the east. Debbie had one of those new digital cameras and was able to capture that moon and enlarge its image until you could see the cow that jumped over it!

Brenna was delighted with the duckling that one of Ramona's hens (as in chicken) had hatched the night before.

The cherry tomato kit I purchased from one of the Stangel girls for a class project is dripping with six plants. You grow them inside a bag filled with potting soil, let the plants grow out through the holes and, when the roots are established, hang the thing on a fence post in the sun. Mine are blooming and promise to look just like the photo on the bag. That is, if I remember to move them when Doug turns Ken's heifers outside the yard to graze the tall grass.

On Sunday mornings, Doug and I have breakfast at the Cheyenne Cafe in Joseph, after which I continue to walk it off by heading home on foot. Doug usually shows up about the three-mile marker. He said the jokes got so bad at the "locals" table, especially after one told by John VanBelle, that everyone got up and left!

That afternoon grandson Chad and his wife, Amy, hosted my children and me to a barbecue at their place on the north highway. It seems Chad had these early family photos put on a disc and needed us to identify them. So, after wading through several hundred, we finished in time to partake of hand-cranked ice cream, grilled burgers with all the trimmings, and Amy's still-warm rhubarb pies. Great-grandchildren Ronan, Gwenllian, and baby Kennon walked, crawled, and ran interference, and were there to lick the dasher of ice cream.

June 12—I weeded my Slope garden and baked a batch of ginger cookies to mail to our Marine grandson Shawn, who is stationed in Iraq. Doug added some jerky and other goodies to his "care package."

This evening I showed my old "Oregon Trail" slides to Phyllis' sorority up at her place. Watching those images projected on one of R's sheets brought back memories of hiking two segments of the Oregon Trail with friends and grandsons.

The next day I hosted our Writers' group here on the ranch, after which we partook of a lunch I'd prepared the night before. Fun recipes, full of fresh veggies, eggs, cheese and topped off with a bread pudding containing rhubarb, strawberries, orange zest, ginger snaps and eggs. There were ten of us and we ate every crumb.

June 14—We aging "CowBelles" met for our annual reunion at the Outlaw Restaurant in Joseph. Nice to see Jeanette Knott, who drove over from Cove to join us. Carol Wallace brought a money tree and we presented it to Jean Stubblefield, who, as I write, is changing her name to Jean Cook.

Congratulations to our local cattle buyer Wayne Cook, who lost his wife, Meleese, and to Jean Stubblefield, who lost her Jim, and are being married as we speak.

June 17—28 years ago today Doug and I were married on our front lawn by a local preacher who pronounced us man and wife while our family looked on and the yellow roses bloomed alongside the bunkhouse...just as they do now.

After an overnight honeymoon at the Horse Ranch—formerly Red's Horse Ranch—we flew back to our lives where, that first summer, we had five teenagers in the house and a huge ranching operation to run, which included the Dug Bar Ranch on Snake River, not to mention the combining of two households. I must admit, there were times I didn't think I'd make it. But I always kept my eye on the so called "light at the end of the tunnel."

My backpack is stuffed with provisions in readiness for our annual backpack trip. We "Syringa Sisters" will be six this year, as friend Kathy and her burro Fancy will be accompanying us on the same Rim Trail hike I took last June.

Things will get a bit frantic around here soon, as I'm also packing to fly to California for a (two years in the planning) family reunion. Doug will drive me to Boise, where I'll meet with daughter Jackie and fly to Sacramento Wednesday.

After returning to Boise on Sunday, I'll hitch a ride home with Jessica and Mary, who will be coming to the ranch to leave the next day on our backpack! Just writing this makes me wonder how it will all happen.

Since we're still experiencing those periodic warm June showers, rainbows sprout over Prairie Creek with great regularity; we enjoyed three yesterday. The poppies and phlox are intense in the wildflower patch. Doug picked the first radishes and strawberries in the garden yesterday, and all my transplanted "pretties" are very happy.

Since the weeds and cheatgrass were winning the war in one of my flower patches, I came up with the idea to plant a hill of my ancient squash. They all sprouted and, hopefully, this weed control method—death by squash—will work. I'm hoping these behemoth vines will choke out the bad stuff.

One hot afternoon, clad in rubber boots, I began to plant my Slope garden. It wasn't long 'till I kicked off those boots and planted the rest of it, wearing only socks. Up there, I have a wagon wheel rim surrounding tomato plants and basil, two rows of sweet corn, a row of beans, squashes, and a patch of wildflowers, and thanks to excellent growing conditions everything is up.

That evening, after fixing hamburgers for supper, Doug hitched up our old Dug Bar boat to the pickup and we spent the evening trolling for kokanee on Wallowa Lake. After considerable advice from the old man on how to reel in and reel out, guess who caught the biggest fish? The next night I fried a batch of corn fritters to go with those tasty land-locked salmon.

While on the subject of second marriages, Doug and I celebrated our 28th wedding anniversary last evening with Fred and Phyllis at Vali's Alpine Delicatessen at Wallowa Lake.

Luckily, the 17th fell on a Saturday this year, which means steak night. Beef: it's what's for dinner, and Mike and his son know how to fix it, just like all the years before when Maggie was there with her unfailing energy, as well as daughter-in-law Dione. This rare family-owned business has been IN business for over 30 years!

Our Mary was in the hospital for tests, but we're happy to say she's home again on Imnaha. Lyman's son Craig is here helping with the haying.

Onward.

July 5—5 a.m. Must get this column wrapped up. The company will be here soon. No time to elaborate on our big Fourth of July get-together at Scott and Kelly's on upper Prairie Creek, or about getting up early to bake two large shortcakes, filling them with strawberries and real whipped cream by 9 that morning to serve to our book group on the lawn, or barbecuing ribs and churning homemade ice cream for our family that evening, the occasion being a visit from the California great-grandchildren and their parents.

And now everything in the garden is ripening at once: peas, straw-berries, beets. The lawn needs irrigating and I made the first batch of raspberry freezer jam yesterday.

Between Chief Joseph Days events, our company will just have to get in the swing of life here on Prairie Creek. Grandson James was here for lunch the other day, entertaining us with dangerous tales of rappelling from a helicopter, putting out a fire, then hiking out of the John Day Wilderness carrying a heavy pack uphill, over fallen logs, during this hot spell. It's known as quick response, so these young men must be in terrific shape.

Perhaps, if it cools down a bit, I'll take our company out to visit Doug at Thomason Meadows tomorrow night. Meanwhile there's lunch to fix, and beds to make.

July 7—A week ago today five weary women and a small burro made their slow way up the final section of a 22-mile round-trip trail. The burro stopped every so often to graze the lush grasses growing among the wildflowers.

The two oldsters, Bobbie (78) and yours truly (72), stopped often too, not to graze, but to rest, and to marvel at the view of Hells Canyon to the east and Imnaha to the west. The youngsters, all in their 60s, beat Bobbie and me to the trailhead campground by a mere ten minutes.

We'd done it!

We were five this year. Mary, who'd recently undergone surgery, had to cancel out. But Bobbie and Barb (from Portland) and Jessica (Boise) and I had all carried our packs on our backs the entire way. Kathy's burro Fancy carried her gear and food.

My plans worked out, in spite of earlier doubts. Doug had driven me to Boise to meet daughter Jackie at friend Jessica's place, where we spent the night and boarded the plane to California the next day.

The following Sunday we flew back to Boise and spent the night. The next day, while Jackie headed home to Challis, Idaho, Jessica and I drove home to Prairie Creek, where we were joined by Barb, Bobbie, and Kathy and her burro.

Tuesday morning we packed up and left in three rigs for the Hells Canyon Overlook, and thence down the long, rutty track to the P.O. Saddle Trail head campground, which boasted a corral for Fancy, who spent little time in it except at night, a state-of-the-art outhouse, a picnic table, fire ring, and cold spring water. It rained lightly in the night, just enough to dampen the dust, and we had the place all to ourselves.

The next morning we packed up our gear and helped Kathy pack her burro—no small feat—and headed toward P.O. Saddle. That high, wild ridge trail, perched on the rim of Hells Canyon, glistened with rain drops. The sun felt good, as it was cool at that elevation of more than 6,000 feet.

The wildflowers were brilliant at their peak of color. Penstemon, larkspur, Indian paintbrush, alpine forget-me-nots, mountain blue bells, flax, balsamroot, and sweet fennel covered the steep hillsides. Tangles of lavender clematis hung from firs alongside shaded sections of the trail. Bushes bloomed fragrant and white; mountain spray, cyanothus, and others I can't identify. Butterflies swam lazily from flower to flower, or sipped puddles left by the rain.

When we glimpsed the first yawning breaks of Hells Canyon, and stared off into endless separations of wild blue yonder, we lost our ability to describe the country and, naturally, when the far-off Wallowas appeared to the west, snow still clinging to their peaks, it was enough to make us temporarily forget our heavy packs.

We'd filled our water bottles on the way out of camp, as we wouldn't have access to drinking water until we reached Himmelwright Springs. After leading the burro for a few miles, Kathy decided to turn her loose, whereupon she followed along like a large pet dog. However, whenever the deer flies pestered her or she wanted to shed her pack, Fancy had the annoying habit of sneaking up behind and pushing us quite forcefully with her head.

On one occasion, she nearly upended Bobbie, who verbally let the burro know she wasn't happy. For some reason that response only made matters worse and, during the entire trip, Fancy picked on Bobbie. So all of us were very protective of our friend, and walked between the burro and Bobbie. Fancy's pack frequently shifted whenever the bungee cords used to tie down the load popped off, which meant packs had to be readjusted along the way and frequent stops made to tighten cinches.

Both Kathy and the burro learned myriad lessons—all the hard way— on their maiden pack trip into the wilderness. The burro DID make for an interesting trip, and she added character to our photographs, although we all wished that instead of carrying tether ropes, hay and grain pellets, and other gear Fancy never used, she could have packed our sleeping bags, food and other heavier objects.

We paused to rest at P.O. Saddle and stare downward into the great blue silences of Hells Canyon. The younger ones reached Salisbury Saddle before Bobbie and I did, and took the low trail, while I remembered the high trail taken last year. Up ahead the two trails converged, we having seen far-off vistas of the Wallowas and ambled through a blue world of enormous patches of larkspur. The trail wound steadily up a hillside flaming with paintbrush, pipsissewa, and flax.

We paused often, staring at the sky as well, which blossomed with clouds the color of polished cotton. After joining up again, we walked a long hogback ridge strewn with deadfall, evidence of great winds cleansing the forests of drying trees. Often we detoured around the fallen logs.

Mushrooms—calf brains and puff balls—have pushed up through the forest duff. Steam rises from the trail. A cooling breeze chases away the deer flies. The smells are of mountain springtime. It appears we are the first to use this trail this season, for we encounter no other signs of humans or horse tracks.

In fact, we will not encounter another soul until we return to the Hells Canyon Overlook on Friday. Then there it is: the trail, barely visible, leading up to Himmelwright Springs. I recognize it by the now-spent mule ears. That huge patch was covered with cream-colored blooms last year, and I'll forever remember sighting them through falling snow.

Wearily, we trudge the final steps to an open hillside above the spring, sling off those cumbersome packs, and sink down to rest in the shade. Revived, we walk down to the spring and fill our water bottles. The burro, of course, goes too. Then we must make a decision. We can spend the night here or continue on to the Marks cabin, which is still up beyond Lookout Mountain.

We eat our lunches and decide to push on. That way we can spend the night in the cabin and return to Himmelwright Springs the next night, reducing the distance on our hike out Friday. Since we have reservations at the Imnaha River Inn for dinner at 6:00 on Friday, where we plan to spend the night before returning to our other lives after breakfast on Saturday, we make the decision to continue onward.

Miles and distances have a way of becoming dimmed by time, and my memory of last year's hike was a bit fuzzy. Especially since the side trip to Barton Heights wasn't in the plans this year, I considered the rest of the hike to be much shorter. Wrong. Mainly because, when you begin to age, your energy level sags in the afternoon.

And that's what we did: we sagged, and slogged our way through that beautiful distance. When we came upon a herd of cows and calves, and a few bulls, slapping their tails at flies near a pond that stood in a wide meadow, I knew we were close. After making our way through thick timber, where I'd remembered great mounds of hail had accumulated last year, we came to the gate Mary knows so well.

Below here we headed up a small rise that led down to the cabin. I'd felt bad when we were climbing Lookout Mountain, forgetting how steep it was; everyone was too tired to walk the short distance for a look-see over the edge. When we were on the final mile of eleven miles, I thought my companions would mutiny, but they didn't, bless them, and soon we approached the cabin.

It was nearly 5:00 o'clock and no abode has ever seemed so welcome. The decision to jettison heavy items we wouldn't need at the cabin—like tents, cooking utensils and such, was a good one. We left them stashed at Himmelwright Springs for our return.

A heavy cloud layer made for an outrageous sunset that evening. The cabin, the surrounding trees, the very air itself was bathed for half an hour in watermelon-colored light. The season's remaining snow banks gleamed white across the canyon from the outhouse, and a cooling breeze blew through the open windows. And we slept on mattresses, our tummies full of Mountain House dehydrated beans, rice, and stew.

On every trip to the outhouse we had a burro in our pocket... she didn't want to miss anything.

The next morning we awoke to the comforting patter of rain on a tin roof. Should we stay another night? Rest up and wait for the storm to pass? Or... since it was a warm rain, should we just head out? We lounged around, fixed breakfast of dehydrated scrambled eggs, oatmeal and hot drinks, and felt so much better that we decided to pack and leave.

This took longer than planned due to another hard-learned lesson on behalf of Kathy and her burro, which had to do with packing on a side hill. But finally we were off up the trail into the warm, softly falling rain.

This time we stopped at Lookout Mountain for lunch, and, with slickers snapped tightly around us, peered off over the edge of the old lookout site where Charley Marks spent his summers long ago, spotting fires across miles and miles of some of the wildest country in North America.

In no time we were at Himmelwright Springs and I was scouting around for a remembered elk camp site. Clouds thickening, Jessica— who'd been in the lead—came up missing, though it turned out she walked right past the place and later had to back track about three miles to find us!

I found the camp, collected fire wood, built a huge fire in the fire ring, and contemplated the construction of a tarp-shelter from Kathy's burro pack, so we could stash everything away from the storm I knew

was coming. Only, Kathy had unloaded the tarp below the hill and then
went looking for Jessica, and so had Barb.

Bobbie and I were the only ones in camp when those clouds opened
up. I mean, thunder rolled and lightning zig-zagged across the sky, and
water pooled everywhere. Trees dripped. We were a soggy outfit in no
time. Bobbie and Barb crawled in the tent, which quickly proved a futile
refuge, as a river ran through it. Jess encased herself in a bivvy thing
that fit over her sleeping bag, while Kathy fled to the tarp, which was
now wrapped around the pack bags.

Meanwhile, the burro and I stood out the storm, me dry under my
long poncho, our backs to the storm while the wind whistled, the rain
drummed down, and the heavens erupted with deafening sounds. I loved
it, as it was a warm rain, and I made occasional trips to throw logs on the
fire... thank goodness for that fire. When the rain slackened, I had water
boiling for tea and we were able to dry out all our clothes and sleeping
bags.

That night the moon crept out, and the stars were magnificent.

Jessica and I spread our space blankets on the ground, then our pads
and sleeping bags. I laid my slicker over that. Everything was dewy
damp, but I slept dry.

At 4 the next morning I was up kindling a fire and staring at the
brilliant morning star, when a chorus of coyotes let loose, their quavering
wails echoing far below in those misty canyons. Water boiling for tea,
we breakfasted on mountain bread, packed our gear, and headed down
the trail shortly after 6.

Much later, driving downriver, we met Lyman and Mary and asked
if they could put up with the burro overnight.

"Sure," said Lyman. "Follow me to the calf lot."

After hugs all around for Mary, we continued on down to the Imnaha
River Inn where we indulged in what I described as "a million dollar
shower." Sandy and Nick were wonderful hosts, and that hot meal, wine,
and relaxation on the deck was a perfect ending to another wonderful,
memory-making trip.

The next morning we parted, wondering where we'll meet next year.

The California reunion was full of emotional experiences as well.
Standing with relatives on a high hill, the intense summertime heat
shimmered off the dry grass while cousin Libby shared stories about our
ancestors buried there in the old White Rock Cemetery. We stood there in
the pioneer Manzanita Cemetery in rural Lincoln, sharing stories about
my mother, father, and stepfather, reciting poems while cows grazed an
adjoining field and the Oleander bloomed pink among the oak trees.

That gathering of the Wilson-Butler clan took place at an old ranch house near Rio Linda, where, under an enormous oak tree's spreading branches, we ate, visited, watched the new generation of babies play with water guns, and read about our rich heritage displayed on a huge placard.

I studied an old photo of Eliza Manning, who cousin Libby said walked great distances. Eliza, Electa, Mary Myrtle, Blanche...all strong women. I looked lovingly upon our remaining Wilson aunt, auntie Carol, and realized she is now the matriarch. Guess who's next in line?

Meanwhile, back at the ranch, the busy summer continues.

Last evening Doug and I drove over to Union County to attend the 60th annual Elgin Stampede, and watched proudly as our granddaughter Adele was crowned queen. As Adele raced around the arena in the new saddle she won, I remembered the little towheaded girl I used to take camping with her brother James. We watched as all but five bull riders got bucked off in the Bull-O-Rama held in honor of Adele's stepbrother Mark Nichols, who lost his life several years ago.

Much more to write about, but time marches on. Summer Fishtrap writing workshops begin Monday, and company's coming for Chief Joseph Days. And then there's the Asotin Trail Ride...

July 24—It's so HOT right now...can't think straight. Gonna shade up a while...be back later.

July 24—Later...9 p.m.—Even though the living room thermostat indicates 87 degrees, it's tolerable here at the kitchen table. Every window in the house is open to the coolness settling over Prairie Creek, after yet another scorching summer day. Doug has gone to bed, anticipating leaving on the morrow in his pickup, hitched to a flatbed trailer full of outhouses, for Cold Springs Ridge. That's where the Asotin Trail Riders will come ridin' in to a place called Frog Pond.

After leaving the Asotin County Fairgrounds Sunday, the trail riders headed cross-country, forded the Grande Ronde River, and are now guiding their horses over rough country into Wallowa County. It will be a long hot ride through steep canyons, and finally up Horse Creek.

Doug and the kitchen crew will move camp each day, to Thomason Meadows the next night, then Tippett Corrals along the Zumwalt Road, and finally across the dry hills to their Joseph encampment, where they will join the Chief Joseph Days parade Saturday. It's like a vacation for Doug. I'd planned to join him this year, but the dates conflicted with company coming for Chief Joseph Days. In fact, the Missourians just called.

"We're here in Boise, the plane just landed... an hour late due to a thunder storm. We'll rent a car and be in Joseph by noon tomorrow."

It's a given. When you live near Joseph, you always have company the last week in July. Most generally, this is the hottest time of year.

To escape the heat Doug and I look forward to evening when the sun sinks beyond the Wallowas and we can sit out on the lawn, watching the wild geese come honking overhead to land in Hough's hay field; the white-tail doe and her twin fawns nibble on the alfalfa as we savor the smell of freshly-mown hay and ripening raspberries, and feel the green coolness from the irrigated fields seep slowly over Prairie Creek.

Yesterday I braved the heat and drove down to Wallowa to attend the 16th annual Tamkaliks celebration staged by local citizens and visiting Nez Perce. I'd arisen early to pick lettuce from our garden to make a huge salad for the Friendship Feast.

On the way I stopped to buy a large watermelon and some fig new-tons. Arriving early enough to witness the Indian church service, I sat there listening to these descendants (from three reservations) of Chief Joseph's Wallowa Band of Nez Perce, keeping their fading culture alive.

A cool breeze wandered above, stirring the silky parachute that provided shade as ancient Nez Perce songs and drum beats echoed off Tick Hill and over the lower valley. Tamkaliks, which means "from where you can see the mountains," is held on land now owned by the Nez Perce. Folks like Bobbie Conner and her brother Bryan, Fred Minthorn, and many others should be commended for their efforts to preserve a culture that can teach us much in a world gone mad. They are returning to a once-beautiful land we are destroying, rather than nurturing.

Later, seated beside some of the elders, I enjoyed meeting and visiting with several Nez Perce women as we partook of the delicious local salmon and buffalo prepared by Joe McCormack, along with salads and other dishes donated by the community; a community that gives so much to support this annual homecoming of the Nez Perce.

Mingling with these people put me in mind of the recent memorial held for the late Alvin Josephy during our Summer Fishtrap, a very touching ceremony held on the scenic Josephy ranch located at the north end of the east moraine. Alvin, a true friend of the Indian, was honored by them in a way he would have loved. His empty chair reminded us of his presence, a presence we honored for 18 years at Summer Fishtrap. Tears were shed by those who, because of Alvin, are now taking pride in their Indian heritage.

My friend Bobbie Ulrich had spent that week of Fishtrap with us here at the ranch. Each morning we arose early to attend our workshops.

This year I signed up for Donald Snow's workshop.

Donald, the Visiting Mellon Professor of Environmental Humanities at Whitman College, has taught workshops in creative nonfiction since 1989, at the University of Montana, University of Wyoming, and now at Whitman. Such a pleasure to get to know this man.

Our class was held outside at the Methodist Camp at Wallowa Lake, and on Tuesday we drove out to the Nature Conservancy's Zumwalt Prairie Preserve, which provided education as well as adventure. And what a classroom! Views of Wallowa County's beloved hills...acres of grass, the last of the wildflowers, a herd of elk wandering into an aspen thicket, calves squealing for their mamas, clouds sailing above in a clear blue sky, and cattle grazing.

Naturally, being a rancher at heart, my writing centered on the favorable impacts of cattle grazing, which were quite obvious everywhere you looked. My words came from the heart, of one who lived on and loved the land. I also addressed the fact that the Nez Perce ran thousands of horses and cattle on this native grassland long before the white man arrived in the early 1870s.

There we were—thirteen of us, from all over the U.S—sprawled in the shade of a ponderosa pine on the side of Harsin Butte, eating our lunches, discussing butterflies, bunch grass, and bugs feeding on cow pies. All the while, we stared off across the rolling prairie as cloud shadows slid silently across the sunlit hills, listening to the quiet. It was pretty wonderful and the effect on city dwellers was something to see.

Most importantly, we all emerged from Don Snow's workshop with an essay that will be published in an anthology.

Well, it's nearly 11:30 and I'm sleepy.

August 7—The kitchen table where I write reflects the season. In addition to stacks of correspondence waiting to be answered, there is the following assortment: the first ripe tomato, a recipe for dill pickles, the County Fair premium book, six quarts of pickled beets, six pints of blackberry jelly, and today's mail, which includes the agenda for the annual Wallowa County Stockgrowers' two-day doin's next weekend. Whew!

So goes our brief, beautiful summer. Doug is outside on this hot afternoon picking MORE raspberries. Weather-wise, a hot breeze blows over Prairie Creek as thunder clouds boil up west above the Wallowas, and east over the rim of Hells Canyon.

Weather forecast: 20 percent chance of thunderstorms.

Left to right, the 2006 Chief Joseph Days court: Queen Tessa Kuppinger, Princess Olivia Soares, and Princess Sara Freels.

Asotin Trail Riders in the Chief Joseph Days Parade. They rode from Asotin, Washington, to Joseph, Oregon. Leading the parade is Wayne Tippett, left, and Vaden Flock, right.

August 8—While I was working on this column yesterday afternoon, a knock at the door brought forth granddaughter-in-law Chelsea, plus a visiting girlfriend from Montana. And since this grandma wouldn't think of missing a chance to chat with two delightful young ladies, she put everything on hold, and sought some cool shade on the front lawn.

Chelsea, who just passed her state boards for nursing, says she'll begin working at our local hospital Thursday. Good news. Her hubby, grandson Buck, is busy seven days a week...changing sprinklers, haying, and helping son Todd move cattle. Not unlike all the other young men still engaged in farming or ranching, who live here in the county.

Like young Robert Butterfield, who's working the Hockett place; and his daddy, Dan, and mom, Lori, who in addition to other leased lands farm the Locke place. And then there's Tyson McLaughlin, who planted a field of grain on Larry Waters' farm. And Greg Brink, who lives south of us, who works with his father to run their large farming operation. And that's just Tenderfoot Valley Road. Encouraging to know some of the younger generation is staying "down on the farm."

Prairie Creek is in mourning this week. We've lost a young farmer. Jim Dawson, son of Malcolm and Jean Dawson, who, for years, farmed the home place on Dobbin Road, passed away while working in his field at age 55. He leaves his wife and helpmate Denny, and three children. Jim's shy smile and dedication to work will be missed. He was truly one of the outstanding farmers in the county. I understand local ranchers Rod and Linda Childers have arranged for the harvesting of the Dawson crops. That sort of says it all about our Wallowa County folks.

While tending my chickens at sunrise this morning, I paused to watch hundreds of wild honkers wing their way overhead and land in the neighboring fields to feed. Irrigated pastures provide great habitat for geese.

In the cool of evening Doug and I sit outside on our front lawn and count the while-tail does and fawns in Hough's hay field. The white-tails don't come to what used to be our hill pasture anymore, as this field has been chemically killed in preparation for planting a fall grain crop.

In my mind's eye I will forever hold dear the beautiful red clover crop that used to grow there. The new owners assure me Doug's old ranch will always remain in agriculture, so for that I'm most thankful, but I'll miss seeing fat cattle grazing lush grasses against our snowy mountains, and later, those fragrant rows of baled meadow hay. Life is full of changes.

After chores this morning, I drove up on Alder Slope and picked green beans, zucchini and crookneck squashes, and pickling cucumbers in the garden I planted, where son Todd and his wife, Angie, live. Then proceeded to Cloverleaf Hall, where our county fair is in progress.

Growing up with 4-H...county fairs will always be a part of me. One look at a premium book and there I am again, entering something. As a child I showed Guernsey cattle and Hampshire sheep, and after I was married and began raising a family, livestock morphed into cakes, bread and flowers. Now, in my golden years, I enter photos of my great-grandchildren and zucchini.

I love walking into Cloverleaf Hall with my freshly-picked veggies to join the other exhibitors, most of whom take this competition VERY seriously. Mainly, the reason I enter, is to provide competition for those outstanding entries that deserve the blue ribbons. Next to mine, they really shine.

Arranging my plate of six green beans just so, I'm told, "You're only supposed to have five." So...I pluck a fat green bean from the blue plastic plate. My squashes aren't uniform; neither are my cucumbers. And the premium book has no category for cucumbers, much less pickling cukes, so I enter them in class 28, *all other vegetables not listed.*

Meanwhile, first-time exhibitors, bless them, proudly clutching cabbages, turnips and kohlrabi, stand in line to be helped by local folks, bless them, who volunteer to work at the fair....most of whom didn't grow up in 4-H.

Amazingly, by 10 a.m. all exhibits are in place and I can imagine all volunteers are very relieved. I passed by Ray Combes sitting in his car waiting for his wife, Pat, to enter her stuff, and we had a good laugh. Laughter is still the best medicine and the county fair is so much FUN!

Arriving a bit late for my weekly Writers Group, hands still smudged with Alder Slope soil and wisps of wind-blown white hair escaping from under my floppy garden hat, I joined three other aging women upstairs in Fishtrap House. More laughter, as most of our writing this morning was of a humorous nature.

Then it was off to Safeway to purchase my weekly groceries, where I ran into hubby and proposed we "do" lunch at Cloud 9 Bakery. We chose a sidewalk table, which was nice because we had a good visit with Grant and Barbara Warnock, up this morning from Imnaha to enter stuff in the fair.

Meanwhile back at what's left of our ranch, I unload groceries, nap, and contemplate working on this column. No such luck. The phone rings: Doug's nephew Casey.

"Lightning...ground strikes in the Zumwalt. I'm headin' out."

I looked out north to see zigzag flashes of light zipping from the darkened skies to those parched hills. Praying for rain, I called the Imnaha Store, where Doug said he would go after picking canning peaches for me at Myrna and Larry Moore's at Bear Gulch. I called Scott and son Ken, as they have cattle grazing our summer range. Ken, on a firefighting crew, was already headed out to Elk Mountain.

Casey kept calling. I told him our pumper was ready if someone wanted to take it. Then Casey called again.

"Rainin' like heck," he said. "Big puddles in the road." Our prayers answered, the danger of grass fires diminished.

Doug returned with two buckets of sweet, sun-ripened peaches, and reported hail at Big Sheep Creek. Rain drummed down on Prairie Creek and great flashes of light lit our bedroom as the angry storm rumbled late into the night.

August 9—This morning dawned damp and clear, with nary a cloud. The air is cleansed and the wild geese, confused in the storm, can't seem to stay in one place. Those peaches wait to be canned.

We survived Chief Joseph Days. Our company, like everyone, was awed not just by Wallowa County's scenery, but by the folks who live here.

For six days I talked with a southern drawl. Mike aka "Augustus" or "Dumplin" and wife, Kathy, plus his side kick Bill, aka "Woodrow" and his wife, Martha, were great fun. Mike is a great fan of Lonesome Dove, says he's watched the video sixteen times!

While Doug was in the outback, pulling those outhouses from camp to camp for those Asotin Trail Riders, Mike, Kathy, Bill, Martha, and I did it all. Rode the gondola up to Mt. Howard, attended two performances of the rodeo, watched both the junior parade and the grand parade, ate two cowboy breakfasts, and attended the Nez Perce Friendship Feast.

Thursday night I took our guests out to join the Asotin trail ride at the Tippett Corrals, where they met Doug for the first time and we ate dinner with the riders, right in the middle of the Zumwalt road. Earlier, we'd watched a herd of elk come running down off the hill just before the riders appeared. Quite a thrill for everyone.

The next night Doug and I enjoyed a prime rib dinner with the Asotin gang. Those folks really know how to put on a trail ride and have fun. Great friends.

Friday night Doug and I, wearing our trail ride T-shirts, sat with the Asotin gang at the rodeo.

On Sunday I attended the cowboy church service in the rodeo arena while Doug drove our guests to Imnaha and Hat Point. A bit shook up over the road, they returned, packed up their rented car, and left to catch their planes in Boise. Back to Mississippi and Missouri, leaving behind unforgettable memories.

Meanwhile, I dealt with towels, sheets and raspberry jam. We had a delightful visit with Richard and Mary Frasch, and son David, over dinner in the Glacier Grill at Wallowa Lake. Summer is so crammed full of activity, I can't begin to record it all…like celebrating Janet (Tippett) Uhler's 75th birthday at Vali's with friends, or cooking those first creamed new potatoes and peas from the garden.

Last evening I savored the first Imnaha tomato. My peaches are calling to be canned.

August 23—A fall feeling in the air this morning, a coastal breeze stirring the raspberry leaves, as the scent of Hough's lush, irrigated alfalfa mingled with smoke from surrounding fires that wafts over Prairie Creek. Three giant sunflowers, growing at the edge of Doug's garden, face the smoke-smeared sun.

The corn is ripening. Chinese lanterns, their bright, orange glow visible now, reflect the seasonal shift. And all those petunias, geraniums, moss roses and Impatiens—potted in cast-off enamel kettles—shout their last hurrah, at their most brilliant now in these waning days of August, as are the hollyhocks, having re-seeded themselves and enlarged their patch beside the bunkhouse, much to Doug's dismay.

Remember that ancient Indian squash I planted for weed control? Well, now it's out of control! This giant plant has managed to grow its way through a hog wire fence and, last I looked, those creeping tendrils were headin' for the horse pasture, away from those weeds I'd hoped to strangle. And the weeds? Well, in a spurt of morning energy, I hacked 'em down with a sharp hoe. And now, each morning, I find myself cheering the advancing squash. Go, squash! Your days are numbered.

Our neighbor's grain crops are ripening. And hay hands, putting up the second cutting in Doug's former fields to the west of the 16 acres he kept, are busy swathing, baling and stacking.

On my frequent trips to town I yearn to make a picture of the long rows of baled hay in the morning light. Haying time in the valley is a beautiful thing. Some bales are round, others shaped like bread loaves, all works of art.

Seven-year-old Aspen Birkmaier smiles after completing in the Pole Bending event at the recent Joseph Junior Rodeo.

Young Harley Miller practices throwing a loop in the Dummy roping at the Joseph Junior Rodeo.

As far as I'm concerned, and the majority of locals will agree, our valley's charm is due to its productive agricultural lands, which include cattle ranches. Most importantly, because we have good soil, grass, water, and clean air, we are able to produce quality products, which not only keep folks healthy but contribute significantly to the economic base of our county. My dream is to sustain agriculture...and welcome new ways to produce local products to be consumed by locals, with the hope these unique products could be marketed outside the county.

Here in Wallowa County we have another crop worth sustaining: our youth. Gone off to college, they return with dreams of making a living in agriculture intact, and they're not afraid to work. Their reward: a lifestyle that not only produces healthful food but allows them to raise their families in this place they've always called home, a place in the heart.

They, as well as others from the OUTSIDE, bring fresh, new ideas on how to make a living, even on small acreages, by producing something grown with good grass—and we do have good grass—that would appeal to outside markets. Grass-fed beef is already an established market. How about eggs with yellow yolks, and fryers, all grown on a small scale, not by the thousands? Is there anything more tasteless than a chain-store chicken? Can you envision cheese made from Jersey cows? It used to happen here. Read the history of our county. It could happen again. If you go to farmers' markets in Portland, they sell out of locally-produced specialty cheeses like goat cheese.

We have excellent soil here. Ted Juve once told me we are missing an opportunity for row crops: carrots, cabbages, peas, and my goodness...even ancient Indian squash! What I'm trying to say, I guess, is: do we want our land to grow houses for wealthy retired folks to live in, three months out of the year, or do we want Wallowa County to sustain what is drawing folks here: open space and the rural character of working farms and ranches? We can have both...but we mustn't ruin our rural landscape in the process. Off my soapbox!

While throngs of people flocked to Joseph to attend the Bronze, Blues and Brews event, our county fair was in progress. Although there was an absence of throngs of people wandering through Cloverleaf Hall to view canned peaches, homemade bread, quilts and zucchini, those of us who did attend were, as usual, impressed not only with the exhibits but with the awesome job it takes to run a fair, mostly by volunteers.

Whether it was in FFA, 4-H, horse show, food booth, awards program, junior rodeo, or fat stock auction, there they were...some our busiest ranchers, donating their time and talent to help our youth. Not all of them were ranchers, either. You saw folks from the entire community volunteering in the food booth, at Cloverleaf Hall or the junior rodeo. The theme for this year's fair was "Made in Wallowa County." And what could be more appropriate than our youth? They are made here, and our unique county fair reflects their accomplishments.

More folks should attend the fair. It's been said that if you want to get a feel for a local culture, attend their county fair. And if you want to have some good old-fashioned fun, volunteer or enter your zucchini.

This year the Joseph Junior Rodeo was held in conjunction with the fair...and it worked. Run by volunteers, it was a far cry from Chief Joseph Days. No loud, blaring music, just Tony Yost—raised on lower Prairie Creek, one of my former 4-H Sourdough Shutterbugs—announcing in his very professional, yet personal way. Tony knows Wallowa County. No carnival, no throngs of people, no ads for beer or chewing tobacco. Just daddies, like Tom Birkmaier from way out on Crow Creek, leading his two little girls on horseback through the pole bending event; or wee but mighty Harley Miller, throwing his loop at the dummy steer head stuck in a bale of straw.

We chuckled at kids wandering through the stands, clutching chickens and ducks they'd caught in the scramble. No matter the rodeo runs a little slow...there's always the kind of drama that makes you feel good, like seeing parents helping children have some good, clean fun, while learning skills at the same time. It's a joy to watch the kids, like those Smith kids, growing up way down at Corral Creek on the lower Imnaha. These and others like them are Wallowa County's future cowboys and cowgirls. Let's just make sure we keep our ranching community healthy for their sake.

Over in Cloverleaf Hall I was shocked to find blue ribbons on my green beans, cucumbers, raspberries, eggs, and photographs. My zucchini didn't fare as well. No award. It had competed with the yellow crookneck...both pretty ugly. Doug and I enjoyed several of those famous food booth hamburgers, as well as visiting old friends we seldom see between fairs.

Each year we miss seeing one of our most precious dwindling resources...our old-timers, who, along with their invaluable wisdom, have passed on.

As usual, the fair ended with the fat stock auction. This year I purchased Emily Ketscher's lamb, after which sweet little Emily gave me a big hug and a note, which read, *Thank you so much for buying my lamb. I really didn't want her to die. See you next weekend, Love, Emily.* Although I "turned" Emily's lamb, perhaps it was comforting for her to know I'd gotten the final bid.

The next week flew by in a blur. Daughter Jackie and husband, Bill, arrived from Challis, Idaho, to spend time with their son Buck and his wife, Chelsea, a visit planned to include Jackie's 30th class reunion at Enterprise High. Of course this provided an excuse for our large, extended family to get together. We gathered here on the ranch for a feast of garden veggies, a large ham from a 4-H hog from last year's auction, sourdough chocolate cake for Buck and Todd's birthdays, and hand-cranked ice cream.

While seated at the picnic table, great-grandson Ronan, who never misses anything, said, "The clouds are growling." Indeed they were. Great zigzag flashes of light zipped from blue-black clouds that boomed and bellowed over East Peak. The rain held off until we'd cleared the picnic table.

On Tuesday, after the cowboys worked a small bunch of cattle where Buck lives, we all squeezed into our van and headed out the north highway to the RimRock Inn, where I treated our family to lunch with a gift certificate I'd purchased at Flora Days to benefit the old school.

Sunday afternoon we met again at Buck and Chelsea's for a farewell, where we barbecued hamburgers—our ranch-raised beef—and ate more of that ice cream. In between all of this, we canned. I taught Chelsea to cold pack peaches and start a crock of dill pickles.

Yesterday Doug cut a row of cabbages and we made sauerkraut. Time to put food by.

Another day, I hosted our Fishtrap Board members to what's become a traditional berry dessert and meeting on our lawn, which meant I spent a good deal of time baking blackberry cobbler and strawberry and blueberry pies, served after brown bag lunches.

After which I joined Doug at the Dawson ranch on Dobbin Road for a celebration of rancher-farmer Jim's life, a life that spoke volumes about our ranching community. In his own quiet way, Jim represented all the values inherent in Wallowa County's unique lifestyle.

You should have seen the outpouring of support. The cars filled a field and lined the county road. Throngs of folks carried food and lawn chairs. But, most importantly, they had left their busy lives to show love and respect for this rural family.

Then there was the annual Stockgrowers weekend, which I don't have time to report on here. What a surprise to see Agri-Times Publisher Sterling Allen and his lively wife, Cheryl, on the Friday tour.

More on that next time; strawberries need picking...again.

Bob Morse, left, last year's recipient of the Grassman of the Year award, presents the 2006 award to Jim and Vera Henderson at the annual Stockgrowers dinner/dance.

Bud and Zua Birkmaier proudly display the Honorary Cattlemen of the Year award.

Jeanie Mallory, right, presents Beth McClaran with the Stockgrowers' scholarship at their annual meeting. Jeanie is the first woman to be president of the Stockgrowers since it was organized in 1936.

September 6—It's 5:45 a.m. and Prairie Creek is bathed in stagnant smoky air. At dusk last evening I was sitting out on the lawn, staring at a great horned owl perched on a fence post, when my eye caught a glimpse of orange fire. It was the September moon, which appeared to swim in a sea of purple clouds that resembled billowing smoke, no different from the billowing smoke I'd witnessed yesterday from my kitchen window.

Suddenly, the wind began to moan, and the owl took flight, sailing silently above me. The eerie wind increased, sweeping away the Ponderosa's dry needles, hurling lawn chairs against the fence and slamming my hanging baskets of petunias. Earlier, between drum rolls of thunder, it had poured down rain, and I imagined lightning strikes igniting still more fires.

Doug and I, pulling our camp trailer, returning from Ollokot Campground at the end of Labor Day weekend, were driving up Gumboot when we noticed the fire. At home we looked south to see a huge cloud of smoke pouring over the ridge. Not until the next morning did we learn we'd seen the beginning of what's now been dubbed the Twin Lakes Complex. These fires would spread so far, so fast, they would necessitate closing all campgrounds between Indian Crossing and Ollokot.

Despite hot, dry conditions, and, thanks to grandson Buck and wife, Chelsea, who reserved a camping spot for us on their way to McCall, Idaho, we had a great Labor Day weekend.

Friday evening at Ollokot, we had a pleasant surprise visit from Wilmer Cook, on his way to Council, Idaho, to celebrate his 90th birthday with grandchildren, along with daughter Joyce, husband Steve and grandson Bret. It felt like old times, when Wilmer and his Mary camped up Dry Creek every Labor Day.

We'd just finished supper of roast beef which I'd cooked at home, corn on the cob from our garden, and some of those yummy Imnaha tomatoes, topped off with apple pie I'd taken from our freezer, when they drove in. We offered them pie, but Wilmer declined, saying granddaughter Amy would have pies waiting in Council. We had a great time recalling those "Sourdough Shutterbug" days, when Wilmer's grandchildren belonged to my 4-H group. All those great kids turned into fine adults raising families of their own.

On Saturday we relaxed, read, napped, and, for the first time in days, I actually had time to write in my neglected journal. Summers in Wallowa County are so crammed with activity, it presents a real challenge for busy gals like me.

Sunday morning we headed up the ridge and down North Pine Creek to Halfway, a ranching community nestled in peaceful Pine Valley. On the way...to Halfway...we noticed miles of scorched hills, clearly the blackened path taken by the recent Foster Gulch fire.

After driving into the quiet little hamlet of Halfway, we followed signs to the "all you can eat huckleberry pancake breakfast" served up by the local Lions. Since it was then 10 o'clock, we wolfed down several of those pancakes with ham, potatoes and eggs, seated across from folks we knew from the upper Imnaha, who told us they were camped at the fairgrounds to take in the Baker County Fair and Panhandle Rodeo.

As in years past, I enjoyed this unique fair. I wandered around in the exhibit building, taking time to savor the locals' colorful flower arrangements and their bountiful harvest of garden vegetables, and photographing a plate of sourdough cinnamon rolls that won Best of Show. The rolls were baked with sourdough more than 100 years old.

The rodeo began at 2:00, and, although it was breathlessly hot, this little community knows how to put on a show. Announcer Lee Daggett informed us that the local community had raised half a million dollars to keep their little fair and rodeo going. Impressive. The theme this year was, "Sow'n' Seeds of the Future." No Indian races this year, so Doug and I couldn't bet a dollar on a horse, but we understand they are working on staging relay races in the future. Since the country surrounding Halfway, including Idaho and Eastern Oregon, is real ranching country, the audience and the contestants were peppered with genuine buckaroos. We saw lots of big hats.

Before we left on Labor Day, Chelsea and Buck stopped in on their way back from Idaho. And while we were building Dagwood sandwiches, here came my hunter/gatherer husband. Returning from his "secret patch"...bearing a pail of huckleberries.

With only one day separating our backpack up Bear Creek and our annual camping trip to Ollokot, I didn't have much time to can the sauerkraut and pack the trailer...'cause, you see, a week ago Monday, Kathy, Phyllis and yours truly, not to mention Fancy, Kathy's burro, and large lab Choco, took off from Boundary Trailhead around 3:30 p.m. on one of the hottest days of the year. Our destination: Goat Creek.

Originally we'd planned to spend Monday night at the Boundary campground and head up the trail in the cool of morning, but two friends wanted to spend two nights in the wilderness. Since most of my energy had been spent that morning—meeting a deadline for our local newspaper, dealing with a dead printer, and other equally frustrating events—I was not looking forward to carrying a heavy sleeping bag, tent, warm clothes, and very little food, mostly uphill, for four miles in the heat of the day. This would prove to be a test for my 73-year-old endurance.

Phyllis Webb (left), Fancy the burro, and Kathy Hunter (wearing a mossy beard) pose like old prospectors while hiking out the Bear Creek trail on a cold late August morning.

It was also Phyllis' first backpacking adventure. Because she was nursing a bad shoulder, she's scheduled for surgery next week, her husband Fred had fixed up a light 15-pound pack for her. Good husband. Therefore, 70-year-old Phyllis surprised herself and did just fine.,..although, at times, she didn't believe there was really a Goat Creek.

62-year-old Kathy, her camping gear loaded on Fancy, who was turned loose on the trail to do as she pleased, plus the large chocolate-colored lab...took off and left Phyllis and me in the dust. Sweat poured down my back and seeped into my eyes. I sipped water often, and carried an extra bottle. The trail followed Bear Creek, sometimes at creek level, then wound high above, skirting rocky precipices. We grazed on thimble berries that brushed against us and grew in great patches. We managed a mile an hour.

The sun had long since disappeared over high, rocky ridge when I glimpsed the bridge that spanned Goat Creek. Kathy, not that far ahead of us, had selected a place to pitch her new tent. We were just about out of daylight. The burro wandered around, rolling in the powdery dust, glad to be free of her pack. The dog ran into the creek, then into Kathy's tent. The burro, jealous of the dog, laid back her ears, bared her teeth and chased the dog into the tent. It was a circus.

Phyllis and I managed, with frustration in the gathering darkness, to put together my old tent that had seen better days. It sagged. I threw a rain fly over it as the skies were clouding up. We tossed in our sleeping bags and clothes, and by this time it was totally dark. Stumbling around, we located some food. I ate a peanut butter and jelly sandwich and drank more water, then tied the food bag up in a tree away from bears—this was Bear Creek, after all.

Exhausted, we all climbed into our sleeping bags. It was still hot. I could have packed a lighter bag.

Several hours later—I couldn't sleep—the burro stepped on my pony tail, which was lying outside the tent... as she traipsed around all night, bumping us with her head. Then I heard this ominous wind whip the tent, and... *whoosh!* Off went the rain fly. Of course, it began to rain. Big drops.

I climbed out—no easy feat, as I nearly stepped on Phyllis' head—and stumbled around in the dark until I located the fly, flying off toward the creek. Phyllis, awake by this time, staggered out, and together we secured the fly to the tent pegs. Of course, it immediately stopped raining. But the burro continued to tromp around our tent all night so I didn't get much sleep.

However, the morning was glorious! The air cleansed by the brief storm, the temperature mild, the happy sound of Bear Creek... no phone, no TV, no worldly cares. We were in the wilderness. Then I heard this crackling noise: Kathy's dog attempting to escape the tent, which was zipped up. Suddenly, Choco burst through into the morning, and here came the burro after him. The day had begun.

We ended up having a wonderful time. Spent that day hiking to the historic Bear Creek guard station, thence on up the creek to the confluence of Dobbin Creek, where the Bear-Minam trail takes off, before switching back to Standley Springs. We returned to camp to move our tents away from a dead tree that was cracking and groaning, leaning dangerously in our direction; then waded in the cold creek, read, studied our map, napped, and dined that evening on dehydrated beef stew and Phyllis' oatmeal cookies with tea.

What a good burro: she carried Kathy's little propane stove.

Slept better Tuesday night, in spite of the fact the burro opted to spend the entire night grazing grasses next to our heads.

The predicted cold front was moving in rapidly, so we made haste to pack up the burro and head down the trail early next morning. Kathy and the burro made it to the trailhead in two hours. Phyllis and I, carrying our packs, made it in three. We felt great. We'd done it! And, to celebrate, we met at the Little Bear Drive-In in Wallowa for big, juicy hamburgers and french fries. We ate outside on the picnic table, still wearing our jackets. The temperature had dropped dramatically and a cold breeze blew. At home, I turned on the heat.

September 7—Outlined in smoky haze, our Wallowas are barely visible today.

It frosted on Prairie Creek the last two mornings. Doug managed to save the garden by running the sprinkler at night, but my ancient squash, the one advancing outside the fence...well, it don't look so good. And now I'm freezing corn, picking peaches down at Bear Gulch, and preparing for Mule Days this weekend, with company coming Monday.

September 25—A welcome breeze wanders through the open screen window where I write on this warm, late-September afternoon. From where I sit upstairs in this large, open-ceilinged log house, seated in front of a sewing machine cabinet that serves as my desk, I can look down upon a lush irrigated field of grass and clover. This green field is in sharp contrast to the dry canyon sides that slope steeply up to tiered basalt rims that scrape the sky. Separating green from dry is the freshly-graded gravel road, which winds its way up the Imnaha River.

My window lets me see every rig making its way up the road. I know Vicky Marks will be returning soon from driving school bus for the little school at the Bridge, the same two-room school were two of my grandchildren attended K-8 not too many years ago. This is the same bus route that Barbara Warnock drove all those years, picking up and delivering her own grandchildren.

Even though the river's winding course is hidden by tall cottonwoods and brush, its water song is always present.

Several mule deer does and fawns have just run, bucking and playing, down the steep canyon side to leap the fence and graze Lyman's green field. Below me, in the kitchen, I can see Cheryl canning the prune plums she just picked off the old tree in the pasture. And I hear that familiar rattling sound: fruit jars boiling away in an old enamel kettle. Seated in her chair next to the wood heating stove, sleeps our Mary, recovering from a knee infection that began last Tuesday night.

Westward Ho! Parade is a big part of the Pendleton Round-Up.

A team of oxen pull wagons during the parade.

September 26—5:00 a.m. It's been a week now since I arrived here at Lyman's ranch, about twelve miles or so upriver from the small settlement of Imnaha. Lyman left last Tuesday for cow camp, to gather in his cows and calves, ship the calves, work the cows, and sort out culls and replacement heifers, so I offered to stay here with Mary.

It's been an eventful week, including three 100-mile round-trips to Enterprise and Joseph... twice to the doctor's office and then, last Sunday I drove out to Joseph to join Doug at our upper Prairie Creek neighbors' Scott and Kelly's 25th wedding anniversary celebration.

After leaving the party, I drove out to our little house on Prairie Creek to pick several ears of corn from the garden, read my mail, and survey our house, which was swathed in foil! There's really no other way to describe it.

Driving down Tenderfoot Valley Road, my eye was drawn to this building that used to be our home. In its place was something akin to a space station. Since Doug decided to have the house sided, I decided to "quit the flats." My house would be turned all topsy turvy and Mary needed me. What better place to flee than the upper Imnaha in the fall? So, after removing all pictures from the INSIDE of the OUTSIDE walls, men pounding nails might send them crashing to the floor, I picked up the phone, canceled a week of my life on the calendar, and packed my bag.

I drove to Enterprise, where I reported in at our weekly writers' group and purchased some things for Mary, and headed down into the canyons. It was raining... a real gully washer. Two inches. Just what the canyons and hills needed. And after the rain, an Indian Summer.

Mary and I loved the seasonal change. We inhaled the golden air that sifted through the screen door and windows, and looked out on the yellowing corn, withered beans, and trailing squash in Lyman's garden. We longed to be up at cow camp and imagined what the boys were up to. Were they finding the cows and calves? Dick Hammond was riding with Lyman and sometimes, in the evening, they would drive to a high ridge where they were able to call on Dick's cell phone to report in and check on us. We said we were holding the ranch together.

Mary improved daily. Lyman's pullets were beginning to lay. I was feeding the cats. Mary was walking again. We'd had company: bow hunters, Mary's old friends. I'd gone downriver to Jerry Witherite's for tomatoes, sorta split after the rain, and canned 14 quarts of them.

Also canned two kettles of prune plums from Lyman's old tree. Cheated the deer out of 'em. Lyman said his cattle were pretty scattered due to last week's early snowfall. Same one that dumped 8 inches

on Marr Flat. Grandson Buck told me he was up there ridin' too, got
stuck in the snow. That was the day it snowed here on Prairie Creek, and
the day sister Mary Ann and her friend Mary departed for Bend, after
their five-day visit.

September 29—The above paragraph was written early this morning
(in my foil house) back here on Prairie Creek. It's the first break I've had
to finish this column since leaving Lyman's ranch on the upper Imnaha.
In the interim, there's been a heap o' livin'... 'cause, you see, after Cheryl
arrived to take care of Mary, I drove out "on top," taking a few minutes
at the top of Sheep Creek Hill to pull over and enjoy the view that lay
before me of Prairie Creek, backgrounded by our beloved Wallowas, still
wearing the season's first snow.

To fortify myself for what lay ahead, I took a sort "power nap," for
what lay ahead included driving directly to Enterprise to purchase beef
and other fixin's for feeding 15 cowboys and cowgirls at cow camp the
next day.

Barbara Warnock would stay on the river with Mary, and a gal named
Margie would be here at 6:30 Wednesday morning to help me. Doug
would stay in the valley until the calves were weighed, then drive his
pickup and stock trailer out to the corrals near Harl Butte, where the
"boys" would be sorting and weaning, eat with the crew, then haul half
of Lyman's replacement heifers back to the river.

Meanwhile, in Enterprise, I ran into my poet friend Cathy, who had
just hit town too. Cathy's a "north ender" who lives near Flora. We
decided to do lunch at the Olde Town Cafe in Joseph, where we sat
outside in a sort of rocked-in patio, in the sunshine. Fun. Then it was
back to the grocery store. Beef on ice—the day was hot—I drove back to
the ranch, where I gathered the eggs, unpacked, fixed supper, and picked
up food and supplies to take to cow camp on the morrow. Doug dug
spuds while I picked corn.

On her way home to Wallowa, Cheryl left off two pies and a coleslaw
Barbara Warnock had prepared to send to cow camp, and Doug went
to bed. I dealt with the beef, which I stuck in the oven and got up at
intervals all night to check. Whenever the timer went off at bedside,
Doug jumped a foot!

Morning came. Doug went to the "office" and Margie showed up as
planned. We visited while I sliced roast beef. Doug showed up to load
the pickup, thank goodness—heavy stuff. And then we were off, loaded
with food to feed a hungry crew.

Beautiful morning. Up Little Sheep, over Salt Creek Summit, down to

Lick Creek and to Harral Butte and Marr Flat: trembling aspen thickets the color of gold coins, dry meadows dotted with cows and calves. Beyond lay the weathered little cabin. Cow camp. Horses sunned themselves near thorn brush thickets the color of coral. The tiny outhouse, so dear and familiar. This is the first year our Mary couldn't come.

Then the work began, and didn't end until Margie and I loaded up the pickup with pots and pans and a very few leftovers. We were the last to leave. The sun had already gone down over the Wallowas. That hungry crew devoured mashed potatoes, gravy, roast beef, corn on the cob, coleslaw, cucumbers, and sliced tomatoes, topped off with slices of Barbara and Joanie's apple pies, and a pot of cowboy coffee boiled in an old enamel pot.

Old-timers Mike Brennan and Wayne Marks visited us in the cabin while we cooked, and Sam Morgan, the vet, was the first one we fed. Sam had the dis"stink"tive job of preg-testing the cows. He left before the other boys showed up.

The rest of the crew included truck driver Dan Baremore; Mike Fluitt and his daughters, Lexi and Ryya, and their friend Hannah; Joe, Charley, and Dan Warnock; Lyman and Doug. During our busy morning of preparing food, Margie and I did manage to hike up to the corrals and ask how long before they were finished. The fall colors were lovely in that meadow, fringed by golden aspen that provided a colorful setting for working cattle in the weathered log corral.

Mike Brennan returned to the cabin with us and hooked up Doug's little propane stove so we could boil the potatoes. The crew didn't finish until 3:30. After they washed their hands in a wash basin perched on a block of wood, they chowed down. It had been a long day for all of us.

After the last horse trailer rumbled away out of sight, Margie and I were alone, far from civilization, with only an occasional grouse hunter coming or going. As we drove home, Margie talked to me so I wouldn't sleep at the wheel.

And now, as Dave and his workers pound the Glacier White siding onto our house, I find it hard to concentrate. And I haven't even reported on how great Mule Days was. Or sister Mary Ann's visit. Just ran out of time.

Buck season opens in the morning. Doug says I can go wit him to the hills. Wish us luck bagging our winter meat.

On Sunday I leave for a week at the Fishtrap Writer's Retreat on the upper Imnaha. I'm ready, and it'll be good to see my friend Mary again.

Back again this year at Hells Canyon Mule Days was Sheryl Curtis of Washington with her two Brown Swiss oxen. She is shown here in the non-motorized parade.

Grand Marshal Bob Casey and wife Jan sit behind Larry Waters (left) and Clay Freels (right) in the Mule Days Parade. Larry Waters handles the reins of his team. Good weather this year brought out a huge crowd.

October 5—Well, here is me again, in my one-room log cabin, snuggled into the canyon side near the mouth of Indian Creek, directly across from the larger log lodge that serves as our Fishtrap Writer's Retreat on the Upper Imnaha River. It is 4:30 a.m. and I didn't get much sleep last night, what with the light of the nearly full "Hunter" moon, as well as the apples dropping from the tree onto the shake roof—*thunk, thunk*—and tumbling down the stairs I must climb to gain entrance to my abode. Lying in my sleeping bag, thrown on a small rollaway bed, I'm always aware of the river's sound. It is a sound that seeps into my soul, and a sound I'll miss greatly when, on Sunday...I must leave, and resume my hectic life "on top."

However, there have been times this past week when it seemed my hectic life followed me to the upper Imnaha. Take yesterday, for example. When Liz, Sarah and I got into a canning marathon that ended when Sarah lifted the last batch of plum/apple butter out of the canner at 11:00 p.m. It's a disease. We jut couldn't let those luscious plums go to waste, nor could we bear to let that flock of wild turkeys eat every cluster of Concord grapes. No, NEVER! Especially because my friend Kathy and I had been the ones to prune the vines last April.

When the day ended, we gals had used every pot in the kitchen; strained and stained and steamed until every grape, plum and apple was turned into either jam, jelly or butter. The aromas wafting from our kitchen carried the very essence of fall on the Imnaha. And the fruits of our labor filled every jar with love...all 39 of them! We printed labels that read "Indian Creek Concord Grape Jelly," or jam, or butter.

Between and betwixt we wrote poems on scraps of paper smeared with purple fruit. Our creative juices were flowing. However, the old stove had HAD it. Only one burner was working and it went out in a blaze of glory. Rich showed up one night with a new one. The old stove sits out on the deck, remembering all the Retreats over the years, having come to rest at last, purple plum juice—like dried blood—running down its side.

It's just been Liz and me this week, except for Sarah, who arrived with canning supplies and spent two nights. Indian Summer has prevailed, which has made it most difficult to concentrate on writing. So we go for long hikes...that is, when we aren't cooking a "moveable feast" to cart across the bridge and thence down to Lyman and Mary's.

One day, one of Mary's long-time hunter friends, Dan, caught us a mess of trout, and I poached them with lemon and shallots; gathered windfalls and baked a dutch oven apple pie; baked Doug's Yukon Gold potatoes. Liz sliced up some of those Imnaha tomatoes and drizzled 'em with balsamic vinegar, and I shucked the last corn from our garden to cook in Lyman's kitchen. It was a memorable feast.

All of this in the middle of buck deer season. Every time we delivered our "meals on wheels" to Lyman and Mary's, here would come one of their visiting hunters with a buck. We were in the thick of it.

We feasted on deer liver from the fat white-tail buck Doug shot here on Prairie Creek on opening day, before I headed to the canyon that next morning. That is, before I arose at 4:00 to can juice from the box of tomatoes Ron dropped off just after Doug shot his buck. I'd ridden to the hills with Doug opening day, but the only horns we saw were on a three-point one of the hunters staying at Doug's place on Wet Salmon had killed.

However, it turned out to be an enjoyable day, clear and crisp, and the coral-hued thorn brush thickets filled the draws with color. Visited along the way with Doug's brother Biden and nephew Casey on Pine Creek, where we ate lunch in the warm autumn sun. Then a short visit with Sharon and Lou in their house out near the Buttes. Glad to hear Sharon is recovering from her horse wreck.

October 9—Monday. Prairie Creek. Here is me... sitting at my kitchen table again. The house is sided white. Glacier White. It looks brand new. My lilacs are gone, all cut down. They used to grow alongside the house, but Doug said they would hinder installation of the siding. I'm trying to get used to it.

It's cold this morning. There's new snow on the mountains. That is, when the cold, misty clouds haven't hidden them from view. I catch glimpses now and then of a winter-like scene.

On our way out from Imnaha yesterday, Liz and stopped at the Hells Canyon Road House for lunch. What a treat to be waited on! And that hamburger with Swiss cheese and bacon really hit the spot, especially since we'd been up before the crack of dawn, packing, cleaning out my cabin and the log house for the next shift of writers. We carted our computers across the bridge and stopped by Lyman and Mary's to say goodbye, then ended up wrapping deer burger and washing up the grinder.

Like I say, we were "mainstreamed" into life on Imnaha, which is not much different from life here on Prairie Creek. When I drove in late yesterday afternoon, Doug had just returned from the woods with a truckload of fence material. In my absence he'd cared for my chickens, covered my geraniums, cut, split and hauled in fire wood, cut and hauled off the six blue spruce trees (sob) that grew at the edge of the garden, cut and wrapped his buck, fed the cats, played cribbage, and kept the home fires burning here on the ranch.

They are still burning, but I'm the one feeding the old Monarch today as Doug, along with Biden and Casey, is out fetching in more fence material. Got to keep those fences mended in the hills, because herds of elk tromp through 'em on a regular basis.

Before we know it, our Land Owner Preference (L.O.P.) tags will (hopefully) be filled. Both Doug and I have one. Perhaps we can reduce those elk numbers a bit. In the meantime, can't have too much fence material.

Well…I must wind up this column. I'm not even unpacked from Imnaha yet. The phone has been ringing off the hook. My life on Prairie Creek has returned. Tomatoes from the Slope garden, picked before the frost, ripen and need attention.

Daughter Ramona and family are visiting granddaughter Tammy and her family in Lodi, California, along with granddaughter Carrie and great-granddaughter Brenna. I understand they are visiting Disneyland with the kids. Hope they have a great time.

Cause for all of us to celebrate…our prayers have been answered. Our Marine grandson, Shawn, is home with his wife, Maria, and children, Jackson and Savannah Rose, in South Carolina, safe after completing his second stint in Iraq. My thoughts are with my great-grandkids in Disneyland, and Shawn and family who, I understand, will be here for Thanksgiving. LIFE IS GOOD. I think I'll plant red and yellow tulips where the lilacs used to grow.

October 23—4:00 a.m. What's with this? Why slip silently, so's not to startle Doug, fumble around in the dark for my socks, then wander down the hall to the stove where I make a cup of Postum, seat myself at the kitchen table, and begin to write this column? Why? Well, let me tell you why. For starters, there's nothing in our bedroom except the bed.

It's a long story.

It all began October 10, when my friend Cheryl arrived to help me catch up on some long-neglected house cleaning. Doug was out unloading a load of firewood into the woodshed. I was asking C. if she could begin by cleaning out our bedroom. All of a sudden, it hit me. With Cheryl's help we could rip up that OLD DUSTY RUG.

Before Doug had a chance to object, C. began to rip. After being gone basically for two weeks, errands in town took up most of my day. When I returned, there was the carpet: rolled up, along with its pad, on the carport. This little bundle of energy had also washed down the walls and the windows, and—in general—made the dust fly.

The next day I inquired at Fashion Floors in Enterprise about installing a laminate wood floor. Well, today is the day. Around 9:00 a.m. Jeff—the same Jeff who put Pergo in the living room and kitchen—will arrive to install our new bedroom flooring.

Last evening Doug and I moved dressers, night stands, chairs—and stuff you can't imagine—out into the living room, and into what used to be my office bedroom. Writing while this is going on is akin to writing while the house was being sided. Impossible.

And why not write tomorrow? Because, late this afternoon, my childhood chum Sandra and her hubby, Fred, will arrive froth California to spend a week with us. This is a long-looked-forward-to visit, and I want time to spend with my friend. Plus, I just looked at this week's calendar and I don't see ANY other time to write this column.

I just stepped outside to breathe in the cold, frosty air, and gaze up at a sky full of crisp, bright stars. We're so fortunate here on Prairie Creek not to have what's called "light pollution." Still lingering in the pre-dawn air is the essence of skunk, the one Doug disposed of under the chicken pen fence yesterday morning, after he returned to the ranch with the "controlled doe hunt" white-tail he'd just bagged lying on the bed of his pickup. The fried liver and onions we had for supper last evening is giving me energy to write at this early hour.

5:30 a.m. Doug just left for the "office" at the Range Rider in Enterprise, where, if you don't get there early, you're apt to miss out on the cribbage game. The old Monarch is snapping and popping, the tea kettle is steaming, and I've finally managed to put words on paper. Doug says he'll probably head to "the hills" to put out salt and check cattle... and elk.

It's been pretty interesting around here since I returned from the Imnaha Writer's Retreat. For starters, I emerged from the canyons a bit rundown, which apparently resulted in a sore throat, recently diagnosed by one of our new local docs as a swollen lymph node. This node is having a hard time fighting off whatever it is that's attacking my body.

Of course, a lack of sleep and keeping up with my busy life isn't helping. I need to rest, drink liquids, take my vitamins, and read poetry. Well that all sounds good, especially the poetry, but there was my calendar... ruling my life. And there was more food to put by for winter: apple jelly to make from the windfalls I brought up from Imnaha, the ripening tomatoes from my Slope garden; not to mention the winter's squash.

On the 11th I lost my voice, but still had plenty of energy so planted those tulips where the lilacs used to grow, and tidied up our yard after the siding operation. Indian summer prevailed, and new snow on the Wallowas contrasted with the golden tamaracks and forested evergreen slopes. I longed to go hiking with my friend Phyllis, but she'd undergone surgery on her shoulder. It was so mild I had all windows, mostly new now, open to the autumn air.

One by one, the busy days were accomplished. I called grandson James in Montana and learned he'd had a great time fishing in Alaska, as well as trout fishing and bow hunting in Montana. Said he was driving over to Powell, Wyoming, to visit his sister, Adele, who is a college freshman there.

Rode out to Salmon Creek with Doug while he helped son Ken, grandson Chad and wife, Amy, gather, sort, and ship a load of steer calves, a couple of cows, and two bulls. A perfect day, very warm, the hills all tinted with autumn. Good thing we'd begun the day with sourdough waffles, as we didn't return to the valley ranch until late afternoon.

Barely made our Fishtrap Board meeting at 4:00…followed by take out Chinese food, followed by a program sponsored by Fishtrap at Stage One of the historic E.M. & M. Bldg. in Enterprise. Gwendolyn Trice wowed us all. Her people came out to the logging camps at Maxwell and we're so glad they did, 'cause now we have the pleasure of knowing this beautiful, educated young lady who is collecting stories about those folks who helped write the history of Wallowa County. Good stuff.

Gone are my geraniums, petunias and everything else susceptible to frost. It got down to 20. A relief, really, not having to cover them every night. And recent rains, followed by warm afternoons, have turned our hills and canyons green as spring. On Imnaha I saw a wild rose blooming on the same limb as an orange hip, and buttercup leaves are appearing on the sunny slopes of the hills.

Phyllis and Fred have a little donkey. Her name is "Roxy." Goodness, now I'll have to get one. Don't know how many more years this old back will support a backpack.

Then there was the "Apple Squeezin'" at Chuck and Chris Fraser's place on upper Prairie Creek. Boy, do they ever luck out. Beautiful weather again, and lots of good folks, all working to press cider, grind horseradish, and then partake of one of the most glorious feasts you can imagine. Barbecued chicken, a whole hog (a la Chuck), roasted to perfection on a spit in a home-crafted barbecue; plus oysters, shrimp, marinated lamb sizzling over a grate, smoked salmon, a kettle of beans

Old-time cider pressing scene at Chuck and Chris Fraser's Ranch.

hanging from a tripod over coals, and the bed of a flat bed trailer loaded with salads, breads, cakes, pies...not to mention that golden apple juice to drink, as golden as the air that day. The very essence of fall.

Chuck supervised the boiling down of apple juice to make syrup, and I can't describe those aromas, the apple pulp pile growing, two little girls playing in it. I'd contributed a persimmon cake, made from some of those California ones I'd frozen last fall, and a kettle of sauerkraut dipped from my crock downstairs.

Folks visited and lingered over the food, or took turns turning the crank, slicing apples, straining juice, filling bottles, and dumping pulp. All hand-cranked this year. Took lots of energy.

Before the sun dipped behind Chief Joseph Mountain, several of us took off on our traditional hike, led by Stanlynn Daugherty, to work off some of that food. Then the fiddle players began to play, young and old alike, until a bitter chill settled over Prairie Creek and everyone drifted toward their cars, carrying apple juice. When Doug and I got home I canned some of that juice.

The next day it rained in the valley and snowed in the mountains.

On the 16th our book group met at Fishtrap House and we discussed our monthly read, *The Chosen*. Doug to the hills to help Scott vaccinate his cows, and then build rock jacks and repair more elk-damaged fence.

On the 17th the snow level kept lowering. Ferguson Ridge ski area is now white. Working intensely now on Mary's book. The end is finally in sight. Met with my weekly writers' group, after an absence of three weeks.

Prairie Creek mourns again. Dana Hough, daughter of our neighbors Don and Lois Hough, passed away in Boise on October 14. She was 46. Our heartfelt sympathy to the Hough family.

My two roosters, Flash and Larry, got into it, and their confrontation resulted in both of them nearly killing each other. To eliminate further bloodshed, I let Flash—the loser—outside the pen. Now every evening he scrambles up the trunk of the willow tree in the yard, where he roosts 'till dawn, at which time he becomes very vocal, right outside the kitchen window.

Last Saturday I met with other members of our Fishtrap Board for a day-long session of meetings. And that night Doug joined me at Fishtrap House, where we were treated to a most elegant dinner prepared by Sharon's daughters, one of whom, Shannon, is an accomplished chef. Words fail when it comes to describing the entire evening. Thank you, Sharon and daughters. A good time was had by all. And the filet mignon continues to give me strength to face today. Beef... It's What's for Dinner... and here in Wallowa County we grow some of the best—beef, that is—in the world.

It's now noon. Jeff has the floor almost in, and Sandra and Fred will be here soon. Got to go.

November 8—At 8:30 a.m. Prairie Creek glistens with melting frost, our mountains are dusted with new snow, a faint breeze wanders across the fields and hills, and the ancient willows, stripped of their leaves by recent wild winds, stand braced for yet another winter. Melville's tractor stands silent in the earthen field which used to be our pasture and hay ground.

Pale November sunlight spills through the living room window, illuminating a wooden bowl of persimmons. Two quartered cow elk carcasses hang in the shop, and the garden sleeps, stunned by cold. A row of carrots has been covered with straw and dirt, giant sunflowers, frosted and brown, hang their heavy heads, storing seeds for the Juncos in the hungry months to come.

What a difference a day makes. Yesterday morning the thermometer on our car port registered 67 degrees! A weird, warm wind whirled leaves and rattled tin roofs, rain splattered my clean windows and freshened the dry hills. It was dark and cloudy all day. Out near Salmon Creek,

Doug was on his way to mend a section of fence, torn down by a fleeing herd of elk, when he ran into Ben, who was hunting his cow elk. Then, he and Ben ran into THEM. The elk. And you know the rest of the story.

Doug and Ben filled their LOP cow tags, which translates into work. The two of them drove in late last evening, covered with mud and gore, and worked late into the night. After calling Pat Combes and explaining why we couldn't attend their "Snowbird" potluck, I concentrated on washing bloody clothing and feeding my exhausted hubby. Hopefully, Doug will return to the hills to mend fence before any cattle get out.

Our phone rang off the hook yesterday, elk hunters wanting permission to hunt Doug's property.

'Tis the season. Elk season that is. Here in Wallowa County everything comes to a halt during this time. It's a big deal. And there's no shortage of elk, not in the hills anyway.

Last Saturday morning we invited grandson Buck and our friends Fred and Phyllis over for sourdough huckleberry pancakes, cooked on our old Monarch range, before we all headed for the hills. Too many hunting stories to tell here, but by day's end I'd bagged my elk, and so had Fred. Plus, Buck and I got in some serious hikin' and stalkin', the way I prefer to hunt.

The other evening, armed with a roaster pan full of barbecued elk ribs for supper, Doug and I took most of my elk up to Fred's to use their grinder to make elk burger. We saved the back strap and enough round to make stew and steaks. Now, we must deal with Doug's huge cow. Good thing we have lots of friends and family to share our good fortune. Elk meat solves the problem of what to give for Christmas.

As usual, the past weeks have been crammed with living. Our new flooring was installed in the bedroom just minutes before my childhood chum Sandra and her husband, Fred, drove in from California. I'd finished my column while Jeff made numerous trips past me at the kitchen table, heading out the front door to saw another section of flooring.

After Jeff left, Doug and I hurriedly moved dressers (and their contents) from the living room to the bedroom, and I swept the floor. While Doug grilled trout on a small barbecue outside, I put potatoes to bake in the oven.

That week whirled with activity, and Sandra loved being part of my life. We did it all. While Fred and Doug played cribbage most mornings, Sandra and I planned our days. And what days!

Our weekly writers' group met at Lynn's place, then we ventured down into the lovely Indian Summer on Imnaha for lunch at Hells Canyon Roadhouse. We purchased bacon at the store next door to take upriver

One of many herds of elk that roam the Zumwalt Prairie. Like cattle, they thrive on nature's bunch grass. Photo by Doug Tippett.

to Lyman and Mary's, and enjoyed the flaming sumac, the brilliant yellowing cottonwoods, the glint of autumn light on the river, the canyons greening like spring. We sighted wild turkeys and one huge mule deer buck, loving the fall. I remembered how my mama loved autumn, and who left us just a year ago this November.

We found Mary, looking pretty spry for a lady 89 years old, fussing around the kitchen, meat roasting in the oven. Mary's never been one to sit still very long. Then we drove to the Writers' Retreat, swaggered across the swinging bridge, and made our way through a yard layered with golden leaves. More leaves drifted down upon us as we shuffled our way to the house, where we delivered supplies to Kathy, Ann and Jenepher. Lucky Melinda was occupying my tree house cabin, now cloaked in yellowing apple leaves.

Back to the ranch to cook up a kettle of potato soup before Fred and Doug returned from fishing way down on the Grande Ronde River at Troy. By 7:00 p.m. we were all seated at the Wallowa Valley Visitors Center, listening to a program that consisted of old-timers narrating tales about living along the Snake River back in the "olden days."

One of the old-timers featured was Doug, who recalled what it what like to spend a winter alone at Dug Bar, when it got down to zero and stayed there for a week. He recounted how he lived on frozen "blue doe," sourdough biscuits and beans.

Then there was Ace Barton and Dick Hammond with equally interesting stories. We celebrated long-time cowboy Dick Hammond's 77th birthday that evening with a birthday cake baked by Nancy R., who works for the Forest Service.

On the 26th, Sandra and I picked up Phyllis and drove way out to the RimRock Inn along the north highway, where we could look off into Joseph Creek and enjoy a most delicious lunch served up by Jessica, a member of our extended family, in honor of Phyllis' 70th birthday.

We took a brief tour of nearby Flora, a ghost town which is coming back to life, what with the restoring of the old school and the presence of a rustic bed and breakfast. Again, autumn colors were at their peak, the day was crisp and lovely, and we seemed to be the only folks out and about.

That evening Sandra stayed home to rest, while I participated in our museum benefit at Fishtrap House. Happy to report that a donated copy of the rare book *History of Wallowa County* sold at auction for $475, the high bidder being Richard and Mary Frasch, who plan to retire here and desire to learn more about our local history. Nice folks, who, although they live in Minnesota, have generously contributed to various Wallowa County projects.

On the 27th Sandra and I head to La Grande to hook up with two of my "Syringa Sisters," Jessica and Mary, who've traveled from Boise; we all proceed to Pendleton, where we meet Bobbie and Barb, who've traveled from Portland. Over lunch at Tamastslikt Cultural Institute, we plan our next adventure and our early get-together, which will be at Wallowa Lake for the 2007 Summer Fishtrap, where we originally met in Bob Pyle's nature writing workshop. A return to Aneroid Lake to spend two nights in Silvertip's cabin is also in the works.

On the 28th, Sandra and I attended the museum thank-you program held at Stage One of the historic EM&M building in Enterprise, where we viewed an old film of early-day Enterprise. The 4-H radio auction took place that Saturday as well, and I ended up the high bidder on Wayne Marks' shelled walnuts. Then it was up to Joseph for lunch at Mad Mary's, after which Sandra "did" the shops and I napped in the car. Another gorgeous day.

That evening, accompanied by our hubbies, we found ourselves seated in a booth at Lear's Main Street eatery, enjoying prime rib and salmon, all the while being entertained by local song writers. Tunesmiths they were, who sang songs they'd written, accompanied by a variety of instruments. It was a most enjoyable time and a wonderful way to celebrate Sandra and Fred's 55th wedding anniversary. Way back in time, yours truly was Sandra's matron of honor. I say matron, 'cause I was already married, with my firstborn babe in my arms.

Sandra and Fred left Sunday morning to drive straight through to Auburn, California. After our company left, Phyllis came over and we drove down to the Writers' Retreat on the upper Imnaha, where we joined Kathy and spent the rest of the day scrubbing, cleaning, and closing up the Fishtrap Writers' Retreat. One last gorgeous day on Imnaha.

Doug had gone to the hills to help Scott and Kelly ship calves. As it turned out, that Sunday ended Indian Summer.

When P. and I topped out on Sheep Creek hill, a chill wind blew over Prairie Creek and fresh snow fell from the darkened skies, spitting against our windshield.

On October 30 it got down to 15 degrees. I attended my friend Jean Ketscher's funeral. It brought back memories of when she and I were in CowBelles together, and her boys grew up on Alder Slope with my children. A wonderful lady, who I've missed ever since she moved from our valley. After Jean's services I drove to Community Connection, where I joined Maxine Kooch in representing the now-defunct CowBelle/CattleWomen, and served the meal at what is now called the Wallowa County Dining Center.

Zero degrees on Halloween. I baked molasses cookies. No trick or treaters came to Prairie Creek.

Last Saturday night, after my successful elk hunt, daughter Lori and granddaughter Lacey drove in from Pendleton and spent the night with us. After breakfast at the Cheyenne Cafe the next morning, they left for home.

The days continue to be filled. Last Sunday evening I attended the Wallowa Valley Chorale at the Enterprise Community Church. Wonderful stuff. Music, the cement that glues our community together. Such a joy to be part of a standing-room-only crowd, listening to those dear familiar folks perform such a variety of songs. My soul was filled with a true sense of community. We should all be forever grateful to live here in this special place.

On Tuesday I hosted our weekly writers' group here at the ranch. It was so warm I opened the windows while we wrote, read, and enjoyed the "elk soup" and homemade bread I'd baked that morning. Next week we'll "brown bag" it at Christine's cabin at the lake.

Fifteen expected for Thanksgiving…be here before we know it.

November 9—I spent from 1:30 a.m. to five writing my last column. Daylight revealed it had snowed in the night. After a brief nap I drove to Alpine House, our assisted-living facility in Joseph, and read for Fishtrap to some of the folks who live there. Among them were Irene McFetridge, Kate Wilde, and Dorothy Waters, all of whom are former Prairie Creek ranch wives.

Between naps I managed to attend our Fishtrap Board meeting, followed by a lecture given by State Librarian Mary Kay Dahlgreen. Biden and Casey came for their heifers today, and Hough's shipped a truckload of cattle.

November 10—Windy. Using the last cabbage from our garden, I cooked up a kettle of soup using ham, carrots, onions, and potatoes. Above the roar of the wind I could hear Melville's tractor moving dirt.

Most of the day was spent working on my photo albums. Hard to believe what we did this past summer and fall. But there it was…our lives recorded in photographs.

November 11—Nancy, her son D.J., Kathy, Andy and I drove 60 miles to La Grande to the Eastern Oregon University Theater to attend the matinee performance of Gilbert and Sullivan's "The Pirates of Penzance," which was just wonderful. The singing, the actors and the stage sets were tops. Nine faculty members and 33 students participated in the production. It was truly a comic masterpiece. There's just something about live theater.

Afterward we celebrated Andy's birthday at Foley's Station, where we enjoyed gourmet dining. During the performance I was remembering a granddaughter Carrie, along with grandson Chad, who once starred in our local high school's version of "Pirates of Penzance."

November 13—I thought most of the day about my mother, who passed away a year ago. Out our kitchen window I watched several white-tails leap over two fences to graze Locke's field, while three coyotes trotted alongside. After they learned I'd just taken a mincemeat pie from the oven, son Todd and grandson Buck drove in. Buck said he'd been riding on the Divide and reported the wind had drifted the snow up there.

November 14—Snowed again today and the roads were pretty icy when our Writer's Group met at Christine's cabin on the west side of the lake.

I hosted "Stitch and Bitch" here on Prairie Creek. While the wind howled outside, we celebrated Sally's birthday with a potluck, after which we retired to the living room to S: and B. Doug returned from the hills to partake of the leftover steelhead I'd baked in the oven.

This evening Doug and I attended a program at the Wallowa Valley Visitor Center where old-timers Mike Brennan, Melvin Brink and Bill Aschenbrenner told stories about life out on the Zumwalt Prairie. So many stories, especially about big Dan Goertzen, a colorful legendary character who lived alone in those hills.

November 17—Jean (Stubblefield) Cook and I served 80 senior citizens at the Dining Center in Enterprise. A turkey dinner always brings out a crowd. Our local Rotary Club sponsored the entree.

This evening I drove to Enterprise to join in the 30th anniversary celebration of the Book Loft. We're all very proud of our little independent book store. We were supposed to come dressed as our favorite literary character. I tried to imitate Willa Cather's "My Antonia." Even though my hair wasn't black and Antonia was much younger, I couldn't help feeling 19 in my heart.

November 18—This Saturday was a busy day. I spent the morning cooking up a large pot of chicken noodle soup to take to granddaughter-in-law Chelsea's baby shower, which was held on Lower Prairie Creek. Loved being included in that lively bunch of young mothers. Babies all over the place, four of whom were my own great-grandchildren. Of course Lucy was there, too, snug in her mommy's tummy. This lucky little gal will be well clothed, I can tell you that!

We were supposed to bring baby pictures of ourselves, which were displayed for all of us to identify. After a most delicious three-soup lunch, topped off with banana splits, Chelsea opened her gifts. It was a gorgeous day, so warm the windows were open to the sun...and there was NO WIND.

From Chelsea's baby shower, I drove to Joseph to join a crowd of old-timers who were helping our favorite "old hand" Mike McFetridge celebrate his 98th birthday. There he was, clad in jeans, boots and hat, that same old smile on his face. Our beloved Mike.

Ken Nash, left, and son Chad sort calves from cows on Salmon Creek in October. The calves were shipped and sold, while the cows and replacement heifers were weaned and hauled to the Wallowa Valley on November 18th. Their average weaning weight was 650 pounds. Photo by Amy Nash.

November 20—Every time the phone rings, another member of our large, extended family announces they'll be here for Thanksgiving. Most recent count...32. This includes eight great-grandchildren, ranging in age from six-year-old Riley Ann to one-year-old Kennon. Actually, the youngest would be Lucy, but she's not born yet. Lucy's expected time of arrival is December 7th, when she will become our 15th great-grandchild. Our family is many-times blessed.

We are especially blessed this year, as our Marine grandson Shawn—home safe after two stints in Iraq—will fly out from the east coast to be with us. Because this is Monday, and Thanksgiving Day is Thursday, my mind is rather preoccupied with how we'll squeeze that many folks in our modest little home. Plan A is to move some of our larger furniture out onto the carport to set up two long tables we've rented from the Fair Board. Doug has already made a trip to Cloverleaf Hall to haul them and ten folding chairs to our shop.

So, if Plan A works, the adults will all be seated at a table, while the youngsters will "picnic" off a tablecloth spread out on the floor in the hall. I hope this works, as there is no Plan B.

After our museum board met last Friday, I drove up Hurricane Creek highway and turned onto Pine Tree Road where, on that frigid afternoon, Peter Donovan's turkey harvest was under way. I likened this experience to tromping through the woods to cut down a Christmas tree. Only there, under those cold, snowy mountains, you could watch your own turkey being butchered.

The scene really put me in the Thanksgiving spirit. However, I'm sure Peter's turkeys didn't share my sentiments. And I doubt his crew did either, as the sun sank over the Wallowas and their breath hung in the cold air. Good for the meat, though. Chilled it out real good.

Hoisting my 22-pound bird, I made for the car and headed back to Prairie Creek. Now, if I can find a roaster pan big enough to cook this broad-breasted free-range turkey, we'll have it made.

With Thanksgiving less than a week away, Peter experienced a bit of bad luck. During one of those fall wind storms that have battered our valley recently, his turkey shed collapsed, killing approximately 30 turkeys. Typically, however, local folks came to Peter's rescue and managed to salvage most of the breast meat.

Those fierce winds wreaked havoc all over the county. Blew a landmark barn down, sucked several window panes out of our chicken house, downed trees, scattered wheel lines, and left us wondering if our houses would blow away. Here on Prairie Creek—where the wind lives—we continued with our lives as great gusts roared down from the direction of McCully Creek.

Today things are calm and mild, with a bit of rain falling. Tonight it may snow.

November 21—12:30 a.m. Since our writers' group meets here at 10, and the rest of my day is pretty full of "getting ready for Thanksgiving," this seems to be the only time to finish my column. Actually, I rather enjoy these nocturnal writing sessions. It's absolutely quiet, save for the ticking of our bird clock and its hourly chirping. The phone doesn't ring, no one appears at our door, and the night belongs to me.

Doug was hauling replacement heifers to the valley and missed the party. After he returned from the hills, we managed to make it to a dinner hosted by Melvin and Mary Lou Brink in honor of our "snowbird" friends who will be heading south after Thanksgiving.

It's now 3:15 and I must get some sleep. Hope you all have a great Thanksgiving.

November 23—Speaking of Thanksgiving…it was wonderful, well worth all the work and planning. We were actually able to seat 26 adults at three tables, one in each room, thanks to Randy, who supplied those Fair Board tables and chairs. Peter's 22 lb. turkey was moist, tender and flavorful, and the eight great-grandkiddies romped around downstairs, just like their parents used to do.

Our Marine grandson, Shawn, made the long flight and showed up, along with two of his buddies, who drove him to Prairie Creek from the Boise airport. I'd been up before dawn, preparing dressing and stuffing two turkeys. Doug spent an hour peeling enough potatoes to fill our canning kettle. I covered the long tables with queen-sized sheets and decorated with Indian corn. Several inches of snow fell the night before, so we had a white Thanksgiving.

It was all pretty emotional for me, being surrounded by so many members of our large family. Lots to be thankful for. Little four-year-old Ronan recited the blessing. Much of the meal was prepared on the old Monarch, and hopefully memories of this special Thanksgiving will remain with the younger generation for the rest of their lives, just like our childhood Thanksgivings did for my sisters and brothers. We'll always remember those times at my grandma and grandpa Wilson's in Rio Linda, California. It was my grandma who taught me how to put on this traditional meal. Somehow, here in my kitchen each year, I feel grandma's presence.

Before everyone left, we grouped ourselves in layers near the living room sofa for a family photo. However, there were so many of us, we had to shoot in increments of three. We had quite a time, too, with the berry cream pie that grandson James requested. Had to hide it.

A week later I had another request from grandson Buck, so naturally, I built him a pie too. Spoiling grandsons is one of the joys of grandmotherhood.

November 24—Spent the day cleaning, distributing leftovers, and simmering the turkey carcasses for future soups. I found enough time to attend the bazaar at the Joseph Community Center, where I purchased a Christmas wreath, plus handmade rugs from Hope McLaughlin and a small table, to seat great-grandkids, from her husband, Harold. This rare couple are truly treasures of Wallowa County. Their handiwork is created with love.

November 25—It snowed two more inches and turned bitterly cold. The white-tails invaded our garden to nibble corn stalks and cabbage plants. I managed to photograph two does through the front room window. There are deer prints all over our yard, and once I observed two young bucks sparring beyond our raspberry patch.

I did steal away to Enterprise and treat myself to a hot mocha...prepared by Andy Fairchild at the Bookloft. I always enjoy visiting folks who wander into Mary's cozy little book store.

The temperature dove to 10 degrees when Doug and I met Phyllis and Fred at Lear's Main Street Pub and Grill tonight to attend another one of those wonderful "Tunesmiths" Nights. I ordered pan-seared wild salmon, and the others chose black Angus beef prime rib. It was all delicious and the music was tops.

After all that Thanksgiving cooking, it was a real pleasure to be waited on and spoiled. Dinner was compliments of Fred, who appreciated being able to hunt and bag his elk on Doug's property in the hills.

November 26—Visibility on Prairie Creek is limited due to blowing snow. Drifts have formed in my chicken pen, between the raspberry patch, and around the woodshed. Snow swirls around the house, and great sculpted drifts fill the borrow pits. Walking up to feed and water my chickens, who are only laying two eggs a day now, I could barely stand upright. Wind-driven snow stung my cheeks and felt like sand in my eyes. A good day to stay home by the fire.

Grandson Buck and wife, Chelsea, stopped by later this afternoon to visit. They'd been out cutting their Christmas tree. Gotta get their tree up before little "Lucy" arrives!

November 27—Doug and I left at dawn to drive to the hills, where we bucked drifts on the Pine Creek Road to reach Ken's cows, which were scattered among the hills in the Deadman pasture.

Near zero that morning so we were really bundled up against the cold. When the sun appeared over the eastern horizon, those snowy hills glittered like zillions of diamonds. After Ken, Jared, Doug and I trailed the cows through the gate onto the Pine Creek Road, I followed behind the herd on foot. There we were, alone in a lonely country locked in winter silence.

That is, until, peering westward, I spied another herd of cows heading south on the Lewis Road, being driven by a lone man on horseback. When it appeared our herd would arrive at the intersection of Pine Creek Road at the same time as those cattle, Ken held ours up until the others had a sizable lead on us. Apparently, every cow in the hills wanted to go home that day, visions of hay spurring them on.

Even Birkmaier's cows were trailing single file on the other side of the fence when what turned out to be Yosts' cattle plodded past what used to be the old Hearing Place. At the fence corner near Dry Salmon

Creek I came upon Tom Birkmaier and his dogs persuading his cows NOT to jump the fence and join us.

Doug was behind me on Salmon Creek, opening gates for the horses that winter out there, and our cows outdistanced me when I. stopped to help Tom. Since Ken and Jared were in the lead, I found myself quite alone and loving it. After the sun's warmth finally took hold, I began shedding layers of clothing. My fleece-lined snow boots were not made for walkin'...and I was wishin' Doug would show up, when I spied two large bull elk peering at me from a thorn brush thicket below the road on Dorrance Grade. Storm clouds gathered over the far-off Wallowas, offering me glimpses of gleaming snow fields.

I was remembering we were supposed to meet Doug's sister Barbara at Cloud Nine Bakery for lunch, when here came Doug, sliding to a stop at the bottom of the icy grade.

We did make it for lunch: hot potato soup really hit the spot. Ken trailed the cattle onto the green corrals where they spent the night along the Crow Creek Road.

November 28—Ken was back out there at 5 o'clock to start the cows to the valley. They arrived here around 10:30 in a snow storm.

November 29—Dick Hammond rode out with Doug today, to haul out two of Dick's horses and bring Ken's back to the valley. Now the roads can drift shut.

The temperatures kept falling. Zero this morning, with a high of 10. I kept a pot of beans or soup simmering on the old Monarch and really burned the wood.

November 30—Doug and I drove to Upper Prairie Creek to the Barciks', where we joined other neighbors for a "No Turkey" party. Cracklin' cold outside but warm and cozy inside; the food, without turkey, was scrumptious. I baked a vinegar pie.

December 5—1:30 a.m. Wide awake again, sitting here at the kitchen table while Prairie Creek sleeps. Just stepped outside to read the thermometer on the carport, which registered a warm 20 degrees. I say warm because we've had several nights when it's gotten down to zero with day-time highs in the teens. The winter-white landscape is bathed in diffused moonglow; beautiful and cold and still.

While viewing the moon, clad in bathrobe and slippers, my eyes wandered north of the shop where I could make out the dark bodies of Ken's cows bedded down near the ancient willows that line the irrigation ditch in a field that used to be part of Doug's ranch. Thank goodness for the presence of cattle. Can't recall a time when I wasn't around livestock of some sort. Still miss my cows.

My thoughts are with granddaughter-in-law Chelsea and her husband, Buck. Could our little Lucy be coming into the world during this full December moon?

The season has definitely shifted from fall to winter. Thanksgiving to Christmas. Only one great horned owl came back this year to roost by day in the ponderosa pine in the yard. What happened to its mate? And what happened to the twenty head of white-tail does, fawns and bucks that sought the shelter of the barn lot, nibbling corn stalks in the garden when it was so cold? Methinks they've congregated on upper Prairie Creek, where I observed several good-sized herds grazing the snowy alfalfa fields in the moonlight as I was driving home from the lake Sunday night.

That was a magical night if there ever was one, returning from the annual Christmas caroling party held at the historic Wallowa Lake Lodge. December's COLD moon illuminated Chief Joseph Mountain and the calm, darkened waters of the lake. Every tree, bush and object was visible on that crisp, clear night. From the foot of the lake you could see the warm glow of Christmas lights at the old lodge, a beacon of warmth and cheer, wherein friends and neighbors had gathered for Gail Swart's popular Christmas sing-along.

There we were, singing those old familiar carols like "Joy to the World" and "Jingle Bells," songs that put you in the Christmas spirit. It was so peaceful there, listening to the Handbell Choir, before we drifted into the gaily decorated dining room to partake of an elegant meal prepared by the staff.

More music followed, performed by members of our talented community, and Rich Wandschneider provided us a reading of "Shorty Pringle's Christmas" while among the singers I recognized familiar faces: Young Will and Alex McCadden, Taylor Darnielle, Duff Pace, Randy Morgan and of course Janis Carper, who sang songs she and Rod Ambroson composed for that event.

The one person who shone most throughout the evening—a quiet-spoken Gail Swart—must surely know by now how much joy she brings our community, and how much our community loves her!

Phyllis and I didn't make it to the annual Christmas Bird Count this year. However, we did take a snowy walk around the ranch, and we counted 1 bald eagle, 20 ravens, 30 sparrows, 2 house finches, 3 red-tail hawks, 1 golden eagle, 3 magpies, a tree-full of starlings, a sky-full of wild mallard ducks...and, of course, the great horned owl in our pine tree. Although things slowed a bit after Thanksgiving, there's still a lot going on around here.

December 6—2:30 p.m. Still no baby, and the sun is shining over the snow. Lyman called last night. "UPS man just delivered a bunch of crab. Need help eating it." So...between and betwixt writing this column, I baked a rhubarb-strawberry cobbler, and pretty soon we'll head for the canyons. Christmas looms. Must get those cards in the mail. And since the next column won't come out until January, we wish all of you in Agri-Times land a very MERRY CHRISTMAS and a HAPPY NEW YEAR.

December 26—'Tis the day after Christmas and all through our house, it's strangely quiet. It wasn't that way yesterday, however. Our little house on Prairie Creek bulged with family, food, and the joy brought on by just being together. At the center of our joy shone 10-day-old Lucy, this long-awaited great-granddaughter who came into our world during the wee hours of a wild and windy morning.

On Christmas Eve I'd driven into Joseph to attend the candlelight service held at the Methodist Church, where I was joined by grandson Buck, his wife, Chelsea, and wee Lucy. The old stone church, with its high ceiling and stained glass windows, was filled with Christmas spirit. Miss Lucy slept through it all.

Our thoughts were with daughter Jackie and her husband, Bill, Buck's parents, who were making their slow way over icy roads from Challis, Idaho, to Wallowa County. Added to our concern was granddaughter Mona Lee, who'd work til midnight, rest up, and drive over more icy roads from Chehalis, Washington, to arrive in time for Christmas dinner.

Earlier in the week, daughter Ramona and husband Charley, braving blizzard conditions while pulling a stock trailer loaded with two 4-H steers for great-grandsons Clayton and Cole, arrived safely to spend Christmas with granddaughter Tamara's family in Lodi, California.

Much of our large, extended family traveled long distances to be with us during the holidays, including our Navy grandson, Josh, and his fiance, Desiree, who had driven straight through from San Diego. Then there was granddaughter Adele, who drove solo all the way from Powell, Wyoming. Good thing this grandma's hair is already white...else you'd notice the new ones.

Everyone made it, however, and for that we are most thankful.

Again we served the traditional prime rib dinner. I'd spent the day before baking long loaves of sourdough bread, mincemeat and wild blackberry pies. With the exception of Lucy, our home brimmed with grandchildren, who have become young adults seemingly overnight.

A pair of white-tail does jumped the garden fence to nibble on the Tippett corn stalks during the recent cold spell on Prairie Creek.

Cows trailing in a snowy storm into the Wallowa Valley from the hills where they grazed all summer and fall. Shown here on Klages Rd, not far from their wintering ground on Prairie Creek.

December was a busy month. Many a cold winter evening I'd hear son Ken unloading truckfuls of hay he'd hauled all the way from John Day. Large bales, now stacked in our hay shed, which will provide winter feed for his cows, pastured north of our house in fields that used to be part of Doug's ranch.

It seems a long way to haul hay over wintertime roads, but hay is in short supply this year. Unlike years past, when hay raised in the valley stayed here, hay now seems to fetch higher prices and, therefore, goes out of the county to those who can afford it. Makes it tough for the locals. Times are changing.

Daughter Jackie and her husband, Bill, are staying with us 'til Friday, when they'll head back to Idaho. Naturally, as much time as possible is spent with their first grandchild, not to mention their two grown children.

This morning Bill left early to join son Buck, who will trailer horses to Big Sheep where they will spend the day in the saddle gathering cows clear up into Squaw Creek. At least the wind isn't blowing. We've had some pretty intense wind storms this month. The only white we had for Christmas were the icy drifts left from former storms.

While Doug played cribbage with the "boys" at the Range Rider and Bill and Buck rode the canyons of Big Sheep for son Todd, Jackie, Mona and yours truly went to lunch at the newly-opened Calderas in Joseph. Local wood artist Steve Arment's beautiful handiwork is very impressive, as is the food. A rare burst of sunlight spilled through the clouds, warming the polished wooden furnishings as we savored our meal.

By the time we left it was snowing. Then it was back to the ranch to prepare a large dutch oven of tamale pie, most of which I sent over to feed the cowboys.

On Christmas day both owls returned to roost in the Ponderosa pines. The white-tail have not, which is good. My little apple tree has suffered from their browsing.

That crab feed at Lyman's on the upper Imnaha was super. We SO appreciate Craig's generosity. No matter how hard we tried, none of us could keep up with Doc Morgan when it came to crab consumption.

December activities filled my calendar: Fishtrap's Good Book Sale, Winterfest in Enterprise, Mid-Valley Theater production of "The Big Bad Wolf" held at the Providence Academy in Lostine, our Write Group meetings here at the ranch and in the basement of the Enterprise Library, a dance program at the OK Theater, and a dinner at Lee's High Country dining compliments of Lee in appreciation for allowing him and his son to bag their bull elk on Doug's property in the hills.

Doug and I, and Phyllis and Fred, went to Day Ridge to cut our own Christmas tree. Armed with a Forest Service permit, Doug and I trudged through knee-deep snow to select the perfect tree, after which we joined Fred and Phyllis to munch our lunch and warm ourselves over an open fire. Fun.

Then there was the traditional potluck for members of our Reader's and Writer's Group and their spouses at our place. Great food, followed by poetry readings, including one read by grandson James, written by son Todd, about a cow dog named "Jiggs." Doug recited a ditty about a dog, which isn't really appropriate for all audiences.

It turns out the bird count held at Minam was a trial count. The official Christmas Bird Count was held on December 17th. It was 6 degrees here on Prairie Creek when I drove that early morning to Enterprise to meet a small crowd of brave birders. Since the turnout was sparse I was assigned to count birds on upper Prairie Creek... by myself, which turned out to be most enjoyable. After the sun burst over the Seven Devils and warmed those snowy fields, various species of birds came to life.

I counted several hawks, a kingfisher, and many ravens and magpies. Most of the birds were close to—and in the case of the magpies, on top of—the cattle. Ranchers were feeding hay from the beds of slow-moving pickups or tractors pulling trailers.

Parking at the foot of the hill, below the steep icy road leading to Kinney Lake, I got out and hiked up to the frozen lake. Halfway up I startled several "Huns" (Hungarian Partridge) that had been feeding under some wild rose bushes.

Slowly making my way down the frozen road, I was awed by what lay before me. The brilliant snowfields of Chief Joseph Mountain, upper Prairie Creek awakening to a "bluebird day," the cobalt sky unmarred by cloud, jet contrail or smoke, silent and still; truly a treat.

We all converged at noon at the Mountainaire Cafe in Joseph, where we tallied our sightings over a hot lunch.

One bitterly cold evening I drove to the LDS church on the hill above Enterprise and observed a live nativity scene. Most impressive. A small burro, several sheep and goats, and of course, Mary, Joseph, and the babe in a manger. Standing out in the cold were the shepherds, standing watch. Inside the church, I found music, supplied by various talented members of our community, and a table laden with cookies.

Now Christmas is over and the new year looms. I wish the best to everyone in Agri-Times land.

December 31—Took a long walk around what used to be Doug's ranch. It was 16 degrees, so I bundled up against the chill. The irrigation ditch was frozen over and coyote tracks led along the old cow paths.

Several hawks called from the leafless willows, and I noticed a dead cottonwood had fallen over the old fishing hole...the same hole where grandson James hooked his first fish. Ken's cows munched their daily ration of hay, as did Hough's cattle across the road.

Returning by way of my milk cow's old pasture, I wished to see them again. Friendly old mama kitty rubbed against my legs as if to say, "You still have me."

My hens are laying again, after their usual winter slump.

Tonight we were honored by a visit from Ben and Jackie Tippett, who now live at the foot of the lake. It was good to see them.

Two cow ponies doze in the warm autumn sunshine in front of the Marr Flat Cow Camp. Not too many days after this picture was taken, however, chilly weather descended on the area.

2007

January 8—The sun's out, it's 32 degrees, and there's NO WIND. Especially grateful is the pair of Great Horned owls, who spend their days perched high among the thrashing, needle-laden branches of the two ponderosa pines in our front yard. Amazing to me how they maintain their balance, much less sleep.

For the first time in many years, Doug and I opted not to visit California this January. Perhaps later on in the spring, when the oak trees sport their new leaves and the foothills are carpeted with poppies and bluebells, we'll head down to where I was raised. Besides, there's just so much going on in Wallowa County.

Like the Big Read. Doug and I are reading John Steinbeck's *Grapes of Wrath,* which is only part of the big Steinbeck celebration. There's a screening of Elia Kazan's "East of Eden" at the OK Theatre, a film montage presented by Dennis Nyback, book discussions, and vinegar pie at the Odd Fellows Hall. There will be a showing of "The Grapes of Wrath" at the OK Theatre, a talk by Dr. Donna Beegle on "The Culture of Poverty" at Stage One, and the finale, a "Hard Luck" dinner and photo exhibit, when Kate Power and Steve Einhorn—Fishtrap's writers-in-residence—will entertain with Depression-era music at the Hurricane Creek Grange Hall.

A large segment of our community, including school children, have gotten involved in this fun project. Next week I'll be busy baking vinegar pies.

That box of carefully-wrapped tangerines, picked by sister Kathryn in her backyard in Roseville, California, arrived in our mailbox during a December blizzard. Hungry for fresh, sweet, juicy citrus, we savored every one.

Backlit by the sun streaming through my kitchen window, four brilliant red Amaryllis blooms add their cheer to this January morning. Great billowing snow clouds cloak the Wallowas, while tattered fragments of cloud drift over Prairie Creek. Snow from last week's storm continues to melt. If it weren't for the occasional drift, the fields, and even the hills, would resemble November more than January.

We did have enough new snow last week to allow Phyllis (on cross-country skis) and yours truly (on snowshoes) to take to the woods. It was very invigorating being out doors after a fresh snowfall, traversing several snowy trails up Hurricane Creek before making our way up the steep driveway to Phyllis' warm kitchen, where we dove into steaming bowls of her ham, bean, and vegetable soup.

Earlier, Don Green and I had spent the morning reading to the patients at Alpine House. Don, also a member of the Fishtrap board, and I really enjoyed listening to the old folks' stories as well.

Speaking of old folks, I had the pleasure of visiting over the phone with our Alder Slope friend Wilmer Cook recently. Doug and I visited Wilmer again when we ate lunch with the "old folks" at the Community Dining Center last week. Wilmer's pretty proud of that new great-grandson, born just before our Lucy and named after him.

Good to see other old-timers as well: Bill Bailey, Ken Kooch, Harold McLaughlin, George Justice, and Wayne Lathrop, all sitting at the same table. The entree that day, chicken enchiladas, was compliments of Richard and Mary Frasch.

Our friend Mary Marks, who has been confined to our local hospital this past week, is now back on Imnaha. She reports Lyman is very busy with the calving. Popular Mary had lots of company last week. Every time I visited, someone else walked in.

Our traveling families made it safely home; always a relief to this worrying mom.

Later, we drove up Hurricane Creek to spend the evening with Fred and Phyllis. Phyllis really outdid herself preparing dinner: baked ham, homemade rolls, scalloped potatoes, and the salad I'd made. Of course, we old fogies were home in bed by 10 o'clock!

Doug treated me to breakfast at the Mountainaire Cafe, the only place open in Joseph, on New Year's morning. Our little town was pretty deserted and quiet. It was 15 degrees, and I suspect most folks were snug in their warm homes. Spent that day taking down Christmas decorations, which always seems kind'a sad.

I drug our little Christmas tree up to the chicken pen to join the other skeletons of Christmases past.

On January 2 our Write Group resumed meeting in the basement of the Enterprise Library, and on the 3rd the "Wolf Moon, or"Hunger Moon" (January's full moon) was so bright I couldn't sleep.

Last Sunday I joined a small group of poets and writers to celebrate Oregon Poet Laureate William Stafford's birthday. Several local poets

*Under the stunning backdrop of Chief Joseph Mountain, these cows antici-
pate their daily ration of hay.*

*From the hills to Prairie Creek, the last of a large herd of cattle make their
way to hay and water, where they will spend the night before completing
their journey from canyon to valley. These are Marr Flat Cattle Co. cattle,
being driven by Angie Nash and her dog, "Dottie." Photo by Chelsea Nash.*

read their favorite Stafford poem, followed by a sample of their own work. Although William has left us, his prolific writing will keep his memory alive.

Time to add potatoes to the venison stew…it's been simmering in the Dutch oven all day.

January 19—I braved the cold again, this time to watch the sled dog races. Doug and I have always been in California during this event, so it was a new experience for us. That morning here on Prairie Creek the temperature registered 10 above, and it was mostly sunny. I spent the latter part of the morning reading to the folks in Alpine House, after which Phyllis and I lunched in Joseph, and then walked and talked our way uphill to the lake and back.

The 12-dog teams were scheduled to leave the starting chute around 4 p.m. at a spot over the hill from the east moraine. After being waved into a parking spot in a rancher's field, I bundled up against the cold, slung my camera around my neck, and struck off to walk the lane where I could watch the start of the race.

Echoing off the mountains was a cacophony of sound—such a wailing, yipping, barking, howling, whining, and whimpering, as I've ever heard. I was soon walking alongside the source of this sound. The sled dogs were lined up alongside the road, waiting to go, not hitched up yet, just snapped to a long rope secured at both ends, between their traveling kennels.

There were folks everywhere. Mushers, helpers, spectators, children, and babes in arms or in strollers. Everyone was watching the leaping, licking, yelping dogs. Dogs lapped water and made yellow snow; these dogs that were greyhound thin and slim, though of all breeds and colors; muscled like athletes, they were trained to pull sleds over snowy terrain.

Finding myself caught up in the drama of the thing, I yearned to be a musher and head off into the vanishing light of evening, following a snowy trail, winding toward night through dark woods in the company of the whisper-soft sound of the sled runners, the warm panting of my dogs, and the silent forest primeval, through a night pulsing with starlight.

I could imagine me, gliding over a starlit, snowy trail, pulled by my faithful dogs.

It was nearing 4 o'clock and a bitter chill settled over the Wallowas as it began to snow. Feathery flakes hovered in the air, settling on my noise and melting there. Then came the loud voice of the announcer.

"Spectators up the road, the race begins soon."

Dean Fairburn of Garden Valley, Idaho, was the first dog team to finish the 200-mile Sled Dog Race.

I trudged up the familiar road where the snow was deeper at that higher altitude. A bright orange plastic fence had been erected to form a chute, over which a banner read: *Start…Finish.* It was too noisy there. I wanted to see the dogs gliding along through a more natural setting. So I kept on walking uphill to a remembered meadow.

For more than 20 years Doug had leased this area to run his fall-calving cows. I had ridden it horseback to gather cattle, hiked it on foot, and cross-country skied the property in winter. After reaching the meadow where the dogs would cross, I climbed a nearby hill and took refuge under a tall ponderosa pine. After what seemed like a long time, I heard the soft hissing sound of sled runners and the barely audible panting of dogs.

I aimed my zoom lens on the meadow, and suddenly there they were in my view finder. I made my picture…and then they were gone, like ghosts melting into the darkening forest. I was losing my light but the snow meant there was enough reflection to work, I hoped. I waited for the next team, hoping for a decent shot.

Because I was alone, away from the noise, it made the experience more real to me. By then it was deadly cold, and I had to walk back to my car and head home. But my heart was with the mushers sledding on into the night, for I knew the route: up Salt Creek, down Gumboot, to Ollokot, Fish Lake and finally Halfway. Then back to the finish, 200 miles in all.

A healthy crop of Suffolk lambs soak up the January sunshine on the Upper Prairie Creek Ranch owned by Charley and Ramona Phillips of Joseph.

January 20—It was 12 above on the 20th, and Phyllis and I gave up watching for the sled dog finishers, but my friend Marilyn snapped a fine photo just as the winning team approached McCully Creek.

Phyllis and I stopped by that day to see daughter Ramona's lambs, all 80 of them. She's been a busy gal lately. One of Ramona's longtime friends from California was there to give her a hand.

We're still all involved in the Big Read, and enjoying celebrating Steinbeck. The vinegar pies? They were a hit.

January 23—Thirty-three degrees feels unseasonably balmy this afternoon. Doug has gone to La Grande to shop for a portable loading chute. My friend Cathy is seated in the living room reading "Grapes of Wrath." Our Writer's Group met this morning in the basement of the Enterprise Library, after which Cathy and I had lunch at Calderas in Joseph. Cathy hadn't planned to spend the night here, but the "funny noise" she'd been hearing in her car was diagnosed as a brake problem. More specifically...a "no brakes" problem. Because she lives way out in the north end of Wallowa County, the mechanic wouldn't let her drive home.

"Your car should be ready by noon tomorrow, if the right part arrives in the morning," he'd informed her. There is a thick layer of dust on the furniture; the jigsaw puzzle, laid out on a card table in the living room, waits for hands to fit the pieces together. The five brilliant red blooms of the amaryllis are wilted, and their short-lived beauty spent.

The first baby calves born to Ken's heifers have made their appearance. Even though the recent severe cold spell has eased, all waterways and ponds remain locked in ice.

Last Sunday afternoon, while I was out and about photographing, I ended up at Wallowa Lake, where I came upon a scene that resembled a Currier and Ives painting: ice skaters in an ice hockey game, while others skated far out on the frozen lake, some two by two, others alone, all enjoying the January sunshine beneath the stunning beauty of Chief Joseph Mountain.

It was 10 below on January 10th. All over Prairie Creek, cold cattle resembled black sculptures, standing still in the frozen dawn. In addition to the daily feeding of hay, Ken continues to break through the thick layers of ice that form on the irrigation ditch to provide open water for the cattle to drink.

To tolerate the cold, I wear a baklava to cover my head, nose and chin, and don layers of clothing when I venture out to tend my chickens or take a walk. The temperature climbed to a high of 8 that day.

On the spur of the moment Doug and I invited Fred and Phyllis to dinner that evening. I'd found a frozen steelhead in the freezer, smeared it with lemon and butter, and poached it in the wood stove oven. Since Fred is learning to bake with sourdough, he contributed a tasty loaf of French bread, while Phyllis whipped up a coleslaw.

After the meal, I draped a sheet over the picture window and projected slides of pack trips taken in the '60s into the Sierra Nevada Mountains when the children were small. Since Fred and Phyllis now own a burro, complete with pack, and plan on a summer filled with packing adventures, they were interested in how we managed way back then.

On the 14th it warmed to 5 above, and it wasn't much warmer when Phyllis and I took a snowshoe (for me) and cross-country ski (for her) up Hurricane Creek. Let me tell you, when the sun slid over the Hurricane Divide, it was COLD. By the time we reached our car we were numb.

Dealing with the cold was nothing compared to what the cowboys and one cowgirl endured, however, while trailing Todd's cows from Big Sheep canyon to Prairie Creek. Ken, who lives on Big Sheep Creek, Todd's wife Angie, and grandson Buck were the brave ones who spent two days in the saddle. With the help of their faithful dogs, the cows—after three days—slowly plodded their way to their wintering grounds south of Enterprise.

That last day the cowboys stayed in their pickups, because the cattle had only a few miles—all on county roads—to reach their destination.

It was below zero that Tuesday morning. I'd arisen early to prepare a large kettle of chicken soup and set a cast iron fry pan of sourdough biscuits to rise in the warming oven, before driving to Enterprise to attend our weekly writers' group.

Excusing myself early, I returned to the ranch, baked the biscuits, and added noodles to the soup. By the time Buck's wife, Chelsea, arrived with little "Miss Lucy", all was ready. So, we three got in the pickup and drove up Echo Canyon just in time to see the herd making its way over the hills. They'd come up Hayden Creek, and the last cows were trailing into Carl Patton's pasture.

We watched while Carl and Buck cut out one of Patton's cows that had somehow gotten in with Todd's along the way. Then we followed along until the cattle trailed into the pasture just north of us, where they would spend the night. The cows immediately turned their attention to the hay Buck had previously spread out for them.

After breaking ice so the cattle could drink, and unsaddling their horses, the weary crew trooped into our warm kitchen. There is nothing more satisfying than watching cold, hungry folks enjoy a hot meal. Soup and sourdough biscuits...their reward for spending two days in a cold saddle. Little Lucy slept through it all, awakening just long enough for a cuddle or two.

Mary Marks is in our local nursing home in Enterprise for a while, until she recovers from a circulation problem with her feet. I try to squeeze in a visit whenever I'm in town, and Mary seems in good spirits. She says there are a few old-timers there whom she enjoys visiting, and the calving is going well on the river.

"Lyman's got lots of calves now," she says.

February 6—It's really hard to stay INSIDE and write, when it's 45 degrees OUTSIDE. However, I've just returned from a three-mile jaunt around Prairie Creek, which has improved my outlook considerably.

Now that Ken's older cows have begun to calve, there's always plenty of activity happening in the lower field. Today a curled-up little black ball stood and began to bawl for its mama...while mama was clear at the other end of the pasture, preoccupied with the birth of her second calf. Then there's the pair of bald eagles perched in the ancient willows, ready to snatch up a meal of fresh placenta.

As I walk, I listen to the birds, many of whom I can't identify, singing as if it were spring; the ice crackles as it breaks up in the irrigation ditches...the very same ditches I walked on top of three days ago.

Yesterday, clad in boots, I slogged my way through the thawing muddy garden to fork the straw and dirt off a row of carrots. Although frost glistened in the soil that clung to the carrots, they were tender and sweet. I steamed some for supper to go with the elk I braised with shallots and garlic, also harvested from our garden.

Since the old Monarch wood stove was kept stoked with wood all during our recent cold spell, I took advantage of the heated oven to bake things like rice pudding, meat loaf, and various breads. Naturally, I utilized that wood heat to bake those old-fashioned vinegar pies.

After that Big Read event, I received several requests for vinegar pie recipes. So...for those of you who wrote, including Irene Walchli, Agri-Times reader from Hermiston, here are two recipes I found in my old cookbook collection. The first was found in an old Grange cookbook given to me by my grandma, Myrtle Wilson, years ago.

Vinegar Pie
Ingredients: 1 cup sugar, 3 tablespoons butter, 2 eggs, 3 tablespoons vinegar, 1 teaspoon lemon extract, 1 unbaked pie shell. Cream sugar and butter, and beat in eggs. Stir in vinegar and lemon extract. Pour into pie shell. Bake in preheated 350-degree oven until filling is firm. Makes a small rich pie.

I got so caught up in vinegar pies, I stumbled across this recipe in an old yellowed cookbook given to me by Mary Marks. This really old recipe assumes you understand basic cooking. Although not called vinegar pie, the recipe calls for it. I suspect this pie was invented by an early-day farm woman who wanted to use up an excess of sour milk.

Sour Milk Pie
Ingredients: 2 eggs, 1 cup sour milk, 1 cup sugar, 1 cup raisins, 1 1/2 tablespoons vinegar, 1 teaspoon cinnamon, 1/2 teaspoon cloves, and 1/2 teaspoon allspice. That's it. I got my wood stove oven pretty hot, poured this mixture into an unbaked pie shell, and baked it until the filling was set. It resembles a sour cream raisin pie. I didn't have sour milk—no milk cow—so I simply added the vinegar to fresh milk, and voila!—Sour milk.

I sent along with my column the following poem written by Todd Nash, of Enterprise, who runs the Marr Flat Cattle Company in the the rugged canyons that include Big Sheep Creek, the Divide and Marr Flat. The story told in the poem is true. Todd's son, my grandson, James, a student at Montana University West in Dillon, helped with editing.

The country Todd's cattle run in is so steep, and ranges over such a large area, a well-trained border collie is worth several cowboys on horseback.

Way Around

I ran as fast as I could run.
The General had given me orders
I ran as fast as I could run

Through ice cold waters up
broken rims covered with snow
My soldiers fell in behind me
but only I was asked to go

The canyon walls at Bristo Creek
are steep with one long bench
As I approach that one flat spot
I smell the cattle' stench

Two thousand feet above
two thousand feet of canyon wall
One hundred cows to gather
I'll do my best to bring them all

I'll swing south to Little Bristo
and get those cows in motion
Bite that baldy on the nose
and cause a small commotion

The troops are still behind
but barely keeping up
Jill has always been there to help me
since she was just a pup

Climbing two more rims
the cattle head for the main ravine
From this higher vantage point
there are four more I hadn't seen

Nearly on the skyline
the General sees the four
and doesn't say a word
He knows that he can send me
and I'll bring the entire herd

Down through Bristo, across the bench
come on cows, let's go
Take it kind of easy girls
with this little skiff of snow

Way off high I hear the cry
from somewhere deep inside
to the uphill side of the last four cows
I push myself with pride

One full mile from the General
and his horse
The other soldiers have abandoned me
this has been a brutal course

The cattle go along easily
as we spiral down the breaks
Slowly following one hundred cows
I feel my age, my pain, my aches

All lined out from bench to bottom
the cows have met defeat
Time to return to my post
my job is now complete

The General's voice is cracking
there's water running from his eye
When he says, "Jiggs, I see the
creator's perfection in you
and that's what makes me cry"

You're the best I've ever seen
you give it all you can
I am humbled in your presence
You're a better dog than I am a man

So that's the way it happened
when I was at my peak
it's what I was born to do
When I gathered Bristo Creek

February 6, later—Ken's first-calf heifers are mostly through calving, and I've worried every birth into this world. Since their calving pasture is close to the house, it provides a much-needed diversion from housekeeping. And to watch those little black babies race around…bucking and playing…brightens my winter days.

On Super Bowl Sunday I joined granddaughter-in-law Chelsea and wee Lucy, in her mama's snuggle pack, along with Callie and her little girl Addie for a walk. It was such a lovely warm day, even though we need more snow. It's hard not to enjoy these bright sunny days.

The "Big Read" goes on. Tonight is the showing, using original old reels, of The Grapes of Wrath at our OK Theater in Enterprise. We've had book discussion groups and lectures by a Steinbeck Scholar, and so many folks are reading other works by Steinbeck.

As an alternative to the Super Bowl, a small crowd of us gathered at Fishtrap House to view an old black and white film entitled "Sullivan's Travels." You oldsters out there, remember Veronica Lake? She was one of the stars.

February 7—Our local OK Theater was filled to overflowing last night as folks munched popcorn and enjoyed a showing of the original black and white film "Grapes of Wrath." Doug and I arrived early for a good seat. It was a nostalgic experience to wait five minutes for a reel change, and listen to the humming of the old projector.

It was a wonderful movie, depicting that epic mass migration of farm families who were forced off their lands during the dust bowl era. Relatively speaking, during this present time of plenty, it's good to be reminded of what it's really like to be poor, to want a job when there are no jobs, and to need a roof over your head when there are none. Like the Joad family, whose dream of one day owning a bit of land to work with their hands and raise their own food. That was all that kept them going.

For days Prairie Creek's morning temperatures hovered around 10 degrees, and that's how cold it was when Doug and I drove into Joseph for breakfast at the Cheyenne Cafe. To walk off my blueberry pancake, I decided to take off on foot for home. After hiking two and a half miles along the Imnaha Highway, I was ready to accept a ride from Doug.

The two owls continue to sleep by day in our pine trees.

Just at dusk one evening, I noticed the smaller of the two owls with its large eyes focused on the ground. The object of the owl's intense attention turned out to be our black cat playing with a mouse right under the owl's tree. The cat would toss the hapless mouse into the air, after which the tormented rodent would hit the ground running…only to be snatched up again by a playful paw. This went on for some time, and I could imagine the owl—hungry by now—wishing the cat would toss the mouse just a bit higher.

Whenever I'm in town I try to visit Mary, who seems to improve slowly. Lyman calls every morning and keeps her informed on how things are on Imnaha.

On Thursdays I read to the folks at Alpine House, who always offer stories more interesting than mine. Like Vinita, who says her father, Earl Prout, used to be a sheep herder.

"He loved working with the sheep," she says. "Spent all summer with them, could hike up a mountain just like a sheep." Vinita says she was born out there at the Buttes. "Doctor came out there to the head of Pine Creek and deliver me, said I wouldn't live; only weighed two pounds. But my mother put me in a shoebox in the wood stove oven and willed me to live, and I did."

Today, 80+-year-old Vinita says it hurts her eyes to read now... but she read books from the time she was a child. She remembered reading *Grapes of Wrath*, and recalled how it was during the Great Depression.

Time to start supper. Have fun with the vinegar pies.

February 20—Our window panes are plastered with snow flakes, gusty winds howl down the stove pipe of the old Monarch, and out in the calving pasture, the cows and calves are all bunched up, backs to the blizzard, patiently enduring this sudden storm.

I've just returned from town, where I joined our weekly Writers Group in the basement of the Enterprise Library, after which we all met for a soup and sandwich lunch at the Cloud 9 Bakery. This snow storm interrupted my plans to visit Mary, who's still in the nursing home and having a pretty hard time of it lately.

On top of her other problems, Mary's now battling pneumonia. She's a real trouper. I drove in yesterday and we had a good visit.

Today is a far cry from Saturday, when the thermometer rose to a spring-like 58 degrees. That's when I decided to walk around our country block. Ken's new calves were stretched out in the pasture, sunning themselves; returning robins hunted the thawing fields for worms, a noisy gaggle of wild geese had discovered a good-sized pool of open water in the ice-clogged Farmer's ditch, and the mountain snow fields were blinding in their whiteness.

Actually, February WAS a pretty mild month. Phyllis and I did a "walkabout" through Wallowa Lake State Park, which is always pretty deserted this time of year. Everywhere, fragrant pine needles, branches, and uprooted trees—the evidence of previous wind storms—criss-crossed our route. We watched a water ouzel (dipper) bob up and down on an icy rock in the river before disappearing into the rushing whitewater. Only a trickle of water drains a high country still locked in winter.

We're through with the yearly tax "thing," great-granddaughter Lucy smiled at me when her mom came over for eggs last week, Doug and I joined the "old folks" for lunch at the Community Dining Center in Enterprise, and one Saturday evening we took in the annual "all you can eat crab feed" at the local Elks Lodge.

Sometimes, on weekends, Ken and son Chad bring the great-grandkids over to help feed. How they love being in the midst of the cattle, and helping grandpa and daddy with the chores. And how I love watching them…remembering when my children and grandchildren toddled after me.

Several Sundays ago, our friend Maurice, who is house sitting this winter, invited Doug and me for dinner. It was snowing heavily that evening as we made our way to Upper Prairie Creek, and by the time we arrived around six inches of new snow blanketed every tree, fence post, and roof. After trudging through the soft white fluff, we left our shoes near the door and were greeted warmly by Maurice, who bade us enter. There's nothing like stepping from a snowy evening into a room full of cheer and light…and being assailed by the aroma of supper on the stove.

"I made us a turkey dinner," said Maurice. "I've been cooking all day!" And indeed he had.

"Not so good at making gravy," he added, however. "I need some help."

So, naturally, I took delight in whipping up the gravy using the nice drippings in the pan. Besides, it was so much fun working in a modern kitchen.

The evening was full of merriment, and the memorable dinner, complete with mashed potatoes, dressing, cranberry sauce, three kinds of vegetables, and a salad, was topped off with Maurice's apple pie. Doug and I first became acquainted with Maurice when he was our good friend Max Gorsline's caregiver. Maurice is looking for another place to stay, preferably in the county, after the first of March. He says he loves Wallowa County, but if something doesn't come up soon, he would consider moving elsewhere.

My friend Phyllis is in Hawaii for a few weeks. I miss our snowshoe hikes and our talks over lunch at her place on the mountain. Doug and I visited Phyllis' husband, Fred, over breakfast at the Cheyenne Cafe last Sunday.

"Heard from Phyllis?" I asked.

"Yeah, said she was sittin' on the beach, drink in hand, watchin' the whales."

I've never been to Hawaii. Maybe some day.

Outsiders often ask what we do for winter entertainment here in this far-flung corner of Northeast Oregon. Well...let me tell you, we don't lack much. For starters, the Big Read filled our calendar, coming to an end with the Grand Finale Hard Luck Dinner at the Hurricane Creek Grange Hall.

Thanks to the Grange ladies, who baked all those pies and helped in the kitchen, and to folks like Tom Swanson, who prepared the meat loaf, mashed potatoes, and gravy; and others, who cooked up a pot of beans, or planned and served the prime rib dinner...the evening was a huge success.

The way it worked, you bought a ticket for five bucks, and took chances on your number being included in a Joad (the poor family in the Grapes of Wrath), a middle class person, or a Rockefeller (upper class). Wouldn't you know, I was one of the 25 Joads. Beans for me. There were 70 middle class meat loaf eaters, and only five Rockefellers, who dined on prime rib while seated at a select table and served by a tuxedo-clad waiter.

Fishtrap's traveling photo exhibit was set up, and our board members wore Depression clothing. For entertainment our songwriters-in-residence, Steve Einhorn and Kate Power, played guitar and banjo and led the audience—who all had song books—in a sing-along of hard luck songs, which included tunes by Woody Guthrie, like "Ain't Got No Home," "Times a-Gettin' Hard," and the "Tom Joad Song" he wrote about the "Grapes of Wrath." We ended with "Good Night Irene," written by Huddie Ledbetter.

Then last Thursday evening Doug and I traveled the 60-mile round-trip to the Imnaha Store and Tavern for "Baby Back Ribs Night." Dave and Sally really know how to put on a feed, and we enjoyed visiting others who had driven down from "on top." Going down Little Sheep Creek we noticed the sap beginning to rise in the red osier dogwood. That familiar burgundy color fairly shouts its message: "Spring isn't far off!"

Last Sunday afternoon, those of us lucky enough to get tickets—seating is limited in the Indigo Gallery—were treated to a rare performance by Wallowa County's beloved Gail Swart and her friend Peter Donovan, who performed a piano recital. They began and ended with duets, and in between played amazing pieces composed by the masters: Chopin, J.S. Bach, Mozart and Franz Liszt.

There, in that beautiful venue, with still life paintings of fruit glowing softly against the walls, the gleaming black piano, and the artists themselves, fingers flying over the keys...a sort of magic took place. So...you see, we may live in the sticks, but when it comes to community, we have it!

Winter Fishtrap Writing Conference begins at the Wallowa Lake Lodge this Friday evening. I'm looking forward to it. One of my "Syringa Sisters," Bobbie Ulrich, from Portland, will join me for the weekend.

After walking out our snowy lane to post this column in our mailbox, I'll continue down the road and check the calving cows. I suspect my retired-rancher husband will be finishing up his cribbage game with "the boys" down at the Range Rider soon.

February 22—I arose early and baked a vinegar pie for those folks I read to at Alpine House every Thursday. It seems they'd heard about me baking those pies for our Big Read, and they wanted to taste one. I showed up the next week with the promised pie.

Last Thursday they told me it tasted so good they wanted another one.

February 25—Rain during the night turned to snow on Friday...which was nice, as that day my friend Bobbie showed up and we were able to work in a wonderful snow shoe trek up past the ski run before the Winter Fishtrap Writing conference, which began that evening.

It was like vacationing in my own county to spend the weekend with Bobbie at the historic Wallowa Lake Lodge. We shared a room on the third floor. The presenters really got us to thinking about the theme this year: "Crossing the Great Divides: Civil Conversation in the West." And Fishtrap is known for civil conversations. It is like food to us.

While frigid February winds blew snow off the trees outside, we gathered together in the cozy Great Room and listened to NPR's Howard Berkes enlighten us on the politics, economics, and culture of rural America. Of course I, being from rural America—living it every day—had some different views. But Howard's perspective was very interesting and made us all think and talk, which is good. We decided that's what's really needed to bridge the great divides: simply put, one-on-one talks with folks of different beliefs and cultures.

One of the attendees told the story about sitting down and talking to a cowboy about birds...come to find out they shared a common interest, and became fast friends.

Bill Bishop, who is currently completing a book on political segregation, really made us think. Bishop and his wife owned a weekly newspaper in rural Texas from 1983-1988, and Bill was a Pulitzer Prize finalist in 1989.

But it was Wyoming's Poet Laureate David Romtvedt who stole our hearts.

Married to a Basque woman, David worked for his father-in-law repairing windmills on a sprawling ranch in Wyoming. Author of the book "Windmill", David writes essays from Ten-Mile Ranch while living in a sheepherder wagon, in addition to other experiences he contemplates, much as Thoreau wrote from his but near Walden Pond.

And David knows music. He was a graduate fellow in folklore and ethnomusicology at the University of Texas at Austin. He's lived in Buffalo, Wyoming, since 1984. And let me tell you, Saturday evening he took his small accordion out of the case and played like no one we'd ever seen. Then he was joined by Steve Einhorn, Kate Power, Janis Carper and one of the attendees.

There were two guitars, one fiddle, and a banjo. We, the audience sang along...remembering words to the old folk tunes of yesteryear. He even had us holding hands in a large circle, teaching us ho to dance the Bulgarian Wedding Feast Dance. Never saw such energy in one person. It came to me that music is the universal language: music crosses the Great Divides.

Cutting my lunch short on Saturday, I drove to Upper Prairie Creek to attend a bridal shower, which was already in progress at daughter Ramona's in honor of granddaughter Lacey. Lacey, a nursing student at Blue Mountain College, will marry her Colin on March 24 in Pendleton. Colin, a good sport, stuck it out until the shower was over, and seemed to enjoy the silly games. I loved seeing my family, which included several great-grandchildren, all making over their new baby cousin Lucy.

Of course, all our meals were eaten there in the large dining room, the delicious menus prepared by the staff of the old lodge. After a Sunday brunch it was back to Beaverton for Bobbie, and back to Prairie Creek for me.

Our director Rich Wandschneider remarked on the subject of the American Divides, "I think David has a key, that maybe small places and small gatherings like this one have something to show larger places and bigger audiences how this can be done."

While I was at Fishtrap, Doug was down on the Upper Imnaha that Saturday evening, helping Lyman and his family and neighbors chow down on another large shipment of crab sent up by Lyman's son, Craig. They even saved some for me.

Mary Marks has her bad days and good days. Yesterday was a bad one. We all wish her well and applaud her efforts to keep on fightin'. They don't make 'em any tougher than our Mary.

Last week I noticed a little bowl of buttercups sitting on her bedside table.

"Wayne Marks found those, and sent them up for me," she said. Mary sounds better this morning. Said she finally got some good sleep.

February 27—Peering out the window during a snow storm, I noticed one of the older cows taking a long time to calve, so I called Ken, who drove over and pulled the husky calf. Why is it cows go into labor at the first sign of a storm?

Last Saturday evening Doug and I drove into Enterprise and out to Cloverleaf Hall to join our neighbors for a roast beef dinner prepared by the Wallowa County Fair Board, after which we sat ourselves down in a chair and took in the Old Time Blue Mountain Fiddlers jam session.

For the first time in many years, Charley Trump and Leonard Samples, both in wheelchairs, didn't play their fiddles. But there they were, sitting in the back row, obviously enjoying the program they have, over the years, contributed much to the success of.

It was Tim Collins' young son who stole the show. I remember this little tow-headed toddler from last year, running around the hall, still in diapers. This year there he was up on stage, standing beneath his tall father, wearing his own little guitar around his neck, strumming away, tapping his feet, imitating everything his daddy did. Give that boy a few years and he'll be fiddling with the best of them. His older brother and sister are already performing admirably.

We're so proud of our Upper Prairie Creek girls as well. Ryya, Lexi and Hannah are ranch-raised gals who've come a long way with their fiddle playing. While waltzes and other toe-tapping tunes were played on stage, several oldsters and youngsters found a place to dance out on the floor. No sense letting that good music go to waste.

The full moon had long since risen over the eastern hills as we headed home, flooding Prairie Creek with blue light. Grandson James, a college student in Dillon, Montana, who reads my column, whoops, did it again, called last week:

"Grandma" he said, "you're using too many parentheses. You don't need to use them where you do, just use a comma." If anyone else would have told me that, I would have taken offense, but not when a grandson corrects me. James made me proud, proud that he is receiving a college education, which his grandma never had.

But then, James says he'll be home for spring break soon and wondered if he and his friends could sample some of my pies. Now, there's where I have a degree. And I earned it in my own kitchen.

March 6—March might have come in like a lion, but six days into the month, our lion has morphed into a kitten. The air is soft and the sun is deliciously warm; warm enough for more buttercups to unfurl. I say more because on the last day of February I struck out over the hills east of here in search of the first drop of golden color...and found one. One small buttercup, shivering amongst the melting snow banks.

The squirrels are out! Squeaking and running hither and yon among the dried sage, nibbling tiny shoots of green grass and scurrying at the slightest sign of a hawk down their holes, which dot the hills where I walk. Today I found an old dried board to sit on, and plunked myself down in the midst of the squirrels. It was so peaceful there I could listen to the quiet. The only sounds, other than the squirrels, were made by birds...croaking ravens, the liquid songs of blackbirds, mallards gossiping in the irrigation ditch, and the faraway cackle of my hens laying eggs.

Only a few thin slices of ice line the ditch banks now, and the water, frozen for so long, swirls happily northward, providing stock water for the cattle on lower Prairie Creek.

On my way home I counted more than 40 calves sunning themselves on the hay Ken tossed out to their mamas this morning. In the leafless willows perch the bald eagles, eyeing yet another cow in labor. These birds are growing fat on afterbirths.

Yesterday Phyllis, all tan and back from Hawaii, and I snowshoed up the snowy road to the Hurricane Creek trailhead. Today's sunshine will have turned that fluffy snow to slush.

Last evening Doug and I joined other friends at daughter Ramona and husband, Charley's, ranch house on Upper Prairie Creek, where we visited old friends Pat and Linde, who now reside in Butte, Montana. They had delivered a buck (sheep) to a neighboring rancher, and were enjoying being back in Wallowa County. The couple had built a lovely log home on Upper Prairie Creek, and Linde, my hiking partner for years, and I recalled our many treks over high mountain trails. Ramona spent the day cooking a roast pork supper, which really hit the spot.

March 8—I rode to the hills with Doug to check our horses and count the elk grazing the new grasses. And did we see elk; hundreds of them. Every turn we took on those winding dirt roads brought into view another herd. Buttercups bloomed on the sunny southern slopes, and the grass was greening.

March 10—Phyllis and I drove to Lostine to attend the Providence Academy drama production of"The Taming of the Shrew." Billed as a weird comedy by Shakespeare, the play was so much fun. The cast was brilliant, as were the costumes and stage settings. We were transported to Italy as we sat through three acts. Those young folks never missed a cue. Kudos to the entire cast, and especially to Benjamin Boyd. The play was presented in the old Lostine School gym.

March 11—Doug took me out to breakfast at the Cheyenne Cafe. Because it was such a fine, warm morning, I decided to walk off that platter of ham and eggs by heading out the Imnaha highway toward Prairie Creek. Usually, Doug picks me up around the three-mile marker, but that morning I decided the walking was easier down in the borrow pit. Consequently, Doug zoomed right past without seeing me. I watched, helplessly, as he turned around and took another route to the ranch.

Later, as I was nearing Tenderfoot Valley Rd. our neighbor Scott gave me a ride. I would have made the remaining distance home, but the morning had warmed considerably and I had no water bottle.

Meanwhile, Doug was combing the roads looking for his wife. After gulping down some water at home, I headed up the road and ran into him.

"I was about to call the sheriff," he said.

I recovered from my marathon walk in time to attend the grand opening of our new Wallowa Memorial Hospital in Enterprise that afternoon.

This state-of-the-art facility is really hard to describe, as was the reception honoring its opening, a huge community effort that really did happen. A beautiful structure with a stunning view of the mountains.

March 12—Drove to La Grande to give a presentation to the Knife and Fork Club.

Last fall Cheryl Hafer had called to ask me to speak after their dinner. As the date approached, I became increasingly nervous. What would I say? When would I find time to put together a slide show? My friend Cathy gave me a pep talk.

"You can do this, Janie," she said. "Just think about all the great memories you have of your camping trips, they'll love

On the way over I did some serious reminiscing, and arrived early enough to visit La Grande's new library, where I met up with granddaughter Carrie, who works in the children's section, and was able to relax with a good book until it was time to drive to the Senior Center.

There, I was greeted warmly by Mr. and Mrs. Hafer, who put me at ease. After the meal I was introduced and the dreaded hour disappeared painlessly. Nice folks, who sat through it all and were most attentive. I spent the night with Carrie and great-granddaughter Brenna, who had waited up for me.

The next morning, after a cozy breakfast visit, I made it back to Enterprise in time for our weekly Writer's Group in the basement of the Enterprise Library.

March 15—I spent all day baking pies and cooking a roast pork supper for grandson James and four of his friends, who showed up hungry as bears after being in the canyons all day. Granddaughter Adele also showed up, so we had a full table. These young college students, on spring break, were so much fun.

And once again I upheld my reputation of belonging to Virgil Rupp's "Pie Hall of Fame." During the main meal, one of James' friends remarked, "Real mashed potatoes."

And, of course, those requested huckleberry-cream and lemon meringue pies were most appreciated.

March 17—This morning—St. Patrick's Day—the phone rang. Phyllis. "It's a gorgeous day, let's hike the east moraine," she said.

"Great," I replied. "Let's seize the day!"

A half hour later, leaving her car at the foot of the lake and mine near the head, we struck off up an old logging road that zig-zagged its way to the top. For over 20 years Doug had leased this land to run his fall-calving cows. I'd spent many hours in the saddle riding these same steep slopes. In the fall, after it snowed up, we would trail the cows and the calves down to Prairie Creek for the winter.

Huffing and puffing, Phyllis and I emerged from the shaded, timbered slopes and gained the open grassy ridge top of the moraine. From there we could see in all directions. Below sprawled the lake, a skim of ice still covering its surface, and above loomed Chief Joseph Mountain's blinding white snow fields, gleaming in the morning sunshine. On the eastern horizon rose the Seven Devils Range in Idaho; northward rolled the Zumwalt Prairie; to the west, the Blue Mountains.

Stumbling our way to a pair of large granite boulders, we sat on one and put our feet up on the other, and rested. From that high vantage point it was easy to envision the glacial action that created the lake, shoving up these lovely moraines for us to hike.

Following an old cow path alongside a fallen down fence, we ambled up and down the gently rolling ridge line. Suddenly, we were walking on a carpet of buttercups.

"Now if we could just see a bluebird," remarked Phyllis, and shortly thereafter...I spotted a flutter of blue. One blue bird! And then another, until we counted five pair, flitting from one granite boulder to another, their color so intense it was as though a scrap of sky had taken wing.

We truly felt alive, infused with new energy. It must have been over 70 degrees, with only a wisp of a breeze off the lake. We did overcome a rather large obstacle when we encountered the high elk fence, and I'll spare the details, but we managed to find a space large enough to squeeze underneath. The sight of two aging women sliding under a fence was not pretty, but we managed.

Winding our way through glacial drift, we surprised several pair of Hungarian partridge and a small herd of mule deer. The deer bounced away on spring-loaded legs, then ran ahead and paused to stare back at us before repeating the process. Phyllis' car remained a small dot in the distance, and we were getting low on water.

We'd stopped to eat our lunches midway, while looking down to an opening in the lake ice where several ducks had congregated. The ice, beginning to shatter, resembled a broken window pane. Finally we came to a draw that sloped gently downward toward the highway and Phyllis' car. We'd done it—we'd seized the day!

The day that was far from over, because that evening, we drove down to the Wallowa's high school to attend the wonderful program presented by the combined symphonies and chorale groups of the Inland Northwest Musicians. A very touching experience, listening to the voices of so many of our friends. A perfect ending to a perfect day.

The next day I spent most of the time in my kitchen, whipping up an impromptu corned beef n' cabbage dinner for family and friends. Fred baked a batch of his famous sourdough biscuits, Phyllis contributed an apple pie. I baked two rhubarb-strawberry pies. Naturally, grandson Buck and son Todd were able to take pie home. Little Lucy slept contentedly on her mama's lap during most of the meal.

March 20—Awoke to two inches of snow on the ground. I baked oatmeal cookies for the grandchildren, due to arrive tomorrow, which is the the first day of spring.

March 26—March is nearly ready to march off the calendar and my life's been so hectic lately, I've scarcely had time to record it...but here goes. Before dawn this morning we were wakened by the hoots of our resident owls, who swooped on silent wings to perch in the ponderosa pine. Carolee and Donna, our house guests from Roseburg, peered out the front window to see the owls outlined against the pale pink sunrise.

A 20-degree morning with thick frost shocked not only the greening grass, but the first purple crocuses blooming alongside the house.

Yesterday, as we drove back to Wallowa County from Pendleton, it rained, and snowed a bit over the Blues, which was a good thing, because the country needs moisture to keep that grass growing. One more month of feeding hay before turnout time.

Saturday morning Doug and I headed over the mountains to Pendleton to attend granddaughter Lacey's wedding. She and Colin tied the knot in the lovely 100-year-old United Methodist Church, with its gorgeous stained glass windows and fine stone work.

Daffodils bloomed outside in a warm sunshine-filled day, as family and friends arrived from far-flung places. Son Steve, wife Jennifer, and children Bailey, Stetson, and Ethan spent several days with us last week, after flying from Alabama to Portland and renting a car.

Naturally, the children were pretty wound up after so much traveling, and stayed that way during their entire visit. Each morning they arose early enough to "help" Uncle Ken feed the cows. While they were thus occupied, I busied myself at the wood range, cooking large amounts of sourdough hot cakes, which they happily consumed.

On Thursday evening Doug and I took the family to Imnaha for one of Sally and Dave's "All you can eat ribs feeds" and, on the way down Sheep Creek, we stopped to watch the big steelhead making their way into the fish facility there. After the family left Friday I was about to clean house for our next company, due to arrive Sunday, when our electricity went out. After it was restored, I attempted to rid the house of hay, cow manure and chicken poop left behind by the grandkids.

After Lacey and Colin's wedding reception at the Elks Lodge, Doug and I spent the night in Pendleton with other members of our large family. It was fun seeing all of them. A pity we must wait for weddings or graduations to get together.

Most of March was unseasonably warm. We let the fire die out, hung clothes on the line, and spent as much time as possible outside.

March 28—Catching up on my column this morning, as the calendar tells me it's March 28. The snow that fell during the night lingers. A cold wind blows across Prairie Creek. Our house guests have been invited to breakfast. It seems grandson Buck was doing the cooking. I sent over a couple dozen eggs.

New spring calves find a cozy spot to warm themselves on a cold morning.

April 1—It rained lightly during the night and we noted new snow on the highest peaks. Low clouds encircled the mountains and it was cold enough for a fire in the cook stove.

Eleven of us at the long wooden table. *Talk, talk, talk.* Delicious potluck, and a lemon-poppy seed cake, baked by our poet Myrna. After Annie and I washed and dried the dishes, we all retreated to the living room to pull out the knitting or embroidery. A fire crackled in the fireplace. Then...the yawns began, as the long day faded into night and six of us had nearly 50 miles to go before we slept.

April 2—It snowed through sunlight again, and I spent the day working on an essay for our weekly writers' group, and baking a plum cobbler from some plums I'd frozen last fall. This evening I watched the full "pink" moon rise, so named because this is the time when pink flowers bloom.

April 3—I hung my wash on the line. Even though it was only 19 degrees that morning, with a heavy frost, the sun was out, and a cool breeze freshened the sheets. Made it to our weekly writers' group, which meets in the basement of the Enterprise library every Tuesday at 10 a.m.

April 4—I left an elk roast simmering in the crock pot, along with plenty of onions, carrots and garlic, made myself a brown bag lunch, and drove to Christine's cabin on the west side of Wallowa Lake, where I met up with other members of our writers' group to "play" with words. There in Chris' cozy kitchen we played Scrabble into the afternoon. Just below us the lake was a dull sheen, not a breath of wind rippled its surface. Steller's jays and flickers took turns visiting Christine's bird feeder.

April 5—Since this was the week we'd planned to be in California I hadn't marked my calendar up with dates, which was nice because it freed me to play. Because it was one of those warm spring days, Phyllis came over and we drove to the bottom of the hill below Kinney Lake.

We hiked up to the lake, which is now free of ice, and kept climbing the hill until we came upon more buttercups and bluebirds. Selecting a sun-warmed rock, we sat ourselves down and enjoyed our lunches.

There's nothing finer, on a sunny day in April, than being in a place where everywhere you look, there are no houses; nothing but rolling hills, sloping downward to the breaks of canyon country, where you can listen to the quiet. Nothing tastes finer than sandwiches layered with lettuce, pickles and a bit of roast chicken. eaten in such a setting.

April 10—Although the snow that fell during the night has melted, its breath lingers in the wind that blows across Prairie Creek this afternoon. Ah, spring!

Well, spring in Wallowa County anyway. When, in April, the first curly red leaves of the rhubarb push up through the soil and daffodils unfurl; when the buttercups on Hough's hill wane, and are replaced by grass widows and Prairie smoke; when the cherry tree and forsythia burst forth, and blizzards, born in the mountains, sweep across the valley.

It's all beautiful and amazing to watch, especially when snow flakes whirl through bursts of sunlight...but now spring retreats a bit. Cattle, hungry for grass, relish their hay again. Stunned by cold, daffodils droop under the snow's weight.

And, lying in bed in our brand new hospital, our Mary looks out the window at her 90th spring. If you read Mary's dairies you'd know it's always been this way. And being a rancher, Mary would say this snow is good for the grass. She's right. All too soon the weather will warm, and the difference between a good grass year and a bad one always hinges on springtime moisture.

Mary's not doing so well. I try to visit every day. Someone brought her a bouquet of birdbills and yellow belles from the canyons—hoping, I'm sure, that bringing a bit of Mary's beloved Imnaha to her bedside would comfort her.

On Easter Sunday I arose early enough to attend the Sunrise service at the Joseph Methodist Church, an experience made special by all those in attendance. Although there was no sunlight to stream through those lovely stained glass windows, there was no lack of joy. This is due, in part, to the joyful voices of the choir, directed by Claudia Boswell, seated there at the piano.

After the service I joined Doug at the Cheyenne Cafe for a blueberry pancake. There we lingered amid the all-male "locals" table, listening to the aging cowboys spin their tall tales.

Easter was different this year. No ham in the oven at home and no little ones to color eggs with. Just happened that our family was otherwise occupied or out of town. Nostalgic, I recalled all those Easter Sundays spent on Imnaha, when the canyons were a-bloom, the air balmy, and the young and old of us played baseball using dried cow pies for bases.

Picnics included homemade ice cream, ham, potato salad and deviled eggs. There we'd be, walled off from the world amid those sunny, green canyons.

Ken has moved his cows and calves to another pasture, one not visible from the house. This provides another excuse to get out and walk, so I can enjoy those growing calves. The hay barn is emptying of bales and soon the cattle will be trailed to the hills.

Oftentimes I walk high on Hough's hills, to watch the progression of wildflowers. On the way I encounter muskrats, mallards and, once, was surprised to see a ground squirrel cavorting about in the irrigation ditch. Overhead fly red-tail hawks, ravens, and blackbirds. Lately, I've been seeing killdeers, and the occasional great blue heron. There is a network of life underfoot: squirrel villages and cavernous entrances to badger dwellings.

Once again a fire burns in the old Monarch. Often a pot of beans and ham hocks simmers there. During the recent "false spring" we let the fire die out, as there was enough warmth in the sun to solar heat the house.

The Sunday we returned from the wedding, after Carolee and Donna arrived, Doug came down with a dilly of a cold. After a recent visit to the Doc he's feeling much better.

Daughter Jackie and her husband, Bill, drove over from Challis, Idaho, and spent that week visiting their son Buck and his wife, Chelsea. Of course the main attraction was wee Lucy. Our little miss is developing her own personality, which provided an excuse to get together and "Lucy Watch."

Monday, Lucy included, we all met for lunch at the new hospital, where sometimes Lucy's mamma works the night shift while her daddy babysits.

After completing another jigsaw puzzle, I took a walk up and down our county roads, collecting trash and cans.

April 12—And now... it's the morning of April 12 and I'm still working on this column. Doug just came in and announced the water has been turned off. He and Ken are putting in a new water line for irrigation.

Last evening I joined six other members of our "Stitch and Bitch" group, and drove to the upper Imnaha Writers' Retreat to celebrate Kathy's birthday. Armed with potluck dishes and knitting projects, we parked near the swinging, swaying bridge that spans the Imnaha, a first for these gals, which had me a little worried some of those carefully-prepared casseroles might end up in the river. But they all made it.

Kathy and three other writers have been at the retreat all week. As always it's like stepping into a different world: bulbs bursting with colorful blooms, the golden forsythia blooming, violets running amok over the lawns, crown imperials bowing their watery eyes, and the apple trees just beginning to bud.

Nothing tastes finer than sandwiches layered with lettuce, pickles, and a bit of roast chicken.

April 16—A soft April breeze wanders down the river, stirring the new green leaves of alder, the deep pink flowering quince, the canary yellow forsythia, the pink and white bleeding heart, the deep orange crown imperials, the yellow tulips, and the wild arrowleaf balsamroot blooming on the sunny slopes above our cabin. The sound of water rose above it all, rushing over rocks.

You guessed it... I'm here to witness yet another spring on Imnaha. The Upper Imnaha to be exact. Here at the Fishtrap Writer's Retreat. We are five this week. Anna drove from Challis, Idaho; Adam flew from Texas to Portland, and hitched a ride with Melissa; Diane drove from Carey, Idaho; and yours truly.

Saturday night's storm left the high rims dusted with snow as white as the cherry blossoms here in our yard. Arriving around noon on Sunday, I lit a fire in the wood furnace, pushed two cart loads of belongings across the bridge, and settled into the downstairs bedroom.

I opted not to take the tree house this time. Our resident owl had left its calling card on the deck, and it was apparent no one had occupied the cabin since last fall. Besides, to be a proper "den mom" I was obliged to be the "tender" of the wood furnace, which turned out to be a wise decision, because cold, rainy weather prevailed during most of the week. Meanwhile, the place was all mine. The other four writers weren't due until later that evening.

The afternoon warmed up enough to enjoy a riverside stroll before the sun slid over the canyon wall. Pausing under an old apple tree, I listened to several wild turkeys gobbling their way up Indian Creek. A few shriveled apples clung to the tree, which was about to burst into bloom. Across the river three mule deer does grazed a high grassy bench, and below, where the river makes a bend barely visible through a copse of leafy brush, I caught sight of Mary's house.

I wanted Mary there, so I could walk over in the morning and find her in her little kitchen, cutting out biscuits, frying tiny deer steaks, or stirring the milk gravy. I remembered fondly how, when she'd see Lyman driving down the hill, she'd pop the biscuits in the oven and set out a pint of homemade apricot jam, and the kitchen would be all warm with the smell of coffee and biscuits baking.

"Here, better have some breakfast," Mary and Lyman would say. And how could I refuse? There wouldn't be much talk while hungry folks ate. Then Lyman would push himself away from the table, saying "Gotta fix fence, or work on irrigation pipe." And off he'd go. Lyman always did the dishes, except when I was there and he sensed Mary and I needed to visit, so we'd chatter away while I washed and she dried.

Now Mary waits out her days in our local nursing home, far from her beloved canyons. I called her yesterday before I left Prairie Creek.

"Headin' for the river," I told her. "That time of year again. Hang in there, Mary, 'til I get back. I'll call you tomorrow."

This afternoon, as I edit the final manuscript of the book I'm writing, I think about Mary's life. I've come to the realization that Mary lived during the best of times here along the old Imnaha. Sadly, as our old-timers leave us, so too goes their culture.

The other four writers came straggling in late. It was nearly dark when Diane showed up at the door. I'd put together a scalloped potato and leftover ham casserole for supper, cooked some green beans, and made a salad using produce left here from the last shift of writers.

The next morning Melissa decided to clean out the tree house. Now everyone is settled in, and this morning dawned clear and sunny, a bit of frost whitening the new, green grass. Dark clouds replace the sun as I write, however, so I feed the furnace with the newly delivered wood we're hauling across the bridge in carts; this is wood that warms us twice.

The day before I arrived at the retreat was a full one. Phyllis and I decided to drive out the Zumwalt Road and catch up with son Todd's cattle drive; the second day of a three-day trailing of cows and calves to Big Sheep Creek. We ran into the herd halfway up OK Gulch. Son Todd, wife Angie, and Julie were bringing up the rear. Cows and calves were strung out over the next quarter mile.

Angie Nash nears the end of a cold two days in the saddle while driving cattle from Prairie Creek to Big Sheep Creek near Imnaha. Photo by Chelsea Matthews.

Ethan Lowe pauses near the top of OK Gulch to turn the cows and calves.

At the top of the hill we met Ethan, who was turning the cattle eastward. Driving on, we met cowgirls Sharon, Sherry, and Rochelle, scattered out in the lead.

Before the first cows plodded their way over a rise, Phyllis and I shouldered our day packs and took off on foot ahead of them. Hiking down a faint road that ended in a grassy draw, we were startled by the sound of pounding hooves. Several horses we'd spotted earlier were heading our way. After satisfying their curiosity, they thundered up to harass the cows and calves. It took many attempts on behalf of the cowgirls to convince the horses they didn't belong in that cattle drive.

Making our way up the draw, Phyllis and I noted a bevy of wildflowers: blue bells, yellow bells, prairie smoke, bird bills, grass widows and cous. A cold breeze greeted us on top of a high bunch grass-covered ridge, and we covered our heads with hoods and caps. Presently, we came to an old gate, and passed through to follow cow paths that headed steeply down South Lightning. This trail would eventually take the cattle down Lightning Creek to the Sheep Creek highway, where they would spend the night in a holding pasture.

Suddenly, far below, two cowboys appear on horseback. They turn out to be grandson Buck and Sherry's husband, Duane, who are riding up from Lightning Creek. Buck has lunches in his truck, which is parked at the bottom of South Lightning.

When I ask Buck how far it is to the barn where the trucks and trailers are parked, he says, "A long ways, grandma, about four more miles." Right then Phyllis and I decide to return to our pickup, eat lunch, and drive around the road to meet up with the herd. Besides, Buck would've had to bring us back to our rig after a long day in the saddle.

Anyway, we'd had enough exercise for the day, so we retraced our steps and soon found ourselves back where we'd started. The weather deteriorated on top but moderated a bit when we reached the ranch on Lightning Creek. Here we waited for the herd to come down South Lightning so I could do some more photographing. They didn't show up until 2:30, and the riders must have welcomed a rest.

Leaving the crew to eat their lunches we slowly made our way through the cows and calves, who by this time were moseying along toward Sheep Creek. Then it began to rain, and it was spitting snow by the time we reached Sheep Creek Hill.

After fixing a hurried supper, I made it to the Enterprise High School in time to spend a wonderful evening listening to a concert staged by the Inland Northwest Musicians. Granddaughter-in-law Amy played first violin, and other familiar faces were scattered among the musicians.

The musicians were a combination of Inland Northwest and Wallowa Valley Orchestras, the Willow Creek Symphony and Singers, and Inland Northwest Chorale. The music was thrilling. I'm still humming "Sweet Caroline," and will never forget the energy in those violin strings during the playing of "Fiddle Faddle." During the end of the performance, after Dane Mickelson, a scarf wrapped around his head, conducted "Pirates of the Caribbean" the audience rose, cheering, to its feet.

April 18—It's been raining all day, which is good for the country and good for writers, else we'd be drawn outside. This morning we noticed the snow line lowered in the night. Halfway down the canyon sides, in fact. From the window where I write, I can look out at the river, which has risen significantly since we've been here.

April 27—I smeared peanut butter on a couple of sourdough biscuits, filled my water bottle, and struck out on foot behind Ken's cows and calves. Because we got an early start, it was nice and cool, and the herd moved right along. This spring I kept up; had to, as we were only Ken on horseback, grandson Chad on a four-wheeler, and me on foot, where I prefer to be when herding calves. A person on foot can get into places better than a mounted one, especially when calves hide behind wild rose bushes or wander into a deep borrow pit.

The day dawned clear, a lovely, fresh April morning. Up early again, I drove out the Crow Creek road and caught up to the herd, which was nearing the old Warnock homestead. Leaving my pickup parked alongside the road, I hoofed it behind the cows and calves again.

Spring in the hills is something to see. Crow Creek flowing with renewed vigor due to recent rains, and the air was thick with the fragrance of new aspen, chokecherry, and alder leaves; the green hills were sprinkled with yellow cous and carpets of pink phlox, and the smell of crushed grass and damp soil as the cows ambled along.

Phyllis appeared at the foot of Dorrance Gulch, so we drove back and left her car, and took the pickup back to the herd. Making our way through the cows and calves we drove on top and parked so I could photograph the cattle trailing up the steep grade, with the far-off Wallowas in the background.

While waiting, Phyllis and I walked alone in a vast, lonely landscape, a world of undulating hills wearing spring green. Dry Salmon Creek is wet. Squirrels have dug holes in the road. Squeaking and staring at us, they dive into the safety of their dens. Greenwood Butte looms ahead, and we are there at the North Pine Road to turn the herd.

Presently Chad's wife Amy and children Ronan, Gwenllian, and Kennon arrive, with grandma Annie. Phyllis and I drive to the Butte Creek pasture and hike to a canyon overlook, taking time to eat our lunches before returning home. By then, I've had enough walking.

At intervals during that day I thought about my Auntie Carol, celebrating her 90th birthday in Sacramento, California. All my siblings and cousins would be there, and I wished to be too. Auntie Carol, the surviving sibling of my mother's large family, was an important role model in my formative years. By example she taught us that a sense of humor can ease the path of life.

April 28—Kathy and I drove to the canyons to check on the Fishtrap Retreat. Despite the chilly morning, we were cheered by the sight of pussy willows along Sheep Creek, and all those wild plums running rampant upriver, their snowy blooms matching the snowy rims above.

Dug out a package of Myrna Moore's peaches from the freezer and baked a cobbler. Mixed up the sourdough jug and set a fry pan full of biscuits to rise in the warming oven, then thawed out some turkey broth leftover from Thanksgiving, added noodles, and put together a salad…and invited everyone to supper. Since our cowboys had been outdoors all that long, cold day, sorting pairs, they nearly fell asleep at the table. Sister Caroline called this evening, wondering when we were coming to California for a visit. Sadly, I told her that, because of Doug's cold, we had decided to change our plans.

April 29—Doug and I drove to the Cheyenne Cafe in Joseph, where I partook of a platter of ham and eggs, which gave me the energy to walk toward home. Nearly made it too. Doug picked me up as I was nearing Bicentennial Lane. Changed my route this time: Highway 82 to Walker Lane to Liberty Road. Waved to neighbor Marian Birkmaier, who was working in her flower beds.

April 30—I arose early to prepare a send-off sourdough pancake/waffle breakfast for our family and guests, who would be pulling out early tomorrow morning. After consuming stacks of hot cakes and waffles, along with bacon, eggs and raspberry jam the cowboys left to feed. While Carolee and Donna did up the dishes, I tended my chickens. By 10:30 we were on our way to the Senior Citizens dining center in Enterprise, where we volunteered to serve the noon meal that Friday.

Rummaging around in my closet, I'd come up with two more Cow-Belle aprons for Donna and Carolee. Those two pitched right in, real troopers they were. Since all the tables were full that day, I really appreciated their help. Afterwards we drove over to Buck and Chelsea's so Lucy could have her photo taken with her two great-grandmas.

Another reason this column isn't finished is because I spent yesterday from noon to 2:30 up at Christine's with our writers' group playing Scrabble again. This time I beat Christine, and that's something.

Time to print this out and get on with my day, which will include spending the afternoon with Mary.

May 1—Today was a warm one—nearly 75 degrees.

May 2—It was raining lightly as I peered out my kitchen window to see a coyote, nose pointed toward a gopher mound, in the neighbor's field. After observing it for a while, I sat down and wrote a villanelle, a form of poetry that has been around for three hundred years. There is a pattern you follow, beginning with a pair of rhyming lines that form the heart of your meaning. Since we are writing villanelles for our writing group, I came up with this one.

A coyote pauses in a field
His nose is pointed toward a mound.
Does the gopher know its fate is sealed?

In a farm house yard the children squealed
Which frightened the gopher in the ground.
A coyote pauses in a field.

In a nearby village the bells have peeled
A sonorous, saddened sound.
Does the gopher know its fate is sealed?

The coyote stands so still and steeled
As if all creation has been found.
A coyote pauses in a field.

A green pasture of grasses yields
to myriad darkened tunnels round.
Does the gopher know its fate is sealed?

Overhead the ravens reeled
And the rodent's heart began to pound.
A coyote pauses in a field.
Does the gopher know its fate is sealed?

The weather turned cold; there's a fire in the old Monarch again.

A good rain fell on the thirsty land as we drove to the Enterprise High School to attend the annual FFA spring banquet. For the first time in nearly 40 years I didn't have a child or grandchild in FFA. Doug and I enjoyed our meal of pork loin, prepared by Steve Lear, and served by Debbie Hadden's home ec girls.

The Enterprise FFA is the oldest chapter in the state of Oregon, and this was its 77th banquet. Former FFA members son Todd and his son, James, were there. The FFA has, over the years, produced many of our community's leaders, which would include a whole new crop of first-rate young people.

May 3—Our hills were frosted with spring snow, but that didn't stop Phyllis and me from hiking up Hurricane Creek. After munching meat loaf sandwiches, we drove up the narrow road, parked, and ambled through the campground, which was at creek level.

Sudden clouds emptied themselves of tapioca-like snow pellets as we poked around. The walk was invigorating and we inhaled the scents of budding alder, red osier dogwood, and snow melt water rushing over rocky Hurricane Creek.

The frost didn't keep Doug from roto-tilling the garden either. He was hard at it when I got home.

May 4—Dawned clear and 25 degrees. Once again the tulips and daffodils were shocked with cold.

Tonight I enjoyed an evening of classical music at the Enterprise Christian Church. A thrilling performance by local talent that included: Peter, Hugh and Grace Donovan, Gail Swart, Hannah Lund, Ashley Morehouse, and the incredible soprano, Helene Hipple.

May 5—Up early preparing deviled eggs when grandson James called. "My friends and I are heading to Big Sheep Creek, we'll be back later this afternoon. Wondered if you had any pie? Been bragging to my friends about you."

So, wouldn't you know this grandma got in and baked a raspberry pie, using a package of frozen berries I found in the freezer. Then, leaving the pie to cool, along with a note to James, I gathered up those deviled eggs and headed out to Salmon Creek, where Ken and his family were branding those calves we'd helped trail out. As usual, here was this grandma, perched on the top rail of the corral, photographing the scene.

One of life's pleasures is watching one's offspring at work and play, and brandings are a chance to be together while accomplishing a task.

At the top of the Dorrance Grade, Ken Nash trails his cows and calves to the hills where they will summer into late fall.

There was young Cutter, toddling around; his mom, Kasey, a veterinarian from John Day, working with the ground crew; his dad, Rowdy, roping calves on a three-year-old colt; Chad, flanking husky calves, and his wife, Amy, numbering ear tags; Todd branding and castrating; wife, Angie, giving shots; Ken everywhere at once; Ronan, Gwenllian and Kennon right in the middle of it all: hot irons in the branding fire, Salmon Creek wandering between willow-lined banks, the bawling of mama cows, and the stench of scorched hair, dust and manure.

All this amid the hills themselves, rolling bunch grass green as far as the eye could see.

Grandma Annie arrived with baked ham, beans, salads, and cakes. The stuffed eggs didn't last long. Little Gwenllian smiled and said, "We're having a picnic." And indeed we were. A tailgate picnic, right there by the loading chute.

Doug arrived later to mend a gate, and we made it home in time to attend the Hells Canyon Mule Days Poetry Gathering at the Liberty Grange Hall, located just to the west of the ranch. The evening music included fiddles, mandolin and Allen Schnetzky on the piano. Proceeds from the event went to the Max Walker Memorial Scholarship Fund. This year $3,000 was divided among Matt Exon, Maggie McClaran, and Toviyah Lowe.

And that raspberry pie for James and his friends? Just one slice left, along with three notes I'll always treasure. Grandmas have always known that baking a pie is just another way of expressing their love.

May 6—This morning Doug and I were back at the Grange Hall devouring Carmen Kohlhepp's sourdough pancakes. This hearty breakfast was prepared by the Liberty Grange members for the ploughing bee going on in the field of our neighbors Larry and Juanita Waters that weekend. What a thrill to see those colorful teams of mules and

Vicki Leonard, of Pendleton, drives her team of Belgian draft horses as they plow a field on the Waters' Ranch on Tenderfoot Valley Road during the Lee Scott Memorial Ploughing Bee.

horses pulling vintage plows up and down the field, and listening to the bells jingle on the collars of Vaden Flock's team as it worked. It was a photographer's dream, and I shot two rolls of film.

As I write, looking back on these past weeks, I wonder, as usual, how we here in Wallowa County keep up with it all. Spring has sprung.

May 8—The morning sun pushes up over Hough's Hill earlier these days. Its welcome warmth seeps into every blade of grass and sprouting seed, and illuminates the brush strokes of pale green worn by the ancient willows that line the irrigation ditches.

The fields are sprinkled with dandelions, and robins have built their nests in barn rafters, old machinery, and trees in our yard. Doug has roto-tilled the garden and pruned the apple tree, Ken has been working on the new irrigation line, Doug has mown our lawn twice, the tulips are still blooming, and the rhubarb is ready for pie. Great clouds of dust boil up on the hill, as seed peas are being drilled into ground that used to grow meadow hay.

Although I was a day late to see Mary Marks one more time, we'd said our goodbyes the week before. Mary passed April 20, and she picked a lovely time to die. The afternoon memorial at the Enterprise Cemetery couldn't have been more special. Although Mary was short on relatives, she was long on friends. Folks from far and near came to pay their last respects to a lady who has become a legend on Imnaha.

On Mary's infrequent trips out "on top" she always marveled at the Wallowas. She would have done so at her memorial. Their snowy ramparts created a glorious presence as the sun shined down on her flower-bedecked casket. Mary was buried beside her husband, Kid, who died in 1987. Mary always enjoyed hearing about my adventures. It brought back memories of when she, too, trailed cattle all those years. Although we'll all miss her, Mary left us a rich legacy of stories.

As usual, it didn't take long to plunge back into life here on Prairie Creek after I returned from my week at the Writer's Retreat. For starters there was the grand marshal dinner to honor Blanche Maxwell, the 2007 Hells Canyon Mule Days Grand Marshal. An amazing lady.

I visited past grand marshals, including Ben Banks, Manford and Vera Isley, Arnold Schaeffer, Bob Casey and Fred Talbot. I remembered Mary was a past grand marshal, along with Joe McClaran. Sondra Lozier and her Hells Canyon Mule Days committee do a bang-up job of promoting this fast-growing, popular event, which is always held the weekend after Labor Day.

Then there's our writer's group that meets every Tuesday in the basement of the Enterprise Library. Poet Cathy Putnam drives the long miles from Flora to attend. If it's snowing or raining on Wednesdays, several of us "brown bag" it at Christine's cabin on the lake and play Scrabble.

And wouldn't you know it? The little hen that's been flying over the chicken pen to scratch in Doug's raspberries is still enjoying her freedom. It seems the hen I plucked from the roost the other night to clip a wing…was the wrong one.

May 10—A welcome rain ushered in the season's first thunderstorm. Great alabaster clouds, like mountains in the sky, grew from tiny puffs of cotton on the horizon in the time it took to walk to Klages' corner and back.

Grandson Buck, wife Chelsea, and wee Lucy stopped by on their way to our neighbor's ranch to mend fence, where they are pasturing their first-calf heifers. Good thing the cookie jar was full of oatmeal cookies. Buck always has the "munchies." Great-granddaughter Lucy, clad in a bird-bill hat just like mom, was obviously enjoying the outing.

Those tulip bulbs planted in the fall are adding a splash of red color to our "glacier white" house. And during that long warm spell it was nice to hang the clothes on the line and let the fire die out in the old Monarch. Life is so much simpler when one doesn't have to bundle up to go outside.

May 13—Mother's Day dawned cool and cloudy, but that didn't stop me from walking home after breakfast at the Cheyenne Cafe. All the usual offerings of affection were bestowed upon me, which makes motherhood worthwhile. They included hugs, phone calls, cards, gift certificates to nurseries, and the gift of a sweet cherry tree, planted for me by son Todd.

I purchased petunias, herbs, a tomato plant, and onion starts with the certificate daughter Ramona gave me, and picked out a colorful hanging basket of mixed flowers with the one daughter Jackie sent me. Doug treated me to pizza that evening at the Brew Haus in Joseph.

May 14—The temperature dipped to 32 degrees and a light frost covered Prairie Creek.

May 15—The mercury rose to 79 degrees, and the frantic growth continued.

This afternoon a friend and I hunted for morels in the woods, and came home with bags full of tasty mushrooms. It was very pleasant wandering around in the coolness of the forest, especially when we could see heat waves rising from the valley below. Among the morels bloomed the pink orchid-like calypsos, and yellow and blue wood's violets.

This evening Doug and I invited Maurice to supper, and I sauteed those morels in garlic butter and served them with juicy pan-broiled rib steaks—Wallowa County beef. It just don't get any better than that.

May 16—Drove into the new hospital to visit our old friend Wilmer Cook, who was suffering a bout of pneumonia. Wilmer, the champion checkerboard maker—and player—is well into his 90s now, and we wish him a safe recovery.

Wilmer told me stories about when he was a young lad living in a tent, out north, in the winter time for six weeks, cutting saw logs with a crosscut saw. He said he and his crew stayed warm because they had a Duckett stove.

May 17—The temps rose into the 70s again as I drove out the north highway to visit my poet friend Cathy, who lives near Flora. I love this drive in the spring. Krebs' sheep grazed the long open meadows, the sheepherders' wagons parked on the hill. The mule ears bloomed golden and the purple-blue haze of camas filled the boggy areas. Then there were those pale green leaves on the trembling aspen, and wild ducks with their young swimming in the stock ponds, all lit by the snowy Wallowas rising to the south.

I pulled in and parked at the Joseph Creek Canyon view point to stare down at the miles of silent draws and ridges, where I imagined the shadowy ghosts of the Nez Perce who once inhabited this land, their ancestral home. The overlook is now an interpretive site, where one can glimpse a spectacular canyon as well as learning a bit of Nez Perce history.

The ghost town of Flora is sparsely inhabited by people, but heavily populated with narcissus that have over the years run riotous among the long-vacated, weathered buildings. It is a lovely sight. For miles around the settlement, north end farmers' fields were sprouting acres and acres of grain, and mule deer bounded across the road or shaded up under ponderosa pines.

After I parked beside a fragrant hedge of lilacs, Cathy came out to meet me, and shortly we were walking up the road. Back in her homey house she served up a kettle of potato soup. All manner of shrubs and trees were blooming in her yard, and two roto-tilled gardens waited to be planted.

As a reward for helping tie up her raspberry canes, Cathy treated me to strawberry shortcake, made with frozen strawberries from her garden.

May 19—I drove out the Zumwalt Road to the Nature Conservancy where, like last year, I had been invited to participate in the preparing of traditional foods for a group that was touring the outback of Wallowa County. My part was to demonstrate hand-cranked ice cream and provide a dutch oven in which to bake an applesauce cake. All went well, and thanks to cook Beth Gibans, the food was delicious.

After making my way out the bumpy road to the Summer House, a set of buildings and barn tucked into a draw at the head of Camp Creek, I took a hike up a nearby hill to view the surrounding country. On top I found myself in a saddle smothered in wildflowers: mule ears, prairie smoke, lupine, pink phlox, and others I couldn't identify. To the south rose the three buttes: Harsin, Findley and Brumback.

Returning from my hike I layered ice and salt in the wooden tub of my ice cream maker and began to crank away. A gal named Penny relieved me, and soon we had a can of smooth, rich, custard ice cream. After draining off the salt water, removing the dasher, and sampling the ice cream, I packed the can in ice. Beth's menu included local beef kabobs, marinated with bell peppers and onions; homemade whole wheat rolls, salad and spelt. Ice cream and cake for dessert. Those visitors to Wallowa County were not only impressed with the country, but with the food.

After an evening of storytelling, I threw my foam pad and sleeping bag down on the floor of a "work-in-progress" building and promptly fell asleep.

Looking up the Imnaha canyon, as seen from Buckhorn Lookout.

Jan Hohmann explains how the Nez Perce peeled away the cambium layer more than 100 years ago on these Ponderosa pines.

Arising early this morning I prepared sourdough hotcakes using the starter I'd brought along and mixed up in a big bowl the night before. Those flap jacks disappeared almost immediately as I flipped them off the cast-iron griddle.

After reading several stories of early settlement in and around the Buttes, I was on my way back to the ranch. A cold rain had begun to fall and, by the time I reached home, the fire Doug had burning in the old Monarch was very welcome.

May 22—Fragments of blue sky are beginning to appear after three cloudy days in a row. And, even as the soft rain continues to fall, rays of sunlight intensify the brilliant greens on Prairie Creek. The seed peas planted on the hill have sprouted, as well as the canola crop that was "no-till-drilled" in the lower field.

Ken hauled his replacement heifers over last week, and they are belly-deep in grass. In Doug's garden the radishes and lettuce are up, and I've baked two rhubarb pies. The snowy blossoms on the apple, plum and cherry trees match that new white stuff on the mountains.

And now, as I write, it's hailing on my transplanted petunias, pinging off the windows, and littering the lawn with ice.

May 23—I've just returned from playing Scrabble all morning outside on Christine's sunny deck that juts out above Wallowa Lake. Christine beat us again. This little lady used to play Scrabble in Alaska, where she lived while she taught school in an Eskimo village. She says her place used to be called the "house of words." A very popular hangout for the villagers who played the long winter hours away.

May 23—A heavy frost blackened my newly transplanted tomato, basil and marigold plants. After having replaced them, there appears to be new life emerging from the damaged plants.

May 24—This morning Phyllis and I climbed aboard the Community Connection bus in Enterprise and joined a daylong tour of Wallowa County's outback. Traveling out the Zumwalt Road, we gazed at acres and acres of bunch grass interspersed with wildflowers, stock ponds, and old homesteads, nestled in draws or anywhere there was a spring. Suddenly a white-tail doe and her tiny fawn appeared out the window. The little fellow, only hours old, bravely wobbled after mom.

After we entered the timber we passed the old Steen ranch alongside Chesnimnus Creek, and past Thomason Meadows we turned onto a narrow road that took us to one of the old Indian village sites. Here, tour guide Jan Hohmann led us on a short hike through a grove of ponderosa pines, several of which had the inner layer (cambium) peeled away years ago. These trees provide a living record of the Nez Perce who used this area as a spring camp.

According to Hohmann, this spot provided a welcome change from living all winter in the Nez Perce pit houses located in the canyons. While camped here they harvested the camas roots, hunted game, and competed in horse races. In the dampened meadows camas bloomed just as it did when the Indians camped there.

It was noon when we rattled up the winding road to Buckhorn Lookout. Indian paint brush, lupine, mule ears and pink phlox bloomed beyond a split rail fence that had been built just down slope from one of the most stunning views in the West. Far below flowed the Imnaha River in its canyon, flanked by side canyons like Horse Creek and Cow Creek. Dinosaur ridges rolled on into infinity, and to the east rose the Seven Devils. Beyond the Snake River divide, the north-flowing Snake creates the wild boundary between Oregon and Idaho.

I was thrilled to see a blue bird perched in the lookout. It was like a flutter of blue sky was trapped behind the glass. After I opened the door, it flew out. Several of us ate our sack lunches in there while gaping at the scenery. Then back to Enterprise by way of Coyote Campground, Red Hill Lookout, and the head of Joseph Creek; onto the Cow Creek Road, up Elk Creek to the Charolais Road, thence to the north highway and back to Enterprise. A huge circle.

The perfect day, with lovely clouds and blue skies, had provided endless photo opportunities.

May 26—We thought of Mary Marks, who would have celebrated her 90th birthday. I rode out to La Grande with Doug that day to purchase sprinkler parts, and we stopped at the Little Bear Drive-In near Wallowa on the way home for one of their famous hamburgers and milk shakes.

May 27—Doug hauled stock salt to the hills and checked the cattle.

On my daily walks I see the canola and peas are growing well in those fields that used to grow hay. Memorial Day continued to maintain its cold weather tradition. The temps dipped below freezing again.

We were invited to a branding at the Triple Creek Ranch that Monday. The cold wind didn't seem to deter the cowboys and cowgirls, who branded 100 calves before the generous hosts provided a most tasty meal served outside on picnic tables. Not your ordinary branding fare, we were served King Crab legs drenched in garlic butter, filet of mignon grilled to perfection, beans, salads, and desserts.

There's nothing like seeing working cowboys enjoy their food. What a treat. Sons Ken and Todd and grandsons Buck and James did justice to those crab legs.

May 29—Doug hitched our boat to the pickup and we drove to Wallowa Lake to troll for kokanee, those tasty, silvery, land-locked salmon. Doug caught two really nice ones, while I lost several but managed to land two pan-sized beauties.

Aside from the fishing it's just plain pleasant to be out on the serene lake, listening to the rippling water slap the side of the boat, while watching the nearly full "once in a Blue Moon" rise at dusk over the east moraine. Catching fish is a bonus.

I can't wait to fry kokanee rolled in flour and cornmeal for breakfast tomorrow morning.

Last week I watched baby Lucy for a couple of hours while her mommy attended a meeting. Everything was going well and we were watching the border collie puppies play when, suddenly, Lucy realized her mommy was gone. She wasn't happy. Luckily for both of us, she fell asleep in my arms before mom returned.

After my weekly writers' group met last Tuesday, Phyllis and I drove out the north highway to look for mushrooms. Phyllis only found three, but we did encounter a cow elk crashing through the timber. We guessed she had a calf somewhere.

On Wednesday our writers' group met at Christine's cabin on the west side of the lake to play Scrabble on her sunny deck. Christine tells us an osprey has made a nest south of there, and she has observed at least two chicks. After eating our brown bag lunches we tackled another game.

June 2—Doug and I attended Sharon's 70th birthday bash at the United Methodist Church Camp at Wallowa Lake. Let me tell you, that family of hers knows how to put on a party. There was live music by "Soul Renovation," Hawaiian leis to wear around our necks, and photos taken of all those in attendance, printed out by son Steve, pasted on a card with something we'd written, and placed in a scrapbook for Sharon.

There was Shannon, Sharon's famous chef daughter, all the way up from Southern California, who, with help from other family members, prepared a feast that included appetizers of shrimp, beef and lox, followed by grilled chicken, pork ribs, salads, and beans.

Dione Vali baked two special cakes and decorated with whipped cream flowers. All in all, an enjoyable evening for the 70 in attendance.

Although temperatures had soared close to 80 that day, it was pleasantly cool under the pines.

The calendar just keeps filling up. We have a Friends of the Museum pie sale during the vintage car show in Joseph this weekend, for starters. Now a wonderful rain is falling as I wind up this column. Son Ken jut stopped by to check his heifers and reports the hills are receiving a good soaking as well.

June 4—Just in the past hour our weather has changed from very hot to very pleasant. Having such hot weather this early in the season has caused frantic growth to anything that was irrigated, and drained energy from those of us who do the watering. Thunder heads boiled up in those wide prairie skies as I headed north yesterday afternoon on the Zumwalt Road. Wildflowers, past their peak now, appeared wilted, yet still colored the hills with yellow and blue.

It was nearly 4:30 when I pulled into the Summer House of the Nature Conservancy to participate in another one of those tours. After repeating my hand-cranked ice cream, Dutch oven, sourdough thing, I told several stories around the campfire before driving those long miles home in the dark.

Among the highlights of my evening were visiting with a young man from Scotland and a young lady from Ireland, both serving as volunteers for the Nature Conservancy this summer.

A thunder shower of short duration freshened things and moved on north before the Beth's meal was served outside on picnic tables. The menu included fajitas, made with Wallowa County beef grilled on the barbecue along with peppers and onions. For dessert, we enjoyed a rhubarb/peach cobbler baked in the Dutch oven and hand-cranked ice cream that required several hands to crank.

Since Doug finally got the sprinkler system going things have greened up considerably. It is comforting to hear the steady *swish, swish* of those long jets of precious water as they irrigate the raspberries, garden, and portions of the lawn. Our recent warm nights, aided by the "Blue Moon," really brought up the garden. Potatoes, peas, carrots, beets and corn are all pushing through the soil.

Our book group is reading Ivan Doig's *The Whistling Season* this month, which I highly recommend if you enjoy reading about one-room country schools. Fans of Jane Kirkpatrick will be happy to hear she has another book out, *A Tendering in the Storm*. This is a novel based on a true story about a woman who finds herself alone and pregnant with her third child. It is set in a remote coastal forest of Washington Territory.

Gregario Cortaberria shears a Suffolk ewe in just three minutes.

June 6—I whipped up a platter of deviled eggs and headed over to Mary Lou Brink's for our annual CowBelle reunion. Shopped at the museum on the way to pick up the old CowBelle scrapbooks, so we could all look at our younger selves doing all those things we used to do. In spite of the years since then, we patted ourselves on the backs for the way we looked.

Survivors we were. Survivors of the changing face of our rural way of life. Leafing through the pages of those years, we could see the changes. Where today large land owners have purchased many of our smaller ranches, there used to be family farms, where we didn't really make much of a profit but continued to live a lifestyle that was very rewarding.

So many changes. Today huge homes or remodeled homes are being built where modest homes used to suffice. However, times change and we must change with them, and often times these newcomers employ our young people, who grew up here, know the country, understand the cattle business and have the skills needed to run a ranch. So not all changes are negative.

It was fun seeing these women again, these women who remember being CowBelles, not CattleWomen; these women who are living proof that eating BEEF is good for you.

Doug burst through the kitchen door. "Put the water on to boil." Oh, oh, another hen flew the coop! So...there I was, after dark, snatching the offender off the roost, and clipping her wings.

June 9—There we Friends of the Museum pie bakers were again, selling our homemade pies on Joseph's main street during the Wallowa Mountain Cruise, a vintage car show. Long tables bore huckleberry, raspberry, lemon, chocolate cream, rhubarb, apple, and raisin cream pies. Yum! Ann and I were sold out by 1:30.

I didn't make it to the pie sale with one of my pies, as Doug purchased it for $20 before it left the kitchen.

This evening Doug and I drove to Cloverleaf Hall where we feasted on a barbecued pork dinner prepared by the Wallowa County Fair Board crew, and then retired to enjoy an evening of fiddle tunes performed by the Blue Mountain Old Time Fiddlers.

That program was a memorial for Charley Trump, the beloved organizer of this event. Charley's wife Nancy carried on as before and the place was packed. I'm sure everyone there felt old Charley's presence, as well as long-time-gone fiddler like Spencer Bacon, who lived way out on Lost Prairie. Spencer's grandson Allan is holding on to his grandpa's tradition, however, and making his fiddle sing. Old folks hobbled to their feet and danced the night away, putting us all to shame.

June 10—We had a long, soaking, warm rain. Fat night crawlers wiggled on top of the ground, and the hills took on a brighter shade of green. Tucker's Mare, the snow shape of a horse on the mountain south of here, has all melted, and the high alpine meadows greened in the rain.

After the rain, the valley was, as my poet friend Amy described it, achingly beautiful.

June 11—I drove out the north highway to deliver two of my setting hens to daughter-in-law Amy. My car radio was tuned to NPR's classical music, which seemed to calm my hens, who clucked contentedly in concert to the violins. Great-grandchildren Ronan, Gwenllian, and Kennon were thrilled with the chickens, and I placed several fertile eggs under the hens.

Home to bake two long loaves of french bread to go with the beef/veggie soup simmering for supper.

On my evening stroll down Tenderfoot Valley Road, I met Larry and Juanita Waters riding their mule and horse. We stopped to chat and remarked how blessed we are to live in this gorgeous place.

June 13—Our writers' group met here at the ranch, and I fed them whole wheat pita pockets stuffed with roasted peppers, feta cheese tomatoes, and spinach sauteed in olive oil. After which we played scrabble. Sharon won…and won. Doug fled to the hills to put out salt for the cattle.

June 14—I planted the Slope garden. Since son Todd had it all tilled, how could I resist? Now sweet corn, beans, and tomatoes are coming up.

This evening, after a Fishtrap Board meeting in Enterprise, I drug a lawn chair in front of the gazebo on the courthouse lawn and, like everyone else, nibbled fresh strawberries and succulent sugar peas from the Farmer's Market while listening to fine blue grass music. These concerts are staged every Thursday evening and provide a place to relax and enjoy fine music.

June 15—Doug and I headed over the Blues to Pendleton to take in granddaughter Lacey's nurses' pinning ceremony. Since I'd never taken the old Emigrant Road that dives off at the top of Cabbage Hill, we decided to take that route. Not a single rig did we see until we arrived at Mission. Lovely views in all directions, and despite the sharp curves, I found it much more relaxing than the freeway.

Since the ceremony didn't begin until 2, we lunched at the Great Pacific and enjoyed tasty sandwiches before making our way to the ceremony. We are very proud of our Lacey, who studied long and hard to achieve her nurse's certificate from Blue Mountain College. Now we have two nurses in the family.

June 16—Dave Kasahan showed up to install the dark green shutters next to the windows on our house. Sure do make a difference.

This afternoon Phyllis and I hiked up Hurricane Creek to Deadman Falls. June is the perfect month to visit this area; wildflowers, plenty of rushing snow melt water tumbling down the creek, and wild water falls at every turn. No dust, no insects, fresh air, warm sun, and all that wilderness, practically in Phyllis' back yard.

June 17—Today was Father's Day, and our 29th wedding anniversary. Daughter Ramona and her husband, Charley, treated us to breakfast at the Mountainaire Cafe in Joseph, which was nice of them, as they departed that afternoon for California to travel to Lodi to watch great-grandsons Clayton and Cole show the 4-H steers they purchased from Papa Charley.

June 18—I arose early and baked a spinach/ham quiche to take to our monthly Readers Group, which met at Phyllis' after a brunch. From Phyllis' living room you can look right out at Sacajawea Mountain. Ivan Doig's *Whistling Season* stimulated a lively discussion.

Then it was home to clean house, and put a marinated pork tenderloin in the oven. My childhood chum Sandra and her hubby, Fred, were due late this afternoon. What fun to see them, and taste the fresh cherries, peaches and apricots they brought from a Farmer's Market in California.

June 19—Up early to deal with those ripe peaches. The ripest went into a cobbler and the remainder were frozen for future cobblers. Is there anything better than warm peach cobbler made from sweet peaches?

On the way to our Writer's Group later this morning, we stopped in to see granddaughter-in-law Chelsea and wee Lucy. When we drove into the ranch, there was mama mowing the lawn with bright-eyed Lucy in a pack on mom's back. Of course great-grandma had to snap a photo.

The reason I mention this is because Lucy has a grandma in McCall, Idaho, who reads Agri-Times, and if I don't say something about Lucy, well, she lets me know about it.

At noon Sandra and I, joined by Doug and Fred, were up at the Forest Service Visitor's Center watching grandson James rappel out of a helicopter as part of his ongoing training for fire fighting. James' dad, Todd, was there too. Made my stomach lurch when he stepped out beneath those whirling blades and shimmied down that dangling rope to the ground.

James seems to have an amiable crew who work hard to man the initial attacks, sometimes in remote areas, where they must hike out, mostly over rough terrain for many wilderness miles.

June 20—I wanted to show Sandra the Hurricane Creek Trail, so we picked up Phyllis and repeated our hike. Sandra wasn't so sure if she wanted to continue after we crossed rushing Falls Creek on two narrow logs, but we assured her there wouldn't be any more such crossings. We ate our lunches while seated on a log that afforded a view of Deadman Falls.

On the way home we stopped at the Hurricane Creek home of Anne and Jim Shelly, who operate Fire Works Pottery in a shop next to their house. Anne told us she had just seen a very healthy bear run through their yard, followed by a lazuli bunting.

This talented pair create their own original pottery and have recently opened a display room. Jim was working on a frog that sat on a lily pad. The frog was a flower holder. Of course, I had to have it. Sandra selected a rose vase.

This evening we joined Fred and Doug in the boat on Wallowa Lake kokanee fishing, and tomorrow we'll have a fish fry.

June 21—The summer solstice. Doug and Fred drove to the hills to move cattle, while Sandra and I walked the streets of Joseph and "did" the shops and lunched at Calderas.

Later in the afternoon we were on the courthouse lawn listening to "The Duelin' Sopranos." Another very relaxing musical interlude, and a good way to end the first day of summer.

June 22—Doug started up the sprinklers again, and Sandra and I packed a picnic and headed for the lake, where we parked and walked across the bridge to the Methodist Camp, then down along the river and back in a big circle, like tourists. We ate our lunch in a sunny clearing near a campfire ring.

This evening we had reservations at the Wallowa Lake Lodge to celebrate our anniversary: prime rib and all the trimmings, and Gail Swart at the piano. It just don't get any better than that.

June 23—Missing my friends after they left this morning, I was cheered by a phone call from granddaughter Adele, who came out for lunch and a visit. Miss Adele tells me she's working for the Forest Service trail crew this summer.

"I get to clean trails, see the Wallowas, and get paid for it," she says. Adele began college in Wyoming and transferred to Blue Mountain, where she is majoring in agri-business management. She says she's getting in a lot of roping practice this summer too, in addition to learning to pack mules. Oh, to be younger!

June 24—Yesterday was grandson James' 21st birthday. Hope my boy had a good one out in fire camp. His present from me: a certificate for a pie of his choice.

Since June has five Fridays it's been awhile since I've sat myself down to write a column. Consequently there's been a heap o' livin' goin' on 'around here to record. June is "Bustin' Out All Over," just like the words in a song.

One of our former cow pastures/hay meadows is glowing gold with blooming canola, and the calving pasture provides a contrast as large bales of fragrant hay repose in long rows. On the hill, tender green seed peas are sending out their tendrils and beginning to flower. Fledgling hawks perch on the edge of stick nests high in the cottonwoods, white-tail fawns hide in the tall grass in Locke's field, and the air is saturated with clover blossom and wild rose scent; we are living on a diet of spinach, lettuce, radishes and onions from the garden, served with beef of course, and every old kettle or pot holds blooming flowers in our yard.

Hanging baskets of lobelia and petunias are suspended from the clothesline poles, and the wildflower patch reverted to pink phlox this year, sprinkled with red poppies. The raspberries and strawberries are dangerously close to bearing fruit, and the first company of the summer just departed yesterday morning.

After Doug and I enjoyed breakfast at the Cheyenne Cafe this morning, I took leave of the "locals only" table and walked out of Joseph, turned east on Walker Lane, and was nearly home when Doug picked me up. A lovely cool morning to walk off biscuits and gray.

Must get this in the mail and hang sheets on the line.

June 26—The temps dipped into the low 30s but our gardens were spared. I packed a lunch for Doug and old cowboy Dick Hammond before they hauled their saddle horses out to Salmon Creek to move Scott and Kelly's cattle into another pasture. After supper I struck off toward Hough's hill and walked along the irrigation ditch.

Pausing midway to rest, I was startled by a *whomp* and a splash. Apparently I'd surprised a large muskrat. The animal reminded me of a beaver. Further along I heard a loud alarmed call coming from a great blue heron, which flapped its large wings and flew off to the pasture below. Hough's Angus cows and calves stared at me as blackbirds pecked around their feet. Mallard ducklings babbled and splashed among the reeds, and overhead, a red-tail hawk screamed.

As the sun dipped over Chief Joseph Mountain, a welcome coolness spread across the land and the wild roses, lining the lane, gave off their delicate scent.

June 27—I baked an "If you don't have enough limes" key lime pie. Obviously, I didn't have enough, so I substituted orange and lemon juice to fill my 3/4 cup. Delicious.

While the pie chilled, Phyllis and I hiked the West Fork of the Wallowa River trail up to within a mile of the Ice Lake cutoff. It was a lovely morning, and we encountered wild orchids, trailing vines of orange honeysuckle, clematis, and the orange blossom-scented syringa.

The trail followed the rushing whitewater of the river that flowed into blue green pools edged in snowmelt froth. Wild thimbleberry, raspberry, and huckleberry brushed against us as we wound through damp sections of the trail. Several waterfalls tumbled down rocky chutes, draining the Eagle Cap Wilderness.

After breaking out our brown bag lunches, we ate seated on a log alongside the trail and the afternoon warmed considerably. Returning, we hiked past enormous rock slides that breathed the coolness captured during our cold spell.

Returning to our car parked at the trailhead near Wallowa Lake, we drove to Mad Mary's in Joseph and ordered chocolate sodas.

June 28—I draped netting over the pie cherry tree son Todd gave me for Mother's Day several years ago. Don't want those birds robbing my pie.

This evening, seated in a lawn chair, I nibbled Rainier cherries and golden ripe apricots purchased at the Farmer's Market on the court-house lawn, whilst listening to Joe Schlick and Janice Carper sing songs they'd composed themselves. There they were, strumming their guitars and singing in the gazebo while families gathered on blankets and pic-nicked, and children played hide and seek. Another wonderful evening in Paradise.

Taking a break from gardening and watering, I hiked around the old ranch, which is quite diversified these days. Fields of peas, grain, canola, hay, and even a pasture full of grazing cattle fill every acre of what used to be hay and irrigated pasture.

June 29—Former CowBelle Maxine Kooch and I served at the Wal-lowa County Dining Center, volunteering for the CattleWomen. It was the June birthday meal. I wore my "Beef. It's what's for dinner" apron, but they served chicken! Always good to see the smiling faces of folks like Wilmer Cook and Hope and Harold McLaughlin. Sorry to hear about Ken Kooch's broken hip.

June 30—Saturday; the last day of June. I looked at my calendar and realized it was the morning of the Lostine River run/walk. So there I was, pinning on my number and boarding the bus, along with the other 5 K runners and walkers, to be transported up the Lostine River canyon.

It couldn't have been a lovelier morning, with a cool breeze to fan us as we made our way along the three-mile course back to the old Lostine school. Sharon and I were the only 70+ participants in the race. So, after Gerald Perren fired the gun, we were off… and quite suddenly alone.

The younger generation had fled. Even the walkers were race walk-ing. Gradually I left Sharon behind, and eventually really was alone. No matter; the coolness gave me a new burst of speed and I finished in 45 minutes, which gave me an average 15 minute mile. I felt great, and could have walked another three miles.

Ken's replacement heifers appear to be bred, looking sleek and sassy and up to their ears in feed. They keep our small acreage grazed down. Doug has finished the second round of pipe setting. At age 75 he is glad not to have all that irrigation to contend with.

Sharon, who walked in crocs, came in later, a really game gal. Phyllis and Kathy appeared, leading "Choco", Kathy's large Lab, who was wearing a backpack. We strolled down Lostine's Main Street and visited the booths of the annual flea market, seeking food. Kathy purchased Walla Walla onions and divided them between "Choco's" pack pockets. Our noses led us to a foot-long hot dog stand and I ordered one with all the trimmings, washed down with real hand-squeezed lemonade.

Then it was back to the ranch to nap and pick lettuce, onions, and radishes from the garden, and build a salad to take to Bernice's barbecue on upper Prairie Creek. And what a party, to celebrate all those over 60.

Bernice's place commands a view of Prairie Creek that extends to the Buttes and the hills beyond. A little creek splashes past the lawn, where we reposed in lawn chairs, listening to live music on the porch and enjoying the smell of barbecued beef ribs drifting in the evening air.

We visited with, and met, several new neighbors, of whom there are many lately. Meeting in that place reminded me of all the great times we had in the past at our friends Pat and Linde's, who built a lovely log home across the road from Bernice.

July 1—Doug and I fortified ourselves with ham and eggs at the Cheyenne Cafe, which was a good thing because Dick, Doug and I drove 25 miles out to the hills to put Scott's cattle back in a pasture they had broken out of.

Probably one of the bulls got to fightin' and knocked down the fence. Luckily, they were only scattered up and down the lane near Salmon Creek, and hadn't wandered too far. The cattle are sleek and fat, and the feed looks good. Appears there was more rain out there than here in the valley.

My friend Kathy decided she didn't want my little rooster "Larry" anymore, so I turned him in with my hens and "Fred." Well, let me tell you, those two really went at it. The testosterone flew in all directions and both roosters were pretty bloody, until one of my big white hens grabbed Larry by the comb and drug him off. This morning the two cocks are pretty subdued and not nearly as robust as they were.

A field of canola in full bloom on Upper Prairie Creek adds a splash of color.

Sally Seymour of Wallowa at the rains is joined by Bernice Bernatot of Joseph for a ride along the county road near Joseph in a gas-saving rig.

Six-month-old Lucy Lee Matthews helps her mom, Chelsea, with chores.

July 2—All of Prairie Creek appears to be encased in a giant greenhouse. The temperature is 69, and the skies are cloudy, sultry and cirrus. Hay is either cut and curing, or baled in the field, grain crops are high as a cow's eye, peas are blooming, and the canola field casts a golden glow that can be seen for miles. Mama kitty crawled into the bottom of a rusty barrel by the shop and birthed a litter of kittens that resemble one of Hough's many tomcats. Her grown daughter went into labor last evening, then disappeared in a clump of hollyhocks. This morning I see more of that tom cat's offspring are nursing a proud curled-up mama.

July 6—Doug took off for Hat Point, unloaded his three-wheeler, and drove to Lord Flat, and brought back sweet apricots to can, stir and stew into jam and nectar.

I would have gone with him, but our half of beef arrived that day. This tasty, nutritious Marr Flat Natural Beef delivered by son Todd, who raises it.

July 7—Today was the Tippett Family Reunion held at Wallowa Lake. We were color-coded as to family. We, of the "Jidge" line, wore yellow. Nice and cool under those tall cottonwoods, with a sweet breeze blowing off the lake.

Tables laden with potluck accompanied barbecued hamburgers, family photos were taken, and lots of visiting went on into the late afternoon. Kind'a nice to take a break from summer and relax.

July 8—I met up with my "Syringa Sisters" at the United Methodist Camp at the lake, where the 20th annual Fishtrap Writer's conference was being held. As in the past, we stayed in one of the yurts, pretty modern ones that boast a shower, bunk beds, sheets and mattresses.

For a whole week we—Jessica, Bobbie, Mary, Barb and I—will be together. This is the 11th anniversary of our meeting in Bob Pyle's workshop, and Bob Pyle is back, so we all enrolled in his class again.

July 9—This morning, after a most delicious breakfast served by the staff, we were walking UPHILL to our workshop, held in Bob and wife Thea's cabin in the pines. We hiked a quarter mile every morning for three days. Thea gathered an armload of syringa and placed the orange blossom smelling blooms in a vase on the coffee table, and we were transported back eleven years ago to Bob's class.

Inspired to write, I produced six pieces of writing that included poetry, fiction, short story and nonfiction. What an instructor, and what a deeply-caring person Bob is.

Since Doug took off in his camper for the Steens Mountains, I came back to the ranch every afternoon to tend to chores and watering. Three days whizzed by, and on the last night I joined Jessica on the deck and slept under the stars. Does and spotted fawns wandered about the grounds, and we breathed deeply of the syringa-scented air. The West Fork thundered past and immersed us in the theme of Summer 2007 Fishtrap: "The River Still Runs."

Even though the place was crawling with celebrities—like Bill Kittredge, Kim Stafford, Ursula Le Guin, John Daniel, John Remember, Molly Gloss, and many others—we packed our gear and moved up Hurricane Creek to a secluded campground.

That Wednesday evening was memorable. There we were, right on the banks of the creek, oil cloth on a long picnic table, tents pitched, roasting ears and kokanee over the coals, sitting in our lawn chairs, remembering summers past. We nibbled the traditional rice crispy treats smeared with chocolate I'd made earlier in the week and sipped coffee, building up the fire as we talked late into the night.

I chose to sleep on the ground outside. The night was so mild my arms were flung out of the sleeping bag 'til dawn.

Before 5:00 a.m. the stars winked out, and I was up building fire for breakfast of bacon, eggs, and toast with apricot jam. Barb's coffee woke the others, and our day was under way, a day that included a hike to Fall's Creek falls, a picnic lunch, and—since Phyllis joined us—she invited us to her mountain home for root beer floats afterwards.

This evening we volunteered for kitchen duty at the Fishtrap Camp and stayed for open mic.

Then we returned to Hurricane Creek and slept like kids at summer camp. Slept so hard I missed the thunder and lightning storm that fateful Friday the 13th...a storm that ignited the fire on Cottonwood Creek. A fire that would cause the cancellation of the Asotin Trail Ride and consume acres of former Tippett land. Due to the extreme heat we canceled our overnight backpack, opting to spend the day where it was cooler.

However, the next morning, I rousted the gang out of their sleeping bags by 5:30. We were on the trail to Slick Rock Creek before the sun broke over Chief Joseph Mountain. We were four, as Mary had a date to meet her sisters in Sisters, Oregon. The trail was deliciously cool, and brilliant fire weed brushed against us, as well as alpine forget-me-nots.

Rain from the night before had dampened the trail dust and cooled the forest. We nibbled wild strawberries and gazed at the whitewater tumbling down the creek below the trail.

Before 9:00 we were already where the trail crosses Slick Rock Creek above its confluence with Hurricane Creek, and I couldn't wait to climb a steep side trail to the third level of falls that spill over solid rock to form pools. In anticipation of a bath, I got down on all fours and crawled through Cyanothus brush. Barb and Jessica, who were following behind, quit me at the second level.

"Too scary," they said, and headed toward the second falls. I kept on...and there it was! A natural bath tub. A thin veil of water fell into a turquoise pool, and just big enough to accommodate my bottom was a sculpted seat in the rock, above which hung a scatter of blooming yellow Arnica, gaining sustenance from a tiny clot of earth in the rock face and watered by the misty falls. The water, warmed by the rocks, was wonderful.

After a brief stop to snack on trail mix, we returned to the trail head and drove to Joseph, seated ourselves at an outdoor table, and treated ourselves to delicious sandwiches and ice-cold drinks at Calderas, where we could look up the canyon from whence we'd just returned.

July 23—Doug is picking raspberries. I can see his hat bobbing through the leafy aisles as he patiently picks his way up and down the rows. Luscious red berries glow in the mid-July heat, which shimmers through a smoky haze; Hells Canyon is on fire.

In that searing hot country forming the border between Oregon and Idaho, the Battle Creek Complex includes names like Barton Heights, Lookout Mountain, Himmelwright Springs, and Grizzly Ridge; all places I've been, when wild penstemon still clung to terraced trails. For days we've watched the advance of these fires; sunrises and sunsets are brilliant paintings etched upon smoky skies.

As summer ripens, activity increases. Wrapped around it all is the urgent need to preserve summer's harvest. My kitchen bubbles and boils, sorts and bags. Raspberry and apricot jams, pesto, and pitted pie cherries roll out into the canning cupboard and freezer. Zucchini and yellow summer squash are sauteed with eggs for breakfast, peas are shelled, and new potatoes dug and cooked in a cream sauce. Tender young beets are steamed with their tops, and lettuce is layered in sandwiches and served in salads.

Yesterday I picked the first ripe tomato, and now the strawberries cry for attention. Irrigation is never ending, and all over the valley haying goes on into the night time cool.

August 7—Afternoon clouds boil up for the third day in a row, the wind rises and flings the irrigation sprinkler's water hither and yon...but

Cutter is the 22-month-old son of Rowdy and Kasey Nash of Mt Vernon, Oregon.

it doesn't rain. Mama kitty's surviving calico kitten has grown large enough to crawl out from the back seat of the old Jimmy pickup, where her mother dragged her from the "birthing" barrel.

The deep, blue Delphiniums have spent their color, and now it's the hollyhocks' turn. The faithful petunias bloom on. Myriad hummingbirds buzz around their feeder, competing with yellow jackets to sip the sugary water. Neighbors Sarah and Mike are out picking raspberries. The eighth picking.

My freezer is full, not only of raspberries, but blackberries which my hunter/gatherer husband fetched from Imnaha. He also returned with a small pail of huckleberries, found, he said, in some undisclosed part of the forest. I got in and picked, podded, and froze the peas, pickled the beets, and processed more pesto. Yum!

While the dew was still fresh on the veggies this morning, I arose to cut one of Doug's large cabbages, pluck raspberries, and snip a basket of herbs: parsley, sage, rosemary...and whoops...basil. Didn't have any thyme. Then I selected three nice specimens of marigolds and threw

Tepee on the edge of Joseph Creek Canyon as seen against a smoky sunrise.
Three tepees are available for overnight stays next to the RimRock Inn
restaurant on Highway 3 between Enterprise and Lewiston.

together an arrangement that was supposed to represent the theme of the
fair, "100 Years of Heritage, 1907-2007," which consisted of old-fashioned
hollyhocks stuck in one of my blue enamel coffee pots, surrounded by a
rolling pin, my old dented canning funnel, and a milk strainer. Kind'a
says it all. Except, in 2007, I still use these old kitchen utensils.

The day before, I'd volunteered from 7:30 to 5 in Cloverleaf Hall
accepting, cataloging, clerking for the judge, and placing ribbons on
a record-breaking number of photo entries. In weak moment I'd told
Nancy Carlsen I'd be this year's photography superintendent. Nancy is
a wonder herself. The exhibit hall would never function without her. If
she was willing to do all she does, I could certainly help out.

Only thing was...I wasn't quite renewed from a three-day pack-trip
to Aneroid Lake and, consequently, was pretty pooped and constantly
hungry. You take three aging ladies—73, 71, and 63—one miniature
Mediterranean donkey, one small burro, a half-Arabian mare, a six-
and-three-quarter-mile steep mountain trail, and you have a recipe for

Gideon (with rope) and twin sister Jada ride uncle Todd's horse at the "cowboy party" on Upper Prairie Creek. The four-year-old reside in Nampa, Idaho, and are the grandchildren of Ken and Annie Nash of Enterprise.

adventure. And that's just what Kathy, Phyllis and I had.

Insisting we leave the trailhead before sunup, I organized the expedition to beat the heat. Doug hauled Kathy's burro, Fancy and my mare, Morning Star, to Wallowa Lake, and Fred helped Phyllis with her donkey, Roxy. We said goodbye to the men and took off up the trail.

The initial introduction of my mare to those "other animals" was a bit exciting, but soon wore off. You can imagine how tiny Roxy's pack outfit was! Phyllis had rigged bags, removed from backpacks, to sling over the miniature saw bucks. The bitty donkey was all but covered with her pack, which was secured by myriad buckles, cinches, snaps and straps. Witnessing the packing of such a pack on such a donkey was vastly entertaining, and a feat we would watch over and over, as the pack slid up on her neck or crawled under her belly.

Fancy, on the other hand, now a seasoned pack animal, went up the trail just fine. My mare carried a pair of pack boxes borrowed from son Todd, slung over an old Decker pack saddle Doug found in our bunkhouse. She was great.

All of our food, sleeping bags and personal gear had to be packed in. A crudely-furnished cabin awaited us. Hot pink fireweed, grouse whortleberries, elderberries, Indian paint brush, and mountain bluebells lined the trail. We stopped often to graze on tiny wild raspberries, and to drink from our water bottles. We strode beneath enormous tumbled rock slides and gazed downward at the rushing East Fork of the Wallowa River. We chose a high opening near the trail to munch our sandwiches, and visited two horseback riders on their way to camp.

Everything was going well, and we were huffing and puffing our way up the steep, rocky trail, when we came to the first water. Immediately Roxy climbed the bank, followed by Fancy.

"No way," their body language told us. So...I left my friends and continued onward, to beat that searing high altitude heat. There was nothing I could do, save let my two friends work out their problem. Three more miles to go—straight up.

Several grouse stood curiously in the trail, then flew to a log and watched us pass. Higher and a higher, the steep talus slopes of the Wallowas rose around us. The air was wonderful, the sky was blue, and a blissful breeze wandered up the canyon.

Morning Star and I came to the green, grassy meadows below Roger Lake. The stream was so clear, you could see the golden sand, and count every rock winding its way through an opening in the forest. We paused, and my mare grazed.

Finally we came to Roger Lake, a turquoise jewel glittering through the firs. It was 11:00 o'clock and I was beat. The trail wound up over solid rock, leveled out, and climbed again before Aneroid Lake's cool waters finally beckoned through the trees. I couldn't have taken another step.

I lead my mare into a log corral, tied her to a hitching rack, and greeted Dennis, the new caretaker, who showed me to Silvertip's cabin and helped me with those pack boxes. After tending to my mare, I stretched out on a bunk and relaxed.

An hour later, here came my compadres, their burro and donkey looking fresh, but Phyllis and Kathy a bit beat. We settle in, in Paradise. Pete's Point rises up to our left and a high ridge of basalt rings us in. A splashing stream tumbles down through a cleft in the mountain, and winds through a grassy, wildflower-strewn meadow to the lake. Historic log cabins lay tucked among evergreens, it is peaceful and calm.

The main event that afternoon was a SHOWER. Yes, a shower. Cleverly constructed of black plastic hose coiled around on a sheet of black plastic and exposed to full sun, leading to a shower head enclosed in a wooden shower stall, with a cement floor and sky for a ceiling... and a dressing room... with a mirror! After long naps on the old ornate metal beds, with mattresses, in the upstairs sleeping loft gained by a series of cut log steps, we were refreshed enough for a stroll across log bridges to the lake.

Phyllis borrowed oars from Dennis and paddled out on the lake to hook us some fish for supper. Except the fish weren't biting, so we sat ourselves down at the log picnic table and ate sardine sandwiches, nibbling on cucumbers with mountain bread and Kathy's healthy cookies. We brewed water for tea and turned in early, leaving the door wide open

I awoke in the night to see our basin flooded by the light of an August moon. Lying in bed I could stare up at Pete's Point and a rock formation that resembles the Madonna and Child.

The next morning dawns bright, clear and deliciously cool. We spend the day reading, relaxing, feeding our pack animals, hiking to the lake, and eating. That night for supper, I fire up the old rusted wood cook stove that sits outside on a rock patio. After sauteeing onions, I brown turkey sausage and heat up chili beans, while Phyllis and Kathy slice tomatoes and cucumbers, grate cheese, and set the ancient log table.

We invite Dennis, who appears with cherries and orange slices, packed in by mules. We feast.

"Too bad we didn't bring stuff for s'mores," says Phyllis, whereupon Dennis vanishes, reappearing with graham crackers, marshmallows, and chocolate bars, plus sticks for roasting marshmallows. Using the coals in the stove, we savor our childhood treats.

Saturday morning we're up early, packing those animals again. More rodeos. Kathy takes off first, and we space ourselves due to the dusty trails. Halfway down, I lead my mare off the trail to allow two riders and nine pack mules to plod past. Below Roger Lake, Phyllis and I pause at the meadow to snap photos. Farther down the trail, Roxy's outfit slips down around her neck and Phyllis has to tie her to a tree and begin all over again.

Far below in the valley, we spot Wallowa Lake, notice a smoky haze, and bid goodbye to the cobalt blue of our mountain air. Phyllis has developed a sore toe, so drops back. The dust is so powdery, I take the lead.

Arriving at the trailhead I locate Kathy and tie up my mare to wait for Doug, who will appear at 2:00. Phyllis comes dragging in an hour later, a bit worse for wear. Fred is there to help her, however, and they leave together. Doug helps Kathy and me load up, and we head to Russell's for a hamburger and iced tea, one more adventure to put away in the old memory bank.

I was so caked with dust and mud, our shower drain nearly plugged up. However, after a few days, I'm ready to go again.

Chief Joseph Days is history and we have our town back again... almost, as it's still the peak of tourist season. I attended three performances of the rodeo, which were great. Sitting there under our Wallowas, watching the wild cow milking as grandson Buck missed his loop, a nearly full "Fire Moon" rose over Hells Canyon and the last helicopter of the evening whirled overhead, carrying its swaying bucket of water.

I turned to Miss Rodeo Colorado—Amy Jo Fields—and commented how great it all was. This gorgeous miss agreed. Amy Jo had earlier, riding son Todd's mare, participated in the Grand Entry. She is the niece of Todd's wife, Angie, and was quite taken with Wallowa County.

We took in Saturday's Grand Parade, and while Doug visited his cussin' cousins, I took my salad over to the Nez Perce Friendship Feast. This was truly a feast, a repeat of last week's Pow Wow in Wallowa. Due to the extreme heat, I headed back to the ranch before the dancing began.

The next morning Doug and I drove into the cowboy breakfast, where I downed a grilled steak while Doug ate ham, eggs and hotcakes. Here, we visited with the Tippett clan, who had canceled the Asotin Trail Ride but managed to camp out for Chief Joseph Days.

Doug returned to the ranch, while I ambled over to the grandstands to take in the Sunday cowboy church. "Soul Renovation" belted out wonderful songs, and wee but mighty Lucy, sitting on her great-grandma's lap, sang the loudest.

There is definitely a shift in the season. The days shorten, the evening skies are filled with goose music, the nights are cooler, and I feel like cooking again.

The other evening our friend Maurice came over to pick raspberries, and we invited him to stay for supper. I fixed a pasta dish, sliced tomatoes, opened a jar of pickled beets and we enjoyed the meal out in the yard.

Now it is Fair Time. Doug just returned from town. His huge head of cabbage won best of show! Tonight Richard and Mary Frasch are treating Doug and me to dinner at the Outlaw Restaurant in Joseph.

August 9—I drove to our county fair, and sure enough, there was that purple ribbon, Best of Show, taped to Doug's humongous cabbage.

Janie Tippett and 'Morning Star', left, and Kathy Hunter and 'Fancy' on the trail to Aneroid Lake.

Riding in the Chief Joseph Days Jr Parade was the 2007 court, left to right: Queen Megan Yost, Princess Amber Shear, Miss Rodeo Oregon Jennifer Steffen, and Princess Shay Lyn Massey.

My herb basket won a blue, but my "theme of the fair" and marigolds garnered white ribbons. Such fun.

After joining Doug for one of those famous fair hamburgers, I stopped by the courthouse lawn on the way home to purchase a box of peaches.

August 10—This morning found me in my kitchen canning peaches, making dill pickles, and freezing chard. Simmering the chard broth with every veggie in my garden, I added pasta, chicken broth, bacon and, *voila!*—soup for lunch.

This evening Phyllis and I attended the "Abridged" version of the complete works of Shakespeare, staged at the lake's open air theater. The three actors, all drama students at Eastern Oregon University, put so much energy into their performance I was amazed. A most enjoyable evening. I mean, where else can you attend a Shakespeare play whilst two enormous mule tail bucks graze the stage's back drop?

August 11—The fires continued to burn, but prevailing winds blew their smoke away from our valley. Today, Saturday, was a marathon of activities at the fair. The watermelon seed spitting contest and chicken scramble in the indoor arena competed with the Joseph Jr. Rodeo going on outside in the main arena.

At 2:30 I wandered over to the exhibit building, dismantled the photo exhibit, gathered up that cabbage, salvaged my herbs to dry at home, and returned to join Doug for the Enterprise FFA barbecue and awards program, after which we sat with a large crowd of buyers who'd come to purchase animals in the fat stock auction.

When young Riley Steen walked into the ring with his hog, I noticed tears coursing down his cheeks. Clearly, Riley was not enjoying the prospect of his pet becoming bacon. And since I didn't have any grandkids showing this year... you guessed it. I adopted sad little Riley. Pretty soon I was up to $4.60 per pound. Obviously, math has never been my strong point.

"Turn it," I told the ring man, after he yelled "sold." So, to the tune of $946, I helped Riley, who was still sobbing when he brought me a photo of him showing his hog. After giving Riley a hug, I vowed to do it again. Some of us are soft touches when it comes to weeping little lads.

August 12—Doug and I joined the "locals" table at the Cheyenne Cafe on this Sunday morning. Our town was just emptying of the Big Bronze, Blues and Brews Festival held at the Joseph Park this weekend. What a contrast to our county fair, I thought. A shame more outside folks don't make their way to one of Americana's fading traditions, where agriculture is showcased so well.

Later that afternoon, the Melvilles continued harvesting peas on ground that for years grew meadow hay. A Fall feeling in the air prompted me to put a pork roast in the oven for supper that evening. Also baked a crisp using some of those wonderful transparent apples.

Since my eggplant is bearing so prolifically, I put together a dish of eggplant enchiladas for the freezer. To keep up with the zucchini and yellow crookneck, I've discovered drying slices of them works well for future soups and stews.

While thus occupied in the kitchen, I looked out the window to see Ken's heifers nibbling the tall sunflowers that hang over the garden fence. Enough of that! I shooed them into another pasture. These heifers are so tame, one pretty bovine looked me in the eye and, with a large sunflower leaf protruding from the corner of her mouth, showed me she really enjoyed her treat.

This evening I stepped out on the lawn to observe the Perseids meteor shower, and was rewarded by one so spectacular it left a long trail of star dust in its wake.

August 13—I cleaned three dozen eggs for my regular customer Idella, who bakes bread for the Farmer's Market. Then I got in and baked a cherry pie for son Todd's birthday, using cherries I picked from the tree he gave me for Mother's Day several years ago.

On the subject of raising and eating local foods, I might mention a book I found most educational, *The Omnivore's Dilemma,* by Michael Pollen. In an ideal world, growing and eating locally grown food would work. Unfortunately, our population is so great and there's so much "mega" everything that most folks don't think along those lines. A pity, as it would benefit the soil, our bodies, our minds, and therefore our communities. All tend to nourish each other.

August 14—I hosted the traditional dessert Fishtrap Board meeting. Since our strawberries haven't survived the heat very well, I substituted a rich devils food cake frosted with whipped cream. Owing to the pure mint extract given to me by one of my fans, who owns a mint farm in Summerville, the cake was quite remarkable. Thank you again, Mr. Royes.

Of course there were also the usual blackberry cobbler and blueberry cream pie. Amazing what 16 people can do to such treats.

By afternoon the fires boiled up again in the hot wind, and for miles the high ridge line that separates the Snake from the Imnaha formed a barrier of smoke.

August 15—Up early picking, snipping, and pressure-cooking the first batch of green beans. Finished in time to attend the Museum Board meeting. Enjoyed visiting Jack Harmon, who told me he showed a Jersey heifer at the Wallowa County Fair 75 years ago. Jack, born and raised in the Leap area, said the judge gave him the prize because his heifer was so well-trained.

Stopped by the Slope garden to check my corn, which is as tall as a bull's eye.

Last weekend was the annual Stockgrowers meeting. Held in Clover-leaf Hall, it appeared the ranchers' attendance was lower this year. Perhaps a lot of them were haying—but let me tell you, they were all there that evening for the dinner/dance. Once again Randy Garnett outdid himself on the barbecued beef, while we Stockgrowers' wives furnished the salads.

After the awards we danced, and even a few old codgers got up and shook a leg. Enjoying himself was Lyman Goucher, all the way up from Imnaha, as well as Dick Hammond, and Jack and Marge McClaran.

August 19—It began to rain today. Blessed rain. Nothing refreshes like a few days of moisture. When the clouds lifted, there was a dusting of snow beneath Twin Peaks.

August 20—Our book group met to discuss the book *Water for Elephants* at Fishtrap House. Then it was home again to preserve more of that bountiful garden. Doug, recovering from dental surgery, is looking forward to eating corn on the cob again.

Must finish this column, as will be leaving with Kathy on Monday for a horseback trip into Minam Lodge, which is near Red's Horse Ranch on the Minam River. Been a long time since I've been there.

August 25—This column is dedicated to my sister Kathryn, who is mourning the loss of her daughter Dawn. Dawn passed away this past week and, because I was unable to attend the memorial held yesterday, I've been keeping in touch by phone. My every thought has been with you, sister, and I know your many Oregon relatives hold you dearly in their hearts. My niece wrote wonderful poetry, and her words live on for us to enjoy.

Once again my kitchen reflects the season.

On the table: jars of canned dill pickles, applesauce, and pickled beets; a large pressure cooker; and, of course, my laptop! Rosemary, basil, parsley and dill dry on the old Monarch range, and the newly-dug shallots are spread atop newspapers on the floor. In a large crock, the sauerkraut Doug and I made yesterday begins its fermentation process. Today Doug will pack the crock down to the basement until it's ready to can.

As fall approaches, and the hours of daylight shorten, the mornings are freshened by a welcoming cool that infuses me with enough energy to accomplish most of my day's work during the mornings. As usual, it's been a busy three weeks.

Doug and I so enjoyed our diner date with Richard and Mary, eaten outside on the patio of Joseph's Outlaw Restaurant. After I commented on how the experience put me in mind of what I imagined it would be like to dine in a sidewalk cafe in Europe, Richard put me straight.

"No way," he said. "This is so much better."

Never having been there, nevertheless I looked at our mountains, smelled the fragrant petunias in their hanging baskets, listened to the water fountain, watched visitors stroll past, and suspected he was right.

Just talked to my childhood chum, Sandra, from Auburn, California, who tells me the memorial service for my niece Dawn was one of the nicest she's ever attended. Just wanted to let my sis know I was with her in spirit, and sincerely hope her lovely Dawn's service will provide a bit of solace during this time of great sadness.

August 25—I drove to Imnaha and joined the standing-room-only crowd in the church fellowship hall to honor our friend Doug "Doc" Morgan on his 90th birthday. All ten of Doug and his deceased wife Betty's children were there.

In addition to the hilarious veterinarian jokes told by son Sam, also a vet, other children told about growing up in the huge house that is today called the Enterprise House Bed and Breakfast. It seems the family had a milk cow and drank the whole milk. Once a visitor asked if the milk was pasteurized, to which one of the daughters replied, "Of course! Our cows live in the pasture; they're pasteurized."

You could sure tell Doc is well-loved in our community. Folks came for miles to honor him. Coyotes yammering wake me in the morning and are the last thing I hear at night.

During my evening walks around the ranch, a great blue heron flaps overhead, a trout in its beak. As darkness descends, we listen to the mournful hooting of the barred owls that inhabit the ancient willows. The hills are parched and the muddied ponds continue to shrink; the elk are back, and Scott and Kelly have already weaned their calves.

Doug spends a great deal of time salting, fence repairing and moving cattle from pasture to pasture. Despite the drought, the cattle look good.

*Doug Tippett displays his "best of show" cabbage at the Wallowa County
Fair. The cabbage was grown in his garden on Prairie Creek, east of Joseph.*

August 27—Kathy and I drove to La Grande and treated ourselves
to a gourmet meal at #1 China Buffet before plunging into the Minam
Wilderness. We headed up the long, narrow road to Moss Springs campground south of Cove, where we pitched a tent near the trailhead, shook
out our sleeping bags, and spent the night in peaceful slumber.

The next morning we were up early to "hoof it" down the trail. Plans
to have horses meet us didn't work out, and Kathy had this heavy pack,
which she decided to leave in her car.

Grabbing a toothbrush and other necessaries, I donned a day pack
and, carrying my camera and two jugs of water, led off down the trail to
Red's Horse Ranch on the Minam River. Our destination: The Minam
River Lodge. Since the days are dwindling down, we decided it was time
we visited this magical place before the snow flies.

The morning coolness lasted until we were nearly at the end of our
eight-and-a-half-mile trek. To me it was perfectly delightful. It'd been
years since I'd hiked or ridden this trail, and I was anxious to see it
again. Too dry for huckleberries, the trail was lined with their bushes,

Barbara Warnock of Imnaha stands beside her blue ribbon scarecrow entry at the Wallowa County Fair.

beginning to redden with fall.

Huckleberry Creek splashed into the Little Minam where we nibbled on thimble berries. At the wooden bridge that spans the Little Minam, we paused to rest, and eat a bite of lunch while seated on a sunny rock. On the other side of the bridge was the cut-off to Jim White Ridge, and the trail then took a turn to the left, angling off to follow the ridge to a hog's back from where we could look down on Red's Horse Ranch.

Far below, simmering in the late August heat, were the landing strip, the old barn, the lodge, the cluster of small log cabins, the pond... and so many memories for me. Since Kathy had never been there, I was eager to show her around. We slowly made our way down the dusty switchback trail to the ranch, then turned left at the bottom to follow a shady trail that led to the Minam River Lodge. Only a quarter mile to go.

It was nearly 3 on that warm afternoon when the old barn hove into view, and soon we were hiking uphill to meet Shelly Steen, who showed us to our cabin and fetched us glasses of cold iced tea. Refreshed, we crossed the meadow to the Minam River, just beyond the landing strip, and dove into the clear, cool waters to wash off the trail dust.

Our stay couldn't have been more satisfying. Shelly cooked our meals in the old lodge, and we partook of hot showers, beds with clean sheets, and a lawn swing from which we contemplated the meadow below and absorbed the quiet of the Minam. What a place to read, write, and dream. Mules and horses wandered around, friendly and curious, and we didn't want to leave.

The next morning we hiked over to Red's Horse Ranch, now owned by the U.S. Forest Service, and met the caretakers who showed us around. More memories. I was happy to see the place being taken care of by folks who love being there.

We walked across the new bridge that spans the Minam River where the trail forks. Downriver lies the old town of Minam, while upriver I used to cook for Red's deluxe elk camp at Elk Creek. It is a wild place beyond, where the spawning salmon wiggle their way up feeder streams, and bears and eagles wait to dine on decaying fish.

After our hike back to the lodge, the smells of barbecued pork, beans, rolls, and strawberry shortcake wafted from the kitchen. Shelly runs the Minam Lodge, while husband Shawn flies in and out with supplies and books hunters for their Indian Crossing and Snake River camps. A very busy young couple, whom I admire greatly.

Since Shelly had to take two saddle horses and two pack mules out to Moss Springs the following morning to bring in more guests, we were allowed to ride out... for which we were most grateful, as the trail, mostly downhill coming in, was uphill most of the way out.

We made it without incident to Moss Springs by noon, where we bid Shelly goodbye and headed down the road to Cove and gobbled down hamburgers and huckleberry floats at a tiny eatery.

Just hours after Kathy and I returned home, a lightning storm started a fire near Moss Springs and the campground, as well as the trail to Minam Lodge, was closed for nearly a week.

Darn. We should have stayed another day.

Home to find Doug and Fred had gone on a successful catfishing expedition to Brownlee Dam on Snake River. Expecting to make soup for Doug—as he'd had all his teeth pulled that day—I found a note saying he was in the hills! These old cowboys are either tough or don't have better sense.

September 10—After three mornings in a row with frost nipping the cucumbers, the temperature stands above freezing. However, there is a crispness to the air that lingers into the afternoon, an autumn coolness in the breeze. Our mountains are outlined in smoky blue, due possibly to Montana fires.

Prairie Creek is quiet today. No tractor, baler, and harvester sounds. Hough's second cuttings of hay have been compressed into giant loaves. Butterfield's hay is baled. The canola in the lower field has been harvested, as have the seed peas on the hill. There's still some grain left across the creek, and cattle graze the pasture next to Ben's place. I hear the call of the Canada geese and mourn the loss of our swallows, those small, joyful birds that slice the air with their happiness. They must've fled south already.

The giant sunflowers alongside the garden fence are as radiant as the sun itself, storing up seeds for winter-hungry birds. Doug and I are attempting to keep up with the ripening garden. I canned the sauerkraut last evening, and the seven-day sweet pickles the day before.

There are only three heads of cabbage left. The corn has been husked, eaten and some frozen for winter. One more picking of green beans awaits for the pressure cooker; squash has been dried, or baked into casseroles and frozen; strawberries made into jam, dill stuffed into pickle jars with garlic and cucumbers, eggplant finding its way into soups and sandwiches, bell peppers used daily, and cayenne dried. After the potatoes are dug, the garden will look pretty spent, save for the carrots.

Ken's heifers wait patiently for us to throw corn husks over the fence to them. As usual, every hour of every day has been filled with living. This past weekend we survived Mule Days and our birthdays, which always coincide.

There we were again, in the grand parade, riding in a mule-drawn wagon down main street, seated on bales of straw along with other past grand marshals: Vern Isley, Ben Banks, Lois Blankenship, and Merle Hawkins, while following behind, riding horses and/or mules, were Dick Hammond, Fred Talbot, Marcel Walker and Arnold Schaeffer. I love listening to Merle tell his stories of when he owned the Layover pack outfit up Lostine, and led pack strings into that wild beautiful country above Red's Horse Ranch.

Mule Days staged their Max Walker Cowboy Poetry Gathering in the indoor arena at the fairgrounds Friday evening, where local cowboys and cowgirls stepped up onto a truck bed and recited or read their poems. Interspersed with words was fiddle music performed by various members of our community.

Louie and Marie Gagnon, of Waitsburg, Washington, stand in front of the rustic log cabin that serves as their home while they caretake Red's Horse Ranch, upriver from Minam River Lodge.

It was the grand finale, however, that brought everyone to their feet. The Reddington family from Cove: Mom on guitar, dad on bass fiddle, oldest son on guitar and mandolin, and younger brother and sister on fiddles. Let me tell you, those strings were smokin'... especially during Orange Blossom Special. Mom and dad must be very proud!

This 26th annual Mule Days was a smashing success. The three-day long-eared celebration was packed with events that ranged from wild cow milking, fast-ass express, pancake frying contests, jumping, a Jim Probert pit barbecue, a horse and mule auction, and a quilt show... just for starters.

Mules brayed during the singing of the Star Spangled Banner when Doug and I were in the grand entry. Nothing could have been more appropriate. Mules stole the show all weekend. And the weather was perfect. Better mark your calendars now for next year's Hells Canyon Mule Days, always the next weekend after Labor Day.

Shawn and Shelly Steen, of Joseph, managers of the Minam River Lodge, on a sunny August morning. This rustic lodge is situated along the Minam River in the midst of the Eagle Cap Wilderness, the largest wilderness area in Oregon.

September 11—Our writers' group helped celebrate my 74th birthday with a chocolate cream pie, compliments of Cathy, as well as poems they'd written 'specially for me. Most appreciated.

September 12—Mary Lou Brink hosted the annual get-together of those of us who used to work at the Wallowa Memorial Hospital in the "old days." We all brought finger food and sat outside in the Brinks' lovely yard, the cattle just beyond the fence, those outrageous mountains ever present as we recalled many stories.

Later this afternoon I met with our Fishtrap Board, which served up fresh sourdough apple cake and feted me with more cards. Darn. Just can't forget my birthday.

September 19—The 16th dawned clear and sunny, with a cool breeze rustling the ancient willows. It was nearly noon when I lifted the last pint of green beans from the pressure cooker. Grabbing my backpack I jumped in the pickup and headed for Lostine. Kathy, accompanied by her burro and large lab "Choco," had a two-hour lead on me.

At Lostine I turned up the South Fork and drove 17 miles to the Two Pan trailhead, where I shouldered my pack and took off up the trail to Minam Lake.

My pack was light: sleeping bag, poncho, sleeping pad, two space blankets, toothbrush, pair of socks and underwear, T.P., cup, spoon, a plastic bag of fire starter—pitch, matches, candle, newspaper—along with lip chap, a jacket, two tuna and two PB&J sandwiches, two oranges, two apples, three ginger cookies, tea bags, some squares of mountain bread, and a can of sardines. This would suffice through Saturday morning, when we would head out.

Since Kathy hadn't hiked this trail before, we had agreed to meet at the meadows near the Copper Creek cutoff. The trail was worn, and wound through fir and alder as it followed the West Fork of the Lostine River nearly all the way. Summer wildflowers were spent, but the lovely lavender asters bloomed in damp places. Thankfully, the trail was mostly shady, as it was approaching the heat of day.

I picked up Kathy's tracks and the trail began to climb, steeply in places, and I found myself negotiating narrow, rocky chutes. The altitude affected my breathing, so I had to rest my back against a log to take the weight of the pack off my shoulders.

The country rose above, fall colors contrasting with bleached white talus slopes, shy pikas squeaked at me, pine squirrels chittered as they created piles of cone midden under the pines, large elk tracks entered the trail, and the West Fork of the Lostine tumbled down over rocks and foamed into turquoise pools, so clear I could count the darting trout.

I was quite alone, never met another soul going in. Around 2:45 I arrived at the junction of the Copper Creek trail. The lovely meadow spread out around a meandering stream. There was a tent...Kathy? Then I spied two men.

"Seen anything of a gal with a burrow and a big dog?"

"Went that'a way," said one of the men, pointing in the direction of Copper Creek. Just what I was afraid of: Kathy had taken the wrong trail. What to do? Well, I followed her tracks, which led to a wide creek, without any way to cross other than get wet. So, I took to the meadow and came across two backpackers who said Kathy and her animals were "over there someplace."

I walked on down the meadow and called, then yodeled, until I heard, "Janie, I'm over here." And here she came from under a copse of pines, followed by her burro and dog. I'd never have found her if she hadn't heard me.

The stream was still between us, so I took off my hiking boots and waded across. Seems Kathy had arrived only minutes before, and was surprised to see I'd made such good time. I sat on a grassy bank and ate my tuna sandwich while my feet dried. I'd skipped lunch and was hungry.

We decided to camp here in the meadow, rather than hiking on up to Minam Lake; a good decision, as the next day we found that trail went almost straight up without a break.

Our campsite was lovely, in the large green meadow beside the clear, cold stream, with a rocked fire pit, level spots to sleep, and grass for the burro.

I helped Kathy put up her tent and opted to sleep outside under the stars. It was an easy choice, because "Choco," who loves to swim in the creek and then roll in burro manure and dirt, is a house dog, and would share the tent. No thanks! That left only the burro to deal with, and this time she behaved herself and didn't step on my pony tail.

When the sun disappeared over the western rims, an autumn chill descended on the meadow, so I brought out my trusty fire kit and soon had us a nice warming fire. No fire danger here, as the meadow was damp and green.

After consuming another sandwich and a hot cup of herb tea, I placed my two space blankets on the ground, laid out my pad and sleeping bag, then spread the poncho over all and snuggled into bed, succumbing to the wilderness night…which was so bright with starlight I could see every tree.

At intervals in the night, I detected a shuddering of Kathy's tent: "Choco" shivering. The second night Kathy put her jacket on him. Other than the sound of the burro grazing—*chomp, chomp*—the night was wonderfully quiet.

At first light I was up kindling the fire. "Choco" burst forth from the tent and the day was on its way. A pack string of mules, packing in bow hunters, plodded past on the trail. And a friendly camp doe stomped into HER meadow and raised a hoof to Choco, at which time the burro chased the deer away while Choco fled to the tent.

That morning was cloudy, and we debated whether to head out or hike on up to Minam Lake. The day warmed, so we set off up the trail, Choco and the burro in tow. And I mean, UP. After a mile or so, I told Kathy I would head back to camp. She and her menagerie could proceed to Minam Lake; I'd already been there.

Four miles up and four back made eight miles, and I needed to save my energy to hike out in the morning. It was a good decision. Back in camp, I napped and nibbled a sandwich, throwing my crusts to a friendly Steller's Jay, who provided just the right company.

Kathy and her entourage returned safely with digital photos to prove they'd made it. Choco curled up and slept, and the burro went to grazing.

That evening, around the fire, we finished up most of our food, drank tea, and turned in early. A heavy dew in the night collected on my poncho, and when I moved, water ran down my neck! Luckily, I'd thought to bring a wool cap for my head, and hadn't suffered from the cold.

Much colder the next morning, we made haste to head down the trail. After helping Kathy pack her burro, I took off in the lead, wetting my feet in that stream, which made me walk faster to keep warm. I made it out to the trailhead by 9:00, and waited for Kathy to help her load the burro.

We agreed to meet at the Lostine Tavern for a hamburger. Let me tell you, food never tasted so good, greasy onion rings and all.

I arrived back at the ranch in time for Ron to deliver my three large boxes of tomatoes. Doug, who'd been fishing with Fred on Snake River, had a nice mess offish frozen in the freezer.

September 23—On this autumnal equinox there is the smell of snow in the air. Blue-black clouds, pushed by a north wind, scud across the sky. The few drops of rain that fell last evening were swept away by that wind. Over to the east, where the Horse Creek fire burns, the sky is deep purple. Let's hope it's raining there.

As each day brings us closer to winter, we prepare for the coming cold. Just finished picking the last green cherry tomatoes. After our Imnaha tomatoes are gone, these little ones will continue to ripen in the house.

To escape the frost Doug carted the larger potted tomato plant from the garden to the bunkhouse. Because he arises in the middle of the night to turn on the sprinkler, the garden has been spared. The Northwood maple is brilliant with persimmon-colored leaves, and the high country aspens are yellowing.

Last evening, armed with potluck and various projects, we "Stitch and Bitchers" descended on Leslie's old farm house up the Lostine River canyon. Leslie was just taking country french bread out of the oven when we arrived. My contribution was bruschetta—sliced tomatoes, garlic, basil, sprinkled with sea salt, and drizzled with olive oil, so we heaped the tomato mixture on warm bread. Thanks to my egg customer Idella who gave me the idea.

Seated around an old oak table we celebrated tomatoes: salsa and chips, Leslie's homemade tomato soup, and Lynn's tomato lasagna accompanied by Nancy's tasty coleslaw with crab meat. The potluck gods were good to us: no one brought dessert.

We created a picture of early Wallowa County after retiring to the living room, where we bent to our early-day tasks: Leslie weaving at her loom, Sally and Nancy knitting, Annie winding yarn into a ball, Chris crocheting, Jan embroidering, Lynn felting, and me writing down names, dates and places under the photographs in one of my albums.

Through the window we could see, amid the old apple orchard, the season's wilting flowers, tall golden grasses, and a glorious patch of cosmos glowing pink in the light of a brilliant autumn sunset. Six-year-old Anna sat in her little chair, weaving her "play" needle work, while we talked about putting food by for winter and listened to each other spin tales of our varied summer adventures.

The following days were spent making salsa, canning tomatoes, freezing roasted tomatoes, and canning old-fashioned chile sauce. A mixture of my garden peppers, onions, tomatoes, spices, honey and vinegar that this 150-year-old recipe instructed me to "simmer for days" on the back of the stove. Well...I did simmer it for 48 hours, at which time the sauce was thick and flavorful. We spooned it on beans. Yum.

When I was putting up salsa we experienced another one of those lightning storms, which started more fires over toward the breaks of

Imnaha.

The next day I followed Doug, who was driving our flat bed truck, loaded with the cat, out to Salmon Creek, where he unloaded it before I brought him home. The following day he and son Ken deepened a pond so it would store more water next year. The drought goes on, and the hills are as dry as any old-timers can remember. Luckily most of our ponds are holding their own.

Grandson James called. He was headed back to Montana after a summer of fire fighting. His sister Adele, who has been working on the Forest Service trail crew, also called to visit.

We are waiting for the birth of our 16th great-grandchild, the wheat has been harvested, and the Melvilles have no-till-drilled winter wheat into the pea fields on the hill. The sweet corn in my Slope garden finally ripened and was worth the wait. I put up the LAST jar of dill pickles from the cucumbers in the garden.

The frost finally fixed the plants last night. Time to mail this.

September 24—I enjoyed a visit from granddaughter Adele, who just finished her summer job, working for the Forest Service trail crew. Said she's learned a lot about packing mules and using a crosscut saw. While she told me stories, I fed her bacon and tomato sandwiches.

Watching grandchildren grow is such a joy, although it happens in a heartbeat.

September 25—I babysat great-granddaughter Lucy, as her daddy was leaving to haul in weaned calves from Marr Flat and her mommy works the night shift at the hospital. Chelsea arrived home before Lucy woke up. Not fair.

From their living room window I was treated to a sunrise that tinted Ruby Peak…well, the color of rubies. By 10 a.m. I was sitting around a table in the basement of the Enterprise Library for my weekly Writer's Group, after which I went grocery shopping for cow camp tomorrow.

September 26—Pickup loaded with moveable feast, I headed up Salt Creek Summit and down past Lick Creek, then up the hill to begin the seventeen gravel road miles to cow camp. Trembling aspen thickets glittered gold against an azure sky, cattle grazed the forest clearings or wandered onto the road, and I noticed an occasional grouse hunter's camp tucked away among the pines. Otherwise, I didn't meet a soul…and there wasn't a soul at the cabin. Inside, the place was so clean you could have eaten off the floor, as Mary used to say.

Janie Tippett on the trail to Minam Lake in the Eagle Cap Wilderness. Photo by Kathy Hunter.

Turns out Lyman had been staying with the Warnock boys, 10 miles back at Mahogany Cow Camp, and Joe Warnock had cleaned the cabin.

Frost on the meadow that morning, so the cabin was cold inside. Lucky for me, Joe had thoughtfully laid a fire in the wood stove. All I had to do was light a match. Soon a granite pot of coffee came to a boil, and by the time my stuff was all packed in, Barbara Warnock arrived from Imnaha to help peel the spuds.

After we got everything organized for the meal, the two of us walked the dusty cow path up through the thorn brush thickets, past the spring, to the corrals—new corrals built by the boys to replace the old rotting log ones.

Amid the melee, we recognized Sam Morgan preg-testing the cows, the Fluitt girls—Ryya and Lexi—pushing cattle up the chutes, the Warnock "boys" driving cows in the corrals, Lyman working the chute gate, and the other fellers doing what cowboys have done for years. Everyone had

Sheryl Curtis of the Old World Living Oxen Company curries one of her huge Brown Swiss oxen. Curtis raised this one from a baby calf.

a job.

Earlier, two semi loads of calves had rattled down the road. Through the dust and bawling of mama cows, we hollered to Lyman to ask when they'd be ready to eat.

"Don't know," he said. "Got 100 more cows to preg."

So...like all the years before, we could only guess.

Doug, who'd headed out to Salmon Creek earlier, as Scott was weaning calves, wasn't able to help this year, so Dick Hammond drove our pickup and stock trailer to Marr Flat to help haul heifers.

Aspen fringed the meadow beyond the corrals, and I guess there's no prettier sight in the fall. This is a scene that's repeated all over Eastern Oregon's cattle country.

Barb and I walked back to the cabin, brought chairs out into the warm autumn sunlight, and while she embroidered, I read a book. Later, here came Ryya and Lexi.

"The guys are coming," they shouted. We were ready. Mashed potatoes, gravy, roaster pan full of sliced roast beef, rolls, Imnaha tomatoes and cucumbers, and Barb's blackberry cream and apple pies.

Between mouth fulls, Sam the veterinarian told stories while everyone filled their empty bellies. Dan Baremore parked the last semi-load of calves alongside the road, and joined the crew to eat. We heated water on the stove, did up the dishes, and put the cabin in order. Barb went on ahead so her dust would settle before I took off.

I swung the old pole gate—that Kid Marks built—behind me, and bounced out the rocky road, all the while thinking of our Mary, who so loved this place. For 27 years she and husband Kid spent spring 'til fall here, when they worked for the Marr Flat Grazing Association.

September 27—Doug went out to help Scott preg-test his cows. It was 70 degrees, real Indian summer weather, but unfortunately a dry wind came up in the afternoon, which caused the Cayuse Flat fire to jump the line. Guess a couple of hunters got out just in time. I stayed home and baked a chocolate mint torte to take to a potluck that evening.

September 28—Kathy and I drove to the upper Imnaha to inventory the Fishtrap Writer's Retreat, where we saw lots of wild turkeys and enjoyed the flaming red sumac scattered all over the canyons. After stopping to say hello to Lyman, we drove out on top, and along the Sheep Creek byway we came upon a small bear, seated in an apple tree, gorging himself on fruit.

September 29—Buck deer season opened this morning, and although Doug could have gotten his buck, he was reluctant to pull the trigger. It was cold and damp, and I guess he thought about all the work ahead if he did shoot his deer. So he'll wait a few days and let it warm up before he decides to get one.

Opening morning, as I watched a nice buck through the kitchen window, a skunk ambled into the raspberry patch.

September 30—This morning Doug and I spotted a pair of sand hill cranes on the way into Joseph to breakfast at the Cheyenne Cafe. Prairie Creek skies are full of wild geese and ducks that feed in the stubble fields and hang out in the irrigation ditches. The wind blew furiously today, and our electricity went out.

Phyllis and I braved the cold—it snowed last night—and wandered around Alpenfest at the lake. After treating ourselves to the traditional German sausage and sauerkraut meal, we hiked to the Wallowa River to watch the "red fish" kokanee make their way upstream to spawn.

After, we walked to the old lodge and took in the Nez Perce Art in the Wallowas show. Most impressive. Very talented artists, the Nez Perce people.

This evening I attended the dinner at the Joseph Community Center. The feast, presented in a professional manner, consisted of hams of roasted smoked buffalo, luscious wild salmon, local vegetables, and huckleberry cheesecake. A memorable dining experience, and an enjoyable evening, highlighted by Ed Edmo's traditional stories.

October 1—It had rained the night before, so I picked the last of the sweet corn in my Slope garden. The hunters called and said a cow had broken through a fence, so I rode out to Deadman with Doug to repair the damage. Although the hills appear dry, the cattle look good. There's still plenty of feed, and water in the ponds.

October 3—I drove out to La Grande yesterday, and treated granddaughter Carrie and great-granddaughter Brenna to dinner at the #1 China Buffet, then attended a Chautauqua at the college. I spent the night with them and returned this morning. It was an enjoyable ride home, as there was a spectacular rainbow arching over Elgin.

This afternoon I drove to the upper Imnaha and joined my writer friends for dinner at the Fishtrap Retreat, after which we stayed up until late reading our work to each other, and I stayed overnight.

October 6—Yesterday's rain, although cold, was welcome. And this morning a light breeze wanders across Prairie Creek, loosening the once-colorful maple leaves.

As the leaves float to the lawn, the movement attracts the kittens, who twirl around on their hind feet in a sort of kitten ballet in their futile attempts to catch the leaves. The half-grown kittens so resemble the leaves in color, it's difficult to distinguish leaf from kitten. Such a joy observing them through the kitchen window.

90+-year-old Helen Willard of Prosser, Washington, just called. Seems she's been visiting our county with a tour group. She called from Wallowa Lake Lodge, where they'd spent the night. This amazing woman, a former reporter and author, decided to write again, for her local newspaper. She says the name of her column is, "Return of the Roving Roza Reporter." Helen, you are truly an inspiration.

Dug some of those yummy red potatoes and fried them up to go with venison liver, heart and onions last evening. Sliced tomatoes, shucked the season's last corn on the cob, and we feasted on the young white-tail buck Doug bagged here on Prairie Creek, fattened on alfalfa, peas, and grain.

It appears Doug didn't make a dent in the local white-tail population. This morning I counted 20 head in our field, including two bucks.

Our mountains are white-washed again, and the tamarack trees, scattered on their slopes, are beginning to lighten. Sparse spaces between

Callie Miller is ready to enter the Keyhole race at the recent Hells Canyon Mule Days show. This year's event broke records for attendance.

clouds appear deep-blue and autumn-bright.

It is a lovely time for our newest great-grandchild to enter the world. And he's here! Welcome to our family, Gavin DeWolf. Gavin's middle name was my great-grandma Electa's maiden name.

As I write, the fire in the wood stove snaps and pops, and radiates a comforting warmth. I'd much rather cook on the old Monarch range than my electric stove. Food just tastes better somehow, and when a kettle soup is cooked, you just push it over to the far side to keep hot. Plus, you can fry, boil, simmer, bake and warm the house at the same time.

October 7—Sunday evening Doug and I, along with Dick Hammond, drove to the canyons again, this time to the lower country, to the Imnaha River Inn—compliments of Lyman, who treated his shipping crew to dinner.

It's always a treat to visit there. The massive log lodge, built above the river, is difficult to describe. You just have to see it for yourself.

We visited over roasted Cornish game hens, wild rice and salad, with warm brownies and ice cream for dessert, drizzled with chocolate sauce. This place is the best-kept secret in Oregon.

If you don't plan to spend the night and just want dinner, you need to call ahead and tell Sandy and Nick. If you come from a distance, it's worth the money to spend a few days. You won't be sorry.

Time to wrap this column up and fix supper.

October 8—Doug took off for the outback to go "wooding." It's what you do here in Wallowa County in the fall. lie returned with a load of seasoned tamarack that should last the winter. I stayed home to stew up the last of the ripening tomatoes into juice. After placing a roaster pan of deer ribs in the oven for supper, I called Phyllis to join me for a walk. And soon we were wandering the winding cow paths over Hough's hill.

October 9—It was breezy enough to dry the clothes on the line. Warmed to 70 degrees and melted some of the snow on the higher peaks. Which didn't last long because it snowed again, the next day.

October 11—Ken and Chad shipped their calves and older cows. Missed going to the hills this fall, because Doug had an appointment in La Grande that day, and I was the driver. It was an enjoyable trip, like driving through a watercolor painting. Fall colors were at their peak in the Minam Canyon and out past Elgin.

October 13—Once again Chuck and Chris Frazier lucked out when they chose today for their annual "apple press'in party." The frosty morning chill soon melted into a splendid warmth that lured you outside. Our mountains, so close there on upper Prairie Creek, were wearing a new snowfall, which clearly defined their autumn clarity. Added to that was the seasonal combination of golden tamarack-covered slopes against the deep blue skies of Indian Summer.

This year there were four antique apple presses. One had the date 1866 imprinted on the iron works. Only a few of us arrived early; Chris and her granddaughter Maya and I began the cranking and pressing that resulted in a flow of fragrant juice. Soon more folks showed up to man the other presses.

Children appeared and began romping amid a growing pile of apple pulp. To slake our thirst we poured glasses of sweet freshly-pressed juice, and tasted the very essence of fall. Delicious cooking smells wafted from various hand-crafted bar-b-cues. A whole pig roasted slowly, marinated chickens browned over briquettes, oysters in their shells steamed in a bed of coals, and beans bubbled in cast iron dutch ovens suspended on tripods over fires.

More neighbors arrived, carrying homemade breads, pickles, cakes, pies, and salads—all the bountiful harvest of the season. The food was spread on a long flat-bed trailer. Some folks peeled horse radish roots, while others turned the crank of an old grinder to grind the chopped roots into a pulp, which was then mixed with vinegar and bottled. This process is best done outside, lest your tears salt the horseradish.

Several men took up their fiddles and guitars, and began to sing for us. A maze had been constructed from large straw bales, much to the delight of the children, who whooped and hollered all this bright, lovely day.

Around 2:00 we begin to heap our plates with food, and I watch the raspberry cobbler I baked that morning disappear. And, by the time I finish eating and visiting, that poor pig is reduced to a pile of bones and skin, its roasted head still intact!

As an excuse to walk off our feasting, Stanlynn, Chris and I strike off over the hill, past a pond, and into the woods. Following Chris, who knows the country, we hike a large loop that brings us back to the festivities. The country side glows with golden cottonwoods and aspen thickets, and a rushing creek tumbles past the house. This is a special time you want to hold forever in your heart.

Already the sun is sinking over the Wallowas, and that familiar chill is settling in. Doug is ready to leave, so we return to our home, which is only a few miles down-country.

October 15—The days have continued on like that, so today I called Phyllis and we decided to hike the West Moraine of Wallowa Lake. Carrying our sandwiches and bottles of water, we found a trail that zig-zagged it's way to the top. The view is always startling when you look down upon the lake, and we were the only humans in sight. A cool breeze blew, but weather-wise it was delightful.

So, aimlessly ambling; a trail here, a fork there, we suddenly realized we were traveling farther and farther from the car. And...it was all up hill going back.

"What'll we do?" asked Phyllis. "Where are we? I'm too pooped to go back."

"Never fear," I said. "Call it an adventure. We'll hike to the lake shore road to Christine's house, and she'll drive us back to the car." Luckily

Chris was home and quite happy to rescue two wandering friends.

October 21—On the 18th we had a wonderful warm rain, and Saturday turned stormy with a bit of snow falling on Prairie Creek. After bidding by phone on items offered for the 4-H Radio Auction, I drove to our new hospital to visit our dear friend Wilmer Cook, who recently suffered a slight stroke. 95-year-old Wilmer is one of Wallowa County's treasurers. We wish you well.

October 22—As the morning sun slowly makes it way down the east-facing canyons, a breeze loosens a sudden drift of locust leaves. Through the sliding glass door that provides a window to this golden October world, a movement catches my eye. Wild turkeys... sauntering along, muttering to themselves as they peck windfall apples.

Indian Creek canyon rises to tiered rimrocks that end in blue autumn sky. Writing here at my table, where I can can observe all this, provides both diversion and inspiration. And you guessed it... we're down here at the Imnaha Writer's Retreat. I say we as, once again, we Syringa Sisters have gathered to write, hike, and enjoy these last golden days of fall.

Barb and Bobbie pulled in yesterday afternoon from Portland, while Jessica and Mary took the Loop road, arriving from Boise via the upper Imnaha. Archaeologist Ken Reid, who has been working on a project all month, is occupying the "tree house." Since he drove out "on top" yesterday to split wood for his father, we've yet to meet him. However, we are most grateful for the large stack of wood and kindling he left on the porch.

I made it down here early enough to feed the wood furnace and tidy the place a bit—last week this place was inhabited by men. No offense. They were busy writing, and that's good.

After lunch I cheated our resident bear out of a bowl-full of apples, and set about baking a deep dish pie. So by the time the first cart came bumping across the swinging bridge, everything was in "apple pie order," and the cinnamony smells coming from the oven would have tempted any visitor. One must watch where they step... especially out past the grapes and under the apple trees. Bear scat, those unmistakable piles of recycled apples, remains hidden under drifts of leaves. So far we haven't spied Mr. Bear, but that's ok.

The river makes a bend here, and across the Imnaha's clear waters sits Mary's house, now occupied by unfamiliar folks. All we have left of her now are memories—as well as, hopefully, a book about her life that should be ready for the publisher soon. Thanks to this special place, where one can write uninterrupted. We at Fishtrap are indebted to the generosity of Dr. Driver and his family for allowing us the use of their lovely log home.

Last evening, after supper eaten at the long, wooden table, we coiled up to the warmth of the rock fireplace to read to each other, share photos of summer treks, and catch up on our varied lives. Although we are aging, our spirits remain young.

October 23—While eating breakfast this morning at the Imnaha Writer's Retreat, while watching the sun make its way down the canyon, we decided to take a break from writing and seize the day.

"Let's hike the Saddle Creek Trail." I suggested. Three years ago we'd made it to the top of Freezeout Saddle; surely we could again. Hurriedly we packed our lunches, filled our water bottles, and drove to the trailhead, which is just up the road.

Mary, who is recovering from hip surgery, opted to stay back and write. We shouldered our day packs and took off up the trail, which wound in and out of fragrant Ponderosa Pines, some of them quite large. Earlier we'd watched a ruffed grouse strutting along, seemingly unafraid.

The trail was steep all the way. Up and up we climbed, with the two youngsters Jessica and Barb far in the lead, and Bobbie, our 79-year-old heroine, and I bringing up the rear. The trail climbs 2,500 ft. in two miles, so you can see we were exerting ourselves.

Finally we began to rest at the corner of each switchback, Otherwise we put one step in front of the other, higher and higher, ascending above the tree line, right in the midst of those soft-shouldered canyons now covered with golden bunch grass. A few cows grazed the area, but did not appear to have made much impact.

Far off to the West rose the snowy crest of the Wallowas. The sky was intense blue, a faint breeze cooled our sweat-soaked brows, and we were so immersed in beauty, we forgot about being tired.

At the top we joined Barb and Jessica, who'd eaten their lunches and were stretched out enjoying the views. Since we were on the Rim Trail, we could gaze down toward Hells Canyon of the Snake River. I'd say "look down at the awesome sweep of country," but we couldn't actually see the river.

Due to recent moisture, and now warmth, the green of new growth was replacing the acres of blackened burn that remained from last summer's raging fires. To the south lay the Marks cabin; to the north Hat Point, and trails lead off in both directions, as well as the Saddle Creek trail that dove off into the depths of the Snake River country. We'd made it! A wonderful feeling.

We took photos of each other at the rock cairn that marked the top of the saddle, before carefully making our way down the trail.

And now, as I put a period to this column...it is raining. A lovely warm rain patters softly on the piles of leaves collected on the deck, drips off the roof, and slakes the canyon's thirst. Far above, the rims are swathed in mists, the green ponderosas marking the course of Indian Creek, and I hear the plop of a falling apple. There's a fire in the furnace, and one in the fireplace—let it rain.

October 27—The "Hunter" moon hovered high over the rims above Indian Creek early this morning when we Syringa Sisters arose to pack up our gear before heading home. I'd mixed my sourdough the night before, so was able to send everyone off with a tummy full of pancakes. After they left, I gave the place a final going-over before locking up and pushing my belongings across the bridge. The temperature dropped dramatically that morning, and frost covered the bridge, which made crossing rather treacherous.

Driving downriver, I noted with a tinge of sadness the changing face of the country. Many old-timers gone, others aging, and ranchers selling out...you can feel it. The Change. I missed seeing Lyman's beautiful replacement heifers near the road by the house. Lyman sold them, along with his cow herd.

When I drove back to our place on Prairie Creek Doug and Ryan were still hunting in the hills. What with unpacking, and cooking up a pot roast supper for the returning hunters that evening, I was plenty pooped by bedtime. It was fun having grandson Ryan here, even though they didn't bag an elk.

October 30—Our museum board hosted a reception for long-time board chairman Caryl Coppin at the conference room in the old Toma's building. Caryl, a very deserving lady, has given hours of her time to the local community.

November 3—Daughter Ramona, the one in our large family who always sees to it that every newly married gal and every new mother has a shower, pulled off another one. This one honored wee Gavin and a soon-to-be born baby boy Nash—they know these days—who lives in San Diego. Although grandson Josh and wife, Desiree, couldn't attend, they were in our thoughts, and our gifts will be mailed to them. I was able to hold my newest great-grandson in my arms, and enjoy some other greats: Ronan, Gwenllian, Kennon, Riley, Ashlynn, and Jada.

Oh yes, and the puppy fit right in.

Every October Chuck and Chris (shown above) Frazier host an "apple press'in party" in their Upper Prairie Creek ranch.

Olivia Woods holds a glass of freshly pressed apple juice at the Fraziers' recent party.

November 5—What's with this weather? Our days are warmer now than they were in October. Clothes are drying on the line, Doug is hauling manure to spread on the garden and raspberry patch, and I've just returned from a long walk around the old ranch. Ken hauled his heifers away last week, and the only livestock left on the place is my mare, Morning Star. But after grandson Buck trims her feet, Doug will haul her to the hills to winter on bunch grass with the other horses. At least I have my chickens to tend to, as well as several cats we keep for mousers.

And then there's my puppy. Yes...a puppy. Which is like adopting a child. Not since my faithful Daisy did I even consider owning another dog. However...for some time now, my children have insisted I NEEDED a puppy. The matter came up each time one of their border collie females produced another litter.

A few weeks ago daughter Jackie called from her home in Challis, Idaho. "Mom, I have this cute little puppy; you'd just love her," and I heard myself say, "I'll take her." What was I thinking?

"Great," replied my daughter. "Bill is coming over next week to go elk hunting with Buck; he'll bring the puppy. She's adorable and only 7 weeks old!"

So it came to pass, on Halloween. Buck's wife, Chelsea, called. "Your puppy's here!" And my life hasn't been the same since.

First off... she IS adorable. No doubt about that. I mean, how could anyone not love this puppy? border collies are very intelligent, and of course Halley, derived from Halloween, is far above average. She's also far above average when it comes to chewing up shoes, ripping clothes off the line, terrorizing kittens, and gobbling down her puppy chow.

But to her credit, she house broke... or rather, "porch broke," herself. Only one mishap, and that was my fault for not letting her out in the middle of the night. Now she sleeps on the carport, curled contentedly in an old blanket with her head resting on an orange-colored teddy bear long abandoned by the grandchildren.

Doug and I drove to Cow Creek on the lower Imnaha yesterday. While Doug fished for steelhead, the puppy and I took short walkabouts. When Halley tired, she sprawled out on the green grass in the sunshine and slept soundly while I read a book.

It felt more like May than November. This place, down there across the bridge, is a very special place, known and loved by many. It's here where the Imnaha enters a five-mile, rugged gorge that ends at the river's confluence with the Snake at Eureka Bar. After crossing the bridge, the road continues its rocky, narrow-rim-hugging route to Dug Bar, where it ends at the Snake River.

Over the hill you come to McClaran's Cow Creek ranch, where a side road veers up a steep canyon. This is the spot where grandson Buck and his dad—who brought my puppy—packed into the Snake River unit to hunt elk. Riding their horses and leading two pack mules, they would have ridden up the Fingerboard Trail into the Snake River country.

How I envied them. Setting up a tent in those glorious canyons, spending a week away from civilization. Even if they don't bag an elk, they will treasure this father-and-son time together, in the heart of the canyons they both know and love so well.

Around 3:45 the sun disappeared over a rocky rim, and shortly thereafter Doug emerged from the shadowy trail that enters the Imnaha Gorge. Apparently the fish weren't biting that day, as I'd observed another luckless fisherman depart earlier. For me, fishing is secondary to just "being" at the Cow Creek Bridge on a warm November afternoon.

We left, jouncing and bouncing our way in the four-wheel drive pickup, past Corral Creek, then up the Horse Creek grade, winding around hairpin curves as we climbed to heights that drop off into those monstrous canyons. From Horse Creek south, nearly to Imnaha, those steep canyons were blackened by last summer's fires.

As for wildlife, we drove past a large herd of mule deer does, grazing new green grass growing near an old corral. Close to Fence Creek we spotted two many-antlered bucks. Leaving the puppy in the pickup, we pulled up to the Imnaha Store and Tavern, where Sally Tanzey fixed us a bite to eat, before we headed back up "on top."

November 29—Doug and I braved a snow storm to drive to the head of the lake to visit our friend Maurice, who for the time being is living up there in a rental cabin. Carrying a casserole of lasagna, a loaf of sourdough bread I'd just baked in my wood stove oven, and salad fixin's, we made our way through deep snow into the warmth of that comfortable, furnished, two-story cabin that a kind friend made available to Maurice until he locates a place to spend the winter. During that recent wild wind storm, Maurice's trailer was completely destroyed by a falling tree.

We arrived early enough to survey some of the uprooted trees littering the picnic area of the park, as well as several homes around the lake that were severely damaged during that freak storm.

November 30—Jean Cook and I, representing the CowBelles, volunteered to serve at the Community Dining Center in Enterprise. After which I walked over to the annual Christmas bazaar, which is always held in Cloverleaf Hall. My purchases included some of Gene Hayes' hand-painted note cards, and a zucchini cake baked by Marvel Eaves. Then I drove up to the Enterprise High School gym to join son Todd, grandson Buck, wife Chelsea and great-granddaughter Lucy, to watch a wrestling tournament. While there, my winning bid during the silent auction to raise money for the wrestling club netted me a fragrant holiday wreath.

This evening found Phyllis and me attending the wine-tasting event held in Enterprise at the Community Dining Center, which was gaily decorated for Christmas, and featured fine wines from the Gilstrap Winery in Cove, food by Holy Smokes, and music by the Lenahans. Proceeds from the auction and ticket sales will help fund the Community Connection dining center for our elderly citizens.

December 2—Fierce winds blew Prairie Creek's loose snow from the fields into enormous drifts. Three-foot drifts blocked my path to the chicken house and curled around the burning barrels. Although we didn't suffer like those living in coastal towns, we were without a phone, even a cell phone, and our driveway was blocked by drifted snow.

Thankfully, we had electricity, but our radio and TV were both out. I cooked on the wood stove, and saved water in the event of a power outage. For two days I was without communication. A weird feeling.

Doug, whose pickup was parked outside the driveway, spent most of that time in Enterprise, at his "office" in the Range Rider, playing cribbage with "The Boys." I took advantage of the lull in my life, and began decorating for Christmas. I baked persimmon cookies and made caramel corn.

December 4—There was this absolute stillness today. No wind. It was 40 degrees, cloudy, and balmy. A small bird perched in the leafless old apple tree sang like it was spring. A bird which, I suspect, should have gone south months ago. It was so mild I opened the kitchen window to the fresh air while I baked sourdough bread in the wood stove oven and simmered a kettle of chicken noodle soup for our writer's group, which showed up around 10.

After lunch, while we were playing scrabble, our phone was restored.

December 5—I baked another loaf of sourdough bread today, and made clam chowder on the wood stove. Eight of us from "Stitch and Bitch" gathered around our kitchen table for soup, bread, and salads. I thawed out Marvel's zucchini cake for Heidi Muller's birthday and we all sang Happy Birthday. Then we retired to the living room to "stitch."

Heidi, who hails from Appalachia, was making a hand-sewn crazy quilt. With sunlight streaming through our windows, it felt more like April than December.

When Ken and Chad trailed their cows into the valley, one old cow bolted from the herd and headed here to the old ranch. This was home and there was no stopping her once she set her course toward Prairie Creek. Ken had to drive her into the corral and haul her back in his trailer.

December 7—Doug and I were invited into Enterprise for supper at Wilma's and, of course, Lyman was there too. We had a great time, and it gave us both a much-needed lift to witness these two love birds.

I purchased one of those fresh fir trees, grown on a tree farm out near Paradise, from the Enterprise FFA chapter, which had just cut them

These cows, owned by Ken and Chad Nash of Enterprise, are being trailed from the hills to the valley, where they will winter. Shown here at the old Dorrance place on Crow Creek. Chuck Dorrance built this barn in 1915.

that zero-degree morning. Now, the tree is all trimmed and granddaughter Adele was here for lunch yesterday. We had great fun recalling Christmases past when she was a little girl... seemingly only a heartbeat ago.

Since I've been sitting here at my word processor from 12:30 a.m. 'til 4:00 a.m. I should get some shut-eye. Need to get those Christmas cards mailed. Merry Christmas and happy new year to all of you in Agri-Times country.

December 10—Gail Swart is playing "The Most Wonderful Time of the Year" and, thanks to her C.D. entitled "Christmas Comes Gently," Gail's professional and heartfelt piano renditions of familiar carols help to "gentle" my Christmas. The cover photo on Gail's C.D. was taken by her father, the late Gwen Coffin, who captured so beautifully a snowy country road.

The same image could have been recorded today. The same listing fence, snow-flocked evergreens, and same snowy meadow with its small red barn, forever backgrounded by our beloved Wallowas.

Driving through Joseph last evening, Phyllis and I enjoyed seeing our home town glittering with Christmas lights. All those brightly-lit shops seemed to warm the snowy streets. We were on our way to the

Janie Tippett took this photo through her window in the room where her cook stove is, looking west. First light always hits Chief Joseph Mountain first, she said. "Even though my zoom lens brought the scene closer, this is how it looks on a cold winter morning."

Wallowa Lake Lodge to attend Gail's annual Christmas caroling party. Due to blizzard conditions last Sunday, the event had been rescheduled.

There, in the white stillness that follows a snow storm, we felt the presence of the cold lake as we approached the rustic lodge.

All festooned with colored lights, the historic lodge beckoned in the night. Snow crystals from the tall Ponderosa pines filled the air as we stepped inside to warm ourselves by the fire. Soon we began to sing: Jingle Bells, Winter Wonderland, and Joy to the World. Didn't matter if you had a good voice or not, your voice mingled with those of friends and neighbors, and the result was joyful.

After the Handbell Choir's magical performance, we wandered into the festive dining room to be served an elegant meal prepared by the staff and served by local volunteers. Still nibbling Christmas cookies, we were treated to more music.

Gail played piano solos, Heidi Muller and Carolyn Gilbert played their dulcimers, along with Janis Carper and her guitar. Helene Hipple, accompanied by Gail, thrilled us with her stunning voice; Randy Morgan played Ave Maria on his trumpet, Carolyn Lockhart's Blue Holiday was great, soloist Rod Ambroson sang Hail Merry Christmas, a song he composed himself; Janis Carper sang a song she wrote for Gail, titled "Holiday Feeling", and Wallowa County's Duff Pace sang two solos. Then we all joined in singing Silent Night, White Christmas, and We Wish You a Merry Christmas.

We who live in this special place are blessed to have so many talented musicians. Thanks to supporters and organizers like Gail and Janis, our valley is filled all year long with song. Music, the universal language that crosses all barriers, nourishes our souls and is as necessary to our being as food.

December 11—My favorite time of day is dawn. I love looking out my living room window as light seeps over the silent snowy fields, observing a lone coyote as it leaps into the air, pounces on a mouse, then devours the small rodent in a single gulp. Oftentimes I watch the deer foraging under the snow for bits of grass.

By mid-morning the finches have returned to feed on the dried sunflowers that droop over the garden fence. And Halley, my border collie puppy, is ready to do something…anything.

One morning she followed me to the chicken pen gate, then slipped inside the pen before I could stop her. Let me tell you, my molting hens haven't been the same since. Around and around she went, chasing first one bird, and then another, until my little flock was so traumatized they flew to their roost, where they spent the remainder of the day.

Halley follows me out to the mailbox every day, and she's as excited as I am when there's a package. One snowy day there was a package from sister Kathryn, who each December sends us some of those sweet tangerines picked fresh from her tree in Roseville, California.

Tucked lovingly in with those juicy tangerines was a plastic bag of what appeared to be fruit leather. WRONG. It was a teething treat for Halley. I'll give it to her on Christmas morning.

Halley is doing pretty well in the gift department. Doug brought home a fancy dog carrier from the Grain Growers store, all decorated with a red bow…which means Halley can go with me when I snowshoe up Hurricane Creek.

December 14—I made a kettle of clam chowder to welcome Carol and Mark DeJong who arrived that evening from McCall, Idaho to spend two nights with us. Carol and Mark are pretty important folks. You see, they are Lucy's maternal grandparents. They'd traveled the winter roads to celebrate Lucy's first birthday on the 15th.

December 15—Today was memorable, because Lucy's great-grandma (me) got to go on the Santa Train. The birthday party boarded the train near the old grain elevator in Joseph. Fare was accepted in the form of canned goods for the local Food Bank.

Lots of railroad history here. The completed Joseph Branch opened officially back in January 1, 1909. On this Saturday there were three "Santa runs" from Joseph to Enterprise and back. This route allowed us to travel through farms and ranches where we watched horses, cattle, and deer eating hay spread by ranchers across their snowy pastures, all backgrounded by our winter Wallowas.

When the birthday girl had her photo taken with Santa, she was more than a little wary of that strange-looking man with the white beard. After boarding the train, Lucy's mamma, Chelsea, informed me that my 17th great-grandchild had been born that very morning, on Lucy's birthday yet! His name is Wyatt Richard, born to Josh and Desiree Nash. Wyatt's daddy is in the Navy, stationed in San Diego, California, which is a long way from Wallowa County where he grew up.

December 17—I got really behind on our Christmas cards this year, but finally managed to get them mailed. Our book group met at Fishtrap House today, and of course everyone brought cookies.

December 18—Windy with snow in the forecast when our Writer's Group met here. I cooked a big dutch oven full of tamale pie, Ruth brought a spinach salad, and we had Sharon's sensational Sherry cake with custard sauce for dessert. Then we cleared the dishes and played Scrabble.

After they left, I put together another salad and drove over to Sally's place to attend the "Stitch and Bitch" Christmas party. Great fun! Cold and snowy outside, warm and cheery inside. A White Elephant gift exchange netted me a knitted Christmas vest, purchased originally at our local Soroptimist Thrift Shop. Despite a missing a button and a bit of unraveling, the vest was very Christmasy and I'll wear it on several occasions.

My poet friend Cathy, who lives way out to Flora, called to say her road was drifted shut.

December 19—Neighbor Beverly Frasch hosted a dinner in her gorgeous log home for seven of us ranch wives who live close by, so she could become better acquainted. It was fun getting together, as our busy lives only allow for brief visits at the grocery store or a wave as we pass on Prairie Creek's country roads.

Interesting to note many of the women living on ranches are school teachers, among them Carol Voss, Nancy Hook, and Karen Patton. Donna Butterfield owns the Art Angle in Joseph, which she wants to ell; Lois Hough is a full time ranch wife, Donna Smith is a rancher herself, and Beverly Frasch's son and daughter-in-law own what used to be Doug's ranch. This makes me a retired ranch wife, a role I'm not really ready to accept. That's why I'm in the market for a milk cow come spring...

While we enjoyed a delicious meal and fellowship inside what used to be the old Bob Perry ranch house, the Prairie Creek wind howled outside and the Christmas lights swayed which way and that in Beverly's wintry yard. The Frasches are very generous folks, and have given much to our community. Richard and Mary read Agri-Times way back in Minnesota and look forward to retiring here in our valley. So, this then, is a letter from home.

December 20—Worked on an outline for my column while a blizzard raged outside.

Doug and I hosted our annual Christmas potluck which featured smoked turkey, given to us by Pete, a hunter friend who lives in Hermiston. Guests contributed yummy side dishes. After feasting we retired to the living room to read poems, tell stories, and bask in the spirit of the season.

December 29—Ranchers from miles around converged in the cemetery on the hill above Enterprise to pay their last respects to Paul Yost today. Yes, we buried another old time rancher, a true rancher who loved the land, especially his lands out on Chesnim. I guess Paul, as he aged, would rather be "on the crik" than anywhere else. Can't say as I blame him. Pretty special place out there.

Paul didn't consider running a ranch to be work. He just was doing what he loved, in a place he loved. He was a good steward of the land. I'm sure the next generation of Yosts will continue the good work. I still miss Paul's wife Gladys, who was a good CowBelle and a friend, who passed away several years ago.

The sun shone on the snow as Paul was laid to rest, Our glorious mountains put on a show more beautiful than any flower-bedecked funeral ever could.

December 30—This column should have been written and sent in last week... but then I wouldn't have had time to spend with my family, and since Christmas is all about family, my column sat on the back burner until this afternoon. For the past few nights I've had all good intentions of arising in the pre-dawn hours to write, but somehow that never happened. So...here goes. Being the matriarch of such a large loving family is rich, rewarding...and exhausting.

Last night was the first time since Christmas Eve that I didn't set the table for five to 14 people. It was great fun! For some reason I was really into the Christmas Spirit this year. Must've been all those wonderful holiday events that filled our calendar, as well as being blessed with such an amazing family. And now, as we approach the last day of 2007 and brace ourselves for a brand new year, my heart overflows with joy.

As I write here at the kitchen table, there is a break in the blizzard that's been raging outside. The juncos and chickadees have returned to feast on the pendulous sunflower heads swaying in the icy wind.

Halley, my puppy, leaps in the air, then lands, front paws planted in a snow bank, to watch the rolling balls of snow she has created. Puppies, like children, love to play in the snow. Doug is working a cross word puzzle and watching a muted football game on TV. I haven't the foggiest notion of what teams are playing.

This time last Sunday I was attending the Community Christmas Concert held at Stage One in Enterprise. This inspiring afternoon of music was organized by the Wallowa Valley Music Alliance, and included Gail Swart, piano; Helene Hipple, vocals; Tommy Hutchison, Hawaiian Slack-key guitar; Carolyn Lockhart, vocals; Janis Carper, guitar and vocals; and Brady Goss and his outrageous piano-playing.

Stage One, in the historic E. M& M. Bowlby Building was packed— standing room only.

The Sunday before, I'd braved icy roads to attend the Mid-Valley Theatre Company's two hilarious comedies, "Shock of his Life," and "Muggsy's Merry Christmas." We were told to bring blankets and wear warm clothing, as the old gym is very expensive to heat. But let me tell you, we in the audience laughed so hard we scarcely noticed the cold. It was another one of Kate Loftus' great productions, held in the historic old Lostine School, which now houses the Providence Academy of Classical Christian Education.

Then we all got in our cars and headed back to the First Baptist Church, which sits on the hill above Enterprise. Since all parking spaces were taken, we latecomers parked in a nearby snowy field. It was another overflowing crowd. Folks left their cozy, warm homes to venture out in the cold to listen to The Christmas Section of Handel's *Messiah.*

Words fail when it comes to describing that evening of song, under the direction of Iva Lindsay and Randy Morgan. Wallowa County's beloved Gail Swart at the piano accompanied several thrilling solos performed by various talented members of our community. Luckily, I found a seat in the second row next to my neighbor Lois Hough. That night the combined voices of our county-wide choir singing the Hallelujah Chorus danced in my head.

December 31—The days have raced by without enough hours to accomplish everything. Our owls didn't return this winter to roost by day in the Ponderosa Pines. I miss them. Loved walking out our snowy lane to the mail box and receiving Christmas cards. One snowy evening our friend Maurice (who is house sitting for the winter on Upper Prairie Creek) appeared at our door with a lovely poinsettia.

Likewise for grandson James, who just left to return to college in Dillon, Montana. It was so wonderful to see James and sister Adele over the holidays. Then there was granddaughter Mona Lee, who along with her parents, my daughter Jackie and her husband Bill from Challis, Idaho, arrived on Christmas Eve to spend a week. Now our Mona is on her way to India to spend three months up near the Himalayas.

Finally, after many family get-togethers, Bill and Jackie made it safely back to Challis.

We made phone calls that stretched from Alabama to Lodi, California, to connect with family members who couldn't be here. After Bill, Jackie and Mona arrived on Christmas Eve, I fed all of us clam chowder before we drove to Joseph to attend a Frontier Christmas play at the Baptist Church, which began at six. Whew! Then we scooted over to the Christmas candlelight service at the United Methodist Church. Both were wonderful! And Bill, Jackie and Mona, who lived here for many years, gave and received many hugs.

Christmas dinner was considerably easier than Thanksgiving, and I roasted the traditional Prime rib. Fourteen of us gathered at two tables, where gaiety prevailed as we put away a kettle of potatoes mashed by son Todd, gravy, two loaves of sourdough bread, and a green salad. We followed the feast with mincemeat, blackberry, and yes, another one of those huckleberry cream pies.

Daughter Ramona and her growing family all gathered in Lodi, California, for Christmas. Phone calls on Christmas morning brought great-grandkids Clayton, Cole, Brenna and Halley Jane a bit closer. We definitely had a white Christmas this year, and our house rang with good cheer, as our family truly loves being together.

So much more happened over the holidays, like the Solstice party hosted by Skip and Liz at their home in Joseph. When Phyllis and I got out of the car and walked to their house we were awed by the mountains which stood clearly defined, bright as day, under the Solstice Moon.

After sampling Skip's gourmet Southwest soups, we drove to Enterprise to view the live nativity scene in front of the LDS Church before we stepping inside the church to enjoy a musical program staged by our community, which included granddaughter-in-law Amy playing her harp while four of my great-grand children sang Christmas carols.

Holding baby Gavin in my arms, my heart overflowed with pride as Gavin's sister Gwenllian and brother Ronan, stood up there with their cousins Ashlynn and Riley Ann, singing their little hearts out. Helene Hipple's rendition of "Mary let me hold her baby" was stunning.

I'll never forget the full December moon, the "Cold" moon, that shone on Christmas Eve.

There were so many fond memories made this season. Like the night we had Lyman and Wilma over for dinner, and I made a casserole of lasagna and baked another loaf of sourdough bread. Christmas is the time to gather around friends and family.

I treasure the visit with grandson James and his dad, who stopped in to have leftover prime rib. One of my proudest moments was reading a story James wrote. And, late at night, rereading poems written by granddaughter Mona Lee.

And now it is 5:30 a.m. on New Year's Eve day and I've been writing since 3:00 a.m., bringing to mind William Stafford, Oregon's poet laureate, who used to rise before dawn to write his poems.

A half moon hangs in a clear cold sky, and from my kitchen window I see the planet Mars glittering above the eastern horizon. Hopefully, I can record this on my memory stick, drive to Enterprise, and e-mail it to Agri-Times before the deadline.

Our friends Phyllis and Fred will be over this evening to help bring in the New Year. We'll build a big pizza and play cards, and most probably fade long before 2008 makes it's appearance.

You all have a happy and prosperous New Year.

Halley, Janie's border collie pup, stands on a drift in the yard. High winds created drifts of snow like these all over Prairie Creek.

2008

January 7—It is late morning, and through the living room window I watch Hough's cattle relish their hay…hay that was put up on their wintering grounds. It's a beautiful thing, this symbiotic relationship with the soil. Winter's accumulation of manure and snow soaks into the ground, and come spring the established permanent pasture responds to another growing season. After two cuttings of hay are harvested, the resulting growth provides enough fall feed to sustain the cattle before they must rely on hay.

When Prairie Creek is locked in winter white, the hay returns as cattle feed before being recycled into natural fertilizer by the cow herself. And so the seasons roll, with the same rhythm that has sustained Prairie Creek's cattle ranches for over 100 years.

In winters past, when wild winds roared across our prairie, we never experienced dirty snow. That is, as long as we were surrounded by permanent pastures. But when the land is farmed, like the hill that used to be part of Doug's ranch, and that protective cover of snow is blown away, the hungry wind eats away at the top soil. As a result, great dirty drifts formed in my chicken pen and built up in our yard. Those drifts melted, then froze, and hardened, and then it snowed again, a quiet snow that fell softly over the land, and there was no wind. And you should have seen Prairie Creek yesterday! It was a calendar photo.

Buried beneath a pristine coverlet of snow, these great open spaces rose and fell under a clean blue sky. The sun blazed down with summer-like intensity and warmed our winter-weary bodies. Truly a "Bluebird" day. How could anyone stay inside on such a day?

Well, daughter-in-law Chelsea, with baby Lucy in a backpack, and Lucy's great-grandma (me) DIDN'T. We hiked up Echo Canyon to watch son Todd and his cowboys, and one cowgirl (Todd's wife, Angie) trail 358 mother cows down out of those snowy eastern hills that separate prairie from canyon. And what a sight it was.

Earlier that morning the cows had been let out of their holding pasture along Little Sheep Creek and turned up Hayden Creek Canyon.

I would have loved to have ridden with the crew as those cows topped out. In my mind's eye I can picture their dark bodies plodding slowly through the snow across that vast expanse of open, gently undulating hills that form the southernmost boundary of the great Palouse Prairie, from which we can gaze at our beloved Wallowas, all blue and white, with not a sign of human habitation as far as the eye can see.

However, Chelsea, Lucy and I were blessed just the same, because we could see up and down Prairie Creek to all the neighboring ranches, backgrounded by those outrageous mountains. And when Chelsea spotted the herd, I was able to do some photographing before the last cow trailed into Frasch's north pasture... the same pasture in which son Ken wintered his cows last year. For one night, at least, there would be cows again.

Here, on pasture land that has been ranched for many years, the cows will dive into the hay that has already been spread over their field. These cows, like Hough's, will most probably eat hay that was raised on their wintering ground. Here too, they will calve out, and come spring those cows and calves will be trailed back to the canyons.

These canyon cattle are rustlers. They're in good shape. These cows haven't been fed any hay, as the lower elevation canyons have provided nutritious bunch grass. Now, the cows must winter where the hay is, because hay is expensive to raise and expensive to haul 30 miles for that many cattle. Because of high fuel costs, it's also expensive to haul cattle in trucks, which is why these cattle are trailed in the old way.

Of course the Nez Perce also wintered in the canyons and summered on top. And, if you are lucky enough to own such a set up, ranchers like Jack McClaran still do, as did Doug when he owned the Dug Bar Ranch on Snake River. Otherwise, today's Eastern Oregon cowmen must rely on Forest Service grazing permits and abide by their rules... rules which are sometimes implemented by good-meaning folks who don't really have a feel for the land, not like the cowboy who rides it, loves it and understands grass.

Oftentimes it is the cowboy, riding alone amid miles of canyon, high plateau and forests, who really understands the relationship between cows, grass, and the land. He lives by the seasons and knows his cows and operates on his own gut feelings.

January 14—Well, I've gotten off the cow path a bit. Where was I? You see I've been seated here at my kitchen table since 1:00 a.m. It is now 4:45 a.m. and the date is January 14th. I started this column on the 7th with all good intentions; however my life got in the way.

I've promised Sterling Allen I will E-mail this column later on this morning, which means I must finish, drive to town with my laptop, and have Richelle at Central Copy do the E-mail thing. Because...I don't. Neither do I do the internet.

No siree...I'd rather be walking behind a bunch of cows like I did this past Saturday, when I joined son Todd and his crew, grandson Buck, friend Ken Hunt, and Todd's wife, Angie, to trail those 358 head of cows from Big Sheep to above Brushy where they spent the night. I suppose I walked nine miles, all uphill on the Imnaha Highway, and I loved every minute of that wonderful day.

The day began at 5:00 am. when I drove over to Buck and Chelsea's house to watch wee Lucy until her mom got home from working the night shift, as she's an R.N. at our new hospital. Normally Lucy's daddy, grandson Buck, tends to her, but he had to leave for Big Sheep. After mom returned, I drove down into the canyons to enter a different world...a world without snow, of mild air and green grass, where the osier dogwood is reddening and Little Sheep Creek splashes merrily along. Behind those cows, a place I most like to be, I walked, talked, visiting Angie and canyon-dwelling artist-cowboy Ken.

I was startled to come upon a bobcat feeding on a road kill deer. And my border collie puppy, Halley, loved her first cattle drive. She's hooked now. As we climbed higher we glimpsed snowy rims, and when the cows were trailed into the holding pasture above Brushy, they ran eagerly to bury their noses in the fragrant hay scattered over the dry meadow.

While the cowboys drove off to haul horses and return to the valley, Angie, Ken and I got in with Ken's wife and rode back to my car. By the time we topped out over Sheep Creek Hill, our stomachs were growling. It was nearing 3:00 and breakfast had been pretty skimpy, so Angie and I rewarded ourselves with a cheeseburger and a side of onion rings at the good old R. and R. in Joseph.

Then, back to the ranch and a hot bath.

Yesterday, before walking up Echo Canyon with Chelsea and Lucy, I'd spent the morning cooking up a big kettle of turkey noodle soup—yep, the end of that 45 lb. Thanksgiving Turkey; I'd frozen the broth. I'd also baked a peach cobbler using some of Myrna Moore's peaches grown there in Bear Gulch, frozen in '06. Yum.

It was 2:00 before we all sat down to eat. So ends another perfect day in Paradise.

You can see why I don't finish the column. How could I sit at my laptop and write, when I could be out there behind those cows experiencing something to write about? Why, you might say, do I continue to

Janie Tippett helps trail cattle from Big Sheep Creek to the Mt Joseph Cattle Company ranch southeast of Enterprise. Her border collie puppy Halley helps on her first cattle drive. Photo by Angie Nash.

write this column in the middle of the night, when all of Prairie Creek is asleep? Because...it's the only time I have to myself.

I also continue because of folks like Nicole Lewis, who wrote me the most amazing fan letter I've ever received during the 24 years I've written "Janie's Journal."

Nicole grew up in La Grande and is presently enrolled in Gonzaga University. Nicole and I walk the same trails. I can't wait to meet her. From her letter I find out she has long blond hair, drives a stock truck, is often seen hiking in Hells Canyon and the Wallowas. I met her dad when I was backpacking out the west Fork of the Lostine last fall.

We also lost another solid citizen and friend to all. Bill Williams was buried while I was walking behind those cows. Bill would have wanted me to do that. I understand the Joseph United Methodist Church was overflowing with folks come to say goodbye to one of Wallowa County's beloved folks.

And now, I must put a period to this rambling, and head to Enterprise. Perhaps Todd and Buck will already have those cows turned into their wintering ground. I'll have to peer through thick frozen fog to see them. Presently it is 20 degrees and everything is coated with hoarfrost.

January 22—It is 6:50 a.m. and I'm seated here in my childhood chum Sandra's living room, where she and her husband Fred live on a high ridge overlooking a vast flood plain, one of northern California's great valleys…the valley of the Sacramento. From my youth, I remember Sacramento as a city unto itself, but as now I stare down into that sea of glittering lights, I see no separations between the towns. Sacramento flows into Roseville and gobbles up Rocklin, Loomis, Newcastle, and these beautiful foothills of the Sierra Nevada here in Auburn.

Like a malignant tumor, Sacramento spreads northeastward and devours my home town of Lincoln, and continues its poisonous path northward, where it has populated the unpeopled places where once great thriving ranches and farms dominated my beautiful Golden State. I remember fields where poppies and baby blue eyes once bloomed in spring, and oak trees, wearing new leaves, dotted the green rolling foothills; where creeks ran clear and our early settler's barns and houses rotted into the same soil in which pestles and arrow heads surfaced after a spring rain.

In this place, Digger Indians ground their acorns in holes hollowed out in large granite rocks, and hunted black tail deer while enjoying the good life, the pleasant climate below the snow but above the fog. They breathed clear, smogless air, and fished Bear River and Coon Creek and Doty's Ravine, where I learned to swim as a child.

My heart is saddened by what I see. After 40 years of living in Wallowa County, I am in shock. Traveling these six lane freeways I panic like a wild thing. In my mind's eye I drive the Zumwalt road, where it's not uncommon to travel 17 miles to the old Dorrance Place and never meet a single rig.

Doug and I didn't travel to California last January; never got around to it. Besides, the main draw was my 95-year-old mother, who passed away two years ago. Now mamma sleeps next to daddy, and Bill, her husband of 16 years after daddy died, in the old pioneer Manzanita cemetery, where a bit of my beloved foothills remains undeveloped. This is a peaceful place where cattle graze, oak trees spread their lovely arms, and bluebells and johnny-jump-ups still bloom in April.

We are here to visit my baby sister Kathryn, who lost her daughter Dawn just five months ago, and to spend time with my sister Caroline and brother Jim, and of course we want to see granddaughter Tamara, husband Matt, and great-grandchildren Clayton, Cole, and Halley Jane.

January 25—Now I'm seated here at sister Caroline's new kitchen counter, typing away again. Caroline and husband Duane have a modest home here in rural Newcastle, where, beyond the swaying limbs of digger pines, huge McMansions rise in enormous gated communities surrounded by iron fences. These pretentious castles dominate every hill top, every view of Folsom Lake, and every creek and hilly ravine. I shudder to think how much of our natural resources these mansions devour.

It has been stormy every day since our arrival on Monday. Cold rain has been soaking the foothills and valleys, bringing much-needed moisture. Even though it's 40 degrees I can't keep warm. Unlike the dry cold of Eastern Oregon, Placer County's damp cold penetrates my very bones. Can you believe I've been wearing long johns? In California, yet! But then when I call home to visit with son-in-law Charley, he informs me it's been 19 below, 12 below and 9 below, with a foot of snow on Prairie Creek. Guess I shouldn't complain.

Doug and I left Wallowa County early Sunday morning and traveled the icy road to La Grande, where we stopped for breakfast. Just out of Imbler we came to a halt to allow 70 head of elk to cross the road in front of us. Led by a many-antlered bull, the herd milled around in a snowy field long enough for me to snap several pictures. We spotted another herd near Ladd Marsh.

The roads improved and we made it safely to Winnemucca; where we spent the night at Scott's Shady Court.

Monday morning—Martin Luther King Day—would be memorable. After fortifying ourselves with one of The Griddle's famous home-cooked breakfasts, we proceeded southward through miles of desert sagebrush toward Reno…where it began to snow. The more it snowed, the faster the cars sped along. There was no turning back.

I sighed in relief as Doug pulled into Boomtown, where we were told that Donner Pass was open, chains and snow tires required. Since a brand new Cabela's, billed as the world's largest outfitter, had just opened only a block away, and I'd never been in one, we walked through massive wooden doors to enter a world where wild bear, elk, moose, fish and waterfowl—once free to roam, fly and swim—now graced the walls, or reposed, fully mounted, in natural-like settings…stilled forever. Swimming lazily about in a huge glass-walled tank, well-fed trout, bass, catfish and carp could be viewed at eye level. There were shops full of fudge and huckleberry jam, and sections full of tents, backpacks, fishing poles and every type of outdoor gear you could imagine.

Taking advantage of their Grand Opening sale I purchased a pair of fleece-lined elk hide slippers. Then, to soothe my soul whilst crossing the snowy Sierra, I bought a CD of Rocky Mountain music, recordings of birds and running water.

However, after traveling several uneventful miles up the eastern slope of the Sierra Nevada mountains, we slowed to a crawl, then to a stop. Three lanes of gridlock stretched up and over the summit. Idling semis drowned out my Rocky Mountain music, and the stench of exhaust fumes filled the mountain air. Three lanes of traffic for as far as we could see.

We called Sandra and Fred. "Don't know when we'll get there, Cal Trans says a two hour delay."

"We'll keep the soup hot," said Fred.

After leaving Cabela's at 2:00 that afternoon, we didn't arrive at Fred and Sandra's house on Hubbard Road until after 7:00 p.m. What normally takes us an hour had taken over five. Needless to say, I was a basket case. When the traffic finally returned to its normal flow, those crazy Californians sped down that mountain going 75 and 80.

We found out from the "locals" that you NEVER cross Donner Summit at the end of a three day holiday. Martin Luther King Day, coupled with the political caucus thing and excellent skiing conditions on Boreal Ridge, had created a traffic nightmare. Who would have thunk it.

When I was a girl, first off we didn't travel to the Sierras in winter on that two lane road, and if we did go to Reno, we could actually see the mountains and smell the air, and hardly meet a car. So, other than peaceful interludes here and there, we've been caught up in the FAST LANE that IS California ever since. Everyone down here is in a hurry. Some large stores even rate their checkout girls as to the speed with which they wait on a customer.

However, being with family has made our trip worthwhile. Yesterday, brother Jim drove us down to visit granddaughter Tamara, husband Matt, and our great-grand children, Clayton, Cole and Halley Jane, in their warm home surrounded by 400 acres of wine grapes. Happy times.

Auntie Caroline and Auntie Kathryn joined us. Clayton and Cole showed us their 4-H steers, hauled down by Poppa Charley all the way from upper Prairie Creek. And Halley Jane still has "Mu Mu," her Emu, as well as a pet chicken, a burro and a horse. The children also have an assortment of dogs. We didn't feel stuck in Lodi; we felt blessed with family, and us three sisters and brother laughed so hard at most anything, we were amazed that Doug put up with us.

After more intense traffic we returned last night to Caroline's, and now I must put a period to this column and e-mail it to Sterling Allen. So much more to tell, however, like the Sled Dog races at Wallowa Lake before we left, which all seems so far away now. Barring another blizzard, we plan to start home Monday.

I miss my pup Halley, but granddaughter Adele is giving her plenty of TLC. This afternoon we've been invited to brother Jim and wife Joyce's place for dinner. They live on what is left of the original 240 acre ranch us Bachman kids grew up on. I'm excited to see it.

Brother Jim is president of the Placer County Farm Bureau and still runs around 30 mother cows. He is a retired carpenter and promises to build me a bird house made from a cedar tree that my father planted. The old tree succumbed to a storm, and Jim had the lumber planed at a mill operated by Caroline's son, Jeff, who lives in Forest Hill. It will be a special bird house.

Outside in Caroline's windy, rain-soaked yard, I can see blooming narcissus, and lemons growing on trees. A birdseed-filled sock attracts myriad finches, and an occasional blue jay screams from the branch of a digger pine.

See you soon back on Prairie Creek.

February 6—Peering out my kitchen window on this cold, snowy afternoon, my heart is gladdened by the sudden appearance of three pair of Red polls perched on the new bird feeder my brother Jim built for me. Daddy would be proud to know his son is using that wood creatively. The fragrant red wood was planed from a fallen tree our daddy planted so long ago, when he and mama lived on what is left of the original 240 acre "Oakcrest Ranch" in Placer County, California, where we five children grew up.

My new feeder, mounted on a wooden pole, is stuck into a 9-ft snow drift that grew up in our absence, in front of the raspberry patch. Beyond that drift, which rises higher each day, the upper Prairie Creek country rolls onward like a scene in the attic, stopping just short of our snowy Wallowas. Nothing moves, save for the wind, in that frozen, snowy winterscape. My whole world is white. Our lane is drifted shut, again, while yet another winter storm watch is posted for Eastern Oregon.

I called my neighbors, Gardener and Tappy Locke, to ask if they needed anything, and how were they managing?

"Fine," said Tappy, "but we'd sure like some fresh eggs." Since the elderly couple were completely isolated, at the end of a long drifted lane, I told her if the wind stopped blowing, I'd snowshoe over the field with a dozen eggs.

"My hens are laying," I said. "Joel Stein, the young fellow who did our chores while we were in California, took good care of my chickens."

However, after I hung up, the wind increased and a "white-out" prevailed. I couldn't even see Locke's house.

Later, their grandson Nathan, who had been plowing alternate routes through snowy fields and across frozen irrigation ditches to his grandparents house, drove over in his truck to pick up the eggs. I'd managed to snowshoe out as far as our mailbox.

Upper Prairie Creek appears even more isolated and drifted-in than us. Local ranchers are plowing county roads, since the Road Department is working overtime to keep the school bus routes open. Hundreds of hungry white-tail deer and elk are raiding haystacks on Prairie Creek and Alder Slope. Using ski poles, I snowshoe up, over, and down enormous drifts to reach my chicken house. Even though, during our absence, granddaughter Adele saw to it that Halley received plenty of TLC, my growing border collie was happy to see me. She has turned into a "snow dog," pushing snow ahead of her with her nose before chasing the rolling snowballs down the drifts.

Our cats aren't at all happy about having Halley back. In fact, they've taken refuge in my old sheepherder wagon, where I now feed them. But that's ok. They're supposed to be barn cats anyway, and keep the mice under control.

Being snowbound is one way of dealing with the high cost of fuel. Doug parks his pickup out on the road, and I stay home. He sees no point in plowing out our lane when it just drifts in again. Consequently, I keep the home fires burning, except on rare occasions when I want to attend a Fishtrap "Big Read" event, or we both must meet with our accountant about the Income Tax. We are saddened this year by the all-too-soon death of our long-time accountant Chuck Roberts.

The old "boys" who regularly meet to play cribbage six days a week at the Range Rider in Enterprise are wandering aimlessly around the county lately. It seems the old Tavern's roof caved in with the weight of the snow. Word has it that the new roof is nearly installed. Methinks the "gang" has been meeting at the Cheyenne Cafe in Joseph; that is, at least those old cronies who aren't snowed in.

It's been quite a winter and it's far from over. Who needs a grocery store, anyway? When I run out of bread, I bake a loaf from my sourdough, and since there's plenty of food put by for winter, we aren't going to go hungry.

On Super Bowl Sunday Doug had just finished plowing out our lane for the second time, when in drove Lyman and Wilma. Their timing was perfect. Not only for a visit, but for sampling the lemon pie I'd just baked, using my fresh eggs with fresh lemons from sister Caroline's tree in California. Lyman and Wilma are still planning on tying the knot. However, the wedding has been held up 'cause Wilma's brother, the preacher who will perform the ceremony, hasn't been able to get from Union to Wallowa County.

The day after we returned from California, Lyman had called.

"Wilma and I are get'in hitched, y'all come around 12:30."

"We can't get out our lane," I said.

"No problem, I'll come pick you up."

Later, he called to say Raymond, the preacher, had only made it to Imbler; had to turn around in blowing snow. Another whiteout.

Like I say, we managed fine. When the electricity went out, I saved water and, since I cook on the old Monarch all winter anyway, we didn't lack for heat. Candle and lantern light works quite well, and lends a sense of warmth.

We were without a TV, yeah, and phone, for awhile, but no big deal. I washed clothes and hung them on a wooden rack in front of the wood stove, and we survived in the same way Prairie Creek ranchers have for years, when wealth was measured by your ample wood pile and hay stack, and how full your canning cupboard, root cellar and freezers were. After 40 winters here I've learned you can never be too prepared.

My old friend Grace Bartlett used to say, "Winter was good for the mind." Nothing better than curling up to re-read Craig Lesley's *Riversong,* Fishtrap's Big Read selection. Speaking of Craig Lesley, he is in the county now, making appearances for our Big Read. I guess there is no finer fellow than Craig. Modest, genuine and sincere, Craig is beloved by all who know him.

Since one of the chapters in *Riversong* is set near Dug Bar, at Robinson Gulch and Deep Creek, there has been a lot of interest locally in Craig's book.

Local bush pilot Joe Spence flew Doug out to Salmon Creek to check on our three horses. Due to the severity of our winter, I was concerned. Doug reports they are pawing under the snow for bunch grass and doing fine, but I still worry. The road from the Dorrance place to Salmon creek is drifted in, not maintained in winter. It must be a white wilderness out there. I wish my mare, Morning Star, was here so I could care for her.

The "Wolf" moon, the "Hunger" moon, has gone, but there is still hunger. Eagles both Bald and Golden can be seen feasting on placentas as the first calves appear in the valley. And the coyotes are mating, creating quite a racket on Hough's hill. As long as there are plenty of deer I don't worry they will come after Halley or the cats.

Hawks, wild geese and ducks, flickers, crows—and, of course, the juncos, Red polls and sparrows, seem always able to find food. Often I see wild honkers eating alongside the cattle. If it weren't for the ranchers' hay, it would be a pretty tough time for our valley's wildlife. Pretty tough on the rancher's pocketbook, however, when $150 per ton of hay is eaten by herds of deer and elk. However, as I write, the great meltdown has begun. That is, until Mother Nature changes her mind again. Here, in Wallowa County they say, "Only fools or newcomers predict the weather."

Our California trip seems like a dream, like it never happened, except when I refer to my daily journal. I still can't believe we crammed so much into such a short stay. All the while it snowed up here and the temperatures dove below zero, it rained in California. However, that rain didn't hinder having a good time with family and friends.

I remember the Hidden Falls hike with sisters Caroline and Kathryn, a wonderful getaway from the frantic life that is California. The rain let up as we hiked the oak-studded foothills to a creek where wild blackberry bramble, Toyan berries and manzanita grew. Where coyote calls replaced the sound of the freeway, and the sights and smells of my childhood were evident all around us.

I can still taste the food at Thai Basil in Roseville, where my sisters and I lunched before shopping. I couldn't believe the sales. Flannel sheets for $20.00! A small travel Scrabble game, small enough to put in a backpack. Trader Joe's—oh my gosh! I treasure the visit to the restored Fruitvale School, where I walked from Clovertop Ranch, where my daddy worked, to the one-room school to attend first grade.

Had lunch one day with my niece Lori at Newcastle Produce; and how could I forget that mouth-watering Tri-tip, bar-b-cued by brother Jim at our old ranch? Jim's wife Joyce cooked all day: potato casserole, salad, bread, pecan pie and chocolate trifle. Yum! Viewing family photos of times past was great fun. Surprised to see beavers working in Doty's Ravine, on Jim's property.

All the while, storm after storm swept over Northern California...and the tiny tree frogs sang sweetly, another memory of my youth.

February 12—On February 3rd we lost another old time cowboy, Sam Loftus, and today he was buried up on the hill above Enterprise. His service was held in Cloverleaf Hall, standing room only. Sam's worn saddle, hat and boots were there, and words hovered in the air, as friends stood up and related stories.

Sam, born on Elk Mountain, spent most of his life on Imnaha, living

Ken Hunt pauses during a cattle drive that trailed 358 head of cows from Big Sheep Creek to Enterprise. The drive took 3 days. Ken lives on Big Sheep Creek, near Imnaha, Oregon. He is a wood carving artist and also braided the reins you see him holding.

a unique life in an era that will never be again. I'll always treasure my own memories of working for Red's Horse Ranch, during that long-ago snowy November elk season, way up there in a cook tent on the upper Minam, at a place called Elk Creek where Sam and I ran the deluxe elk camp. Sam, who suffered for such a long time, a victim of Parkinson's disease, is now at rest.

There is so much more to write about, like the finale for Fishtrap's Big Read, held at the Hurricane Creek Grange, where Craig Lesley talked to us about his books Riversong and Winterkill, and Joe McCormack bar-b-cued salmon, the Grange ladies baked pies, and folks brought potluck. The place was packed.

The old Ira Pace barn, built in the early 1900s, has weathered many Prairie Creek winters. Chief Joseph Mountain is in the background.

February 16—I want to tell about the baby calves being born to son Ken's cows near Alder Slope, and how I drive up there sometimes, and park to watch the cows and calves. And how, on the way to Enterprise, I enjoy seeing the increase of calves on the Mt. Joseph Ranch, born to those same Marr Flat cows I helped drive from Big Sheep. I enjoy seeing son Todd and grandson Buck feeding, and watching the growing calves romp on the hill.

Then I want to talk about taking granddaughter Adele to lunch on Valentine's Day, a day before her 20th birthday. And how Adele is helping me with my housework. Yeah! And how son-in-law Charley delivered me a bale of leafy alfalfa hay for my chickens, and now they are laying five eggs a day. And how my neighbor Tappy Locke is buying eggs from me every Thursday.

Then there was that February moon, the "Snow" moon, in full eclipse, as viewed from our living room picture window. A miracle of sorts. I wanted to report that Doug hauled hay on his four-wheeler to our stranded horses way out in the hills on Salmon Creek. Been a tough winter.

Most importantly, when I delivered some of my sourdough starter to

Todd Nash, manager of the Marr Flat Cattle Company, relaxes with two of his cow dogs after turning 358 head of mother cows into a pasture for the night.

Jan, who lives up on Alder Slope, she showed me Snow Drops blooming alongside her house. I remember reading in Mary Marks' diaries, and how she never failed to note the blooming of the first snowdrops.

Jason Cunningham, the young cowboy caretaker of Richard and Mary Frasch's cattle operation on Doug's old ranch, moved some cows into the same pasture where Ken's cows calved out last winter, and where Ben calved out our cows for over 25 years. When I went for a walk yesterday, I saw two calves.

One day I made a big kettle of homemade beef soup and took it out the north highway to grandson Chad's family who have all been sick with the flu. I feel so sorry for the little ones, who are a long time recovering.

One morning I picked up the phone and called one of my first cousins Pam, who lives in Georgia and reads this column, sent to her by another cousin Janet who lives in Sacramento, California. Thus, this column continues to be a letter from home.

Next time I will write about two recent funerals, the Blue Mountain Old Time Fiddlers program that took place in Cloverleaf Hall while the

One-year-old Lucy Matthews has a birds eye view of a recent cattle drive.
Shown here with her mom, Chelsea Matthews. Her daddy Buck Matthews
was one of the cowboys. Lucy is Janie Tippett's great-granddaughter.

Joseph Eagles won the title of State Class 1-A Championship in Baker
City; not to mention all those events that will transpire on a daily basis.

For now, I want to say goodbye to Jackie Tippett, beloved wife of Ben
Tippett, who lost her battle with cancer. Jackie was a loving wife, mother,
and grandmother, and will be missed greatly by her many friends.

February 25—Last week six male red wing blackbirds appeared at
my bird feeder. I'd been hearing their familiar liquid notes floating from
the tall willows for several days. These ancient willow trees, watered by
the irrigation ditch that meanders just beyond the bunkhouse, provide a
haven for hawks, owls and numerous song birds. The blackbirds, with
their red-tinged wings, have been sharing the feeder with myriad juncos,
chickadees, and the first returning robin.

While volunteering as a CowBelle, along with Jean Cook, at our

Senior Dining Center last Friday, I ran into—literally—Wallowa County's infamous bird lover, Van Van Blaricom, who informed me that the male red wings arrive three weeks ahead of the females, to stake out a place to nest. Interesting. Since five foot snow banks encircle the house, my bird feeder is still stuck in the snow, and subsequent snowfalls continue to add to our already impressive drifts.

Checking in on Lyman and Wilma I was surprised to learn they'd eloped. Yep, got hitched. Since the preacher, Wilma's brother Raymond, never did make it into Wallowa County, the couple drove out to Union. Congratulations, you two love birds. Lyman tells me he and Wilma will be movin' down to the river soon, that is, when they both get over the flu.

"And," says Lyman, "After the second cut'in of hay is up, we're planning a whing ding at the ranch on the upper Imnaha."

More good news—our friend Maurice located a place to park the large trailer he recently purchased. He'll be living down at Lou's place, the old Warnock ranch, downriver from Lyman's ranch.

Doug and his cribbage-playing buddies are happy to be back in The Range Rider again. I understand the roof is repaired and it's business as usual. While on the mend, I attended our Winter Fishtrap Conference, held on February 22-24 at the historic Wallowa Lake Lodge. I spent Friday and Saturday night there, sharing a room on the third floor with my friend Kathy.

This year's theme was "Living Right: Empathy, Charity and Responsibility" and featured Debra Dean, author of *The Madonnas of Leningrad*, and Michael Rohd, founding artistic director of Sojourn Theatre in Portland, and Sisters of the Road, a Portland-based Cafe that's celebrating it's 27th year of providing a haven for anyone "down on his or her luck." We were blown away by these presentations.

Quotes from Sisters of the Road brochure include, "Sisters isn't a restaurant, it's a friend. I always feel better after I leave here, the whole rest of my day improves. It's part of the reason I'm not doing drugs and alcohol, and why I've started back to school."

"I can come here even though I'm mentally ill, and people don't judge me and are not afraid of me."

"I'm not looking for a handout. Sisters lets me earn my meals by working for them. It has really helped my self esteem."

It was heartening to listen to these fine folks who are quietly going about their work to improve humanity. Since our Book Group had just finished reading Debra Dean's book, wherein she addresses art and Alzheimer's, it was a real treat to meet and listen to her read. Debra, an extremely gifted gal, is currently the visiting writer at the University of Miami.

The weekend passed all too quickly, and even though the presentations were pretty intense, the food, conversation, and relaxing atmosphere did a lot to heal my winter-weary soul. During free time, Sharon, Chris, Kathy and I played scrabble there in the historic great room, using the little "travel Scrabble" set I purchased in California. While outside, feathery flakes of snow swirled around the old lodge, the wind stirred the limbs of the tall Ponderosas, and the snow sifted quietly down. Beyond lay the silent frozen lake.

On Sunday morning the sun streamed through it all, and humongus icicles began to drip, loosen their grip, and then crash like broken glass onto the deck. The large, frozen, sculpted fountain glowed blue-green in the morning sunlight, and the deer came to eat apples handed to them by some of the attendees who had traveled by Moffit bus from Portland. Those folks thought they were in fairyland. And we, who live here, KNEW we were.

For over 20 years now Fishtrap continues to work its magic. We all went away a bit wiser to the ways of an increasingly complex world.

March 3—Temperatures have warmed considerably this afternoon. Water drips from our roof as an accumulation of snow begins to melt. Prairie Creeks reeks of "false spring." The back of winter appears to be broken, and from now on the snow will be soft and full of moisture. Just today, I sensed the change. In my mind's eye I pictured a spot of bare earth on Hough's hill, where the sun-warmed rocks provide just the right conditions for the unfurling of the first buttercups...and I sense the eternal stirrings of Spring.

I'm impatient to heal, be strong again, to strike out over the thawing fields, to climb the hills with Halley forging ahead, sniffing the squirrel breath that wafts from every muddy den. However, I must be patient. Two weeks ago I came down with what I suspect might be the AH3N2/Brisbane-like strain of flu, obviously not the strain I received a shot for last fall. Two strains of the flu are presently running rampant in Wallowa County. The bad one I have produces a deep, wracking cough, high fever, and weakness.

So, on top of being snowbound, I was homebound...which wasn't all that bad. Actually, it was a relief to pick up the phone and cancel my life. I needed a rest, have gotten myself a bit run down. So, I drank a lot of tea, made chicken soup, and read several books. However, as my health improved, it didn't take long to get caught back up in my active lifestyle.

Consequently, this column, began on February 25th, is just now being completed during the wee hours of March 3rd.

March 15—As evening descends on Prairie Creek there appears to be a break in the hail, sleet and snow squalls that have come and gone all day. At some point this afternoon there was a period of brilliant sunshine, which generated enough heat to melt the new accumulation of snow on our roof. As I write, water streams down our window panes. Typical Wallowa County March, still roaring with its lion-like entrance. Hopefully, the proverbial lamb will appear soon.

Peering out my kitchen window I see Halley, my rapidly-growing border collie pup, standing next to the bird feeder, which is still stuck in a snow drift. I hope she's not eating the bird seed! Meanwhile, perched in the old apple tree, two robin red breasts, three red-winged blackbirds, and a Rufus-Sided Towhee, wait patiently for her to leave. And she does, after I open the window and scold her.

I dread cleaning our yard after the big meltdown. Winter's flotsam, including Halley's teething toys, will be exposed. Actually, there is only one TOY—her favorite—a very chewed-up gift from sister Kathryn. Her other treasures include a pair of holey hiking boots, bleached deer ribs, same deer's antlers, worn gloves, broken plastic buckets, my torn-up flower planter, and what, I suspect, might be a fossilized placenta buried years ago by my old dog Daisy.

Needless to say, Halley is a very busy girl. And very smart. She understands seven words now, like ball, walk, cats, chickens, chores, birds, and fetch—oh my, can she fetch, you never saw such gusto.

As I was driving past the Eastern Oregon Nursery one morning last week, my eyes were drawn to something colorful. Primroses! I did a U-turn and drove back to take a closer look. After living in a winter-weary landscape so long, I just had to sit and stare. Long story short, I drove out with 20 of the prettiest primroses you ever saw. But what was I thinking? What about Halley? She'd eat them! So I gave them away, to my granddaughter and great-granddaughter; to my friend Kathy, who recently underwent surgery on her wrist; to Carolee at KWVR radio, who has the flu; and to friends I met in town. Much more fun than planting them just to watch Halley seek and destroy.

Now I'm thinking window boxes and hanging baskets. How long does puppyhood last, anyway?

Doug and I just returned from Joseph, where we attended a memorial service for Chuck Roberts, who passed away of lung cancer on January 28th. Chuck's celebration of life was held at the Joseph United Methodist

Church. Chuck was our accountant for years, and taken from us too soon. However, as the Reverend Dr. Craig Strobel summed it up, "Chuck embraced life" and, although he won't be around to grow old, he made the most of life while he was here.

We'll always remember Chuck's gentle smile and genuine desire to help us through those difficult tax times when Doug still owned his ranches. I like to think it was a gift from Chuck when sudden sunlight streamed through those lovely stained-glass windows of that old stone church, as Claudia Boswell played Irish tunes on the piano.

By the time we returned to Prairie Creek, it was snowing again. Time has been trotting along so fast I scarcely know what day it is. Why is it, the older we get, the faster it moves? Day break. Sunset. Winter. Spring.

On Thursday afternoon, after attending two back-to-back board meetings, I met granddaughter Adele and fled to La Grande, where we joined daughter Ramona, granddaughter Carrie, and great-granddaughter Brenna at the #1 China Buffet. Four generations of females gabbing and gobbling up Chinese food. Fun.

On the way over we'd experienced cloud bursts of rain, sleet and snow, followed by brief shots of sunlight. Then Adele and I made it to the Schwarz Theatre on Eastern Oregon University campus in time to purchase tickets for the performance of "You Can't Take It With You."

Eastern's version of this Pulitzer prize-winning classic was hilarious. Of course, my worldly Adele, who, at the age of 17, was a Rotary Exchange student to Argentina, has seen musicals in places I can only imagine. That doesn't stop me from living vicariously through my grandchildren, however. There we were, second-row seats in a small, intimate theatre. It was fun being there with my lovely 20-year-old granddaughter.

After the play ended we drove a few blocks away to granddaughter Carrie's house, where we spent the night. I slept in great-granddaughter Brenna's bed, and four-year-old Brenna slept with her grandma, my daughter Ramona, while Adele took the sofa.

The next morning I was up visiting Carrie before she left for her job at the new Cook Memorial Library. It was like a slumber party. For breakfast we munched on yogurt, strawberries and granola, then watched a 2006 DVD of our Wilson/Butler family reunion in Rio Linda, California. We loved being there in Carrie's cozy little house, whilst hail stones pattered on the pavement outside.

Around noon, a pleasant surprise: granddaughter Chelsie showed up with four more of my great-grandchildren. What fun! Seems they were in La Grande shopping for cake decorating supplies. Chelsie, who lives in rural Joseph, says she's going into the cake decorating business.

Naturally, everyone was hungry, so we sent Adele out for pizza. Watching Riley Ann, Ashlynn, twins (Gideon and Jada) and Brenna, little cousins, seated around the kitchen table, made my day.

Leaving her children with us, Chelsie went shopping while Adele, Ramona and I played scrabble with the little "Travel Scrabble" I purchased in Roseville, California. Meanwhile, those five little cousins paraded back and forth wearing costumes they'd found in Brenna's magical closet.

It was late afternoon when Adele and I drove to the library to tell Carrie goodbye, and headed home to Wallowa County.

Back at what's left of Doug's ranch, Halley was wondering where I was, and Doug was hungry. So, I cooked up a kettle of clam chowder and wasted little time tumbling into bed. I really haven't taken enough time to fully recover from the flu. Consequently, I'm still coughing and tire easily. My calendar, however, just keeps filling up.

It seems we've gone to more than our share of funerals lately. There was Sarah Juve's grave side service at the Enterprise Cemetery. Sarah was only 32. Then, Ben's wife Jackie Tippett, another victim of cancer. Taken in the prime of life. Somehow it's hard to think Jackie is gone.

That evening, after Jackie's funeral at the L.D.S. Church in Enterprise, Doug and I attended the Blue Mountain Old time Fiddlers program at Cloverleaf Hall. Actually, the event was a Memorial to Charley Trump who was one of Wallowa County's treasures. A kind, gentle man, who, for years, organized the fiddle events in Cloverleaf Hall.

Thankfully, Charley's widow Nancy keeps his tradition alive. What a balm to the soul was that fiddle music, from two and a half-year-old Ariana to her grandpa Leonard Samples, who fiddled from his wheel chair. We sat next to another veteran music maker, native Wallowa Countian Lester Kiesecker, who recently broke a hip. In spite of getting around with a walker, Lester couldn't contain himself when his son Tim tucked his fiddle under his chin and began to make music.

"Let me out!" said Lester, and—holding his walker with both hands— this agile aging man proceeded to dance in time to his son's fired-up fiddle. Songs like "When the Cactus is in Bloom," "Boil The Cabbage Down," "Drowsy Maggie," and "Milk Cow Blues" filled the air there in Cloverleaf Hall. And even though most of Wallowa County was OUT of the county, down to Baker City to watch the Joseph Eagles win the Class A State Basketball Championship, we, who remained, felt very blessed.

Randy Garnett and the Fair Board cooked up a bar-b-cued pork supper that was pretty popular, and the proceeds went to helping run our Wallowa County Fair. A very worthwhile cause.

We enjoyed listening to various members of the Collins family, and a group known as "The Pot-Bellied Trio." Of course we cheered our own "Prairie Creek Girls," Ryya, Lexi, and Hannah. Then there was the old fellow who climbed on stage to play his fiddle saying, "I ain't played this piece for anyone. 'Cept my wife and dog." After deciding it was time to become a member of the Old Time Fiddlers, I paid my dues, and was delighted with my miniature wooden fiddle, a reward to the first new member that evening.

After two funerals in two days my spirit was restored. Music, the best medicine.

Since my hens are laying again, I've been baking old-fashioned cup custards, which taste so good when one has the flu. The soup kettle is always on the old Monarch these days as well. I took another pot of soup over to grandson Chad and Amy's family, who really appreciate grandma's homemade chicken noodle soup. "Ronan ate three bowls," reported Amy. "Gwenllian two, and Kennon two." And, to this very deserving young mother of four, the soup raised her spirits as well.

Because of my lingering illness, and more snowfalls, I never did hike up Hough's hill to search for the first buttercups. However Doug, on one of his trips to the hills, dug a cluster of them, and presented them to me in a rusted can. I transferred those buttercups, still growing in their fragrant prairie soil, to a blue enamel pan, where they continue to bloom.

On several occasions I managed short walks down Tenderfoot Valley Road with Halley to see Jason's new calves. All over the valley, the pastures smell of birth. And, perched in the old cottonwoods, the bald eagles wait for their next meal of fresh placenta.

Taking time to drive to Enterprise and visit old timers Mike McFetridge and Wilmer Cook, who were hospitalized with pneumonia, I was surprised to see our local radio announcer there too. Yep. Another pneumonia victim. Lee came down with "the bug" while he and wife Carolee traveled miles to cover all those out-of-town basketball games. Carolee carried on down at the radio station, and that's why I gave her some of those primroses.

I saw Wilmer down at the Community Dining Center last Friday, and Mike—who will turn 100 in November—was sitting up and taking nourishment. Yeah!

Received a surprise phone call from grandson James, back in the county during Spring Break from college at University of Montana West, in Dillon.

"On my way over," he said. "Have a present for you" which turned out to be a "state of the art" backpack, a super light one I can't wait to use.

Several nights later we had James, his dad (my son Todd) and wife Angie, grandson Buck and great-granddaughter Lucy over for supper. I'd spent a good deal of time in the kitchen baking sourdough bread and a "made from scratch" lemon pie, preparing a large dutch oven full of tamale pie, tossing a salad, and fixing chicken fried steak. We missed Lucy's mom Chelsea, who works the night shift at our local hospital. Wee one-year-old Lucy wowed us, almost as much as James did with his wild pig-hunting stories.

Doug drove home his new/used pickup/camper the other day. Does this mean we'll go camping?

My friend Phyllis just returned from her cruise to Portugal and Spain. Since tomorrow is St. Patrick's Day, we're having Fred and Phyllis over for Corned Beef and cabbage. I suspect we'll hear all about it. We understand while Phyllis was away, Fred caught two steelhead in the Grande Ronde River.

Sharon and I went to see "The Bucket List" at the OK Theatre in Enterprise. A wonderful movie. We should all have a list of things to do before we "kick the bucket."

Lyman and Wilma stopped by on their way back from "the river" the other day. I fed them homemade chicken noodle soup to help Wilma feel better. Lyman got over his flu, but, like me, Wilma's seems to be lingering on. What we all need is a little sunshine.

March 26—Through my open kitchen window I hear the springlike trilling of birds, which seems unnatural owing to Prairie Creek's frozen landscape. The only other sound this morning, save for a ticking clock and a popping fire, comes from one of Hough's old trucks, chugging along in low gear as their hired man tosses hay to the cows.

My window is open because the old Monarch is fired up to cook a pot of pinto beans that are now simmering with the ham bone left over from our belated Easter dinner. I say belated, because we waited until Monday evening to prepare our traditional dinner. The reason being, daughter Jackie and husband Bill, pastor of The Assembly of God Church in Challis, Idaho, were expected to arrive that evening.

Jackie and Bill's arrival prompted many impromptu family get-togethers that naturally revolved around food. That's where this grandma shines. She loves to cook. That Monday evening after Easter was especially joyous, as we were entertained by one-year-old Lucy and her four-year-old cousin Brenna. Once again we were four generations gathered around the kitchen table, helping ourselves to baked ham, scalloped potatoes, home-canned green beans, Angie's fruit salad, fresh-from-the-oven french bread, and Ramona's mango bars.

With the exception of a few sunny afternoons, March, thus far, has been its typical and fickle self. Snow flurries come and go, mornings are frost-tinged and frigid. Although they appear to be shrinking, those snow drifts that encircle our house, are still very much in evidence.

Bill and Jackie, Lucy's grandpa and grandma, are visiting here in Wallowa County, on their way to Seattle, to meet their daughter Mona, who will be flying in from India Friday night.

March 28—And now it is Friday night, and I wait for a phone call from Seattle. Our carport thermometer registered a chilly 19 degrees this morning, and, later this afternoon, sudden sunlight filtered through a layer of cold clouds to illuminate more swirling snow flakes. Ah, Spring! Wallowa County style.

Miraculously, a clump of lavender crocuses continue to bloom next to the house, where it's warmer and free of snow. And, on Hough's hill, the waxy golden petals of the buttercups hug a carpet of winter-killed cheat bloom amid myriad squirrel holes, sage, and rotting patches of snow.

On the first day of Spring we experienced one of those rare sunny afternoons, so Halley and I braved thawing fields, two snow-covered irrigation ditches, and three fences, to emerge at the base of a snow-filled draw. Scouting around I found a weathered board next to a rockjack, sat myself down in a patch of buttercups, and dozed off in the delicious warmth of the sun. Meanwhile, Halley entertained herself by investigating every squirrel den in the area.

While seated at my kitchen table on the morning of the 26th, just beginning this column, a knock on the door produced Phyllis' husband Fred, who was closely followed by Doug. Suspecting Fred was here to help Doug with his Direct TV problem, I continued to write. Six hours later Fred was still here, and he hadn't gotten around to Doug's TV yet—rather, Fred was DETERMINED to get me "dialed up" to the internet so I could e-mail my columns.

"This won't take long, we're almost there," was a phrase I heard often during the course of the afternoon.

Meanwhile, this column was put on the back burner, while I attempted to keep ALL burners of the wood stove hot in order to cook those beans, as well as make chicken stock for a kettle of noodle soup.

Since Jackie and Bill were staying with their son Buck, wife Chelsea and granddaughter Lucy, I had invited them over for supper so we could visit. This meant I was having to juggle "hands on" E-Mail lessons, poking wood to the fire, stirring beans, unplugging phones, dragging cords from the kitchen to the front room, cooking noodles, baking cornbread, setting the table, and (when the phone was plugged in) answering myriad calls from my family.

In other words, I was alternately elated at having the e-mail set up and frustrated by numerous delays, all the while scrambling to have supper on the table by 5:30. It was after 5:00 when Fred finally addressed Doug's TV problem, which turned out to be UNsolvable. I had also invited Ben Tippett, Doug's cousin, who worked all those years on Doug's ranches, and who recently lost his beloved wife Jackie. Ben showed up, as did our Jackie and her family, and we had a wonderful evening. Food was consumed and stories were told.

Ben said he wouldn't have met his future wife if he hadn't gone to work for Doug. You see, Doug had hired Jackie Kingsford to help with the cooking when he owned the Dug Bar Ranch on Snake River. So it was only natural that the handsome young cowboy took a shine to the pretty blond girl with the beautiful smile. As the story goes, the young couple stayed out longer and longer each night, "checking the first-calf heifers." What could be more romantic than a canyon setting?

After everyone left, I did a sinkful of dishes and fell into bed. The column stayed on the back burner.

The next day I met daughter Jackie and granddaughter Adele for lunch at the Cloud Nine Bakery. Adele had just returned from visiting her brother James who attends college in Dillon, Montana. Jackie and Adele shared stories of when Jackie was on the Chief Joseph Days Court, and Adele was Queen of the Elgin Stampede.

March 29—It was nearly 9:30 when the phone rang last night—daughter Jackie reporting in. Thankfully, our Mona landed safely in Seattle on the same day she left India. You figure it out! A relief to me that Jackie and Bill made it over the Pass in that March blizzard. Wouldn't you know, it even snowed in Seattle.

Just sitting down this morning to continue the unending saga that is my life, when Fred, as in WEBB, not WEB-mail, showed up with Doug in tow again. The "boys" at the Cheyenne Cafe had obviously exhausted their stories for the day, so Fred said he was here to finish hooking me up to the e-mail. Well, let me tell you, Fred just left, and it's 2:30 in the afternoon. Somehow I'd managed to brown a pot roast, slide it into the wood cook stove oven, fix lunch, and write down a step-by-step process to "do" e-mail. Do I really want this? Too late now; I'm hooked. Up, that is.

And since we're now into the weekend and my column's still not finished, I must wait until Monday morning to see if this thing works. Having expended so much energy on technology, I don't have enough *oomph* left to elaborate on the wonderful Easter Sunday Church service, where I joined four great-grandchildren for the Good Friday evening service at the Joseph United Methodist Church. I'll always remember that full March moon though, the "Worm Moon", rising in the east as we made our way down the stone steps to our cars, and how it swam ahead of me as I drove back to Prairie Creek.

Then there were those Scrabble games and lunches at the new hospital with my writer's group. A pleasant way to spend these lingering cold days of spring.

On Easter Sunday Doug drove to Dug Bar. Said the road was bad. So, what's new? Said he wet his line in the Imnaha (no keepers) and reports the Sarvis is blooming at the lower elevations.

Frasch's cows are calving in what used to be Doug's lower field, and a pair of Bald Eagles reside in the cottonwoods that line the irrigation ditch.

Doug and I attended the annual Wallowa County Grain Growers annual dinner/meeting in Cloverleaf Hall on March 27th. I enjoyed visiting old-timers Ruth Baremore and her friend Aleta Neal, both of whom used to ranch out near Promise. Also visited my neighbor Lois Hough, as well as Ann Hayes, Shandon Towers, Maxine Kooch, Shirley Parker and Mary Lou Brink.

Must put a period to this "slice of life" and peel potatoes to go with the pot roast for supper. Tomorrow morning, Phyllis and I will meet with other Friends of the Museum at the Minam Motel for a history lesson before boarding the Eagle Cap Excursion Train to Rondowa. I'm ready for a little R. and R.

March 30—Phyllis and I ran into a spring blizzard as we drove through the Minam canyon that cold morning. By the time we parked in front of the Minam Motel to walk the railroad tracks and board the "History Train," a freezing wind wafted feathery flakes of snow in our faces. As the engine returned from transporting steelhead fishermen downriver, we boarded.

We didn't notice the cold as much after Jan Hohmann from the Friends of the Wallowa County Museum introduced Agnes Roberts and

Two-and-a-half-year-old Ariana Samples stole the show at the recent Old-Time Fiddlers program in Enterprise. She is the third generation to play the fiddle. Ariana's father is Caleb Samples and her grandpa is Leonard Samples, both accomplished fiddle players. Ariana was accompanied by her uncle Tyson on the bass fiddle and Dave Murrill on the mandolin.

The old Jean Butler barn off Airport Road in Joseph. The roof damage is due to violent fall windstorms. Photo by Doug Tippett.

Barbara Raines, who entertained us with stories of what it was like to live there in Minam when it was a small town that revolved around a sawmill. Much of the logging took place way up the Minam River, and in those early years, teams of horses were used to drag the logs to a splash dam located 30 miles upriver. Old-timer Merle Hawkins pointed to where a huge horse barn once stood, and Barbara showed us an old photo of the structure.

"Stalled 20 head of horses," said Merle. "And there was a platform built down the center so men could pack a string of mules and not have to lift those heavy loads of supplies." These long pack strings were led up the Minam River, 25 miles to what used to be Red's Horse Ranch and another five to the Splash Dam, bringing supplies to the loggers who camped up there. To me the unsung heroes of those early day logging ventures were the horses and mules. Without them there would be no jobs.

Merle, former Hells Canyon Mule Days Grand Marshal, guide and packer, married Red Higgins' daughter. Two of Merle's daughters, Nora and Mary, accompanied their dad on the train ride.

Barbara showed us old photos of what the town looked like when her family lived there. Both she and Agnes set up housekeeping under the crudest conditions, but admitted they had fun. They recalled dances and told stories about moonshine, chickens, milk cows, snow slides and ice jams. The women said 21 families once lived in the little town of Minam.

It was nearing noon when our engine came around the bend, pulling the HEATED dining car. After all connections were made, we wasted no time filing into the warmth of the dining car, where we munched our brown bag lunches, all the while staring out at the Wallowa River swirling along on one side, and melting icicles clinging to colorful rock formations just inches from us on the other.

Soon we arrived at the old logging railroad siding known as Vincent, where an old road led to the former logging community of Maxwell. Here, Howard Creek, the color of snowmelt, splashed into the Wallowa River. As we chugged our way to lower elevations, the country appeared to green up, and there was an absence of snow. Joyfully, we spotted brilliant blue bells, and golden buttercups clinging to rocky clefts in the canyon walls.

We stopped at Kimmell, another junction, to pick up several fishermen who lugged their gear and coolers full of fish into the warm car. Eventually we arrived at Rondowa, where we parked on the bridge while the engine swapped ends. From our vantage point we gazed down the Grande Ronde as it made its way to Troy. Eventually this river empties into the Snake at Rogersburg. From the other side of the car we looked down at the confluence of the Wallowa River and the Grande Ronde.

April 6—Noth'in's as lov'in as someth'in from the oven, is what I'm think'in this morn'in. That "someth'in" be'n a cake, bak'in in the old Monarch oven.

You see, yesterday Doug and I drove down to Imnaha in separate rigs. He driving, or rather "herding" his old Dodge pickup ahead of me, while I followed in the smaller pickup. Doug was delivering the ancient truck to our friend Maurice, who is now living in his new/used trailer, which is parked in Lou's yard at the old Warnock place. Since Maurice was looking for a truck big enough to tow his trailer, Doug let him have the old Dodge.

While the men discussed truck wheels, I wandered around, admiring the daffodils and primroses blooming in Lou's yard. Spring was happening along the Imnaha, and my winter-weary heart was gladdened by the greening canyons. Leaning against the garden fence, soaking up the sun, while staring dreamily at the whorls of red rhubarb emerging from the moist soil, made me yearn to pull weeds. Our garden is still buried beneath a layer of snow.

On our way upriver to Lyman and Wilma's, where we'd been invited for dinner, we spotted a flock of wild turkeys. Typically, the gobblers were strutting around with their tail feathers all fanned out, showing off for the hens. As we arrived Lyman was coming off the hill driving his tractor with a load of rocks in the bucket. Said he was building one of those large round rock jacks to anchor his fence.

Wilma welcomed us into their rustic log home, and pretty soon here came Lyman. We spent a most pleasant afternoon visiting, before sitting down to feast on broiled salmon. Lyman gave his son Craig credit for catching the fish and showing him how to cook it. Every bite was moist and flavorful. With the salmon we had steamed rice, a tossed salad I'd put together after we arrived, and french-cut green beans.

Lyman's bride told us she'd seen 50 head of elk from their kitchen window that morning. While washing the dishes my gaze wandered upward to those high green benches, where I counted 20 head of deer grazing Lyman's hay fields. As we were leaving, Lyman gave us some frozen applesauce. Said he'd made it from some of those apples grown upriver. So, that's how come I made the applesauce cake.

Lyman's applesauce reminded me to hunt up an old faded handwritten recipe, one I discovered years ago, hidden inside a rusty coffee can perched on the window sill of an abandoned cabin. That simple recipe never fails when baked in a wood stove oven.

Later, after topping out on Sheep Creek Hill and gazing down upon Upper Prairie Creek, still locked in winter-white, made canyon living seem all the more appealing. Especially this Spring. Locals might be right when they say, "Be August 'fore we get into our mountains."

And now it's nearly noon, the cake is cooling, and Doug has just returned from the Cheyenne Cafe where he and the "boys" have been telling tall tales. Weather-wise: same 'ol, same 'ol, daily blizzards interspersed with sleet, hail, bursts of sunlight, and wet spring snow…followed by melting and freezing.

I still haven't mastered the e-mail thing, but friends assure me I'll eventually get the hang of it. Thanks to granddaughter Adele, I was able to receive two stories her brother James had previously e-mailed. How can words fly through the air? Too weird for this grandma to figure out. My mother always said I'd be kicking and screaming my way into the 20th century.

April 11—We "Stitch and Bitchers" met at the Cougars Den in Wallowa for yummy pizzas before walking up the street to the high school

Triple Creek Ranches hay barn on Upper Prairie Creek on an early April morning. Portions of Wallowa Valley are still locked in winter white.

Mary Hawkins, left, and Nora Hawkins, right, pose with their father, Merle Hawkins during the "History Train" ride at Minam, Oregon. Merle, a past Hells Canyon Mule Days Grand Marshal, used to be a guide into the Wallowas. He remembers lots of history about the old logging operations.

gym, where we attended a performance by the Inland Northwest Musicians: The Wallowa Valley Orchestra and the Willow Creek Symphony and Singers. One of our S. and B gals Nancy played the violin. A wonderful evening of music.

Granddaughter Adele just delivered me one dozen roses. It's time to put a period to this column.

April 13—Son Todd and his crew of cowgirls and cowboys started the Man Flat cows and calves to Big Sheep. A three day drive.

April 14—A gang of us Fishtrappers converged at Dr. Driver's cabin on the Imnaha River for a working weekend. Pam and I were in charge of organizing meals, as well as pitching in and helping with this job we'd volunteered for.

Since I was the first to arrive, the amount of clean-up appeared daunting. What were we thinking? Decks and lawns were cluttered with heaps of rotting shakes and tattered tar-paper. The old shakes were being replaced with metal roofing. Because Fishtrap is indebted to Dr. Driver and his wife, Kathleen, for allowing the use of their wonderful place for our spring and fall writers' retreats, we had offered to help.

While several folks dedicated themselves to the "roof mess," others tackled routine spring chores. Don pruned the grapes while his wife, Rosemary, vacuumed and deep-cleaned the living room furniture. We emptied the ashes in the wood furnace and fireplace, and helped separate tar-paper from shakes.

Since the weekend was clear and sunny, the river was up the next morning—and there we were, hard at it again, pausing only long enough to fuel ourselves with Jim's hearty breakfast. Due to our prolonged cold spring, the forsythia was just beginning to bloom, as were several brave daffodils. The lawn, where it was free of debris, was a carpet of white and lavender violets. Normally the apple orchard would be a froth of pink and white blooms, but not this year. By noon most of us began packing our sleeping bags across the swinging bridge and heading for home.

On the way downriver I stopped to say hello to Lyman and Wilma, informing them the Spring Writers' Retreat will begin in mid-May this year, and how I was looking forward to a visit.

April 15—My young border collie Halley and I joined Todd's crew below Peek-a-boo, where the herd had bedded down for the night, and helped drive the cattle past Bear Gulch on foot. It was a perfect morning for trailing cows and calves; cool, with bursts of sunlight that made for great photo ops for me, and now Halley thinks she's a cow dog.

Since I had a 2:30 meeting in Enterprise, Halley and I hitched a ride back to my car with Dan Warnock. Nice thing about the road to Imnaha, sooner or later a Warnock or one of the Moores shows up.

This evening found Doug and me seated at a table, along with other past Hells Canyon Mule Days grand marshals, in Joseph's Outlaw Restaurant. The event honored the 2008 grand marshals: the Ulacia sisters, Maria (Marge) Onaindia and Juana Malaxa. Both are very deserving women, and wives of former grand marshals Joe and Gus, who used to own and operate the Cherry Creek Sheep Company.

There were many interesting stories told that night. Hells Canyon Mule Days is always held the weekend after Labor Day.

April 16—Our "Stitch and Bitch" gals celebrated Kathy's birthday with a potluck supper here.

I baked two loaves of french bread, and put together a seafood pasta casserole. Others brought salads, and Nancy baked a chocolate cake. We were thrilled to have Heidi Muller and Bob Webb sing and play for us. Heidi and Bob, visiting from West Virginia, are both well-known folk music artists. Heidi sang a couple of songs she'd written recently, inspired by her stay here in Wallowa County. She's been busy teaching a dulcimer workshop to our local folks.

April 19—Forty of us from Wallowa County boarded one of Reamer's large excursion boats at Clarkston, Washington, and sped up the Snake. On board with us was Craig Lesley, author of Fishtrap's Big Read book, and Bobbie Conner from Pendleton. In spite of the unseasonably cold weather, which even invaded the normally milder canyons, I enjoyed the trip—a trip cut short before we got to Deep Creek, which disappointed most, as a visit to this historic site was the purpose for our planned Snake River venture. One of the chapters in Craig's novel *Riversong* features the fabled Chinese Massacre, which took place at Deep Creek.

However, we did make it to Dug Bar where our young navigator pulled into the back water eddy to read the interpretive sign, a historical marker that describes the Nez Perce Crossing when Chief Joseph's Wallowa band of Nez Perce, along with their hundreds of horses and cattle, babies, children and elders, forded the Snake, swollen in spring flood, and crossed to the Idaho side, where they sadly began their trek to the reservation. That is—until the confrontation at White Bird, which turned the Nez Perce retreat into a war.

I was well-acquainted with this crossing because my husband used to own the Dug Bar ranch, as did his father before him. I had spent many hours sitting on a rock above the eddy, thinking about how hard it must have been for these native people to leave their ancestral home.

Memories of the short time I knew this place came to me from the time before Doug sold out to the government, before Doug's Forest Service permit land was included in the Hells Canyon National Recreation Area, an act that forever changed cattle and sheep ranching in the canyons. Today there is no more deeded land along that portion of the Snake.

It was heartening, however, to see cattle grazing the Forest Service permit land at Dug Bar. Those grassy slopes benefit from the cloven hoof, as well as the manure, which adds to the nutrients of the soil. I remembered the alfalfa field, where hay was put up on the bar itself. Mostly though, I remembered early springs, when snow lay deep on top and a new crop of healthy calves lay sunning themselves on that long bench above the ranch buildings. It was a sweet place to calve out cows. The elevation at Dug Bar is only 1000 ft.

The cement block ranch house, which Doug's family built to replace the wooden one that burned so long ago, stood vacant and forlorn.

Leaving Dug Bar behind we surged on upriver through foamy, malt-colored rapids toward Deep Creek. Then suddenly, our navigator-guide headed for a section of slack water and allowed the motor to idle, said he had to "check something," which turned out to be a broken fuel line in one of the motors. Good news and bad news. We did have one motor left to putter slowly back to Clarkston, but not enough power to get us to Deep Creek...and we were so close.

Our final stop would have been the historic Kirkwood Ranch of *Home Below Hells Canyon* fame, a must read by Grace Jordan about her life in the Snake River Canyon on her husband's sheep ranch.

There were lots of disappointed folks. However, I'd been there many times and was thankful we had enough power to ensure our safe return. After all, there we were, 60 miles upriver in the heart of Hells Canyon. Of course, I would have been perfectly happy to stay at Dug Bar.

Since it was noon, we gladly accepted the lunches handed out by the mate. Later, as we had on the trip up, we docked at Heller Bar and de-boated to tell stories as we enjoyed a brief sunny rest stop on the deck above the river. Listening to Bobbie Conner talk about her people, the Nez Perce, about their overwhelming sadness at leaving their beloved Wallowa country, made us much more aware of what that experience was really like.

My face pressed to the window, I savored our leisurely return. More time to contemplate golden arrowleaf balsamroot, brilliant pink Clarkia, wild mountain sheep, eagles, hawks, ospreys and wild honkers. More time to study the confluence of the Imnaha at Eureka Bar, the Salmon, and the Grande Ronde. Not to mention the lesser waterways: Cherry Creek, Jim Creek, Doe Creek, all places that held memories.

The day was fading when we finally docked at Clarkston. After searching out a Thai restaurant in Lewiston, we wolfed down a family-style meal before heading across to Anatone, then down Rattlesnake and up Buford into the snow country again. In spite of this prolonged cold spell, spring in Wallowa County is business as usual, and that translates to BUSY. So busy I scarcely take time to notice the weather.

April 21—Last night's full moon—April is the Pink Moon—shone over a landscape glittering with frost. Nothing was pink. And then I remembered the pink Clarkia (or was it phlox?) blooming in the Snake River canyon. April seems even colder than March. Mud puddles freeze solid, and our daily blizzards of dry powdery snow, or sleet, are borne on chill winds.

April 25—Prairie Creek was white again this morning, but like old-timer Mike McFetridge says, "Snow don't lay long on green grass." And the grass appears greener every day. Our neighbors are busy harrowing, plowing, fertilizing and seeding.

Doug just left for the hills to haul in my mare. It's been a long winter. Be good to see her again.

Lyman called one morning: "Hey! Got four hens, need a rooster." Then I remembered Kathy had a rooster she'd named Studley; said she wanted to find a home for him. So I gave Kathy a call.

"Sure," she said. "I'll bring him up when I come to my birthday party."

And so it came to pass next morning, we were awakened well before dawn by "Studley," crowing in outrage at being left in a cat cage all night on our carport. Thankfully, Lyman and Wilma showed up that afternoon, plunked the rooster into a gunny sack, and took off for Imnaha.

One rare sunny afternoon Phyllis and I struck off across the fields, making our way carefully across a snow bridge that spanned the irrigation ditch, and later emerged at the base of Hough's hill. Between the snow-filled draws and rock outcroppings we spied the first grass widows and yellow bells, blooming among masses of buttercups. At the top of the hill we breathed in the fresh spring air and gazed down on Prairie Creek, all backgrounded by our glorious mountains.

Helping on a cattle drive from Enterprise to Big Sheep Canyon—a 3-day drive—are, from left, Hannah Schaafsma, Ryya Fluitt, and Buck Matthews.

At the top of the snow-covered north slope, I reverted to being kid again by sitting down on my jacket and sliding clear to the bottom of the hill. Makes for a cold bottom!

"You're nuts," said Phyllis. She'd brought her pup, Tic, along, and naturally she and my Halley had a great time running free over the open hills.

Since those huge snowbanks in the garden have finally melted into the ground, Doug has been doing some cleaning and raking. I see the garlic is up, and he dug the remainder of the carrots that have been covered with straw and dirt all winter.

After his morning cribbage game, he's been piling willow limbs and harrowing pastures. Of course, when it snows again, like today, those jobs seem less appealing, so he spends most of his time in Enterprise at Ye Olde Range Rider with "the boys."

May 9—About a month ago, while talking on the phone with Grandson James, he mentioned that he was presenting his thesis on May 6th. Then I heard myself say, "I'll be there." Although James, a Literature major at The University of Montana Western, won't graduate until December 2009, he decided to fulfill his thesis requirement now.

"I'm excited about you coming Grandma. See you then," said my

21-year-old grandson, and hung up.

The week before I was to leave, Doug decided to stay home. So, I went by myself. My plan was to drive to Challis, Idaho, stay with daughter Jackie and husband Bill until Tuesday, when granddaughter Mona Lee (just back from India, and visiting her parents) would accompany me to Dillon, Montana.

All worked out as planned, and this road trip will forever remain in my memory, in that I traveled through some of the wildest, most beautiful country in the Pacific Northwest.

I began on May 4th, on the road by 4:30 a.m.

After a brief stop in Island City, I didn't rest until Garden City, Idaho. I followed rivers: the Snake to the Payette, to the South Fork of the Payette, to the Salmon. These miles of high wild country are just awakening from a long winter. Leaving Farewell Bend and following the Snake, I took 201 on back roads that wound through irrigated farm lands and sagebrush hills splashed with shades of yellow arrowleaf balsamroot and cous.

At Horseshoe Bend I followed the Payette northward, then turned up its South Fork at Banks. Soon I was driving through Garden Valley, with its great greening open meadows, before climbing higher on that less-traveled route, where recent enormous slides continued to shed rocks on the road. Far below, full of snowmelt, the South fork of the Payette dashed through its wild, rocky gorge. At Lowman, still following the river, and never having passing a single vehicle, I wound my way up to 6,260 ft.

Stanley, Idaho. Where snow stood three feet deep and large melting meadows appeared blinding white in the sudden sunshine. Misty clouds hovered around the base of the sharp-bladed Sawtooths. I stopped to photograph. The White Cloud mountains were equally brilliant on the opposite side.

Turning north I followed the Salmon River all the way to Challis. Traveling through the small settlement of Clayton, I relaxed; only 27 more miles. It was 1:30 p.m. when I pulled into Challis, population 900, an old mining town that sprawls on the edge of a large arid basin. I say arid because the basin escapes the rain shadow of the surrounding Salmon River Mountains and the Lemhi Range. To the southeast rears 12,662 ft. Borah Peak, Idaho's highest.

At 5,283 ft, Challis' air is dry and pure. Crude log buildings, constructed long ago, remain perfectly preserved. Daughter Jackie and husband Bill pastor the Assembly of God church in Challis, and Jackie works at the local high school. From main street I turned onto Challis Creek Road, and drove out into the country to where my daughter lives in a modest log home, surrounded by pastures and small acreages. And there, running to greet me, came two smiling border collies—Halley's parents!

Weary of driving, I plunked down in a lawn chair and soaked up the sunshine and mountain views while visiting my daughter. Soon granddaughter Mona Lee and her dad pulled into the yard in a pickup. They'd been feeding their horses and mules, pastured down along the Salmon River. Jackie said water had just been turned into the pipeline, all gravity-flow from Challis Creek, so Bill slipped into his boots and started the irrigation in several nearby hay fields.

That evening, while sipping chai tea, I was transported to India via Mona Lee's creative slide show.

The next morning the weather continued spring-like and pleasantly warm. Took another walk, this one with Mona Lee, after which we returned to sort through Jackie's photos and organize them in a photo album. Around noon we took sandwiches to the school where Jackie works, sat at picnic table and enjoyed the sunshine.

That evening Jackie took me for a walk around the large Bauchman ranch, which sprawls outward from Challis Creek, where several hundred head of cattle had wintered in the shelter of numerous cottonwoods and willow thickets near the creek. These folks also raise hay, horses, and Clydesdale draft horses. Jackie says they put up all their own hay. She tells me hay grown in the area stays there, isn't shipped out like hay in our valley. I was impressed with the amount of leftover hay on most ranches, especially after this long winter.

Early next morning, Mona Lee at the wheel, we headed north toward the town of Salmon. Cottonwoods along the river were beginning to leaf out, and we noticed lots of wildlife. Surprised to see a pair of geese nesting on a high rocky cliff above the road. Sandhill cranes waded in the river shallows, and wild turkeys roamed the meadows. In Salmon the climate appeared milder, and several fruit trees were in bloom.

Turning southeast, with the Beaverhead mountains rising to our left and sage brush hills to our right, we followed the Lemhi river as it wound through miles of cattle country. It gladdened my heart to see so many cattle ranches, and therefore lack of "development." I prefer the acres of open range, where cowboys were out riding horses instead of four-wheelers, and vast areas of river bottom produced hay and provided wintering grounds for calving.

At the little store in Tendoy, smaller than Imnaha, a kindly lady informed us that Lemhi Pass wouldn't be open until the first of June.

"About 27 miles down the road you'll come to Leadore; take Bannock Pass, it's open." she said. "Good luck."

So we continued on and found the gravel road that led over the Continental Divide into Montana. Up and around we wound, through sagebrush hills, following a maintained gravel road that led to 7,681 ft. Bannock Pass, where we spotted several head of antelope. At the bottom we rattled over a cattle guard—and there in a soggy meadow stood an old Beaver slide hay stacker. I stopped to photograph the first of many Beaver slides we'd see in Montana. Again, we didn't meet a single rig. Sure glad we didn't have car trouble.

At the Clark Canyon reservoir we were surprised to see two pelicans swimming amid wild ducks and geese. Driving through country saturated with Lewis and Clark history, we turned north onto Highway 15 to Dillon. Mona Lee got her cousin James on the cell phone, and he said he'd be waiting on the other side of a bridge that spanned the Beaverhead River, to direct us to his place.

After showing us his apartment, James joined us for lunch in downtown Dillon. Always aware of his sense of place, James pointed out the numerous mountain ranges that ringed his college town there in Beaverhead County. Their names rolled off his tongue like poetry: The Sweetwaters, Rubys, Tobacco Roots, Pioneers, Snowies and Black Tails. Proudly James showed us around his college campus. Mona Lee and I were impressed with the people we met, especially his English professor Alan Weltzien, whom we visited in his office.

After securing a motel for the night, we returned to James' place, where the little boy I taught to fish showed his grandma how to roll cast, using a fly he'd tied himself, into the swirling waters of the Beaverhead river.

"See those little insects flying over the water?" asked James. "They're caddis flies. And see that dark water over there? That's where the fish live." And then James proceeded to "catch and release" four native German Brown trout.

"They don't plant the Beaverhead," said James.

I hadn't even seen a native German Brown trout since the 1960s when James' dad, my son Todd, along with my other three children and their dad, packed into the Desolation Valley Wilderness area in California's Sierra Nevada Mountains. How lucky can this grandson be, to have a famous trout stream in his front yard?

That evening Mona Lee and I met James, known in Dillon as Jim, and professor Alan at the Black Tail Restaurant for a gourmet meal. With full tummies we found our way to the "Cup," an eatery located on campus, to listen to James present his thesis.

The four short stories were inspired by his Wallowas, the country that shaped the boy. Never a prouder grandma. Where did the years go? How could this poised young man be standing there reading stories he'd written, when just a heartbeat ago we'd traipsed across the pastures—poles in hand, grasshoppers in a can—to fish for trout in the irrigation ditch that flows out of Wallowa Lake?

Saying our goodbyes, and wishing James (Jim) well, Mona Lee and I returned to our motel. Since we'd be leaving early in the morning, we wasted no time tumbling into bed. I wouldn't see James again until the end of summer, as he begins training next week for the Forest Service helicopter rappelling Fire Crew out of Salmon, Idaho.

The next morning it was raining as we traveled north by west on Highway 278, which headed up 7,681 ft. Badger Pass, then down, and up again over 7,639 ft. Big Hole Pass before leveling out into the old town of Jackson. There we found ourselves in the Big Hole Valley, with a river of the same name winding through it.

I remembered this "Valley of 10,000 Haystacks" where, in 1970, I rode horseback with 300 other riders, all mounted on Appaloosas, through the huge Hirschy Ranch. That year we'd lopped off 100 miles of the Chief Joseph Trail Ride, a ride that began at Wallowa Lake and ended at the Bears Paw Mountains in Montana. That summer we'd ridden from Darby, Montana, across the Continental Divide, and ended up in the Lemhi country.

After Mona and I passed through the small town of Wisdom, we stopped briefly at the historic Big Hole Battlefield monument. Since the interpretive site was closed, and it was beginning to snow, we didn't stay long. Deep snow lay in the forests and clung to the evergreens, but didn't stick to the pavement as we crossed the Continental Divide at 7,264 ft. Chief Joseph Pass. For those Big Hole ranchers, it was still winter. I felt sorry for the cattle. The memory of one old cow still haunts me. She resembled Charley Russell's famous painting entitled "The Last of The Five Thousand."

After heading south at the pass, we lost elevation and suddenly found ourselves below the snow line. Near Gibbonsville, we spotted a large herd of elk. In no time we were back in Salmon, following that wild river back to Challis.

By 4:30 the next morning I was on my way home. At first light, between Challis and Stanley, I encountered hundreds of elk. They were everywhere. The small town of Stanley was still asleep, and the Sawtooths appeared ghostly, shrouded in clouds. Once again, on the long lonely stretch to Lowman, I encountered nary a vehicle.

Just outside of Lowman, along the Payette River, a grey wolf stepped out in front of me, then turned suddenly and melted into the forest from whence it came. Hungry by the time I reached Garden Valley, I pulled up to a small cafe and devoured a half-order of biscuits and gravy. The conversations at the "locals" table resembled those at Joseph's Cheyenne Cafe.

I picked a scenic route through small Idaho towns that led to I-84. However, freeway travel is not my thing, so beyond Baker City I took the North Powder exit. This took me past steaming Hot Lake and on into the quiet town of Union, where I ate a sandwich before heading to La Grande and home. Halley was beside herself, wondering where I'd been.

In my absence Prairie Creek had greened up. My tulips, daffodils and grape hyacinths were all a-bloom, Doug had roto-tilled the garden, and our 42-year-old refrigerator had died.

The next morning I was up and away by 4:45 to meet granddaughter Adele for breakfast at the "Friends" restaurant in Enterprise. Adele had her car all packed. She was headed to Austin, Texas, where she begins Culinary school next Wednesday. I'll miss her, but I know she'll make me proud, just as her brother did.

And now it's Saturday, and tomorrow is Mother's Day. I've already received cards in the mail. Doug is mowing the lawn and the sourdough bread is baking in the oven, to go with the pot of chili simmering for supper. I must gather the eggs and toss some hay to my mare, who seems to have survived the winter.

May 26—Here is me on this Memorial Day, seated at a table in the downstairs bedroom of this large log house, peering over the top of my laptop out an open window, to a leafy lightness which appears more intensely green each hour. Due in part to the natural progression of Spring, coupled with sporadic warm rains that continue to bless the upper Imnaha, I feel like I've been plunked down in the midst of full blown SPRING. You guessed it...I'm here at the Fishtrap Writers Retreat.

Normally we inhabit this magical place during the month of April, but that month and most of May has seen a great transformation in the log house Dr. Blackburn built so long ago. Workers have replaced the weathered cedar shakes with a metal roof, and constructed a new deck to replace the rotting wooden one. Despite the upheaval of accomplishing these improvements, Spring rules. The fragrance of lilacs permeates air filled with birdsong and watersong. The Imnaha was just under

16-month-old Lucy helps her dad, Buck Matthews, feed heifers at the Mt Joseph Ranch near Joseph.

flood stage when I pushed my cart across the swinging bridge yesterday morning.

As I write, my brain is fueled by great breaths of water scent. The old Imnaha smells sweetly of the high country it drains. I imagine the trickle beginning under Hawkins Pass; the rotting snows charging down the South Fork, the Middle Fork, the North Fork; and all the lesser creeks flowing in as the Imnaha roars past us here at Indian Creek. I can see it now, flashing through the leafy alder beyond the overgrown lawn where lavender Columbines tremble in the breeze.

In the orchard, tiny apples and cherries are visible among the leafy limbs, while across the road older varieties of apples continue to bloom. The shoulders of the soft, grassy canyon sides are ablaze with the golden arrowleaf balsamroot. Such a show, I've never seen.

Waterfalls splash down rocky draws, and the feed is every cowman's dream. Great thunderheads build above the rim rocks, thunder rolls down the canyons, and warm rain patters on the roof...before sunlight and rain-scoured skies of purest blue prevail, at least until the next shower.

This Spring we are three. Eileen and I from Joseph, and Anna, en route from Challis, Idaho, where she is the editor of the local paper. Anna was the first recipient of the Sally Bowerman Memorial Scholarship, awarded to a working woman by Fishtrap. Anna lost her husband in a helicopter crash in Alaska and has been making her own living for a number of years.

While in Challis recently, I dropped into the newspaper office to say hello to Anna, whose arrival has been delayed due to the illness of a sister.

May 27—Naturally, returning here always brings back memories of walking over to visit Mary, joining her and Lyman for breakfast. Mary's little white house is being rented out now, and I have no reason to go over there. But my mouth waters for Mary's hot biscuits and gravy, and for Lyman's tiny deer steaks for breakfast. Well, guess what? This morning I drove down the river to Lyman's place.

His new bride Wilma was just putting the biscuits in the oven, and Lyman was frying some "dead deer" in a cast iron skillet on the wood cook stove. Between the two of them the gravy got made, the biscuits baked, and the sizzling steaks made it from the frying pan to the table. And so did we. It was nearly 10:00 a.m. and food never tasted so good, especially since I'd hiked upriver this morning. We polished off the biscuits by slathering them with apricot jam and honey. Lyman also served us some of his homemade chunky applesauce, and a glass of pure grape juice…a real Imnaha ranch breakfast. I'm so full, it's a wonder I can write.

Lyman's garden is all up and responding to the warm rains.

On the way back I happened upon one of the Warnock boys moving cattle. Not on a time schedule, I pulled onto a wide spot along the road and waited until the cows and calves were corralled. What's the hurry? It's not every day you can take time to contemplate Springtime canyons. Chokecherry blooms line the river.

Lots has happened "on top." My 42-year-old fridge died while I was gone. Doug drove to Elgin and purchased a new fancy one with a pull-out freezer on the bottom, then decided I needed a new stove as well.

Son Todd came by with a black cherry tree for us to plant, his traditional gift to me. Daughter Jackie's lovely hanging planter spills over with blooms on the front overhang. Pretty nice Mother's Day for me. First new stove I've ever had. Bakes and cooks like a dream.

Our Book Group and Writer's Group met on two separate occasions at Idella Allen's lovely home on Barton Heights in Joseph. Idella and her husband Herb have a garden second to none. Idella had just taken cinnamon rolls out of the oven when we arrived for our Writers Group, and she baked rhubarb crisp for our Book Group. Surrounded by hundreds of blooming daffodils, staring out at Chief Joseph Mountain on those two lovely mornings was a special treat.

We've been enjoying the first spears of asparagus from our garden, and the rhubarb is nearly ready. Doug has most of the garden planted and tells me the peas are up. The other day he drove out to the Livestock Auction in La Grande and hauled back 22 yearling steers to graze the grass growing all over the place.

"Halley thinks she should"herd' the steers," says Doug, who had to get after her. He also started the sprinklers during that hot spell.

Our mamma kitties birthed kittens, one in a barrel and the other in a box in the woodshed. Doug went to the Big Loop Rodeo in Jordan Valley. Took off in his camper/pickup. Said it was a good rodeo, but awfully hot.

I drove to La Grande to attend great-granddaughter Brenna's fifth birthday. Little cousins ran through the sprinkler on that hot day.

May 28—I drove out "on top" to join Doug and attend Linde and Pat's 25th anniversary. This couple used to live in a lovely log home they built on upper Prairie Creek, and they'd driven all the way from Butte, Montana, to be with old friends for their special day. Daughter Ramona and husband Charley hosted the potluck, and wouldn't you know, it rained. So the whole neighborhood crammed into Ramona and Charley's little house on the Prairie, which didn't dampen any spirits. The stories were as good as the food.

The next morning I returned to the raging Imnaha, crossed the swinging bridge, picked some juicy stalks of rhubarb in the rain, and set about baking a pie. Then I hauled a wheelbarrow full of wood to start a fire in the fireplace. We'd invited Wilma and Lyman for supper. Around five o'clock here they came.

Wilma, despite being a little alarmed at crossing that narrow foot bridge over the swirling waters of the river, clung to Lyman's arm and managed a brave smile. It was her first crossing.

Inside the old log cabin it was cozy and warm, and it didn't take us long to polish off a steaming platter of Marr Flat beef steaks, roasted veggies, and salad. Lyman had seconds on pie, then stood up from the table, walked over to the sink, and washed all the dishes. What a guy!

May 30—My watch died and, since there's no calendar down there, I allowed myself the luxury of ignoring times and dates. That's what writer's retreats are for.

So, after spending the morning writing, I took a long walk downriver to Lyman and Wilma's. It was a lovely afternoon. Enormous cottony clouds collided over the rims, but held their rain. All was quiet around

THE OLD AND NEW: "It was so startling to look across the road and see the juxtaposition," photographer/writer Janie Tippett of Joseph said. "Quite frankly, the 'old' looked more appealing—no dust—and today that crop is beautiful and green." Julie Kooch of Enterprise with her two mules prepares the soil for planting the old way at the annual old-time plowing bee at the Larry and Jaunita Waters ranch on Prairie Creek. Directly across the road from the old-time plowing bee, Prairie Creek farmer Robert Butterfield works his ground the modern way.

"It was so startling to look across the road and see the juxtaposition," writes Janie Tippett. "Quite frankly, the 'old' looked more appealing—no dust— and today that crop is beautiful and green." Julie Kooch of Enterprise with her two mules prepares the soil for planting the old way at the annual old-time plowing bee at the Larry and Juanita Waters ranch on Prairie Creek. Directly across the road from the old-time plowing bee, Prairie Creek farmer Robert Butterfield works his ground the modern way.

the Goucher Homestead. I suspected it was nap time. After resting up on their deck, I headed back upriver.

Before I got to Mary's old place, it began to rain, a warm mist that reminded me of the old song, "Walking in the Rain."

May 31—This morning I carted my stuff across the bridge for the last time, pausing midstream to gaze around me at the rushing river, the canyons rising upward, a Kingfisher flying low over the water. Halfway up a steep hillside, a cow bawled for her calf. It's always hard to leave this place, where one can simply take the time to savor each moment and feel no guilt.

Anna drove out this evening to attend Tunesmiths Night with me at the Outlaw Restaurant in Joseph. Tunesmiths are also wordsmiths, who add the wonderful element of music to their words. That night was a celebration of their newly-released CD, "Songs From The End of The Road." Tunesmiths Janice Carper, Heidi Muller, Rodd Ambroson, and Carolyn Lockhart performed to a standing-room-only crowd, and Heidi Muller's song "In Wallowa" strummed the heart strings of those of us who live here.

June 1—To celebrate June 1st, Phyllis and I embarked upon a wild mushroom hunt...which didn't produce any mushrooms, just plenty of wild. Somehow we ended up on Ferguson Ridge, where we could look down on Kinney Lake. Prairie Creek spread out, emerald green as far as the eye could see. The view extended beyond the Buttes clear to Zumwalt. We didn't spy any morels, but came upon other fungi and numerous emerging wildflowers, including Indian Paint Brush, Lupine and the delicate orchid-like Calypso.

I was remembering all those winters past, when Linde and I cross-country skied this ridge. In that mountain stillness I imagined the sound of our skis gliding over the snowy trails along the Papoose Lake Loop. Suddenly, blocked by melting snow, we took off on foot and wandered farther from the car than intended. All uphill back to the car—oh well, our guys would just have to wait for supper.

June 3—After our Writer's Group met this morning, we headed out the North Highway to the RimRock Inn to celebrate Sharon's birthday. "Dining on the Edge" is what you do there, because you are seated in front of large windows that look out over the lip of Joseph Creek Canyon. The view, seen through a thin veil of rain, resembled a watercolor painting. We were entertained by a variety of hummingbirds sipping at a feeder suspended from the deck.

Dessert was a version of Wilma's famous mud pie—yep, Lyman's Wilma used to own the RimRock Inn. This house dessert is "on the house" for birthdays, candle and all.

More watercolor paintings on our return. A solitary sheepherder wagon, the herder leading his horse in the rain, and those enormous bands of sheep; green Aspen thickets, ponds brimming with water, long grassy meadows, and creamy mule ears blooming everywhere.

June 4—We were allowed a brief glimpse of our mountains, just enough to see a layer of new snow. There was enough of a lull to allow Doug and Dick Hammond to brand and work Doug's new steers. I stayed indoors, fed the wood stove and baked a rhubarb pie.

June 5—The sun shone on a soggy, green Prairie Creek, and I don't know what possessed me, but I washed windows.

June 6—We lost our old cowboy, Mike McFetridge, who didn't quite make his 100th birthday. Born on Elk Mountain, Mike spent his entire life in Wallowa County.

My wish for you, old pardner, is that you have a good horse to ride, and a long trail to follow, behind a bunch of cows head'in for those everlasting springtime hills.

So long, Mike, we'll never forget you.

June 9—Although Prairie Creek appears intensely green, it is a dull cloudy day, in a succession of them. Apple blossoms drift like snow past the window, while up on the mountain it IS snowing. A cold breeze scatters dandelion fluff over the fields and makes the blooming Bleeding Hearts shiver. Doug's young steers, belly-deep in grass, graze their days away, converting all that abundant feed to beef.

Due to frequent rain showers, most of the ranchers have turned their sprinklers off, while many haven't even begun irrigating. Anyone changing pipes this morning has my sympathies, as having to slog through ice-encrusted fields would not be fun.

Yesterday Doug and I attended birthday parties. The first was the result of a "hear ye, hear ye" invitation in our local paper to honor two popular Wallowa County couples: Wayne and Jean Cook, and Tip and Ruth Proctor.

On the occasion of the men turning 80, and their wives 70-something, Enterprise's First Baptist Church overflowed with folks socializing and eating cake.

Had a nice visit with Wilmer Cook, who has long since passed the 90 mark. Also Zua and Bud Birkmaier, who is very close to 80 himself, who tell me they faithfully read this column. Then we drove over to granddaughter Chelsie's place to celebrate son Ken's 55th birthday.

Since the weather smiled on us, and the sun shone warmly until it slid behind the mountain, we cranked two freezers full of homemade ice cream. Plenty of strong arms, as well as little arms, took turns cranking. Uncles appeared late from brandings, and played with their nieces and nephews—my great-grandchildren—and Ken's sister Ramona baked him a rhubarb pie with candles on it. Mighty good with ice cream. It was fun taking time out, during a busy spring, to be with family.

June 12—Now I must put a period to this column. Doug has the boat hooked up and we're headin' for the lake to hopefully hook some Kokanee. It's a lovely warm evening, the June moon is growing, and the fish are waiting.

P.S. Doug limited out! Nice fat ones. Since I didn't have my license yet, I was the official netter. Just as the sun slid over the mountains, a migrating loon wailed and we headed for the dock.

June 23—"Nothing so rare as a day in June," a well-worn phrase that aptly describes this Prairie Creek morning. Sunny skies, acres of green, rain-cleansed air filled with birdsong, and the chomping sound of Doug's steers mowing down the high grasses growing in the lane.

Doug and I took advantage of the morning cool to hoe weeds in the vegetable garden. It's been a challenging time for Wallowa County gardeners, what with a winter that wouldn't end, and a spring that sprung directly into summer.

Eventually seeds did sprout, especially the beans. Goodness, you should see the beans!

Normally, the corn is as high as my border collie's eye by the end of June. Not this year. The second planting is just breaking through the soil. Potatoes, onions, cabbages, garlic and shallots are all thriving, however, and I picked the first strawberry this morning.

Due to frosts as recently as last week, not to mention hail and snow, we are, for the time being, grateful for what we have. As far as flowers go, there aren't many. Just perennials. This will be the year of allowing Halley to lay in the flower beds.

Next year, hopefully, puppyhood will have fled. If not, hanging baskets work really well.

Speaking of flowers, a fragrant bouquet of fresh-cut snapdragons, daisies, baby iris and carnations gladdens my heart as I write here at the kitchen table. A gift from our children for our 30th wedding anniversary. The old-fashioned roses that grow alongside the bunkhouse, the ones that have faithfully bloomed every June since our wedding day, didn't this year. Me thinks heavy snow drifts did them in. Some of the bushes are showing signs of life; perhaps next June they'll bloom again.

Our anniversary was special because my child hood chum, Sandra, and husband, Fred, drove all the way up from Auburn, California, to celebrate with us. As usual we squeezed in the maximum amount of fun—and the minimum amount of work—while they were here.

When they arrived late Monday afternoon, I was putting together a hot potato salad to go with the fresh Kokanee (landlocked salmon) Doug and I had just caught in Wallowa Lake. Rhubarb pie for dessert. Fred brought us freshly-picked, sun-ripened apricots, and dark sweet cherries from his neighbor's foothill orchards. A rare treat, as much of our local fruit was hit by frost.

After supper Sandra and I took the first of what would become a daily walk up Tenderfoot Valley Road. Halley looked forward to these outings and forged ahead of us, sniffing wild critter trails in the nearby fields. white-tail does stared at us in that golden evening light, and we sensed their fawns were hidden in the lush grasses.

On Tuesday morning I took Sandra with me to our Writer's Group, which meets every week in the basement of the Enterprise Library.

Then, armed with the deviled eggs I'd whipped up that morning and packed on ice, we drove to Mary Lou Brink's lovely home for the annual get-together of our surviving Wallowa County CowBelles. Great fun seeing all the gals, nibbling finger food, and poring over old scrapbooks I borrowed from the Museum.

"My," we murmured, "the energy we expended to promote beef! And were those young slender gals smiling from those pages really us?"

We returned to the ranch to find the guys, who had spent the day fishing from our boat on Wallowa Lake, cleaning kokanee.

On the 18th Sandra and I drove up Hurricane Creek to Phyllis' mountain home, where she joined us for a hike to Fall's Creek Falls, which was worth the effort. Not only were the falls spectacular, with vast amounts of snowmelt spilling down that solid rock face, but water cascaded down every chute on the Chief Joseph Mountain side of Hurricane Creek.

Due to record amounts of snow, we could hear the creek thundering its way down the canyon below us. Indian Paint Brush, Clematis, and Larkspur lined the trails, and we noticed many downed trees.

Sandra and I stayed up that night to watch the full June "Strawberry" moon rise over Locke's hill. Worth the wait, when that pink glow below the skyline morphed into a brilliant full moon.

On the 19th we "did" the shops in Joseph, wandering up and down the brick sidewalks, gawking at the life size bronzes that grace main street, popping into art galleries, and admiring the hanging baskets overflowing with colorful petunias. Why is it, when you show a visitor around, you look at everything differently? Perhaps we're seeing it through their eyes. Kinda fun being a tourist in your own town.

Weather-wise, it couldn't have been a more perfect day, which seemed to magnify the brilliance of Chief Joseph Mountain's gleaming snowfields. We lunched on "Mad Mary's" Turkey Lurkey sandwiches, then drove to the lake, where Sandra purchased gifts for her family. After treating ourselves to huckleberry ice cream cones at the Matterhorn Swiss Village, we found a table in the shade to "people watch." Sandra loves to photograph the Mule deer bucks sporting their velvet antlers. She wasn't disappointed. We discovered two obliging bucks in the campground.

On the way back we spotted our hubbies out on the lake again. Two more limits of kokanee later they returned. That evening, Sandra beat me at Scrabble.

To celebrate the Summer Solstice, Phyllis, Sandra and I headed out the North Highway to see what we could see. Just out of Enterprise Sandra was able to photograph Stangel's buffalo herd up close; cows with their new calves nursing, shaggy bulls sparring with their large pointed horns. Our destination: the RimRock Inn, where we sat ourselves down on the sunny deck and munched a light lunch, all the while gazing off into the green depths of Joseph Creek Canyon.

To the north, at the edge of the timber, bloomed a golden patch of Mule Ears. To the east rose the snowy tips of the Seven Devils Mountains in Idaho, and the three tepees pitched in the meadow below brought back memories of last summer, when we "Syringa Sisters" spent the night in one of them. Another photo for Sandra when we happened upon Krebs' sheep grazing those long, aspen-fringed meadows, not far from Snow Hollow Hill.

That evening we had reservations at Vali's Alpine Delicatessen at Wallowa Lake to officially celebrate our anniversary. Over flaming beef shish-ka-bobs, served by Maggie, my girlfriend and I recalled the year 1951. Sandra had chosen me, an 18-year-old mother, as her matron of honor when she and Fred were married in her parents' home there in the Mt. Pleasant District, amid the Sierra foothills where we'd spent our childhood.

Our friends left Saturday morning with kokanee frozen in ice, and memories of yet another pleasurable visit. Halley and I missed Sandra's company on our morning walk.

Grandson Buck showed up to trim my mare's feet, and later that afternoon, through the dust of a sudden thunderstorm, I watched great-grandchildren, twins Gideon and Jada, come busting out of the chute in the mutton busting event at the Broncs and Bulls rodeo at the W.C. Fairgrounds.

A busy summer stretches ahead. Our California family is here now, as well as our Marine grandson Shawn, wife Maria and children, Jackson and Savannah Rose, all the way from North Carolina. Daughter Ramona and husband Charley's little house on the Prairie is bulging at the seams.

Friday we'll all get together, and crank more ice cream.

June 30—A hot wind blows over Prairie Creek, setting adrift the "summer snow" that forms on willows and cottonwoods this time of year. It is 80 degrees in our living room and nearly 90 outside. Cottony thunderheads sporting dark purple bellies build to the east like they did yesterday. During the early morning hours it sounded like a civil war around here, what with thunderous explosions and brilliant flashes lighting up our bedroom.

The garden loves this heat, especially the warm nights, and, all over the valley "the boys" are busy haying. Used to be you didn't hay 'til the Fourth of July. Not this year. One day Spring, the next Summer. It looks to be a vigorous crop. Irrigation has been intense and, thanks to a good snow pack, the ditches are brimming with precious water.

Our neighbors have been installing one of those center pivot irrigation systems. What has been a source of entertainment for us, must surely be a frustration to them. Since the area within the sweep of this enormous circle contains myriad ditches and fences, there have been subsequent days of delays while dump trucks, backhoes and sweating men deal with these obstacles that lie in the wheeled monster's path. It seems strange now, looking east; where once pipe changers moved hand lines, mostly hidden beneath chest high meadow hay, we now see this high arching piece of machinery tracking its way over newly-constructed bridges and through newly-installed fence gates.

Yesterday, this product of man's invention rolled its way halfway up the sagebrushy hill. I've noticed several more of these automatic irrigation systems going in around the county. Possibly, the day will come when ranchers can't find "pipe changers." It's nearly come to that now. Gone will be the sound of early morning and late evening four-wheelers zooming up and down Tenderfoot Valley Road as young boys and girls head to the fields to change pipes.

Forty-two members of our family, several neighbors thrown in, gathered at daughter Ramona's last Friday evening. You guessed it. "Camp Runamuck" was in session again. Tents were pitched on the lawn and cousins camped out during those first mild nights of summer. The children look forward with great anticipation to this annual gathering—a get-together in which parents really have no say, and Grandma Ramona and Poppa Charley allow kids to be kids. This means most anything can happen, and often does. There's nothing like a ranch on upper Prairie Creek to let kids "run-a-muck."

My contribution, as usual, was lugging the wooden ice cream freezer with all the fix'ins up there, and being responsible for the finished product. Since everyone was preoccupied with other Camp Runamuck chores, my only help came from great-granddaughter Savannah Rose, who stayed with me 'til the ice cream was hardened. She, of course, got to lick the dasher.

Granddaughter Chelsie baked one of her specialty cakes to honor her cousin Tamara and husband Matt's anniversary. Each summer new babies appear, and the other children grow a little taller. And overnight, it seems, they are grown with children of their own. Ramona outdid herself organizing what has become a tradition; not to mention the food: fried chicken, potato salad, a kettle of beans, and everyone contributing side dishes. Grandson Shawn bar-b-cued hot dogs, everyone heaped their plates, and we all hunkered down on the lawn to eat. No thunderstorm to drive folks inside this year.

Children climbed the ladder to the tree house in the old crab apple tree and picnicked among the leaves. Camp Runamuck was bathed in that golden, low evening light that lit the green fields and the east moraine, and accentuated the weathered outbuildings, survivors of the Homestead era. In other words, it was the kind of evening we dream about all winter long.

Ramona introduced the founding members of Camp Runamuck, then handed out bags of goodies to every child there, which included baby Gavin DeWolf, the youngest of our 17 great-grandchildren. Two-year-old Cutter and his mommy, Kasey, had traveled all the way from John Day. Daddy Rowdy didn't make it; mom said he was in the middle of haying.

After the sun sank behind the mountain, we sat around the campfire, holding sleepy little ones in our laps until it was time to go home.

Trolling for Kokanee continued good. One evening I pulled in a 15-incher, which provided supper for two.

Later, as I had another landlocked salmon on my hook, I heard *keer-splash* and was surprised to see an osprey dive from the sky to snatch a fish swimming alongside our boat.

One evening Doug invited Clayton, Cole, Halley Jane, Savannah Rose, Jackson and Brenna, along with their parents and grandparents, to go fishing. The fish were biting and everyone was kept busy baiting, netting and reeling in nice fat kokanee. Although Doug's old "Dug Bar" boat wasn't as shiny and new as some of the others, it was, for sure, roomy and sturdy enough to hold "Camp Runamuckers."

The next afternoon was a scorcher when Doug and I joined a crowd of fans on the north side of the Harley Tucker Memorial arena to take in Wallowa County's first-ever Ranch Rodeo. Although these events lacked the glitz and glamour of professional rodeo, the show didn't lack for excitement. I mean to tell you, these were real cowboys who'd come to town to do what they did every day on their ranches. Loops were thrown, cattle branded, critters penned, and broncs ridden. It was WESTERN.

Take those Baremore boys in the team roping. When Cody's horse went down, no problem. Cody simply rode him back to his feet and threw another loop. Teams were represented by local ranches. Son Todd was on the Marr Flat/Rocking J team that tied for third. The crowd cheered as rancher Jill McClaran showed the boys how it's done, and won the team branding event.

That evening we had enough pep left to take in the Blue Mountain Old Time Fiddlers show in Cloverleaf Hall. The Wallowa County Fair Board whomped up one of Randy Garnett's famous roast beef dinners, followed by a toe-tapping evening full of fiddle music and songs. Before retired rancher Dick Ervin stood on stage to play the fiddle, he announced that he and his wife were visiting Wallowa County because he'd read so much about it in Agri-Times' "Janie's Journal."

After Dick played "the Wreck of the Old '87", he and his wife purchased a membership in the Blue Mountain Old Time Fiddlers, which meant they won Denny Langford's special stew. Denny opened up the box and displayed all the ingredients for the stew, along with the recipe.

A fellow by the name of Bob Waless showed up with a belt full of harmonicas. He could sure make those mouth harps sing. The "Prairie Creek Girls," Hannah, Lexi, Ryya, and Landra, thrilled us with "Orange Blossom Special." Then there was faithful old Len Samples and his son Caleb, who must make daddy pretty proud. Not to mention tall and lanky Alan Schnetzky of Enterprise, a chip off his granddaddy Spencer Bacon's old block, who not only wowed the audience with his fiddle tunes but his honky-tonk piano playing as well.

On Sunday the many friends of Mike McFetridge gathered at the VFW Hall in Enterprise to celebrate the life of Wallowa County's Old Hand.

Mike would have turned 100 in November. It was a hot afternoon but that didn't stop folks from remembering Mike. Many stories were told, and many work-toughened hands reached for their handkerchiefs. A similar thread of respect stitched all their stories together. Everyone agreed Mike was hard-working, gentle, caring, adept with horses, humorous, and above all, humble.

One early morning, to beat the heat, Phyllis and I set off to hike the East Moraine. Later, on top, seated on a rock, we stared across at Chief Joseph Mountain's melting snowfields and took in the shimmering lake below. Serenaded by a Meadow Lark, we opened our brown bag lunches. It just don't get any better than that.

July 2—Grandson Ethan is visiting. I baked a rhubarb pie this morning, and soon we'll be hitching up the boat to take Ethan fishing on the lake. Enjoy your summer!

July 4—Today we gathered with friends and family at Scott and Kelly's on Tucker Down Road. After a well-timed potluck bar-b-cue in their yard, moist thunder heads boiled down off the mountains and plundered across Prairie Creek, treating us to a preview of Mother Nature's pyrotechnics before we experienced Man's version later. Just as we were carrying picnic tables into the garage, an immense cloud, rent asunder by streaks of lightning followed by thunder, emptied its contents on our picnic.

Then, as so often happens, a shaft of sunlight sliced through those dark clouds and gifted us with another light show, bathing a herd of curious cows across the road in the reflected light of a brilliant rainbow.

Later, from our vantage point midway up the east moraine, we were further awed by Wallowa County's traditional fireworks display, launched from a floating dock on the lake below. Chief Joseph Mountain echoed each boom, and it seemed the night sky was full of exploding stars.

That morning I'd driven to the Lower Valley to take in Wallowa's Old Time Fourth of July Parade. Lots of red, white and blue decorated dogs kids and horses, and here came the vintage tractors, a line of McCormick Deerings driven by the farmers who'd restored them, proudly *putt-putt-putt*-ing down Main Street. There was our neighbor, Tom Butterfield, sitting in the driver's seat steering his John Deere.

Reigning over all were the 2008 Grand Marshals, Reid and Marilyn Johnson, both descended from early Lower Valley pioneer families, waving to us from a mule-drawn wagon.

Suzan Hobbs, left, and Angie Nash of Marr Flat Cattle Company grill their Natural Beef burgers at the recent Lostine Flea Market. The burgers were a success: they sold out. Angie and Suzan, who were in charge of sales, work hard to promote beef.

July 5—At the Lostine Flea Market I spotted Angie and Susan selling Marr Flat beef burgers, and made a note to eat lunch there. Glad I did. After strolling up and down Main Street and mingling with the Fleas, I partook of one of those burgers. Nothing like the smell of frying onions and beef on the grill to draw folks to some of Wallowa County's finest natural beef.

Doug headed south that morning to attend the Haines rodeo, where some of our family were entered in various events.

Later, I learned grandson Buck had been drug around the arena by a mad cow. Or something. I really didn't want to know.

July 15—On the 6th, Friends Bobbie and Dick showed up at our house, to spend the week of Summer Fishtrap as our guests. The three of us were signed up for writing workshops scheduled from Monday through Friday. This year I took Brenda Miller's creative non-fiction workshop. Our class met in Brenda's rustic cabin, a short walk up the road from the Methodist Camp.

On the banks of the West Fork of the Wallowa River, where the sound of water and the sight of floating cottonwood fluff inspired us as we wrote out on the deck. We had homework, so each day I returned to Prairie Creek to complete my assignments, tend chickens, water the yard, and fix supper.

In class that first morning, one of the gals interrupted Brenda. "Sorry," she said, pointing a few yards away. "But isn't that a bear?"

Sure enough it was. A shiny black yearling bumbled along, sniffing garbage cans. Apparently these yearlings are sort'a on their own, as mamma is busy raising her new cub. Of course, bear sightings dominated our lunch conversations.

The theme of 2008 Summer Fishtrap was "Speaking Truth"—and this we did, producing some pretty amazing discussions and myriad writings as a result. Of course, with presenters and authors like Oregon poet Laureate Lawson Inada, Luis Urrea, Kim Stafford, Peter Sears, Jan Vandenburgh, Tom Spanbauer, Paulann Petersen, Peter Chilson, Robin Cody, music by Marv and Rindy Ross, and entertainment by Greg Keeler and Jim Hepworth, how could we not be inspired?

It was quite a week.

To relax, we visited over meals eaten outside, and took hikes upriver to a refreshing falls. This year Amy Minato conducted a children's writing workshop. Writings, as well as photos, taken by the children, were tacked to various tall Ponderosa trees that grew at the edge of camp. One afternoon the children read their pieces at the podium. Heartening to see youngsters interested in creative writing.

As in years past, new friendships were forged and old acquaintances renewed. Fishtrap has become, over the years, a sort of family reunion for writers. We all noted that a goodly number of us are aging. It was my 21st Summer Fishtrap.

Now, the July moon, the "Buck Moon"—so named because it's time for male deer to grow their antlers—will be full tonight. I think Phyllis and I will drive to Tamkaliks, at the Nez Perce Homeland in Wallowa, and take in the colorful dancing.

July 18—It was a perfectly lovely evening as Phyllis and I drove to the Lower Valley. Just out of Enterprise, at the S-curve, we spied a herd of elk grazing a green meadow. Their coats were bronzed in late Summer light, and several young calves were standing on their hind feet, sparring with each other.

At Tamkaliks we took a seat to watch the colorful dancers, presided over by the Whipman and Whipwoman, step to the drum beats as they made their way around the dance pavilion. The soft rays of the Westering sun back-lit eagle feathers, beads, bells, and delicate doeskin. A soft breeze billowed the parachute cover overhead, and the effect was both spiritual and magical.

Phyllis suggested we hike down the path along the river, to the Tick Hill trailhead, so we did. As the drum beats grew fainter, and disappeared altogether, so did the sun.

"We'll just go up a little ways," I said. However, the trail was so inviting, we just kept going. As the final light bled out of the western sky, we gained the top and found ourselves in chin-high rye grass that all but obliterated the path. We talked about returning…that's when our spirit of ADVENTURE kicked in, and we decided to see if we could complete the trail down the other side to where our car was parked.

Well, let me tell you, we had no idea what we were getting into. Just then, in the east, that Buck moon pulsed its way into the sky ahead of us. At that point we lost the trail and found ourselves on a rocky maintenance road that serviced a cell phone tower. We imagined every dark shape to be a cougar. We encountered deer, which were curious at first, their silhouettes outlined in the moonlight, but who then bounded away at the sight of two elderly women stumbling along in the dead of night.

I won't go into the stickery, muddy, manurey details, but it was after 11:00 pm when we rolled under the last of many fences and staggered our way to the car. The drums were still beating as the Nez Perce danced on into the night, and it was midnight when I crawled in beside my husband, who had no idea of what his 74-year-old wife had been up to.

Then there was the Big Bash on Imnaha Sunday for Lyman and Wilma, but that's another story for another time.

This Sunday Jessica and I head for Central Oregon to join the other "Syringa Sisters" for our 11th annual get-together. Or is it the 12th? After Chief Joseph Days, we "Syringa Sisters" will meet south of Bend at my sister Caroline's home near Sunriver. We'll be celebrating Bobbie's 80th birthday.

We lost another old-timer. Attended Al Fregulia's funeral on the 15th. Al and his wife Minnie helped move my family to Wallowa County forty years ago. Goodbye, old friend.

July 20—Early on my walk with Halley this morning, I sensed Prairie Creek's maturing summer in ripening wheat, the dew-dampened smell of timothy hay, the *swish-swish*-ing of a wheel line, chattering starlings, and soaring hawks. The warm sunshine released sweet clover blossom scent and my laying hens discussed the contents of the chicken bucket, *buck-buck-buck*, as Halley sniffed a coon track and the purifying smell of sage wafted from the dry hills.

A white-tail doe's ears protruded above the wheat, her fawn's spots fading. Mamma kitty's kittens tumbled around the wood shed. I sense the season in the burgeoning garden, in the sweet onions, red leaf lettuce, spinach, parsley, tender baby beets, and those first ever-bearing strawberries.

Up on the mountain, Tucker's mare, the snow-shape of a horse, has melted away. We are on the cusp of a busy time, one last hoorah before the season shifts.

Old-timer Mike McFetridge used to say, "It's all downhill after Chief Joseph Days," and Chief Joseph Days begins this coming week. As soon as we pick up all the litter left by hundreds of visitors and our town returns to normal, the days will shorten, the tempo will slow, and the blackbirds will gather on the fence rows to announce the beginning of Fall.

The first cuttings of hay have been put up, a goodly portion of which has been loaded on semis in the field and hauled out of the County. The crops have been good. Doug has finished the.second sprinkler irrigation on our remaining acreage—all hand lines. The steers are sleek and shiny.

August 1—Well, I've put it off long enough. Must sit down on this hot August afternoon and begin my column.

July has galloped off the calendar in less time than it takes to trot to the mailbox. It seems only yesterday that Chief Joseph Days ended. Daughter Lori and husband Larry showed up for the weekend, which was not only crammed with rodeos, parades and cowboy breakfasts, but another one of Ramona and Charley's impromptu family bar-b-cues in honor of visiting relatives Deb and Nancy. We all had another great evening outdoors, the little cousins running helter skelter over Prairie Creek pastures before gathering at sunset around the campfire to toast marshmallows and slap together sticky s'mores.

Saturday night's performance of the Chief Joseph Days rodeo was memorable, even though we listened to it over KWVR, our local radio station. Grandson Buck and his mugger Joel won the Wild Cow Milking. Pretty impressive belt buckles they're wearing these days. Earlier in

Doug Tippett hoes a row of beets

the week, great-granddaughter Riley Ann captured second place in the Mutton Busting event.

Jessica arrived Saturday afternoon, July 30th, from Boise, and by 5:00 a.m. Sunday we were on our way to Sunriver to meet up with our other "Syringa Sisters." Near the S-curve between Enterprise and Lostine, we stopped to watch a herd of elk, their calve playing in the early morning cool.

After an uneventful trip down the Columbia River, we exited at Rufus and headed south to connect with Highway 97. Soon we were driving through rural communities with names like Grass Valley, Moro, and Shaniko while viewing Eastern Oregon's high desert country. Briefly stopped for lunch in Madras before braving traffic that clogs the roads from Redmond to Bend.

South of Bend, a mile past the entrance to Sunriver, we turned west on Vandevert Road. Following sister Caroline's directions, we arrived at our destination along the Deschutes River around 4:00 p.m. All the roads were named for waterfowl.

On Snow Goose Road we watched for Canvasback Drive, and soon we located the house we'd call home for a week.

Sister Caroline and husband Duane, who live in California, had graciously offered their vacation home for our stay. We barely settled in before here came Bobbie, Barb and Mary. There we were again: our

Lyman Goucher and his bride, Wilma, dance in the dirt during a wedding feast at his ranch on the Upper Imnaha River.

Marr Flat Cattle Company is located in Joseph.

12th Summer meeting. Barb fixed a yummy tomato, feta cheese, basil concoction on phyllo dough for dinner, and we tumbled into bed to rest up for a fun-filled week of adventure.

The next morning, up early, we traipsed to the dock to plunk down on a sunny bench along the banks of the Deschutes River, coffee and Jessica's "dunk'in" biscotti in hand. A mamma mallard and her downy ducklings kept us company. As the lovely Deschutes swerved around a bend, we were entertained by all manner of wildlife, including a bald eagle. Thusly we begun each day, relaxing in this wild setting.

Later that morning we met another one of my sisters, Mary Ann, a permanent resident of the area, who accompanied us to the Benham Falls trailhead. The trail takes off from a parking lot bordered by tall Ponderosa Pines, and follows the Deschutes River to cross a large wooden bridge, where it resumes its way to a rocky gorge where cold mountain water now runs over what was at one time red hot lava flows. In fact, the eastern bank of the river stops short of an enormous lava moonscape. The contrast is startling.

Mary Ann joined us for lunch beyond the falls, after which we hiked to Slough Meadows, which we renamed Mosquito Meadows. Nevertheless it was a scenic walk, and we were able to soak our feet in the eddy of the river before returning. Enormous patches of Alpine forget-me-nots tinted the river banks a pale blue color. Indian Paint brush and a brilliant yellow snapdragon-like wilding lined the trails.

That evening we feasted on another gourmet meal. Bobbie's turn, featuring Shrimp Pilaf and a fresh peach pie we ate warm from the oven with ice cream.

The next morning finds us quietly puttering down the Deschutes in a pontoon boat piloted by Mary Ann's friend Marie, who has generously agreed to give us a tour of the river. Sipping coffee and eating donuts, we admire the lovely homes along the banks and wave to folks working or relaxing in their yards. After our boat ride, we visit more of Mary Ann's friends, one of whom is a very talented wood carver, who gives us a tour of his work, displayed in his equally interesting home. His wife was waterproofing their dock. Glen and Mary Lou are avid readers of Agri-Times and "Janie's Journal."

Back to our "Snow Goose Bungalow" to pack a lunch and drive north to the High Desert Museum, where we spend the afternoon hiking traits that lead to various exhibits, including a live otter viewing area, a Raptor exhibit, where we watched two owls fly from a nearby tree to perch on the handler's wrist, and a girl lead a badger out on a leash. So much to see here: Desert Indian exhibit, reptiles, recreated homestead and sawmill, and one of the most impressive Basque museums I've ever seen. We ate our lunches in the shaded patio of the Rimrock Cafe.

Later, after showers and Jessica's fabulous broiled chicken salad, heaped with fresh fruit, we planned the next day's adventure.

The next morning we headed to Smith Rock State Park, another one of Central Oregon's geologic wonderlands. While Jess and Barb (the youngest of us) climb Misery Ridge, Mary, Bobbie and I hike the summit trail that takes us to a landmark rock called Monkey Face.

Words fail when it comes to describing this steep-walled canyon where the Crooked River flows through some of the most awesome rock formations in the West. At every turn we'd see rock climbers swinging from ropes, or clamping their feet into ledges and groping their ways up sheer rock faces. We met the gals at a connecting trail, and ate our lunches along the river before returning to our cars.

Not far from Smith Rock we brake to a screeching halt: The Hard Rock Ice Cream hut! Huckleberry ice cream cones all around.

That evening, sipping cold Moose Drool beer, I prepare my dinner of Kokanee, fresh from Wallowa Lake, frozen in ice.

On the way back to the house, we'd stopped at a Sunriver outdoor market to purchase fresh corn on the cob. Using lettuce from our garden, we build a salad. During the long, golden evenings we'd work on a jigsaw puzzle (began by sisters Caroline and Kathryn), play scrabble, read and write.

The next day Bobbie consults her hiking guide and we discover several trails that follow Fall River. One trail dead-ends at a place that is rather magical. Three springs bubble up from the ground to form a creek, where Alpine forget-me-nots and green grass abound. The water is so cold it numbs our fingers. Downriver we encounter great floating islands of wildflowers, like floating wild gardens. Yellow monkey flowers grow from rotting logs that fell years ago into the river.

Home to see our resident Mule deer doe in the yard nursing her twin fawns. On Thursday, we serve up all the leftovers for supper. Since Friday is our last day, we make the most of it, piling in the car and heading up to the Newberry Crater to hike the Obsidian trail that is carved from pure obsidian. We take in lovely views of Mt. Bachelor and Broken Top, not to mention Paulina Lake, so blue it appears like an inverted bowl of sky. Nice cool breeze at that high altitude, and interpretive signs explain the massive upheaval that created the obsidian deposit.

After, we drive to Paulina lake and hike a steep path to Paulina Falls, where we choose to eat our lunch. The falls are enormous, an 80 ft. drop from the lip of a rocky gorge, where wildflowers, clinging to wet ledges, shudder from the thunderous waters while rainbows dance in shafts of sunlight.

Back at Paulina Lake we bask in the warmth of the sun as clouds are forming and a cool wind begins to blow. The lake fades from turquoise blue near the shore to deep blue in the middle, and we watch several women kayakers beach their boats. Then it's back to Snow Goose to clean house and pack up.

That evening we treat Mary Ann and Bobbie to dinner at a gourmet Italian restaurant in Sunriver. To honor Bobbie on her 80th birthday, we order Tiramisu cake for dessert and sing Happy Birthday to our amazing friend.

Mary and I hitch a ride home with Jess. We decide to return on Oregon's back roads. Winding through Prineville we relax and observe coyotes and deer amid ranchers putting up hay along the creek bottoms. It was a lovely, restful drive with no traffic. We stop in Mt. Vernon to eat in a place that reminds me of Joseph's Cheyenne Cafe.

We continue on past old homesteads, through miles of open country full of sagebrush and juniper, northward to Long Creek and Ukiah, and finally La Grande. Mary and Jessica spend the night here, and leave for Boise the next morning.

August 6—Doug's zucchini and lettuce won blue ribbons at the fair. My herb basket and delphinium did too. This evening we bar-b-cue again, as granddaughter Mona Lee returns to Chehalis, Washington, and daughter Jackie and husband Bill return to Challis, Idaho. And so goes our Summer.

Hope all of you in Agri-Times land are enjoying yours as well.

August 12—Doug and I donned crazy hats and weird attire to attend Dave and Andi's wedding feast, held at the Wallowa River Camp, which is located next to the Joseph City Park. Over 100 folks gathered from near and far to feast and celebrate this union. An enormous grill, presided over by a friend, sent aromas of barbecued beef, pork and chicken swirling out across the lawns. In a picture-perfect setting, large tables sagged under the weight of salads, baskets of bread, polenta and pies. In a huge suspended iron kettle bubbled a pot of beans.

There was music and dancing, wherein old and young held hands, formed a gigantic circle, which wavered into the shape of a heart and corralled the bride and groom. Then we danced around and around, greeting new friends and smiling at familiar ones. Children scampered in and out of the circle, and babes-in-arms, carried by proud grandparents, added to the musical mix.

As evening descended, merriment and music increased. A real old-fashioned Wallowa County wedding feast. Where else can you wear an elk tooth necklace?

August 13—Doug returned from his annual blackberry-picking foray into the canyons of Imnaha bearing 4 gallons of dark purple berries for our freezer.

August 14—Our Fishtrap Board met here for the traditional berry dessert meeting. Up early, I whipped up a made-from-scratch lemon meringue pie, a large blackberry cobbler, and a nectarine/strawberry/cream pie. Board members brought their brown bag lunches and, since it was a warm August noon, we ate outside in the yard. I barely managed to salvage one serving of cobbler and a slice of pie for Doug that evening.

As usual, we were distracted by several hummingbird wars at our feeder, and Halley couldn't believe all the attention she received.

August 16—A warm breeze whipped the sheets on the line and it was in the 80s.

Our annual Stockgrowers meeting was held this morning and afternoon, followed by the dinner/dance this evening. Richard Frasch, our afternoon speaker, enlightened us on "Food versus Fuel: Impact on Agriculture." Richard is Senior Vice-President of Cargill and reads Agri-Times back in Chanhassen, Minnesota. He and wife Mary plan to retire in Wallowa County, and Richard's mother Beverly, one of our neighbors, contributes mightily to our community, as do Richard and Mary. The couple now own the ranch we continue to live on, minus our house and the immediate land that surrounds it.

Nice to see our neighbor Tom Butterfield receive Grassman of the Year, and Alder Slope ranchers, Dave and Shirley Parker, garner the Honorary Cattleman award. Doug and I were presented with our certificates and pins for winning the Diamond Pioneer award from O.S.U. a year ago. Since we couldn't make the luncheon in Corvallis to receive our awards, our local extension agent John Williams did the honors.

Nice to see a good turnout of Stockgrowers and their families. Especially the new crop of young adults at the helm, not to mention their offspring running around the dance floor. Once again, Randy Garnett and crew prepared one of their famous beef barbecues. We Stockgrower wives provided side dishes and salads.

We all welcomed back former Wallowa County ranchers Carol and Ed Wallace, who drove over from Clarkston, Washington. This couple used to ranch on Trout Creek, off the North Highway. Due to Ed's health issues they sold the ranch and moved where he could receive dialysis treatments.

August 17—Our family met again to celebrate three birthdays today. Son Todd, grandson Buck, and grandson-in-law Justin. Everyone arrived bearing food at granddaughter Chelsie's place at the base of Chief Joseph Mountain. Son Todd barbecued Marr Flat sirloin, and there were Angie's famous beans, Annie's creamy potatoes, and enough salads and desserts to feed over 30 of us. Chelsie, our young baker, baked a chocolate cheesecake and a peanut butter cake.

August 18—Halley and I had just begun our daily early morning walk when we looked up to see eight head of elk standing regally in a row in a grain field that used to be our hill hay field. Only yards away, we could smell them. Very rarely do we see elk here, so it took both us and them by surprise.

Two large spikes raised their heads, whipped around and, with the cows behind them, dashed downhill to leap over the fence onto the road in front of us. They swiftly jumped another fence and raced across the fields, clearing two more fences and irrigation ditches until they zigzagged up Lockes' hill, paused on the skyline, then melted over the ridge. What a sight!

Later this morning our book group met at the home of Bernice Bernatot on upper Prairie Creek, where we relaxed in her lovely yard under the tree near a running stream, to discuss this month's book, Robin Cody's *Ricochet River*. Robin was one of our workshop instructors at Summer Fishtrap. A very good read, we all agreed.

Then it was home to spend the afternoon preparing for our company, Christopher and Debbie James from Challis, Idaho.

This evening we seated ourselves outside at the picnic table and partook of the meal I'd spent all afternoon preparing: broiled Wallowa Lake kokanee, creamed new potatoes and peas from the garden, pickled beets, coleslaw from our first cabbage, and homemade bread—with apricot cobbler for dessert. The Jameses are friends of daughter Jackie and husband Bill, who also live in Challis.

August 19—This morning we took Christopher and Debbie off to Imnaha. At Fence Creek we found more ripe blackberries and picked enough for a cobbler, then headed up the Dug Bar Road, just far enough so our visitors could get a feel for the canyons. That's when a Bighorn ewe and her lamb walked our midst. Lots of photo-ops.

On the way out we stopped to visit the Imnaha Store and Tavern, with its carved wooden Indians out front, and its multitude of dollar bills tacked on the ceiling. We purchased T-shirts imprinted with "Where In The H* Is Imnaha?"

I pointed out all the places Bill and Jackie used to live, the church they helped build, and the school where their children, Mona and Buck, attended K-8 grades.

We made one more stop along Sheep Creek to pluck a few ripe peaches we'd been given permission to take at Myrna and Larry Moore's place. A warm peach fresh from the tree is hard to resist. Then we returned to Joseph, and on to Wallowa Lake where we saw two huge 6-point Mule Deer bucks, still in the velvet, wandering among the tourists.

This evening we returned to the Lake and dined at the Glacier Grill. They serve a tasty fish and chips. We really enjoyed having this couple visit. Debbie and I got in two games of scrabble, and Christopher enjoyed watching Olympics on TV with Doug.

August 20—Debbie and Christopher left Wednesday morning. I washed clothes and helped Myrna and Larry pick raspberries between rain showers. Doug's sister Barbara came out for lunch, and we loaded her up with garden veggies to take home.

August 22—Last evening daughter Ramona and husband Charley treated us to the Michael Martin Murphy concert at the OK theater in Enterprise. The place was packed. Over 300 folks came out of the woods to listen to the lone cowboy sing his songs. A thrill to hear "Wildfire" as well as old songs like "Little Joe the Wrangler," with only an aging cowboy singer, his guitar, and two saddles straddling bales of hay for props. It was truly a Wallowa County Heartland evening, and Michael touched a lot of hearts.

Son Ken and wife Annie also joined us. Tomorrow is Ramona and Charley's 39th wedding anniversary, and so goes the summer, which is just about gone. I'm getting this column out early so Kathy and I can load the burros and head to the high country. We plan to take the trail up the West Fork of the Wallowa River to Six-Mile Meadow, camp, then take day hikes to the Lakes Basin. Hope the weather cooperates.

August 23—On this near perfect afternoon I am making frozen peach pies and Doug is mowing the lawn. From the open kitchen window wafts the scent of ripening raspberries. Earlier, lacking sufficient strawberries for a batch of freezer jam, I substituted raspberries. The result was "berry" good.

Various members of the family, as well as friends, have helped with the picking of our prolific raspberries, which only seems to encourage their production. In the vegetable garden I've managed to freeze every pea Doug has podded, as well as pickled beets and dill pickles. I'm afraid to look at the green beans—Doug planted so many of them!

Of course, it's a given that visiting friends and family go home loaded with zucchini.

Weather-wise we've gone from sweltering in 90 degree heat to wearing rain coats due to cooling rain showers that caused our morning temperatures to dip into the 40s.

Our County Fair ended with a flurry of chicken scrambles, mutton busting, and goat-tail-tying Junior Rodeo events, followed the awards program that afternoon. All was capped off by the fat stock auction. I was there at 2:30 to take down the photography exhibit.

Daughter Lori and husband Larry were our house guests Saturday night, as they'd traveled from the Tri-Cities to attend Lori's class reunion. It took a few days to get rested up from that week.

August 25—Yesterday afternoon Phyllis and I went huckleberry'in. Got enough to flavor the sourdough pancakes this morning, with enough left for the freezer. By the looks of things a very large bear had been grazing our patch. Luckily, we only saw its sign.

This morning I picked green beans and pressure-cooked eight pints, then canned four pints of apricot jam. And, since it's now raining and our trip has been delayed a day, I decided to use the sourdough again. Biscuits are in the oven.

Bretta Wentz of Swamp Creek in rural Enterprise won the coveted Jidge Tippett Memorial Award for the best beef project at the Wallowa County Fair. Shown here with Jidge's son Doug Tippett, Brenda displays some of her other awards.

August 26—Our Writer's Group treated one of our members, Cathy, to lunch at the RimRock Inn on the occasion of her birthday. Always an adventure to travel out the North Highway. This time we stopped to watch Krebs' herder and his dogs drive the ewes and lambs across the road to a corral to be sorted. A joy to watch those dogs work.

Our meal on the edge of Joseph Creek Canyon was unique, as usual, and the traditional Mud Pie was served up with much merriment.

August 29—The morning of the 27th, I was up early to meet other Kathy at the West Fork of the Wallowa River trailhead. We spent a good deal of time loading her two burros, Fancy and Donkey Hoatey, before packing into the Wilderness. It was Hoatey's first trip, and we took turns leading him. Fancy was loose most of the time, and we were thankful for the coolish weather as we made our way higher and higher into the mountains.

All went well until we were almost through a cleared section of trail that had been carved through a most impressive snow slide. Then Fancy's pack caught on a protruding limb, and she went tearing off through the forest, spilling the contents of our camp along the way. Donkey Hoatey

Packed to head out of Six Mile Meadow in the Wallowas is Janie Tippett and burro "Fancy." Photo by Kathy Hunter.

got into the act, which meant his pack had to be retied as well.

A couple of backpackers ahead of us snapped our photo holding the burros under the sign that read *Lakes Basin*, with an arrow pointing to the right, and *Hawkins Pass*, with an arrow pointing left. We'd made it! Our destination: Six Mile Meadow. Which we had to ourselves, save for three gals, all backpackers, who were camped beyond the meadow.

They pulled out the next morning and we were able to savor the quiet, which was lucky, because on our trip out we met mule and horse pack strings, llama strings, and large groups of backpackers who were all planning to camp at Six Mile Meadow.

The camp we chose sported a fire ring, log benches, a stump table, a cold clear nearby stream, and a stunning view of the mountains that ringed us. The last of the summer snow was still visible at this high elevation, and the weather was crisp, clear, and sunny. We had frost the first morning but none the second.

We dined on the frozen stews and soups we'd prepared at home. The creek kept our food cold, and our tent and sleeping bags kept us warm. Thanks to the burros who carried it all in for us.

The next day I took a day hike up towards Hawkins Pass and Glacier Lake, while Kathy stayed in camp to look after the burros, who tended to wander in search of greener grass. Wishing we'd brought along a fishing pole, as we watched a woman day hiker catch some fat trout.

Midway out the next day, we turned the burros loose to wander up and down the trail while we picked huckleberries. It was an amazing patch. We simply sat on a log and picked two bags full. A mile from the trailhead at Wallowa Lake, my toes began jamming in my old hiking boots, and I was mighty glad to dig in the packs and don my crocks. And let me tell you, the Glacier Grill serves up a mean hamburger when you've been hours on the trail.

August 30—This morning I met Myrna Moore out on the Imnaha Highway to pick up the three boxes of peaches she had for me. She had a pickup load to sell in town. Since the fruit was plenty ripe, I got right to them: 14 pints canned, two quarts brandied, 8 1/2 pints of peach honey, one cobbler, three gallons of frozen slices, and a crock of peach brandy going in the basement later.

Our table was so filled with canned peaches, along with pickles I'd made from the cucumbers in the garden, we had to eat in the living room.

It is a time of plenty. Doug returned with more huckleberries than fish from Snake River, I pulled the shallots in the garden, we picked more strawberries and raspberries, and Doug cut the cabbage and shredded it while I layered it with salt in the crock.

The hiking trip made me strong enough to endure all this "putting food by." Of course I had to whip up a batch of baking powder biscuits so we could try out the peach honey. Yum.

September 1—We had our first killing frost last night, but Doug put the sprinkler on around midnight so the garden was spared. The first snow of the season fell, and the white stuff was visible on the higher peaks when we woke up to September.

This morning Doug and I headed over the mountain to Halfway, and made it in time for the Lion's Club huckleberry pancake breakfast, which was followed by the parade down Main Street that morning, and the Baker County Fair and rodeo that afternoon.

As usual it was a Wild West affair there in picturesque Pine Valley. Mule races, wild cow milking and ranch horse bronc riding were just a few of the many events. Of course we had to try out those juicy fair hamburgers before heading up North Pine Creek to return via the Wallowa Mountain Loop Road, a scenic route that brings us down Sheep Creek Hill to Prairie Creek and our back door.

September 2—Temperatures zoomed downward this morning, and the corn and sunflowers were sheathed in ice but spared again.

September 3—I helped Doug sort his 31 steers to be shipped to the Livestock Auction in La Grande. We held three head back to stay here.

This afternoon I joined Phil Brick from Whitman College and his "Semester In The West" students, who are traveling all over the West in a sort of traveling classroom. Was most impressed with the quality of the students, who were from all over the U.S. They camped at our neighbor's place, sleeping in the loft of the old Blue Barn.

Kept busy attending the Museum Board meeting, writing up the minutes, baking zucchini bread, sending out cards to my multitude of grand, and great-grandchildren, and writing.

September 5—My sister-in-law Barbara paid a visit and brought along lunch, which we ate out on the picnic table before she picked beans. Doug drove over to Clarkston to attend Lois Tippett's Memorial. Lois, Ben Tippett's mother, has been a role model for so many of us. She was a grand lady.

I stayed home to prepare for the Cowboy Poetry Gather'in that night at the showbarn on our Wallowa County Fairgrounds. This annual Gathering is part of the Hell's Canyon Mule Days Celebration. Smoke Wade, Doug's nephew, M.C.'d the evening, which included poets from all over the northwest.

When it was my turn, I felt a bit intimidated being the only female and all, but things went better after I recovered from forgetting my glasses. Luckily they were in my purse held by Barb in the stands. We had to step up onto a flat bed trailer and lay our papers on a bale of straw, then speak into a microphone.

The grand finale was listening to the Reddington family from Cove. My goodness, you never heard such music. Those young'uns can play with the best of them. Two sons and a daughter, with mom and dad in the act too. "Orange Blossom Special" really made those fiddles smoke. The crowd went wild! And Smoke Wade (aka Bob Fauste) was tough enough to wear a pink shirt.

The proceeds of this Max Walker Memorial Poetry Gathering all go to the Mule Days Scholarship Fund, a good cause.

September 8—Today was Doug's 77th Birthday, which means fall is here. Ah! September. My favorite time. The golden fields of wheat are being harvested, the sauerkraut is fermenting in the crock, the raspberries have ceased their bountiful harvest, the first frosts have nipped the zucchini (but not slowed it down much) and Houghs are swathing their third cutting of hay.

And there we were today, Doug and I, riding in a mule-drawn covered wagon with other past Mule Days Grand Marshals, in the Hell's Canyon Mule Days annual parade down the Main Street of Enterprise. The weather couldn't have been better for this weekend event, which broke records for attendance. Angie and Suzanne were there selling those Marr Flat Natural Beef burgers and I understand they sold out.

There was so much going on. A Dutch Oven cookoff Sunday, a rodeo on Saturday, followed by one of Jim Probert's pit-barbecued pork dinners, eaten outside with music by "Soul Renovation," and a horse and mule auction that also broke records.

It was a *hee-haw*-ing good time for Wallowa County, and today I'm feeling a bit weary. The amount of volunteers it takes to pull off this annual event is staggering, but as usual Wallowa County was up to the task. Beautiful scenery and beautiful people.

Ran into John Groupe at the Cowboy Poetry night, and he said my column was too long. He's right. Too much show and tell.

We were gladdened to read a report from Roger Pond. We've been missing you Roger.

OK, John, this is it. See you next time.

September 9—The phone rang off the hook for my birthday. Our children, friends and my sisters all wishing me a happy 75th. My writing group met that morning, then treated me to lunch at the "Happy Garden" in Enterprise. We had a "happy" time over tasty Chinese food.

September 10—Another frostless morning. After those first few days, we've been lucky, and the garden is producing with renewed vigor. I lined my hen's nests with clean straw in the chicken house, and cooked up a kettle of French onion soup, using those Walla Walla Sweets from our garden.

September 11—I rode to Walla Walla with friend Kathy who had a doctor appointment. After which she treated me to lunch at Merchant's, where we sat at a sidewalk table and savored Reuben sandwiches. We squeezed in a visit to "Andy's" to purchase bulk foods before returning via Tollgate to Wallowa County.

September 12—Received a call from grandson James. He and his other grandma, "Nanna" McAlister, were coming for dinner that night. Since James was between fire fighting and returning to college in Montana, this grandma baked his favorite pie—huckleberry cream—using the huckleberries Kathy and I picked alongside the trail coming out from Six

Mile Meadow. I also baked sourdough bread, and heated up some of our fresh sauerkraut with sausages. Was nice to see them both.

James' sister Adele called from Austin, Texas, this morning; says she's doing well in Culinary school. She mentioned the traffic was thick, with folks fleeing Hurricane Ike.

September 14—Yesterday I canned dilled green beans, then picked all the Transparent apples from our young tree and canned applesauce, freezing a few slices for pie. Tonight I was tricked into going out some-where for my 75th birthday. And, after taking me on a circuitous route to Alder Slope, Doug swept through Enterprise and ended up at Cloverleaf Hall…where all seven of our children were waiting, along with nearly 150 friends and other relatives. SURPRISE! It was a bit overwhelming.

Son Steve had flown in from Alabama, Linda from Salem, and Jackie from Challis, and there followed big hugs and grins. The hall was deco-rated with homemade quilts, and flowers spilling out of pots from the kids' yards, and old milk cans and antiques. Randy Garnett and family catered a yummy tri-tip dinner, granddaughter Chelsie baked one of her specialty cakes, and I was roasted and oded, and myriad photos were snapped of our huge family. I was one proud mamma.

The out-of-town children spent the night, and the next morning Doug treated them all to breakfast at the Cheyenne Cafe in Joseph, before they scattered, like quail, back to their busy lives.

September 15—I drove with two other gals down to Kathy's in Lostine for our monthly book group, where we discussed the book *Auntie Mame.* Later Kathy drove up here and together we headed to Imnaha to pick pears and blackberries down at Lyman and Wilma's.

On the way home, along Sheep Creek, we stopped to purchase two boxes of heirloom tomatoes.

This evening I put up 6 pints of blackberry jelly.

September 16—Began by roasting those delicious tomatoes with garlic, olive oil, basil, salt and pepper for three hours before canning them. Yum.

While I was in the process of doing this, Ed and Carol Wallace, from Clarkston, Washington, drove in for a brief visit.

Then James stopped in on his way back to college, and I loaded him up with larder from my canning cupboard. He was pretty proud of his new dog. It seems he found the dog on the internet, in a pound in Madras, where his step father just happened to be at the time. He said the dog was perfect, and brought it home. Now that's fate, not to mention, a girl working at the pound had been hiding the dog on the kill day for three weeks. I think James named him "Fatefull."

This evening the full Harvest Moon pushed its way up beyond Hough's hill, and my heart was as full as that moon.

September 17—The coyotes were quite vocal. Must be the moon.

On a whim, I asked Phyllis if she would like to help me use two passes I had for the Gondola. It was a lovely morning, and we were at the lake shortly after 10:00. Soon we were floating up the slopes of Mt. Howard in one of those little cages, staring down at the lake and across at the waterfall spilling out of Ice Lake. At the top we hiked 2 1/2 miles along trails that offered views to the heart of the Wallowas, the canyons, and the valley, where we pinpointed our homes.

We dined out on fish and chips on the sunny patio at the Summit Grill. Life was good.

September 18—Doug hauled the last three steers to the auction in La Grande. I pressure-canned cream style corn, started the seven-day sweet pickles, and cut some little roses to take to Christine Anderson, who broke her hip, and is in our new hospital.

September 19—Doug and I started the day off with sourdough huckleberry pancakes, and later I baked a loaf of sourdough bread. You see, I'd carried some of that pure sweet water back from the summit of Mt. Howard, where I'd captured it from a spring that bubbles out of the ground up there. My sourdough loves wild water.

September 20—A sudden gust of wind, of short but powerful duration, shook the old apple tree last night, and loosened the ripest fruit. Today my kitchen smells of sauce bubbling from those golden windfalls.

Far into the night we heard the sound of Dan Butterfield's harvester as it chomped its way up and down the ripened rows of wheat. He dumped the last row of grain into the truck just before the first drops of rain fell. This morning on my walk with Halley, the air was saturated with the pleasant odor of dampened stubblefield.

A warm, drizzling rain continues to fall as I write—a welcome change from the dry, hot days we've been experiencing. It's been a busy two weeks.

Phyllis was here to pick strawberries, and brought me some plums, so I baked a cream cheese plum clafouti.

This evening was the "Pink Tie" affair at Cloverleaf Hall to raise money for a digital mammography machine for our new hospital. The event was a HUGE success. The community raised over $550,000!

Two Saturday nights in a row at Cloverleaf Hall, for two totally different functions. The hospital benefit was so elegant, chairs covered with white cotton covers with pink bows and the same for the tables, with fresh flower centerpieces, and an enormous punch bowl full of shrimp on ice. Music was by Janice Carper, Rod Ambroson, and Carolyn Lockhart; the prime rib by Holy Smokes, and the silent dessert auction was a feast for the eyes as well as the palate, full of items too numerous to mention—and our friends all dressed up! Pink ties on farmers yet! All for a good cause.

September 21—Doug and I were having breakfast at the Cheyenne Cafe when we ran into Jan Thompson and Joan Byr, classmates that were staying at Wallowa Lake for a class reunion. Jan is a faithful reader of Agri-Times.

September 22—The Autumnal Equinox. After two days, the clouds have lifted to expose a fresh dusting of snow on the mountains. Phyllis, Kathy and I are planning to take my mare and their burros to Aneroid Lake Wednesday morning, and we'll be com'in down the mountain Friday. Wish us luck.

September 23—28 degrees. Our garden encased in ice, but the sprinkler saved it. Packing up for a trip to Aneroid Lake tomorrow. Kathy backed out, so it's just Phyllis and I.

Baked two apple pies, one for Doug, one in a small tin to pack to Aneroid Lake. The pack boxes I borrowed from son Todd are all loaded, ready to go.

September 26—Lovely cool morning on the 24th, mostly sunny with a few clouds and no frost. Doug drives me, my mare Morning Star, and border collie Halley to the trailhead at Wallowa Lake, where we meet up with Fred and Phyllis who are packing up their miniature donkey "Roxy."

I fill out the wilderness slip: Two people, two pack animals, one dog. Destination: Aneroid Lake, six miles, all uphill.

And we're off...well, that is, until Phyllis discovers she's lost a glove. I wait until she finds it along the back trail, and my mare is chomping to go. We climb through yellowing trembling aspen thickets, pick our way through giant rock slides where shy pikas shriek, and stare at dashing whitewater thundering down the East Fork of the Wallowa River. It warms up, brilliant shafts of sunlight streaming through the fir forests, and we are warmed by the exertion.

2008 grand marshals of the Hells Canyon Mule Days parade were Maria Onaindia, left, and Juana Malaxa of Enterprise. These two Basque women and their husbands, Joe and Gus, ran the Cherry Creek Sheep Company on Snake River for years.

Phyllis calls from the rear. "I've got to take off my long johns!" I elect to keep going and don't see her again until lunch time, where I've stopped to eat a sandwich near an opening in the trees. I stuff Phyllis' extra clothes under the tarp, on top of my mare's pack. We approach the familiar sign which reads "Inbound and Outbound" where the trail splits.

We take Inbound, a high narrow trail that looks far down to the headwaters of the East Fork. Soon we approach the meadows, all golden now in autumn, with their meandering stream. Since Phyllis has fallen behind, we wait until she catches up. Then, there is Roger Lake, and one more final pull to Aneroid, a high alpine lake sparkling blue through the trees in the late afternoon sunshine. The climb took us from 4,650 ft. to 7,500 ft. elevation: we've done it, one more time.

Caretaker Dennis and his nephew Jordan lead us to our quarters in the wilderness. Dubbed "the Benson," the log cabin is crude, built in

Mike Brennan, son of the late movie actor Walter Brennan, was honorary grand marshal of the 2008 Hells Canyon Mule Days. He lives on a ranch in rural Joseph.

1920—and our home for two blessed days and nights. We settle in, build a fire in the wood stove, sip hot tea, tend to the pack animals, and rest.

That evening we invite Jordan and Dennis for a supper of German sausages, my homemade sauerkraut, corn on the cob, and apple pie. A fire in the stone fireplace provides a cheery light to eat by. We were asleep early in the loft, warm sleeping bags spread on comfortable mattresses, starlight glittering through cracks in the ancient logs amid absolute quiet. We are the only guests.

The next morning dawns clear and cold, with the sun bursting late over the talus wall of rock to the east. Reddened Lambs Quarter marches up the draws, and the sky is as blue as a bluebird's wing. A whisper of mist over the lake's clear skin. Clark's Nutcrackers scold us from a nearby snag. After breakfast, a hike around the lake, reading, and (for me) writing, we played scrabble and soaked up sun on the upper deck.

That evening, we pan-broiled steaks on a cast iron griddle over the wood stove. Fried potatoes in the dutch oven kept hot in the fireplace, and we finished off the apple pie.

Later, we play Scrabble with Dennis and Jordan late into the night.

The next morning the meadow is white with frost as we load up the pack animals and head down the trail. Halley says this is the most fun she's ever had. This wild country is full of wild smells, and she has the

Rick Hagen, of La Grande, stirs his stew while his bread bakes during the Hells Canyon Mule Days Dutch oven cook-off.

Phyllis Webb, left, with donkey Roxy, and Janie with her mare, Morning Star, and border collie Halley packed up, ready to leave Aneroid Lake after a two-night stay in an old cabin built in 1920.

freedom to run, run, run.

We make it back to the trailhead by 2:30 and Doug soon arrives to take us home. I've been reading this book, written by Robert Morgan, entitled *Boone,* a biography of Daniel Boone. Wonderful writing. I can identify with Old Daniel. Some of us just can't get enough of wilderness living.

September 27—I canned the seven day sweet pickles, and Doug peeled apples which I turned into sauce and apple butter. Then we drove to the Lake to treat ourselves to one of those German sausage kraut sandwiches washed down with a glass of dark draft beer. Warm Indian summer prevailed. Even though it isn't known as Alpenfest anymore, and lacked the Bavarian dancers, the event was a success. Enjoyed visiting with John Groupe, who presented me with a copy of his book, *Eastern Oregon Horse Pack Trips.* This is a great guide to backcountry trails.

Our days are so full. Cooked up a batch of apple chutney, the pungent odor of which lingered in my kitchen for days. Then there was the Halibut feast at the Enterprise Community Church. Yum!

October 1—September's 30 days HATH fled. Kathy and I made another run to Imnaha for tomatoes. Can't have too many canned tomatoes.

"The Benson" cabin in the Wilderness at Aneroid Lake. The log cabin was built in 1920. Janie is soaking up the September sun on the porch in front of the sleeping loft.

Also froze several containers of tomato soup base.

October 2—Rode out to Marr Flat with Doug to haul in a load of son Todd's weaned calves. Lovely out there on that high, wide, grassy plateau, with its old corrals, views of the far-off Wallowas, and steep breaks of Big Sheep. The huckleberry bushes were reddening, the aspen yellowing, the cows in good shape, and the calves fat.

October 3—I remembered giving birth to my oldest child 59 years ago in Medford, Oregon, that beautiful, bright-eyed baby girl, Ramona Jane.

Next Sunday I head to the writer's retreat on the upper Imnaha for a week of putting the finishing touches on my book.

October 4—As early morning clouds lift, the Wallowas, dusted with yet another fresh snowfall, come out of hiding.

On my walk with Halley this morning, we paused alongside the irrigation ditch to listen to the wild wailings of coyotes hunting Hough's hill. You can pick out the young pups from the parents. Their yammering echoes across Prairie Creek as sounds are amplified by the phenomenon we call Echo Canyon.

The October air has a crisp clarity and smells of spent summer: fermenting apples, wet wheat stubble, rotting leaves, and yellowing willow and cottonwood. As fall advances, the red delicious apples, hanging heavy on the young tree son Todd gave me on Mother's Day several years ago, redden; the sunflowers loose their showy bloom and concentrate on maturing seeds, the last three cabbages hunker down and stop growing, corn stalks rattle in the wind, and Prairie Creek heaves a sigh and relaxes.

The last fields of wheat, hay and straw have been harvested and baled, the hay barns are full, and outside stacks are tarped. Locals drive old pickups, pulling old trailers loaded with seasoned wood from the forests, and I'm still canning plums, now Italian plums from Imnaha. I have a Zwetschgenkuchen (German Plum Cake) in the oven, my contribution to the "Stitch and Bitch" Potluck at Kathy's this evening.

Occasional rifle shots boom from the hills, as it is opening morning of Buck deer season. I put the word out that I need a venison neck to make mincemeat.

Neighbor Tom Butterfield showed up at our back door the other evening with a tub of whole wheat.

"For your chickens." he said. He'd cleaned out his harvester.

By comparison, the slice of hot apple pie I gave Tom seemed a mere token of appreciation, since I've been paying a fortune for my chicken wheat.

Had a nice phone visit with my little sister Kathryn Jean, who lives in Roseville, California, this morning. She says it's finally raining.

Took a bowl of applesauce over to great-granddaughter Jada this afternoon. Little Jada just had her tonsils out and applesauce is one thing she can eat. In fact, I've been giving applesauce to all of our Wallowa County families, to assure none of those heirloom cooking apples go to waste.

October 8—Phyllis and I headed to the canyons to pick up windfall golden delicious apples to use for the annual "apple squeez'in." After filling our buckets, we walked down the road to visit Myrna Moore, who lives up Bear Gulch.

Myrna was in the middle of freezing bell peppers from her garden, so we pitched in and helped, after which she warmed up a kettle of homemade tomato soup and we three sat around a table in her little kitchen, chatting and savoring that flavorful soup.

Since Myrna was also canning her soup, I copied the recipe and, utilizing some leftover tomatoes, I put up several pints after I got home.

October 9—It was spitting snow as Halley and I walked along Tenderfoot Valley Road this morning. I was feeling sad, as I could see the old willow trees that line the irrigation ditch quivering before succumbing to the chain saw. I imagined the sky was full of frozen tears. As each ancient willow crashed to the ground, it felt like an old friend was dying.

October 10—Prairie Creek was white with the first snowfall when I bundled up to walk with Halley.

At noon I met sis-in-law Barb at Calderas, where we savored a steaming bowl of Nancy's tomato bisque soup. Calderas is an experience. Not only is the food created from Nancy's wonderful Sheep Creek garden, but the place itself is so interesting. There's Chuck Fraser's blacksmithing iron work staircase, and Steve Arment's beautiful wood carvings.

October 11—Still cold when a big crowd gathered for the annual apple squeez'in party at Chuck and Chris Fraser's. A freezing wind blew while we took turns cranking the antique apple presses that grind and squeeze out the sweet golden juice. But Wallowa County folks are a hardy lot, and the reward to all this labor was the gourmet potluck served in Chuck's blacksmith shop.

Folks gathered outside by warming fires over which oysters steamed in the shell. An enormous handmade iron rotisserie, dripped with juices from a haunch of bear, venison, and 30 chicken halves basted on Lyle's homemade grill; fresh shrimp served with cocktail sauce, homemade salads, kettles of beans, baskets of breads, pies, cakes, cobblers. I added my apple crunch pie and dutch oven full of sauerkraut and sausages to the groaning table in the shop.

"The Bunk House Band" played old timey fiddle tunes, folks danced, tools hung on the walls, and Chuck's latest work in progress provided the back drop. Children romped in the pulp pile, the aspen along the creek trembled gold, the snow remained on the ground, and our Wallowas were covered with it.

Returning home, I got in and canned the apple juice, saving enough for making mincemeat later.

October 20—I was on my way the morning of the 12th to the upper Imnaha to spend a week at the Fishtrap Writer's Retreat. With the exception of drizzly rain the first day, the weather was fair. Crisp and frosty in the mornings, then warming as soon as the sun spilled over the eastern ridge and down the western rims around 10:00 a.m.

Wild turkeys and mule deer paraded past our windows, apples plunked to the ground with every gust of wind, the river slid musically past, the colors deepened, and inside we WROTE. During that week I was able to complete the final editing and placing of photos for my book.

Of course, we also prepared gourmet meals. Writers are good cooks. Bobbie and Barb had driven from Portland, and Ruth and I both live "on top." One evening we had Lyman and Wilma for a supper of chicken enchiladas, salad, and Bobbie's warm peach pie. Wilma made it over the swinging bridge like an old pro this time.

On our walks up and downriver, we watched the sumac turn fiery red, the cottonwoods yellow, the thornbrush blush coral, and purple clusters of elderberries ripen. We spotted great piles of bear scat in the yard, but no bear sightings. We spent our relaxing evenings reading to each other around the fireplace, and Ruth and I even worked in several games on my little "travel scrabble". set.

The week sailed by all too fast, and soon I was back "on top."

In my absence Doug dug the potatoes, tended my chickens, and cared for Halley and the cats. A few days later he hooked up the boat and drove to Snake River, where he met up with friends for several days of steelhead fishing. He returned a day later with good news and bad news: a delicious steelhead fish and a broken prop on his boat. Darn rocks.

October 27—Outside beckons. There is a golden quality to the October air. It's as though the very air reflects the glow from the golden tamaracks growing on the slopes of the mountains, and the cottonwoods and yellowing aspen that line our creeks. Jars of venison mincemeat and canned venison are stored on our canning cupboard shelves in the basement. The rest of Doug's deer, fattened on alfalfa and wheat fields, has been cut, wrapped and frozen. And, when the winter squash is canned, I'll be through "putting food by" for the long winter.

As I write, I hear the steady drone of a very large tractor pulling a very large piece of earth-moving equipment in our former hay field on the hill. My, the activity for such a small field. To begin, with huge trenches were dug, pipe and electric line laid, powerful pumps installed, concrete pads poured, and enormous center pivot irrigation systems assembled like giant erector sets. Now these behemoth wheeled sprinklers dominate the skyline.

Every morning on our walk Halley and I notice something new, like the enormous boulders that have been unearthed from the hill. The lower fields are undergoing the same transformation. The now defunct wheel lines repose forlornly against the fences, the pump houses torn down, the ancient willows (sob) that once lined the creek now reduced to a sad-looking pile of trunks, limbs, and browned leaves.

Progress. It's happening all over the valley.

Somehow I miss the old tractors, the handlines, the flood irrigating; seems to me one could pay a pipe changer pretty good wages and it would still be cheaper than the cost of a center pivot system. I understand one of those babies cost as much as we USED to pay for a small ranch. We now live in a different time.

Last Saturday, to escape all this activity and fill my soul with a bit of wildness, I hiked with my friend Phyllis and my dog Halley up Hurricane Creek to a place called Slick Rock. It couldn't have been a more perfect day, and along the trail we met others who live here in the valley. We were surprised to find not a drop of water in Falls Creek. We simply walked across the dry "crik" bed.

After huffing and puffing our way up to where we could look down on Hurricane Creek, and thence to our highest mountain, Sacagawea, I paused to snap a photo of the scene.

The air was crisp and clean, the trail a carpet of tamarack needles, and views from the open meadows could rival any scene on earth for beauty. The solid rock formations that create the Hurricane Divide leads the eye to the sky. Waterfalls are dry this time of year, save for Slick Rock, where water cascaded down over summer-slimed rock. We ate our lunches alongside the creek, where sunlight warmed our skin, and the creek's water sound relaxed us. A perfect way to savor Indian Summer.

On Tuesdays lately our Write Group has been meeting at Chris' cabin on the West side of Wallowa Lake, because Chris is recuperating from a broken hip. We all pack a lunch and enjoy watching the reflections of the water on the living room walls, and staring out at the lake.

October 29—Phyllis and I hiked the East Moraine of Wallowa Lake today. A day made in Heaven... warm, the lake like glass, breeze on top. We ate our lunch sitting on glacial boulders, staring down at flocks of migrating geese. Halley loved it.

Looking west we gazed across to the slopes of Chief Joseph Mountain. To the east we could see the Seven Devils of Idaho and the Divide, the

Shipping and weaning calves on Marr Flat in Wallowa County, left to right: Todd Nash, Buck Matthews, Doug Tippett. Marr Flat Cattle Co. calves did well this year averaging nearly 600 pounds.

cut that marks the Imnaha Canyon road; out north lay the Buttes and the Chesnim country, where hunters were hunting elk. The town of Joseph; Upper, Middle and Lower Prairie Creek; it was all there.

Halley played with a small red fox, and sniffed numerous game trails. At the south end we met Dan Warnock, checking his cattle that graze that beauteous pasture, the same pasture Doug rented all those years. I remembered riding horseback in November, bringing down our fall calvers in a snow storm, and driving them up again in the spring. Dan said they were gathering the cattle the next day.

Again, we who live here, are so blessed. May we never forget that, and pledge ourselves to being good stewards of what we have.

October 31—While I was dipping apples into a gooey caramel mixture for our expected "trick or treaters," I remembered it was just a year ago that Halley came into my life. How such a small bundle of black and white energy can steal one's heart is amazing. Thank goodness puppyhood is behind us, but I hope my border collie never loses her youthful spirit.

At noon I joined Jean Cook at the Wallowa County Dining Center, donned my CowBelle apron, and served a roast pork dinner to a full house. The delicious pork was compliments of Richard and Mary Frasch.

Our senior citizens really appreciated the treat.

This evening, when spooks and goblins were ghosting about Prairie Creek, here came Riley Ann, Ashlynn, Gideon, Jada, Ronan, Kennon, Gwenllian, Gavin, and Lucy—all decked out, as were their parents, in a variety of creative costumes. Very entertaining to have great-grandchildren living close by. Those caramel apples, as well as cookies, were whisked into little bags.

"Thank you grandma and Poppa Doug," was our treat.

November 1—The first day of November was wild, windy, warm and overcast. After our walk, I heated up the griddle, fried sourdough hotcakes, and drizzled 'em with real maple syrup. Then set more sourdough to rise for bread that evening.

Later this morning, Kathy and I were on our way down into the canyons to close up the Writer's Retreat on the upper Imnaha. After cleaning out refrigerators, emptying ashes, washing sheets, and locking everything up in that leafy world of falling apples, we drove downriver to 90-year-old Wayne Marks' place, where we visited this interesting old-timer. Since Wayne had an English walnut tree, he let us rake up a bucket full of fallen nuts.

Doug returned from the hills to report he'd seen a thousand head of elk. Naturally, they were on land that is off limits to hunting.

Baked apples, drizzled with apple cider, made the kitchen smell like fall.

November 2—We're back on Standard time, which always seems weird. Hard to stay up late after darkness settles in.

I baked an apple/pear/cranberry tart to take to the potluck held up Hurricane Creek at Fire Works Pottery, where our potter friends Jim and Ann Shelly had hosted a day-long open house sale. After which folks gathered in the Shelly's studio where, midst their works of clay, we enjoyed food as creatively prepared as Shelly's art.

November 3—I was wondering what to do with this enormous banana squash I'd purchased from Lyle Davis, who grew the vegetable in his Milton-Freewater garden. I decided to bake it in the oven, stuff it into jars, and pressure can it. So, taking a meat saw, I went at the squash and soon had it cut into manageable chunks, saving enough for supper. Now, when I want to bake a pumpkin pie: *voila!* canned squash in the basement.

Also baked a mincemeat pie, and son Todd stopped by on his way back from Marr Flat to take a slice home.

It was a cold stormy evening and Todd started a fire in the old Monarch, which was cozy, since it had begun to spit snow. While I husked the walnuts and stained my hands, Doug cracked up a winter supply of nuts that had been drying in the shop.

November 4—Our writer's group met at Ruth Wineteer's home on the hill above Enterprise, where Ruth served us steaming bowls of squash soup, after which we played scrabble until it was time to leave and drive to the Enterprise grade school, where I read every Tuesday to my two students in the SMART program. A very worthwhile program, and one that Fishtrap is now directing locally. Many volunteers make this possible.

November 5—This morning was sunny and crispy cold. Phyllis and I bundled up and strolled around Joseph, gathering colored maple leaves that I later pressed between magazines to decorate our Thanksgiving table.

Back to the ranch to capture three of my old hens. While Doug chopped off their heads, I carried scalding water outside to dip them. Soon feathers were flying and three fat hens were all plucked. However, it took 'til midnight for those old girls to get fork tender.

November 6—I arose early to remove meat from bones, stuff the chicken and broth in jars, then set the timer for 90 minutes. While the pressure cooker sizzled and spit, Halley and I headed over the hill for our morning walk. Called grandson James, who has been ill, and was relieved to know he is on the mend.

November 9—On the 7th, Pam, Nick and I headed to Portland to attend a weekend strategic planning meeting for Fishtrap. The colors that border the Columbia River Gorge were truly gorgeous. Suddenly we were in the city and checking in at the Mark Spencer Hotel. My room was on the third floor, where I was to join my friend Kathy, who hadn't yet arrived.

By some quirk of fate, Pam and I were given tickets for the opening night of the opera "Fidelio" that night, to be performed at the Keller Auditorium, several blocks away from our hotel.

After dining on Italian food, we struck off along the leafy streets, taking in the golden maple leaves, backlit by street lights as we walked beneath those skyscraper buildings. Far above, the November moon sailed free of watery clouds. The opera would be hard-pressed to beat that show, I mused, but it did.

It was my first live opera and we had third-row seats, where we could literally feel the vibrations of those magnificent voices. This, Beethoven's only opera, was sung in German and the words projected in English over the stage. The place was full to capacity with people, every manner of humanity, dressed in every manner of clothing; more people in that auditorium, it seemed, than the entire population of Wallowa County. It was a thrilling experience.

After the Opera ended, Pam and I walked a couple of blocks to where we had been told to board a trolley...only it was the wrong one. Turns out a couple from Bend, also lost, were standing next to us, and also staying at our hotel. Unreal. An eavesdropper understood our plight, directed us get off at the next stop, and guided us to the right trolley. It was after 11:00 when we tumbled into bed that first night. I was so keyed up I couldn't sleep.

The next day we attended intensive meetings at the nearby Governor's hotel. That night, our local Fishtrap Board met at a Thai restaurant and "pigged out" on gourmet food before walking back to our hotel.

The weekend also included a visit to Powell's Books, only a couple blocks from our hotel. An entire city block of books. Oh my!

I found a copy on sale of *The Guernsey Literary Potato Peel Pie Society,* and a pie cookbook. Pam and I had to get out of there or we would have needed a wagon to haul our books back to the hotel.

The drive home on Sunday was pleasant, and the roads were good. It rained hard in Portland, but by the time we reached Eastern Oregon the weather turned cloudy and warm. Halley was one big grin!

Portland offers opera, food, and other big city hype, but Wallowa County is where my heart is.

November 10—What began as a damp dreary morning has morphed into a mostly sunny afternoon. Recent rains have soaked into the soil and accompanying winds have all but stripped away Autumn's color. Regardless of weather, Halley and I strike out each morning for our walk. We were greeted this morning by a large flock of geese flying low over Locke's field, and the sound of bawling cows. Weaning time.

Our mountains are blanketed with snow again, which is the way we're most used to seeing them. Refreshed from my walk, I got in and canned the pears I'd brought back from my last trip to Imnaha.

November 11—Our "Write Group" met here and, after spending the morning writing, I treated them to braised lamb shanks, cooked in my dutch oven. Those tasty shanks were courtesy of Sharon, who had purchased a 4-H lamb at the county fair fat stock auction. Phyllis brought

Phyllis Webb enjoys the view from the East Moraine of Wallowa Lake.
Highway 82 is seen far below.

along a warm apple pie and we feasted. Cold weather does turn one
indoors and inspire cooking.

November 12—Pat and Ray Combes invited the gang (those of us
who haven't gone south) to a barbecued rib dinner. Pat is an excellent
cook, and she and Ray are the hostess and host with the most'ess, in
their lovely new home located in rural Joseph.

November 14—It was sunny but windy when seven of us "Stitch
and Bitchers" carpooled and headed to La Grande, then sped southwest
to Lehman Hot Springs. Once again we'd reserved the apartment over
the pools. Our carload, the first to arrive, wasted no time jumping in.
Ahhh, there's nothing like it.

This evening I lit the mesquite briquettes in the small bar-b-cue

Janie Tippett and her border collie Halley lunch on Hurricane Creek in the Eagle Cap Wilderness. Photo by Phyllis Webb.

I'd brought along, and grilled some of those Marr Flat T-bones. Nancy warmed up her pre-baked potatoes in the microwave, Angie tossed a green salad, and Annie sliced her home-baked bread and brought forth the sinful chocolate cake she'd baked for Sally's birthday. Of course we were ravenous after spending all afternoon in the pools.

We were back soaking again after dinner, seven gals dissolving in the mists. These natural hot springs originate in the nearby pine forests, and the steaming water is piped to the fenced-in pools where it trickles down over rocks. In a crevasse among the rocks blooms a solitary rose, one pink blossom quivering in the steam.

That night was the full November "Beaver Moon" and it was pure magic after the lights were turned out. Even though the moon was obscured by clouds, its diffused glow was sufficient to illuminate the pools and lighten our walk back to the apartment.

The next morning, I arose before dawn to softly, so as not to wake the others, make my way down the outside stairs, step gingerly across the frosted pool-side, and slip into steamy Heaven. Immersed in steam, I floated and stared up at that leftover moon, still high in a crystal sky. I remained submerged until the dark line of evergreens to the West turned gold in rising sun, and the moon slipped out of sight.

By then the others straggled out, and later we gobbled down slices of Sally's delicious quiche. Driving home I was thinking how many precious memories we are making, memories to cherish when we are confined to rocking chairs. NEVER.

November 15—Phyllis and I drove to the historic Wallowa Lake Lodge, where we joined a full house of folks who had come to listen to Steve Einhorn and Kate Power perform their wonderful ballads. Kate on banjo, Steve on guitar, and sometimes harmonica, backed up their unique voices as they sang songs they'd written themselves. This husband and wife team are truly friends of Wallowa County, and many of their songs were inspired here.

Driving home that night along the lakeshore, the moonlight reflected Mt. Joseph's snowy shoulders.

November 16—I was thrilled to receive several poems from Grandson James, who is a student at University of Montana West in Dillon. No grandma could ever be prouder.

Using some of those walnuts Doug cracked, I baked a walnut pie. Also pulled more of those beets to cook, then freeze.

November 17—Our book group met at Fishtrap House to discuss November's read, which was the great book *Three Cups of Tea*. In the afternoon I planted crocuses, hoping Halley wouldn't dig them up.

For dinner I concocted a homemade chowder using ingredients I had on hand, which included corn, potatoes, bacon, clams and parsley. Yum.

November 18—After our Write group met, I took a long walk around Alder Slope, until it was time to meet with my two young girls for the SMART reading program.

November 19—A salmon-colored sunrise tinted the sky as Halley and I wandered Hough's hill and startled a covey of Hungarian Partridge. And now, it's almost Thanksgiving, and we'll only have eleven as compared to 32 last year. I purchased the turkey today, a fresh one, remembering that monster I stuffed in the wood cook stove last year.

Sharon Gibson, of Joseph, pauses for the camera during a recent cattle drive up Sheep Creek Hill. Sharon and her twin sister, Sherry, are capable cowgirls for local cattle ranchers

You in Agri-Times land will have already eaten your turkey by the time you read this. Happy Holidays just the same. We all have so much to be thankful for.

November 23—Our thermometer on the clothesline post registered 10 degrees when Halley and I set out on our morning walk. One of our coldest mornings yet. The November sun had just burst over Locke's hill, and Prairie Creek glittered with frost. The sky, cleansed by cold, was bluebird blue. No wind. Perfect. That is, if you are bundled up—and I was.

Crunching through the frozen grasses that line the irrigation ditches, I thought about the wonderful cozy evening we had down at Lyman and Wilma's log home on the upper Imnaha yesterday. Doug and I were invited, along with other friends, to "help" them eat the generous amount of iced, fresh crab that Lyman's son Craig had shipped via UPS from McKinleyville, California. Our contribution was seashell macaroni salad and beer.

The old wood stove provided its share of warmth, and the rest was generated by the simple camaraderie of neighbors and friends getting together to enjoy this crab feed, which is becoming a tradition. Once again, 91 yr. old Doug ("Doc") Morgan won the prize for cracking and eating the most crab. Doc lives with his son Hank at "The Bridge" near the Imnaha Store and Tavern, and is beloved by all who know him.

When we stepped outside to drive home, the stars glowed like cut diamonds in that blue-black, cold canyon night. As I write, a pair of flickers are busy in the old apple tree pecking the last frozen apples clinging to the limbs. Halley, basking in the sun, is dreaming about tomorrow morning's walk. A neighboring rancher has just driven a herd of cattle past our place, and my young border collie was snoozing so soundly, she didn't even notice.

Doug is off cow elk hunting again. Yesterday he and grandson Buck left early for the hills, and I'd left my warm cocoon of covers to fill them up with sourdough hotcakes, fried ham and eggs for breakfast. Buck, who says he eats more in cold weather, put away an amazing amount of pancakes. Although they spotted thousands (literally) of elk, once again, the wily wapiti were off limits to hunters.

I must say, after being dragged kicking and screaming into the age of technology, I am enjoying the e-mail from my 91-year-old Auntie Carol, who lives in Sacramento, California. She says she still drives, takes water aerobics, reads voraciously, plays bridge, still lives in her own home, and "does" the Internet.

November 30—Our 18th great-grandchild made her appearance in the Central Oregon community of John Day, Born to Grandson Rowdy and wife Kasey. Welcome to our family, sweet little Nevada Dawn.

Our calendar was filled with holiday bazaars, where you could purchase a piece of 92-year-old Harold McLaughlin's wood work, or some of wife Hope's hot pads, then, "for the person who has everything, or the one who has nothing," a gift package of Marr Flat Cattle Company Natural Beef steaks, a fragrant Christmas wreath, some of Gene Hayes' beautiful hand-painted note cards, Christmas ornaments, and all manner of homemade crafts and goodies.

From the kitchen wafted the smells of chicken noodle soup and freshly-baked cinnamon rolls, and Santa—clad in his itchy attire—presided 'neath the Christmas tree.

Jane Kirkpatrick sent me a copy of her soon-to-be released book, *Aurora*, which is beautifully done and features never-before-published photos of antiques and treasures kept by descendants of the Aurora Colony of Oregon's Willamette Valley. I sat down in one evening and read about the old quilt patterns, and the stories woven through them, that created the fabric of that community's ordinary lives, lived in the early settlement of Oregon.

December 1—A flock of Cedar Waxwings wheeled, then flew into our Mountain Ash tree. They stayed long enough to peck every last orange berry hanging heavy on the limbs before flying off to find another tree.

Just this morning I see the Red polls are at the feeder my brother Jim built for me last January.

December 3—I drove to the Enterprise Elementary School to listen to great-granddaughters Riley Ann and Ashlynn sing Christmas songs with their classmates. Let someone's child sing in a Christmas program, and every aunt, uncle, grandma, cousin and parent shows up. It was standing room only. And, of course, this great-grandma, along with countless other kin, were extremely proud, craning our necks to pick out our loved ones as they, hair curled, dressed in their finest, waved to us.

Prairie Creek ranchers have begun feeding hay to their cattle. Every morning I look forward to hearing the old truck motor grinding its way over the fields, as Hough's hired man pushes flakes of summer-cured hay off to a long line of Black Angus.

Early this snowy morning I watched grandson Buck catch and load his two horses in the trailer, then head off for a day of checking cattle down on Big Sheep.

December 8—Halley and I just returned from our morning walk. Finally, snow. Slogging slowly in my rubber chore boots, I watched Halley as she leap-frogged over the white fields, leaving tiny snowballs rolling in her wake, pausing just long enough to sniff a fresh set of deer prints.

At last, everything's as it should be in December. Golden fronds of fall grasses, bent with their burden; cottonwoods traced in black and white; snow hissing in the creek; the *whoosh* and *croak* of a Great Blue Heron taking flight; that cold fresh smell of newly-fallen snow.

Magically, it began last evening while we were singing songs like "I'm Dreaming of a White Christmas," "Silent Night," and "I Wish You a Merry Christmas." Wallowa County's beloved Gail Swart accompanied us on the piano in the Great Room of the Rustic Wallowa Lake Lodge. Between songs, Gail peered out the windows and exclaimed, "Look! we made it snow." And indeed we had, as rain morphed into white feathery flakes, drifting softly as they transformed our world.

Earlier, when we first arrived, the Hand Bell Chorus performed their hauntingly beautiful Yuletide tunes. Peace seemed to flow over the listeners in that perfect setting as the bells, played by members of our community, chimed out those familiar carols.

Soon we were seated at long tables in the lodge dining room, buttering hot rolls, nibbling fresh greens, and greeting our neighbors before diving into a stuffed and roasted Cornish Game hen. Another large Christmas tree, festooned with lights, glittered in the lakeside corner of the dinning room, and the piano was been moved in.

While we munched an assortment of Christmas cookies—baked by Gail—and sipped savory coffee, we were treated to more music: "A Rossetti Christmas Birthday of a King," played by Gail Swart; "White Star Christmas," sung by mother/daughter duo, Monica and Dawn Hunter; "Good King Wenceslas, sung by Gracie and Emma Carlsen;"Holiday Feeling" and "Solstice Bells," written for this caroling party by Janis Carper; "Christmas Son" and "Noel of the Birds," sung by Carolyn Lockhart.

Nick Yahn entertained us with "A Visit from St. Nicholas" and a duo trombone version of "It Came Upon a Midnight Clear." Young and lovely Erica Bailey sang a song she composed, "Healer of Hearts," and lastly came Duff Pace, who told us that "45 years ago, when he couldn't carry a tune in a bucket, his teacher Gail Swart persuaded him to think otherwise." Therefore, Duff was able to stand in front of us last night and sing "Oh Holy Night" and "In This Very Room." Duff says singing comes from the soul, and there's no doubt HIS does.

Before we all stepped out into the snowy night, we sang "White Christmas" and "Silent Night" one more time. As in years past, my heart overflowed with gratitude on the drive home over snowy roads back to Prairie Creek. For we, who live here, ARE truly blessed.

December 12—It was foggy overnight, and that means hoarfrost coats every object within a person's visibility…which is limited. It was an eerie world to walk in, muted, silent, and cold.

December 13—On this Saturday evening, Doug and I drove into the Cloverleaf Hall parking lot, where I climbed up onto a long flat-bed trailer to join 10 of my great-grand kids and ride in the Winterfest Parade. What fun! Surrounded by the kiddies and their parents, all perched on bales of straw. We waved to the old folks in the Nursing Home before heading to Main Street, where the kids threw great gobs of candy to the onlookers.

Son Ken pulled us along from the driver's seat of his huge yellow grader, which was all a-twinkle with colored lights. Other floats consisted of lighted tractors, trailers festooned with bright lights, a huge floating Santa, a real Santa, girls on horseback, and half-barrels fashioned into small cars. At Warde Park, where a giant tree lit the night with more cheer, we turned back toward the fairgrounds. The candy was all gone.

Then there was the Fishtrap Good Book Sale, where great books sold for a dollar and the proceeds went toward the Alvin Josephy Library.

Another worthwhile event, dubbed "A Winter Tale," a fundraising for our local SMART reading program, was held in Stage One of the old Bowlby Building in Enterprise. A catered meal by Steve Lear, entertainment, and a silent auction, consisting of baskets filled with goodies that revolved around a theme of a children's book.

I must get this column finished as son Steve, his wife Jennifer, and their little hats, Bailey and Stetson, are due here today. They flew all the way from Alabama to spend a few days with us. Must bake bread and a raspberry cobbler, then put a pot roast in the oven.

Merry Christmas to every one in Agri-Times Land.

December 15—Our book group met at Fishtrap House to discuss the book *A Thousand Splendid Suns* and, wouldn't you know, there was a cookie exchange. Our "Write People" group met at Ruth's where, after writing, we potlucked on open face sandwiches, pickles and nothing SWEET. We remembered the late Sally Bowerman, as she always contributed tuna sandwiches.

After lunch we got involved in a very competitive game of scrabble until it was time to read to my SMART girls at the Elementary school in Enterprise.

If a person wasn't yet in the Christmas spirit, I'd recommend attending the live Nativity Scene, erected in a lot across from Safeway this year. Grandson Chad and his helpers had created a splendid replica of that long ago Holy Night in Bethlehem, including a manger with Mary, Joseph and the babe, wise men, shepherds, a real donkey, a goat, a pen of sheep, a pony, corrals, and drop dead cold provided by Mother Nature.

Chad, one of the shepherds, endured the bitter cold for two and a half hours along with the other actors, after which the public was invited to the LDS church on the hill above Enterprise for a wonderful musical evening. The performance included Chad's wife Amy, playing the harp and singing as a pageant in songs and slides was played out. The children's choir included six of my great-grandchildren.

December 20—I sit here at my kitchen table, cup of hot tea to my right, blank screen in front, and the thermometer hovering around zero outside.

On this snowy Saturday afternoon before Christmas, I reflect on our annual get-together of friends and family last night. Thanks to Doug, who charged up his old tractor and plowed out our drifted lane, folks were able to make it to our back door without trudging in on foot.

Although the Winter Solstice happens tomorrow, winter has made itself known on Prairie Creek. I fired up the old Monarch, heated up the soup base I'd made the day before, and, as each guest arrived bearing scallops, shrimp and white fish, plunked them into the rich simmering broth. Snowy boots, caps, coats and mittens were piled in a corner, and folks helped themselves to the hot mulled wine simmering on the wood stove.

We sliced two loaves of sourdough bread still warm from the oven, opened jars of dilled green beans and seven-day sweet pickles, and feasted. Some sat at the kitchen table, while the overflow gathered around a card table in the living room. The lemon cream pie I'd baked that morning, and Annie's coconut rice pudding, provided the perfect desserts.

Full and warm, we retired to the living room, formed a circle, and began reciting or reading poetry, telling stories, and reading excerpts from books. It was very special having grandson James here, reading one of the poems he recently wrote in college.

His dad, son Todd, also recited a poem he'd written about his cow dog, "Jiggs." Outside, bitter cold bore down on Prairie Creek, stars crystallized in a clear sky, and colored lights, strung on the blue spruce outside the picture window, glowed softly against the snow. We'd invited our new neighbors Don Harker and Nancy Knoble, who recently purchased the old Hockett Ranch, to make them feel welcome.

The group of writers, gathered in our living room, was extremely diverse and interesting. They included a woman mountain climber, who had climbed Denali, among other famous peaks around the world; a fellow who once belonged to the Legislature in West Virginia; a couple who had herded sheep for a living in the rugged Snake River Country; a cowboy who had been raised on Joseph Creek; a young man who'd spent a year in Norway, and wrestled in Berlin; a woman who was raised in Germany and had owned a place in Troy; a cowboy who ran cattle on one of the largest and most remote ranges in Wallowa County; a woman potter who, with her husband, had operated two restaurants; a professional writer, whose book on a Southwest artist has just been published; an anthropologist, who described Christmas in Taos Pueblo, New Mexico; and yours truly.

Rather amazing how life's trails had led us all to this warm room, in a ranch house, in a valley sheltered by the Wallowa Mountains, on a snowy December night, here in the far Northeast corner of Oregon.

At one point during the readings, James' dog Fate began to bark, which set Halley off too.

This morning I found tracks in the road and, later, hiking over the hill and down through our old hay fields, Halley jumped three coyotes. My fleet-footed border collie took after them until one veered off in the opposite direction and Halley wisely drifted back to me. Coyotes have been known to lure dogs astray, while others close in for an attack. I imagine these wild creatures are hungry. Hunting mice under the snow is more of a challenge during this severe cold.

Hiking through deep snow is invigorating, and the world was white and pristine this morning, the sunshine almost blinding. The small creeks are frozen over now, and covered with snow, and the "murdered willows" pile harbors China pheasants, who crouch beneath those massive trunks for protection from the bitter cold.

Last week our house was alive with the presence of two very active grandchildren, Stetson and Bailey, with their Alabama accents. "Yes Mam, no Sir." Wilmer Cook will be happy to know a great deal of time was spent playing checkers on the board he made for us.

At 5:30 in the morning Stetson would appear bright-eyed. "Want to play checkers, Grandma?"

Speaking of Wilmer, we wish him well, as we understand he's in the hospital as a result of a recent fall.

Doug treated son Steve and family to a breakfast of sourdough hot cakes one morning, and the last evening they were here, we all piled in the car and drove around Joseph looking at all the bright Christmas decorations, of which there were many. We did enjoy having the family around, even though, as their dad quipped, "Stetson has the attention span of a goldfish!"

It's been a week of riding on the Holiday Merry-Go-Round.

There was my dear friend Edna Roundy's 90th Birthday Party, held at Russell's at the Lake. Also The Cowboy Christmas Party at Darlene Turner's, where we dove into steaming bowls of elk stew and nibbled cornbread in Darlene's Christmas house. Every nook and corner was filled with animated Santas and his helpers. Words fail when it comes to describing this magically decorated home. Darlene loves Christmas, and her grandchildren must be very happy she does.

I was asked to read cowboy poetry, which I did, selecting poems written by a very talented 90-year-old cowgirl poet from the Great Plains. Outside, the full December moon, the COLD moon, glittered off the snowy ramparts of Chief Joseph Mountains, lighting the valley like day.

December 22—Yesterday afternoon I attended the Wallowa Valley Music Alliance's Christmas program at Stage One in the old Bowlby building in Enterprise. Each year this just gets better. We are so lucky to have all this local talent. We even have an orchestra!

Last night I baked a tamale pie casserole, and braved the deep snows to drive to Skip and Liz's house, where a Solstice Party was in full swing—complete with a campfire and a stove full of steaming kettles of soup. Skip, a gourmet cook, loves to prepare Southwestern dishes. Needless to say, we feasted our way out of the shortest day of the year.

Today I'm baking more of my traditional sourdough Christmas breads to give away as gifts. And on Wednesday I'll be busy preparing for our family Prime Rib Christmas dinner here. By the time you read this, 2008 will be history, so Happy New Year to you and yours.

December 30—We had a heartwarming family Christmas. Jackie and Bill arrived in time to attend Christmas Eve services at the Joseph United Methodist Church. It was snowing heavily when we bucked huge drifts that plugged Tenderfoot Valley road to get to Joseph, but we made it. Colorful lights, streaming through the stained glass windows, reflected on the snow outside the old stone church. Welcoming us inside, where we joined friends and neighbors for the traditional candlelight service.

Earlier, I'd cooked up a kettle of clam chowder to fortify us against the cold. Although there were only nine of us around our Christmas dinner table, we made a serious dent in the 20 pound prime rib, mashed potatoes, gravy, salad and sourdough bread. Not to mention blackberry and mincemeat pies.

That night Jackie and I stayed up until 12:30 a.m. to welcome Mona Lee, who had to work both Christmas Eve and Day. She'd gotten stuck in the snow in her driveway in Chehalis, and then when she reached our lane, found it too plugged to drive in! I think of her, driving all those lonely miles at night, getting stuck at both ends of her trip.

Bill and Doug were kept busy plowing out our lane so folks could come and go. The younger generations organized a sledding party on Upper Prairie Creek after stuffing themselves full of sourdough huckleberry pancakes.

Later that week I treated several female members of our family to lunch at Calderas in Joseph, where we sat at one large table and enjoyed savory soup, salad and sandwiches, while the sun glowed off the warm wood carvings and blown glass art. When grandson Buck, wife Chelsea, and great-granddaughter Lucy returned from McCall, Idaho, where they'd spent Christmas, we lost Jackie and Bill. Of course, the attraction was Lucy!

Then, so all of the Wallowa County family could visit with the out-of-towners who weren't here for Christmas dinner, I rolled up my sleeves and roasted three chickens, used them to simmer a rich broth, dropped in some homemade noodles, and invited 18—and they all showed up. The soup disappeared at an alarming rate, but it was worth the effort to see everyone enjoying themselves.

By then we were in the midst of a big thaw. Fields were awash with snowmelt, and milky-colored water sluiced over icy creeks. The warm breath of a Chinook wind blew our snow away, leaving frozen drifts.

Today we had a visit from grandson Ethan and his family. Wilmer, once again, your checkerboard was the center of attraction. Buck, Todd and Bill spent a couple of days riding Big Sheep Creek, checking Marr Flat cows. Those cows have been rustling and doing well on natural bunch grass; however, they will be trailed to the valley sometime next week.

December 31—We invited Phyllis and husband Fred over for homemade pizza after which we played dominoes. I must say it's the first time Doug and I have played this game by the rules. Pretty intense. However, we only made it to 10:00 o'clock.

After they left and Doug went to bed, I curled up in my chair and watched the New York Philharmonic Orchestra, live from Lincoln City Music Hall on OPB, until midnight.

Angie Rubin, of Wallowa Lake, holds the lead dogs during sled check at Ollokot Checkpoint.

2009

January 1—Today is the day I dismantled Christmas, which is always a bit sad. Our little spruce tree is propped up in the snow drift outside the living room window.

Grandson James and classmate Amber stopped by for a visit. I just happened to be baking sourdough bread. You can guess what happened to that loaf!

January 3—Between 8:00 and 9:00 a.m., seven days a week, a lone figure makes its way uphill in our old hayfield in all kinds of weather. Sniffing tracks, occasionally glancing back to watch the human figure, a young border collie bounds joyfully ahead. Yep, that would be Halley and me. So far, for over two months or more, we haven't missed a morning.

There have been many mornings lately, like today, when I peer from my warm kitchen to watch blowing snow sift across the fields, knowing temperatures are well below freezing, wondering if this is the morning I won't go. Then I spy Halley waiting, tail wagging in anticipation. So, after donning countless layers of clothing—two caps, mittens, glove liners, ski pants, and the new insulated boots Doug gave me for Christmas—I step out into the winter world of Prairie Creek.

All in a week's time, I've had to deal with light snow over solid ice, soft snow drifts, thawing slush, mud, rain, and frigid winds so strong they blow you sideways. This morning was treacherous. Freezing wind blowing snow across large patches of solid ice or the windswept bare ground where granules of topsoil sift over the hill, resting for a moment on ice before they skitter away to who knows where. The hills are a desolate, uninhabited moonscape.

But then, after a snow storm in the night, comes a Blue Bird morning when the skies are polished by cold and a winter sun bursts over Locke's hill, illuminating the brilliant snow fields of the Wallowas, the rolling hills, and the voluptuous folds of the East Moraine. And there's no wind! Those are the mornings I could stay out all day.

On my kitchen table, where I write, four full-blown red amaryllis blossoms hover over my laptop.

The tantalizing odor of braised short ribs, roasting in my dutch oven, seeps from the stove. The bird clock ticks on, every hour announced by a recorded bird call. Juncos, chickadees, red polls and sparrows chatter at the feeder my brother Jim made for me, just outside the kitchen window. Hough's Angus cattle eagerly lick their daily ration of hay off the frozen fields, fat flakes of snow drift in the air, and the wind has laid down. My mare Morning Star is having an easier winter this year. She's here, where I can keep an eye on her.

Always thankful to hear that most of our traveling family made it home safely after the holidays; Granddaughter Mona Lee to Chehalis, Washington; daughter Jackie and husband Bill to Challis, Idaho; and daughter Ramona and husband Charley, plus granddaughter Carrie and great-granddaughter Brenna from Lodi, California.

Now we have to get grandson Josh, wife Desiree, and great-grandson Wyatt home to San Diego, and grandson James back to Dillon, Montana. James is in Walla Walla as we speak, where he is scheduled to have his tonsils removed tomorrow. That is, if he was able to exit Wallowa County. According to KWVR, our local radio station, all roads leading out of here were closed this morning.

January 4—Phyllis and I drove up Hurricane Creek, where I donned my snow shoes and she her skis. The snow was perfect and we made our way almost to the trailhead, where we found the road blocked by a huge snow slide. Apparently, during our warm spell, the snow broke loose far up the mountain, slid down a creek bed, and plugged the road.

Back in Phyllis' kitchen, seated next to her wood cook stove, we broke out the cheese and crackers and sipped steaming bowls of soup. Temperatures dropped dramatically.

Next week will be an adventure. Along with other volunteers, I'll be snowmobiled into Ollokot Campground, where a check point for The Eagle Cap Extreme Sled Dog Races will be set up. I'll be spending two nights in a wall tent there on the upper Imnaha, cooking for the mushers and crew. Wish me luck!

P.S. James did make it out of the county over the Blues in that blizzard, and is now tonsil-less. We sincerely hope he is feeling better real soon. We also hope his dog Fate improves from being hit by a car.

Sometimes life gets tedious, but this too shall pass.

January 19—Words from an old song, "What a Difference a Day Makes, 24 Little Hours", wandered through my mind as I slogged through fresh snow to climb the hill this morning. Yesterday morning, on this

Women's sleeping tent at Ollokot Checkpoint.

Sled dogs ready to embark.

same hill, I was thankful for long johns, two caps, glove liners, wool mittens and a heavy coat. It had been ten below zero.

This morning, however, in 30 degree temps, I began to shed clothing. By the time I'd completed my walk around the old ranch, I was hatless, gloveless, carrying my jacket, and wishing I could jettison the long johns!

Those of us who braved the cold last week, serving as volunteers for the Eagle Cap Extreme Sled Dog Race check point at Ollokot campground, didn't do much shedding of outerwear, not even inside the tents. The only clothing items that came off when I crawled into that frigid sleeping bag were my insulated boots. But then, not much time was spent sleeping. Not with dog teams arriving and departing at all hours of the night, with mushers to feed, crew to feed, fires to feed, and the myriad other chores we all pitched in to do. What a ride!

After hitching a ride with daughter-in-law Angie and granddaughter Becky, I left Prairie Creek the morning of the 15th. Traveling the upper Imnaha road as far as the Palette Ranch, we parked our rig and tossed our personal gear onto a growing mound of musher's dog bags and other camp equipment.

On that clear, crisp, sunny morning we waited where the county road ended and a snow-packed trail began. Winter ruled the backcountry. Presently, we heard the sound of approaching snow machines.

"Cooks go in first," announced our leader, and soon, there I was, clinging to his waist as we flew up the trail, towing a sled full of gear, snow flying in our wake. It was exhilarating. The cold air on my face, the icy river dashing below the trail, the snow-burdened evergreens, and yes, the element of danger. The fish weir flashed past and then we were at the mouth of Gumboot. Six miles flew by.

We cruised into Ollokot campground, a dear familiar place Doug and I had spent many Labor Day weekends camped in our fifth wheel trailer. The encampment that greeted me there that day was a far cry from what I'd ever known at Ollokot, however. A huge hospitality tent had been erected the day before, dubbed the "Ollokot Hilton."

Inside, already on the job, the communications crew, headphones in place, were taking messages from Race Central in Joseph. The race began at 1:30 p.m., and from then on words would fly back and forth between Ollokot, Ferguson Ridge, Salt Creek, and—later—Fish Lake, Trinity and Halfway. This amazing network is set up for the safety of the mushers and volunteers, who would be scattered along a 200 mile course of Wallowa County's snowy wilderness.

The Ollokot Hilton was equally impressive. A huge barrel stove that featured a flat cooking surface and a hot water tank, with a spigot yet, glowed with welcome heat.

Boxes of every size and shape occupied most of the remaining space. Not to mention folding chairs, a long table, and a small two-burner propane stove. I made a mental note that before the first meal could be prepared we'd have to create some semblance of order.

First, though, we had to "stomp" snow. Yep, stomp snow, in an area big enough to accommodate our wall sleeping tent. After a large plastic tarp was laid on the stomped snow, we "assembled" the tent, color coded as to which part of the frame went where. You know how that goes. In spite of us, with the help of those who understood, the tent was raised.

Then we noticed a sheepherder stove had been dumped near the tent's entrance. Mary Rose, Angie and I had it together in no time, poked the stovepipe up through the tent hole, and *voila*, a stove. But no fire. There arose a challenge that would employ all of my backcountry skills. What wood we had was wet with snow. On bended knee I nursed some pitchy bark, dry needles and toilet paper cardboard into a tiny flame. Keeping the coals alive with my breath, until dry kindling (thrust under the tent flap by a pair of masculine arms) arrived just in time.

Later, as the stove heated, its left legs listed. In spite of the fireproof board beneath the stove, the snow and ice under the tarp was beginning to melt. Lopsided or not, that little stove kept us from freezing to death. Us gals never let that fire go out.

That done, we concentrated on the first meal. Wonder of wonders, we organized the boxes, locating cooking utensils and ingredients for our supper soup. I hooked up the propane stove and began browning onions and hamburger. Then we discovered three crockpots. Crockpots? Yep, we had electricity. Off somewhere in the distance, a generator hummed, and below the cooking table we found extra outlets… even one for the coffee pot. I'd never had it so good.

That evening, and long into the night, remains a blur in my memory. After feeding the crew, we heard, "Musher coming!" which meant I had to dash out in the cold and hold the lead dogs during the sled check. By the light of my headlamp I peered down past the 12 dog team to watch the musher.

When he bobbed his headlamp, the signal to release the dogs, that meant you had to think fast or get run over. Down the trail they flew, on to Becky and her crew of dog handlers.

Meanwhile, back in the tent to feed more folks who drifted in; three veterinarians, sweepers (on snowmobiles that swept the backcountry to be sure no one got lost or off the trail), the local press, plus the Oregon

Public Broadcasting crew and driver, snowmobilers who volunteered to haul gear, and lastly but not least, the musher. Over 30 folks.

Then the other teams arrived, back to back. More lead dogs to hold between a dash to the tent to warm up. After a rest, the first team headed out toward Fish Lake, and ultimately Halfway, on the 200-mile course. Other teams arrived and departed for Ferguson Ridge in the 100 mile race. Bitter cold descended along the Imnaha river and the stars were brilliant. Later, the waning "Wolf" moon rose above the dark Ponderosa forest.

Returning from the outhouse, I remember seeing the cook tent glowing softly from within, strung with colored lights, and how my breath wreathed my face like smoke. A surreal scene. I also remember climbing into my sleeping bag, hearing the crunch of ice and snow under the thin tarp, and pulling the cover over my bag around my capped head. No sleep, just rest, because a "drop dog," one that had come up lame, pointed its wolf-like nose toward the cold stars and howled mournfully 'til dawn for its teammates.

I remember hearing the whisper of sled runners outside the tent on the packed trail as a late night musher departed just inches from my head.

The next morning: 8 degrees. Still, clear and cold, a blur of mixing hot cake batter, flipping flapjacks, and filling hungry bellies. Angie fried sausages on the wood stove. All of us slumped in chairs, stealing sleep when we could. The day blurred. Lunch fix'ins laid out on the table. Cooking dinner that night. Waiting for teams to arrive from Halfway, imagining them out along that long cold trail in the middle of the night. Up at five the next morning, entering the Hospitality tent to find the communications crew, plus our official timer, Angie Rubin, had been up all night.

The last two teams arrived at dawn for a makeshift breakfast, eaten on the go. We brewed gallons of coffee. One team hit the trail for Ferguson Ridge, and the last musher "scratched" from the race, his lead dogs lame. Heartbreaking, as the young man is so close to the finish.

The huge camp comes down as we all pitch in. Cooks are first down the trail on the trip out. Home. Hot shower. Rest.

At the musher's banquet that night, held at the Joseph Civic Center, most of the Ollokot crew is missing. Turns out the last load of gear, not to mention drop dogs, arrived at the trailhead around 9:00 p.m. But those of us in attendance were proud of our Ollokot team, especially when the mushers told their stories and mentioned how well they were treated. A real tribute, as Wallowa County's race has become an Iditarod qualifier and these were very experienced mushers.

That meal, prepared by other hands, was most appreciated.

January 20—Doug and I attended our local Stockgrowers "Dollars for Scholars" fund raiser at Cloverleaf Hall this evening. Randy Garnett's "Apple Flat Catering" whomped up a mouthwatering prime rib dinner. The lemon meringue pie I'd baked for the dessert auction fetched $140; Grandson Buck and son Todd bid Doug up. Angie traded a huge slice of chocolate cake for a wedge of Doug's lemon pie.

January 22—On a cold afternoon Phyllis and I hiked a snowy upper Prairie Creek road to visit daughter Ramona, who showed us her new Suffolk lambs. Said she'd been up most of the night, ended up pulling a big, husky lamb. Mom and baby were inside the barn under a heat lamp, doing fine.

January 23—Yesterday morning found Halley, my young border collie—a year older now—and yours truly—likewise—hoof'in it up Sheep Creek behind son Todd's 400 cows. We'd joined the drive at Bear Gulch and stayed with the herd till they got to Hayden. It was a lovely day, made more so when the sun broke free of those high rims long enough to warm us. Sap was rising in the Red Osier dogwood, ice clung to Alder limbs that dipped in the creek, and Halley was in Dog Heaven.

Ken, Angie and Renee, all on horseback, took turns walking. Todd in the lead, Buck bringing up the rear. After the last cow trailed into the overnight pasture at Hayden, where hay had been scattered, Angie and I scrunched in Ken's pickup along with our two dogs for a ride down to our rigs.

This morning, while the cowboys and cowgirls trailed the cows up Hayden canyon, I spent the morning in my kitchen, rolling out home-made noodles, simmering a huge kettle of chicken soup, and baking a wild blackberry pie. Out our living room window I watched the lead cows plod slowly down Echo Canyon.

About then, Buck's wife Chelsea, and great-granddaughter Lucy arrived, so we sampled the soup. It was 2:00 o'clock before the hungry crew gathered around our kitchen table and filled their bellies. The soup disappeared, and the pie cut into large wedges and served with scoops of ice cream on top. Then there followed the telling of tall tales.

After everyone left, Doug and I headed down into the canyons to meet up with Lyman and Wilma, plus Jim and Carolyn Maasdam at the Imnaha Bed and Breakfast, where Lyman treated us to a barbecued steak dinner. Always a special treat, just being inside that immense log home, with its polished juniper staircase and beautiful wooden craftsmanship throughout.

We flopped down on comfortable sofas in front of a roaring fire in the rock fireplace. Good friends, a glass of wine, and waited on by our hosts Nick and Sandy, who served us a delicious meal. It just don't get any better than that.

Later, we ventured out in the foggy, cold night to drive 35 miles back to Prairie Creek, which was completely coated with hoarfrost.

January 24—Buck and Todd showed up early this morning to trail the cows to the Snyder place just south of Enterprise. As the herd completed their three-day trip, it began to snow. For the remainder of the winter, those cows, thus far wintering on nutritious canyon bunch grass, will be close to the hay pile. They will remain on top until after they calve, and as soon as the grass has a good start they'll be driven back down to Big Sheep, eventually working their way up to Marr Flat by early summer.

January 26—The air was filled with diamond dust, or so it seemed. 16 below in Joseph! Tonight our book group experienced the North Country cold, as we met at the Outlaw Restaurant in Joseph to discuss Jack London's *Call of the Wild*, Fishtrap's Big Read book. After eating a bite, we viewed the movie version of the book, which was very well done.

Jack London writes in *Call of the Wild* that Buck was fully alive when he was running free. I understood what London meant when he wrote those words. I, too, feel truly alive, living here in Wallowa County in the midst of winter. This is the first winter in years that Doug and I haven't traveled to California in January.

How could I miss all this living?

January 30—Ruth Proctor and I, representing the CowBelles, served chicken fried steak with all the trimmings (compliments of Richard and Mary Frasch) to a most appreciative crowd at the Community Dining Center in Enterprise. We missed long-time CowBelle Jean Cook, and wish her well.

February 1—We readers joined a crowd of folks who gathered at Fishtrap House for Renee Fleming's entertaining and informative presentation, which centered around her participation in what's known as Alaska's Serum Run Sled Dog Race. Renee, formerly of Alaska and now living in Wallowa County, is a musher in her own right, having participated in two of those races. This talented young woman, who was also a bush pilot guide to Denali, in her later life elected to return to college and earn a degree in Veterinary Medicine. Renee was one of the official vets at our Ollokot check point. The following week she rode grandson Buck's horse and helped with the cattle drive from Big Sheep to Enterprise.

Renee's account of those historic sled dog teams, who transported lifesaving serum to Nome, in 60 below temps, to save a village of children stricken with Diphtheria, was riveting. Especially meaningful to those of us who recently worked with dog teams and mushers, some of whom would compete in Alaska's famed Iditarod.

One weekend daughter Lori and husband Larry paid us a visit. Along with a pot of beans simmering in the crockpot, I seared some T-bones in my cast iron skillet, and baked a pan of cornbread. That evening I mixed up the sourdough jug, and we feasted on huckleberry pan cakes with ham'n eggs for breakfast the next morning.

After the couple left, on that Super Bowl Sunday, I worked on the income tax, while Doug watched the game.

February 2—This evening a small group of readers discussing Gary Paulsen's book, *WinterDance*, at the Outlaw Restaurant in Joseph. After a bowl of soup, we nibbled popcorn and viewed the movie "Balto," an animated film version of one of the heroic sled dogs that led its team over those frozen miles to Nome.

Moments before parking in front of the Outlaw, I'd stopped at a crosswalk to allow six Mule deer does and one buck to amble across the street!

February 3—Ten degrees; clear, sunny and COLD. After my walk with Halley I drove to Enterprise to join our writing group, where we read, wrote, ate our lunches, and played scrabble. At 2:30 I joined other SMART volunteers who meet every week with two grade school children, and listen while they read to us. Latest findings suggest the best way to enlarge your vocabulary is to READ. Even in our age of technology and the internet, I'm of the opinion that nothing takes the place of curling up with a book to make a friend you can store on a bookshelf, and read over and over again.

One sunny day Doug drove his pickup to Cow Creek to try his luck at Steelhead fishing. No luck, but said he'd enjoyed the canyons.

February 5—Phyllis, Ruth and I drove to Wallowa to view the screening of "The Logger's Daughter," an OPB documentary that was subsequently aired on "Oregon Experience." Gwen Trice, who has been in Wallowa County for several years, searching for her African-American roots, found some of them when she discovered her father, Lucky Trice, had arrived in a box car along with other loggers from Arkansas, to work for Bowman-Hicks Lumber Company, where, in the remote forests north of Wallowa, in a settlement called Maxville, there were two schools for loggers children: one for black, one for white.

Gwen should be commended for recording the histories of those still alive who once lived there. There is only one building left at the site of Maxville today, but thanks to Gwen, many stories of that once-thriving logging community have been documented.

February 6—Sally, Nancy, Kathy and I drove to Lehman Hot Springs. Although misty rain clouds dampened our day, the weather was mild, and nothing could spoil a soak in that relaxing place. At noon we spread our picnic lunches on an inside table, where it was warm, and while we ate, we watched steam rise above the pools, then drift on into the dark forests where the hot springs originate.

On the way home we treated ourselves to Chinese food in La Grande, and wished those Hot Springs were closer to home. Rain turned to snow in Enterprise, and a good three inches of slush covered our roads here on Prairie Creek.

Meanwhile, Doug, had been invited to another one of those crab feeds down at Lyman and Wilma's, so he'd just gotten home. Speaking of crab, Doug and I joined a huge crowd the next night at the Elks Club in Enterprise, for their annual all-you-can-eat crab feed. Yum!

Better clean house. Two of my sisters from California. are due next week. Can't wait.

February 9—Snowflakes, aloft in the wind, drift past my window on this cold February morning. Well before dark last evening I happened to glance toward the eastern hills, just as the nearly full "Snow Moon" broke free of a dark purple cloud bank. Guess that moon magic is happening today.

Wouldn't have believed it yesterday afternoon, when Phyllis and I were trudging up and over snow drifts, climbing the steep road to Kinney Lake. Skies were outrageously blue, brilliant sunlight bathed all of upper Prairie Creek, and the clarity of the stunning white Wallowas was a scene out of Alaska. A lone Bald Eagle stared at us from a bare-limbed cottonwood, and a small bunch of Angus heifers trailed behind, treading a well-worn path that led to open water in a nearby creek.

Angie Nash, left, and Renee Fleming trail Marr Flat cattle from Big Sheep to Enterprise. Border collies Halley, front, and her cousin Dotty, help too.

Janie Tippett holds lead dogs for Eagle Cap Extreme Sled Dog races. Shown here at Ollokot Checkpoint. Photo by Angie Rubin.

Each step we took loosened a scatter of snow crystals, as we followed a very large dog-like track that led to the lake. What was this animal? Naturally, we speculated, imagining all manner of wild beasts.

Although the frozen surface of Kinney Lake was criss-crossed with wild animal trails, nothing moved. Locked in winter, the landscape revealed no sign of life, save for those monstrous tracks. The eagle was still on its perch when we reached our car, and the Angus heifers, having slaked their thirst, had returned to their pasture.

After bundling in layers, I braved this morning's blizzard with Halley, who anxiously awaits these daily rounds of the old ranch.

Later, ambling along the creek I heard *keer-splash*. Peering downward, I watched my drenched border collie claw her way up the icy bank, having broken through the thin ice. Every day she learns something new. After several vigorous shakings, Halley continued hunting mice tunnels as if the incident had never happened. Made me shiver; the temperature hovered around 25, not counting wind chill.

These cold midwinter days provide an opportunity to feed the mind. I've been feasting on books related to Wallowa County's Big Read. During the past weeks, in addition to Jack London's *Call of the Wild*, I've devoured *White Fang*, *To Build a Fire*, *Never Cry Wolf*, *Into the Wild*, *WinterDance*, and *Hatchet*.

February 25—Outside my kitchen window, a flock of Red-winged Blackbirds are in the midst of a feeding frenzy. Birdseed, scratched out by sparrows, has drifted from a wooden feeder onto a shrinking snow drift. Providing competition for these shiny blackbirds, with their startling red and yellow wings, are the red polls and sparrows. More harbingers of Spring were the numerous robins Halley and I happened upon on our walk over the hill this morning. They appeared to be gorging on kernels of wheat, exposed now, that the snow has melted from the stubblefield.

Yesterday afternoon I glanced out our living room window and did a second take. Our horse pasture had turned into a lake! Due to temperatures in the 40s, aided by rain and warm wind, winter's accumulation of ice (that has clogged the culvert) was melting. A large chunk of ice, lodged inside the culvert that lies under our lane, was slow in breaking up, causing water to back up like a beaver dam.

The skies were alive with waterfowl. Seemingly from nowhere, honking geese and quacking mallards appeared, wheeling low over Prairie Creek's sodden pastures before splash landing. False Spring!

Those Marr Flat cows, pastured just east of Enterprise, have been calving for some time now, which means the bald eagles have returned to gorge on fresh placentas.

On my walk this morning, I thought about my sisters, Kathryn and Caroline. I missed their company. I missed their laughter, their joy, their sense of wonder at every turn we took along that beloved route on Doug's old ranch.

"Look at the light on the snowy mountains! Watch Halley leap for a field mouse! Sky so blue, air so fresh, moraine so close, miles of open space, the rolling hills, the sound of silence." Caroline lives in Newcastle, and Kathryn's home is in Roseville.

The California Sierra foothills, where we grew up, are no longer rural. We knew silence as children. We could hear a cow bawl without the roar of traffic. We climbed oak-studded hills, looked down on small pastoral farms and ranches, listened to water flowing in the creeks, watched Black-tail deer nibble acorns, and discovered Indian grinding holes in large granite rocks where wild blackberry bramble grew alongside Doty's Ravine, where gold was discovered, and our father unearthed remnants of wheel barrows left by the Chinese who dug all those ditches.

Mt. Pleasant was, indeed, pleasant. There were uncultivated fields of poppies and lupine, sweet-scented clover pastures where our Guernsey cows grazed, and blooming orchards that buzzed with bees in the spring, and bore pears, peaches, and plums in summer. The narrow country roads were free of traffic. There were no McMansions.

Today, every hill is dominated by a pretentious house, light pollution prevents star gazing, those self-sustaining farms and ranches are now hobby farms occupied by the wealthy, or by those who sought the solace of the country and who commute to work in nearby cities. Sacramento to Auburn is now a solid sea of humanity. My soul still aches for those foot hills.

For days I looked forward to sharing Wallowa County with my younger sisters. On my walks, I imagined them enjoying every turn in the trail, every view of moraine and mountain, frozen stream and bare-limbed cottonwood and willow. True happiness is always sharing what you love with those you love. You want them to experience what you feel. And that's just what they did. Every day was an adventure.

They arrived at noon on the 17th, and it couldn't have been more beautiful. A Blue Bird day, snow on the ground, blue skies, sunshine. I'd finished cleaning house, sourdough was bubbling, and clean flannel sheets waited on the beds. After hugs all around, and enthusiastic greetings by Halley, they unloaded boxes of fresh oranges, lemons and grapefruit, all picked from their yards.

While I opened a jar of sauerkraut and grilled Reuben sandwiches, they settled in and became more acquainted with Halley, who loved them from the get-go.

Kathryn, who should have remained a rancher, plunged right into life on Prairie Creek. She kneaded the bread, checked on the chickens, and tended to my mare, Morning Star. Soon, both sisters were refreshed by the beauty I'll NEVER take for granted. While the bread was rising we went for a walk around the old ranch. The first of many, in all types of weather.

That evening I lit a pile of mesquite briquettes on the carport, and grilled some of those Marr Flat T-Bones.

"It's been so long since I've had a good steak," said Caroline, as Doug and I watched those Californians devour Wallowa County's Natural Beef. They even gnawed the bones clean before tossing them to Halley. The warm sourdough bread and tossed salad provided a perfect compliment.

On February 18th, it was 33 degrees with fresh snow on the ground and dramatic clouds shifting over the Wallowas. Doug left for the "office" at ye old Range Rider, and we three sisters reverted back to our childhood. The intervening years disappeared. Caroline practiced her flute and Kathryn tended my chores, then baked a pecan pie using nuts she brought along from the tree in her yard. She also spoiled Halley with a new toy and treats.

After our walk, we slapped together sandwiches made from leftover steak and sourdough bread, and toured upper Prairie Creek, which looked like a picture postcard. Noon found us picnicking at Wallowa Lake while watching cross-country skiers glide over fresh snow that covered the lake's frozen surface. Then it was lattes at Mad Mary's in Joseph on the way home to Prairie Creek to put a small turkey and beef roast in the oven.

That evening, the majority of our extended Wallowa county family arrived, bearing more food. Altogether, 24 of us! Including nine little great-grandchildren, who ate their meal, seated on an oilcloth, spread on the living room floor. They'd all gathered to see the "Aunties."

Grandma Angie had news! My 19th great-grandchild had been born that morning. A baby boy, Ryder Todd, born to grandson Josh and wife Desiree, who live in San Diego, California. Josh is stationed there in the Navy. Our family loves an excuse to get together, feast and have fun, and my sisters enjoyed connecting with their Oregon relatives.

February 19th was another lovely day, clear, and cloudless. Turkey sandwiches in my day pack, we drive to the foot of the lake, park near the boat ramp, and hike the East Moraine. Using ski poles we gain the ridge top, which affords a magnificent view of Chief Joseph Mountain and the frozen lake below.

We continue along a faint trail that eventually takes us to where a panoramic view of upper Prairie Creek leads the eye further east to Idaho's Seven Devils Mountains. The girls go nuts photographing. Although the west-facing slopes are free of snow, the high trail is not. We leave our boot prints in the snow.

At noon we munch our sandwiches in the lee of a glacial boulder. Then it's back to the ranch in time to leave for the canyons, as Doug is treating us to Baby Back ribs at the Imnaha Store and Tavern. It's still daylight, so the girls can see the tiered rim rocks and steep canyon draws on the drive down along Sheep Creek.

Dave and Sally really put on a feast for the locals: those ribs, plus biscuits, beans, and salads, washed down with a pitcher of dark beer. Dee-licious. No visit to Wallowa County is complete without a visit to the Imnaha Store and Tavern. Where else can you find dollar bills tacked to the ceiling, a running rattlesnake count, shelves stocked with stables, walls adorned with stuffed moose, elk, bear, and many-antlered bucks, and a pool table, all the while enjoying the homey warmth of a barrel wood stove? In an ever-changing world, this place is truly unique.

Early on the morning of the 20th, we three gals gathered in the kitchen and, using those fresh lemons, put together a lemon meringue pie. Noon found us attending a luncheon, staged by Fishtrap, for author Roderick Nash, held at the Enterprise Community Church. Here we three joined others over a tasty lunch, which featured salmon and corn chowder, catered by Erin Donovan, with desserts provided by Fishtrap Board members. Needless to say, our lemon pie vanished before I got to the dessert table.

Rod Nash, who would be a presenter for Winter Fishtrap, due to begin that evening at Wallowa Lake Lodge, was very well-received.

By 4:00 that evening Caroline and I were registering for Winter Fishtrap at the historic Wallowa Lake Lodge. After a delicious sit-down dinner, we listened to the weekend's presenters: Kathleen Dean Moore, Roderick Nash, and Jack Turner.

Leaving Kathryn to hold down the fort at home, Caroline and I drove to the lodge the next morning for breakfast, followed by all-day sessions, which included writing, group discussions, and talks by the presenters, all of which centered around the theme "Reimagining The Wild." A very interesting and timely topic.

It was good to see 95-year-old Helen Willard there from Prosser, Washington. Helen is an inspiration to us all. Caroline and I returned to

Prairie Creek that evening to pick up Kathryn, who had attended a baby shower for granddaughter-in-law Chelsea that afternoon. The three of us enjoyed a salmon dinner served in the lodge dinning room, before retiring to the Great room for Saturday Night's program.

Winter Fishtrap ended with an open mic session on the 22nd, followed by final wrap-up by the presenters. A noon Kathryn appeared with a picnic, and we sisters fled to the deserted marina at the head of the lake, where we listened for the groaning and breaking up of the lake ice. We noticed a young fisherman walking toward us across the frozen lake. As he approached, he showed us the two fat kokanee he'd caught through a hole in the ice.

The wind began to blow as the weather changed, and it was quite cold, but we decided to have our "picnic" anyway. Discovering a newly-constructed gazebo, we retreated to its shelter to shiver and eat our lunch. We'd been fascinated with the sound created under the ice, a faint sort of booming noise.

To warm up, we stopped at Mad Mary's, and became a bit MAD ourselves. We ordered hot fudge sundaes with caramel sauce, whipped cream and a cherry on top! You only live once.

On that foggy cold morning of the 23rd, Katelyn Claire Matthews was born in our new hospital in Enterprise. Her mom Chelsea, daddy Buck, and sister Lucy were very excited—as were we all. Baby Kate makes my 20th great-grandchild. Unfortunately, I caught a flu bug that was making the rounds hereabouts, so the girls spent that Monday running errands and having lunch with daughter Ramona. Doug saved the day by picking up a pizza for supper at the Embers in Joseph. I spent most of the day sleeping.

My sisters left the next morning, leaving a very large hole in our lives. A pity they live so far away. Halley misses them still.

February 26—Mini-blizzards sweep across Prairie Creek. Sunshine, wind, blowing snow, and temperatures dropping. Feeling better today, back to my morning walk with Halley. Today, Doug is home with "the bug."

Grandson James called from Dillon, Montana, where he is a student at the University of Montana Western. He said Oregon author Craig Lesley visited his literature class today, and will read tonight in the same room where James read his thesis last Spring.

This grandson will be back in Wallowa County next week for Spring break. Look forward to seeing him.

March 11—It's COLD! For the third morning in a row, temperatures in Joseph's rural areas have hovered around zero. Our Wallowas rise like frozen white sentinels, forbidding yet outrageously beautiful, especially just before sunup, when they are bathed in pale pink Alpenglow. Their cold breath seems to hover over Prairie Creek, which feels colder now than it did in midwinter.

Due to the cold, I waited until 10:00 O'clock to walk with Halley this morning. By then the sun's warmth took the edge off the chill. I feel sorry for the new little lambs and calves being born during the night time hours, and just as sorry for those folks on duty for night check.

This morning the sky is a cold blue, but snow clouds swirl around the highest peaks as I write. Our still, cold nights are bright as day, lit by the full March moon, the "Worm Moon".

Yesterday morning I rose before the sun to bake a lemon pie. You see, grandson James, his friend Kyle, here during Spring break from college, plus his dad, Todd, and Todd's wife, Angie, were invited to supper. And you know how grandmas are. They love to cook for their children and grandchildren. Besides, home cook'in draws 'em here like bees buzz'in to honey.

I enjoyed preparing that pie: grating lemon peel, squeezing juice from those fresh California lemons, using the first fresh eggs my hens decided to lay, beating the whites into a high frothy meringue, and spreading it over the luscious filling… all the while imagining how my loved ones would savor every bite. My Farm Journal Five-Star lemon pie recipe is worth the effort it takes to create.

Leaving the pie cooling on a rack, I tended my small flock of chickens, mailed a birthday card to one of our daughters, stopped to pet my mare Morning Star, opened the gate to our former calving pasture, and struck off with Halley on our daily rounds of the old ranch. I still mourn the ancient willows that used to line the irrigation ditch. I miss the calving cows, too, and the eagles who perched in the bare-limbed trees to clean up the placentas.

The Red Wing Blackbirds miss those massive willows as well. Often those trees were alive with their singing, not to mention the nests for Robins and cow birds. I'm most grateful for the old Cottonwoods and willows left standing along my route. There is always a hawk, an owl, or a flicker in them, and when Spring does come, these trees will smell of new leaves, as the buds swell, open, and turn green again.

By the time Halley and I gained the hill above our house, the first car pulled into our driveway. Members of our weekly writer's group were arriving. I'd left a note on the door, *Come on in, coffee's on, Halley and I are out walking.*

After a productive morning of reading our work, followed by a writing exercise, we heated up our lunches and gathered around the kitchen table to eat and chat. While the gals cleared the table, then dove into a serious game of scrabble, I whomped up a tamale pie in my cast iron dutch oven.

Leaving them battling with words, I took off for the Enterprise Elementary school to meet with my two young girls who are participating in the SMART reading program, now sponsored by Fishtrap.

Meanwhile, back at the ranch, Doug returned from his "office" to find a group of aging women seated around our kitchen table, playing scrabble! So, what's new! In due time, I returned to put a chicken in the oven, along with the tamale pie, thaw out a loaf of sourdough bread, toss a salad, and set the table.

"Who won the scrabble game?" I asked Doug.

"Christine." he said. No surprise. Christine is 86 years young and generally ALWAYS wins. She tells us she used to teach Eskimo children in Alaska how to play scrabble, when, in earlier years, she taught in places like Good News Bay.

Years ago Christine taught grades 1-8 in the one-room school at Imnaha. Her life has been very rich and full. She was a graduate of Vassar and raised in New York, then married a Colorado cowboy, raised four children, moved to Wallowa County, and, after her husband died, taught school in Alaska. She's also sailed all over the world on container ships, learned to fly an airplane, and designed, then had her own modest home built on Wallowa Lake, where she continues to live. There are some amazing women in our group. But I digress from my story.

My family arrived bearing large appetites. After hugs all around, Kyle and James heaped their plates and dug in. These two college students had spent that cold day re-roofing a cow barn. The day before, they'd hiked from the Cow Creek bridge, following the Imnaha gorge trail, to Eureka Bar on the Snake River. They'd been steelhead fishing. Kyle said they came home with one keeper.

Son Todd, of course, with help from grandson Buck, is in the midst of calving. He was mighty thankful to be in out of the cold. I had the old Monarch fired up that night. That lemon pie, so lovingly created, was reduced to a single crumb of pie crust in less time than it takes to write about it. An entire pie!

James says "Grandma, you're famous in Dillon."

"How's that?" I ask.

"I tell all my friends about your pies, and how you belong to the 'Pie Hall of Fame.'"

And that always brings to mind the late Virgil Rupp, who, on November 14, 1985 issued to me a certificate, wherein it states: *Janie Tippett has been welcomed into the Agri-Times Pie Hall of Fame.* To this day, it hangs, framed, on my kitchen wall.

It was pretty easy to obtain this honor. Virgil loved pies. So, if you baked a pie of his choice and he liked it, you were pretty much assured. Virgil was a wonderful person. He came up with the idea of Agri-Times, a small regional newspaper that has endured the test of time.

My column has run in Agri-Times since the newspaper began in 1984. For 26 years this month, I've sat myself down at this same kitchen table and come up with a "Janie's Journal." In that time, I've gone from a Smith Corona to a Dell laptop, from mailing my column in our rural mailbox to e-mailing it out into cyberspace. Over the years the column has documented our life on a ranch, to life AFTER the ranch, and it has provided a tool for connecting with loved ones and friends who are scattered all over the U.S. Writing it has improved my skills and provided much satisfaction, not to mention myriad friendships.

Doug and I still live on 16 acres of the old ranch, and I miss the ranching lifestyle, but there comes a time to retire. Doug is enjoying his hard-earned leisure time, but I'm still looking for a milk cow!

Another one of our precious old-timers passed away last week. Harold McLaughlin lived a long life of 92 years. He was born in what he remembered as the "Little Dust Bowl" of Eastern Colorado. He used to tell me stories of that life, how hard it was, but that life honed Harold, made him tough yet gentle.

Harold was my friend. I loved listening to him talk about wood. He loved wood; loved the different grains and colors, and could describe the tree each piece came from. Harold fashioned stools, benches, tables, cutting boards and many other objects from the wood he collected. He was an artist with an artist's sensitivity. He was passionate about his work, about fanning, about old machinery, and about music.

Once, during Alpenfest at Wallowa Lake, where he and wife Hope had their booth set up, I found Harold seated near the weathered log porch, listening to a talented singer belting out familiar tunes of a bygone era. I couldn't resist bursting into song, and neither could Harold. So, there we were, singing our hearts out. A special memory.

Later, I purchased a tape of those songs and let Harold and his wife Hope listen to them in their own home on Alder Slope. I'll miss Harold. He always had a joke and a song in his heart. He was a good person.

On Saturday evening Doug and I attended the Blue Mountain Old Time Fiddlers jam at Cloverleaf Hall. We took in the entire show, beginning with a mouthwatering roast pork dinner, served up by Randy Garnett and the Wallowa County Fair Board. Randy is famous for his bar-b-cue sauce, a product he is now marketing. It is being distributed by Apple Flat Catering in Joseph, Oregon. Yum.

The fiddle music was just what we needed, foot-stomp'n music by old and young timers. The Prairie Creek girls, Ryya, Lexi, Hannah, and Landra, brought down the house. Good to see the Samples family. Leonard left a hospital bed to attend, and grabbed the mic to tell us that sweet little girl with the toy fiddle was HIS granddaughter. Folks came from miles around: Lost Prairie, No Name City, Baker, Cove, La Grande and Walla Walla.

When we stepped out of the warmth of Cloverleaf Hall it was snowing and freezing. You could hear the sound of folks scraping their windshields all over the parking lot. Temperatures were falling, *brrr.*

So much more has happened, like the Poetry and Piano program at the lovely Enterprise Bed an Breakfast on Sunday afternoon. This Fishtrap-sponsored event honors Collier, our Writer-in-Residence. Gail's piano-playing was like meditation and allowed us to unwind from our busy lives.

Fishtrap Board members supplied light fare. I'd sliced some of that Marr Flat Beef and served it with thin slices of sourdough bread and horse radish sauce.

Then things like holding baby Kate, snowshoeing up near Fergie Ski area, cross-country skiing with daughter-in-law Angie and friend Phyllis at Wallowa Lake, and preparing Farley Mowat's recipe for "creamed mouse" for the finale of the Big Read.

Speaking of which, the finale of the Big Read was something else. Everyone had a howling good time. The sourdough biscuits I took were gone before I got in line, as were other sourdough breads, baked by members of the community. The bar-b-cued venison, donated by locals, was a hit, as were the pies contributed by the Grange Ladies. The historic Hurricane Creek Grange was filled to capacity.

And wonder of wonders. The photo, taken by Janis Carper, of yours truly reading "Call of the Wild" to Halley, won the Grand Prize for the "Reading Jack London to Your Dog" contest. And the creamed mouse? No one touched it. Halley ate it when I got home.

March 12—This column still isn't sent in. Too much time spent on the above. Must close and hike the hill east of us. The weather has

Prairie Creek Girls: Hanna Schaafsma, Ryya Fluitt, and Landra Skovlin.

warmed. Time to look for Buttercups.

March 13—I baked a raspberry pie to take to grandson Buck for trimming my mare's feet, and for an excuse to catch a second glimpse of baby Kate.

This afternoon Phyllis and I skied and showshoed up into the woods east of the Fergi Ski area. The snow, and the day, were perfect. Perhaps the last good day, as it was so warm the snow was melting everywhere.

Doug treated me to a rib steak dinner at Ye Olde Range Rider. He redeemed a gift certificate, purchased at the 4-H radio auction last fall.

March 14—Discovered the first patch of Buttercups, at the base of Hough's hill.

Drove to Alder Slope to visit my 96-year-old friend and Neighbor, Wilmer Cook, who is now living with his daughter and son-in-law in their new house, which has been constructed just above Wilmer's old home. Mostly we talked about the "olden days" when we both had our milk cows.

March 15—I cooked up the traditional corned beef and cabbage dinner, and we invited friends and neighbors.

March 16—We woke up to six inches of snow and it was still snow-ing! Soft, wet, spring snow. Halley and I sloughed through it on our morning walk. I also discovered some sort of varmint was feeding on my chickens. Only ten left now, but they are laying.

March 17—For St Patrick's Day, I simmered a pot of soup made with leftover corned beef and cabbage, and served it, along with another loaf of soda bread to our Writer's Group.

We lost another old-timer, 92-year old former Cowbelle, neighbor and rancher's wife, Irene McFetridge, who lived for many years on lower Prairie Creek, passed away at our local care center. Irene was the matriarch of a very large ranching family.

March 18—Awoke to a heavy frost. Stunned by cold, the buttercups shivered.

March 21—Is there a better place to experience the first day of Spring than Imnaha? Liz, Kathy, Pam and I are convinced there isn't. 'Cause that's where we were when the Vernal Equinox worked its magic. We three gals were Pam's guests.

My friendship with Pam Royes goes back many years. You see, Pam, her husband Skip, and their children, Luke and Hope, lived on Imnaha during the same era that my daughter Jackie, her husband Bill, and their children Buck and Mona were there.

The two young families worked on ranches that stretched from Dug Bar to Hat Point. They raised their children in cow camps, tents, and trailer houses that were scattered in some of Wallowa County's most remote and rugged areas.

Their children attended K-8 grades at the "Bridge" school under the Rim Rocks, and those canyon children grew up on sourdough, elk, venison, fish, and Imnaha's bounty of fruit and vegetables. They lived with rattlesnakes, rim rocks, outhouses, pack rats and, the river. They learned to ride, rope, fish, hunt, and work cattle at an early age. They attended the first church on Imnaha, a church their parents helped build.

Those children are grown now. The boys, Buck and Luke, continue to live in Wallowa County, Buck and wife Chelsea, who market Natural Beef, are raising their two little girls, Lucy and Kate, on a ranch. Chelsea is an R.N. at our local hospital.

Luke and wife Callie built their own house in the country, and are in business for themselves. Callie milks a cow to help feed their three children, Addy, Lilly and James. The two girls, Mona and Hope, have graduated from college and are making their way in the world, Mona in Chehalis, Washington, and Hope in Bend, Oregon. Whatever jobs they tackle, their canyon upbringing serves them well.

As usual, I digress.

Yesterday morning Kathy and I drove to the upper Imnaha to check on the Fishtrap Writer's Retreat, to see how the place survived the winter, take inventory, and do a bit of cleaning. After making our way over the swaying wooden bridge that spans the river, we unlocked the house... and shivered. The place was cold. A winter's worth of cold, stored deep in the weathered logs. Bundled in layers, we hurriedly completed our tasks.

Although we noticed buds beginning to swell on the fruit trees, the air was anything but spring-like. By the time we drove downriver to Pam's place, however, the weather had warmed and the sun was out. Our spirits lifted at the sight of violets scattered over Pam's lawn, and a clump of snow drops blooming alongside the river made me think of Mary Marks, who never failed to note the appearance of the first snow drops in her daily diary.

What a treat to spend time in this peaceful place, which Pam and husband Skip have lovingly built over the years. From a small piece of riverfront property, and a crude cabin, this couple have created a unique hideaway with their own hands and lots of sweat, including rock walls and path ways, a fertile garden space, a modest home, an awesome view of the river rushing past; all in the heart of those awesome Imnaha canyons.

After sipping cups of tea, Pam led Kathy and me on a circular hike that took us into those mysterious canyon draws, to waterfalls that spilled over steep rims and where we had to scramble up narrow chutes to reach a high grassy bench, from where we gazed westward to Middle Point and downward to the Imnaha, flowing north. We discovered buttercups and yellow Cous blooming on the sunny slopes, as well as fresh elk sign. Truly a wonderful hike.

That evening we turned the shrimp, potatoes, shallots and corn I'd brought along into a kettle of chowder, and baked a loaf of Irish Soda bread to go with it. That's when Liz showed up. For dessert we had Kathy's squash pie. After doing the dishes we relaxed and read our writings to each other as darkness descended on the canyons. My bed was upstairs in a small alcove that afforded views of river and canyons. The narrow pathway of sky was sprinkled with stars, and the breath of Spring was in the air, so mild I opened my windows.

March 22—The first day of Spring dawned mild and clear. After rising above the eastern rims, the sun took its time sliding down the western walls. The air was filled with birdsong as Pam simmered dried apples, adding oatmeal and roasted walnuts. After breakfast we packed up and left. Life awaited us "on top."

Signs of spring! The break up of frozen Wallowa Lake.

Another sign of spring were the numerous baby calves sunning them-selves in pastures along Little Sheep Creek. This morning I discovered the first blooming crocuses alongside our house. Then I grabbed my bird book to identify a large cream-colored bird with a black ring over its neck, which turned out to be a Ringed Turtle Dove. Go figure! There it was among the Red Wing Blackbirds, pecking seed spilled from the feeder.

The snow is all melted, save for the large banks that have lined the irrigation ditch all winter. Hawks were nesting in bare-limbed cotton-woods, and the liquid notes of blackbirds filled the air around us.

March 23—Woke to a snowing and blowing blizzard. Wet snow, didn't stick.

This afternoon I drove to Lostine to take in the Mid-Valley Theatre Company's production of "Steel Magnolias". All of us in the audience took along blankets and dressed warmly, because you can't hear the actors when the heat system is running, and so the heat is turned off.

We are so lucky to have talented Kate Loftus in our valley. She's a pro. The audience was transported to Truvy's Natural Beauty salon in Chinquapin Parish, Louisiana in the 1980s. All the drama you'd expect, laughter mixed with tears.

Must get this in mail. Doug and I leave for California on Tuesday. So excited. Haven't seen a Placer County Spring in 40 years!

March 26—California; we made it! As I put a period to this column, I'm looking out on the newly leafed-out oak trees, and hummingbirds at a feeder outside the window of my childhood chum's living room window. It's 70 degrees and everything is GREEN. But that's a story for next time.

April 9—Just returned from my morning walk with Halley. Sure, I could've had this column written earlier in the week, but I know my priorities, and my daily walks are at the top of the list. My usual route is off limits, for the time being anyway. Some sort of herbicide has been applied to the greening fields that used to be cow pastures and hay fields.

Doug's former ranch can better be described now as a farm, though we continue to live on the 16 acres he still owns. Our "mini ranch" includes a bunkhouse, woodshed, chicken house, milking parlor, box stalls, hay storage, machine shed, calving barn, hay shed, corrals, chutes,

Border collie Halley accompanies Janie along a daily walk of Doug Tippett's former ranch. Chief Joseph Mountain is in the background.

Signs of spring! Break-up of frozen Wallowa Lake.

tin salt house, modern shop, an older shop, a former potato cellar, and our modest house.

Fenced permanent pastures fill the remaining space and a small ditch wanders through three of the pastures, sustaining several ancient willows and supplying water for Doug's irrigation system. There is a large, fenced garden plot, a raspberry patch, two large flower beds presently claimed by weeds, and a spacious lawn, large enough to warrant Doug's recent purchase of a riding lawn mower.

My half Arab Mare "Morning Star," who has all three pastures to herself, appears to have wintered well. The varmint feasting on my laying hens has been discouraged from further visits to our chicken house by an electric wire Doug hooked up to the chicken wire. In spite of my hens being OLD, they keep us in eggs. If, and when, one of my hens decides to set, I'll order some chicks to slip under her at night. Aracuna pullets. I love their blue-green eggs.

This morning being mild, with no frost, my retired rancher is out in the pastures, driving his old tractor, harrowing. Earlier in the week he lit a match to the dry grass that fills the borrow pits and lines the lane. Happens every April.

Where to hike? Preferring not to walk the county road, I head toward the hills that rise east of us, on property owned by our aging neighbors, Don and Lois Hough, who (bless them) continue to operate a large cattle ranch.

After traipsing through Locke's hay field, Halley and I make our way over the new head gate that spans the Silver Lake Irrigation ditch, then amble through two cow pastures to a smaller irrigation ditch. It is negotiated by crossing over a narrow plank placed there years ago. After climbing through a hole in the barbed wire fence, I enter Hough's hill pasture.

Beneath the sagebrush and cheat grass, between the squirrel holes and rocks, lays a carpet of golden Buttercups. The sun spills down through a break in the clouds, the air is moist and mild, and nothing can stop Spring now. Not even the soft wet snow, that will, inevitably, fall into June.

Halley is in dog Heaven. Squirrels squeak, taunt, then elude her by disappearing into their holes. Following a cow path, as I have since childhood, I gain the top of a rocky hill and pause to catch my breath. There below me lies Prairie Creek, the place I call home. The fertile prairie itself, dotted with small ranches, stops short of the Wallowas, brilliant snow fields disappearing in cloud. There is a faint greening upon the hills, as well as the fields below.

I watch Hough's hired man push hay off the bed of his truck to a small bunch of Angus cows and calves. I spot Doug, far away, still harrowing. I see Hough's old ranch house, the Liberty Grange Hall, and daughter Ramona and husband Charley's ranch. I see Alder Slope, where sons Todd and Ken live, where they raised their families. I see the Prairie Creek Cemetery, where grandson Bart is buried, there at the base of the East Moraine.

Halley flushes a pair of Hungarian Partridge. Everything is pairing up: Mallards, Canadian Honkers, Herons, Pheasants. Two rotting snow banks cling to the shaded north of a steep draw.

Back at the ditch, I hear a *plop* and a muskrat swims upstream. As I climb over the rock jack onto the county road, I wave to a passing neighbor.

Meanwhile, back in our kitchen, my laptop stares at me. Clothes need to be washed and hung on the line. Our lawn is strewn with winter's flotsam of bones, broken doggie toys, a dehydrated dead tom cat, a goose wing, numerous dried cow pies, and my border collie's favorite object, a 5-gallon plastic pail she's rolled around so much with her paws and nose, it's all but shredded.

Doug and I returned safely from our California trip on April Fools Day. Having left Wallowa County in a blizzard, we returned to Prairie Creek just before another one swept down out of the North. After waking up the next morning to several inches of soft Spring snow, Placer County seemed but a dream. Halley was ecstatic at seeing us. Grandson Buck had faithfully tended my chickens, and cared for Halley and the cats.

Our brief trip south, to Placer County, California, where I was raised, proved to be everything I'd hoped for. Golden California Poppies, shiny new leaves on those beloved old oak trees, and my foothills of home, wearing their April green. For most of our stay we were blessed with cloudless sunny days, in the 70s.

As planned, on the evening of March 23rd, daughter Jackie and husband Bill arrived from Challis, Idaho. I'd spent the day preparing enchiladas, baking a berry cobbler, and, at the last minute, inviting family over. It was one of baby Kate's first outings. After everyone except Bill and Jackie left, I hurriedly packed my suitcase.

Up early the next morning to fix sourdough huckleberry pancakes for all of us before departing. Bill and Jackie would stay here and caretake our place until Friday, at which time they would return to Challis.

Doug and I spent that first night at Scott's Shady Court in Winnemucca, and the next morning found us eating breakfast at "The Griddle," which always brings to mind former A.T. editor, Virgil Rupp, who used to rate hotcakes during his travels in and about the West. I remember Virgil saying he'd rated "The Griddle's" right up there with the best. I ordered one.

It turns out the longtime owner was there, seated at the counter, eating a pancake. So, I told him about Virgil, whereupon he disappeared into the kitchen to make sure my pancake was special. And, it was!

Thus fortified, yours truly at the wheel, we sped across miles of Nevada's high desert to Reno, where Doug took over the driving. I don't do traffic.

After a brief stop at Cabela's, where we did a bit of shopping, we headed up and over Donner Summit to the western slope of the Sierras, thence to Auburn, where we were catapulted into full-blown SPRING! Daffodils, Forsythia, pear trees and tulips bloomed profusely. Oak trees glowed softly with new leaves, and the grass was GREEN. Alongside the roads bloomed California poppies as well as other wildings. Recent rains contributed to the greenness.

Doug took the Bell Road exit and I breathed a silent prayer. Off the freeway, at last. Relax. From there we made our winding way through the hills above Auburn to Hubbard Rd, where Doug let me out to walk the final miles to Fred and Sandra's home.

Perched high on a scenic ridge near the end of a dead-end road. Fred's parents at one time owned much of the surrounding country, which was, when he was a child, truly wild. That high ridge and canyon, with Coon Creek running through it, is now dotted with new homes and mini-ranches.

However, the country still retains its rural character, and several ranches have not subdivided, so there are large chunks of hill land where livestock continues to graze the scattered pastures, and where wild turkeys strut about and feed on fallen acorns. Where, in deep woods, Johnny-Jump-Ups grow next to patches of Baby Blue eyes and carpets of scrambled eggs. There are still ferns growing in crevices of large granite boulders, and Nevada Irrigation Ditches wind through the country side and water the cow pastures.

Sandra, my childhood chum, was still at work, but her husband Fred greeted us warmly. That evening we dined on homemade soup and the traditional Lemon Pie, baked in a pie plate Doug gave Sandra years ago. After spending hours in our car, and leaving Wallowa County in a blizzard, it was pure magic to experience SPRING. My senses were filled with the sights and smells of my childhood. 40 years is a long time.

Early the next morning, there I was, seated at my laptop, finishing my column. I would e-mail it from sister Caroline's place, as Sandra doesn't own a computer. I was anxious to be outside, walk without a jacket, breathe in the scent of oak woods, search for wildflowers, and stare at the views from Hubbard Ridge.

All too quickly, the days flew by. Doug and I lunched at Newcastle Produce, before driving to sister Caroline's, where we gaped at lemons clinging to a tree, and a newly-mown lawn. Caroline proudly showed us her "garden" planted in a wagon, so she could bring it in at night to foil the deer, who would've eaten all her lettuce and herbs.

Later, during our stay, she served a salad, grown in her moveable garden. Too many experiences to record: Sitting in Sandra's lawn swing for hours, soaking up sun. Writing, reading, relaxing. Enjoying Fred's scrumptious chicken supper that evening.

Lunch at the "Flower Farm" with my sisters Caroline and Kathryn, and friend Sandra, where we dined outside on a sunny patio next to a pond that featured an old wooden water wheel. Whilst all around, things bloomed!

Then we drove to Oakcrest Ranch, where we five children were raised, to visit our brother Jim, who still owns 75 of the original 240 acres. We walked through the woods and cow pastures to the pond, stocked with bass, and shaded by large weeping willows. Little Ditch Creek flowed into the pond and everywhere were lovely oak trees, Digger pine, and Buckeye, sporting shiny new leaves.

We walked past the old dredger piles, left by the 49'er gold seekers, and followed a cow path to Doty's Ravine, where we'd all learned to swim, and saw where a beaver had chewed on the cottonwood trees. I photographed BIG TOP, the hill that was my childhood mountain until I moved to Wallowa County! That day ended with a Chinese dinner at Twin Dragons, compliments of our friends Fred and Sandra.

On March 28th, Doug drove me to Roseville to spend time with sister Kathryn. Our hours together were filled with shopping in book stores and walks around the neighborhood, all a-bloom with Azaleas.

That evening, attending our Cousin Bob Clifford's 80th Birthday Party, held in what used to be called "The Brown Cow" in the nearby town of Penryn. Cousin Bob is the only link to our father's side of the family. Not only was my salmon dinner delicious, it was fun meeting so many shirttail relatives.

Early next morning Kathryn and I walked the quiet, tree-lined streets in her charming old Roseville neighborhood. My baby sister led me to a park, where she plunked herself down on a piece of cardboard and slid down the long, curvy, scary cement slide.

"Come on" she chided. "Nothing to it."

So, her 75-year-old sister...DID—heart in her throat—and found it rather exhilarating! Glad no one was watching.

Kathryn drove me to Caroline's, whereupon my two younger sisters led me on a scenic hike through the oak woods. The trailhead began at Rattlesnake Bar, located near Folsom Lake. I'll always cherish the memory of us three sisters sitting in a sunny clearing scattered with wildflowers, staring down at the lake, watching wavelets sparkling in a warm breeze.

That afternoon Caroline and I drove to the Del Oro school to attend a musical production of Beauty and the Beast, staged by the Rocklin Youth Theatre Co., in which one of my nieces, Jeanelle (my brother's granddaughter) sang and danced.

I spent the night with Caroline, and husband Duane, who live in Newcastle.

On March 30th Caroline took me back to Fred and Sandra's, where Doug had been staying. That afternoon Doug and I drove to brother Jim's ranch to visit Jim and wife Joyce, who later join us for dinner in Lincoln, my old home town. We dine in a fancy Italian restaurant, which used to be Jansen's Feed Store when I was a girl!

The next morning we said goodbye to Fred and Sandra, and to spring, and headed up into the snowy Sierras.

And, as I put a period to this column, it is now late afternoon on Easter Sunday, and Doug and I have just returned from a delicious ham dinner prepared by daughter Ramona. Granddaughter Carrie was there with great-granddaughter Brenna, who made Easter special. She showed us her baby chicks, a baby kitten, and an Easter basket brimming with goodies.

Early this morning I attended the Sunrise Service at the Joseph United Methodist Church. It was a lovely service with the sun streaming through the stained-glass windows, and the smiling faces of friends.

April 20—Here is me again, on the Upper Imnaha River at the Fishtrap Writer's Retreat. April is being kind, gentle and warm, on the cusp of bursting into bloom. The Forsythia already has, its brilliant yellow blossoming lighting up the east lawn. The buds of the flowering quince are just beginning to redden, a few stray daffodils nod their heads in the breeze, and lavender and white violets run rampant.

On the steep sunny hill sides the first arrowleaf balsamroot punctuates the greening bunch grass with its sunflower-like blooms. Indian Creek spills over blackened basalt, just up the canyon from its confluence with the Imnaha.

A rancher feeds hay to his cows and calves on a ranch located between North Powder and Union. The snows are melting and on this sunny day it feels like spring.

I've just returned from a solitary walk, one that leads up Indian Creek canyon. It's the same trail I've taken for years, a game trail; a cow trail. Ever alert for rattlesnakes, out now after winter hibernation, I scrambled up the steep rocky trail to reach a high bench, where I found myself in a sunlit patch of pink filaree. A common weed, remembered from the foothills of my youth. As the filaree matures, it forms slender green spears, from which, after all these years, the child in me continues to create tiny scissors.

From my high vantage point I gazed down upon the weathered log house that comprises our Writer's Retreat. A dear familiar place, nestled amongst the trees, where the river, over the years, has carved a horseshoe bend. I could see Julianna and Richelle, notebooks in hand, escape to the sunny lawn near the river.

After their long drives from Portland, Oregon, and White Salmon, Washington, these women (both song writers and poets) are unwinding from city life. This place must seem like Paradise. Nothing to distract them but the river's song.

By the time I return to my own writing alcove, it's just plain HOT. Hard to believe, after such a long cold season. From my sliding glass door I can see the last of the winter snows clinging to the shaded norths of the South West canyon. The high country snows are rotting and the river is rising. Yesterday's riversong was a murmur, but today's is a roaring concert of rolling boulders and the river's color has changed from turquoise blue to chocolate malted milk.

On the 19th, I arose early on Prairie Creek to pack my car before driving to Joseph to pick up Darlene, a new member of our Writer's Group, who would be spending the week at the Retreat. This was Darlene's first trip to Imnaha.

Spring was very much in evidence by the time we reached the "Bridge." Cherry and numerous wild Plum trees were bursting into bloom. The air was balmy. I knew in my heart, we writers would wax poetic with words of praise for the upper Imnaha. And, when it came time to leave, a part of us would forever remain in that magical place in time.

As in Aprils past, it was like coming home for me. Pushing my cart across the swinging bridge; breathing the water-scented, violet-scented air, and hearing the river's song, the noisy cawing of nesting crows, the Kingfisher, the Dipper and the *see-fee-bee* sound of an elusive little bird. I felt the warm sunshine caressing my winter-white skin, the river's presence washing away all life's travails for that moment in time, as I stared up at the tiered canyons that rise above Indian Creek.

By evening there were five of us. The Retreat was a new experience for Darlene, Juliana and Richelle. Melissa had been here two years ago.

As usual, it was hard to concentrate on writing when the resident mule deer buck—antlerless, this time of year—wandered into our midst, or a friendly crow came swooping down to snatch bits of bread we tossed its way. When Mergansers rode the wavelets, bobbing two by two until they disappeared around the bend.

The morning sun washed slowly down from the high western rim to ignite the first golden arrowleaf balsamroot. It requires absolute commitment to sit in front of a laptop and write when that game trail calls, says to you, *put on your hiking shoes, grab your walking stick, fill your water bottle, shoulder your camera. Follow, follow...* and that's what I did. I submitted to its siren call.

So, it was a week of following not only that game trail but many others, including the Saddle Creek trail to Freezeout Saddle, where three of us stared down into the depths of Hells Canyon.

It became obvious I wouldn't finish this column, but to me the siren song was priority. At age 75, I don't have that many sunny days left.

On the morning of our departure, the high rims were dusted with snow. It had rained most of Saturday night. I arose at 4:00 a.m. to complete this column.

Sherrie VanLeuven, left, of Union, and Sharon Gibson of Joseph, twin sisters, were raised on the Divide in Wallowa County. Here they help trail several hundred cattle pairs for Marr Flatt Cattle Company from Enterprise to Big Sheep Canyon, a three-day drive. They're shown here on Lower Prairie Creek the first day.

The freezing Prairie Creek wind blows and sleet stings their faces as Buck Matthews and his uncle Todd Nash bring up the rear as they head to Big Sheep Creek near Imnaha, where the cattle will summer on Marr Flat. The feed looks good this year due to plenty of moisture.

After the gals left, Liz, who had joined us on Tuesday, had gone out "On Top" to fetch fresh supplies, then returned Sunday morning to take my place as "Den Mom" for the final shift of writers. The others got in plenty of quality writing time, and songs and poems—inspired by the magic of that place—will live forever. I was privileged to spend a week with five extremely creative women.

Because Darlene and I spent so much time cleaning house for the next shift, my column remained unfinished. And since it was already afternoon when Darlene and I pushed those carts full of stuff across the bridge for the last time, and said our goodbyes to Liz and Kathy, we stopped on the way home at the Imnaha Store and Tavern for a hamburger. Then headed up Sheep Creek, thence to Joseph, where I delivered Darlene.

Back on Prairie Creek, Halley was very glad to see me. Doug was gone. He returned later in the day, having driven all the way down to Dug Bar, to visit his old ranch. Naturally, on the way home, he, like us, had stopped at the Imnaha Store and Tav. "Had chicken strips," he said.

April 27—Cold here on Prairie Creek. There's new snow on the mountains and in the forecasts for the rest of the week. The 16 new heifers Doug purchased while I was gone last week are grazing the lower pasture. Melville's have no-till-drilled most of Doug's old hay fields and cow pastures; daffodils and tulips, now in bloom, droop forlornly in the cold, stunned by a recent frost. Got down to 15 while I was gone.

There is so much more to write about. Son Todd's crew trailed 350 pairs over three days to Big Sheep Creek. Halley and I joined them on the last day for the big branding up Big Sheep.

But it's all going to have to wait for another time. Halley is waiting for her walk, I'm not yet dressed, my chickens need attention, and Doug is down at Ye Olde Range Rider, playing cribbage with "the boys."

April is nearly gone. A week from Thursday we'll be on our way to pick up granddaughter Adele in Spokane, where she is flying in from Austin, Texas, to join us driving on to Dillon, Montana, where we'll attend her brother James' graduation from college. I can't wait.

Life is good.

May 3—As I sit here at my kitchen table, wondering how to begin this column, the earlier snow flakes have melted and been replaced by a cold drizzly rain. It was still snowing when I walked down to the barn to tend to Morning Star. Halley and I look in on her every four hours or so, to offer her water and soaked hay. You see, my beloved little mare foundered while I was down at the Writer's Retreat.

This is the second time she's suffered from what is known as Laminitis, caused from gorging on green grass after a long winter of no hay, only mature grass that she pawed through the snow to eat. Perhaps this condition could have been prevented by putting her in a dry lot before the grass became so lush.

The year previous, my little gray mare spent the winter in the hills, and by the time we were able to drive out to Salmon Creek, she was barely able to walk. That first time she was so ill, Doug contemplated putting her down, but our friend Dick Hammond suggested dry lotting her, feeding nothing but grass hay. It took several weeks, but slowly Morning Star recovered enough to run around like her old self again. Last fall I was even able to pack her into Aneroid Lake.

This year she wintered here on Prairie Creek and seemed to be doing fine until green grass appeared, and things went from bad to worse.

May 8—It's 1:30 a.m. and this is the first chance I've had to complete this column. I will leave around 7:30 a.m. and drive to Alder Slope where I will join son Todd, who will drive us to Dillon, Montana, where we'll meet up with grandson James, who is graduating from The University of Montana Western tomorrow. Also present for James' graduation will be his sister Adele, whom we haven't seen since last summer, when she departed for Austin, Texas to attend Culinary School. We'll return on Mother's Day. Can't think of a better gift than being with family on such a happy occasion.

Meanwhile, back at the ranch, all three mamma cats have given birth to their usual spring litter of kittens, including Halley's sleeping partner, the nameless black stray that wandered into our midst last spring. Halley, who graciously surrendered her dog house when mamma kitty decided to birth her babies there, now sleeps on a large pillow covered with the soft blankey sister K.J. purchased for her from Second Best. The two kittens are growing fast and Halley seems as proud of them as their mother.

Old Mamma Kitty had her babies in a cardboard box Doug placed in the woodshed for that purpose. Meanwhile, the other Calico hid hers in the hay shed. It takes a lot of kittens to supply our growing herd of great-grandchildren.

It did stop raining or snowing or hailing long enough for me to wash windows, clean out flower beds, and rake limbs, dog poop, horse poop (drug onto the lawn by Halley), bones, chewed doggie toys, and winter's accumulation of debris into piles. And now, if it will ever stop raining, we need to mow the lawn. Daffodils and tulips, blooming alongside the

Branding scene up Big Sheep Creek. Marr Flat Cattle Company's annual event. A large crew worked 350 calves and 400 cows in one day. A family affair with cowboys gathering from miles around. Tyson McLaughlin on horse in foreground.

house, are alternately happy when the sun is out, and sad when it snows and dips into the teens.

All in all, I can't complain. It is, after all, moisture, whether in the form of rain or snow, that puts a smile on ranchers' and farmers' faces. That is, if you were lucky enough to get your seed in the ground before this prolonged wet spell. I envision a beautiful display of wildflowers in the Zumwalt hills in June.

During a recent hike on Hough's hill, I discovered the first pink Grass Widows. Any day now, Yellow Bells and Prairie Smoke will appear. I spotted a sandhill crane in the lower field, and the ring-necked dove is back at the feeder.

Last week a pair of Canadian Honkers landed on the tin roof of the old hay shed, and yesterday evening mallard ducks cavorted in the rain right in the middle of Tenderfoot Valley Road. The rain put a damper on the annual Lee Scott Memorial Ploughing Bee, scheduled up the road at our neighbors Larry and Juanita Waters' place.

Doug did attend breakfast that Saturday morning at the Liberty Grange Hall. He said Heather Flock was there flipping hot cakes, and frying sausage and eggs, and Carmen Kohlhepp was there, too. Carmen's our grand marshal for the 2009 Hells Canyon Mule Days, which is always

Grandpa Ken Nash, of Enterprise, with granddaughter Riley Ann Gray at a recent branding up Big Sheep Creek near Imnaha.

Buck Matthews headin' and heelin' at a branding up Big Sheep Creek. Buck works for Marr Flat Cattle Company in Wallowa County and also runs cattle of his own.

held the weekend after Labor Day. Guess Vaden Flock headed home to Anatone with his team of mules.

Although I didn't make the breakfast (tending my mare and other chores) I did, later, receive a call from Doug. "Could you pick me up at the grange hall? Steering's out on my pickup."

I had planned to elaborate on that wonderful warm spring day when our family, along with many other families met to help with the branding on Big Sheep Creek. Good thing I took lots of photos, as haven't had time to write about it. Then I also had in mind to report more about the Writers Retreat on the Upper Imnaha.

Oh well, it's nearly 3:30 a.m. and I must get more sleep. A big day ahead. Our prayers continue to be with son Steve, who recently underwent back surgery in Alabama, where he and his family live.

Also in our thoughts is Lyman Goucher, who undergoes heart surgery in Spokane today. And Wilma, thanks for the rain dance outfit!! It fits. Methinks it'll be an exceptionally wet spring.

May 28—Last week I was all set to sit myself down and write this column, when I discovered there are five Fridays in May. The reason I know this is because we CowBelles serve at the Senior Meal Site whenever there is a fifth Friday in a month, and that's happening tomorrow. And, since Agri-Times comes out on the first and third Friday of each month, that meant I had another week to think about it.

As usual, I procrastinated until I suddenly found myself immersed in the crush of spring "things," and now here it is 9:30 p.m. on Thursday and I'm just now free to write.

This was our first really hot day, so our windows are open to capture the evening coolness that descends upon Prairie Creek after the sun sinks over the Wallowas. Today Ben helped Doug brand the heifers he purchased several weeks ago to graze our small pastures. Seemed sort'a like old times. We had him to lunch afterwards. Faithful Ben also shows up early of a morning to change Doug's hand lines.

It's been unseasonably hot and dry lately, and, although it threatens, no appreciable rain fell. Consequently, most of the "boys" (as some are girls) have started up their irrigation systems. I see Hough's center pivot marching slowly across their fields, and, in other Prairie Creek hay fields, I notice wheel lines are still doing the job, as well as hand lines.

On my way to Enterprise, I noticed an irrigator with a shovel in his hands, flood irrigating, a dying art these days. Hoorah for him.

My mare "Morning Star", though much improved, is still plenty stiff from her foundering episode. I keep her in a dry lot down by the corrals,

Scene out Janie Tippett's kitchen window: East Peak, Wallowa Mountains to the right. Doug Tippett's heifers graze the first grass of spring.

Doug Tippett, 2005 Hells Canyon Mule Days grand marshal, shares a joke with 2009 grand marshal Carmen Kohlhepp during a recent dinner in Carmen's honor, at the Outlaw restaurant in Joseph.

which means I must toss grass hay to her and make sure she has fresh water on a daily basis. Two of my broody hens are setting on fertile eggs—if Fred the rooster is doing his job. According to my calculations, baby chicks should appear any day now.

The stray black cat, who gave birth to two babies in Halley's dog house, got run over by a speeding pickup last week. Luckily our great-grandma Calico cat, who birthed HER kittens about that same time in the wood shed, willingly adopted the orphans. All five kittens are healthy and tumbling about in the morning sunshine, cute as kittens can be. Much to the delight of our myriad great-grandchildren, who all want to take one home, in spite of repeated objections voiced by their parents.

I've been busy weeding, digging, shoveling, and hauling manure to what Doug refers to as my "weed patch." Determined to turn this area into a thing of beauty, I decided to construct a flower bed like the one I'd admired at my friend Idella's when she hosted our monthly book group last week. After lugging a rusted iron bedstead found leaning against the shop, down to my flower garden, I placed boards along the sides, and *Voila!* A real flower BED, get it?

I constructed the bed around a cluster of Red Icelandic poppies, and when they finish blooming I'll plant some perennials like Foxglove or Bleeding Hearts. I also planted petunias in every pot I could find, and created planters of Wave Petunias from last Spring's hanging baskets.

As a result of all this effort, my 75 year old body protested. Wilma suggested I might have a twisted gut, and you know what they do to horses with that condition, and Doug kept saying, "Go to the doctor." So, I relented, and let him drive me to Winding Waters clinic, where one of our local docs, Theresa Russell, probed around a bit, asked questions, then declared I was suffering from a condition known as Costachondritis.

This means I have torn the cartilage loose under my rib cage, and somehow suffered a couple of cracked ribs. Cracked ribs are a familiar feeling, as I associate it with getting bucked off a horse, and I distinctly remember when this present injury occurred. While hoisting a heavy basket of frozen meat from the bottom of our chest freezer, which I was defrosting, I felt something give way. After which, I did all that digging in my weed patch. Now, the Doc says not to lift anything heavy, or use a shovel, or pull a stubborn weed, nor push a wheelbarrow until my Costachondritis has a chance to heal itself. And it's Spring!

Our lawn is ready for its third mowing, those brilliant green leaves have popped out on the Northwood Maple, and the ancient apple tree is in full bloom, as are the plum and cherry trees I planted in the chicken pen. Buck and Chelsea's two horses are grazing the lush grasses that grow in the area between the yard fence and the vegetable garden, which is all planted, thanks to Doug, and the radishes are up. The Walla Walla Sweet onions are transplanted, as are the cabbages.

Ben helped clean out the chicken house, and granddaughter Chelsie helped her grandma clean house last week. A mother Starling laid her eggs in a metal chicken feeder hanging on the wall in the chicken roost, and her five babies are ready to fly away as I write. For the great-grandchildren's sake, I was able to stop Doug from doing the birds in. He does not share my love for ALL birds.

The rhubarb is ready for pie, and the forsythia Mary Marks gave me is a cascade of golden blossoms. Barbara Warnock sent me a lovely African Violet, like the one I admired when I was down helping Wilma take care of Lyman, after his daughter Vicky brought him home from Spokane where he'd undergone open heart surgery, on the day son Todd and I headed to Dillon, Montana, to attend grandson James' graduation from college.

Now, that's a run-on sentence!

Lyman turned 80 the day after he came home, so I baked him a wild blackberry pie. I stayed until Lyman's daughter Judy arrived from California to take over. It rained during my stay there, and Lyman gives me the credit, so does Mike Fluitt and all the farmers who wanted me to do the rain dance so their newly-planted fields would sprout. Now, rain is needed again, but I can't fit into that teensy weensy bathing suit Wilma picked up at Second Best, to wear during my rain dance, due to my Costachondritis. Actually, I couldn't fit into it before my malady, but now it would surely aggravate my condition, so I'm not even go'in to try.

May 29—11:00 p.m. I'm supposed to leave with Pam and Liz by 8:00 tomorrow morning, to drive to The Dalles to attend Fishstock, a gala money-raising event for Fishtrap. After which we gals will spend the night with our friend and fellow Fishtrapper, Mary Schlick, who lives in Hood River. We'll return on Sunday.

Son Todd and I did travel to Dillon on Friday, via Lobo Pass into Montana, then south and east over Chief Joseph Pass, down into the Big Hole Valley, through Wisdom, and on into Dillon. We passed through miles of beautiful, wild high country, still wearing patches of winter snow. Most of those Big Hole Valley cows were just beginning to calve on numerous cattle ranches with their great hay meadows, where large wooden Beaver slides turn gray with age and all those brutal winters, reminding us that draft horses once provided the needed power to stack hay.

The next morning, watching grandson James graduate cum laude with a degree in Literature and Writing, during the 112th Annual Commencement of the University of Montana Western, triggered tears of pride and joy. Seated in back of her brother was granddaughter Adele, who had flown all the way from Austin, Texas, where she's enrolled in Culinary School. Adele was given the honor of placing the traditional cloak over her brother's graduation gown.

The Commencement address, given by author John Maclean—son of the late Norman Maclean, well-known author of *A River Runs Through It*—was truly inspiring. John's advice to the graduates boiled down to three things he deemed necessary to live a successful life: work, faith and family. In my opinion, John was right on!

After the ceremony, we followed James out to the Dillon airport, where he has been living as of late, and there, near the runway, my Wallowa County grandson tossed some of his dad's Marr Flat Top Sirloin on the grill. Soon other friends showed up bearing potluck, and we dove into the food.

After driving in rain, sleet, hail and snow to get there the night before, we were blessed that afternoon with perfect weather. Under wide Montana skies we soaked up that welcome sunshine. From where we feasted, on what James's Literature Professor described as "Serious Beef," we could view the mountain ranges that surrounded us, mountains James identified as The Rubys, Tobacco Roots, Black tails, Pioneers and Sweet Water. Their distant snowy presence provided a startling backdrop to our unique picnic.

It was 3:00 o'clock by the time James' freezer, saddle and other gear was loaded in Todd's pickup and we left for Challis, Idaho, to visit daughter Jackie. Todd had never seen any of that country before, which turned out to be the same route granddaughter Mona Lee and I had traveled to hear James present his thesis just a year ago. Up and over Bannock Pass, down into Leadore, thence to Salmon, and then south along the Salmon River to Challis. A very scenic route.

Jackie and husband Bill, having driven in from a family reunion in Bend just minutes before our arrival, welcomed us warmly.

Also there from Wallowa County, where she'd stopped over to visit during her move from Chehalis, Washington, to Challis, Idaho, was granddaughter Mona Lee. This granddaughter would be working for the Challis National Forest on the Rappeller Fire Crew for the summer. It was fun being with family.

The next morning, May 10th, was Mother's Day. Todd and I bid goodbye and headed south to Stanley, where we found those wide open meadows buried under several feet of snow. Down we dropped to the South Fork of the Payette River, past Garden Valley to Banks, then south to Horseshoe Bend, thence to Ontario, where Todd treated his mom to a Mother's Day dinner.

Home just in time to drive to the upper Imnaha and help Wilma with Lyman, which was followed by several brandings, including one out on Salmon Creek at Doug's old place in the hills, and another on upper Prairie Creek for Scott Shear, who manages Triple Creek ranches. More on these events later.

Then there was Mike and Maggie Vali's 35th anniversary of Vali's Alpine Delicatessen at Wallowa Lake, where I contributed three dozen deviled eggs to the burgeoning table of goodies created by Mike Jr. and his lovely Dione.

So much more has transpired since last I wrote, but Halley is howling at coyotes on Hough's hill, Doug is snoozing in the bedroom, and I'm tired; need to get some rest before another big adventure happens tomorrow.

June 11—Prairie Creek's resident rainbow has just faded away. Chances are its pastel bow will appear again tomorrow, when that low evening light filters through another misty rain. June rains. Remember them? Well, let me tell you, there's been plenty this year. And it's all because of Wilma and that itsy bitsy bikini.

I hear Lyman and son Craig are trying to bale their first cutting of hay on the upper Imnaha, but it won't stop raining. Prairie Creek and the hills are so happy, emerald green for as far as you can see. Petunias, Lobelia and Moss Roses, planted in my blue granite ware pots, are reviving after being pounded THREE times with hail stones and frog strangler cloud bursts.

For many days now, lightning has zippered the clouds, thunder has rolled down from the Wallowas, and Hells Canyon and the Seven Devils have been swathed in deep purple rain shadows.

Because it's been more than a little crazy this past week, I'm just now sitting down to write the column I intended to have written before my childhood chum Sandra and hubby Fred arrived Monday evening. Due to unfortunate circumstances, Doug and I haven't seen much of our friends. You see, Fred suffered a heart attack during their first night here, and subsequently ended up in our local hospital, after which he was transported by ambulance to another hospital three hours distant, in Richland, Washington.

Now we've learned that Fred is being released tomorrow (Saturday) so Doug is planning on driving over to bring Fred and Sandra back to Wallowa County. Needless to say, Fred's episode has disrupted their visit, however, uppermost in our minds is the fact that Fred was able to receive efficient, professional medical attention at our new Wallowa Memorial Hospital.

If our week had gone as planned, the four of us would be seated at Vali's Alpine Delicatessen tonight celebrating Doug's and my 31st wedding anniversary. Over the years it's become a tradition that Fred and Sandra help us celebrate this occasion by enjoying a gourmet meal prepared by our friends Mike and Maggie Vali in their homey Wallowa Lake eatery.

58 years ago, as a new 18-year-old mother, I was Sandra's matron of honor at her and Fred's wedding, which was held in the home of Sandra's parents in the foothills of Placer County where we both grew up. In the blink of an eye, the years have flown, and now here we are, what we are, in this place and time.

In addition to bustin' out all over, June has been an extremely busy month. Not only for us, but everyone, or so it would seem.

Our trip to The Dalles, although rushed, was entertaining, and provided just the right break from our frantic lifestyles. Three of us Fishtrap Board members—Liz, Pam and I—left the morning of May 30th, and drove directly to Hood River, where we stretched our legs after that long drive by wandering up and down the quaint tree-lined streets in brilliant spring sunshine.

At the top of a scenic hill, which afforded a view of the mighty Columbia, we lunched outside on the patio of the Three Rivers Restaurant. Sipping iced tea and nibbling cool salads, we relaxed and agreed to come back to revisit Hood River. A charming little town.

A breeze off the river wafted to us the sweet scent of roses, which bloomed profusely all about town. Returning to our car, we paused "to smell the roses." Fishstock, held at the historic Civic Auditorium in The Dalles, was a huge success, reflecting months of planning by our Fishtrap Staff and board members.

During the silent art auction five of us gals, who'd spent a week together at the April Writer's Retreat on the upper Imnaha, presented a short reading. Great fun meeting up with Melissa, Julianna and Richelle again, and Julianna, backed up by husband Barry, performed one of the songs Julianna wrote while she lived in the tree house. The title, "Imnaha's In Love," was inspired by Imnaha's bursting into spring. There followed an evening of readings and music, performed by some of Oregon's Best—Mary and Rindy Ross, Kate Power and Steve Einhorn, Craig Lesley, Molly Gloss, Joe Schlick, Rodd Ambroson, Carolyn Lockhart, and Janice Carper.

It was late when the program ended, and later still, when we wound our way up the Mt. Hood Highway to Mary Schlick's hide-a-way home. Mary and Kathy were already in bed and we wasted no time finding ours.

The next morning I looked out the window to see a blooming dogwood tree, and later, as we sipped tea on the deck, the sight of snowy Mt. Hood gladdened my heart. Mary's house is nestled in a fragrant forest, where recent rains had freshened the wildflowers.

Our gracious hostess, Mary Schlick, who authored the beautiful book *Columbia River Basketry,* is a longtime Fishtrapper, having attended many conferences over the years, as well as spent time on Imnaha at the Retreat. Mary is known for her own basketry as well, so spending time in her company was a rare treat.

After stopping in The Dalles to pick up Gail Swart, we girls talked our way back to Wallowa County in no time.

My ribs and torn whatever have improved dramatically, and so did my foundered mare. Great-Grandma Kitty and her five kittens are happy in the woodshed, and the kittens are at that adorable stage where you wish they'd just stay, while the great-grand children are choosing what color kitten they want.

Our vegetable garden is recovering from three violent spring storms, and today the shredded cabbages don't look quite so sad. My "Weed Patch" flower garden, with it's REAL Flower Bed, is such a joy, and the resulting beauty is worth the effort. Icelandic Poppies are beginning to bloom, and the potted petunias will assure a colorful summer.

The baby starlings in the chicken house flew away, Ben finished the first irrigating, and we hired our friend Cheryl Cox to help with the spring house cleaning. Cheryl also stacked the wood, which Doug purchased at a benefit auction, that had been delivered and left in a pile in front of the woodshed. That gal can get more done in a short time than anyone I know; a real worker.

Doug's heifers are fattening up on all the lush grasses, and Buck and Chelsea moved their horses to our neighbor's pasture. These two horses did a great job of grazing the tall grasses between the garden and machinery shed; very friendly horses, who were in my hip pocket whilst I tended my myriad chores.

My two setting hens sat and sat and sat, and alas, their eggs weren't fertile. It would seem "Fred" the Cochin rooster was all show and no virility. Little but mighty in appearance, he was never destined to sire baby chicks. Darn, and my two hens are still setting and hoping.

However, one must never look a "gift rooster in the mouth." Dismissing Fred, I ordered baby chicks from a hatchery in Caldwell, Idaho. And, on June 23rd, the Joseph Post Office will be filled with the sound of peeping chicks, cause that's when my order of 25 Aracuna pullets will arrive. I sincerely hope my hens are still setting, else I'll become a mother hen myself. Since the minimum order is 25, and I only wanted ten, anyone in Agri-Times land who would like some Aracuna pullets (they lay green and blue eggs) should let me know.

Then yesterday, grandson James came by with a girl from England and turned a new rooster in with Fred and his harem. I wasn't here, so missed the fight; needless to say, Fred was defeated in the third round and banished to a corner of the chicken pen. Turns out the new rooster, given the un-chicken-like name of "Piglet" by James' English friend, is a son of the infamous "Larry," so named for our neighbor Larry Waters, who left him in my chicken pen after one of our County Fair Chicken scrambles.

This long story has been previously told in this column, and it's not worth repeating, except to say that James informed me that Larry sired three sons, who all grew up and murdered their dad. Not a pretty story, but in Chickendom these things happen.

June 13—Doug is on his way home with Fred and Sandra, who originally planned to leave for Auburn this morning. Doug is picking up "Take Out" Chinese food at our local "Happy Garden" on the way back here to Prairie Creek. It will be good to see them again, and we wish Fred the best.

This morning I delivered the apple pie I baked yesterday to a pie sale staged by our local Friends of the Wallowa County Museum. Business was brisk when I left, and the town of Joseph was ALIVE. You see, this weekend was the Wallowa Mountain Cruise, the annual vintage car show, and lots of folks were apparently hungry for homemade pies.

Leaving Joseph behind, I headed to the old Snyder Ranch, where I joined my great-grandchildren, Lucy and baby sister Kate, at a small branding. My lazy J brand has been transferred to grandson Buck and his wife Chelsea. Of course, I had to photograph the event. Mom Chelsea jumped on her horse, roped a few calves, then it was back to nurse baby Kate on the bumper of a pickup. That's ranch life in Wallowa County.

While I rode herd on Luke and Callie's two little girls and Lucy, Callie watched baby James and baby Kate. Thunder clouds threatened but held off until the small bunch of calves were worked.

June 14—Now it's 9:00 p.m., and Sandra and Doug are playing cribbage at the kitchen table where I'm attempting to finish this column. It's not easy! A light rain is falling outside and the day is over. I've been up since 4:30 in order for Sandra and I to make Vali's Continental breakfast and savor one of Mike Jr's freshly made twists.

By 10:00 a.m. my friend and I were seated in the Joseph United Methodist Church for a special service, made especially memorable due to Pastor Sharon, who recently walked from Enterprise to Joseph to raise money for the restoration of the church's 100-year-old stained glass windows. Not to mention the soul-stirring music of the well-known group, "Sky in the Road".

June 15—1:30 p.m. on this Monday, and Fred and Sandra just left for Winnemucca, Nevada, where they will spend the night before returning to their home in Auburn, California. Our prayers are with them. God Speed.

June 23—I baked two Birthday pies. Huckleberry cream for James and rhubarb for Ethan. James turned 23 today, and Ethan's 14th birthday was on the 15th. Then I got on the phone and invited family. James' dad arrived bearing flank steak and tri-tip beef, which he then bar-b-cued to perfection. I'd also baked a large loaf of sourdough bread and put together a large salad...using our local Farmer's Market romaine lettuce.

Mother Nature smiled on us and it was a lovely evening, so we ate outside on a picnic table. Having great-granddaughter Lucy there with baby sister Kate made it special. Todd's hired hand, Ty, who lives in Colorado and spends the summer here helping with ranch chores, along with Ethan and James, displaced those pies in rapid order.

Last Wednesday, grandson James and I drove out to Billy Meadows to check out the kitchen facilities where I will be cooking for the upcoming Fishtrap Outpost Writing Workshop, due to begin on July 6th. I'll be heading out there with the food on July 5, which is rapidly approaching.

On Thursday of that week, I'll be returning to the United Methodist Camp at Wallowa Lake to join in the annual Summer Fishtrap Gathering. Therefore, I must get this column emailed so I can concentrate on my menu and planning. Billy Meadows is a long way from a grocery store.

James and I really enjoyed the ride out. We saw lots of wildlife, including a bear, and a Mule Deer doe and baby fawn. Lots of wildflowers coming down Red Hill, too. It's incredibly lovely in Wallowa County's backcountry, due to our wet June. Miles of forests, meadows, and silence broken only by birdsong. We who live here are truly blessed.

June 27—It's 9:30 p.m. and here I am again, seated at the kitchen table wondering how to begin a column that should have been completed earlier in the week. As in weeks past, there haven't been enough hours to squeeze in writing time. 'Tis the season for activity. After our long winters, we Wallowa Countians seem to fill every waking moment with living.

Today was no exception. Grandson Ethan, who lives in Cottage Grove, Oregon, is spending the weekend with us, and this afternoon we took in the Second Annual Ranch Rodeo. This year's event was held at the Harley Tucker Memorial Arena and began the countdown for the famous Chief Joseph Days Rodeo to be held in this same venue during the last weekend in July.

Don't know who had the most fun, spectators or contestants. You see, a ranch rodeo is one wherein our own working cowboys and cowgirls come to town and demonstrate the skills they use everyday on their ranches. These seasoned hands merge to form teams that represent their brands or cattle companies. Outfits that are scattered all over Wallowa County. They're REAL. They ride the outback, the windswept divides, steep canyons draws, high grassy plateaus, remote mountain meadows, and acres of forested lands so far removed from civilization they can ride all day and never see a soul.

Places like Promise, Marr Flat, Harral Butte, Big Sheep, Imnaha, Lookout Mountain, Salmon Creek, Prairie Creek, and the Chesnimnus country. These cowboys and cowgirls hold spring brandings in timeworn corrals nestled in canyons and hills. Mounted on good ranch horses, they head and heel and keep the old ways alive. Everyone has a good time, even the women folk who transport food over miles of rutty roads to feed the branding crews. It's a family affair, where the younger generation learns from the oldsters.

This year's teams competing were Baremore Ranch, Broken Arrow Cattle Co., Circle P Ranch, Corriente Cattle Co., Dawson Ranch, Marr Flat Cattle Co/Rocking J, Quail Run Ranch, Triple Creek Cattle, and Yost Quarterhorse.

The rodeo began this afternoon with the ever-popular Mutton Busting event. Two of our great-grandchildren, Gideon and his twin sister Jada, came busting out of the chute riding mature Hampshire bucks. Brave little Jada got dumped, while her brother hung on, even after being dragged around the arena for longer than he wanted to. Not good, but Gideon's suffering paid off. He scored an 80 and won the buckle!

Of course, our family cheered for the Marr Flat Cattle Company's cowboys, son Todd Nash, grandson Buck Matthews, Ethan Lowe and Colin Cunningham, who comprised the winning team. All got buckles. However, any one of Wallowa County's real cowboys deserved to win. Dan Warnock gave it his all, as did the Baremore boys, and of course our hero was Ethan Lowe, who rode a saddle bronc.

Grandson James, mounted all afternoon on a horse, worked the arena, as did myriad other volunteers who gave generously of their time to stage this action-packed community rodeo. Doug and I enjoyed visiting former Wallowa County ranchers Ed and Carol Wallace, who had driven over from Clarkston, Washington, to attend. Ed used to do his share of team roping when he and Carol operated a cattle ranch up Trout Creek.

Carol and I had fun remembering way back in the 70s, when we won the Wild Cow Milking at Wallowa County's one and only All Girl Rodeo! In fact, we wished they'd had such an event today; we would have entered. Of course our speed these days would be a gentle little Jersey, not a wild crossbred range cow.

Finally, today actually felt like summer. After weeks of rain, albeit good for the country, we are finally getting a break. For days now the soggy vegetable garden begged for sunshine. We are eating radishes and strawberries, and soon the succulent leafy lettuce will be ready. The kittens romp around the woodshed, awaiting the time they'll go to new homes with the great-grandkids. My mare, Morning Star, is grazing the machinery yard, and my flowers beds have never been more colorful.

Doug's former ranch, planted to grain crops, has become showy fields of brilliant green. Due to the rains, the shiny, new, behemoth center pivot irrigation system remains silent, resembling an elongated metal dinosaur on wheels, sprawled across the hill. Tucker's Mare, the snow shape of a horse, is still visible west of East Peak.

Our friends Fred and Sandra made it home safely to Auburn, California, where Fred seems much improved. Thanks to daughter Ramona and husband Charley, we DID make it to Vali's to celebrate our anniversary last Friday evening.

Grandson Shawn, wife Maria, and their children Jackson and Savannah Rose flew out from South Carolina for a brief visit, a surprise Father's Day gift for Papa Charley. We savored Flaming Beef Shish Kabob and enjoyed visiting Maggie and her wonderful family. Shawn, one of our Marines, leaves this fall for Afghanistan, as does another grandson, Josh, who is stationed at the naval base in San Diego. Yet another grandson,

James, has been Accepted into flight school in the Marines and will be leaving in September for Florida. Although our Wallowa County boys scatter to far places, Wallowa County remains in their hearts.

Last Saturday was quite a day. To begin with, grandson James and I participated in the Amy Hafer run/walk for Breast Cancer. It was a nice cool morning with sun breaks and a course that led uphill toward the Ant Flat Dump. Wild blue flax lined the road and the views of the Wallowas from the hill above Enterprise were breathtaking. James, of course, ran, while I maintained a fast walk in the 70-plus category. Didn't notice any folks my age, however.

I finished the 5-K Women's walk in under 55 minutes. There were over 250 walkers and runners, and since it's mostly uphill to the turnaround, it meant an easy return to our new Wallowa Memorial Hospital, where we were treated to a lovely brunch.

At 2:00 o'clock I was seated in the Mormon church attending memorial services for Marvel Eaves, an old friend who once owned the restaurant at Pete's Pond, and who was a member of our writing group. Later, at Marvel's brief graveside service, a ray of sunlight burst forth through the clouds, illuminating the area over Pete's Pond. Snowy Ruby Peak rose above the town of Enterprise, thus providing a fitting tribute to a remarkable lady. Marvel had just celebrated her 80th birthday.

Then it was back to Prairie Creek to join Doug in attending Tom and Donna Butterfield's 50th wedding anniversary. Tom and Donna are neighboring ranchers. Their family did a super job of pulling off this celebration. A large farming/ranching family with roots that go deep in Prairie Creek soil, back at least four generations.

The rains fell again, and the water ran in rivulets when Doug and I turned in our lane.

Later, out on the carport, I was cranking our old wooden freezer to make ice cream for a family bar-b-cue, planned for upper Prairie Creek at the Phillips Ranch, in honor of Shawn and family—when in drove several cars. It was apparent the bar-b-cue had been rained out. So here they came, bearing sodden pork chops, fresh off the grill, fried chicken, salads, rolls, and cakes. Carload after carload of family and neighbors, and before I could blink an eye, nearly 30 souls filled our home. Oldest son Ken took charge of cranking the ice cream. Daughter Lori and husband Larry, who had driven over from Richland, spent the night. As usual, everyone had a rollicking good time, and that ended a mighty long day.

Well, those 25 Aracuna pullets, the day-old baby chicks, arrived at the Joseph post office on the 24th, and since then I've all but taken up residence in the chicken house. After endless labor and many intensive hours spent making my small flock happy about this increase in population, things are finally settling down.

Luckily, my two hens were still setting. When I slipped those little peepers under them that night, they fluffed up their wings and began making motherly clucking noises. Thank goodness! My smaller hen adopted ten chicks, and the larger one accepted the remaining fifteen. Piglet, my new rooster, struts around as though he were responsible, and indeed he could be. My poor hens get very little rest these days.

The banished Fred has the run of the place OUTSIDE the chicken pen, and for excitement he and Piglet spar between the chicken wire. Fred and Halley also do this boxing thing. I tell you, this place is a zoo!

And now I've been up since 1:30 a.m. and it's 3:30, and I'm going back to bed.

June 28—5:00 am. Up and at it again. Must end this column and check my chicken family. Ethan is asleep downstairs, and Doug is hanging out with the "boys" at the Cheyenne Cafe, if you know what I mean.

July 2—Quite the opposite from my last column, this one will be finished a week ahead of the deadline. The reason being, I can see NO TIME in the coming days and weeks to write. Summer is definitely here. Temps are supposed to climb to 84 today. Heat and I don't do so good, and that's unfortunate, cause I'm extremely BUSY

I must arise early, this morning at 4:30, to check the mother hens and make sure they've kept the chicks warm all night. Because this is a high mountain valley, the temps do fall during the nights, especially during the early morning hours. The smallest hen has taken to roosting in her nest, leaving her chicks to huddle together in a corner of the chicken house. So, I get up and make sure she is covering them during the chilly time.

This morning I needn't have worried. At first light, "Piglet" my new rooster, had awakened all of Prairie Creek with his lusty crows, and the chickens, young and old, had already begun their day.

While I'm up, I water the mare, feed the kittens and mamma kitty, and play with Halley. By this time I'm wearing down, 'cause I was out hoe, hoe, hoeing in the garden 'til dark last evening.

While I'm napping, Doug leaves with the boat to meet our California great-grandkids, Clayton, Cole and Halley Jane, and their Poppa Charley, at the lake by 6:00. They say if you want to catch Kokanee, better go early in the morning, that's when they're biting now. The kids are visiting their Poppa Charley and Amamona, and that means the Phillips Ranch annual Camp Run-A-Muck is in session.

Clayton and Cole recently showed, and sold their 4-H market steers in Lodi, California, and sister Halley took second in 4-H goat showmanship. This young Miss tells me she got $7.00 per lb. for her goat! The boys did equally well, and all three children say they've socked the money away for college.

After finishing my chores, I drove to the foot of Wallowa Lake and spotted my family fishing out of Doug's old Dug Bar boat. Since it was such a lovely fresh morning, I decided to hike up the trail to the East Moraine. From there I photographed the fishing party against Wallowa County's number one tourist attraction. The smell of sage, after the brief thunder storm the night before, gladdened my heart, as did the blooming Lupine.

I returned to the lake just as Doug was bringing the boat into the dock. Soon, there they were, lugging a bucket of Kokanee. Halley said she caught the most and the biggest. By this time everyone was ravenous, including me, so I treated my family to breakfast at the Cheyenne Cafe in Joseph.

This afternoon I will grocery shop for the Fishtrap Outpost Writing project out at Billy Meadows. My list is made, and our front room is stacked high with cooking pots, dutch ovens, and camping gear.

July 15—On July 4th, Grandson James and I ran/walked the Lostine River Run, which is held in conjunction with Lostine's famous Flea Market. James won a third place ribbon and a day pack to boot. After he made it in, he came running back to accompany his grandma over the finish line. I completed the three miles in just under an hour, and won a blue ribbon. Of course, I was the only one over 70!

After the race, we walked up Main Street Lostine and chowed down one of those Marr Flat Hamburgers that Susan and Angie were serving hot off the grill with onions. Yum!

Then it's home to load the pickup and make a salad to take to daughter Ramona's for the annual Fourth of July bar-b-cue at the Phillips ranch. I'll leave before the fireworks, as have to get up early and head for Billy Meadows, where I cook until Thursday, at which time I'll return to Prairie Creek, unload and make it to the continuation of the Summer Fishtrap conference at Wallowa Lake, which ends at noon the following Sunday.

Meanwhile, Doug leaves today for Asotin, Washington, and the Tippett Family Reunion, followed on Sunday by his brother Jack Tippett's 90th birthday, also in Clarkston. Doug will be return on Sunday, the day I leave. Such a summer!

Maintaining the vegetable garden, the chicks, watering the flowers and lawns, tending the dog and cats and my mare, not to mention the 22 heifers, and irrigating the pastures will take up quite a bit of Doug's time. I will have my great-granddaughter Halley Jane come to water the flowers in all my little containers and baskets.

Granddaughter Adele called yesterday from Austin, Texas. "Hi grandma, be flying to Boise on the 22nd and be here for Chief Joseph Days." Really looking forward to seeing this gal, who's nearly through Culinary School.

Her brother James has been in Florida for some sort of Marine training meeting, and is due back today. Grandson Shawn has now been deployed to Okinawa, so he and his wife are putting their home in South Carolina up for sale and moving with their children to Japan.

Grandson Josh is off to Afghanistan, and son Todd and wife Angie just returned from San Diego to visit their son before he ships out. Josh leaves behind wife Desiree and two sons. Our prayers are with our young men, as well as all the others who are serving our country.

At the end of Chief Joseph Days, I will be leaving with our "Syringa Sisters" to hike 8 miles from Moss Springs into Minam Lodge for a week, where we five aging gals also plan to backpack five miles up the Minam River Trail, camp two nights, then return to the lodge and ride horses out on Friday morning. After a mandatory soak in the hot springs at Cove, we'll return to our lives—that is, if we survive.

And that will take us into August and the County Fair. So much more to write about, like the birthday dinner we planned to have at the RimRock Inn, only it was closed, so our writing group drove down Buford to Boggan's Oasis, where Farrel Vail cooked us a yummy lunch with ice cream with candles for our birthday gals, Sharon and Lynn.

The drive down to the Grande Ronde river was very colorful with blooming Mule Ears, Indian Paint Brush and Lupine. The river was roiling with frothy snowmelt. One of our group, Cathy, met us out there as she lives near Flora. The drive out the North Highway in June is just lovely: green meadows, ponds brimming over with water, new leaves on the Aspen trees, and Krebs' sheep grazing. Always the Wallowas in the distance. Stangel's buffalo were calving out, and we spotted many calves along Trout Creek.

This afternoon Doug and I will meet on the Courthouse lawn to listen to The Prairie Creek Girls perform some good old fashioned fiddle tunes. Also on the Courthouse lawn, I'll purchase fresh lettuce and produce at the Farmer's Market to take to Billy Meadows. Hope everyone in Agri-Times land had a safe and Happy Fourth of July while we here in Wallowa County continue to enjoy our brief beautiful summer.

Marr Flatt Cattle Co. Team won high point team at the recent Ranch Rodeo
held at the Harley Trucker Memorial Arena in Joseph. L-R: Buck Matthews,
Ethan Lowe, Todd Nash and Colin Cunningham.

July 19—Once again, the kitchen table where I write reflects the
season: six quarts of canned Imnaha apricots, four pints of apricot jam,
the schedule for Tamkaliks and Chief Joseph Days, sticky notes that
remind me to pick lettuce, water garden, answer letters, check e-mail,
call sister Mary Ann, begin column, write in daily journal; the notes
are scattered among photographs, labels, and guidelines for the Fishtrap
anthology.

'Tis a lovely morning. Cooler than yesterday, which is nice. We've
been experiencing some pretty hot weather lately. Good for the boys
haying. They needed it, as some of those heavy tops of alfalfa and
meadow grass hay got drenched during one of our recent thunder storms.

It is a lovely time here on Prairie Creek. Such a lushness when sun
follows rain. Fields of timothy, oats and wheat create a mosaic of greens.
Early of a summer morning, a new crop of young coyote puppies yip
and yowl over Hough's hill. Halley cocks her ear and joins them. "Piglet,"

the new rooster, startles the morning stillness with his crowing, which is followed by the bellowing of one of Hough's Angus bulls. Summer mornings are full of birdsong: Robins, Killdeer, Doves, Ravens, Hawks, Pheasants, and Red Wing Blackbirds.

The Billy Meadows Outpost Writing project was wildly successful, and other than being exhausting for me, was also very fulfilling.

On July 5th, I headed out the North Highway with Amy Minato and her two children, Ruby and Mateo, in tow. We took the Charolais Road to Crow Creek, then up Red Hill, past Coyote, and finally to Billy Meadows. Sorted through our food stuffs, put things away, and began preparing to feed 20 folks that evening.

Halfway through grilling hamburgers, a thunderous summer storm ensued. Billy Meadows creates its own weather. We witnessed an extremely violent show of hail, rain and limb lashing wind. Since we didn't use electricity, we weren't concerned with losing it. I simply moved inside and finished grilling those hamburgers on my heavy cast iron griddle, placed on a propane cook stove. Sure glad I thought to bring it, 'cause it came in handy for sourdough hot cakes, french toast, and whole wheat toast for breakfasts.

I felt fortunate to have such handy facilities. Many of my former outdoor catering ventures, when I was much younger, were accomplished under primitive conditions. Billy Meadows, a Forest Service complex, consists of a module home and a historic ranger cabin, built by the CCC boys. I did use that rustic log cabin kitchen to bake my sourdough bread, cobblers and cookies, which required that I traipse back and forth carrying fragrant bakery items.

The meadows themselves were brilliant green in the morning sunlight, and speckled with blooming False Hellebore, Cinquefoil, Lupine and Penstemon. In the evening elk and deer appeared at the meadows edge, and a tiny creek held pollywogs and frogs, much to the delight of the children.

The next day, Sunday afternoon, Amy and I, with help from the kids put together a potato salad. Ruby and Mateo had just finished shucking corn when the van full of workshop writers arrived, set up their tents, and filed into the kitchen for the first of many meals. Several included my specialty: cast iron dutch oven cookery, utilizing the coals of a wood fire built in a well-constructed rock fire pit. Nothing compares with dutch oven pot roast, or chicken cacciatore. That dramatic storm, the mountain meadow setting, the cabin in the pines, and authentic outdoor cooking, provided the desired fodder for writing. It also produced appetites. Never saw folks eat so much. No leftovers.

After breakfasts we'd set out fixin's for lunches and the writers made their own, leaving me ample time to bake and get organized for the night meal. One sunny afternoon I even stretched out in a lawn chair, relaxed, and jotted down notes in my journal. Also worked in several relaxing walks in the woods with friends.

I'll never forget Tuesday night, when we were all seated around the fire, listening to Amy's husband Joe explain about the phases of the moon—all the more interesting because that was the night of the full "Buck" or "Thunder Moon," so named for the male deer, as they begin to grow their antlers this time of year. The "Thunder Moon" takes its name from the intense summer storm season. We could attest to that.

During this time, poems were read, someone played a guitar, and songs were sung; the youngsters roasted marshmallows on sticks to make s'mores, and firelight shone on the faces of city folks who will never forget this circle of friends.

On Thursday, after breakfast, and lunches made, I was extremely grateful for workshop instructor Kim Stafford and Billy Meadows writer-in-residence Charles Goodrich, who organized the troops and made quick work of disassembling camp and loading my pickup.

We headed for Buckhorn Lookout, where we perched on the lip of the breaks of the Imnaha and stared down at that tiny curve of river flowing north through miles of rim rock canyon country. We listened to the sound of silence as we ate our lunches. Although the Penstemon, Indian paintbrush and Lupine had faded into summer, those blue canyon distances fed our souls.

Home via Thomason Meadows, the old Steen Ranch, Zumwalt Prairie, and Prairie Creek, where, as we drove down Tenderfoot Valley Road, I looked for Halley and Doug. We arrived at Wallowa Lake Camp in time for the Outpost Writers to present their readings, as the 2009 Summer Fishtrap Gathering began that evening. It was late when I returned to the ranch with my pickup still loaded with cooking gear.

The next morning, Anne (bless her) was here before 7:00 to help unload my pickup. Then it was back to the lake to join Kim Stafford's last class with the Billy Meadows participants. Fun. I was able to complete several submissions for our Fishtrap Anthology.

The Gathering ended Sunday. Another successful Summer Fishtrap, wherein we explored the theme, "Usual and Accustomed Places." This is a theme very familiar to me, as I continue to write this column about place.

For the next few days I put things away, weeded the garden, attended the Tamkaliks Friendship Feast at the Nez Perce Homeland site in

Wallowa—which is always wonderful—and suddenly it was Chief Joseph Days.

I also took time to assemble my backpack for our 13th annual "Syringa Sisters" trip to Minam Lodge, which was approaching rapidly. We'd been planning this trip since last year.

Chief Joseph Days remains a busy blur in my memory. My great-grandchildren won first place in the float division of Friday's Kiddie Parade. Eleven of them accompanied a covered wagon, either walking alongside or riding inside. Daughter-in-law Annie had been busy at her sewing machine for days. All the little girls wore bonnets and Prairie dresses, and the boys were dressed in fringed buckskin. Printed on the covered wagon were the words *JOSEPH OREGON, THE EARLY YEARS.*

Hung on the wagon sides were pioneer items such as kettles, water buckets, shovels, and washboards; inside stood a wood cookstove, treadle sewing machine, butter churn, and six-month old Nevada Dawn, visiting from Mt. Vernon, sitting in a high chair, happy as a lark. Riley Ann and Ashlyn rode inside, tending baby Nevada, and trailing along the wagon were Brenna, Jada, Gideon, Ronan, Kennon, Cutter, Gwenllian, and two-year-old Gavin bringing up the rear. All Nash cousins.

This great-grandma, busting her buttons with pride, ran alongside in a most undignified manner, snapping photos…which proved to be next to impossible, so I followed the contingent to the end of the parade for a group photo. Kudos to the parents who helped pull this float off. It was a total surprise to me—not to mention, it was my first glimpse of baby Nevada Dawn.

Then there were those professional rodeos, wherein great-grandson Ronan won the mutton busting one night, and his dad, grandson Chad, and Colin Cunningham, won the wild cow milking event. Son Todd and grandson Buck placed in several other go-rounds of that wild event. And if you count this grandma, cheering in the stands, there were four generations of us participating in those fun events, which feature local cowboys.

Doug and I took in the Grand Parade on Saturday morning, after which we visited several out-of-town Tippetts before returning to the ranch to sit in the shade, visit Doug's nephew and niece, cowboy poet Smoke Wade and his sister Sharon, while waiting for Syringa Sisters Bobbie and Barb from Portland, and Jessica and Mary from Boise.

After their arrival, we "plucked" most of our dinner from the garden. I cooked up some Kokanee I'd found in the freezer, and we ate outside on the picnic table. We proved to be too many giggling females for Doug, who fled to the canyons of Imnaha to hunt rattlesnakes.

Early the next morning, Barb and I took our loaded packs to the Enterprise airport, where we saw bush pilot Joe Spence take off in his plane. Destination: Minam Lodge.

Back to the ranch to breakfast on egg/zucchini scramble with cheese and Jess's fruit salad, then off to attend Cowboy Church, held each year in the Harley Tucker Memorial Arena. Earlier, Barb and I popped into the Cheyenne Cafe in time to see Doug show off his bucket full of rattlers (dead) to the "locals" table. Much to the horror of the waitress.

Later that afternoon we all headed to Cove, where we chomped down our last fast food, before ascending the long dusty road to Moss Springs Campground. Where we "car camped" literally (the mosquitoes were hungry) before hitting the steep nine-mile trail to Red's Horse Ranch and Minam Lodge by first light the next morning, to avoid the heat.

We are older now. Bobbie, still 80, doesn't want me to say she'll be 81 next month; yours truly nearly 76; Mary 72, Jessica 69, and Barb 65. The trail is cool at 5:30 and the sun has yet to appear over the eastern rim. We drop down and spot a lone Syringa blooming between an earth-filled large boulder.

It is an omen, the only Syringa we see. The trail is steep, elevation at Moss Springs trailhead is 5,800 ft and we will experience a 2,200 ft. drop in elevation by the time we reach Red's Horse Ranch. We cross the Little Minam on a long wooden bridge, and are halfway there. Ahead looms Jim White Ridge, and soon we're traversing the Hog's Back, looking down at the landing strip at Red's. Though this is a new adventure for my city friends, my memories come flooding back.

It's hot as we hike the long switchbacks to the meadow. The trail takes longer for Jessica, who has fallen and twisted her knee. Finally, we reach the bottom. The sign above the gate reads, "Red's Horse Ranch."

We take a left in the trail and stumble the final mile to Minam Lodge, the familiar golden meadow shimmering in late July heat. Shelly has iced tea and fixes us pulled pork sandwiches. We rest and secure two cabins. Some choose to sleep outside...we all are in Paradise.

Hot and dusty from the trail, we traipse across the meadow to the Minam River, clear and cool, refreshing our tired bodies.

Back to relax on the deck, sip more iced tea and take notes on our adventures. Other guests appear on horseback. Supper is grilled steak, cooked to perfection by Shelly. Hot biscuits, veggies, and chocolate cake with coffee. We retire to the deck, stare down the meadow and long landing strip, to where a small herd of horses graze. We are in the heart of the Minam Wilderness.

The stars are brilliant, a new moon grows, and we sleep well. The next morning we hear the sound of a plane landing. It is Shelly's husband, Shawn, bringing in supplies and a guest: 89-year-old Ted Grote, from Joseph, a former helicopter pilot and fellow Prairie Creek rancher. Over hot cakes, scrambled eggs and coffee, Ted feeds me tales about Red Higgins, former owner of Red's.

After breakfast we pack a lunch and head off down the landing strip to Red's. Caretaker Patti shows us around Red's private quarters near the river, where, 31 years ago, Doug and I spent our honeymoon. We tour the old log cabin where daughter Jackie and husband Bill spent the winter as caretakers, the kitchen where I baked pies and bread, the firepit where I prepared my fly-in bar-b-cue, and the trail to Elk Creek where, years ago, I was the deluxe elk camp cook for the Horse Ranch.

The swimming hole was still there and we (not all) dove in. After the initial shock, the water was refreshing, and I dog paddled like a kid again.

August 2—Crept out of bed at 11:30 p.m. and worked until 2:30 a.m. on my column.

August 3—7:00 in the morning. Must put a period to this. Time is running out, per usual. Will resume recording our trip to Minam Lodge next time. You see, when I returned to the ranch there was a very large box of cherries to can that Doug purchased for me in Imbler; plus washing to do, and all the catching up from being gone.

The morning after I returned, I got in and canned all those cherries. Also put up pickles. The cukes had multiplied in my absence.

By noon I was at daughter Ramona's on Upper Prairie Creek, attending a baby shower and luncheon for one of my granddaughters, Deanna, who is expecting her first baby. Deanna is one of many adopted granddaughters.

This morning I will assist Sue Coleman in accepting the photography at our annual Wallowa County Fair. She is the superintendent this year; I'm just the helper. That way I can enter some of my own photography.

It's been HOT, terribly hot, and already it is fire season. Stay cool, enjoy life. Soon those gorgeous days of fall will be here. Must e-mail this column and get myself to the fair.

August 11—Yesterday I was just sitting myself down to begin this column when Doug appeared at the door.

"Could ya come and help me get that heifer?" It seems one of his heifers has been taking up residence in our neighbor Don Hough's herd.

Two-year-old Lucy and her baby sister Katelyn take a ride on great-grandma Janie's mare, Morning Star. Daddy Buck Matthews "helps."

The hired man had her in a corral.

We drove down the lane to where the heifer, along with a pair belonging to another neighbor, was penned. I won't go into all the details, but my job was to slam the trailer door when I heard the heifer jump in. The heifer, or what I assumed was the heifer, ran in the trailer, so I slammed the door. Wrong critter. From my vantage point all I could see was feet.

The next time I heard, "slam the door, lady." The hired man's voice—so I did. We had her.

The rest of the day continued pretty much like that, and now it's the 11th and late in the day, and things haven't calmed down much. Granddaughter Chelsie and her four children were here to pick raspberries this morning and Gideon got "bitten" by the electric fence near the chicken pen. I baked a strawberry pie, weeded the garden, tended the chickens, and spent a good deal of time attempting to e-mail submissions for various anthologies. I say attempting, because the folks at the other end weren't receiving my work.

Technology, for all its so-called time-saving, in my opinion does NOT save time. I find it extremely frustrating, and am ready to revert to the simple act of putting pen to paper, where you write something, seal it in an envelope, and walk out to the mailbox. What happened? I used to spend far less time doing this stuff. E-mails take time—time I don't have.

I must say, though, when it comes to e-mailing this column, that seems to work. However, I don't know what goes on at the other end. Perhaps they too are frustrated.

Those hot days morphed into cooler ones, and numerous thunder storms dumped over an inch of rain here on Prairie Creek. Unreal. Subsequently, the garden has taken off. It's almost tropical here. My famous baking squash plants have strangled the apple tree and climbed the garden fence, their tendrils now reaching for the house. As I write, myriad green runners, sporting huge yellow blossoms, have smothered a row of carrots and are attempting to overthrow the crookneck. Soon it will do battle with the zucchini...

The County Fair is history. It was fun and, thankfully, rained, then cooled off. I always feel sorry for the animals and kids when it's so hot. I did well on my photography entries, and appreciated Sue Coleman, who took over my job as Superintendent. As usual, I just couldn't help myself, 'cause there I was Tuesday morning...entering veggies and flowers. Heartening to see so many folks entering produce from their gardens this year.

Thanks to Nancy Carlsen and her crew, there was a very attractive exhibit in Cloverleaf Hall. Due to this present economic crunch, County fairs, like ours, have had to deal with limited funding. Nothing shows off, or represents, our local culture more than the County fair. It's so very important for a community, and if it weren't for all those generous, committed volunteers, our fair would cease to exist. It's a tradition we must all work to maintain.

On Saturday I joined a packed grandstand to watch the various Scrambles. Oh my goodness! Chickens flew to the rafters, escaped to the sheep barn, skittered under the bleachers, and dove behind panels with a herd of youngsters hot on their tails. My great-grandchildren grabbed their share of squawking poultry.

That evening, after the awards, Doug and I partook of the yummy bar-b-cue put on by our local FFA chapter, which was immediately followed by the annual fat stock auction in the covered arena. Since no Wallowa County great-grandchildren are old enough to sell market animals yet, I purchased a 225 lb. hog from Joseph FFA member Riley Steen. Riley's parents, Shawn and Shelly Steen, manage the Minam Lodge in the Eagle Cap Wilderness.

Riley and I had a discussion about his hog a couple of weeks ago, when he flew into the Minam with his dad. So, now we have some good-tasting bacon, ham, sausage and pork chops coming. At four dollars per pound, it ought'a taste real good.

Back to our Minam Trip.

On Tuesday we spent the day exploring Red's Horse Ranch. For dinner we enjoyed more of Shelly's great cooking, chicken paprika, and homemade coconut cream pie. Then we retired to the deck to visit other folks who had ridden their horses down the long trail from Moss Springs. A flock of wild honkers appeared to graze the meadow with their nearly grown brood, along with several mule deer. It was a peaceful scene.

The next morning dawned cool, but quickly warmed up. After breakfast we made our lunches, shouldered our day packs, and took off down the now familiar mile-long trail to Red's. After crossing the grassy landing strip meadow, we entered the woods and came upon a wild turkey hen and her half grown youngsters. I was searching for a remembered lost lake, one I hadn't visited for over 30 years. In a roundabout way we found it, hidden in the forest—a real Wilderness lake, where we sat on a long flat rock in the shade of a fragrant Ponderosa, ate our lunches, wrote in our journals, and watched a pair of ospreys feed their young in a high stick nest across the lake.

Earlier, we'd stumbled onto a Forest Service cabin, built in the early days from logs cut on the site. After all that hiking it was back to our refreshing pool with its sandy beach on the Wild Minam River.

That evening Shelly treated us to dutch oven cookery, simmering in her cast iron kettles a mixture of chicken, sausage, potatoes, cabbage and carrots, swimming in a rich gravy and served with hot-from-the oven biscuits. A delicious coolness wafted up from the meadow as soon as the sun sank over the western rim, and we retreated to the deck to visit other guests who frequently appeared, and left, via horseback.

Evidently, we five women were the only ones who hiked in on foot. The rugged Minam is, after all, horse country. Shelly commented that we were only HALF crazy, as we planned on riding horses out!

On Thursday we were up early, first to the lodge for tea and coffee, followed by a hardy breakfast. Planes landing and taking off delivered more folks for breakfast. Many of these interesting folks knew people we did.

After preparing lunches, we struck off down the familiar trail to Red's, then crossed the Minam on that long wooden bridge that leads to the upper Minam River Trail. Lovely morning, lovely trail, but the day warmed rapidly, so at noon we paused to eat our lunches, then backtracked to the lodge, where we got in some writing time and cooled off in the river. We'd originally planned to backpack to the Splash Dam, but due to Jessica's twisted knee, thought it wise not to.

Shelly treated her guests to a delicious Salmon dinner that night. All the meals were great, and so were our appetites, what with all that hiking and swimming. That evening we gathered ourselves under the pines next to the tepees, where Mary, Bobbie and Barb opted to spend their final night, and read to each other. We also packed our gear to hit the trail in the morning.

On Friday after breakfast, Shawn shuttled our packs to the corrals, where he skillfully loaded it all on two mules. Soon, with the aid of a handy rock, we gals mounted our horses and headed up the trail to Moss Springs. My four friends, who hadn't ridden much, were real troopers. After switchbacking our way up the long dusty trail to the Hog's Back, our stirrups were soon brushing against those laden huckleberry bushes we'd nibbled along the trail on our hike in.

About halfway, Shawn pulled the pack string across the Little Minam river and we women splashed behind to a hunting camp area, where we dismounted and stretched our legs. Fortunately for us, a rather long string of horses and riders chose that moment to pass on the trail above us. Shawn expected them, and hoped we wouldn't meet on a steep narrow trail somewhere beyond. In unison, we too, sighed in relief.

Then it was back on our horses to hit the steep, rocky trail to our cars, parked at the Moss Springs trailhead. Arriving around 1:00 p.m, in what was to become an extremely hot day, we were all pretty frazzled and stiff from the long ride, so we drove down the long dusty road to the little village of Cove and cooled our tired bodies in their clean, refreshing pool.

The goodbyes followed; Bobbie and Barb departed to Portland, Jess and Mary to Boise, and me home to Prairie Creek. Thus ended another "Syringa Sisters" saga. This one took a lot of planning and, I must admit, there were times when I had my doubts. After all, we aren't getting any younger, and this trip proved to be one of our most ambitious adventures.

A busy weekend coming up, the annual Stockgrowers meeting followed by a ranch rodeo this year.

On Saturday Doug will be a pallbearer for our dear friend Wilmer Cook, who at the age of 96, was killed in a car wreck in Council, Idaho. Wilmer, along with his family, was visiting his grandchildren at the time of the accident. Wilmer, you will never be forgotten. I think of you when I pick our raspberries, remembering you and your Mary up there on Alder Slope, on your Dairy, Berry and Apiary, working on your "Too Rocky To Hoe" place. So long, old pardner.

Since I'm running short of time, and the deadline nears, I must get this in the "e-mail."

2009 Chief Joseph Days Court: Queen Sarah Butterfield, center, flanked by
her princesses, Serena Hopkins (left) and Meagan McKenzie.

Next time I'll report on Wilmer's Memorial Service, and the Stockgrowers first annual Ranch Rodeo and World Championship Rock Jack
building contest, complete with photos. It was quite the weekend.

Summer wanes, as the days grow shorter, the nights grow colder,
and the garden slows a bit... thank goodness.

August 26—It is very pleasant on this late August afternoon. Not
too hot. Halley is snoozing on the shady porch, the kittens are hidden in
the Holly hocks, and my young Aracuna pullets are leaping for bugs in
the chicken pen. Speaking of pullets... anyone need some? These young
girls are nearly ready to lay now, and eating ravenously. I only needed 10
replacements for my old hens, but the minimum order was 25. I hadn't
really planned on going into the chicken business!

Doug and I got in and made the sauerkraut a couple days ago, and my
seven-day sweet pickles are in their second day. That amazing baking
squash has all but smothered the dwarf apple tree in the garden, and
it's quite startling to see squashes hanging next to apples. Friends and
family have been picking strawberries, and, thankfully, the raspberries
have slowed. I froze those lovely peaches Myrna Moore brought me from
Bear Gulch, and canned the apricots her daughter Jenny let me pick last
week.

Our longtime friend Wilmer Cook's funeral, held at the Enterprise
Baptist Church, proved to be a fitting tribute to an extraordinary man.

Carmen Kohlhepp, of Joseph, rides a mule in the Chief Joseph Days Parade—Carmen is the 2009 Hells Canyon Mule Days grand marshal.

Ashlynn Gray of Enterprise shows off her chicken caught in the chicken scramble at the Wallowa County Fair.

Alex McCadden, Enterprise FFA winner of the all-around FFA Showmanship award at the recent Wallowa County Fair.

A man who lived his life simply and honestly. A man who possessed a strong faith and work ethic. During the late 60s and early 70s, my family lived on Alder Slope, and Wilmer was our neighbor, as well as our rural mail carrier. If he forgot a piece of mail, he'd turn around and bring it back that same day, even if it was just an advertising flyer.

Wilmer served his time in World War II and became a patriotic citizen of Wallowa County, the place where he was born. He loved to read and was extremely well-read. As he grew older, he loved to record music, the good folk tunes, the western singers of a bygone era, who sang from the heart, onto tapes which he gave away to his friends. Also, in his later years, Wilmer fashioned checker boards from local wood. Those too, he gave away, including several he donated for money-raising events.

Wilmer loved camping, and teaching his children and grandchildren how to pan for gold, pick huckleberries and enjoy the simple things in life. In that way, Wilmer was rich. This humble man left an impact on all who knew him, a fact demonstrated by the many folks who attended

Eleven of Janie's great-grandchildren pose beside their winning entry in the Chief Joseph Days Junior Parade: Chad Nash, Janie's grandson, holds his son Gavin. Six-month-old Nevada Dawn Nash is held by her mom Kasey Nash (hidden).

his funeral. Cars filled the church parking lot, and lined up and down Highway 82. A more good-hearted soul never lived. My memories of Wilmer are dear, an image comes to mind of this aging man, his beloved Mary gone, still carrying his old milk bucket to the barn to milk his Jersey cow.

During my final visit with Wilmer, we talked about the old times and how we missed our milk cows, how those hours in the barn were among the happiest of our lives. There, in the old Alder Slope Pioneer Cemetery, Wilmer, just shy of his 97th birthday, was laid to rest beside his Mary. Many tears were shed as this fine man's handsome grandchildren filed past the coffin and laid sprigs of huckleberries on top.

After the military honors, performed by V.F.W. Post 922, the U.S. flag was folded and handed to Wilmer's eldest son, John. I glanced up at Ruby Peak, which was, at that moment, shrouded in cloud, then looked beyond the granite fence posts to this place known as Alder Slope, with its small ranches and fertile fields, peaceful in the welcome morning sunshine that follows rain. This, the place Wilmer so loved, in which he felt at home.

The "Syringa Sisters" minus Janie, who took the photo, alongside the Minam River between Minam Lodge and Red's Horse Ranch. From left, Jessica White, Bobbie Ulrich, Mary Smith, and Barbara Funkhouser.

I remembered an especially vivid rainbow had formed over Prairie Creek the evening of August 9th, the day Wilmer died in Council, Idaho. Looking to the east toward Idaho, I'll always think it was Wilmer's final goodbye to us in Wallowa County.

My own eyes still brimming with tears, I hurried to our local fairgrounds, where the first ever Wallowa County Stockgrowers Ranch Rodeo was already in progress. I missed the stick horse race that great-grandson Cutter from Mt. Vernon had entered, but did make the World Championship Rock Jack Building Contest.

The morning had begun with the annual Wallowa County Stockgrowers meeting and breakfast held at the VFW Hall in Enterprise. After a short business meeting, the Stockgrowers then concentrated on the rodeo, proceeds of which were to be used for scholarships and other Stockgrowers' projects.

This was definitely something new this year. Jeff Parker, president of the Wallowa County Stockgrowers, and 2nd Vice President Todd Nash, Rodeo Chairman, were ably assisted by a crew of hard-working volunteers. All of the events filled, including, in addition to the Rock Jack Building Contest, Team Sorting, Team Branding, Wallowa County working dog event, Team Doctoring, Horse Roping, and an old fashioned

Historic Red's Horse Ranch in the heart of the Minam Wilderness. Now managed by the Forest Service—accessible only by horseback, foot or plane. Visitors are welcome.

horse race.

A running commentary throughout the Rodeo was performed by two of Wallowa County's own old-time ranchers, Mack Birkmaier and Duke Lathrop, who proved to be very entertaining. Duke told a few of his well-worn jokes, like this one:

"Want to find out who loves you the most, your wife or your dog? Well, you lock the dog and wife in the trunk of your car for three hours. When you open the door you'll know by which one is happiest to see you."

The rodeo was well-attended. Not only was the first ever World's Championship Rock Jack Building Contest a huge success, but this unique event instilled in the spectators a new respect for our local fence builders, those unsung heroes of Wallowa County's remote canyons and prairies, where shallow rocky soil discourages digging post holes; hence the need for sturdy rock jack supports to anchor the wooden stays that cover miles of rugged terrain, some so steep and removed from roads, all fence material must be packed in on mules or pack horses.

Bryan Baquet knows. This young man, employed by the Marr Flat

Cattle Company, builds and maintains fences in a vast lonesome area of Wallowa County.

The crowd's sympathies were with Pat Dougherty, however, who, even though he took a half hour to build his rock jack, forged doggedly ahead. Exhibiting patience and persistence, Pat never faltered, despite his bad draw of a stubborn, stringy log. Eric Borgerding of Big Sheep Creek, and Tom Birkmaier of Lower Crow Creek, placed 2nd and 3rd. Both of these fellows have built miles of fence.

Judges were Larry Moore of Bear Gulch and Gene Bieraugel of Courtney Butte.

That evening in Cloverleaf Hall the Championship Rock Jack was auctioned off, and the winning bid of $375 was bid by Jim Probert of Lower Prairie Creek. Casey Tippett, who ranches with his father on Pine Creek, was the artist who fashioned a miniature Rock Jack trophy that was presented to the winner Bryan Baquet.

The remaining rock jacks were auctioned off and the total proceeds of $2,600 were donated to help with medical expenses for Ryan and Jessi Bacon Mattison's baby son on Lost Prairie.

Jeanne Lathrop, a very deserving ranch woman, won the Cattleman of the Year award this year, She received a standing ovation. Jeanne can be seen driving in all seasons to the hills to tend her cattle. Her cattle are in demand due to the care they receive. Jeanne is a Wallowa County native who lives on upper Prairie Creek.

Steve and Trudy Allison, former neighbors of ours here on Prairie Creek, were the recipients of the Honorary Cattleman Award. A traditional Randy Garnett tri-tip meal was served by the Fair Board that evening to an overflow crowd. Cowboy rodeo contestants came as they were, spurs a'jingl'in on dusty boots. Heartening to see young folks attending now.

"Perhaps, having participated in the rodeo, some of these young ranch hands will eventually become members of the Stockgrowers," commented chairman Todd Nash. President Jeff Parker and all the other volunteers deserve kudos for pulling off this first-ever event. Not only did the ranch rodeo raise money, it provided an opportunity to have some good old-fashioned fun, Wallowa County style.

A western dance followed. Several of the old-timers, kicked up their heels, including Mack and Marian Birkmaier, but mostly it was the younger generation.

That same Saturday was our neighbor Gardner Locke's 90th birthday party, held that evening at the Locke Ranch just up the road from us. Too much going on. We missed that one.

Monday our book group met to discuss our August read, Molly Gloss'
Jump Off Creek.

Daughter Jackie and husband Bill from Challis, Idaho, spent that
week visiting. Jackie picked berries and we had a "jam session" in our
kitchen. She also made a trip into the canyons to pick blackberries, so
returned to Challis with a winter's supply of berries.

September 9—Our garden survived the first frost, which happened
yesterday morning, thanks to Doug, who arose in the middle of the night
to turn on the sprinklers.

Yesterday was Doug's birthday, and today is mine. We'd just as soon
cancel birthdays from here on out, however. I mean, what difference
does it make? You can't stop time, but you can enjoy what time is
left. With that in mind, Doug and I took off late Sunday morning in
his camper pickup and drove to the upper Imnaha, where we located
a vacant campsite in the Ollokot Campground. It sure looked different
from the last time I'd been there, which was during the January Sled Dog
Races.

Earlier, we'd pulled into the campground at Lick Creek to eat our
bacon and tomato sandwiches. While there, we noticed several bow
hunter camps, as well as what we supposed were grouse hunters. Driving
down Gumboot, we noted the yellowing of the Thimbleberry bushes and
cottonwoods, accented by bright orange berries hanging heavy on the
Mountain Ash. The woods were colorful too, what with the rust-colored
ninebark and reddening huckleberry bushes. A lovely fall day, with a
nip in the air that precedes the first frost.

We spent the remainder of the day draped in lawn chairs amid a
sunny clearing above the gently flowing waters of the Imnaha. I've been
reading; nearly finished a good book.

Supper was simple: Marr Flat Beef hamburgers, smothered in Walla
Walla Onions, and juicy slices of Imnaha tomatoes. Apple pie for dessert.
After clearing the high eastern ridge, the Harvest moon shone coldly
through dark Ponderosa boughs, however, we slept warmly in our cozy
nest. Well before the sun spilled over that high ridge, we were sipping
coffee and preparing to leave. Breakfast was an hour away, at Halfway.
Nice thing about a camper: you just take off.

Early morning, no traffic, the forest fragrant and fresh. We climbed
the hill past the Hell's Canyon Overlook turnoff, then wound down
North Pine Creek to join the Highway west to Halfway. Driving into
Pine Valley is always pleasant; cattle grazing long green meadows, the
distant "Baker County view" of our own Wallowas, nostalgic weathered

barns, and laden apple and plum trees, scattered wild across the country side.

We took the turnoff to Halfway, a quiet little town not yet awake on a Labor Day Morning, and found the Baker County Fairgrounds, past horse trailers, horses, campers, pickups; past the cemetery, where the old-timers sleep, onto Main Street, where a sign read, "Lion's Club All You Can Eat Huckleberry Pancake Breakfast", with an arrow pointing to the right.

We followed that arrow, our stomachs rumbling in anticipation. Soon we were buttering our huckleberry pancakes, slicing our ham, and salt and peppering our eggs and taters. Yum. Pine Valley is proud of their produce, and you can help yourself to the fresh cantaloupe, honeydew, and watermelon at the melon bar.

Surprise!—we are seated next to readers of Agri-Times! Nice folks. I hug a sweet older woman, who says she enjoys all my columns. Tummies full, we drive the short distance to the fairgrounds, park our camper, and in a relaxed manner take in the 88th Annual Baker County Fair. This year's theme: "Cultivating Good Times, 2009."

While Doug visits an old-timer about the antiques he has on display, I wander into the small Exhibit Building. Nothing fancy, but chock full of what Pine Valley is about, including a photography exhibit that reflects the rural beauty of the area, home-sewn quilts, enormous cabbages, baking squashes, tomatoes, apples, berries, grains, alfalfa hay, apple pies, chocolate cakes, breads, cookies, zinnias, marigolds, sunflowers, dahlias and petunias. Old timers comment on how proud they are of their exhibit building and the amount of entries this year. Blue, red and white ribbons are attached to the exhibits and folks wander around exclaiming, "Aunt Sally got a blue on her pumpkin, and mamma got a red on her apricot jam."

Next door in a huge metal building, the Fat Stock Auction is going strong. That's where the action is. A loud speaker blares, "Selling hogs now...this young man has done a great job on his pig, what'll ya give me? 3.00 dollars, do I hear $3.50?—Sold!" as the lucky buyer anticipates his homegrown bacon, ham and pork chops.

We found a comfortable bench situated in the September sunshine and "people watched" until it was time for the Panhandle Rodeo to begin. Doug and I selected our usual seats, high in the grandstand for the back rest. After a WEE girl, mounted on a BIG horse, sang the Star Spangled Banner, and Queen Megan and Princess Chelsea galloped around the arena, the rodeo action began with Saddle bronc, Ranch Bronc, Bareback riding, calf roping, breakaway roping, steer wrestling, Ribbon roping, and Mutton busting.

Staged between events were three Mule Races. It's always been our tradition to bet on the Mules. Prior to each race, Doug picked the sorrel mule and I chose the gray. Obviously not a "gray day," however. Doug's sorrels took the lead in every race. Oh well. I drowned my sorrows in a fair hamburger, and enjoyed the show anyway.

As the sun sank lower in the West, and our long drive home loomed ahead, we opted to leave before the bull riding, the wild cow milking, and the cowhide race events. Back at Ollokot we pulled into a deserted campground and polished off that apple pie.

It was dusk, and the white-tails were grazing the alfalfa fields on Tenderfoot Valley Road when we pulled into our lane. Halley was glad to see us.

Last week I invited Juana, Marge, and Marge's daughter-in-law Bobbie, as well Doug's sister Barbara out for lunch. We ate outside at the picnic table, as these late summer days are so marvelous. Thanks to our garden and chickens, we feasted on egg salad sandwiches, lettuce, pickled beets, cucumbers and onions in vinegar, assorted pickles, and a fruit and cheese platter prepared by Bobbie. The laying hens cackled, a soft breeze blew over Prairie Creek's pastures, and the sun was warm. It was so pleasant under the willow tree, we lingered all afternoon.

Juana and Marge were the 2008 Grand Marshals of Hell's Canyon Mule Days. It's always a treat to listen to their stories of when they and their late husbands, Joe and Gus, ran large bands of sheep down on Cherry Creek and up in our mountains.

It's always fun to entertain when the weather is favorable. One evening we invited Lyman and his bride Wilma up from the canyons for supper. We sampled some pork spare ribs, which I bar-b-cued with my own sauce, corn on the cob from the garden, pickled beets, potato salad, and strawberry shortcake from those freshly-picked strawberries. Lyman did the dishes, then they had to go 'cause Lyman had to be down at Bear Gulch to pick pears at Moore's before dark.

I spent last week putting food by; canned the sauerkraut, froze corn, put up more pickled beets, canned the seven-day sweet pickles, put up dilled green beans, pulled the onions from the garden to dry, and gathered wind falls to make pies and applesauce.

Yesterday, Jason Cunningham and his pretty wife Emily and their three children drove in to pick up their pullets. A fun time for the youngsters, who delighted, along with Halley, in the catching of the chickens. Such a ruckus. Finally the last pullet was placed squawking in the dog carrier and the door latched. What a nice little family, who join a growing number of young folks raising a fine crop of children in Wallowa County's North End.

Grandson James was here one evening, and I fed him tacos and more of that strawberry shortcake. Those ever-bearing strawberries just keep on ripening. Speaking of James, he called last night after eight o'clock.

"Grandma, what's the quickest way to climb down off Ruby Peak?"

"Well," I replied, "you should climb down the way you came up, that's the safest route," presuming he'd climbed up the ridge from Scotch Creek Saddle. "Where are you?" I asked.

"On top of Ruby Peak." he said. Knowing the waning Harvest Moon was a long way from slipping over the Seven Devils Range in Idaho, I asked how he was going to see.

"We have flashlights, we'll be fine, grandma." And then I was envious. Of course he'd be fine. He's like his grandma. Oh, to be young again.

Doug sold his heifers this week. Halley and I miss them. Halley especially, as she teased them and sat by the hour wishing she could herd them. The oats planted on the hill, and the wheat in the lower fields is ripening. Soon be time to harvest. Doug and Ben finished the last irrigating, and soon the garden will succumb to frost.

Halley and I walk around the old ranch of an evening and are there when the white-tail doe and her fawn come out to nibble the oats. And often we see a pair of young owls come flying out of the ancient willows in the horse pasture.

Last Saturday we joined other friends and family to help neighbors Darrell and Ann Perkins celebrate their 50th wedding anniversary at the Joseph Civic Center. Good to see their children, who grew up with mine.

And now the 2009 Hell's Canyon Mule Days is in progress and I'm due to tell a story at the Max Walker Memorial Cowboy Poetry Gathering tonight at the fairgrounds. Gotta' go.

September 23—The seasonal change we call the Autumnal Equinox happened yesterday. There's definitely a golden quality to the light. Perhaps it's being filtered through the yellowing raspberry leaves, or simply drenched in sunshine. At any rate, these precious "golden days" are being savored and stored, like the preserved jars of plenty that fill my canning cupboard shelves. Such a bountiful harvest. I'm still canning!

Since the garden survived a second frost, and the cucumbers kept on producing, I put up several jars of Mary Marks' recipe for Sliver pickles. Then a box of tomatoes a friend picked for me from her Imnaha garden suddenly became over-ripe, so I water-bathed a batch of tomato sauce.

Of course, every little breeze plops down another shower of windfall apples, so I've dealt with them: apple dumplings, baked apples, apple-sauce cookies, pies, stewed applesauce and apple butter. Is there anything that defines the essence of fall more than a batch of apple butter simmering all night in the crock pot? I don't think so. Of course it's always fun when a grandchild pops into the kitchen when grandma's cooking. Never a more appreciative taster.

Last Sunday Doug and I drove down into the canyons and picked blackberries at the mouth of Big Sheep Creek. Which made us hungry, so we chowed down on chicken strips and french fries at the Imnaha Store and Tavern. Then, after the 30-mile drive home, I got out my potato masher and, you guessed it: seven pints of blackberry jam. Perhaps, as we slather that tasty jam on hot buttered biscuits this winter, we'll recall that September afternoon, crickets singing in dry grasses, the green coolness of Sheep Creek, our stained fingers plucking sun-ripened berries beneath ancient rim rocks that scrape a cloudless and windless blue sky.

Melvilles have harvested the wheat in the lower fields, including Doug's former calving pasture. The oats are higher than my waist, and every morning, and sometimes at dusk, Halley and I—accompanied by the two kittens—follow four-wheeler tracks that lead up and down the hill and along the irrigation ditch.

Often, we surprise white-tail deer nibbling ripe oats, while overhead the skies are filled with goose music. Large V's of wild geese honking their way to and from storage ponds to feed in farmer's fields. Red tail hawks, flickers, ravens, magpies and enormous flocks of blackbirds inhabit Prairie Creek during this season. Second and third cuttings of hay are going up without rain damage, and farmers are frantically busy planting fall grains, harvesting mature crops, baling straw, and trucking hay from the fields.

Our neighbors the Houghs got their second cutting of alfalfa and meadow hay all cut, raked and compacted into their "bread loaf" stackers.

Our giant sunflowers droop under their own weight, and my un-fortunate dwarf apple tree growing in the corner of the garden has all but surrendered to the baking squash. Suspended from its strongest branch, next to a limb-full of red apples, dangles one of those humongous squashes. Others scattered among the carrots and sunflowers are ripening at an equally frightening rate. My petunias are enjoying one last glorious burst of beauty, having survived the second frost.

Mule Days broke all records for attendance and participation. The weather was picture perfect, which helped. However, due to Sondra

Lozier and her Top Hands (husband Kent and son Christopher) plus a willing crew of community volunteers, this 29th Annual Hell's Canyon Mule Days was well organized. The Max Walker Memorial Cowboy Poetry event was so crowded they had to set up chairs in the arena.

Proceeds from this event provide scholarships to deserving young folks in our County. 2009 recipients were Caleb DeBoie, Danielle Walker, and Ayesha Wortman, who each received $1,000 scholarships.

That Friday evening the lineup of poets included 3-and-a-half-year-old Bailey Vernam on her fiddle, Peggy Brennan, Bonnie Shields, The Prairie Creek Girls, Alisha Young, Jim Aasen, Bill Henke, Stan Kvistad, and Agri-Times' own columnists J.R. Groupe and Janie Tippett. Andy Bales was M.C. We performed on the back of a flat bed trailer decorated with straw bales and wagon wheels. It was fun being there with such an appreciative audience.

Saturday morning found Doug and I seated on straw bales in a covered wagon pulled by a team of mules owned by Julie Kooch. Actually, the bales of straw were taken up by other past Mule Days Grand Marshals, Mike Brennan, Juana Malaxa, Marie Onaindia, Dick Hammond, and Gene and Bonnie Westberg, so Doug and I dangled our feet out the back of the creaking iron-wheeled wagon as it made it's way down Main Street as part of a non-motorized parade full of mules, burros, horses, and others, like "Bull Whack'in Kass" leading her pair of yolked-together Brown Swiss oxen.

Along the parade route we were entertained by former Grand Marshal Fred Talbott, who rode behind us on his ornery mule. As if on cue, Fred's big white mule brayed so loudly it nearly drowned out the parade announcer's words. Behind Fred rode another former Grand Marshal, Arnold Schaeffer, and his sister, both well into their senior years. Arnold rode his mule, and his sister a gaited horse. Way to go.

After the parade Doug and I wandered over to where vendors booths were set up on the lawn, and ordered one of those Marr Flat Hamburgers that daughter-in-law Angie and Susan Hobbs were grilling. Seems those beef burgers were pretty popular. The two gals sold an impressive amount of them during that big weekend.

After watching a few arena events, we returned to Prairie Creek and rested up.

I went back that evening for another one of Jim Probert's pit bar-b-cues. While I was waiting in line, here came "Bull Whack'in Kass," who insisted on buying my meal. Doug had opted to stay home.

The mule auction followed. Lively bidding and many good mules and horses sold to a standing room only crowd.

The next day Doug and I took in more arena events, which included wild cow milking, cow hide racing, and more mule races.

Totally oblivious to Mule Days, my 21st great-grandchild decided to make his way into the world. Baby Lochlan Edward Nash was born on his brother Kenon's birthday in Moscow, Idaho. Lochlan will be coming home soon with his family to Wallowa County.

On September 14th grandson James called.

"How can I find the trail to Thorpe Creek Basin, grandma? Cory and I are going to climb Sacagawea, then scramble over to the Matterhorn and down to Ice Lake, then take that trail to the West Fork of the Wallowa River and end up at Wallowa Lake."

"Wow," says I, the grandma, who years ago, climbed Sacagawea with my good friend Linde, when she and husband Pat, and Doug and I, were camped in Thorpe Creek Basin. "All in one day, huh?" I asked.

"Yep" replied my mountain-climbing grandson, who has been running up mountains to keep in shape for the Marines. I told him how to locate the trail, and offered my suggestions as to the safest approach to Sacagawea.

"Thanks grandma," said James, and hung up.

At 2:30 I got another call. "Hi grandma."

"Where are you?" I asked.

"Top of the Matterhorn," replied my 23-year-old grandson. "Everything's awesome from up here." And I could envision just what he was talking about.

"Want to come for supper?" I asked.

"You bet." replied James. "See you this evening."

So, this grandma got busy, simmering tomatoes into a pasta sauce full of eggplant, mushrooms and pesto, mixing a huge kettle of meat balls, then baking a cherry pie from some of those pitted cherries I'd frozen this spring. The pasta was cooking when Cory and James arrived, along with Holly, Cory's girlfriend, who'd dropped the guys off at the trailhead that morning and picked them up at Wallowa Lake.

Nineteen mountain miles in seven-and-a-half hours. Watching those young fellows eat was worth the effort of preparation. Another reward was listening to the telling of their great adventure. Oh, to be young again.

Made me homesick for the mountains, so Chris and I are planning on heading up to Aneroid Lake for one final pack-in before the snow flies. Grandson Buck is loaning me his little mule he named "Slowly", the one great-granddaughter Lucy calls "Lowly." My mare Morning Star's

Serenade Garbett and Shayla Garland, Enterprise, brought their little burros to town for the Mule Days Parade.

second bout of founder has left her too stiff to stand the six mile steep trail. Wish us luck, and enjoy the fall.

October 5—Well, the snow DID fly before Chris and I could hit the trail to Aneroid Lake. As I write, in spite of a goodly amount of melting, at least four inches remains here on Prairie Creek. Our Wallowas are whitened with several feet of early snow. Just as well, 'cause I got a phone call Thursday night.

"This is Wes Gorbett. I work for the Eagle Cap Pack Station. I was setting up a hunting camp at Frazier Lake today, and your son and grandson were camped there. They asked about a weather report, and I told them it was supposed to snow heavily on Saturday, and turn very cold. They helped me set up camp, and after I left, James came running down the trail and asked if I would call you and Doug. They've decided to come out two days earlier than planned. Wondered if you could be at Indian Crossing tomorrow?"

A very relieved mom and grandma hung up the phone. We, of course, were very much aware of the predicted cold front moving in, with heavy amounts of snow in the forecast. We knew father and son had already experienced some cold and early snow high in the wilds of the Eagle Cap Wilderness. We knew this because James had "texted" his sister Becky from the top of Carper Pass.

"Snowing here, very cold, do you have a weather report?" Becky received his message, but in spite of James holding the phone high into the air, he was unable to receive Becky's reply. So they'd continued on in hopes the weather would improve.

On Friday the 25th of September, Doug and I had arisen before daylight to drive the long way to Cove, then up the winding gravel road to Moss Springs Campground with son Todd and grandson James. We saw them off at the trailhead. Todd was riding his horse and leading two pack horses, while James was afoot.

"See you at Indian Crossing in nine days," they said, and disappeared down the steep dusty trail to Red's Horse Ranch on the Minam River. The weather was perfect, the days warm and the nights cool. No appreciable rain had fallen during the entire month of September.

Doug and I drove to Island City and ordered breakfast before returning to Prairie Creek, pulling Todd's stock trailer. All the way home I thought about my son and grandson, and mentally traced their route: Red's Horse Ranch, North Minam Meadows, Green Lake, Copper Creek trail, Minam Lake, Carper Pass, Frazier Lake, over Hawkins Pass down the South Fork of the Imnaha, under Cusick Mountain, following the Imnaha past the turnoffs to Bonner Flat, the North Fork and Middle Fork, past the Blue Hole, and finally, Indian Crossing.

James and Todd would be traveling through some of the most rugged and beautiful country in the Northwest. A trip of a lifetime.

That next morning, after Wes's phone call, this grandma busied herself around the kitchen, stuffing a picnic basket with egg salad and roast beef sandwiches, jars of home-canned dill pickles, peaches, apple cider, fresh tomatoes, and rice crispy marshmallow treats.

After his cribbage game with "the boys" at Ye Olde Range Rider, Doug stopped by the Cloud 9 Bakery and picked up four fresh apple fritters. After filling two thermos bottles with hot coffee, we headed up Sheep Creek Hill and took the Loop road to Indian Crossing. It was a lovely drive.

A killing frost that morning had finished off our garden. Luckily, I'd picked those huge baking squashes, the crookneck, zucchini, tomatoes, peppers and green beans. Also the remaining sweet corn, which I froze for winter meals.

It was 11:30 by the time we arrived at Indian Crossing trailhead with the stock trailer. With no knowledge of whether the pair had broken camp at Frazier Lake and headed up and over Hawkins Pass yesterday, or this morning, we could only guess at their time of arrival.

Noon came and went. We ate our lunches, napped in the autumn sunshine, and watched deer hunters set up camp in a nearby campground. The afternoon passing, I made various forays up and down the trail, hoping to see the guys. No sign. I crossed the bridge that spans the Imnaha and searched for, and found, a faint trail that led to Duck Lake.

Late in the afternoon, I hiked toward the Blue Hole and, on my return, took a stick and wrote in the dusty trail: MOM AND GRANDMA with an arrow pointing toward the trailhead. The sun sank behind a high rim and the light faded. No sound of hooves pounding a dusty trail.

Cold descended along the river, the hunters started a campfire, and then, a movement at the trailhead: James! Followed by Todd, riding his horse and leading the two tired pack horses. Eighty-six miles throughout the Wallowas. Their grins said it all as they thanked us profusely for being there.

After unpacking and loading up the horses, they climbed in the pickup and opened that picnic basket. Let me tell you, it didn't take long for that food to disappear. James said he'd dreamed of apple fritters hiking down Hawkins Pass.

On the way home they relived their adventures; the bear by the waterfall, racing down the trail to catch their runaway horses, waking that morning to see Frazier Lake covered with a skim of ice, snow falling on them at Carper Pass, the long cold night at Minam Lake, the awesome beauty from Hawkins Pass and the dramatic change from Alpine lakes to the Imnaha drainage.

Each new experience added to their knowledge and respect for the high country, how suddenly the weather conditions can change and how unforgiving that outrageous beauty can be. They were grateful for the wall tent they'd borrowed from Doug, and a camp stove a friend had loaned them.

Cold rain spit on the windshield as we drove down Salt Creek Summit, and by the time we reached home, snow whirled in the air.

That next morning Prairie Creek was buried under several inches, Leafy limbs all over the upper valley began to sag and break under their burden. The mountains were cloaked with snow clouds.

The next evening our electricity was out. Suddenly, like the weather, due to fallen tree limbs on power lines.

I lit a candle. Our world, reduced to a puddle of glimmering light, was so quiet. No refrigerator hum, only the pop and crackle of the wood burning in the old Monarch stove. Doug went to bed while I lingered at the kitchen table writing in my journal.

That Thursday, before we saw James and Todd off at Moss Springs, Doug had picked the last crop of strawberries, which I'd turned into one of those famous strawberry cream pies. The word leaked out before James and Todd stopped by to ask if we could shuttle them from trailhead to trailhead. Doug and I DID need help eating that pie.

Looking back on that experience is like looking back on summer. The last of the garden, the last warm days, the last colorful flowers. My strawberry pie was a celebration of the seasonal shift. I'd also picked the first crop of prune plums off my little tree in the chicken pen, and turned them into a tangy bar-b-cue sauce.

On September 26th, daughter Ramona hosted a baby shower for granddaughter Lacey, who is presenting us with our 22nd great-grandchild somewhere around Thanksgiving. It was one of those last lovely sunny days, so the affair was held outside on the ranch lawn. We feasted on Ramona's fried chicken and potato salad, as well as additional salads and beans provided by the guests. Granddaughter Chelsie contributed a decorated chocolate cake. Lacy received many useful gifts and a good time was had by all.

Grandson Ryan rode his motorcycle over from Pendleton to visit his Grandpa Doug. Daughter Lori, who lives in Richland, Washington, spent that night with us. The next morning Doug treated Lori and me to breakfast at the Mountainaire Cafe in Joseph.

The weather changed again, and a wild wind raged over the country. Grain dust rose in huge clouds over Melville's harvester as they roared up and down the oat fields. Dust, however, was not all that billowed up. Over Sheep Ridge appeared another cloud... smoke billowing high into the sky, moving north, out of the Eagle Cap Wilderness, where the fire had began on August 29th after a lightning strike. Fanned now by the south wind, the fire quickly consumed 2,000 acres and continued to burn until the recent snow storm slowed it to a smoldering burn.

Doug and I made another trip to Imnaha to pick prune plums at Jenny Moore's. A lovely drive, with the Sumac reddening now, and the cottonwoods along Little Sheep Creek beginning to turn. Of course we ate lunch at the Imnaha Store and Tavern. Good to see Sally and Dave, and learn Dave is through with his treatments.

Lots of tourists down there, wanting directions... to anywhere, from what they perceived as complete isolation.

Home to can those luscious plums. That night, a chorus of coyotes kicked up a great ruckus close to the house. Halley barked at something down by the calving shed. The next morning mamma kitty's newly-born litter was gone, "Gobbled up by the coyotes", Halley's eyes told me.

Dug some carrots and potatoes from the snowy garden, browned some beef, added garlic, onions and broth, and placed the lid on the dutch oven. Stew. Cold weather fare.

October 7—A pair of Rufus-sided towhees are scratching around under the frozen raspberry leaves, and a covey of Hungarian Partridge has taken up residence near the chicken pen. I found another buyer for my pullets, and am happy with the eight I have left.

Flocks of Red-Winged Blackbirds feast on the leftover corn in the garden, fattening up for their migration southward. Halley and I, accompanied by the two nearly-grown kittens, traipse through the stubblefield each day. The white-tails are wary now. It's Buck deer season.

Last week Grandson Buck was working nearby, conducting a weed survey along Prairie Creek's irrigation ditches, when I called him. Since it was nearly noon, I invited he and Heath for a lunch of hot roast beef sandwiches, mashed potatoes and gravy, a pan of squash, and zucchini chocolate cake. One of life's simple pleasures, as we grow older, is to cook for a grandson.

Called Lyman and Wilma the other evening, and son Craig answered. He was there for Buck deer season, as well as working on the winter wood supply. Yep, they'd gotten their bucks.

"Eat'in liver and onions for supper," he said. Yum. 'Tis the season.

October 17—I baked a squash pie, and Doug and I drove to Upper Prairie Creek to Chuck and Chris Frazier's place to attend the annual "Apple Squeez'in party." It was a wild and windy Saturday, but that didn't keep folks away. Gallons of apple juice was cranked out of those wooden presses, and that traditional mouth-watering food was prepared, including a whole hog roasting inside a handmade metal bar-b-cue.

Lyle presided over his sizzling chicken halves, broasting them over coals and squirting them with a mixture of apple cider and vinegar, among other secret ingredients. The oyster man was there, prying them open, handing you an oyster on the half shell. I added my squash pie to the long tables of desserts, salads, beans and breads. The children romped on top of, and around, a straw bale maze, while the fragrant apple pulp pile grew taller and taller.

I leave for the Imnaha Writer's Retreat tomorrow.

James and Todd Nash's camp at Frazier Lake.

A smiling James and his dad, Todd Nash, arrive safely at the trailhead at Indian Crossing on the upper Imnaha.

*Aspen Birkmaier, granddaughter of Mack and Marian Birkmaier of Crow
Creek, wears her prairie dress in the Mule Days parade.*

October 20—As in Octobers past, here I am again, seated in front
of my laptop, pausing mid-sentence to watch a flurry of colorful maple
leaves drift by my window. Looking down at the far end of the lawn,
past the row of grapes, I notice the old apple tree's leafy branches nearly
conceal what we refer to as the "tree house." Above and beyond rises
Indian Creek canyon, with its tiered basalt formations, its wild rose
bushes dotted with bright orange hips, its scattered stands of Ponderosas,
and its highest rims catching the first rays of the morning sun.

Often the noisy conversations I hear turn out to be our resident
flock of wild turkeys, who periodically wander down the canyon to
scratch around and peck the numerous wind fall apples. Warm autumnal
sunlight has been scarce since the five of us arrived here Sunday on the
upper Imnaha for the Fall Fishtrap Writer's Retreat.

On those rare occasions when the sun does shine, it always takes
awhile for it to creep down those steep tawny slopes to warm us here at
river-level. As usual, the view from my room provides both inspiration
and distraction. Writing now, my eye catches a movement—Vicky Marks,
horseback, chasing a few head of cattle that have strayed down the draw.
Typical of women ranchers here in the canyons, Vicky wears many hats.
She drives the Imnaha school bus and tends the cattle, in addition to her
role as mother and homemaker.

I watch her now as she tops out on a high rocky bench above us. Skylined, a young woman on a horse, I envy her. I also envy Julianna, who is making her way up a game trail below Vicky. Unlike past retreats, when hiking was an important part of my daily routine, this time I'm staying close to the cabin, avoiding strenuous activity, for fear of relapsing into the nasty cold I had prior to arriving.

Since the weather has been more conducive to staying indoors, I haven't been all that tempted. I love watching trails of moist mists wrap themselves around rim rocks from my warm cozy room. Rain drumming on the roof is a comforting sound, and my window to the world reveals the ever-falling display of leaves and three Mule deer does, who silently appear all floppy-eared, nibbling apples before melting back into the wet thornbrush thickets.

My ears are tuned to the muted sounds of Kingfisher and Water Ouzel flying low over the river, or the Lewis Woodpecker *rat-a-tat-tat*-ing in the plum tree, and, of course, the song of the river itself.

Naturally, cooking is an important part of our Retreat experience, and we all love to sample each others culinary efforts. When it was my turn in the kitchen, beef stew was my choice. I began by baking a loaf of sourdough bread in my dutch oven, then used the same cast iron utensil to cook the stew. Our garden carrots, shallots, garlic and potatoes simmering in a thick, meaty gravy. After chopping some of our last garden cabbage for coleslaw, I gathered enough of those windfalls to bake an apple crisp. Nuthin's as lovin' as country cookin'.

Thanks to young Clancy Warnock, who lives downriver, we are keeping warm. Clancy delivered us a cord of seasoned tamarack, all split. Craig and Deb have carted it all across the bridge and stacked it in the wood shed already. Since this large log home is heated with a wood furnace, it requires a good supply of fuel.

Each night I check in with Doug. I'd left a pot of beans and ham hocks cooked for him, as knew he'd bake his own sourdough biscuits. One evening he reported that he'd caught two steelhead in the lower Imnaha.

"Keepers," he told me. Can't wait to sample some of that fresh fish.

At this time of year the Imnaha runs low and sluggish, occasional riffles catch the light, and rusted red and yellow leaves swirl in its eddies, its song is muted now. Late afternoon's great cottony clouds boil up over the highest rims before dissolving in that narrow void of canyon sky.

Dappled shade and sunlight defines windfall apples on green grass, where deer step lightly, nibbling as they go. When I tire of writing, I stride with a purpose into the orchard, armed with a long mop, to dislodge the last purple plums, carry them to the kitchen, and bake a Plum Kuchen.

In early afternoon, with a warm rain drumming on the tin roof of our log abode, that yeasty fruity aroma wafts through the house. The Kuchen is fragrant with fall.

October 23—Raining; steady rain. I watch as smoke curls upward through the leafy old apple tree. Mariah, our poet, is back from her daily run up Freezeout Creek, and has kindled a fire in her little wood stove.

October 28—Life resumes "on top." The Saturday I returned to Prairie Creek, Doug and I attended the 80th Birthday Party for old time local cowboy Dick Hammond, which was held in the Hurricane Creek Grange Hall. Folks came from miles around to honor Dick, who was born on Grouse Flats, way out in Wallowa County's North End.

Sunday morning found Doug and I seated at a long table in the Cheyenne Cafe in Joseph, where we were joined by other Tippetts, some of whom had traveled over from Clarkston, Washington, to attend Dick Hammond's birthday bash.

This morning I was in my kitchen early, flipping sourdough huckleberry pancakes, frying sausage and eggs, and putting together lunches for Doug and grandson Buck, who are, as I write, out in the hills hoping to fill their Land Owners Preference cow elk tags. Its bitterly cold, with a skiff of snow on the ground.

High today is supposed to be 34. What happened to Indian Summer?

October 29—I entered my chicken house on this raw cold morning and was surprised to hear a motherly clucking sound. Since I hadn't noticed a setting hen anywhere, I was puzzled. Then I heard frantic cheeping. Could this be? At the end of October? The sound persisted...but no chicks.

The peeping seemed to be coming from the roost area, but I searched in there. Nothing.

Then I heard the sound again, coming from above. Could it be? Yep. That little hen had used the same feeder, hanging from a nail on the wall, that the starling used this spring to hatch out her brood of baby birds!

Little Henny Penny, who had followed me, was calling her kids down. Only they couldn't follow. The newly-hatched chicks were trapped inside the round metal feeder. I reached up and lifted the feeder down, and there they were. Two tiny black chicks were especially vocal. I laid the feeder on its side and lectured Henny Penny.

"Don't you know enough not to make babies with a Wallowa County winter coming on?" And I left the family to their own fate. I had a 10:00 a.m. meeting in town.

When I returned, there wasn't a sign of a chick. Nary a feather. Several unhatched eggs were obviously rotten. Just as well. I hadn't relished the idea of bringing mother and babies into the house.

October 30—Phyllis helped me serve for Cowbelles at the Community Dining Center in Enterprise. Richard and Mary Frasch provided the delicious ham entree. This very generous family has donated unselfishly in many ways to our community, which is most appreciated.

Doug, who'd gone fishing that day, returned with two large Steelhead he'd caught in the Imnaha River.

October 31—On the morning of Halloween I got in and baked a huge batch of old-fashioned molasses cookies for our little ghosts and goblins. This evening Grandson Buck and wife Chelsea, all decked out in costumes, along with Katelyn and Lucy, appeared at our door for trick or treat.

Later in the evening, just as we were preparing for bed, here came Riley Ann, Ashlynn, Gideon and Jada: three little pigs and the big bad wolf. Mom and dad—our other Chelsie and hubby Justin—really got into the costume thing. We hardly recognized them.

It was the end of the line, and the wolf, weary of being bad, was yawning. The cookies and poppa Doug's spooky candy proved very popular with the kiddies as well as the parents.

November 2—Phyllis and I drove to the Hurricane Creek trailhead. Since the sun was shining, we left our gloves in the car and carried our lunches up the trail. It was crisp and cool, mostly clear, and soon we were stepping across a log that spanned Falls Creek, which was barely running. As usual, the views of Sacagawea and the multi-hued rock formations of the Hurricane Divide were awesome, and we were quickly in real wilderness. How lucky we are to be minutes from such surroundings.

We came to an open meadow above the creek and seated ourselves on a log...and that's when the weather changed. So fast. Clouds scuttled across the sun, a freezing wind came sweeping down the canyon, and our hands turned to ice. Ever try eating a sandwich with frozen fingers? We'll never do that again.

Hurriedly we gobbled our lunches and, stuffing our hands into our pockets, we made haste down the trail to the warmth of our car. Racing down that trail I remembered back 58 years ago, when I was matron of honor, for my childhood chum Sandra as she married her Fred, there in the foothills where we both grew up. Happy 58th, you two!

November 4—The Indian Summer we missed in October caught up with us today, so Phyllis and I decided to hike the east moraine of Wallowa Lake. Following an old logging road, we wound through Ponderosa Pine and Douglas Fir, these evergreens contrasting sharply with brilliant golden Tamarack. At the top we looked directly across the lake to the blinding snowfields of Chief Joseph Mountain.

Since it was past noon, we hunted up a flat granite boulder, sat down to enjoy the view, and ate our lunches. It must have been 65 degrees, and the sun felt warm on our bare arms. Then we heard an odd honking, and were thrilled to watch a flock of Tundra Swans land on the lake. This time of year the lake provides a stopover for hundreds of migrating waterfowl, and it was covered with wild geese and ducks. From far down near the head of the lake we heard the haunting call of a loon.

How incredibly lucky we were to be in that special place and time.

November 5—The day dawned cloudy and cold, and the Wallowas were hidden in snowy mists.

One morning last week I delivered two loaves of sourdough french bread, fresh from my oven, to Mary and Joe Stangel, who won the winning bid during the recent 4-H Radio Auction broadcast on our local KWVR station.

And now it's late afternoon. Been snowing for two hours. Halley didn't get her daily walk, but this column is finished.

November 11—On this Veteran's Day our thoughts are with all the young people serving in the armed forces. Along with many others from Wallowa County, we pray for our own boys, Grandson Josh, a Navy helicopter gunner in the U.S. Navy, who is en route to serve in Afghanistan, and grandson SSgt Shawn Phillips, U.S. Marines, recently sent to Okinawa, with possible deployment to Afghanistan. Another grandson, James, will be leaving after the first of the year for the Marines.

The day is dull and gray, unlike yesterday, which was full of soft autumn sunshine. It's pretty quiet here on Prairie Creek. Farmers have done all they can do to their fields now, putting everything to sleep for winter. Most of the ranchers have weaned their calves, which means the bawling has ceased.

Early of a morning, the white-tails nibble the oat stubble, then cross the road to Locke's hill, Hungarian Partridge scratch around under the raspberry canes and Magpies break the silence with their squawking whenever Halley discovers them pecking at her elk bones.

"These are mine!" she says.

Our mountains are cloaked in heavy clouds, and the smell of snow is in the air. I saw four cock pheasants in the barley stubble yesterday morning, and Frasch's weaned Angus calves are fattening up on leftover grain in the fields. Recent wild winds have stripped the Willows and Cottonwoods of their leaves, and Prairie Creek is devoid of color.

Doug was able to fill his Land Owners Preference (LOP) elk tag, and yesterday he finished boning, cutting, wrapping and freezing the meat. We had a good feed of backstrap the other night for supper. Served with sourdough biscuits and milk gravy, this is one of our favorite cold weather meals.

Last evening I hacked one of those prolific squashes open, and baked several chunks with brown sugar and butter. Especially sweet this year.

November 12—Attended the history program put on by the Friends of the Wallowa County Museum and others, held at the Hurricane Creek Grange Hall. The early years of Alder Slope came alive through the stories told by several natives to the area. The historic Grange Hall was full to overflowing with both old- and young-timers, come from afar to learn more about some of the first Alder Slope inhabitants who lived in those simpler times before cell phones, internet, and fancy cars.

After the program, guests were treated to cookies, baked by the Grange ladies, and coffee.

November 13—12 degrees on Friday the 13th. A writer friend, who has been staying in Joseph all month, drove out for a visit. We bundled up and took our dogs for a walk down Tenderfoot Valley Road. The mountains were stunning under a clear, cold sky, and the golden oat stubblefield on the hill provided a pleasing contrast. I'd baked a loaf of sourdough bread that morning, and when Melissa and I returned to my warm kitchen, we got in and made potato soup. A pleasant way to spend a cold November morning.

This has been a good month to read. I've finished six books so far.

November 14—It snowed all morning, and the thermometer registered 26 degrees. I cleaned kitchen cupboards.

November 15—15 degrees. This evening Phyllis and I drove down to the old Presbyterian Church in Lostine and took in the Christmas musical "Amahl and the Night Visitors," performed under the direction of Claudia Boswell, Iva Lindsey and Randy Morgan. This was the first opera commissioned especially for television. It premiered on December 24, 1951 in New York City. The 100+ year old Presbyterian church wasn't New York, but it sure got us in the Christmas Spirit before Thanksgiving. And our local talent is amazing.

November 16—Salmon-colored sunrise over Locke's hill. Met this morning with our book group to discuss Ivan Doig's *Prairie Nocturne*.

November 17—A ferocious wind storm knocked all power out in Joseph for the entire day. A Chinook wind that swept snow from the fields and filled the barrow pits with drifts. Every Tuesday our Writer's Group meets at Ruth's home high on a hill above Enterprise. Where we share our writing, write some more, then have lunch After which we play scrabble late into the afternoon, thus blanking out those terrible winds that howl without.

November 18—This morning three coyotes ran down off the hill and nearly collided with Halley and me.

An inch of new snow turned Prairie Creek white again. Doug climbed a ladder and screwed down a flapping piece of tin on the old chicken house roof. Made me nervous to watch, but he got the job done. Good thing, too, as the wind returned.

November 21—Phyllis and I drove to the Providence Academy in Lostine to take in a wonderful performance by the Inland Northwest Musicians, with R. Lee Friese conducting, and our own Randy Morgan as associate conductor. Many of the musicians were local folks, familiar faces. Perhaps the venue, there in the old Lostine School gym, wasn't as elegant as a city theatre, but the music was superb.

And, now, as our world returns to winter white, my thoughts turn to Christmas, and a hot turkey sandwich.

November 24—Our 22nd great-grandchild was born today, a girl. Seely Jo Hemphill, born to granddaughter Lacey and husband Colin, who live near Pilot Rock. Welcome to our family, Seely Jo.

As I write, a scatter of sparrows have flocked to our bird feeder and Halley wants me to come out and play. The cats are curled up on a rug in the woodshed, and Buck and Chelsea's three horses are grazing the dried grasses around the hay shed. This month is nearly gone.

November 27—In stark contrast to yesterday, when sunlight streamed through the kitchen window as I peeled potatoes for our Thanksgiving feast, this morning seems dull and gray. Earlier, a light breeze blew in a bone-chilling fog, and now it's snowing. My world has shrunk to just beyond the garden fence. There are no mountains to be seen.

Yesterday, the homey aroma of roasting turkey filled our house. I was in the kitchen early, to chop celery and onions and brown them in butter before adding the mixture to the bread cubes prepared the night before. I then rubbed some dried sage over the dressing, sprinkled it with salt and pepper, and added just enough hot broth to make it moist. To hold it all together, I broke a couple of eggs over the top, mixing them in with my hands, before stuffing our 20 lb. turkey—just like my grandma Wilson used to do. No packaged dressing mix for me.

When I'm cooking Thanksgiving dinner, I always think of grandma bustling about the kitchen, wearing an apron over her dress, her work-worn hands peeling potatoes, stirring gravy; she always taking time to listen to her herd of grandchildren, making us feel loved. After simmering the giblets, she'd grind them using one of those old hand grinders women used in their kitchens.

Later she would add the ground giblets to the rich pan drippings to make gravy. I'd made the cranberry sauce the day before, cooking the whole berries 'til they burst their skins. I'd also baked the traditional pies, made from those squashes that ran wild in our garden, and mincemeat pie made with home canned mincemeat that contained elk neck, apples, cider, raisins, vinegar and spices. Then there were the yams, baked in a mixture of dark brown sugar and butter.

Family began to arrive in early afternoon. I had lots of help: son Ken to mash potatoes, Doug to carve the turkey, Angie contributing fruit punch, Sandy a tossed salad. James entertained us with his Montana hunting stories. My small kitchen hummed with talk and activity. Soon the steaming turkey was lifted from the oven, the fragrant dressing scooped out, the gravy stirred, turkey sliced, potatoes mashed. We circled the table, holding hands while Ken led the Thanksgiving blessing, not only for us but for those who couldn't be with us. Then we fell to eating a meal that had taken two days to prepare.

Always worth the effort, and the love that went into it's preparation was gratefully received. Angie and Becky did the dishes while I tended to leftovers. We were only twelve this year, as many members of our large family were out of town visiting extended families.

December 9—Very cold evening. I drove up the hill above Enterprise to the Latter Day Saints Church and attended "The Night of the Nativity," an annual celebration open to the public. Words fail when it comes to describing this musical program.

Gail Swart played a hauntingly beautiful Christmas medley on the piano. Then there was the Wallowa Children's Choir, the Rose family and Helene Hipple and Marilyn Soares, performing a marvelous rendition of "Christ Child, Christ Child." Amy Nash played her harp and sang "We Three Kings," and Janis Carper sang "O Holy Night." Austin, Heather, and Rebecca Lenahan closed the performance with a string trio that was as professional as it gets.

After, we all joined in singing "Silent Night" before nibbling cookies, visiting friends, and stepping out into the frigid night. Of course this great-grandma was proud of four of her great-grandchildren singing together with the primary group.

December 10—Below zero, but that didn't stop us from having a Museum Board meeting this afternoon. Then it was home to bake cookies for various Christmas functions.

December 11—Below zero again and Doug returned early.

"Water pipes froze at the Cheyenne Cafe," he said.

Bundled up to walk around the old ranch with Halley, then worked on the Christmas cards. Elk steak, mashed potatoes and milk gravy for supper. Curled up with *Two in the Far North* by Margaret Murie, a wonderful book sent to me from Portland by Agri-Times fan Leslie Labbe, who also owns a ranch in Troy.

December 12—It was snowing when I got up to feed the fire in the wood cook stove.

Delivered cookies this morning to Anne and Jim Shelly, who own Fire Works Pottery up Hurricane Creek, for their annual sale and potluck.

This evening I drove to Lear's Restaurant in Enterprise to attend Tunesmith Night. My friend Julianna Waters and her husband Barry performed original songs they'd written. Julianna, who spent a Spring and Fall week with me at the Writers Retreat, sang a song she'd written for me. Julianna has a lovely voice, and she and Barry's CDs are very popular.

Today our 23rd great-grandchild was born. Baby Jacob wasn't due until March. Born prematurely, due to a life-threatening condition for mamma Maria, Jacob weighed a mere two pounds. Jacob's daddy, grandson Shawn, a Marine, is stationed with his family on the tiny far-off island of Okinawa, Japan. Our prayers have been winging their way across the oceans to Shawn's family.

December 13—The snow that fell today didn't amount to much, already melting when Doug and I drove to the ranch where Buck and

Chelsea live. It was great-granddaughter Lucy's 3rd birthday. Quite a celebration. Mommy baked Lucy a "Horse Head" cake, and served us chili, rolls, and eggnog.

The entryway to their modest home was heaped with snow boots. Fun watching Lucy's little friends all growing up together, just like their parents did.

Doug purchased a tree from the Joseph FFA this morning, and this afternoon I finished decorating it.

December 14—I baked cupcakes with cream cheese filling, took a walk around the ranch with Halley, and cleaned house. It was snowing in the mountains when our Writer's Group arrived for our weekly session. After writing and reading our work, we sat down to homemade clam chowder and a loaf of warm sourdough bread I'd baked that morning, then played scrabble into the afternoon.

December 16—Grandson James came over for lunch and we visited. James will leave for the Marines early in January. He told me about the snowshoe hike he took up the steep Murray Gap trail last week, and how he's been chopping ice so the cattle can drink. We were both pleased to see his poem published in the Eastern Oregon Anthology, *A Sense of Place.*

This afternoon I drove to the Enterprise Elementary School and spotted four great-grandchildren as they sang in the school's annual Christmas concert. I think every relative to every child was there. I had to park two blocks away. Gail Swart accompanied them at the piano.

"I'm in my element." she commented. For years Gail has been responsible for instilling music in the hearts of our local young people.

Later, while shopping at Safeway, I noticed grandson Chad helping construct the live Nativity Scene in the vacant lot across the street.

December 17—A box of the sweetest tangerines arrived from Roseville, California. Freshly-picked by sister Kathryn, from her back yard tree. Yum!

December 18—Freezing fog this morning. While walking along the creek, I heard scratching sounds on the ice, and peering through the fog I was startled to see Halley and a large muskrat engaged in a boxing match. It was hilarious. The muskrat would attack my border collie, who would, in the nick of time, leap up over the rat. Finally, the muskrat escaped into a lead of open water and disappeared under the ice.

Doug and I joined the "old folks" at the Community Dining Center and partook of a turkey dinner, compliments of Richard and Mary

Frasch. This annual Christmas dinner was well attended, and deliciously prepared by the staff.

December 19—With Christmas less than a week away, the freezing morning fog has retreated this afternoon, our icy roads have thawed, the sparrows have eaten their fill at the bird feeder, the hardened snowdrifts have softened, Hough's cattle are licking up the last of their hay, and temperatures have warmed considerably. I've just given Doug a haircut— yes, bald men need haircuts too. And although it's still gloomy outside, our Christmas tree, stockings hung by the fireplace, and nativity scene create their own warmth inside.

December 20—Didn't participate in the annual Christmas Bird Count this morning. Too foggy and icy. However, while walking with Halley around the old ranch, I conducted my own bird count—35 sparrows, 10 starlings, 1 Northern (Red Shafted) Flicker, a flock of pigeons, a Great Horned Owl, several LBBs (Little Brown Birds) singing in the Cotton- woods, and 1 Red tail hawk.

By the time you read this, Christmas and New Years will have come and gone.

At this writing Baby Jacob is holding his own, and Grandma Ramona flies out of San Francisco on Christmas Eve, to join her son's family in faraway Okinawa and be with them during this difficult time. Daugh- ter Jackie and husband Bill, and granddaughter Mona Lee, will arrive Monday. Our young Texas chef, Adele, is flying in from Austin.

December 21—On this, the day of the Winter Solstice, a warm south wind has melted all but the hardened drifts.

Our book group met this morning to discuss our most recent read and exchange cookies. Then it was home to bake German Christmas breads for friends.

December 22—Icy roads today. Cooked up two of those large steel- head Doug caught in the Imnaha for our Idaho family, who arrived last night.

This morning son Todd had trailered saddled horses, along with son-in-law Bill, and grandson Buck, out to the Divide, and left them off near Coyote. They were to hunt for cows and push what they found to Big Sheep. Todd would pick them up that evening.

By the time the cold and hungry cowboys finally arrived for dinner, they were mighty glad for that hot meal. They'd found 20 head of cows and driven them 15 miles through steep, icy canyons.

December 23—The temperature had dropped to 15 degrees when I drove to Enterprise to pick up the prime rib I'd ordered for Christmas dinner.

December 24—Christmas Eve. Daughter Ramona flies to Honolulu today. I baked two loaves of sourdough bread and made pies. Huckleberry cream and mincemeat. Then I built a couple of pizzas and tossed a salad, then we were off to the Joseph United Methodist Church for their Candlelight Service, which has become a tradition. Shivering our way from the car to the warmth of the old stone church, we joined a packed house to sing and celebrate the real meaning of Christmas.

After, wreathed in our own frigid breath, we made our way back to our cars. Over Prairie Creek myriad stars glittered diamond-bright in a cold clear sky.

December 25—Christmas morning dawned clear, 15 degrees and sunny. I filled everyone up with sourdough huckleberry pancakes and waffles before concentrating on the meal for late that afternoon. Grandson James, who had driven to Spokane to meet his sister Adele's plane and drive her home on Christmas Day, had come down with a throat infection and had to be taken to Walla Walla this morning. He was understandably absent at our dinner.

In spite of missing various family members, we enjoyed our traditional prime rib. I had lots of help. Bill mashed the potatoes, I made gravy, Mona made the salad and set the table, Doug sliced the roast, and we feasted. Holding hands, we said a prayer for those who couldn't join us.

December 26—It dropped down to 8 degrees and Bill and Jackie packed up and left by 6:30 a.m. to drive straight through to Challis. I put together some prime rib sandwiches to eat on the way. Granddaughter Mona stayed on for a longer visit.

December 27—The morning dawned clear and in the single digits. Our ancient willows were encrusted with frozen fog, as was every frond of grass and weed, fence post, and strand of barbed wire, not to mention the frozen surface of the creek. It was one of those rare Blue Bird Days, sunshine bright, mountains glorious, and due to the intense cold, even the very air sparkled with ice crystals.

Mona recorded our walk on her camera. When we returned to the warm house, I heated up hot chocolate while Mona scribbled a poem in her writing tablet.

This evening I roasted those ribs for supper.

December 28—This morning I spied a pair of Bald Eagles in the cottonwood tree on Bicentennial Lane. The leftover rib bones went into a kettle with garlic, shallots, carrots and barley, to simmer into soup.

May everyone in Agri-Times land have a happy, healthy New Year, and count your blessings.

Just Yesterday
by Mona Lee Matthews

Today, with my Grandma, I grow younger, knowing
she was there from my beginnings.
I'm surprised I don't fall when I walk, just to be set right again
by her strong hands, which are the same as my mother's.
It seemed odd that we would be conversing as adults, when
just yesterday I could barely reach the corner,
when me and her big, stuffed bear
could both fit in the rocking chair,
reading about the fox stealing the chickens.
We saw one today on our walk, leaping across the field
with its bushy tail tipped white.
We walked by the irrigation canal
I thought was so big, just yesterday,
by the tall cottonwoods, which are still big
with the great roots and limbs we played on.
Grandma stomps across the snow to show
it won't break and I snap a picture.
Just yesterday, she held the camera, and we talked of
yesterday as if it were a long time ago
when I could still take baths in her sink,
and sat, on the floor before this one, to watch
Mr. Rogers, the Smurfs, the Little House on the Prairie.
We finished our morning walk,
and I'm still surprised she doesn't need to
hold my hand as we stomp off the snow.

Janie Tippett and granddaughter Mona Lee Matthews.

Index